W9-BQZ-037

SCIENTIFIC INVESTIGATIONS IN COMPARATIVE EDUCATION

SCIENTIFIC INVESTIGATIONS IN COMPARATIVE EDUCATION

edited by

MAX A. ECKSTEIN
Queens College,
City University of New York

HAROLD J. NOAH
Teachers College,
Columbia University

The Macmillan Company
Collier-Macmillan Limited, London

First Printing

Library of Congress catalog card number: 69–17349

The Macmillan Company
Collier-Macmillan Canada, Ltd., Toronto, Ontario
Printed in the United States of America

The lines on the opposite page are taken from "voices to voices, lip to lip" copyright, 1926, by Horace Liveright; renewed, 1954, by E. E. Cummings, and are reprinted from his volume, *POEMS 1923–1954* by permission of Harcourt, Brace & World, Inc., New York, and MacGibbon & Kee, Ltd., London.

(While you and i have lips and voices which
are for kissing and to sing with
who cares if some oneeyed son of a bitch
invents an instrument to measure Spring with?

                              e. e. cummings

PREFACE

During the past decade, a new genre of work in comparative education has made its appearance. Diverging quite sharply from the predominantly philosophical and historical tradition of the field, it borrowed heavily from the social sciences. The new approach demands the application of complex techniques of investigation and is predicated on a number of crucial assertions: a priori assumptions about the nature of man and his institutions are to be avoided; facts in and of themselves are meaningless, for only in the context of explanation can facts take on significance; research should be concerned with systematic attempts to test hypotheses within a more general framework of theory; and theory bereft of the possibility of empirical testing is little more than metaphysics.

This book is intended to make more widely available some recent studies along these new lines. Taken together, the articles reprinted here illustrate the basic characteristics of the scientific, empirical approach to the study of education and society using cross-national data. Explicitly stated hypotheses are tested against the evidence of the real world, concepts are transformed from the realm of nominal definitions into measurable categories, and conclusions are carefully weighed both for the limits of their reliability and for the power of the inferences drawn from them.

Observance of the methodological proprieties was the single most important criterion for inclusion of an article, but the selections were also considered for their substance. Apart from the first section of the book, which is devoted to matters methodological, each of the remaining articles reports an investigation into the relationship between some aspect of education and some specific dimension of society: its economy, its political and social structure, its culture and beliefs, and so forth. In addition, the articles present and compare data from at least two national or subnational units, and some of the studies employ "global" data drawn from all the countries for which information was available. The editors hope that the collection will serve as companion reading for their book, *Toward a Science of Comparative Education* (Macmillan, 1969), especially by providing examples of the strategy and tactics of comparative investigation advocated there.

We are indebted to the publishers and authors who have given permission to reprint their copyrighted works. We would also like to acknowledge the valuable assistance of Mr. Richard Noonan in the preparation of the manuscript.

M. A. E.

H. J. N.

CONTENTS

ix

3 The Economy

4 Social Differentiation

5 The Culture

6 National Development

SCIENTIFIC
INVESTIGATIONS
IN
COMPARATIVE
EDUCATION

Part I

METHODOLOGY

REFLECTIONS ON COMPARATIVE
METHODOLOGY IN EDUCATION
1964–1966

George Z. F. Bereday

The author reviews goals and methods in comparative education and discusses, with examples, the recent growing concern with methodology.

SINCE THE appearance of *Comparative Method in Education* in 1964 (1), a lengthy log of writings about method has accumulated. This concern is healthy in view of the weakness of comparative method in all social sciences and the continuing difficulty of arriving at a good definition of comparative education in relation to other academic fields. Contributions from Great Britain, Germany, Japan, France and Belgium, Spain and Venezuela, and USSR and Poland continue to explore the methodological frontiers and the history of method in the field (2). Similar efforts in the United States are represented by a sizeable literature (3). In view of a closely knit relationship and continuous interchange of ideas across national frontiers (4), it is difficult to distinguish which ideas are stimulated by thought from abroad and which originate on the American continent.

On April 29th–30th, 1964, there came together a 'state of the field' conference at Teachers College, Columbia University attended by some twenty-five researchers in comparative education in the United States. At that time the following list of methodological questions was submitted for discussion at their request:

1. What are the basic tools of comparative education? It is concerned with education and it operates in international perspective and it is concerned with social forces responsible for educational happenings and it uses comparative method; that much we all know. But what is the basic discipline it should use? Economics, sociology? Government? History and Philosophy? Combinations of these? It is less and less satisfactory that comparative education should be a grab bag in which any and every approach is as good as any other. We never seem to get sufficient depth in this way. Could we not agree on some irreducible elements that lend themselves best to study by one social science and then insist that all researchers in addition to anything else they may have, have also basic training in *that* field?

2. A related question: What are the delimiting lines between comparative education and other 'foundations', history of education, sociology of education, philosophy of education, etc.? Is the following sentence, "Training in academic subjects creates white-collar expectations," comparative education or sociology of

REPRINTED FROM *Comparative Education*, Vol. 3, No. 3 (June 1967), 169–187, by permission of George Z. F. Bereday. © 1967 by Pergamon Press.

education or both? Or does it cross the threshold from sociology to comparative education only when we say, "The evidence obtained in the Soviet Union, Indonesia, Japan and several other countries suggests that training in academic subjects creates white-collar expectations?"

3. What is the proper balance between qualitative and quantitative studies? Between theorizing and empirical approach? Our tradition has been almost entirely qualitative and theoretical. Recently Foshay and his associates and also Perkinson have been urging us to shift emphasis towards empirical and quantitative studies (5). What are the respective merits of the two approaches? If both will be used, what is the optimum ratio of each? Examples: juvenile delinquency must be studied both quantitatively (incidence of crime), and qualitatively (definition of juvenile crime). How could causes of juvenile delinquency (specifically role of the school in causing or preventing it) best be studied?

4. Where does the area study end and comparative study begin? Here are some sentences illustrating the gist of this question:

All Soviet schools are coeducational.

Slavs are on the whole against coeducation.

Polish and Czech schools became coeducational after World War II.

Uzbek schools should not be coeducational.

Mass cultures have coeducational schools.

The Afghan noted with interest that Soviet schools are coeducational.

In Omsk as well as in Tomsk, I found the schools are coeducational.

It will not surprise us that Soviet schools are coeducational.

Americans note with approval that Soviet schools are coeducational.

Which of these sentences fall within area studies and which belong to comparative studies?

5. What is the relation of comparative education and development studies? Are they one and the same thing? Are these two complementary areas of concern? Or are studies on education and development a part of comparative education, indeed, a new frontier in comparative education? Is the same true of international education?

6. If we are to aid planning, what is the place of recommendations in comparative analysis and how do we preserve the line of demarcation between recommendations and moralizing? Traditionally much of comparative education has been exhortation. Some of the recent development studies have been exhortatory too. What can we do to try and avoid it? Should we avoid it? How can we identify it or even detect it when it appears in the literature? For instance, which of the sentences listed under 4 are overtly or covertly normative?

7. What are the language skills that researchers need? Should everybody have French and German, the first because it is an international language, the second because so much is written in German on comparative education? Can one study an area, be it Russia or Guinea, without the knowledge of respective languages? Does one need to be a general polyglot to do global studies in comparative education?

Not all of the above questions have been either discussed or subsequently worked upon. But the developments of the last two years confirmed that these are, indeed, some of the main lines of methodological inquiries in comparative education. For the purpose of discussion, these questions can be grouped under two headings: first the attempts to refine methods by 'internal' probing into the nature of the comparative process, and secondly, a similar effort at refinement of method by 'external' parceling out of responsibility for different aspects of international studies in education.

Towards the Strengthening of Comparative Method in Education

Of immediate importance to professional researchers in the field of comparative education is the first question, namely the efforts to improve methods of cross-cultural analysis. The last two years saw a welcome increase in attempts to analyze educational problems in 'simultaneous comparison' (6). Methodological refinements of analyzing simultaneously data from different countries must keep coming from actual comparisons rather than, as is sometimes the case with beginning writers, from formulations of pious theoretical schemes as recommendations for others to follow.

Comparative Method in Education proposed two steps to simultaneous comparison: juxtaposition and comparison. Experience has shown that these steps can be further subdivided. Attempts could be made as below, to distinguish between tabular and textual juxtaposition and between balanced and illustrative comparisons.

What Is Juxtaposition?

Juxtaposition could be defined as preliminary matching of data from different countries to prepare them for comparison. Such matching has to include the systematization of data so that they may be grouped under identical or comparable categories for each country under study. The process also includes a search for a hypothesis. No doubt a general purpose of the research was defined before materials for comparison were first looked for altogether. But the formulation of a tight and rigorous hypothesis must follow the preliminary classification of these materials. In fact, the hypothesis must be made in terms of what the assembled data are likely to permit one to prove. Sometimes final hypotheses are minuscule and represent bitter retreats from the grand design originally envisaged as researchable.

The simplest form of juxtaposition is tabular or vertical. In spite of its simplicity and usefulness, tabular treatment of data is, however, less popular than the second form, the textual or horizontal listing. In tabular juxtaposition materials to be compared are set side by side in columns. In horizontal setting, they are written down one under another. Vertical arrangement is, of course, particularly useful when comparative statistics are being prepared. It is also well adapted to present details of administrative structure of school systems. In general, descriptive facts or 'static' details lend themselves well to tabulation. 'Dynamic' details, descriptions of changes and trends can occasionally be put in tables but show up better in horizontal listings. In horizontal juxtaposi-

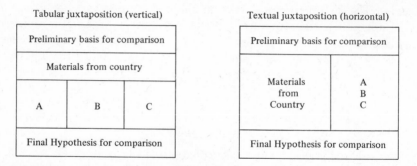

tion, by being written up and placed visually one country under another, the arrangement of the material allows for less stereotyped treatment.

Juxtaposition is simply a process of ordering material for comparison. It permits 'rendering of stewardship,' a review, at a glance or at length, of essential practices in world education. Tentative formulation of laws, later to be tested by full-scale comparison can be attempted by juxtaposition since it identifies the persistent elements throughout these practices. Of course it also tentatively identifies systematic variations which permit the construction of typologies which, if regular, are in themselves laws. Examples of tabular comparisons can be found in *Comparative Method in Education* (7) and in articles in *Comparative Education Review* (8).

Figure 1 is an illustration of one such comparison, in this case a set of diagrams on two African educational systems, Ghana and Dahomey. (Prepared by Misses Mary Ann Brauninger and Barbara Sims of Teachers College, Columbia University.)

The following is an example of textual juxtaposition:

Preliminary basis of comparison: The task is to examine student demonstrations in several countries in order to see why they occur and whether the reasons advanced for them in America hold true in world perspective. One must look for countries in which causes of unrest are sufficiently distinct to permit comparability.

Juxtaposition of data: Review of student unrest in different countries in the last fifteen years suggests a variety of causes. A tentative typology of recent cases would run as follows:

Domestic Cleavages: Buenos Aires
   Students of the University of Buenos Aires took over the University the day after Peron fell in 1956. Decanal offices were sealed by the students who then forced the new government to recognize their demands which included participation in the election of the new rector, dismissal of Peronista professors, stiffening of the curriculum and removal of abuses such as absences of the professors.

International Cleavages: Tokyo
   Students of the University of Tokyo joined other students organized by the Zengakuren, the Japanese students union, in opposing the signing of the Japa-

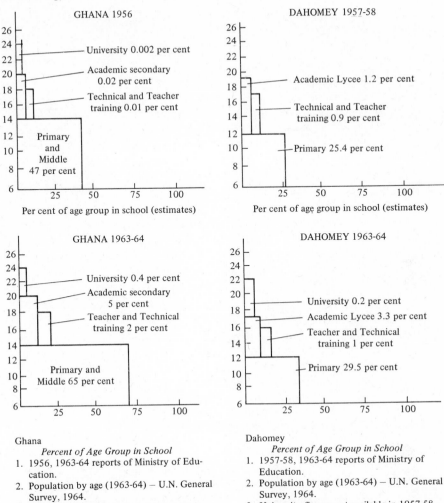

GHANA 1956

University 0.002 per cent
Academic secondary
    0.02 per cent
Technical and Teacher
    training 0.01 per cent
Primary
and
Middle
47 per cent

Per cent of age group in school (estimates)

DAHOMEY 1957-58

Academic Lycee 1.2 per cent
Technical and Teacher
    training 0.9 per cent
Primary 25.4 per cent

Per cent of age group in school (estimates)

GHANA 1963-64

University 0.4 per cent
Academic secondary
    5 per cent
Teacher and Technical
    training 2 per cent
Primary and
Middle 65 per cent

DAHOMEY 1963-64

University 0.2 per cent
Academic Lycee 3.3 per cent
Teacher and Technical
    training 1 per cent
Primary 29.5 per cent

Ghana
Percent of Age Group in School
1. 1956, 1963-64 reports of Ministry of Education.
2. Population by age (1963-64) – U.N. General Survey, 1964.
3. University figures include only students in Ghana. 1964 estimates, 5,000 Ghanaians were students overseas.

Dahomey
Percent of Age Group in School
1. 1957-58, 1963-64 reports of Ministry of Education.
2. Population by age (1963-64) – U.N. General Survey, 1964.
3. University figures not available in 1957-58. University figures for 1963-64 include only those on government scholarships. Total estimates would be double.

FIGURE 1.

Preliminary basis of comparison: *The task is to review in comparative but also in historical perspective, the extent of educational opportunity in Ghana and Dahomey at independence and ten years after.*

nese-American security treaty in 1960. By attacking U.S. Press Secretary Hagerty after his arrival in Tokyo, they effectively prevented the visit of President Eisenhower to Japan and brought about the resignation of the government of Premier Kishi.

Economic Cleavages: Paris
Students of the University of Paris struck in November 1963, the largest of a series of strikes protesting against the inadequate financial provisions for the

universities by the government. Government subsidies have actually increased substantially but the number of students grows faster and their demands include requests for a 'salary' while studying, which the government is unable to satisfy.

Religious Cleavages: Barcelona

Students of the University of Barcelona protesting lack of freedom of their organizations were turned out by the police of a monastery in which they convened a protest meeting in 1965. This breach of sanctuary caused young priests to rally to the students' cause. Attacks upon the demonstrating priests by the police caused tensions between the government and the senior church hierarchy on one side and public opinion on the other.

Ethnic Cleavages: Montreal

Students at McGill University were forced to choose in December 1965 between joining the Quebec French-speaking union of students or remaining in the Canadian English-speaking and Federal association from which the Quebec union withdrew. A referendum was taken as a result of which McGill remained outside the French union, thus accentuating the animosities between the English-speaking and the politically very active French-speaking students.

Racial Cleavages: Ibadan

Students of the Ibadan University College broke out in open disaffection in 1958 when the University authorities, who were overwhelmingly English, attempted to place wire fences around the entrance to women's dormitories. This action was considered racially insulting and followed upon many other real and alleged charges of discrimination. The University closed its gates in protest but was forced under pressure from the government and public opinion to reopen without reprimanding culprits.

Social Class Cleavages: Warsaw

Students of Warsaw Polytechnic were identified after the October Revolution of 1956 as the exponents of the new liberal communism. The suspension of a liberal magazine 'Po Prostu' in 1958 caused them to riot against the government. Students of the University of Warsaw, who are of a somewhat humbler social background, did not join the riot. When working class youths joined the riots on the fourth day of disturbances all students withdrew and condemned them.

Educational Cleavages: Rangoon

Students at the University of Rangoon have developed a tradition of going on strike and rioting against the University and the government. In 1953 the announcement that vacations would be cut in half, added to an already turbulent semester, caused a student strike. Police force was used to break up the strike on the second day.

Hypothesis for comparison:

The causes of student demonstrations are sufficiently diverse to be suspected of being accidental. A review of educational, social, and psychological patterns suggests, however, constant elements as follows:

1. There exists latent alienation of the younger generation from their elders due to growing up and adjustment to adulthood, but this alienation is at a low level, and is not sufficient by itself to trigger off demonstrations.

2. There exists a small group of students who, for several reasons, are strongly alienated from society and who have the capacity to act as leaders in riots.

3. Manifest immediate causes of dissatisfaction raise the general level of alienation of the student body at large and thus permit the leaders to seize initiative. They act only if assured of a sufficient backing of a larger student body.

The hypothesis, such as it is, has defined a relation between social and educational circumstances of student unrest (9). The task of subsequent comparison will be to determine whether this relationship really holds true in the manner indicated in all the above cases. The comparison will work out in detail the materials which in the stage of juxtaposition were looked over only superficially. To further clarify juxtaposition, one simply needs to say that it is preliminary comparison or a confrontation of partners to comparison. Its purpose is not to draw comparative conclusions, but to determine whether comparison is possible at all. Juxtaposition is really intended to provide an answer to the question, "compare in terms of what?" The search here is for what Robert Ulich has called the *tertium comparationis*. Juxtaposition is designed to establish comparability or basic consistency of data. The connections reached for may be spacious and macrocosmic: one could claim on one side that Japan and England are two vigorous island nations offshore great continents; hence, their school systems could be compared for this insularity (10). On the other side, Philip Foster has argued (11), that comparison should be microscopic and that only countries as close as Ivory Coast and Ghana which share common ethnic stock and at the same time have different colonial histories, present a sufficiently uncomplicated set of variables to warrant comparison. Whether one accepts or rejects macrocosmic comparisons, through juxtaposition the stage is set for a systematic exploration of differences (and of similarities) which is the proper subject of comparison.

Comparison

Simultaneous comparison follows juxtaposition and can also be divided into two types. One might call one a 'balanced' and the other an 'illustrative' comparison. Probably the greatest amount of work at present needs to be done to develop the former. Balanced comparison is a symmetric shuttling back and forth between the areas under study. The essence of this method is that every type of information from one country must be matched, 'balanced,' by comparable information from other countries. Such emphasis has the merit of developing the habit of searching for equivalent materials across national frontiers. It is thus particularly useful in the training of students. Altogether too many papers purporting to be comparisons consist of disquisitions on one country only to be climaxed by an ominous final section, paragraph, or even a sentence to the effect that "the other country is different."

Balanced comparison can be of varying degrees of intensity. When one alternates chapters or sections as in the diagram below, the procedure is structurally similar to juxtaposition.

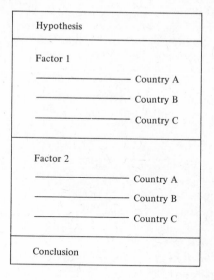

Essentially the same model is reproduced when several countries are treated together, not in sections but in paragraphs or sentences. The systematic crossing and recrossing of national frontiers in the interest of highlighting comparative factors is at the core of this method. The meshing of information in single paragraphs or sentences marks the passage from comparison by rotation to comparison by fusion. Balanced comparison by rotation means that each country is listed consecutively to illustrate the operation of the social factor under scrutiny. In the case of fusion the discussion is truly simultaneous. Countries are not rotated through consecutive sentences, but instead are discussed together even in the same sentence. To illustrate the point in an abbreviated form, we would say something like this in comparison by rotation:

In England, juvenile delinquency is a social class phenomenon. The very word 'Teddy boys' is derived from the style and cut of clothes. The long coats and narrow trousers worn by 'Teddy boys' date back to the Edwardian era and the delinquents have been nicknamed after the gay monarch, the son of Queen Victoria. The remarkable fact is that precisely the same cut of clothes is worn by the occupants of the Royal enclosure at the Windsor Horse Show. Consciously or unconsciously, delinquency is linked with the fury of the angry young men against the Establishment.

In the United States, delinquency is more apt to have an ethnic or racial basis, although, of course, these too are forms of class stratification. Current talk of 'Black power' notwithstanding, the delinquency of immigrants and Negroes is not a voice of protest but an escape. Delinquents, if they know or seek to know it at all, will reject, even jeer at the pattern of life of the upper class. They develop their own patterns and their own subcultures by way of compensation.

What is quite remarkable about racial or ethnic delinquency in the United States is the frequency with which delinquency disappears at eighteen. The gang leader rejoins society and becomes a corporal or a foreman. But for an accident of birth, he would have been a leader in the Boy Scouts in the first place.

To fuse the information contained in the two foregoing paragraphs, one would have to rewrite them as follows:

The poor deviant boys in England and the 'cool kids' of American slums have their delinquency in common, but it is generated by different social causes. The English 'Teddy boys' lash out at the Establishment and its constraints. American Negro and immigrant kids attempt to side step the old society and plunge into a world of values of their own making. At the basis of English delinquency is social precedence. At the basis of American delinquency is race and ethnicity. The narrow trousers and long coats of the 'Teddy boys' go back to the Edwardian era. It is the name of Queen Victoria's son that gave the delinquents their nickname. No distinctive clothes are worn in America that share the cut and style with those worn in the Royal Enclosure at the Windsor Horse Show. On the contrary, the black leather jackets and the bluejeans are symbols of their own, the latter, in fact, copied and worn by the rest of society. American delinquents frequently disappear from view at eighteen, rather than to find their way into the adult delinquency of Soho. Gang leaders become corporals or foremen and would have been Boy Scout leaders in the first place had not color or accent marred their chance of absorption into the mainstream of American life. Their lives are not sufficiently remote from the rest to make them lash out, as do young angry Englishmen, at those who block their path.

It will be seen at once that though the separate paragraphs in the alternating version contain substantially the same information, an attempt at fusion elicited more detail of description. No black leather jackets were mentioned for American delinquents in the first version; it was the necessity to balance the description of the English mod dressers that called it into being. The necessity to balance materials for two or more countries calls for more precision. It forces an appropriate focus in a field where random and imperfect comparisons have been permitted to flourish.

Balanced comparison is, however, not without problems. When students strain for symmetry where there is none, an attempt at balanced comparison may result in an imbalance of judgement. Symmetry is not pedantry, and in comparative dissertations many aspects of school operation have to be relegated to the appendix because they uniquely belong to one country and cannot be matched by others. A few years ago a comparative study of discipline in English and American schools was completed at Teachers College, Columbia University. In surveying pupil self-government in England the author was confronted with the prefect system. Being committed to balanced comparison, he at once cast about for an equivalent in American schools. But since there is nothing comparable in America, the writer was intrigued by the possibility of comparison of the English prefects with American traffic monitors. The results of that comparison could be published only after the basis for it has been broadened enough to reflect elitist as against popular ideals inherent in the two school systems (12).

There continues a dispute about the merits of such broad gauge comparisons. In several areas of education there are no equivalents. When a comparative analysis is attempted in such areas the results may be forced and unreal. On the other hand, there are several areas where balanced comparison has not been attempted but where the need for comparison seems overwhelming.

Balanced comparison must be pushed even against heavy odds when, in the absence of serious analysis, *ad hoc* comparative judgements have instead been made and used. One of the areas in which equivalence studies are most urgently needed is the sphere of equivalence of senior secondary school certificates and of university degrees. There is now so fantastic a traffic of university students and graduates between several countries that some measures other than *ad hoc* evaluation of individual credentials is imperative (13). Poor comparative work in this area may bring tragic consequences to thousands of individuals whose credentials are wrongly evaluated. As an example we may cite the Mellor study (14). In 1957–58, the author came to the United States to carry out the 'equivalence' comparison between British and American university degrees. Though the study took apparently two years to execute, it became a subject of intense controversy. Its conclusions were that American college degrees are vastly below the British degree and that no equivalent standing could be accorded to them. All cautions notwithstanding, the book was adopted as guiding policy at least by one education department, that of Hong Kong, apparently because it was 'better than nothing'. Thus hundreds of Hong Kong Chinese who endure sacrifices of travel and study in the United States find themselves upon return to Hong Kong classified as non-university graduates. If they enter public school teaching their pay and promotion is that of teachers without college education. That as late as 1961 an alumna of Radcliffe or Wellesley should be classified and paid as if she were a high school graduate only, while her colleague graduated from the University of Hong Kong or for that matter Birmingham should enjoy the prerequisites of a university graduate is absurd. Apparently the best American colleges have been now recognized by Hong Kong, but the danger of equating the training even at lesser British and Commonwealth universities with that at the University of Michigan or Wisconsin continues.

Equally perplexing are the problems of equivalence in international exchanges. The Lacey-Zarubin agreement, for instance, provided for an exchange of an equivalent number of students between Soviet and American universities. The Americans sought to send holders of the B.A. degree envisaging the year in the Soviet Union as a year of graduate research. But the American B.A., which is in most cases a general education degree, takes four years to achieve. The Russian 'Diplom' is a specialist degree and takes five years. There was some ground for the Soviet argument that American students in Moscow and Leningrad should be fifth year rather than graduate students. But such a solution was understandably unacceptable to Americans. Fifth year students, like all Soviet students, must attend compulsory lectures on Marxism–Leninism. Eventually Soviet authorities accepted the American B.A. as equivalent to their diploma for exchange purposes. Here is an example of how national pride and political considerations impinge upon the business of comparison. A solidly balanced equivalence system is needed and multiple attempts must be made to attack the problem.

When balanced comparison is impossible or inadvisable, another type of comparison can be resorted to. For want of a better name, one might call this type 'illustrative'. In this method, educational practices in different countries are drawn at random as illustrations of comparative points suggested by the data. In illustrative comparison no generalizations are possible, hence no laws can be arrived at or deducted. Illustrative comparison, one might say, is 'inferior' comparison, at least when set side by side with the 'balanced' version. In illustrative comparison the analysis is derived from comparative data only by implication. Very often what passes for erudition is no more, however, than intuition. Comparative 'examples' are selected to support one's points of view, and as everybody knows, there are few points of view or values in educational theory and practice that cannot be supported by some examples.

With such warnings in mind, however, illustrative comparison should not be denigrated unduly. What would be otherwise an abstract or at least tentative and unrelated sociological analysis becomes enriched and strengthened in depth by the back-up of comparative illustrations. Often, too, the data are too imprecise or nonexistent to attempt a fully balanced treatment. How does one balance the schooling of mentally retarded children in the U.S. compared to treatment of the retarded in the USSR when information from the latter country is scarce? How does one make numbers of students in the two countries mean something comparable when in the former country one half of all the students attend junior colleges while in the latter one half study by correspondence? The difficulties are serious, but illustrative comparison may lay groundwork for a balanced comparison. Below is an example of one such process in the making. The write-up presented describes a research proposal on the subject of race relations in education.

This project is a study by the comparative method of social stratification in education, especially its racial aspects. Four countries: South Africa, the United States, New Zealand, and Brazil have been selected because they offer a clear picture of the different kinds of race relations in education. South Africa on one side and New Zealand and Brazil on the other represent the static models of extreme segregation and integration. The United States is at the middle point between these two poles and is in a dynamic situation.

Because the United States has been moving from segregation (formal in the South, and informal in the North) to integration, an examination of the integrated school model can help much in formulating appropriate plans for the American schools. Two such models will be studied. Brazil represents a unique model of a unified school system. Except for census purposes color is ignored in school planning and educational opportunities are the same regardless of the degree of Indian or Negro blood. New Zealand, on the other hand, has established racial equality while maintaining a dual system of European and Maori schools. Significantly enough both types of schools are attended by a mixed population of Europeans and Maoris. A comparison between the New Zealand schools and Brazilian schools offers the opportunity to estimate the 'integration effectiveness' of a single and a two track school system.

The other extreme of segregated schools, is adequately represented by South Africa, a clear model of racial discrimination which affects Asians and the Cape colored as well as the African groups, who find themselves obligated to attend separate institutions.

To carry out the second phase of the project, the observation of racial relations in the schools of these countries is necessary. The first phase has been completed in five years during which time a doctoral seminar on the race problems in education was held and much valuable documentation was accumulated. In the United States, the second phase of the observation has also been completed including various visits to schools in Alabama, Tennessee, Texas, New Mexico, California as well as teaching in the public schools of Harlem and many visits to segregated areas in the northern states. The preliminary work about the American schools has been published in a chapter "Race Problems in American Education" in Bereday and Volpicelli (eds.), *Public Education in America* (New York: Harper and Row, 1958).

It is necessary now to make the appropriate school inspections in each of the remaining countries and apply methods of history and sociology to the pedagogical data thus collected. The precise plan of inspection will vary according to the degree of general hospitality in each country. South Africa in particular will necessitate exceptional tact. In each country it is planned to spend a minimum of one month for general orientation, interviews and school visits, and a minimum two months in a selected representative school, if possible on the teaching faculty (15).

Race problems in education are a good example of study in which an illustrative comparison only is possible. There is no racial problem in education in all or even in a majority of countries. To fit data for balanced comparison is difficult. Can the Maoris be considered comparable to the Bantu? Are American Negroes and Liberians to be equated because the leaders of the latter are the descendants of the returned Southern slaves? Are Jamaicans in Britain comparable to *favela* dwellers in Brazil? And what of the Japanese 'etas' or the Indian untouchables? What of ethnic minorities which are treated as racial minorities? Should Jews in Nazi Germany be included in racial comparisons? Confronted with such questions the best one can hope for is an illustrative typology from which no global rules as to the treatment of racial minorities in schools can emerge.

COMPARATIVE EDUCATION AND RELATED FIELDS

The search for a systematization of comparative methods is not confined to education. In some fields, for instance literature or law, relatively little headway has been made thus far, and most so-called comparative studies are, in fact, area studies (16).

By contrast tremendous strides have been made in comparative work in the newer social sciences, especially sociology and political science. In political science the advances from qualitative to quantitative work can best be illustrated by comparing Charles W. Merriam's *The Making of Citizens* (ed. Bereday, New York: Teachers College Press, 1967) which originally appeared in 1929 with G. Almond and S. Verba's *The Civic Culture: Political Attitudes and Democracy in Five Nations* (New Jersey: Princeton University Press, 1963). In sociology, which has had major significance on political science and history, the comparative studies are also enjoying vigorous revival (17).

The development of these methods has once more raised the problem: which is the best parent discipline for comparative studies in education. There has been a tendency in the United States to push comparative research training to the post-doctoral level and to recommend single discipline and single area concentration for graduating students. Experience with doctoral dissertations during the last two years has revealed certain heartening elements: the caliber of the present generation of students in the United States is improving due at least partly to increasing recruitment of candidates from academic undergraduate fields but also in part thanks to the upgrading of training in education. New opportunities for travel, such as the Peace Corps, have meant that the majority of candidates can now offer work in the language of the area they choose for doctoral study and have had at least one year of residence there.

In the past, however, American comparative educators have attempted to define the training of comparative researchers in education as cross-disciplinary. The result has been doctoral dissertations written by 'mules' who somehow cannot compensate for the loss of depth in each discipline by the breadth of insights gained from more general overviews. To forestall this, there has begun a movement (related to a similar movement in development education) to train doctoral students in one area and in one discipline and to encourage them to branch out into other disciplines and other geographical areas only after completion of doctoral training and only in supplementary fashion. This movement would imply that simultaneous comparison, treatment of world problems, etc. would not now be attempted by doctoral students but only by working academicians.[1] Needless to say such a movement cannot get under way without inciting opposition. Fear has been expressed that this 'treason' from the notion of a cross-disciplinary approach might im-

---

[1] The present trend in the Department of Philosophy and the Social Sciences (the old Department of Social and Philosophical Foundations of Education) at Teachers College, Columbia University is to recognize six specializations: philosophy, history, sociology, anthropology, economics and political science. In each of these specializations students can major in comparative and international education. Half of the students in the department do so in fact.

ply the entire disappearance of comparative education as a field. Vigorous attempts are being made anew to define in the manner reminiscent of the thirties the field of 'education'. This is done in the hope of raising education to the status of a research field or even discipline, thus finding a mooring for comparative school studies without continuous reliance on other social sciences.[2] This movement has affinities with development education which has inaugurated search for similar definitions of education in order to facilitate planning.[3]

The mention of development education requires now the discussion of the splinter groups that have appeared alongside the study of traditional comparative education. The most vigorous area of these activities is in fact development education. In answer to the interest of economists in manpower studies and hence in education, there has arisen a field concerned with the dynamics of modernization, particularly in the newer nations. Economists, planners, and politicians have come to regard expenditure on education not as a service and consequently a marginal budget expenditure, but as an investment and hence a primary budget item (18).

This new interest coincided with the renaming of the UNESCO-sponsored

[2] On this subject, Dr. John Laska of Teachers College, Columbia University has written as follows:

"The view of one member of this so-called 'opposition' may be succinctly stated. Most academics in the field of comparative education are, I believe, concerned with two major tasks: (1) scholarly research on the frontiers of knowledge; and (2) the teaching of students, most of whom will become primary and secondary school teachers or school administrators. In preparing for the first task, rigorous training in one or more of the traditional disciplines would appear to be desirable, if not essential. The second activity, which is no less important than the first, is concerned with the effective transmission of a body of knowledge. The need to integrate and make accessible this body of knowledge must, therefore, not be ignored in the preparation of prospective comparative educators. This is not to be construed as an argument that 'education' is or should be a 'discipline'; that is a matter involving the organization of academic departments in the university and is quite different from the question of the existence of a body of knowledge on education. The fact that the study of education is not now generally conducted within a distinctive academic department of the university does, however, give rise to an important additional requirement in the teaching of comparative education. In other fields that have a comparative aspect—such as political science and sociology—the teacher in the comparative branch can assume that his students will come to him well prepared in the general content of the field. But for comparative education such an assumption is not possible: students are not now able to acquire from any single course or academic program a general introduction to the scholarly study of the educative process. Because of the absence of a field of study devoted to the totality of the educative phenomenon, it is incumbent upon the teacher of comparative education to recognize this deficiency. Actually, this will not entail any major change in the role of the comparative educator, since the boundaries between a comparative branch and the main field always overlap—and may, as in the case of economics and anthropology, not even be necessary. It does mean, however, that the comparative educator should be aware of the importance of enlarging and systematizing the body of knowledge on the educative process; without this, there will be very little 'education' for him to 'compare.' "

[3] This movement is pioneered, among others, by the UNESCO Institute for Educational Planning directed by Philip Coombs.

fundamental education movement as development education. Henceforth, the concerns with the manpower flow through schools, with planning for and financing of educational expansion, and with the relationship of education to the political power structure and political decision-making, have, among others, become part of development education. Workers in development education are concerned with the dynamics of school-society relations, and though such concerns have always been a part of traditional comparative education, they have preferred to eschew the name and, indeed, often the connection with comparative education.

Thus the center for comparative education at Stanford University has been renamed Stanford International Development Education Center. Harvard abandoned courses in Comparative Education after the retirement of Robert Ulich (the last course was given by this writer in the summer of 1964) and established instead a Center for the Study of Education and Development with Adam Curle as the first Professor of Education and Development. New posts established at the University of Indiana for Nicholas DeWitt and at the University of Wisconsin for Andreas Kazamias were named the Directorship of the International Survey of Educational Development and Planning and Professorship of Educational Policy Studies (19) respectively.

If rule of thumb distinction can or should be attempted, it would be that comparative education concentrates on a comparison of the statics of education while development education is concerned with its dynamics. Comparative efforts are efforts to set together systems of educational phenomena arrested in point of time, or time sequences or sets of events or trends. Only such entities are comparable. Development education is not bound so rigorously by rules of comparison, but is concerned instead with modes of action or making educational policy more intelligent and immediate.

The second specialization, apart from comparative education, has been international education. Long-standing concerns of comparative education in 'international understanding' have emerged under this heading as sustained studies of the crosscultural flow of ideas, movement of men across national frontiers, and of the organizations created to coordinate them.

The flow of foreign students has received particular attention. Organizations such as the United Nations and UNESCO demand full-time efforts of persons studying the international fluctuations of university populations. Cultural efforts of nations abroad, surveys of the diffusion of values, and the more historically orthodox mapping out of educational influences abroad have also become a part of international education. International education, like development education, is concerned with dynamics, but with the dynamics of interaction between cultures and countries rather than, as the former, with the interdependence of schools and other social institutions (20).

Several other efforts concerned with foreign education could be listed under the heading of International Studies in Education. Research on the teaching of English as a foreign language is one. Preparation of materials for teaching international understanding or world history in schools is another. Internationalization of history textbooks is yet another. Preparation of administrators for foreign school management, research of anthropologists or psychologists on foreign child-rearing and many others 'belong' whether with or without the conscious acquiescence of their authors.

As a result of the emergence of these fields, the 'old-fashioned' concept of comparative education is likely to be revised in one of two possible directions. Either, as is often the case at present, the term comparative education will be used interchangeably with the term International Studies in Education while development education and international education will be considered parts of the field, though probably not without much protest from its devotees. Or, as is perhaps more likely and more proper, comparative education will concentrate on school systems, while abandoning the concerns appropriated by the other specialties. Another way of saying it might be that comparative education will approach educational problems primarily with the tools of political sociology, while development education will use those of economics and international education those of anthropology. There will of course be inevitable overlaps in such a formulation, but these cannot and probably should not be avoided. For instance, in a final analysis, it would be risky to say that comparative education is concerned with the statics while development and international education with the dynamics of educational life. In a sense there are no statics in education, only trends, even if caught in a series of still pictures for the purpose of comparison.

BIBLIOGRAPHY

1. GEORGE Z. F. BEREDAY, *Comparative Method in Education* (New York: Holt, Rinehart and Winston, Inc., 1964), 302 pp. Third printing, March 1966. Spanish translation by Editorial Herder, Barcelona; Italian translation by Editrice La Scuola, Brescia; and Japanese translation by Fukumura Publishing Company, Tokyo, now in preparation.
2. The following is a comprehensive though not complete list of relevant writings from several countries:

   Great Britain: ALAN ELLIOTT, Comparison and Interchange: The Relevance of Cultural Relations to Comparative Education, *Comparative Education*, 2, pp. 63–70 (1966). BRIAN HOLMES, *Problems in Education: A Comparative Approach*, Part I (London: Routledge & Kegan Paul, 1965), pp. 3–93. BRIAN HOLMES and SAUL ROBINSOHN, *Relevant Data in Comparative Education* (Hamburg: UNESCO Institute for Education, 1963), 143 pp. BRIAN HOLMES and SAUL ROBINSOHN, Relevant Data in Comparative Education, *International Review of Education*, 9, No. 2, 134–157 (1963–64). EDMUND KING, The Purpose of Comparative Education, *Comparative Education*, 1, 147–160 (1965).

   Germany: OSKAR ANWEILER, Von der pädagogischen Auslandskunde zur Vergleichenden Erziehungswissenschaft, *Pädagogische Rundschau*, 20, No. 10, 886–896 (1966). KARL BROICH, Die Situation des ländlichen Bildungswesens im internationalen Vergleich, *Pädagogische Rundschau*, 20, No. 4, 349–361 (1966). GOTTFRIED HAUSMANN, A Century of Comparative Education, 1785–1885, *Comparative Education Review*, 9, No. 1, 1–21 (1967). GOTTFRIED HAUSMANN, Ludwig Natorps Schrift über Andreas Bell und Joseph Lancaster—ein Beitrag zur Vergleichenden Erzichungswissenschaft aus dem Jahre 1817, *Pädagogische Rundschau*, 20, No. 10, 897–903 (1966). FRANZ HILKER, Internationale Pädagogik, *Bildung und Erziehung*, 17, No. 5, 317–330 (1964). FRANZ HILKER, *La Pédagogie Comparée: Introduction à son Histoire, sa Théorie et sa Pratique*, Mémoires et Documents Scolaires, Brochure No. 1964 (Paris: Institut Pedagogique National, SEVPEN, 1964), 124 pp. FRANZ HILKER, Was kann die vergleichende Methode in der Pädagogik leisten? *Bildung und Erziehung*, 16, No. 9, 511–526 (1963). FRANZ HILKER, What Can the Comparative Method Contribute to Education? *Comparative Education Review*, 7, No. 3, 223–225 (1964). WOLFGANG MITTER, Vergleichende Erziehungswissenschaft an der Pädagogischen Hochschule, *Bildung und Erziehung*, 19, No. 6, 426–435 (1966). SAUL B. ROBINSOHN, Von den Voraussetzungen einer 'Erziehung zu internationaler Verständigung,' *Pädagogische Rundschau*, 20, No. 10, pp. 936–943 (1966). HERMAN RÖHRS, Das Ausländerstudium als Bildungshilfe und seine hochschulpädagogische Problematik, *Pädagogische Rundschau*, 18, No. 8, 719–728 (1964). HERMAN RÖHRS, *Schule und Bildung im internationelen Gespräch* (Frankfurt am Main: Akademische Verglasgesellschaft, 1966), FRIEDRICH SCHNEIDER, Toward Substantive Research in Comparative Education, *Comparative Education Review*, 10, No. 1, 16–17 (1966).

Japan: TAKAO ANDO, *Hikaku-Kyoikugaku Genron* (Theories of Comparative Education) (Tokyo: Iwasaki Shoten, 1965), 224 pp. SUSUMU IKEDA, Hikaku-Kyoikugaku no Kano to Genkai ni tsuite-1 (Some Notes on Possibilities and Limits in the Comparative Study of Education-1) *Kyoto University Research Studies in Education*, 12, 138–174 (1966). SUSUMU IKEDA, A Note on the Comparative Study of Educational Administration Systems, *Japanese Journal of Educational Research*, 33, No. 3, 195–203 (1966). TOSHIAKI KUWABARA, Hikaku Gakko Ho Kenkyu Josetsu (1)— M. A. Jullien no Hikaku-Kyoikugaku, (Introduction to the Comparative Study of School Regulations (1)—M. A. Jullien's Comparative Education) *Studies of Education*, No. 3, 1–11, (1964). I. MATSUZAKI and M. ISHIKAWA, "Selected Bibliography on Comparative Education," *Japanese Journal of Educational Research*, 33, No. 3, 246–272 (1966). SADAMI MONZEN, Jullien no Hikaku-Kyoikugaku ni kansuru Koso, (Jullien's Ideas on Comparative Education) *Bulletin of the Faculty of Education, Hiroshima University*, Part I, 13, 83–94 (1964). MASATOSHI ONO, Hikaku-Kyoikugaku no Hohoronteki Doko: Shikago Gakuha o Chushin to shite, (Recent Trends in Methodology of Comparative Education: Laying Stress on the Chicago School) *Journal of Hokkaido Gakugei University*, Section (1C), 15, No. 1, 41–54 (1964). (Materials collected through the courtesy of Professor Tetsuya Kobayashi of International Christian University, Tokyo).

France and Belgium: G. DELANDSHEERE, Education comparée et dynamique culturelle, *Répères* (Paris), No. 3, 64–79 (1964). RAYMOND POIGNANT, *L'enseignement dans les pays du Marché Commun*, Introduction

(Brussells: Report of the Commission of the European Community Institute for University Studies, 1966), pp. 27–40. ALEXANDRE VEXLIARD, L'education comparée et la notion de caractère national, *Revue de Psychologie des Peuples*, 20, No. 2, 179–203 (1965).

Spain and Venezuela: JOSE A. BENAVENT, La Methodologia comparativa de George Z. F. Bereday, *Perspectivas Pedagogicas*, 5, No. 17, 63–76 (1966). GUSTAVO F. J. CIRIGLIANO, Stages of Analysis in Comparative Education, *Comparative Education Review*, 10, No. 1, 18–20 (1966). PEDRO ROSSELLÓ, Concerning the Structure of Comparative Education, *Comparative Education Review*, 7, No. 2, 103–107 (1964). PEDRO ROSSELLÓ, Difficultés inhérentes aux recherches d'éducation comparée dynamique, *International Review of Education*, 9, No. 2, 203–214 (1963–64). JUAN TUSQUETS, El Instituto de Pedagogia Comparada, *Perspectivas Pedagogicas*, 4, No. 16, 7–12 (1965).

USSR and Poland: Sravnitelnaia Pedagogika, *Sovetskaia Pedagogika*, No. 2, 148–149 (1965). Problemi Sravnitelnoi Pedagogiki, *Sovetskaia Pedagogika*, No. 2, 153–154 (1965). BOGDAN SUCHODOLSKI, Egalité et éducation: Problèmes, méthodes et difficultés des recherches comparées, *International Review of Education*, 9, No. 2, 182–195 (1963–64).

3. The following are sample writings from the United States:

ARTHUR FOSHAY, The Uses of Empirical Methods in Comparative Education: A Pilot Study to Extend the Scope, *International Review of Education*, 9, No. 3, 257–268 (1963–64). MYRON GLAZER, Field Work in a Hostile Environment: A Chapter in the Sociology of Social Research in Chile, *Comparative Education Review*, 10, No. 2, 367–376 (1966). ANDREAS M. KAZAMIAS, History, Science and Comparative Education: A Study in Methodology, *International Review of Education*, 8, No. 3–4, 383–398 (1963). ANDREAS M. KAZAMIAS and BYRON G. MASSIALAS, *Tradition and Change in Education*: A Comparative Study, Part I (New York: Prentice-Hall, Inc., 1965), pp. 1–15. A. H. MOEHLMAN, *Comparative Education Systems*, Chapter 1 (New York: The Center for Applied Research in Education, 1963), pp. 1–14. GORDON C. ROSCOE and THOMAS W. NELSON, Prolegomena to a Definition of Comparative Education, *International Review of Education*, 10, No. 4, 385–392 (1964). URSULA K. SPRINGER, Sinn und Gehalt von Vorlesungen über Vergleichende Erziehungswissenschaft, *Pädagogische Rundschau*, 20, No. 10, 877–885 (1966). I. N. THUT and DON ADAMS, *Educational Patterns in Contemporary Societies*, Chapter 1 (New York: McGraw-Hill, 1964), pp. 1–23.

4. Apart from extensive informal channels and formal cooperation such as the *World Year Book of Education*, four Comparative Education Societies have recently made strides forward. The Comparative Education Society in America was founded in 1956 and had from the beginning opened its membership to non-Americans. Currently (1967) four persons from outside the United States serve on its Board of Directors and five persons are members of the Editorial Board of the *Comparative Education Review*. The Comparative Education Society of Europe which was launched in 1961 was at first reluctant to admit non-Europeans. From the beginning, however, the Society's annual meetings were attended by a sizeable number of American observers and the Society now has opened its door to non-European members, and has in fact invited several American comparative educators to join. Special note needs

also to be taken of the very cordial collaboration that has come into being between the English journal, *Comparative Education*, published at Oxford and the American *Comparative Education Review*. Members of the editorial staff of the two journals have recently exchanged publications. (See W. D. Halls, The Education of the Academically Gifted in Europe: Some Comparisons, *Comparative Education Review*, 10, 426–432 (1966) and GEORGE Z. F. BEREDAY, A Memorial to Isaac Kandel, 1881–1965, *Comparative Education*, 2, No. 3, 147–150 (1965), and also this article.) The Comparative Education Society of Japan (Nippon Hikaku-Kyoiku Gakkai) was established in September of 1964. It held its first meeting in Hiroshima in April, 1965 and its second meeting in Tokyo in August, 1966. In 1966, plans were begun to establish the Comparative Education Society of Canada.

5. In an article "Comparison of Educational Programs: A Methodological Proposal" in *School Review*, 70, 314–331, 1962, HENRY J. PERKINSON urged comparisons of the content of the curriculum in various countries. One such pilot study was made by Robert Jolly in "Elementary Schools in Geneva, Switzerland and Oakland, California," *Comparative Education Review*, 5, No. 1, 67–68 (1961). The major study now in execution is being carried out by an international consortium known as The International Evaluation of Educational Attainment. The relevant publications of this project include at the time of writing: Arthur W. Foshay, et al., *Educational Achievements of Thirteen-Year-Olds in Twelve Countries* (Hamburg: UNESCO Institute for Education, 68 pp. (1962) and Torsten Husén, (ed.), *International Study of Achievement in Mathematics*, 2 vols. (New York: John Wiley & Son, 672 pp. (1967).

6. The following may be quoted as examples:
   MUNIR A. BASHSHUR, Higher Education and Political Development in Syria and Lebanon, *Comparative Education Review*, 10, No. 3, 451–461 (1966). M. A. ECKSTEIN, Ultimate Deterrents: Punishment and Control in English and American Schools, *Comparative Education Review*, 10, No. 3, 433–439 (1966). JOHN GEORGEOFF, Nationalism in the History Textbooks of Yugoslavia and Bulgaria, *Comparative Education Review*, 10, No. 3, 442–448 (1966). W. D. HALLS, The Education of the Academically Gifted in Europe: Some Comparisons, *Comparative Education Review*, 10, No. 3, 426–432 (1966). STANLEY D. IVIE, A Comparison in Educational Philosophy: Jose Vasconcelos and John Dewey, *Comparative Education Review*, 10, No. 3, 404–416 (1966). PAUL NASH, Authority and Freedom in Education: Some Anglo-American Comparisons, *Comparative Education*, 3, No. 1, 13–20 (1966). M. USHIOGI, Changing Higher Education Population in the Process of Industrialization: An Aspect of the Comparative Study of Education, *Japanese Journal of Educational Research*, 33, No. 3, p. 223 (1966). HANS WITTIG, Moderne Bildungspolitik und europäische Bildung, *Pädagogische Rundschau*, 19, No. 9, 595–601 (1965). T. YAMANOUCHI, Comparative Perspective on the Recent Reform of Secondary School Curriculum, *Japanese Journal of Educational Research*, 33, No. 3, p. 214 (1966).

7. BEREDAY, *Comparative Method in Education*, op. cit.

8. HENRY CHAUNCEY, Some Comparative Checkpoints Between American and Soviet Secondary Education, *Comparative Education Review*, 2, No. 3, 18–20 (1959). DIXIE LEE HARRIS, Education of Linguistic Minorities in the United

States and the U.S.S.R., *Comparative Education Review*, 6, No. 3, 191–199 (1963). VICTOR N. LOW, Education for the Bantu: A South African Dilemma, *Comparative Education Review*, 2, No. 2, 21–27 (1958).

9. A preliminary work on this hypothesis has been done in GEORGE Z. F. BEREDAY, Student Unrest on Four Continents: Montreal, Ibadan, Warsaw and Rangoon, *Comparative Education Review*, 10, No. 2, 188–204 (1966).

10. This was in fact the interesting idea conceived by Joseph Katz of the University of British Columbia and submitted for publication in the *Comparative Education Review* some years ago. After the mutual submission of a preliminary manuscript Professor Katz was extended an invitation to work out the topic in greater detail.

11. PHILIP FOSTER, Comparative Methodology and the Study of African Education, *Comparative Education Review*, 4, No. 2, 110–117 (1960).

12. MAX ECKSTEIN, The Elitist and the Popular Ideal: Prefects and Monitors in English and American Secondary Schools, *International Review of Education*, 12, No. 2, 184–195 (1966).

13. MARTENA SASNETT, World-wide Exchange of Information on Education, *Comparative Education Review*, 10, No. 3, 508–510 (1966).

14. BERNARD MELLOR, *The American Degree; A Comparative Study for British Students*, 2nd Edition (Hong Kong: Hong Kong University Press, 1961), 65 pp. Also, BERNARD MELLOR, American Degrees and British Students, *Oversea Education*, 30, No. 4, 147–159 (1959) and JOHN D. LEWIS, American Degrees and British Students, *Oversea Education*, 32, No. 3, 97–102 (1960).

15. Translated from JOSE A. BENAVENT, "La Methodologia Comparativista de GEORGE Z. F. BEREDAY," *Perspectivas Pedagogicas*, 5, No. 17, 63–76 (1966).

16. The writer was a Carnegie Fellow in Law and Political Science at Harvard Law School in 1964–65 and 1965–66 and devoted himself to the study of Western European and Soviet law. As practiced and taught at present, subjects such as Conflict of Laws and International Law are more comparative in nature than Comparative Law which is for the most part confined to area studies. New directions in comparative law are developed by books such as Jerome Hall, *Comparative Law and Social Theory* (Baton Rouge: Louisiana State University Press), 167 pp. (1963).

17. A summary of these can be found in EDWARD SHILS, Seeing It Whole, *The Times Literary Supplement*, 647–648 (July 28, 1966) and in the syllabus of a course 'The Comparative Study of National Societies' (G4058X) taught since 1965 by IMMANUEL WALLERSTEIN and TERENCE HOPKINS at Columbia University.

18. Sample publications in this field include:
C. ARNOLD ANDERSON and MARY JEAN BOWMAN, (eds.), *Education and Economic Development* (Chicago: Aldine Publishing Co.), 436 pp. (1965). COLE S. BREMBECK and EDWARD W. WEIDNER, *Education and Development in India and Pakistan* (East Lansing, Michigan: Michigan State University College of Education and International Programs), 221 pp. (1962). FRIEDRICH EDDING, *Ökonomie des Bildungswesens: Lehren und Lernen als Haushalt und als Investition* (Freiburg im Breisgau: Verlag Rombach), 440 pp. (1963). FREDERICK H. HARBISON and CHARLES A. MYERS, *Education, Manpower, and Economic Growth; Strategies of Human Resources Development* (New York: McGraw-Hill), 229 pp. (1964). FREDERICK H. HARBISON and

CHARLES A. MYERS, (eds.) *Manpower and Education; Country Studies in Economic Development* (New York: McGraw-Hill), 343 pp. (1965). ALEXANDER L. PEASLEE, Primary School Enrolments and Economic Growth, *Comparative Education Review*, 11, No. 1, 57–67 (1967). THEODORE SCHULTZ, *The Economic Value of Education*, (New York: Columbia University Press), 92 pp. (1963). INGVAR SVENNILSON, FRIEDRICH EDDING and LIONEL ELVIN, *Targets for Education in Europe in 1970*, 2, Policy Conference on Economic Growth and Investment in Education (Washington, D.C.), 125 pp. (1962). JOHN VAIZEY, *The Control of Education* (London: Faber and Faber), 263 pp. (1963). JOHN VAIZEY, *The Costs of Education* (London: Allen & Unwin), 256 pp. (1958). JOHN VAIZEY, *The Economics of Education* (New York: The Free Press of Glencoe, Inc.), 165 pp. (1962). MYRON WEINER, (ed.), *Modernization: The Dynamics of Growth* (New York: Basic Books, Inc.), 355 pp. (1966).

19. See also the discussion of the respective position of comparative education and development education by ANDREAS KAZAMIAS in Editorial, *Comparative Education Review*, 7, No. 3, 217–218 (1964) and by JOHN SINGLETON in Editorial, *Comparative Education Review*, 9, No. 3, 249–252 (1965).

20. The following are sample publications in international education:
FREDERICK C. BARGHOORN, *The Soviet Cultural Offensive: The Role of Cultural Diplomacy in Soviet Foreign Policy* (Princeton: Princeton University Press), 353 pp. (1960). FREDERICK C. BARGHOORN, *The Soviet Image of the United States: A Study in Distortion* (New York: Harcourt, Brace & World), 297 pp. (1950). GEORGE S. COUNTS, *American Education Through the Soviet Looking Glass* (New York: Bureau of Publications, Teachers College, Columbia University), 48 pp. (1951). CORA DuBOIS, *Foreign Students and Higher Education in the United States* (Washington, D.C.: American Council on Education), 221 pp. (1956). DENISE KANDEL and GERALD LESSER, *Parental Relationships of Adolescents in the United States and Denmark*, Harvard University, Center for Research and Development in Educational Differences, Unpublished. W. H. C. LAVES and C. A. THOMSON, *UNESCO, Purpose, Progress, Prospects* (Bloomington, Indiana: Indiana University Press), 469 pp. (1957). RICHARD I. MILLER, *United Nations' Trusteeship System and Educational Advancement*, Ed.D. dissertation (New York: Teachers College, Columbia University), 287 pp. (1958). CHARLES W. MORRIS, *Varieties of Human Value* (Chicago: University of Chicago Press), 208 pp. (1958). FILMER S. C. NORTHROP, *The Meeting of East and West: An Inquiry Concerning World Understanding* (New York: The Macmillan Co.), 531 pp. (1946). FRIEDRICH SCHNEIDER, *Geltung und Einfluss der deutschen Pädagogik im Ausland* (Munich: R. Oldenbourg), 358 pp. (1943). ROBERT SARGENT SHRIVER, *Point of the Lance* (New York: Harper & Row, Publishers), 240 pp. (1964). HILDA TABA, *Cultural Attitudes and International Understanding*, Occasional Paper No. 5 (New York: Institute of International Education), 84 pp. (1953). THOMAS PERRY THORNTON, (ed.), *The Third World in Soviet Perspective* (Princeton: Princeton University Press), 355 pp. (1964). J. R. USEEM, *Western-Educated Man in India: A Study of His Social Roles and Influence* (New York: Dryden Press), 237 pp. (1955). J. WATSON and R. LIPPITT, *Learning Across Cultures; A Study of Germans Visiting America* (Ann Arbor, Michigan: University of Michigan), 205 pp. (1955).

BEATRICE B. WHITING, (ed.), *Six Cultures, Studies of Child Rearing* (New York: John Wiley & Son), 1017 pp. (1963). All studies published in Minneapolis by the University of Minnesota Press: R. L. BEALS and N. D. HUMPHREY, *No Frontier to Learning: The Mexican Student in the United States*, 148 pp. (1957). J. BENNETT, H. PASSIN and R. K. MacKNIGHT, *In Search of Identity: The Japanese Overseas Scholar in America and Japan*, 369 pp. (1958). RICHARD D. LAMBERT and MARVIN BRESSLER, *Indian Students on an American Campus*, 122 pp. (1956). RICHARD T. MORRIS, *The Two-Way Mirror: National Status in Foreign Students' Adjustment*, 215 pp. (1960). FRANKLIN SCOTT, *The American Experience of Swedish Students: Retrospect and Aftermath*, 129 pp. (1956). WILLIAM H. SEWELL and OLUF M. DAVIDSEN, *Scandinavian Students on an American Campus*, 134 pp. (1961).

METHODOLOGY OF COMPARATIVE EDUCATION

C. Arnold Anderson

This article recommends a more empirical approach to research in comparative education and urges the collection of better data. The writer discusses the construction of models or typologies in education, the use of hypotheses, and the difficulties and potentialities of the field.

INTEREST in comparing educational systems, which enlisted the efforts of educational scholars and statesmen a century ago, bids fair in our day to become an academic fashion. Clamorous discontent with the operations of present-day schools in nearly every nation supplies much of the impetus for the present revival of comparative studies. What is more natural than to believe that in some other country the shortcomings of our own schools have been avoided? And through the services of Unesco and the International Bureau of Education it has become easier to examine educational practices around the world.

It is the aim of the serious scholars in this field to discipline the speculations of their more vocal associates. Belatedly education has become an active area of investigation for all the social sciences. An integration between education and the social sciences is emerging as systematic comparison makes use of today's more mature social science methods to add greater rigor to these inquiries. On the level of policy, the end of colonialism and a world-wide passion for economic development are stimulating a fresh appraisal of what

REPRINTED FROM *International Review of Education*, 7 (1961), 1–23, by permission of the author. © 1962 by C. Arnold Anderson.

education does or might do towards enhancing the contribution of the human factor.

Enthusiasm alone, unfortunately, does not bring forth scholarship, nor do heaped-up facts make a science. Anyone who follows the flood of articles and books on comparative education must ask whether today's more general concern with these questions has yielded commensurably deeper insight than Stowe or Arnold provided. Too many writers are using archaic tools for shaping the larger supplies of facts into generalizations. Yet signs of growing maturity of scholarship are not lacking.

I would contend that we do not need some novel method to refine the data but only application of dependable social research techniques guided by more appropriate and acute questions. Methods for comparative study have been undergoing refinement in several disciplines. There remain genuine difficulties, to be sure, and in so complex a field as education we must contrive strategies that balance technical refinement with theoretic subtlety, always tempered by recognition of the serviceability of even approximate answers.

I. Contrasting Conceptions of Comparative Education

Two broad but complementary approaches have been espoused since the earliest writing on comparative education; each writer tends to favor one or the other. One group of investigators confine their attention largely to strictly educational data, treating education as if it were an autonomous social system. For example, the scope of compulsory attendance laws is related to levels of literacy; variations in curricula are examined to see why pupils drop out of school; teachers' methods are correlated with pupil achievement. These sorts of correlation are indispensable for comparing educational systems.

The second approach relates traits of educational systems to other features of society; much of this type of research has naturally been carried out by non-educators. One may, for example, relate levels of urbanization to secondary enrollments or changes in laborers' incomes to persistence of their children in school, to use simple examples. This approach is no more comparative than the first one, but it does have the advantage of enlisting the cooperation of other social scientists and it does give greater attention to the social context of education.

1. *Intra-Educational Analysis*

This first perspective was implied in one of the definitions produced by a conference on "Comparative Education", held at the Unesco Institute for Education, Hamburg, in 1955: to identify the problems of education and their presuppositions and to examine these by cross-reference to the experience of other countries. This viewpoint does perhaps give undue latitude to description at the cost of generalization and it threatens to end in ever larger filing systems. Yet the task of correlation cannot be taken up until descriptive data have been codified. Though a vast amount of this kind of information is in the heads of a few educational statesmen, little of their knowledge is available to the rest of us.

This approach is particularly appropriate, as Connell [1] points out, for studying the interchange of educational elements and for tracing out the impact of a new practice upon other features of a school system. Thus one can plot the spread of external, centralized examining and observe the feedback upon curricula. This work resembles a plant explorer's search for viable specimens to be tried out at home. Comparative education in its early days was indeed largely a search for assimilable ideas already exemplified in other systems. Such exploration is not limited to identifying solutions to familiar problems but can also suggest new questions (Holmes, Eckleberry).

Upon the foundation of these collections of "specimens" one may undertake the taxonomic ordering of many aspects of educational systems (Dottrens, Hochleitner). This sort of survey need not use complex statistical methods, though eventually complex factorial designs will be used. Guided by an educational theory that is broader than educational psychology, we can identify the implications of particular practices, for not all combinations of characteristics are possible in any given type of school system.

Many parallels to this first kind of comparative analysis can be found in other fields of scholarship. Different combinations of specialization and economic control entail different modes of resource allocation, income distribution, and production cycles. Certain patterns of family residence are associated with certain role patterns and kinship obligations. Some ways of arranging the interaction of co-workers in a factory diminish conflict. Certain types of electoral systems facilitate decisive outcomes while others foster splinter parties.

2. Educational-Societal Analysis

This second, interdisciplinary approach was also proposed at the 1955 Hamburg conference: to diagnose and study the problems and determinants of education and their implications in a given society and to interpret them in the light of parallel data from other societies. Connell speaks of examining practices which may be comparable from culture to culture. Havighurst stresses the study of actual and possible educational solutions for problems created by diverse underlying social conditions. Certainly each educational system has its present character, as Lauwerys puts it, "not only because it has developed in a certain manner, but also because it corresponds to and is adjusted to social realities". And it is this second approach that most fully meets Kandel's stipulation: analysis of the determining forces of educational systems.

Certainly we must use this second approach if we are serious about examining the "functions" of education. In this context one will assume a more reserved position about the degree to which educational features are transferable to other systems than one is likely to do when one uses what has been here termed the "intra-educational" approach.

[1] All works referred to by names of authors are to be found in the list of bibliographical references at the end of this article.

At the present time investigators seem unable to undertake comprehensive assessments of the interrelations between education and society and must be content to deal with more circumscribed problems. Thus in recent years there has been a flood of studies on social class selectivity in education and on the allocative functions of schools. There is at present a surge of interest in studying the relevance of education for economic development. A few political scientists are beginning to investigate political socialization and the significance of schools for the shaping of ruling elites.

Intra-educational and education-societal inquiries are complementary and not substitutes. The ultimate aim of comparative education, like that of any other analysis of the social world, is knowledge of causation—if so quaint a word may be tolerated. Ultimately it will have both practical and theoretical significance insofar as it succeeds in providing reliable maps for locating congruent educational practices appropriate to coping with the tasks laid upon schools by a society.

In its broadest sense, comparative education might be defined as crosscultural comparison of the structure, operation, aims, methods, and achievements of various educational systems, and the societal correlates of these educational systems and their elements.

II. WHAT WE CAN LEARN FROM THE OLDER COMPARATIVE DISCIPLINES

As White has argued, there are three points of view in the cultural disciplines: historical, functional, and evolutionary. Historians look at the whole network of circumstances in which a particular complex occurs at a particular time and place and at the particular circumstances associated with its modification. Functionalists focus upon patterns comprising abstracted social systems, exploring relationships of essentially undated and often timeless nature. The evolutionist, like the functionalist and unlike the historian, is a generalizer. He is interested in processes that emerge and develop through time, but his time is often undated and represents a variable through which the forms and functions that make up classes of events or systems undergo sequential modification.

It is not the aim of comparison to assemble a museum of social practices to enable idle observers to contemplate their wondrous variation. Neither an ethnographic survey nor an historical description is comparison, but either can provide the starting point for using comparison to identify patterns of relationship. At times comparison may enable the historian to identify and date, as when a philologist traces the filiation of languages. Artifact designs can be compared in order to determine relative dates and paths of diffusion. Comparison may be a substitute for documents; one could be persuaded that Latin did not descend from French without dated documents. But one would not normally use the comparative method for problems (as most of those in educational history) where documentation is abundant.

Extreme historicism as manifested in refusal to concede the possibility of ordered and repeated patterns of social change is being increasingly supplemented by conceptions of stages, levels, and types of development. In both theoretical investigation and in policy formation reliance is being placed increasingly upon models. Search for repetitive patterns leads toward the evolutionary conception and use of comparison; historical and comparative are not polar methods.

Comparative research assumes that study of one system will not suffice to reveal all the relationships within the given realm of phenomena. Human minds, not being omniscient, must explore variations in relationships under diverse conditions.

Just as extreme historicism is on the wane, the comparative method is also being freed from earlier assumptions of unilinear evolution; in Irving's words, "the use of a comparative method and an explanation in genetic terms are not necessarily related". Nevertheless, the contemporary reinvigoration of comparative research in several disciplines has been associated with a revival of social evolutionism in a new and more sophisticated version. In economics, the new interest in development has revived comparative economics and concepts of economic stages (Hoselitz). As those using the evolutionary approach become more adept at causal analysis, their work merges into a functional approach (Steward).

Comparison is a tool, not an end in itself. Beyond seeking schemes of stages and complex typologies, therefore, we use comparison to throw light on processes abstracted from time and even apart from conceptions of stages. Thus comparative philology revealed the principles of shifts in pronunciation, and from kinship analysis we learn about patterns of reciprocity and the influence of symmetrical and asymmetrical relationships upon group cohesion. One of the most important roles of comparison in functional analysis is its contribution to distinguishing stable relationships from erratic ones. Comparison does not oblige us to stress either likenesses or differences; where data are abundant and theory is mature, as Thrupp points out, "intensive comparison" weaves a subtle counterpoint between these extremes.

Indeed, when we speak of "comparative" education, the denotation is as much conventional as logical. Assessment of the merits of part versus whole learning would not be called comparative, for then the method would be coterminous with scientific method. By convention the comparative method deals with relations among complex systems. We can use two cases to test, for example, whether a stable political state can exist on the basis of a feudal order; but analysis may encompass successively larger numbers of details or of societies.

The comparative method is one of the numerous imperfect substitutes for experimentation. Ethnographers who pioneered in developing the method also discovered its hazards. We cannot put isolated examples together in sequences or combinations by uncontrolled imagination. Account must be taken of the surrounding milieus without committing the opposite fault of indulging in aesthetic contemplation of unique situations.

We cannot escape the tension between individualizing and generalizing points of view. We hear often that this is a false issue, but cursory reading of historiography impresses one with the stubborn adherence of historians to a "full-bodied" treatment and their suspicion of schematic approaches. The individualizer is impatient with "reckless generalization" and "unrealistic abstraction"; the generalizer casts out the mass of "insignificant detail" impeding his path to compact summaries. Comparison is logically impossible without abstraction, but it is nevertheless scientifically imperative if we are to rise above the particular.

Herskovits attacked comparison as "a denial of cultural reality . . . comparing facts, torn out of their cultural context, with little reference to meaning". Strict observation of this warning would make all social research wholly descriptive, for every instance would stand alone. A historian in actuality does tear facts from their context; only a trivial portion of relevant events are noticed; there is selection and abridgement. The historian's abstraction, we might say, selects from all events those needed to develop the plot of the story; this plot would not be changed by adding the omitted items. In the generalizing disciplines, however, abstraction does not omit "less important" events that are isomorphic with the included ones (as in history); rather, it deals only with certain perspectives or with certain aspects of phenomena: economic but not political, linguistic but not religious—commonly also neglecting habitation of time and place. Those "meanings" of French education that are truly unique are best left to the historian or essayist, but to talk in a comparative vein about French secondary education presupposes that there are parallels with Soviet or British practices.

It would be a timorous conception of comparative education to conceive of it as merely juxtaposing facts about French and Indian and Danish and American education. There can be no comparative education without looking at different systems, thus breaking down our provincialism, alerting ourselves to possibilities not to be found at home, and freeing ourselves from our traditional pieties. But this is only a beginning.

The purpose of comparative education is to go further, to deal with complex systems of correlations among educational characteristics and between these and traits of social structure, with little reference to the individuality of the societies from which our data were derived. By convention, resting on solid methodological grounds, comparative study involves correlation across the boundaries of societies—whether these societies represent different centuries in one area or spatially distinct societies and sub-societies. What Nadel says of co-variation applies also to comparison.

Now the method of co-variations presupposes three things. First, in a technical sense, it presupposes some preliminary hypothesis or suspicion as to the kind of correlation likely to prove relevant . . . Secondly, the method of co-variation implies the general postulate that social situations are not made up of random items, but of facts which hang together by some meaningful nexus or intrinsic fitness . . . My third point concerns the fact that the study of co-variations is bound up with judgments on the identity and difference of social facts . . . more specifically, with judgments on similarity and partial identity, the very concept of variations implying a sameness of facts which yet permits of some measure of difference.

Three sorts of correlations are steps on the road to comparison-in-depth, whether the data be qualitative or quantitative. We need, firstly, to identify patterns of relationships among various aspects of educational systems—illustrations of which were given above.

Secondly, we need to develop a typology of educational systems. This is one procedure for summarizing vast quantities of data that have already received a preliminary ordering in the first step. In the process, moreover, we will do some fresh thinking about the fundamental features of diverse educational systems—about how combinations of these features vary systematically with shifts in the key elements characterizing a system and with different overall levels of complexity or maturity. By thus compressing many patterns of data into simplified constructions we can pursue the third step more intensively and at a higher level of abstraction. We may then begin to understand better how education is related to types of economy or policy.

Thirdly, we need to display the relationships between various educational characteristics and associated sociological, economic, or other non-educational features. Along this road we will approach a more systematic knowledge of the functional implications of different patterns of education as well as the societal determinants of educational systems. There are two excellent models for this kind of comparative analysis: Murdoch's study of kinship and Udy's study of economic organization.

III. The Major Missing Link in Comparative Education

The gap at present existing in our fund of educational data is revealed when one turns the pages of a book on "comparative economics". The economist has a fund of indexes to the operations and the outcomes of many economies. We in comparative education have few data other than descriptive reports. Scholars always crave more and better data; this shortcoming is more acute in new fields. But comparative education is crippled especially by the almost total absence of information about the outcomes or products of educational systems. We are restricted for the most part to manipulating various independent variables without being able to relate these to definite dependent variables.

Enumerations of enrollments or graduates of various stages of schooling are crude indexes to extent of schooling, but they tell us little about the influence of schooling upon pupils. When classified by ethnic group, residence, or social class, such data tell more about the factors that affect the extent of schooling than about its results. That American youth receive more years of schooling than youth elsewhere tells us more about American society than it does about how our schools work.

This problem has two parts:1) we must identify goals or potential products of education and measure the extent of their realization in various societies; 2) we must factor out the part played by schools in these "products" of different social systems. The amount and quality of education is both a dependent variable, determined by other factors, and an independent variable in turn acting upon them, and through time upon itself.

Each society imprints its members distinctively, and there are additional variants by religion or social class. Even a tourist senses these imprints impressionistically. With some qualities we assume, at least tentatively, that we are observing specific outcomes of schooling; for other traits we would be quite uncertain how much influence should be attributed to schools. Of the first sort would be knowledge of arithmetic, and of the second, initiative; mechanical skills or music appreciation would be intermediate.

One may ask whether different educational systems have a common effect —such as lowering the age of marriage—even though that is not the specified goal of any system and might be deplored. One may ask to what extent different systems achieve a certain outcome, such as "correct" speech, that is a primary goal of some systems and a low priority aim of others. Or one may ask whether a particular school system is contributing, and in what degree, to achieving the ends viewed as most important by citizens of that society. In every instance some outcomes will be intended, some unintended and perhaps unwanted; intended outcomes may be forthcoming to an insufficient degree or not at all.

The distinction between manifest and latent functions (Merton) is related to but not identical with the distinction between intended and unintended outcomes. Manifest functions involve results that are generally recognized or believed to occur, and therefore include attainment of planned goals, but they may include also recognized but unanticipated results that were not goals. Latent functions or outcomes may be no less important and just as much (or as little) desired or approved when noticed, but they are not as often perceived to occur. What is a manifest function for one society may be a latent one somewhere else. This contrast in part reflects the degree to which goals are explicit, but it is also a reflection of other traits of the societies compared. For example, schooling that aims to inculcate social conformity may have the indirect (and undesired) latent effect of reducing willingness to take creative risks. Schools designed mainly to supply certain vocational skills may have the latent (undesired) effect of facilitating vertical mobility, as in Tsarist Russia. Wide diffusion of Bible reading may lay the (latent) mass base for higher economic productivity.

Another useful way of examining the results of education is to distinguish results at "levels" closer to or more remote from the educational process. An ultimate or high-level aim or value may be to raise productivity of the worker or the society. But between study in school and productivity in the factory there are intermediate ends: arithmetic skill, facility in foreign language, adeptness in locating information, reasoning ability. These latter traits are lower-level results and more universally manifest functions. Any given lower-level outcome may contribute to more than one "ultimate" end such as political intelligence or productivity. Other lower-level products, or a different combination of them, may be more contributory to a different "ultimate" end such as producing a cultural elite. Ends may be mutually reinforcing or inhibiting in varying degrees. The comparative educator cannot cut through this means-end maze in all directions; he will focus on those relationships most pertinent to educational policy or to evaluation of school outcomes. He should not, however, confine himself to examining only lower-level ends or only manifest functions.

It is the educator who must assess the more direct, lower-level outcomes of schooling and focus particularly upon intra-educational evaluations. It is his task to estimate what children exposed to different modes of schooling actually learn preliminary to deciding how much of this results directly from formal teaching. Our present indirect measures do not suffice; there are too many intervening variables between school operations and adult library usage or quality of radio programs. Sophisticated achievement testing must be employed to supply this missing link in comparative education. Despite all the arguments asserting that such data are not comparable between societies, until we have such data we cannot go much beyond description. And crude test scores must quickly be supplemented with measures of other skills such as comprehension of principles or application of knowledge to new situations (Bloom). In due course more subtle outcomes, such as social adjustment, can be evaluated. But we will have made one gigantic leap forward when we know how much learning of arithmetic or mother tongue is to be found among graduates of different school systems.

At present we use rubber rulers to compare school systems. One can learn little about one level of schooling by counting the numbers of people proceeding to the next level, for these ratios are equivocal with respect to performance at both levels. Impressionistic reports about graduates of schools in different societies are tantalizing (Sadler). English children master their mother tongue better than American children. French children are better "thinkers". American youth are especially adept at applying what they learn, while German children are disciplined to work. Even if these impressions are accurate, they mean very little because "children" in each of these assertions have a different referent, associated with various sorts of selection and differentiation. We must find the means for procuring definite cross-cultural measures of achievement, and for comparable groups, before we can interpret information about curricula or teaching methods. Only when we have these data can we begin to approach the task of identifying the influences of schools on political behavior, economic productivity, or leisure activities.

IV. A SCHEMATIC GUIDE TO ANALYSIS OF EDUCATIONAL-SOCIETAL RELATIONSHIPS

One of the foremost tasks of comparative education is to identify what education contributes, after partialling out other factors, to various traits of societies. Before imputing to schools an effect upon economic productivity we must disentangle education from physical-capital investment or extra-school socialization. We find it difficult to estimate the income yield from different amounts of schooling since much of the income-education correlation reflects the association of both with parental status or native ability. How much "life adjustment" training is a functional substitute for how much mathematics learned by what percentage of an age cohort, in determining productivity?

Indispensable in any attack on problems of this kind are data with regard to critical elements in the cause-effect interaction patterns, and use of techniques of analysis of co-variation. But problems of measurement and statistical techniques aside, the first and most basic element in analysis is necessarily the formulation of the hypotheses to be tested. In fact, selection of data and their manipulation in one way rather than another involves some set of assumptions. Breaking through the association patterns to "explain" requires hypotheses concerning causation, and their testing by examining association matrices —including the introduction of leads and lags (and sometimes their reversals). Formulation of effective research plans therefore requires specification of models or typologies that include hypotheses concerning interaction processes and their causal web or nexus. However complex, such models are inevitably abstractions, though they may begin with a few very simple elements to which more and more modifications are added to capture relevant aspects of the concrete reality.

It is my judgment that the most fruitful approach in formulating the basic framework of hypotheses is one that combines the evolutionary and functional approaches. This will be illustrated shortly. However, it may be helpful first to note briefly the reasons for discarding two alternatives: the means-end scheme and the Gestalt thesis.

In the familiar means-end scheme, education would appear as an intermediate link that is both an end and a means in turn. The fact that education is a means to multiple, and possibly in part conflicting, ends complicates the problem; but this complexity is inherent in the "reality" that we are exploring and is not a reason for discarding the means-end approach. Neither is the fact that diverse and multiple means may be involved in attaining education as a goal or an intermediate end. The real difficulties with this approach are two: that it tends to encourage a one-directional analysis, and that it rests too exclusively on the underlying notion of purposive action. The first of these difficulties could be overcome by extending the means-end concept to a circular or spiral scheme in which the final end becomes in turn a means that contributes to education as an intermediate end, and so on. Much more serious is the fact that this approach focuses too exclusively on purposive action; unplanned results and latent functions too easily escape notice.

Very different is the Gestalt conception of causal processes. Stating this approach in an extreme form, everything affects and depends on everything else and all the time. Instead of a scheme focusing on selected directions of interaction among societal variables, all interconnections are multidimensional. Although such an approach has theoretical completeness in that ultimately all things are undoubtedly related to all others, it ends up in being no theory at all. From such a mixture it is impossible to get pragmatic leads for approaching even a single society, let alone comparing different societies. By a round-about route we have come back to something operationally, though not philosophically, similar to extreme historicism. We would be better served by a system that generates tentative hypotheses about salient interconnections, that differentiates the strong from the weak relationships, and the predominantly dependent from the predominantly independent variables in given interconnections.

The type of construction suggested here incorporates aspects of both the foregoing approaches, but is neither. Value attitudes are included as both dependent and independent variables in the causal nexus, but the stress on purpose that characterizes the means-end approach is set aside (or perhaps put in its "proper" place). Multi-directional influences are drawn in from the more Gestalt way of looking at things, but there is deliberate hypothecation concerning degrees and directions of influence. This may perhaps be clarified by outlining two highly simplified and contrasting typologies: Type A for a status-selective educational system, and referring only to the elite segment of the society, and Type B for an equalitarian, mass system. Other types could, of course, be constructed, embodying different sets of hypotheses, or modifications toward intermediate types that contained elements of both A and B in varying combinations and proportions.

Since our concern is with what affects education and how, and with how education affects other things, we may start with attributes of the educational system as a central focus. For Type A, which is concerned with the elite only in a status-selecting system, this central focus becomes the "amount and quality of education"; for Type B it is the "universality, amount, and quality of education". In both instances the content of education (curriculum, nature of emphasis, etc.) is also involved. And in both cases it is assumed that the amount of resources devoted to education conditions its quality and amount, though not in any direct way its content.

Turning to some of the further hypotheses involved in Type A, the following interconnections and directions of influence are hypothesized:

1. as the amount and quality of education received by the elite is raised, this exerts an influence that encourages devotion of more resources to education, etc.;

2. as the amount and quality of education is raised, so is what might be termed "high culture", which again contributes to stress on education as a value and so on;

3. more and better education within the elite (confined to the elite) enhances individual prestige and power status, which again encourages stress on education as a value and so on around the circle;

4. there is a two-way interaction between the content of education and "high culture";

5. the content of education contributes positively to enhancement of individual prestige and power status;

6. the initial income and wealth differential between the elite and the rest of society plays a relatively minor role, though it contributes positively when it exercises any influence on the amount of resources devoted to elite education. The amount and quality of education received need not exert a positive effect on the income and wealth differential; it could conceivably even exert a negative effect. And income and wealth may operate in either a positive or negative direction on attitudes stressing education as a value.

Setting aside the possibility of negative effects in interactions involving income and wealth differentials, the interconnections specified here would suggest a continuing upward spiral in the amount and quality of elite education. However, this is because we have not specified the nature of the functions involved, and we have excluded from the model any interaction between the elite and the rest of the society except as this is involved in "individual prestige and power status" (which is not the same thing as status of the elite as a whole). If each of the functions is assumed to be characterized by diminishing returns, which is undoubtedly applicable at least to the prestige and status variable, the model would predict a slowing down of the rise in amount and quality of education and of all the other variables. Thus overall, a construct involving a logistic, ogive, or Gompertz growth pattern could be hypothesized.

The evolutionary-functional character of this typology, or model, should be immediately evident. It is not merely a timeless association matrix; it involves implied sequential processes even though they are not specifically dated. It implies also functional elements in the processes and influences dealt with.

Type B, the equalitarian system, may be constructed in a similar way. Though the minimal number of variables that must be considered even in an outline sketch is much larger, our summary must be brief. The amount of resources devoted to education is assumed to depend primarily upon high economic productivity and stress on education as a value. An increase in the extent and quality of education will in turn increase the stress on education as a value, will raise economic productivity directly, and will advance technology which further raises economic productivity. The content of education supports this technological and economic productivity effect. Furthermore, the more universal the education, and the greater its amount, the more will it support equalitarianism as value and practice, and this in turn strengthens the value placed on universal education. It is hypothesized also that there is a positive, but weak, impact of rising educational levels and quality on "political intelligence" and that the latter has a positive effect on education as a value. "High culture" occupies a minor place in this type, in contrast to its importance in Type A. While a rise in the extent and quality of education may have some positive influence on "high culture", no such hypothesis seems justified so far as content (aside from quality) is concerned. To round out this model, three other important variables may be introduced: (1) a political history favorable to equalitarianism and widespread "political intelligence", which operates through the latter, through content of education, and by enhancing (2); (2) favorable economic motivations and initiative. These in turn contribute to raising economic productivity and technology, the educational system aside. Thus, through their effect on productivity they facilitate devotion of further resources to education. And they contribute to (3), the strengthening of economic-instrumental views of the value of education. This third variable, influenced also by high economic productivity, in turn raises the stress on the importance of education and hence the efforts and resources put into the educational system.

As in Type A, this second model would imply a continuously rising sequential spiral, but again no mathematical functions for the processes or influences have been specified. A reasonable suggestion in this case might be a rising and then a falling impact of economic productivity on the economic-instrumental view of education, associated with a falling and then a rising importance of the relationships in which "high culture" is involved: this would entail a developmental change in the effects of both education and economic levels on higher culture and the content of education.

These models, like any others, can be criticized for what they include and for what they omit. But this is not the point. They constitute a preliminary attempt to present in abbreviated form a systematic set of hypotheses derived from a combination of empirical observations (at a crude level) and deductive reasoning. This kind of formulation can help guide research whether the hypotheses involved turn out to be correct or not. Their testing requires comparative data and application of appropriate techniques in analysis of co-variation. Thus two methodological approaches are involved: the use of typologies and analysis of co-variation.

Most typologies are inherently static in that they focus on stable patterns of relationships. Even though the two types presented here implicitly embody sequential influences and development through time, they are still to some degree static in that basic features of the system remain unaltered. Specification of the shapes of the functions linking the various variables as the system moves through time are a step in the direction of dynamizing such a model; the comments concerning economic-instrumental emphasis in education and "high culture" in Type B provide an illustration. But such modifications are only a small step unless the emphasis is shifted to the structure of such functions, including possible associated reversals in the nature or direction of influence that can substantially alter the system. Basically, there are three ways of using typologies to facilitate analysis of developments through time. One of these is clearly illustrated by the types presented, with their implications of rising quantities and qualities of education and associated variables within a given abstracted system of relationships. The second resembles what economists have termed "comparative statics". Starting from models that emphasize tendencies toward one or another equilibrium state, one may note deviations from such equilibrating tendencies and infer the kind of change that these disequilibrating forces are likely to bring about or the other types toward which a system in transition is moving. Third, typologies that focus on processes of change may be constructed.

It is worth pointing out that multiple correlations are not merely ways of explaining more and more of the variance. Factors that in zero-order correlations appear to have a positive effect, may turn out in a more complex matrix to have a negative effect, or vice versa. How many commonly accepted false assumptions concerning the nature of the interactions between education and other societal traits will be refuted in this way remains to be seen when we have conducted the necessary comparative studies.

V. METHODOLOGICAL COMMENTS ON ILLUSTRATIVE PROBLEMS IN COMPARATIVE EDUCATION

The remaining pages will consider some of the difficulties and potentials of research in comparative education in relation to a few broad aspects of education.

1. *Identifying potentially critical intra-educational relationships: the school as a social group.* An agency for drilling children in a few basic skills—such has been the traditional conception of the primary school throughout most of the Western world. Since children from privileged families customarily branched off into middle schools leading toward university, elementary schools often resembled reform schools for the "lower orders". Secondary schools displayed the companionship of a community, and discipline was self-justifying, if rigorous. Stimulated both by the heterogeneity of elementary classes and by the results of psychological research, primary schools adopted more relaxed methods, which gradually crept up to the secondary schools as they became mass enterprises. Numerous questions concerning the nature and effects of interaction processes in these various settings call for comparative analysis.

Teacher-pupil relations take on distinctive moods, which in turn influence the learning process. Presumably classroom climates affect children's attitudes toward their subjects, toward learning, and toward the place of learned men in society, but in what ways and to what extent? How are these effects modified by external examinations, patterns of selectivity in the schools, societal expectations for different types of school, and forms of social class etiquette? It is easy to generalize and to note paradoxes. Americans think of their society as strongly competitive, yet strict grading in school courses seems to be less emphasized than in societies with more stabilized status systems. English society, by contrast, is honeycombed with "go slow" tactics, but it has accepted a ruggedly selective school system. European students, presumably with more rigorous educational backgrounds, frequently find American graduate schools very difficult. These sorts of impressionistic generalizations need to be tested and explored by replicated group dynamics experiments.

Teachers are not solely instructors but serve also as models for identification, and herein lies an important latent function of schools. Attitudes toward teachers carry over into adult intellectual habits, cultural tastes, and vocational aims. This relationship explains why only part of the talent of even capable pupils is aroused (Rossi). Since, however, it is so difficult to demonstrate just how teachers influence learning in the narrow sense, it is not surprising that we have made so little progress in delineating these more subtle relationships or in tracing out their principal variations from one society to another.

Recent research by Coleman and others on "school climates" indicates that in similar communities or at equivalent levels of financial support some schools encourage high performance and intellectual zeal. Patterns of student leadership play a key role, yet "good" patterns take root quickly under the stimulation of charismatic teachers; they can be torn down as quickly if the most admired teachers emphasize athletics. Diversity among schools in these respects in the United States reflects local control, absence of external examinations, and the power of parents; similar, if less extreme, variations apparently are to be found in other countries.

Some readers may think it pointless in a discussion of methodology to mention this elusive kind of problem about which ignorance is almost total when elsewhere I underline the need for humdrum quantitative data on pupil attainment. But learning goes on in particular classrooms, and interpretation of results from parallel achievement testing must be in terms of teaching situations. Variations in classroom atmosphere will almost certainly be found to reflect many traits of school systems and to be reflected in the pupils who emerge from the schools.

2. *Problems of non-comparability and factor isolation: schools as social and psychological selection mechanisms.* It is difficult to avoid the indictment of superficial generalization from non-comparable data and to abnegate our duty by awaiting the day when data will be adequate. But in any absolute sense, this day can never come. Meanwhile, problems are urgent and policy decisions will be made on the basis of available information; approximate solutions must be utilized. We shall never escape from the task of isolating particular factors amidst heterogeneous evidence about schools and societies scattered over the world.

The educational literature in recent decades is filled with publications on the common theme that in even the most democratic nations education beyond the elementary years remains a luxury. In no society do social classes, religions, or ethnic groups enjoy statistical parity in university, or even secondary, attendance.

For a few countries we have abundant historical information on the changes in school selectivity (Floud, Bereday). Research on the contemporary situation reveals how difficult it is to secure comparable data about equivalent schools. But the road to more precise research has been laid down. There seem to be clear parallels between countries in the ways children from different levels of home select their curricula (Stephenson). The distribution of university students by social origin has been delineated for several countries by the editors of the 1950 Yearbook of Education and the present writer. Children from upper strata predominate nearly everywhere, but this social profile is unique in each country. To be sure, opportunities for lower-class youth are greater in some countries, but the degree of privilege or handicap for any stratum reflects particular national traditions and social structures. In one country opportunities are relatively good for farmers' children but poor for laborers' children, while in another nation the situation is reversed; in some places both groups have comparatively good chances, elsewhere both are handicapped. There are similar variations for other groups such as businessmen. Nor does the social composition of universities respond in some simple fashion to rising enrollments or to changes in the economy. These diversities are clues for a more penetrating functional analysis of higher education.

A major contribution of these studies is the establishment of a continuum to which the profile of social selection in still other nations may be related. Also a broad congruence between these patterns of educational selection and other features of society has been observed. Through these studies, and related inquiries, we are learning more about the culture-bearing role of educated families in all complex societies.

Efforts to build upon this evidence about educational opportunity in order to evaluate the role of education in social mobility are frustrated by lack of data. From the little evidence available one infers that above a certain degree of diffusion of schooling, the influence of schooling upon maintenance or change of individual social status diminishes. Children from workers' homes in the United States have distinctively good educational opportunities, yet we do not find a commensurate increase in vertical mobility (Lipset and Bendix). One infers from inadequate evidence that both the correlation between schooling and intelligence and that between schooling and occupation is higher in Europe. Since the latter may reflect a higher initial correlation between parental occupation and schooling, it does not necessarily imply a greater role of schooling in mobility. In any case, irrespective of the contribution of schooling to individual mobility, the aggregate effect of a population's training upon productivity may be enormous. The macro-functions of education are quite distinct from the micro-functions.

There are further complexities lurking in this problem, as Floud has pointed out. When schools are operated to provide deliberate selection among children with a view to their later occupations, a society may succeed in making "all careers open to talent" and in ending educational discrimination. But this outcome is quite different from one in which schools aim to insure the optimum personal development of children, whatever their potentials in degree or kind. In the first situation the correlation of intelligence with years of schooling would be closer than in the second situation, as would the correlation between amount of schooling and adult occupation. Education without social class selection, it is clear, conceals additional variants of selection, each having its distinctive societal function.

It is in this area of research that the potentialities of enlisting economists in the work of comparative education become exciting. Thereby our functional analyses of education take on more depth and become more adapted to guiding policy decisions.

3. *Norms, functions, and evaluations of the performance of education in the socio-economic system.* There are two reasons for coming to closer grips with the task of comparing the ideological components in educational systems. If one views ideologies as epiphenomenal, lacking significant causal force, we must identify this component in order to separate such functionless material from the "real" factors in education. On the opposite assumption that philosophical assumptions are the distinguishing features of an educational system, it becomes even more essential to devise techniques for analyzing this cluster of influences. Indeed, it is widely believed that comparison cannot be comprehensive because each educational system derives its coherence mainly from its particular ideals.

As Hans has taken so much care to demonstrate, there is an intimate connection between the development of the nation-state and schools. Economic integration among regions and the demands of citizenship press for uniformity in education. The modern nation and the social cadre of ideologues arose together, and the latter have been prime movers in expansion of school systems.

In the Western world, and elsewhere by diffusion, conceptions of nationhood became linked to individual conceptions of self-identity, which form so salient a component in philosophies of education. Though nations emerged from a congeries of prior groups—orders or estates, guilds, classes, regions, and religions—these groups continued as major themes in national life. Out of their struggles emerged the familiar ideologies of the past century revolving around the association of schooling with intellect, intellect with social class, and class with education.

Industrialization and urbanization have strengthened the traditional notion that schooling must play a central role in economic development. Nowhere has it been possible to view this task clearly because of the confusions of information and attitude concerning the distribution of abilities among social strata, uncertainties as to how knowledge becomes practice, and disputes about the importance of knowledge as against personality.

That there is no one-to-one correspondence of these ideologies with variations in societal structure is clear. Soviet educators oppose the idea of "native intelligence" and testing, an opposition related to, if not fore-ordained by, Marxian theory. But Soviet pedagogues tend to use "laziness" where others use "stupidity". There are few distinctive Soviet educational practices, as distinct from ideologies. In the United States emphasis upon practicality and suspicion of intellectuals led to diffuse and indefinite conceptions of the function of schooling. This ideological vagueness has contributed to American casualness about the contradiction of large variations in educational opportunity and our equalitarian ethos. In large measure we have viewed education as a "consumption good" to be widely distributed, without being too concerned as to the rationale for its provision or distribution. In few other countries is the correlation of social status and speech, for example, so loose as here.

A first step in comparative analysis of educational ideologies would be simply to map them. We could exploit the fund of public opinion poll data to obtain a preliminary survey of expectations about education in different countries. Combining these data with content analysis of views among legislators, leaders of opinion, and educational philosophers, would help us to relate contrasts in school systems to differences in aims. One notices that arguments used to justify or attack school programs take both similar and different patterns in various countries, but this knowledge is inchoate.

These findings might then be related to the quantitative measures of norms, as suggested by Fernig and Idenburg. When we have correlated ideological variations with observed differences in the accomplishments of schools, we can then go on to relate those conclusions to data on social structures and develop a more refined functional interpretation of education.

Floud contrasted two manifest functions of schools: direct selection for mobility and individual development. Whether latent or manifest, selection of individuals for vertical mobility is always an important function of schools (Sorokin). Traditional liberal education has always been a kind of vocational training, and the idea that mass education aids economic development is not a new one. Perhaps the status functions of schools have been more salient in Europe than in the "colonies", where schools have been expected to devote much of their effort to cultural assimilation of "internal barbarians". Corresponding activities in Europe did not usually wear an ethnic cloak. At the upper end of the cultural scale, it has been less acceptable in the United States to regard universities as preservers of a treasured and esoteric heritage. We have defended higher education more in terms of practical results, though we have usually been quite uncertain as to what the connection was. And American schools have consciously raised aspirations for material living, whereas in Europe they tended rather to preserve traditional levels and patterns of consumption.

Americans residing in Europe sense that citizens there have roots in their country. Americans seem often to have been heaped up from everywhere by chance; they have had to build consensus rather than inherit it. This is undoubtedly part of the reason American schools so often serve as a collective representation for the local community—and why athletics form a nucleus for this loyalty. In Europe, individual secondary schools and universities tend to be distinctive communities, each being a collective representation for a section of the society, for a class or a religion.

In comparing European with American higher education, one always comes up against the problem of identifying equivalents, in the resolution of which a distinction between explicit and implicit effects may assist. Is a "maturity examination" comparable with completing an American junior college? If measured by average knowledge of language, history, or mathematics one would render a different decision than if measured in terms of skill in applying knowledge "in life". European certificates would carry more prestige. Suppose, however, one correlated amount of schooling with relative income or vocations of graduates. In some degree this would give us a functional index; yet in other respects the "product mix" of various levels of schooling within the economy differs considerably among societies. To go further and take account of subtle outcomes like etiquette or social maturity of graduates raises problems we cannot handle yet. How, finally, does informal education relate to formal schooling in various societies?

The basic elements in a functional approach are not abstruse, and this is not a recent addition to social research (Bredemeier). But it does offer one promising way to develop more refined comparative evaluations of educational systems. It alerts us to the risk of confusing policies with accomplishments. It spurs us to search for concealed and indirect consequences of various educational practices. It can improve our understanding of the devious interactions between educational and other social forces. Emphasis upon functions, both manifest and latent, reveals many similarities beneath the apparently incomparable surface contrasts among educational systems.

BIBLIOGRAPHICAL REFERENCES

ANDERSON, C. A., "The Social Status of University Students in Relation to Type of Economy". *Transactions III World Congress of Sociology*, 1956, V: pp. 51–63.

BEREDAY, G. Z. F., "A Comparative Approach to Social Status in English Education" in: *Essays in Honor of Robert Ulich*. Cambridge, Mass.: Harvard University Press 1958, pp. 121–39.

BLOOM, B. S., *Taxonomy of Educational Objectives*. New York: Longmans 1954.

BREDEMEIER, H. C., "The Methodology of Functionalism". *American Sociological Review* 20: 1955, pp. 173–80.

COLEMAN, J. S., "The Adolescent Subculture and Student Achievement". *American Journal of Sociology* 65: 1960, pp. 337–47.

CONNELL, W. F., "The Methodology of Comparative Education" (unpublished).

DOTTRENS, R., "Pédagogie Expérimentale, Pédagogie Comparée, et Plans d'Etude". *International Review of Education, Festschrift for Pedro Rosselló*. Hamburg 1959, pp. 64–72.

ECKLEBERRY, R. H., "Comparative Education Once More". *School and Society* 33: 1931, p. 303.

FERNIG, L., "The Global Approach to Comparative Education". *International Review of Education, Festschrift for Pedro Rosselló*. Hamburg 1959, pp. 87–99.

FLOUD, J., "Education and Social Class in the Welfare State" in: Judges, A.V., ed., *Looking Forward in Education*. London: Faber 1955, Ch. 2.

HANS, N., *Comparative Education*. London: Routledge 1949.

HAVIGHURST, R. J., Unpublished lecture.

HERSKOVITS, M. J., *Cultural Anthropology*. New York: Knopf 1955, p. 438.

HOCHLEITNER, R. D., "Utilizacion de la Educacion Comparada en la Planeamiento Integral de la Education". *International Review of Education, Festschrift for Pedro Rosselló*. Hamburg 1959, pp. 100–10.

HOLMES, B., "The Problem Approach in Comparative Education". *Comparative Education Review* 2 (1): 1958, pp. 3–8.

HOSELITZ, B. F., "Theories of Stages of Economic Growth". *Theories of Economic Growth*. Glencoe: Free Press 1960, Ch. 6.

IDENBURG, PH. J., "Die Bedeutung der Statistik für die vergleichende Erziehungswissenschaft". *International Review of Education, Festschrift for Pedro Rosselló*. Hamburg 1959, pp. 73–86.

IRVING, J. A., "The Comparative Method and the Nature of Human Nature". *Philosophy and Phenomenological Research* 9: 1948, p. 548.

KANDEL, I. L., "The Methodology of Comparative Education". *International Review of Education, Festschrift for Pedro Rosselló*. Hamburg 1959, pp. 14–24.

LAUWERYS, J. A., "Methoden der vergleichenden Pädagogik". *Bildung und Erziehung* 11: 1958, p. 71.

LIPSET, S. M. and BENDIX, R., *Social Mobility in Industrial Society*. Berkeley: University of California 1959, Ch. 2.

MERTON, R. K., *Social Theory and Social Structure*. Glencoe: Free Press 1957, Ch. 1.

MURDOCH, G. P., *Social Structure*. New York: Macmillan 1949.

NADEL, S. F., *Foundations of Social Anthropology*. Glencoe: Free Press 1951, p. 224.

ROSSI, P. H., "Social Restraints on the Development of Talent among Middle and Upper Class Youth" (Unpublished).

SADLER, M., *The Outlook in Secondary Education*. New York: Teachers College 1930, p. 4.

SOROKIN, P. A., *Social and Cultural Mobility*. Glencoe: Free Press 1960.

STEPHENSON, R. M., "Stratification, Education, and Occupational Orientation". *British Journal of Sociology* 9: 1958, pp. 42–50.

STEWARD, J. A., "Evolution and Process". *Anthropology Today*. Chicago: University of Chicago 1953, pp. 314–24.

THRUPP, S. L., "The Role of Comparison in the Development of Economic Theory". *Journal of Economic History* 17: 1957, pp. 554–70.

UDY, S. H., JR., *Organization of Work*. New Haven: HRAF Press 1959.

UNESCO. *Comparative Education*. Hamburg: Unesco Institute for Education 1955.

WHITE, L. A., "Evolutionary Stages, Progress, and the Evaluation of Cultures". *Southwestern Journal of Anthropology* 3: 1947, pp. 165–92.

Yearbook of Education 1950, Section VI. London: Evans Brothers.

FORMS OF CONTROLLED INQUIRY

Ernest Nagel

It is by means of the controlled experiment that the physical sciences have gained much of their power to explain phenomena. The social sciences, Nagel argues, have an analogous alternative, "controlled investigation." Here, though the researcher cannot manipulate at will the variables under study, he can investigate systematically and scientifically the variety of cases provided by the real world.

O N THE assumption that the paramount aim of theoretical social science is to establish general laws which can serve as instruments for systematic explanation and dependable prediction, many students of social phenomena have tried to account for the relative paucity of reliable laws in their disciplines. We shall examine some of the reasons that have been suggested. The reasons to be discussed call attention to difficulties confronting the social sciences, either because of certain alleged distinctive features inherent in the subject matter studied, or because of certain supposed consequences of the fact that the study of society is part of its own subject matter. These difficulties are generally not mutually independent, so that the issues they raise do not always differ sharply. It is nevertheless convenient to list and examine the problems separately.

Perhaps the most frequently mentioned source of difficulty is the allegedly narrow range of possibilities for controlled experiments on social subject matter. Let us first state the difficulty in the form it receives when a very strict sense is associated with the term "controlled experiment." In a controlled experiment, the experimenter can manipulate at will, even if only within limits, certain features in a situation (often designated as "variables" or "factors") which are assumed to constitute the relevant conditions for the occurrence of the phenomena under study, so that by repeatedly varying some of them (in the ideal case, by varying just one) but keeping the others constant, the observer can study the effects of such changes upon the phenomenon and discover the constant relations of dependence between the phenomenon and the variables. Controlled experiment thus involves not only directed changes in variables that can be reliably identified and distinguished from other variables, but also the reproduction of effects induced by such changes upon the phenomenon under study.

However, experiment in this strict sense can apparently be performed at best only rarely in the social sciences, and perhaps never in connection with any phenomenon which involves the participation of several generations and large numbers of men. For social scientists do not usually possess the power to

REPRINTED FROM *The Structure of Science* by Ernest Nagel, pp. 450–459, © 1961 by Harcourt, Brace & World, Inc., and reprinted with their permission.

institute experimentally designed modifications into most social materials that are of scientific interest. Moreover, even if such power were theirs, and moral scruples did not stand in the way of subjecting human beings to various changes with unforeseeable but possibly injurious effects upon the lives of men, two important problems would arise concerning any experiments they might perform. The exercise of power to modify social conditions for experimental purposes is evidently itself a social variable. Accordingly, the manner in which such power is exercised may seriously compromise the cognitive significance of an experiment, if that use of power affects the outcome of the experiment to an unknown degree. Furthermore, since a given change introduced into a social situation may produce (and usually does produce) an irreversible modification in relevant variables, a repetition of the change to determine whether or not its observed effects are constant will be upon variables that are not in the same initial conditions at each of the repeated trials. In consequence, since it may thus be uncertain whether the observed constancies or differences in the effects are to be attributed to differences in the initial states of the variables or to differences in other circumstances of the experiment, it may be impossible to decide by experimental means whether a given alteration in a social phenomenon can be rightly imputed to a given type of change in a certain variable.[1] In addition to all this, the scope of experimentation in the social sciences is severely limited by the circumstance that a controlled experiment can be performed only if it is possible to produce repeatedly observable modifications in the phenomenon studied—a possibility that seems clearly out of the question for those social phenomena which are ostensibly nonrecurrent and historically unique (such as the rise of modern industrial capitalism, or the unionization of American labor during the New Deal).

These claims as to the restricted scope of controlled experiment in the social sciences raise many important issues. However, discussion of them will be confined for the present to the following two, others being reserved for later examination: (1) Is controlled experimentation a *sine qua non* for achieving warranted factual knowledge, and in particular for establishing general laws? and (2) Is there in fact only a negligible possibility in the social sciences for controlled empirical procedure?

1. Inquiries in which controlled experiments can be instituted possess familiar and undeniably great advantages. It is indeed unlikely that various branches of science (e.g., optics, chemistry, or genetics) could have achieved their present state of advanced theoretical development without systematic experimentation. Nevertheless, this conjecture is obviously unsound if extended to all domains of inquiry in which comprehensive systems of explanation have

---

[1] This difficulty also arises in sciences dealing with nonhuman materials. It can usually be overcome in these domains by employing a fresh sample in each repeated trial, the new samples being homogeneous in relevant respects with the initial one. In the social sciences the problem cannot be resolved so easily, because even if an adequate supply of samples is available, they may not be sufficiently alike in pertinent features.

been established. Neither astronomy nor astrophysics is an experimental science, even if each employs many assumptions that are patently based on the experimental findings of other disciplines. Although during the eighteenth and nineteenth centuries astronomy was rightly held to be superior to all other sciences in the stability of its comprehensive theory and in the accuracy of its predictions, it certainly did not achieve this superiority by experimentally manipulating celestial bodies. Moreover, even in branches of inquiry nowhere near the theoretical level of astronomy (e.g., geology, or until relatively recently embryology), lack of opportunity for controlled experiment has not prevented scientists from arriving at well-grounded general laws. It is in consequence beyond dispute that many sciences have contributed, and continue to contribute, to the advancement of generalized knowledge despite severely limited opportunities for instituting controlled experiments.

However, every branch of inquiry aiming at reliable general laws concerning empirical subject matter must employ a procedure that, if it is not strictly controlled experimentation, has the essential logical functions of experiment in inquiry. This procedure (we shall call it "controlled investigation") does not require, as does experimentation, either the reproduction at will of the phenomena under study or the overt manipulation of variables; but it closely resembles experimentation in other respects. Controlled investigation consists in a deliberate search for contrasting occasions in which the phenomenon is either uniformly manifested (whether in identical or differing modes) or manifested in some cases but not in others, and in the subsequent examination of certain factors discriminated in those occasions in order to ascertain whether variations in these factors are related to differences in the phenomena—where these factors as well as the different manifestations of the phenomenon are selected for careful observation because they are assumed to be relevantly related. From the perspective of the logical role which empirical data play in inquiry, it is clearly immaterial whether the observed variations in the assumed determining factors for observed changes in the phenomenon are introduced by the scientist himself, or whether such variations have been produced "naturally" and are simply found by him—provided that in each case the observations have been made with equal care and that the occurrences manifesting the variations in the factors and in the phenomenon are alike in all other relevant respects. It is for this reason that experimentation is often regarded as a limiting form of controlled investigation, and that sometimes the two provisos are not even distinguished. It may indeed be the case that the second of the above two provisos can be satisfied more easily when experiments can be performed than when they cannot; and it may also be the case that, when experiment is feasible, relevant factors can be subjected to variations which are rarely if ever found to occur naturally, but which must nevertheless be obtained if general laws are to be established. These comments direct attention to matters of undoubtedly great importance in the conduct of inquiry, but they do not annul the identity in logical function of controlled experiment and controlled investigation.

In short, although it is possible to make scientific headway without experiment, either controlled experimentation (in the narrow sense we have associated with this phrase) or controlled investigation (in the sense just indicated) appears to be indispensable. We shall say that an inquiry using one or the other of these two procedures is a "controlled empirical inquiry." [2]

2. In consequence, it becomes pertinent to ask whether in the social sciences the scope for procedures that either are strictly experimental or have the same logical role as experiment is as close to the vanishing point as is frequently portrayed. The claim that this scope is quite small commonly rests on some misconceptions which we shall now briefly discuss.

a. Although John Stuart Mill was a foremost advocate in nineteenth-century England for employing the logical methods of the natural sciences in social inquiry, he was convinced that experimentation directed toward establishing general laws was not feasible in the social sciences. He held this view essentially because he saw no prospects for applying in these latter disciplines either his Method of Agreement or his Method of Difference, the two of his five "Methods of Experimental Inquiry" which were for him definitive of what it is to be an experiment. According to the Method of Agreement, two instances of a phenomenon are required that are unlike in *all* respects but one (which may then be identified as the "cause" or "effect" of the phenomenon); and according to the Method of Difference, two situations are required, the phenomenon being present in one and not in the other, that are otherwise alike in *all* respects but one (which may again be identified as the "cause" or "effect" of the phenomenon). Mill apparently took for granted that theoretically significant social experiments must be performed upon historically given societies in their entirety: and since he believed with obviously good reasons that no two such societies actually conform to the requirements of either of his two Methods, as well as that by no contrivance could they be made to do so, he denied the possibility of social experimentation. [3]

Mill's account of experimental method suffers from the serious defect that he underestimated if he did not ignore the crucial point that, since two situations are *never* either completely alike or completely unlike in *all but one* respect, his Methods are workable only within some framework of assumptions stipulating which features (or respects) of a situation are to count as the relevant ones.

But even if Mill's analysis is corrected on this point, his reasons for denying

[2] It is of some importance not to confuse what is frequently called "controlled (sensory) observation" with controlled empirical inquiry in the above sense. Observations are usually said to be "controlled" if they are not haphazard but are performed with care and are instituted for the sake of resolving some question and in the light of some conception concerning the requirements for reliable observation. Controlled observation in this sense is essential to both controlled experimentation and controlled investigation. However, controlled observation is only a necessary but not a sufficient condition for controlled empirical inquiry.

[3] Mill recommended what he called the "Concrete Deductive Method" as the appropriate one for social inquiry. According to this method, various consequences derived from some set of theoretical assumptions are verified by observation.

the possibility of social experimentation remain inconclusive. For his contention is based in part on the supposition that controlled experimentation (or for that matter, even controlled investigation) requires the occurrence of variation in just one (relevant) factor at a time—a notion that is commonly held but is nonetheless an oversimplified view of the conditions for competent empirical analysis. The supposition does indeed state an ideal of experimental procedure, often realized at least approximately. It is well to remember, however, that the question whether only a "single" factor is being varied in an experiment, or even what is to count as a "single" factor, are matters that depend on the antecedent assumptions underlying the experiment. It is beyond human power even in the most carefully run laboratory to eliminate completely variations in all but one circumstance of an experiment; and the point has already been emphasized that assumptions concerning the changes to be singled out as relevant are implicit in every inquiry. Furthermore, to illustrate the point that special assumptions may be involved in judging a factor to be a "single" one, although in many experiments changing the quantity (e.g., the number of grams) of chemically pure oxygen counts as a variation in a single factor, in other experiments this is not a satisfactory way of specifying what is a single factor because of the assumption, relevant in this second class of experiments but not in the first, that there are isotopes of oxygen. For, since the proportions in which these isotopes are contained in different quantities of chemically pure oxygen are not constant, varying the quantity of pure oxygen may significantly alter the proportions.

In any event, there are areas of inquiry in the natural sciences in which it is not possible to vary one at a time even the relevant and admittedly "single" factors in an experiment, but in which we are not thereby prevented from establishing laws. For example, in experiments on physicochemical systems in thermodynamical equilibrium it is not generally possible to vary the pressure exerted by a system without varying its temperature. It is nevertheless possible to ascertain what constant relations of dependence hold between these variables and other factors in the system, and what are the effects produced on the system by changes in just one of these variables. Moreover, modern statistical analysis is sufficiently general to enable us to cope with many situations in which variables do not vary one at a time, even in the case of phenomena for which theory is far less advanced than it is in physics or for which only techniques of controlled investigation but not of strict experimentation are available. For example, the size of the crop produced in a given cornfield is affected by both temperature changes and variations in the rainfall, though these factors cannot be varied independently. Nevertheless, statistical analysis of data on their simultaneous variations enables us to isolate the effects of rainfall upon crop yield from the effects of temperature. In short, the injunction that factors are to be varied one at a time represents a frequently desirable but by no means universally indispensable condition for controlled inquiry.

b. Accordingly, the field for controlled empirical inquiry into social phenomena is in principle much larger than unduly narrow conceptions of what is essential for such inquiry may lead one to suppose. But let us survey briefly the main forms in which controlled empirical study actually occurs in the social sciences.

i. Despite widespread claims that experimentation in the strict sense is not feasible, several types of experiments are in fact employed in the social sciences. One of them is the laboratory experiment, in essentials similar to laboratory experiments in the natural sciences. It consists of constructing an artificial situation that resembles "real" situations in social life in certain respects, but conforms to requirements normally not satisfied by the latter in that some of the variables assumed to be relevant to the occurrence of a social phenomenon can be manipulated in the laboratory situation while other relevant variables can be kept at least approximately constant. For example, a laboratory experiment was devised to determine whether voters are influenced by their knowledge of the religious affiliations of candidates for office. For this purpose, a number of clubs were created, whose members were carefully selected so that none were previously acquainted; each club was asked to elect one of its own members to an office, and information about the religious affiliations of the members was supplied to half the clubs but withheld from the others. The election results indicated that a goodly number of voters who were given this information were influenced by it.

Laboratory experiments have been employed in increasing numbers in many areas of social inquiry. It is evident, however, that an extensive class of social phenomena does not lend itself to such experimental study. Moreover, even when social phenomena can be investigated in this manner, it is generally not possible in a laboratory to produce changes in variables that compare in magnitude with changes sometimes occurring in those variables in natural social situations. For example, the sense of crucial importance frequently generated by issues in political elections cannot easily be provoked in subjects participating in a laboratory vote. It is a misguided criticism of laboratory experiments in social science that, since a laboratory situation is "unreal," its study can throw no light on social behavior in "real" life. On the contrary, many such experiments have been illuminating; for example, a number of experiments have been made on the behavior of children when the conditions under which they engaged in play activities were varied. However, it *is* a sound observation that no generalizations concerning social phenomena based exclusively on laboratory experiments can be safely assumed without further inquiry to hold in natural social environments.

ii. A second type of experiment is the so-called "field experiment." In such experiments, instead of an artificially created miniature social system, some "natural" though limited community is the experimental subject in which certain variables can be manipulated, so that one can ascertain by repeated trials whether or not given changes in those variables generate determinate differences in some social phenomenon. In one such field experiment, for example, changes were made in the way groups of workers in a certain factory were organized, the various types of organization being defined in the inquiry. It turned out that those groups in which more "democratic" forms of organization were introduced were eventually more productive than groups organized less democratically.

Field experimentation has some clear advantages over experimentation in the laboratory, but it is equally clear that in field experiments the difficulty of keeping relevant variables constant is in general greater. For obvious reasons, moreover, the opportunities for instituting field experiments have thus far been relatively meager; indeed, most of the experiments performed have been undertaken in connection with problems that are only of a narrowly practical interest.

iii. But the bulk of controlled empirical inquiry in the social sciences is not experimental in the sense we have associated with this term, even though such inquiries are frequently designated as "natural experiments," "ex post facto experiments," or are qualified in analogous ways. The aim of these investigations is in general to ascertain whether, and if so in what manner, some event, set of events, or complex of traits is causally related to the occurrence of certain social changes or characteristics in a given society. Examples of subjects discussed in such inquiries are human migrations, variations in birth rate, attitudes toward minority groups, the adoption of new forms of communication, changes in interest rates by banks, differences in the distribution of various personality traits in various social groups, and the social effects of legislative enactments.

Inquiries of this type can be subdivided in various ways: those seeking to ascertain the social effects of phenomena, as distinguished from those concerned with their causes; inquiries addressed to individual actions, as distinguished from those investigating group behavior; inquiries directed to relations between traits occurring more or less simultaneously, as distinguished from those dealing with traits manifested in some temporal sequence; and so on. Each of these subdivisions is associated with special methodological problems and techniques of inquiry. But despite such differences, and despite the fact that the variables assumed to be relevant in these investigations cannot be manipulated at will or that variations in such variables may not even have been planned by anyone, the investigations satisfy to a greater or lesser degree the requirements for controlled empirical inquiry. In a fairly representative study of this type, for example, the problem was to ascertain the influence of television upon the church attendance of children. For this purpose, a sample survey obtained answers to questions concerning the church attendance, age, and sex of each child in the sample, whether or not the child was a television viewer, and the church attendance of the child's parent. When the answers were classified according to whether a child who attended church was or was not a television viewer, the proportion of children attending church in the class of those who were viewers was found to be smaller than the proportion of children attending church in the class of those who were not viewers; and these proportions remained substantially unaltered when children with similar sex and age were compared. On the other hand, when the sample answers were further classified according to the church attendance of a child's parents, in the class of children who were viewers and whose parents attended church, the proportion of children attending church was not significantly different from the proportion of children attending church in the class of those who were not viewers but whose parents also attended church. Analysis of the data in the sample thus supplied some evidence that the church attendance of children is not influenced by their watching television.

. . . Let us make explicit what it is in investigations of this type that qualifies them as in some degree controlled empirical inquiries. Since by hypothesis the relevant factors cannot be overtly manipulated in these investigations, the control must be effected in some other manner. As the above example suggests, this control is achieved if sufficient information about these factors can be secured, so that analysis of the information can yield symbolic constructions in which some of the factors are represented to be constant (and hence without influence upon any alterations in the phenomenon under study), in contrast to the correlations (or lack of correlations) between the recorded data on variations in the other factors and the recorded data on the phenomenon. Accordingly, the subjects manipulated in these investigations are the *recorded (or symbolically represented) data of observation* on relevant factors, rather than the factors themselves. These inquiries therefore attempt to obtain information about a phenomenon and the factors assumed to be relevant to its occurrence, so that by subjecting the recorded data to the manipulations of statistical analysis it may be possible either to eliminate some of the factors as causal determinants of the phenomenon or to provide grounds for imputing to some factors a causal influence upon the phenomenon.

However, the difficulties associated with basing causal imputations upon investigations of this type are notorious. There are not only serious and sometimes intractable technical problems generated by various special areas of social research, for example, problems concerning the identification and definition of variables, the choice of relevant variables, the selection of representative sample data, and the finding of enough data to permit reliable inferences to be drawn from comparisons of various classes of data in the sample. There is also the crucial general problem concerning the nature of the evidence required for ascribing validly causal significance to correlations between data. The history of social study amply testifies to the ease with which the familiar *post hoc* fallacy can be committed when data about sequentially manifested events are interpreted as indicating causal connections. This general problem, as well as the rationale for distinguishing spurious from genuinely causal correlations, will receive attention later. We shall conclude for the present with the observation that much empirical research in the social sciences does not even attempt to be controlled inquiry, and that investigations of this type differ considerably among themselves in the completeness with which they satisfy the conditions for such inquiry.

THE COMPARATIVE METHOD
IN THE SOCIAL SCIENCES

Gideon Sjoberg

The author considers the difficulties of comparing sociocultural systems according to the canons of empirical social science. He discusses the problems arising from difficulties in sampling, attempts to standardize the researcher's observations, and the development of universal categories.

1. Introduction

American social scientists, with the possible exception of the anthropologists, have typically been ethnocentric in their writings and research. Most of their studies are simply unique to a particular institutional complex, possessing little generality beyond a single socio-cultural system. Nevertheless, social scientists nowadays are evincing increased interest in comparative studies. They are coming to realize that many of their generalizations may be found wanting when tested in the laboratory of world cultures. For the solution of many significant problems cross-cultural comparison seems essential—the relationships among the variables involved must be examined under diverse cultural conditions.

An attempt is made herein to survey the principal obstacles to a comparative science of society. Three problems seems to be of primary concern. First, the question, "What is going to be compared?" immediately introduces a number of issues. Then there are impediments to cross-cultural comparison stemming from difficulties both in the sampling process and in attempts to standardize researchers' observations. This paper further demonstrates how these problems are interrelated and suggests procedures which might help to resolve some of these difficulties. Most of the examples for this discussion have been drawn from anthropology and sociology, although the principles enunciated are applicable to other social sciences as well.

Several kinds of comparison are possible. Comparison can be made within a single socio-cultural system of "units" from a given time period or of units from different time periods. Neither approach is given special attention in this paper. Instead, emphasis is placed upon the comparative study of different socio-cultural systems (or segments thereof) without spatial or temporal restrictions. Unfortunately some of what comes under the rubric of "comparative" social science is hardly comparative at all. This is to a considerable extent true of the field which is referred to as "area research"; here studies are often conducted in non-Western cultural settings, but little effort is made to relate the

REPRINTED FROM *Philosophy of Science*, 22: 106–117, © 1955, The Williams & Wilkins Company, Baltimore, Maryland, 21202, U.S.A.

findings to those obtained from other areas. Those social scientists who seem to regard area studies as the only possible kind of "comparative" research neglect some of the fundamental issues pertaining to comparative social science.

2. THE BASES OF COMPARISON

As Clyde Kluckhohn (3) has observed, ". . . genuine comparison is possible only if nonculture-bound units have been isolated." Certain "invariant points of reference" or "universal categories" [1] are required which are not merely reflections of the cultural values of a particular social system. Comparable and relatively stable units must be consciously perceived if comparative study is to progress. Only through the use of invariant points of reference is it possible to test adequately various hypotheses in a cross-cultural setting.[2] None of the social sciences seems to have attained the level of sophistication developed, for example, in the field of linguistics, where more satisfactory universal categories (i.e., phonemes and morphemes) exist. It has often been remarked that more adequate theoretical formulations are sorely needed in the social sciences. Here the problem is the development of a theory of a special type: one which would make possible cross-cultural comparison.

One fundamental assumption must be made by all those who seek to establish invariant points of reference. This is that limits are imposed upon human behavior, whether by biological, geographical, or socio-cultural factors. And as a result only a limited number of stable patterns can arise. Social scientists who reject this premise also will not accept the fact that a science of society is an objective possibility.

Although much of social science inquiry has been relatively unconcerned with the construction of universal categories, some progress has nevertheless been made in this direction, especially in the fields of sociology and anthropology. One of the earliest efforts was Wissler's "universal pattern," (15) a crude empirical catalogue of culture traits which supposedly occur in all social orders. This formulation has proved to be inadequate. Murdock (8), following in much the same tradition, although starting from somewhat different as-

---

[1] In this study problems of terminology arise which are on occasion resolved in a rather arbitrary fashion. The terms, "invariant point of reference" and "universal category," are herein used synonymously. However, as becomes apparent from the discussion below, something may be "universal" simply to a special universe—e.g., that of industrialized social systems—but not necessarily to all socio-cultural systems (although the achievement of the latter appears to be a most desirable goal). Also, it seems obvious that reference points which are invariant within one frame of reference may be variable in another.

The employment of the adjective, "invariant," is not intended to invest universal categories with absolutism. Thus "probability" might be allowed for in the construction of some of these. In fact, von Neumann (13) seems to have done just this with his concept of the minimax in his *Theory of Games*.

[2] Studies of single socio-cultural systems, if they are to have any real significance, also should utilize general categories. For the "unique" takes on meaning only insofar as it can be related to the "general."

sumptions, has sought to isolate certain "common denominators" of culture which may serve as guides not only to research but to cross-cultural comparison as well. This, too, is a systematic listing of rather "empirical" categories,[3] although it represents a definite advance over that presented by Wissler.

In contradistinction to the aforementioned scholars are those who have sought to establish "abstract" categories for use in cross-cultural analysis. For example, Malinowski (5) claims to have isolated seven universal institutions which he believes are functionally necessary to meet the biological requirements of human beings. In a somewhat similar vein, Aberle *et al.* (1) have pointed up certain basic patterns which they contend are functional prerequisites to the survival not only of individuals but, more particularly, of social systems. Two other abstract theories will be discussed in somewhat greater detail. Florence Kluckhohn has set forth five invariant points of reference around which she believes all cultural systems revolve. Through these, cross-cultural comparison of a certain kind is held to be possible. She writes (4):

The five common human problems which are tentatively singled out as those of key importance can be stated quite directly in the form of questions: (1) What are the innate predispositions of men? (2) What is the relation of man to nature? (3) What is the significant time dimension? or What is the direction in time of the action process? (4) What type of personality is to be most valued? (5) What is the dominant modality of the relationship of man to other men? The problems as stated are constant; they arise inevitably out of the human situation. The phraseology of them is variable but variable only within limits.

The limits of the variability, suggested here as at least a testable conceptualization of it, are three-point ranges for each of the main orientation dimensions.

Perhaps the most extensive approach on the abstract level to be offered by an anthropologist or sociologist in recent years is that of Talcott Parsons and his colleagues (10), who have constructed a system around what they term the pattern variable schema, the core of a rather complex theory.

. . . a *pattern variable* is a dichotomy, one side of which must be chosen by an actor before the meaning of a situation is determinate for him, and thus before he can act with respect to that situation. We maintain that there are only five *basic* pattern variables (i.e., pattern variables deriving directly from the frame of reference of the theory of action) and that, in the sense that they are *all* of the pattern variables which so derive, they constitute a system. Let us list them . . .

1. Affectivity—Affective neutrality.
2. Self-orientation—Collectivity-orientation.
3. Universalism—Particularism.

---

[3] The use of the term, "empirical," is not meant to imply that no abstraction is involved here. It is simply intended to convey the idea that this kind of category (or concept) is more "closely associated" with empirical reality than is an abstract category.

4. Ascription—Achievement.
5. Specificity—Diffuseness.[4]

Without embarking upon a detailed analysis of this schema (this would lead us far afield), suffice it to say that Parsons *et al.* have contended that these pattern variables enter into consideration upon the personality, societal, and cultural levels, although they are inherently patterns of cultural value orientation—culture being a more generalized concept than society or personality. Inasmuch as these basic "dilemmas" occur in all cultural situations, and inasmuch as they are logically exhaustive, they should, Parsons argues, facilitate cross-cultural comparisons. More specifically Parsons seems most interested in testing hypotheses which concern the relation of values and social structure, the former being viewed as the "independent" variable.

The preceding discussion serves as an introduction to some pertinent observations. The first is that a number of systems of universal categories have been suggested as possible solutions to the general problem of cross-cultural analysis. Only some of the more significant have been mentioned. Some social scientists become sceptical when confronted by a variety of categories. But different theories may well require different invariant reference points. Put in other terms, an economic or technological determinist who attempts to correlate various aspects of social organization with his most generalized independent variable may necessarily have to select a different set of categories from the social scientist who takes as his focus of study the interrelationships between a society's value system (viewed as the independent variable) and its social structure. So, too, a psychologist starting from different assumptions and faced with different problems would employ still other categories. And it appears that even those who take the same independent variable as their point of departure may be justified in developing different invariant points of reference, depending upon their assumptions and whether the problems to be considered are of a special nature (e.g., if they are treating some limited subuniverses). This practice does not appear to be out of line with that in the

---

[4] Parsons unfortunately has developed a somewhat "private" vocabulary. The following brief discussion, therefore, suggests the meanings given these terms. Each is considered here from a cultural point of view. Affectivity is the normative pattern which grants an actor permission in a given situation to take advantage of an opportunity for immediate gratification without regard to evaluative considerations; affective neutrality is the converse of this. Self-orientation is that pattern which permits an actor to pursue his private interests without regard to the interests of other actors; collectivity-orientation is the converse of this. Universalism obliges an actor to be oriented toward objects (e.g., persons) in the light of general standards rather than in the objects' possession of certain properties related to those of the actor; particularism is the converse of this. Ascription is the pattern which prescribes that an actor should, in his selection of differential treatment for social objects, give priority to attributes they possess over their performances; achievement is the converse of this. Specificity is that pattern which prescribes that an actor should confine his concern with an object to a specific sphere; diffuseness is the converse of this.

physical sciences, which also must resort to various theoretical systems to explain different phenomena. Although the ideal is the development of a unified theory, this is far from reaching fruition not only in the physical but especially in the social sciences. The latter must be wary of relying too heavily upon a single theory and a single set of reference points. The fact that different theories (and the different hypotheses which stem from these theories) may require different universal categories has direct bearing upon the nature of comparative research, a fact which is indicated below.

It should be stressed that the isolation of invariant points of reference is not an end in itself. Nor should these be used simply to classify various social phenomena. Rather they should permit the testing of hypotheses in a cross-cultural setting. Before Max Weber could "demonstrate" relationships between the religious system and the economic system, it was necessary that he isolate certain "trans-cultural" reference points which would facilitate comparisons among European, Chinese, Indian, and other societies (9). Furthermore, only when invariant points of reference have been isolated is prediction possible. Because of their intrinsic importance, much more attention needs to be given them by the researcher.

Now, various problems arise in the selection of universal categories. First, should the social scientist choose concrete (empiric) or abstract categories? Although no sharp division exists between these two types of concepts and the choice to be made is to a degree a function of the particular research project, certain general issues appear. Many social scientists have sought to employ categories which are relatively concrete in nature. Their studies possess the very definite advantage that their generalizations have empirical meaning and content. On the other hand, we find numerous instances in contemporary social science where this procedure has led to some startling contradictions. The use of the concept, "divorce," as a category for examining family or societal solidarity in various cultures seems to be a case in point. Miner, in his recent study of the city of Timbuctoo, took as his working hypothesis the assumption that all urban centers exhibit a degree of secularization and/or disorganization (6). His choice of divorce as a criterion of disorganization was in accordance with the practice of students of European and American urban life. But for a cross-cultural study such as Miner's the choice was a rather unfortunate one. The result is that Miner has implied that the sacred writings of the Koran, which justify divorce in Moslem society, are not sacred at all. Actually, divorce in one society may be an institutionalized and a highly orderly and acceptable procedure, whereas in another it may represent a form of societal disorganization. As an invariant point of reference for this kind of research it displays inherent limitations. Other social scientists who have used the concept of divorce in cross-cultural studies as a reference point for familial disorganization have been faced with similar contradictions. This is just one example of the social scientist's capture by culture-bound concepts; still others could be enumerated. In fact, it may develop that most of the categories currently employed in socio-cultural inquiry are quite inadequate for comparative analysis. It should never be assumed that reference points which hold for one cultural setting are applicable to all others.

In an effort to resolve the contradictions which seem to be inherent in highly empiricized concepts, social scientists such as Florence Kluckhohn and Parsons have been searching for more abstract categories. This is in line with the trend in all the sciences toward utilization of abstract concepts to circumvent problems arising on the "common-sense" level of inquiry. The disadvantages of abstract conceptualization, however, seem apparent enough. Some of the concepts employed by Parsons, e.g., universalism and particularism, and the universal categories offered by Florence Kluckhohn are so general that they are subject to numerous interpretations on the part of the investigator. They require empirical indicators—or better yet certain specified "operational" procedures—which will relate them to empirical reality. Otherwise these invariant reference points will be part of a "neat" theory the empirical relevance of which is negligible. The charge of "over-abstraction" has been leveled against many social scientists—not only verbal theorists but also logico-mathematical "model builders" like the econometricians—who often lose sight of the empirical relevance of their models. Certainly if any theory is to be of value in comparative research the universal categories employed must be established in a manner which will permit their use in the testing of specific hypotheses. Although it is apparent that for some time to come much of cross-cultural research will be dependent upon rather loose and somewhat impressionistic conceptualization, social scientists must strive for a more rigorous approach.

A number of writers have stressed the need for a compromise between the strictly empirical and the rationalistic conceptual schemes. Nowhere is this requirement more strongly felt than in efforts to establish invariant points of reference for cross-cultural research. The use of abstract or concrete categories can not be an either/or proposition. Actually the co-existence of these two approaches serves as a check upon the abuses to which each is susceptible. The process of constructing an adequate set of invariant reference points must, then, be one of continual trial and error and, fundamentally, one of self-criticism. For it appears that most of the systems currently employed in the social sciences will serve merely to "clear away the underbrush" for future scholars; not only are present-day categories unsatisfactory for predictive purposes but they are inadequate for most descriptive purposes as well.

Still other problems present themselves. Invariant points of reference, if they are to be meaningful, should be integrated into a logically consistent system.[5] Few of the early comparative social scientists such as Spencer and Sumner were particularly concerned with this question. Their premises were not clearly stated nor did they attempt to relate their "categories" logically one to the other. In recent years attempts to improve this situation have occurred in the verbal as well as in the logico-mathematical traditions. Among verbal the-

---

[5] Also, whenever categories are developed for a "limited universe," e.g., a kinship system or a class system, they should in turn be related to a still broader frame of reference.

orists Parsons has been a pioneer in that he has stressed the need for logical consistency. However, it is doubtful that he (or anyone else) has developed a satisfactorily consistent verbal theory. For example, Parsons' pattern variable schema does not appear to be homologous; by his own admission its categories do not appear to be derivable from a single principle, but rather from three (11, p. 66). Yet, through his effort the attention of social scientists has been directed to the need for more rigorous analysis in cross-cultural research.

Possibly the logico-mathematical tradition will give the greatest impetus to the formulation of a more rigorous set of universal categories. Although as presently constituted many logico-mathematical deductive models seem to have little empirical import, this does not appear to be an inherent limitation of the approach. Some effort is currently being made, especially through the use of "qualitative" mathematical models, to adjust these systems so that they will conform more closely to empirical reality. The classic work of von Neumann and Morgenstern (13) is an example of a mathematically derived model which has definite implications for cross-cultural research of a special type. The concepts developed—the minimax, coalitions, and randomized strategy— seem applicable to the study of conflict and competition under a variety of cultural conditions. Even when this mathematical model is translated into verbal form it offers some major advances in insight and rigor over previous formulations in the field of social conflict (12). The proliferation of the logico-mathematical approach within the social sciences would do much to further cross-cultural research.

3. SAMPLING AND THE STANDARDIZATION OF OBSERVATIONS

Let us turn our attention for a moment from the question of universal categories or invariant points of reference to problems of a more technical nature. First, just how are we to proceed in selecting "cases" for the comparative study of diverse socio-cultural systems or sub-systems? Here we might profitably take Murdock's recent work (7) as a starting point for this discussion. His comparative analysis of kinship systems is one of the studies which has drawn upon the data amassed by the Human Relations Area Files (at New Haven, Conn.) on numerous literate and nonliterate societies. Murdock's contribution is significant here for his use of sampling and probability statistics in comparative research (we shall not be concerned with his conclusions). Although this procedure can serve as a profitable implement to social science research, certain difficulties arise when probability statistics are applied on a cross-cultural basis. Murdock's sampling design with respect to world societies invites some serious criticisms. Just what is the universe from which his sample has been selected? The fact that he has included within his sample some historically "extinct" societies means that his universe embraces all societies which have ever existed. But we lack sufficient knowledge about this universe. It consists of societies for which we have adequate data, others upon which our knowledge is limited, and finally those about which we really know noth-

ing. There is no way of determining how societies for which we lack information are related to those upon which we have information. Under these
circumstances it is most difficult to consider his sample as "random"; some
major "biases" may in fact be present. And if a random sample is not employed, extreme caution must be exercised in interpreting (if not actually in
applying) inductive statistical techniques—e.g., the chi-square test which
Murdock utilizes to generalize from his "sample" to the universe. Too often
social scientists employ statistical procedures without examining the assumptions upon which their analyses necessarily rest.

Not only is it difficult to determine the nature of a universe, but problems
are encountered in establishing the boundaries of societal or cultural systems.
Many of these are interrelated historically. Are they to be treated as one, or
separately? For example, should the Chinese in Malaya be classed as a separate socio-cultural system or as part of the Chinese social order? To a degree
this is a function of the particular research problem. Yet historical interrelationships among socio-cultural systems serve to complicate the drawing of a
sample by introducing the question of the "independence" of sampling units.
The situation is made all the more confused by the absence of convenient
standards for delineating the sub-systems of a social order. Some formalized
procedures are certainly required if sampling is to be utilized in cross-cultural
research.

Sampling units must also be comparable. If such units as household or community are employed, these can be subject to different cultural interpretations.
A "household" in one socio-cultural system may be quite different from a
"household" in another. Here, too, we are confronted with the need for
"trans-cultural" or "nonvaluational" categories. Still another source of confusion—one of a logical nature—appears often in the literature. It seems fash-
ionable nowadays to take the "community" as a unit for comparison. But can
we really compare the Tikopia of Oceania (a nonliterate "community" which
is co-terminous with the "society") with Yankee City or Chicago? In many
instances this kind of comparison can lead to some questionable conclusions.
Whereas the Tikopia constitute a functionally self-sufficient system, American
communities such as Chicago are only partial systems. A primitive community logically needs to be compared not with an urban or rural community but
with the total society of which the latter are integral parts. Yet comparison
between sub-systems and total systems is common practice in the social sciences.

The application of statistical techniques in the face of the aforementioned
problems might be rationalized by the investigator in certain types of cross-
cultural studies. However, due consideration must be given to the limitations
of using random sampling and probability statistics in most cross-cultural research. In fact, as is indicated below, even social scientists who make comparisons within a single socio-cultural system are plagued by similar handicaps,
although this is not often recognized.

Not only do pitfalls appear in the sampling process but considerable difficulty is encountered in standardizing the observations of researchers working in diverse cultural settings. Social scientists must strive toward the attainment of some degree of standardization: otherwise each field worker will record impressions which can not be validated by others. To be sure, rigorous research designs, sampling procedures, sociograms, and questionnaires have all contributed toward making social science research more than an individual venture. Possibly the greatest advances have been in the field of microscopic research —i.e., the study of small groups—where the situational factors seem somewhat more easily controlled. Nevertheless, some crucial aspects of the problem of standardizing observations, especially in cross-cultural research, remain relatively untouched. There is particular need for standardizing and objectifying the procedures by which imputations are made concerning the "subjective" aspects of human experience, data which are not directly observable. Just how to standardize the imputation of meanings to human action is a pressing issue in all the socio-cultural sciences. When a person enters a place of "worship," just what "meaning" is to be attached to his action? One can observe and record the act easily enough, but imputing meanings to it is another matter. At times it can prove quite trying for social scientists to reach a consensus concerning the meaning of certain acts in their own socio-cultural system, to say nothing of other cultural settings. Yet some standardization within this sphere nevertheless seems possible of attainment.

Another troublesome area, interrelated with that just mentioned, concerns standardizing the imputations of observers about the mechanics of large-scale, complex social systems—e.g., a governmental bureaucracy. Although considerable effort has been given to refining questionnaires and similar research tools, these have proved to be of very limited value for analyzing the functioning of complex social structures. There is clearly a need for standardizing the observations of participant observers in this kind of setting. Furthermore, efforts to standardize researchers' imputations from published records concerning the functioning of large-scale social systems (e.g., through the use of content analysis) are still far from satisfactory. Too many inconsistent interpretations concerning the nature of large-scale social systems have been put forth. Even a partial solution to these problems would do much to enhance cross-cultural research.

4. Possible Directions

At this point it seems appropriate to seek out the relationships among those facets of cross-cultural research discussed above—namely, invariant points of reference and the more strictly methodological problems of research as sampling and the standardization of observations—and through this means to uncover possible solutions to some of the aforementioned difficulties. In order better to perceive their functional interrelationships some slight digression seems necessary. In comparative research it appears that in the selection of cases (whether these be total systems or sub-systems) for testing hypotheses, social scientists must accept the fact that a crude statistical approach, or more often than not some kind of qualitative analysis, is required. This is probably all that can ever be achieved on a cross-cultural basis (especially on the macroscopic level) for some time to come. Among other factors, data simply are lacking on too many societies; therefore, reliance must be placed in most instances upon some kind of "judgmental" sample. This principle should be followed: utilize quantitative and other rigorous procedures where these are required and can legitimately be employed (especially within case studies, e.g., that of a single community), but recognize that certain kinds of problems can not be treated in a rigorous statistical fashion, especially through the use of probability statistics, at the present time. Unless the social scientist is willing to accept this obvious limitation, the whole of comparative study (which appears to form the basis of social science) must be conceded to have no future.

Even granted the limitations imposed upon research in comparative social science, the situation is not without hope. One approach might be pursued to advantage—i.e., the giving of increased emphasis to deviant or unique cases. Such a step may point up some hypotheses which should be rejected—or perhaps define more precisely the conditions under which the original hypotheses are valid—or even demonstrate the need for a broader hypothesis to cover the deviant cases. It is through deviant case studies that reference points can best be perceived or those already in use sharpened and clarified. Some social scientists seem to hold to the view that intensive knowledge of our own culture is required before we are justified in attempting analyses of other socio-cultural systems. But this brings us to a major impasse: the general and stable elements in our own culture can best be understood when the latter is compared with divergent cases.

The physical sciences took centuries to formulate and refine their invariant points of reference, and it seems unlikely that the social sciences will uncover any convenient short-cuts to this goal. Therefore, instead of merely searching for confirmatory evidence, as some social scientists prefer, it seems necessary purposively to gather contraditory evidence, then, in light of this, rework and reformulate the so-called invariant points of reference as well as the hypotheses being tested. A number of social scientists implicitly recognize the value of this procedure. However, there is need for more explicit recognition of its *essentiality* in cross-cultural research. This procedure, incidentally, is in conformance with the ideas of such philosophers of science as Popper and Wisdom (14), who argue that one can only disprove, never really prove, scientific hypotheses, and that the scientific method therefore basically embodies a negative approach.

Not only do carefully-designed case studies, especially deviant ones, sharpen invariant points of reference, but certain other facts should be noted. To the extent that invariant reference points or categories have been isolated for a particular research problem, a case study (whether of a society or community or other social group) takes on added significance. Not only can we perceive its general aspects but we can appreciate more fully the significance of its unique features.

The essential role of case studies for comparisons within a single socio-cultural system is also often overlooked. It is common practice nowadays to use the community as a setting within which to test various hypotheses concerning the functioning of the class structure, ecological system, kinship organization, etc. And it is a relatively simple matter to apply random sampling within this "primary" universe, if this is desirable. However, the community is still only a case study with respect to other communities in the total social order, to say nothing of in the world. It is considerably more difficult to draw a random sample of communities and to study a number of these even within a single socio-cultural system. Thus, social scientists usually take a case study of community life and generalize freely from it to other communities. But they give all too little attention to the question: Is the community representative both *spatially* and *temporally* of other communities within the socio-cultural system? Generalization from one or only a few cases is often necessary, but this is valid only if certain invariant reference points have been isolated. Put in more concrete terms, research projects in such communities as Yankee City and Middletown are significant for an understanding of other communities in the United States to the extent that their findings have been related to certain general and comparable categories.

Some other relationships between research and invariant points of reference merit attention. Social scientists should recognize that different theoretical systems may require different invariant reference points and that descriptive data for various case studies need therefore to be collected with this in mind. The practice of limiting observations to a single set of categories (as well as to a single hypothesis) can be far from satisfactory. If the need for a broader perspective were more explicitly recognized by researchers interested in comparative analysis, their case studies of societies, communities, kinship systems, etc. would be greatly enhanced. We can not be certain which set of reference points will prove to be most adequate: those which we now use are just too approximate. Why, then, gamble on collecting data simply in terms of a single set of categories? If more than one is consciously employed, more of our existing reference points can be sharpened or perhaps discarded, or the need for new ones clearly seen. Also, some comparative work must necessarily be done by non-field workers—the sheer impossibility of one individual ever conducting research in more than just a few cultures during a life-time seems obvious enough. There must be specialists to correlate these findings from various socio-cultural settings.

Finally, a few remarks about standardizing observations. This, too, is strikingly interrelated with invariant points of reference. For to the degree that relatively stable reference points have been isolated, standardization of observation becomes a more objective possibility. Observation necessarily takes place, whether implicitly or explicitly, in terms of some particular theoretical structure. If a researcher is dealing with universal and comparable categories, he is more likely to observe the same kind of social phenomena as do other researchers. This is especially true for studies of large-scale social systems. It seems to this writer that one of the principal reasons for the research difficulties encountered in the last-named area is that no really satisfactory invariant reference points have been isolated. Techniques alone can not resolve these issues.

This is not to imply that all that is required is the construction of conceptual categories. Measurement and operational procedures also have a place. Scales and indices are currently being developed and applied with the expectation that these will somehow standardize observations. And to a degree they may succeed. Unfortunately, however, these devices are often utilized without attention to general and comparable categories. The following question must be kept in mind: "What is going to be measured?" Sociologists are attempting to construct indexes and scales which will aid in depicting, for example, the American class structure or urban ecological patterns. But they are plagued by numerous discrepancies, one reason being that so much attention is given the "unique" rather than to universal reference points.

It is also the writer's contention that social scientists should employ less "stereotyped" methods in attempting to standardize observations. One such deviant approach is suggested by Firey and Belknap (2). They argue that society itself has refined techniques for imputing meanings to social action; one of these is the "jury system" with its judges, witnesses, advocates, etc. Social scientists, they believe, might well utilize some of the principles embodied in this approach as an aid to standardizing the imputation of meaning to social action. This is just one example of how a deviant technique might be employed to advantage, particularly if it is used in relation to sets of universal categories.

5. SUMMARY

It should be emphasized that most social science research evinces no real effort to generalize beyond single socio-cultural systems, the United States in particular. There is a marked tendency to lose sight of the basic function of science—i.e., to generalize. Although the social sciences may never achieve the "predictability" of the natural sciences, a deeper understanding of society than is now apparent seems possible through the comparative method.

Given the intrinsic importance of comparative study, cognizance should be taken of the problems encountered in cross-cultural research. This paper has sought to isolate three of the most significant. Perhaps the major emphasis should be given to developing more satisfactory invariant reference points or universal categories. *In order to test the relationships among variables in various socio-cultural settings, certain comparable and relatively stable categories must be employed.* Some of these invariant points of reference, of course, might be applicable only to limited universes. Also, attention has been called herein to two pressing methodological problems, sampling and the standardization of observations. But even these, as has been shown, are interrelated with invariant reference points; the social scientist should keep this in mind when he seeks to resolve problems in cross-cultural research.

REFERENCES

1. ABERLE, D. F. *et al.*, "The Functional Prerequisites of a Society," *Ethics*, LX, 1950, pp. 100–11.
2. FIREY, WALTER and IVAN BELKNAP, "The Problem of Standardizing Observations in Sociology," *Proceedings of the Southwestern Sociological Society*, I, 1951, pp. 60–67. (mimeo.)
3. KLUCKHOHN, CLYDE, "Universal Categories of Culture," in A. L. Kroeber, *Anthropology Today*, University of Chicago Press, 1953, pp. 507–23.
4. KLUCKHOHN, FLORENCE, "Dominant and Substitute Profiles of Cultural Orientations: Their Significance for the Analysis of Social Stratification," *Social Forces*, XXVIII, pp. 376–93.
5. MALINOWSKI, B., *A Scientific Theory of Culture*, University of North Carolina Press, 1944.
6. MINER, HORACE, *The Primitive City of Timbuctoo*, Princeton University Press, 1953.
7. MURDOCK, GEORGE P., *Social Structure*, Macmillan Co., 1949.
8. MURDOCK, GEORGE P. *et al.*, *Outline of Cultural Materials*, 3rd rev. ed., Human Relations Area Files, Inc., 1950.
9. PARSONS, TALCOTT, *The Structure of Social Action*, The Free Press, 1949.
10. PARSONS, TALCOTT and EDWARD A. SHILS (eds.), *Toward a General Theory of Action*, Harvard University Press, 1951.
11. PARSONS, TALCOTT *et al.*, *Working Papers in the Theory of Action*, The Free Press, 1953.
12. SJOBERG, GIDEON, "Strategy and Social Power: Some Preliminary Formulations," *Southwestern Social Science Quarterly*, XXXIII, 1953, pp. 297–308.
13. VON NEUMANN, JOHN and OSKAR MORGENSTERN, *Theory of Games and Economic Behavior*, 2nd ed., Princeton University Press, 1947.
14. WISDOM, JOHN O., *Foundations of Inference in Natural Science*, Methuen & Co., 1952.
15. WISSLER, CLARK, *Man and Culture*, Thomas Y. Crowell, 1923.

Part 2

COGNITIVE LEARNING

THE INTERNATIONAL COMPARATIVE STUDY OF ACHIEVEMENT IN MATHEMATICS

C. Arnold Anderson

An account of the first major attempt to measure school achievement in mathematics cross-nationally, and to relate achievement differences to parental, school, and student variables. The sample comprises twelve industrial nations.

THE LACK of achievement data for pupils in different nations has been called the missing link in comparative education.[1] When we have measures of outcomes of instruction (cognitive, non-cognitive, or other) to serve as dependent variables we can then proceed with attempts to explain the varying outcomes in terms of the operations of schools and the characteristics of their social milieu.

At that same time a group of educational psychologists from several countries were moving toward a similar proposal. These converging research interests were crystallized by a representative of the curriculum field who directed a pilot study.[2] On its successful completion, plans were made for a more rigorous investigation. An Office of Education grant supported the international portion of the work and the testing within the United States. Each participating country bore its own internal costs. For obvious reasons mathematics was chosen as the initial area of testing. The two-volume report is now published.[3]

REPRINTED FROM *Comparative Education Review*, 11 (June 1967), 182–196, © 1967 by Comparative Education Review. The writer is serving only as rapporteur to bring the results of this important international study to the attention of the Comparative Education profession. His part in the study has been modest; the task has been mainly one for psychometricians. Only a few of the findings are dealt with here, and the writer's conclusions may not correspond in all details to the final report. Professor Torsten Husén of Sweden served as technical director of the study and as general editor of the report.

[1] C. Arnold Anderson, "The Methodology of Comparative Education," *International Review of Education*, 7 (1961), pp. 1–22.

[2] A. W. Foshay, et al., *Educational Achievements of Thirteen-Year-Olds in Twelve Countries* (Hamburg: Unesco Institute, 1962).

[3] T. Husén (ed.), *International Study of Achievement in Mathematics. A Comparison of Twelve Countries* (Stockholm: Almquist and Wicksell and New York: John Wiley, 2 vols., 1967). The completion of this first comprehensive international testing project must be credited to unstinting collaboration, firm administration, and skillful programming. The report contains full details on all operations, and it is candid in admitting mistakes. The full responses (rather than averages only) are in a data bank, the use of which is open to qualified investigators.

The Office of Education has made a new grant to support planning for additional testing in other subject areas and perhaps in additional countries. Another smaller grant from the Office will bring together representatives of social science disciplines to explore ways of inaugurating interdisplinary studies of differences and similarities in the "productivity" of education.

The basic population tested was 13-year-olds; at that age, attendance is universal in each of the twelve participating countries.[4] Tests were given also to students in the last year of secondary school (at which point many countries give a "maturity" examination). These secondary school students were divided into two groups: those taking courses of study with heavy emphasis upon mathematics, and the remainder.[5] Headmasters supplied much information about their schools, and both teachers and pupils responded to an extensive list of factual and attitude questions. A "case study" of descriptive materials was prepared for each nation.

Although the national differences in mean scores on the mathematics tests are of great interest, the project was designed primarily to test specific hypotheses.[6] An extended range on many independent variables affecting educational outcomes can be obtained only by drawing data from different national systems. Many plausible conclusions about the effectiveness of educational practices can be tested only by ascertaining whether a given practice elicits the same pupil performance in different systems and whether correlations of pupil achievement with given factors are stable among countries.[7] It is important to find out also whether the proportionate contribution to variation in pupils' scores by given factors is similar from country to country or from one to another type of school or system when the same associated factors are controlled. At the present stage it was a distinct advantage that all of the participating countries were "developed" and broadly similar in economic-technological pattern.

The outcome of the regression analysis with some two dozen independent variables is summarized in Table 1 and fuller identification of each variable is

[4] Most countries also tested the pupils in the grade that normally includes 13-year-olds and a few countries gave tests to an intermediate population around age 15. Responses were obtained from over 5300 headmasters, 13,000 teachers, and 150,000 pupils. The details of the complex sampling designs are given in the report.

[5] In some countries the second population of secondary students has more prestige and comes from more restricted social backgrounds than the first. The proportion of preuniversity enrollment included in the mathematics curricula is three-fifths or more in Sweden, Australia, and the Netherlands; about half in Finland and France; two-fifths in England and Germany; less than a third in Belgium and Scotland; a quarter in the United States; a seventh in Japan. In ratio to the age cohort, however, these proportions are quite different: 15–20 per cent in the United States, Sweden, and Australia; 7–8 per cent in Japan and Finland; about five per cent in the other countries.

[6] The computer analysis was programed in terms of the hypotheses, but a 54 × 54 correlation matrix for each country and population permits exploration of other relationships.

[7] To take a simple example, it was found that in countries where pupils begin school at age five, learning is not augmented, nor is it greatly handicapped by entry at age seven.

TABLE 1

Contribution to Prediction of Mathematics Scores
by Given Categories of Factors *

	MEAN COUNTRY	HIGHEST COUNTRY	LOWEST COUNTRY	UNITED STATES
13-year-old Population				
Parental Variables	4.8	11.9	.2	10.7
Teacher Variables—Total	5.7	23.5	−.9	2.6
Opportunity to Learn	1.5	22.4	.0	2.1
School Variables-I	1.4	5.1	−1.1	2.1
School Variables-II	3.7	13.4	.4	.4
Sex	.1	3.4	.0	.0
Age	.2	1.4	−.6	1.4
Level of Instruction	14.5	42.9	.0	6.5
Interest in Mathematics	7.5	15.1	3.6	3.6
Percentage of Variance Explained	40	67	28	28
Preuniversity Year: Mathematics Curriculum				
Parental Variables	1.9	8.2	.0	8.2
Teacher Variables—Total	5.2	15.7	1.8	4.8
Opportunity to Learn	2.6	13.2	.2	3.5
School Variables-I	4.3	15.0	.3	3.6
School Variables-II	6.7	26.2	.9	6.2
Sex	.6	2.8	.0	.8
Age	1.3	2.6	−.5	2.4
Level of Instruction	5.6	11.5	2.0	6.2
Interest in Mathematics	13.2	23.4	7.2	11.6
Percentage of Variance Explained	38	46	23	44
Preuniversity Year: Nonmathematics Curriculum				
Parental Variables	2.6	11.9	−.2	11.9
Teacher Variables—Total	3.8	7.5	.5	.5
Opportunity to Learn	.6	4.0	.2	.1
School Variables-I	2.1	4.8	.2	1.3
School Variables-II	3.3	8.3	−5.4	5.3
Sex	5.5	13.3	.0	.0
Age	.8	2.9	.0	2.9
Level of Instruction	7.3	19.9	.0	1.4
Interest in Mathematics	8.2	12.9	2.7	2.7
Percentage of Variance Explained	32	40	25	28

* The variables were dealt with step-wise. In any of these tables, "—" means that the variable was of no importance, while "0" means that the weight was about zero, but that the variable was not eliminated in the processing. "Percentage of total variance explained" is identical with the squared multiple correlation coefficient.

TABLE 2

Correlation of Mathematics Test Scores with Individual Independent Variables:
Mean of Country Correlations, Range of Country Correlations,
Number of Positive and Negative Correlations [1]

	13-YEAR-OLD POPULATION				PREUNIVERSITY: MATH POPULATION				PREUNIVERSITY: NONMATH POPULATION			
	MEAN R	RANGE OF R'S	NO. OF R'S +	NO. OF R'S −	MEAN R	RANGE OF R'S	NO. OF R'S +	NO. OF R'S −	MEAN R	RANGE OF R'S	NO. OF R'S +	NO. OF R'S −
I. Parental Variables												
1. Mother's Education	18	28	10	0	09	25	7	0	08	25	6	0
2. Father's Education	21	34	10	0	09	36	7	1	03	37	3	3
3. Father's Occupation	24	37	10	0	08	28	7	1	06	28	4	1
4. His Occupation Scientific [2]	15	26	10	0	05	20	6	2	03	24	3	3
5. Residence [3]	03	30	6	4	08	47	5	2	07	33	4	2
II. Teacher Variables												
1. Sex	02	34	4	6	−06	15	2	6	−09	27	1	3
2. Length of Training	08	42	9	1	05	34	6	2	01	27	3	1
3. In-Service Training	05	27	8	2	02	25	3	5	01	18	3	1
4. Teacher's Autonomy [4]	00	26	4	6	02	26	6	2	01	18	1	1
5. Pupils' Description of [5]	07	14	8	0	−03	17	1	6	−05	10	1	3
6. Opportunity to Learn [6]	17	59	6	1	20	53	5	1	11	32	2	1

III. School Variables—I

1. Hours of All School Weekly	02	53	4	5	−00	31	3	4	−06	33	2	4
2. Hours of Homework	19	39	9	1	01	30	3	4	04	23	3	3
3. Hours of Math Teaching	−02	69	5	5	14	70	5	1	07	39	2	2
4. Math Homework Hours	02	21	5	3	11	28	7	1	07	21	4	1

IV. School Variables—II

1. Pupils on School Roll	16	42	9	1	15	50	5	2	07	30	5	1
2. % of Teachers Male	10	52	8	2	06	22	7	1	16	21	6	0
3. No. Subjects in Grade 8	−02	21	2	6	—	—	—	—	—	—	—	—
4. No. Subjects in Grade 12	—	—	—	—	02	36	3	3	−04	34	3	2
5. Salaries Per Pupil	09	54	6	3	07	11	7	0	06	32	4	1
6. Educational Differentiation [7]	02	40	3	5	06	57	4	3	−04	29	1	4

V. Student Variables

1. Sex (− = Boys Better)	−09	18	0	10	−12	24	7	0	−26	34	0	6
2. Age	09	26	9	1	−10	35	1	6	−06	27	1	5
3. Level of Instruction [8]	37	74	9	0	32	36	5	0	23	51	5	0
4. Interest in Mathematics	30	22	10	0	41	23	8	0	30	23	6	0

Decimal points omitted.

1 No indication has been made for significance of the coefficients.
2 If father's occupation is scientific-technical.
3 Size of community of parental residence.
4 Teacher's reported degree of freedom or autonomy in work.
5 Pupil says teaching is inquiry-centered or not.
6 Teacher's estimate of whether pupils had become familiar with processes tested.
7 Within the particular school, amount of division of programs.
8 A 9-point scale: only arithmetic, some practical geometry and simple equations, etc.

provided in Table 2.[8] Of the total variation among pupils in scores, only a minor fraction has been accounted for. The characteristics of individual pupils are important, apart from the component attributable to family background. The values in Table 1 allow for the effect of other factors; taken singly (as discussed below) correlations of scores with particular independent variables can be larger or smaller. The level of instruction (the difficulty of the content offered to pupils), the pupils' interest in mathematics, and the teachers' judgments of whether pupils had an opportunity to learn the specific processes tested together accounted for over half the explained variance in scores.[9]

The proportion of total variance in scores explained differs widely among countries and populations of pupils: from 67 per cent for the 13-year-olds in the Netherlands to 23 per cent for the preuniversity mathematics students in England. In view of the great disparity in the residual variations, one can hardly have recourse to "genetic" explanations. Nor would one conclude that all of the characteristics of schools or curricula are manipulable in any given country. Yet clearly improvement of educational operations in each country is attainable. This inference is supported also by the wide variation among the countries in the influence of each factor dealt with.

Holding other variables constant, in Japan and in the United States, the parental variables accounted for over ten points of the variation in scores, but their effect ranged down to less than one point in Finland and France. Family background was perforce of slight statistical effect in the preuniversity populations that had been subjected to educational selection, though it remained important for the heterogenous secondary schools of the United States.

Most of the effect in the "teacher variables" was accounted for by "opportunity to learn"; however, the effect of the other teacher variables was not negligible in every country.[10] The first group of "school variables" dealt with time given to school work and to mathematics in school or in homework. For the youngest population, only total homework had appreciable effect. Among preuniversity mathematics students subject instruction and homework were important but in the other preuniversity population total instruction and homework were salient. The second set of school variables (see Table 2) is mixed, and they were usually of modest effect although in particular countries individual variables stood out. School characteristics other than the allocation

---

[8] The numbers in Table 1 add to the total only for the illustrative country, United States, though they add approximately for the mean country (within rounding errors).

[9] A re-analysis without these three items did not appreciably alter the relative importance of other factors.

[10] The percentages of teachers who were males in the schools of the 13-year population range from 46 (United States) to over 70 (Netherlands and Japan) and in the preuniversity mathematics population from about 60 (France and United States) to 90 in Japan and the Netherlands. The teachers' sense of professional autonomy was low in some high-scoring countries (Belgium) and high in some low-scoring ones (Sweden). Teachers of the 13-year population trained in "normal" schools only were comparatively numerous in some high-scoring countries (Belgium and Netherlands) but few in some low-scoring countries (England and United States).

of time to study have more influence at the preuniversity than at the 13-year level.

Turning to the "student variables," boys get slightly better scores everywhere. The pupils' interest in mathematics is important, as is the level of the mathematics offered to them.

There is, to repeat, abundant opportunity for educational improvement in each country without going beyond the effectiveness attained in some of these countries.

Table 2 summarizes the zero-order correlations between scores on the international mathematics test and the individual variables. For each population tested it shows the mean of the individual country correlations (correlation for the mean country) and the range in these coefficients among countries. The number of positive and negative coefficients indicates the consistency of relationship for each variable among the countries. Scanning these correlations (which make no allowance for the effect of other variables), the general impression is one of very modest relationships.[11]

The range of coefficients taken over the whole set of independent variables and countries is from over +.7 to over −.4, yet half the coefficients are within ten points of zero. On fewer than a fifth of the variables is the disparity in coefficients among countries below 20 points; for the 13-year-olds and the preuniversity mathematics population, about a fifth of the variables display at least a 50 point spread in coefficients among countries. On several variables even the sign of the coefficient changes among countries, but these are usually variables on which the all-country or pooled relationship is low. The range of coefficients is large also for any given independent variable; this range is largest for the 13-year-olds and least for the pre-university nonmathematics population. Particular interest, however, lies in the pattern of coefficients for given variables or countries.

It has been mentioned that the zero-order correlations between pupils' scores and parental characteristics are moderate in size and also disparate among countries.[12] Those countries that differentiate pupils late have larger proportions of laborers' children in the preuniversity year as do countries with large percentages of the age cohort remaining in secondary school. The latter relationship is almost an arithmetic truism. But it is not similarly a truism that

[11] Indications of the statistical significance of all values can be found in the full report. The design called for distinguishing verbal from computational and low from high-level processes; the results did not uphold those distinctions clearly. The tests proved to be quite difficult although they were constructed specially by representatives of the participating countries. Pupils in a given country were not equally adept on all topics; for example, German pupils did better on calculus than on algebra while Belgian pupils displayed the opposite capacity. The common denominator of mathematics topics offered to pupils is surprisingly small.

[12] Despite the high proportion of the age cohort enrolled in Japanese secondary schools, the parental coefficients are low there also in contrast to the United States. There was no consistent urban-rural difference. Apparently level of content offered to pupils (which is correlated with urbanization) absorbed most of the effect of the urbanization variable.

countries with comparatively small percentages of the age cohort in secondary schools have larger percentages of secondary students from upper-status homes —though this does tend to occur. However, neither of the foregoing correlations is close.[13]

Just as the parents of preuniversity students tend to be of higher occupational status than those of the 13-year-old pupils, so are the former also possessed of more schooling. For example the fathers of preuniversity mathematics students in Australia average .5 of a year more schooling than do those of elementary pupils, and the former display a 20 point excess in the percentage coming from high-status occupations. For France, by contrast, the two gains are 3.6 years in education of fathers and 29 points in occupation. For the several countries the percentage of fathers from high-status occupations for each one-year rise in paternal schooling was as follows: France 8, Sweden and Japan 10, Netherlands 13, Finland 19, United States 20, Scotland 25, Belgium and England 27, Australia 40. Perhaps in some countries the social selection accompanying persistence to the preuniversity year is fixed more closely upon intellectual than upon occupational criteria, or perhaps in some countries pupils' abilities are identified more validly independent of family status.[14]

Among these countries the mathematics scores of secondary students were correlated, but not closely, with the proportion of students having high-status or better-educated fathers. However, the scores of preuniversity mathematics students have only a weak negative relationship with the national proportions of the age cohort persisting to that year in school. At the 13-year level, the father's occupation is more closely correlated than is his schooling with pupils' scores in five countries (plus one tie) but more closely correlated with mother's

---

[13] The proportion of the age cohort completing secondary school is only slightly correlated with either national per capita income or with the level of industrialization within the range of these variables displayed by these countries. Countries retaining larger proportions to the preuniversity year do have larger enrollments in "comprehensive" secondary schools. The foregoing index of shift in paternal occupational status takes account only of the upper strata. The index of dissimilarity (proportion of cases that would have to be shifted in the preuniversity mathematics population, for example, for it to match the 13-year-old distribution) was computed after setting farm parents aside as not fitting well into the occupational hierarchy. These indexes are as follows (beginning with the country showing the largest degree of social selection for secondary students): Germany 53, Scotland 45, England 44, France and Netherlands 42, Finland and Sweden 35, Japan 24, United States 22, Belgium 21. Except for Belgium these results correspond to usual impressions. There is no close relationship of these indexes to the proportion of the age cohort retained in school to the preuniversity year.

[14] It is of interest that in all countries (except the United States) the variance of the distribution of paternal education was appreciably larger for both preuniversity populations than for the 13-year-old population. By this test, social selection accompanying secondary school attendance did not produce a socially homogeneous school. By inference, educational selection for secondary school gave opportunities for many able children from non-elite homes. Even in the 13-year population pupils varied as among countries in the standard deviation of paternal education; dispersion was above three years in United States, Netherlands, Finland, and Belgium; about 2.5 years in Sweden, Japan, and France; two years or less in Scotland, England, Australia.

schooling than with father's occupation in seven countries. Mother's schooling equals or outweighs the father's in two countries and has about the same influence in two more (Table 3).

A fascinating question (but one that was difficult to deal with on technical grounds) concerns the amount of gain in mathematics proficiency from the 13-year population to the end of secondary schooling. By a complex use of bridge tests given to more than one of the populations, such estimates were made (see the foot of Table 4). The gain in score for France was about 70 per cent larger than that for the United States and that in England was nearly as large as in France; no other country had anything like so small a gain as the United States. By comparing these gains with the mean scores for the 13-year and preuniversity mathematics populations it is apparent that the increase in score was closely related to the performance of the secondary pupils. These gains in mathematics scores are more closely correlated with the rise in proportions of high-status fathers ($r = .62$), comparing one country with another, than with increases in paternal schooling from the younger to the older population of pupils ($r = .54$).

The recurrent references to the parental variables arise not only from the intrinsic interest in effects of family background upon pupils' school performance. Directly or indirectly children's social backgrounds do affect their school careers, but the degree and pattern of this influence is by no means the same in every country (as Table 3 makes clear). As would be expected, pupils from high status homes outscored others, but that superiority was considerably smaller among the educationally selected preuniversity students than among the 13-year-olds. The size of the difference varied among the countries in each population. But of much greater importance is the fact that low-status pupils in some countries out-scored high-status pupils in other countries. The curriculum, school programs, and incentives for high achievement elicited better performance from comparable pupils in some countries than in others.

The level of the mathematics materials set before the pupils appears to have been important in this connection.[15] Paternal status appears also to have been mediated through effects upon pupils' aspirations and especially upon plans for further schooling; definite plans were associated with higher test scores. Interest in mathematics, on the other hand, had only a tenuous relationship to paternal status, as was true also for the amount of mathematics homework performed.[16]

---

[15] On the nine-point scale for level of content offered to pupils the countries were comparatively uniform at the 13-year stage; the level was distinctively high in Japan, however. In the preuniversity mathematics population the level was lowest in the United States and highest in Finland, Japan, and Scotland; for the parallel nonmathematics population the United States level was intermediate and Scotland was highest, followed by Japan.

[16] Even in the 13-year population, pupils from high-status homes were comparatively more often enrolled in academic than in general programs, and those in the academic programs scored higher on the tests. However, scores were less closely correlated to paternal status within the academic than within other programs.

Table 3

Zero-Order Correlations Between Individual Variables and
Mathematics Scores of 13-Year-Old Pupils by Country

	AUSTRALIA	BELGIUM	ENGLAND	FINLAND	FRANCE	JAPAN	NETHER-LANDS	SCOTLAND	SWEDEN	UNITED STATES
I. Parental Variables										
1. Mother's Education	04	05	24	12	14	32	27	12	16	29
2. Father's Education	06	13	24	13	19	33	40	14	16	30
3. Father's Occupation	22	24	38	01	19	25	33	27	20	28
4. His Occupation Scientific	05	14	27	01	09	27	16	12	18	18
5. Residence	05	-01	-07	05	-10	20	03	-07	07	18
II. Teacher Variables										
1. Sex	-05	-17	-06	17	-11	02	-01	02	-03	01
2. Length of Training	10	09	32	03	03	-04	-10	08	09	08
3. In-Service Training	04	09	02	-15	10	-02	12	12	06	10
4. Teacher's Autonomy	-09	-06	09	-04	17	03	-06	-02	-05	03
5. Pupils' Description of Teaching	01	—	09	15	—	09	13	10	14	02
6. Opportunity to Learn	—	—	55	04	26	09	—	56	-03	19

III. School Variables-I

Variable										
1. Hours of All School Weekly	-01	-10	03	06	-34	04	19	00	-04	-04
2. Hours of Homework	26	24	32	-06	26	11	33	20	07	14
3. Hours of Mathematics Teaching	-09	25	10	-15	-41	03	-20	28	-02	02
4. Mathematics Homework Hours	06	10	04	-08	12	00	00	04	-09	-01
IV. School Variables-II										
1. Pupils on School Roll	10	15	09	26	12	11	41	27	-01	06
2. Percent of Teachers Male	08	07	08	04	18	04	45	-07	21	01
3. No. Subjects in Grade 8	-03	-11	-02	00	08	-13	00	-10	07	-03
4. No. Subjects in Grade 12	—	—	—	—	—	—	—	—	—	—
5. Salaries Per Pupil	-03	—	20	16	14	-02	41	06	-13	10
6. Educational Differentiation	00	02	24	00	-16	-01	15	-02	-01	-01
V. Student Variables										
1. Sex (− = Boys Better)	-03	-19	-10	-10	-14	-10	-17	-04	-03	-01
2. Age	—	—	—	—	—	—	—	—	—	—
3. Level of Instruction	46	46	27	35	61	—	74	20	32	31
4. Interest in Mathematics	30	24	36	27	27	42	31	30	38	20

Decimal points omitted.

TABLE 4

Mean Mathematics Score and Standard Deviation

| | | | | PREUNIVERSITY POPULATION | | | | | |
| | 13-YEAR-OLDS | | | MATHEMATICS | | | NONMATHEMATICS | | |
COUNTRY	MEAN	S.D.	% HIGH[1]	MEAN	S.D.	% HIGH[1]	MEAN	S.D.	% HIGH[1]
Australia	20.2	14.0	16	21.6	10.5	5	—	—	—
Belgium	27.7	15.0	34	34.6	12.6	32	24.2	9.5	12
England	19.3	17.0	21	35.2	12.6	35	21.4	10.0	8
Finland	24.1	9.9	15	25.3	9.6	8	22.5	8.3	9
France	18.3	12.4	12	33.4	10.8	24	26.2	9.5	16
Germany	—	—	—	28.8	9.8	12	27.7	7.6	17
Israel	—	—	—	36.4	8.6	36	—	—	—
Japan	31.2	16.9	43	31.4	14.8	31	25.3	14.3	27
Netherlands	23.9	15.9	25	31.9	8.1	17	24.7	9.8	11
Scotland	19.1	14.6	15	25.5	10.4	9	20.7	9.5	5
Sweden	15.7	10.8	6	27.3	11.9	15	12.6	6.2	0
United States	16.2	13.3	9	13.8	12.6	4	8.3	9.0	1
Total	19.8	14.9	—	26.1	13.8	—	21.0	12.8	—

*Increase in score between the 13-year-old and the
preuniversity mathematics populations* [2]

Australia	2.38	France	3.16	Sweden	2.82
Belgium	2.88	Japan	2.45	United States	1.83
England	3.08	Netherlands	2.86	All Countries	2.60
Finland	2.61	Scotland	2.71		

[1] Approximate percentage of the country sample exceeding +1 S.D. of the composite distribution for the given population.
[2] Estimated by use of tests given to both populations.

A crucial hypothesis of the study originated in the controversies about "streaming." It was hypothesized that differences in scores between pupils from homes of contrasting status would be least where students attended schools marked by high variability of paternal occupation. Scores were computed for four categories of paternal occupation within each status-variability category. Pupils from high-status homes excelled, to be sure, especially at the 13-year level. Within each category of paternal status, however, achievement was lower among pupils in the little-variability schools. Moreover, low status pupils in heterogeneous schools outscored those from all but the highest status homes who were enrolled in socially homogeneous classes. Similar patterns prevailed at the preuniversity level although the contrasts were smaller. Comprehensive education receives considerable support from these findings.

Along with measurement of mathematical proficiency, the investigation sought to elicit expressions of pupils' attitudes and interests relating specifically to mathematics but also to other aspects of their educational experience. The details of the various attitude scales and questionnaires used can be found in the report and only summaries of certain findings are included in this paper. Among the 13-year-olds the mathematics scores showed an overall correlation of .22 with the desire to take more mathematics; the correlation with the status of the desired adult occupation was .18 and with the expected occupation .20. The scores were more closely related to the amount of additional education desired and expected: .38 and .42. No doubt in some degree these correlations reflect a tendency of those doing well in mathematics to display more interest in it or in activities using it.

Guttman-type scales were constructed on five attitude dimensions. The inter-country rank correlations between mathematics scores and these attitudes were as follows: For the 13-year population the correlation with viewing mathematics as process rather than as a fixed body of knowledge was $-.70$, with the difficulty experienced in learning mathematics $-.32$, with believing that mathematics is important for society .15, with favorable attitudes toward school .48, and with the view that men can control their environment .65. The corresponding coefficients for the preuniversity mathematics students were: $-.41$, $-.43$, .45, .20, .38 and for the parallel nonmathematics secondary students: $-.61$, $-.23$, .88, .56, .15. These attitude patterns tend to be consistent over all three school populations within individual countries. It is perhaps disconcerting to discover that viewing mathematics as an open system is less prevalent among the older pupils who have taken more mathematics and in those countries scoring highest on the international mathematics tests. There was some evidence that pupils who had taken some "new math" adopted a less stereotyped view of the subject. Students with the most exposure to mathematics and those making the highest scores were less impressed with the importance of mathematics to society. Liking for school-work and optimism about men's capacity to control the environment were least frequent in the English-speaking countries.

Pupils' ratings of mathematics lessons with respect to their being "inquiry directed" showed only a slight relationship with the test scores; among the secondary students the higher scores accompanied the most rigid teaching. The cognitive and the affective outcomes of instruction seem not to be closely associated. However, interest in mathematics accompanies continuance in the subject and is higher in countries with the highest scores.

I have deferred giving the mean scores for pupils in different countries until some of the underlying determinants were outlined. As Table 4 shows, the disparity in performance among countries is very large in each population of pupils. In the 13-year group the Japanese mean is about three-fourths of a standard deviation above and the United States a quarter of a standard deviation below the grand mean. In the preuniversity mathematics population, the upward divergence is about equally great (Israel being highest) but with a much larger downward spread. On both that and the other preuniversity population the United States is nearly a whole standard deviation below the grand mean.[17] The relative scatter among the means (average deviation of country means from the grand mean divided by the grand mean) is almost identical in all three populations. The relative scatter among the standard deviations, however, is .13, .21, and .28, respectively; performance in some countries is distinctly more uniform than in others and is more uniform at the 13-year level. With a few exceptions countries display the same rank position with respect to variability of scores in the two preuniversity populations. Countries that retain a large proportion of youth through secondary school tend also to manifest comparatively large dispersion in the scores of their preuniversity populations.

Many clues to the bases for the wide differences among countries in mean mathematics achievement are scattered through the published report and some of them have been summarized here. In the light of the prevalently low correlations for most factors, opportunity to learn the subject and motivation loom as major explanations.

The central focus of this investigation, however, lies less in the achievement of pupils than in the mathematical competence of national populations. To be sure, as rates of secondary school attendance become more uniform among countries the two measures of proficiency converge. It was hypothesized that in countries retaining larger proportions of an age cohort in school to the preuniversity year, the higher scores would be achieved by a smaller proportion of enrolled pupils *but* by a larger proportion of the age cohort. Retention of pupils through secondary school does vary widely among these countries, and the crude correlations of mathematics scores with retention were negative: —.62 for the mathematics and —.36 for the nonmathematics populations completing secondary school. The mean scores for the sample populations given earlier support the first part of the hypothesis.

In order to test the second half of the hypothesis, the mean mathematics scores were computed for a constant proportion of the age group in all countries; these averages are given in Table 5.[18] The inter-nation range in average performance for the new constant sized subpopulations was smaller than for the total preuniversity populations (except for the anomaly of Japan in the nonmathematics set). Yet the hypothesis is supported only partially, for

[17] The rank order of country means is quite similar for the 13-year and preuniversity nonmathematics populations, somewhat less close between the two preuniversity populations, and least similar between the 13-year and secondary mathematics populations.

[18] Since Belgium had only 4 per cent of the age cohort enrolled in the preuniversity mathematics curriculum, the top 4 per cent of scores were taken for each other country. Similarly 3 per cent of the scores were taken for each nonmathematics population since Netherlands had only 3 per cent of the age cohort in that population.

TABLE 5

Mathematics Scores of Total Sample of Preuniversity Students
Tested and of Equal Age-Cohort Samples and Percentages of
Each Category Reaching International Norms

| | MEAN SCORES | | PERCENTAGE EXCEEDING THE INTERNATIONAL NORM | | | |
| | | | 50TH PERCENTILE | | 95TH PERCENTILE | |
	TOTAL SAMPLE TESTED	EQUAL AGE-COHORT SAMPLE [1]	TOTAL	AGE COHORT	TOTAL	AGE COHORT
Preuniversity: Mathematics Students						
Australia	21.6	33.7	37	5.2	1.1	.15
Belgium	34.6	34.6	70	2.8	21.0	.84
England	35.2	39.4	79	3.9	12.0	.60
Finland	25.3	32.1	48	3.4	1.2	.08
France	33.4	37.0	69	3.4	9.0	.45
Germany	28.8	31.5	63	3.0	2.0	.09
Japan	31.4	43.9	63	5.0	10.0	.80
Netherlands	31.9	34.7	77	3.8	1.3	.06
Scotland	25.5	29.4	44	2.4	3.7	.19
Sweden	27.3	43.7	53	8.5	3.1	.50
United States	13.8	33.0	18	3.2	3.6	.65
Preuniversity: Nonmathematics Students						
Belgium	24.2	34.9	63	5.6	2	.18
England	21.4	30.2	53	3.7	2	.14
Finland	22.5	29.9	57	3.9	1	.07
Germany	27.7	34.2	81	5.3	1	.06
Japan	25.3	51.7	60	29.4	12	5.90
Scotland	20.7	32.7	50	6.3	1	.13
Sweden	12.6	21.8	10	.7	0	.00
United States	8.3	30.7	12	6.2	1	.52

[1] Upper 4% of age cohort for preuniversity mathematics and upper 3% for nonmathematics population.

the correlation of the original and the new subpopulation means is .45 for the mathematics and .54 for the nonmathematics students. When this recomputation of scores was carried out, several countries shifted their relative positions. Thus when the same superior proportions of the age cohort are compared, countries differ less in mathematical proficiency than when all enrolled students are compared. The best students in all countries are rather similar in performance. Wide disparities in the outcomes of schooling are more conspicuous at lower or intermediate than at higher levels of achievement. Clearly the contrast is not mainly between selective and comprehensive systems for there is considerable dissimilarity among Japan, Sweden, and the United States.

The testing of the second part of the hypothesis was pursued also in another way. International "standards" of proficiency were set up by computing the mathematics scores at the 95th, 90th, and so on, percentiles of the all-nation distribution.[19] Each country should have five per cent of its students reaching the 95th international percentile, and so on. Table 5 shows for each country the percentage of all pupils tested and the estimated percentage for the whole age cohort who attain the international median and 95th percentile scores.[20] The correlation between the percentage reaching the two international norms and the degree of retention as among countries is shown in Table 6.

TABLE 6

Correlation Between Percentages Reaching International Norms and Degree of Retention among Countries

	MATHEMATICS POPULATION		NONMATHEMATICS POPULATION	
	50TH	95TH	50TH	95TH
Tested Poulations	−.72	−.35	−.28	.38
Age Cohort	.55	.10	.95	.81

Considering the first row of coefficients, on the whole, high retention goes with poorer performance. However, the most able students are not greatly handicapped by the presence of less proficient schoolmates—not at all in the nonmathematics groups. Countries were, however, by no means uniformly outstanding or poor; for example, Netherlands students do well in the midrange but not so well at the upper range. Scotland places no more of its mathematics students above the 95th percentile than the United States or Sweden despite the fact that the latter countries have three times the Scottish proportion of youth in secondary school mathematics courses of study. Japan and Sweden enroll equal proportions in mathematics curricula, yet Japan places eight times as many above the 95th percentile. Students reaching the 99th percentile were found only in Sweden, England, and the United States.

---

[19] This was done despite the demonstrated divergence in the preuniversity populations for age and family background. These students were more than two years older in some than in other countries. Moreover, in some countries students carried nine subjects as against only three elsewhere.

[20] The United States, for example, had 18 per cent of the age cohort enrolled in preuniversity mathematics and 52 per cent in nonmathematics curricula; for Germany these percentages were about 5 and 6 respectively.

From the proportions of tested students reaching given international norms it is possible to estimate also the proportions of the total age cohort doing so. Some of the countries with low means for the enrolled students retain very large proportions of all the age cohort through secondary school. As the second line of coefficients in Table 6 shows, the age-cohort proportions scoring high are positively correlated with the percentages of youth remaining in school to the pre-university year. On this basis some countries with high retention (as the United States) produce a larger fund of superior mathematical proficiency than some other countries with highly selective secondary schools. In this sense, high enrollments do not bring lower proficiency for the age cohort as a whole even if the enrolled students do less well than in some other countries.

It is tempting to move on to speculate about the wider ramifications of these contrasting national mathematics scores. But any general assessment of the outcomes of schooling in different countries must wait on similar test scores for other subjects. While one would not anticipate that a country ranking low on one subject would display compensatory superiority on other subjects, or vice versa, neither would one expect the correlation among countries for different subjects to be near unity.

Even with such additional assessments in hand, it will prove difficult to trace out any definite relationships between pupils' achievement-test scores and national characteristics in extra-school life. The total pattern of a nation's life is exceedingly complex and by no means homogeneous. A ranking of nations for readership of books or newspapers is not the same as for school enrollments, patents granted, or scientific discoveries. The quality of city government does not correlate very highly with that of TV programs or output of scholarly books, and neither may show much correlation with pupils' test scores.

As the next phase of this and other international testing programs moves forward, we will gain some additional insight into the relationships between education and society. But already it is clear that the possibilities for the improvement of schools are numerous and that each country has practices meriting adoption elsewhere.

SCHOOL ORGANIZATION AND STUDENT ACHIEVEMENT

Neville Postlethwaite

After discussing the growing scope of comparative education and the purposes and potentialities of the international study of mathematics achievement, the author summarizes the results of his own research based on data from the IEA project. The four problems he investigates are the variations among countries in school retentivity, differentiation, specialization, and age of entry.

I. Frame of Reference

COMPARATIVE education as a discipline is concerned with the study of cross-national or cross-cultural variability in the domain of education. Until the beginning of the 1950's it consisted mainly of separate descriptions of various systems of education; many of the comparative education text-books of that time consisted, with few exceptions, of a collection of chapters, each describing a particular nation's system of education. In the fifties, parts of one system were placed side by side with similar parts of another system and were described in more detail than when the systems as a whole were compared. Bereday (1964) has called this the "juxtaposition" stage. The emphasis has been on the exchange and collation of descriptive material. International agencies such as *UNESCO, O.E.C.D., I.B.E.* and the Council of Europe's *Council for Cultural Co-operation,* have helped to intensify this exchange and collation, with the result that there exists a wealth of data relating to different patterns of educational organisation, curricula and teaching methods. However, where any analyses of these data have been undertaken, these have been of a qualitative nature and usually within countries.

It has become increasingly evident that formal education plays an important part in the social, economic and technological development of a country; at the same time, the scarcity of resources has made it impossible both in developed and developing countries to satisfy the growing demand for educational expansion and this, in turn, has underlined the need for a critical inquiry and reappraisal of some of the educational practices in existence today. Anderson (1961) has indicated the need to introduce into comparative educational studies established procedures of research and quantitative assessment, so as to gather information not only about the "efficiency" of various types of educational systems, but also about the "efficiency" of various educational practices within them. Bereday (1964) too, has emphasised the need for an

REPRINTED FROM *School Organization and Student Achievement* by Neville Postlethwaite, (Stockholm: Almqvist and Wiksell, 1967), 11–22, 128–131, by permission of the author. Copyright © 1967 by Neville Postlethwaite.

analytic (qualitative and quantitative) stage in comparative education—the post-juxtaposition stage. As a result of such cross-cultural analyses it should be possible to draw conclusions on the basis of inductive reasoning.

The efficiency (in terms of optimum production of learning—both cognitive and non-cognitive) of schools in various nations is attacked and defended usually without solid evidence to support the claims of either attackers or defenders,[1] with the result that policy is often made on the basis of assumption and impressionistic and incomplete evidence. A United States admiral, in a widely publicised article in 1965, contended that one school year in the United States would be worth only two-thirds of a school year in Europe, but, as yet, no evidence has been gathered by which this impressionistic statement can be confirmed or rejected. The type of statistics which have so far been collated and classified concern "input" variables to the school system (e.g. statistics concerning teachers, buildings, financial expenditure per student, curricula, etc.) but no systematic measures of qualitative "outcomes" have been made (cf. Harbison and Myers, 1964).

Thus, in order to examine the "efficiency" according to certain criteria of systems as a whole, or of particular educational practices, it is necessary to have measures of the "outcomes" of the various systems. This implies that internationally valid cognitive and non-cognitive measures (in the form of tests, attitude scales and questionnaires) are used, so that comparable data are obtained about a number of educational systems at the same time.

Such data are of special value:

1. when one wishes to study the relationship between certain variations in educational practice and educational achievement, but the practices and school structures one wishes to compare are not well represented within a single country,

2. when it is desirable to test the generality or universality of a relationship that has been found in some country.

One illustration of the former would be an inquiry into the relationship between the age of commencing formal schooling and subsequent achievement. How does achievement at, say, age thirteen, compare for students who entered into formal schooling at age five, age six, or age seven? The uniformity of practice within a single country almost precludes any study of this question within national boundaries. It would be extremely difficult, if not impracticable, to set up an experimental situation within a single country. Furthermore, it would necessitate changing many of the cultural assumptions and values held by teachers, students, parents and society for the various experimental situations. Such variety, however, already exists internationally and an international study would reveal the diversity of practice in different countries and make data on this point readily available.

An illustration of the second type of relationship is the allegation that boys

---

[1] Cf. Carnegie Quarterly, Volume XIV, No. 2, 1966: "The Gross Educational Product: How Much are Students Learning?"

do better than girls in certain subjects. Is this a general phenomenon, or is it limited to certain countries? If the latter is the case, what are the characteristics of the cultural patterns and of the educational systems in which boys do better and of those in which girls do better?

Thus, an international study of education must centre on the kinds of questions that can be answered best (or solely) by comparisons of the achievement of students in different countries, and that can be answered poorly, if at all, by studies of students within a single country. The school systems of the world represent a series of environments in which human beings learn, and as a group are much more varied and contain far greater differences than can usually be found or created in any one system. Thus, educational quasi-laboratory situations exist in which many of the important questions concerning human learning can be studied objectively, though there is still a great deal of difficult work involved in specifying such environments with reasonable accuracy and in comparable and meaningful ways.

The design of the international research study reported here is of the survey type using random probability sampling techniques. As implied earlier on, the survey approach has the advantage of examining practices as they exist, and with the surrounding philosophies and values concerning those practices held by the students, teachers, parents, and other members of society. Degrees of association between certain independent (input) and dependent (output) variables can be measured, as well as between certain of the independent or dependent variables themselves. Although it is more difficult to infer cause and effect relationships than in a controlled experiment, it can be argued that it is extremely difficult to set up a controlled experiment in the educational field for examining certain problems (cf. Carroll, 1963, Kish, 1965). For example, for a controlled experiment involving an examination of streaming, it is important that teachers teaching streamed classes should believe in the principle of streaming and vice-versa for those teaching non-streamed classes. In practice, this is difficult. On the other hand, it is well known that there will always be teachers of differing philosophies teaching both sort of classes. A survey research can look at the situation as it exists and evaluate streaming versus non-streaming in their various contexts. This is obviously of more value than an examination of the problem in an artificially set-up experiment. However, it must be borne in mind that only experimental studies allow conclusions of cause and effect relationships. Any notion of cause and effect from survey research is strictly inferential.

The present study has drawn from the data gathered by the IEA Project (see Husén et al., 1967) where educational research centres or institutes from twelve countries: Australia, Belgium, England, Federal Republic of Germany, Finland, France, Israel, Japan, the Netherlands, Scotland, Sweden and the United States, participated in a cross-national study of a comparison of the outcomes of mathematics instruction. . . . The educational practices chosen for study in the present book are those where wide variation occurs between educational systems. They, therefore, concern data where a study is made of the relationship between certain variations in educational practice and educational achievement. . . . However, it must be made quite clear that these problems are being examined in terms of only *one* aspect of student achievement—mathematics. Whether the results would be the same in other subject areas is a matter for future research.

Retentivity [2]

Retentivity is a term used to describe the proportion of an age group being retained in full-time schooling in a system to the end of secondary schooling. Thus, the United States system, since it retains nearly three-quarters of an age group in school through to the end of twelfth grade, is described as a "highly retentive" system, whereas England, retaining only twelve percent of an age group, could, in 1964, be described as a system with "low retentivity."

In the United States and Japan, which are highly retentive systems, there would appear to be a deliberate policy of encouraging as many students as possible to continue through to the end of secondary schooling. In many European countries, there has been a policy of gradually selecting out a small élite which has been allowed to continue through to the pre-university year. Theoretically, of course, each child is allowed to continue through, but usually on condition that various academic (and selective) hurdles are overcome. In the last decade in Europe, as steps have been taken to broaden the opportunities for secondary and higher education, the objection has frequently been raised that, if more students are allowed through either to the pre-university year, or to the university, this will mean a "lowering of standards." Unfortunately, when asked for an operational definition of "standards," those who use the term are either at a loss to supply one, or suggest, that "standards" refer to the minimum requirement for a "pass" mark that has emerged over the years (cf. Husén, 1966).

By the use of internationally valid mathematics tests, it is possible to compare the outcomes of students both studying and not studying mathematics in the pre-university year. It is possible to compare the outcomes from various points of view. First, it is possible to compare the average performance; it is often asserted that the "standard" of performance of the students in the pre-university year in the European low retentivity systems is higher than that of the United States twelfth-graders—is this true or not? Secondly, it is possible to examine the relative performances of students at different parts of the distribution of scores in each system. Thus, for example, how do the top five percent in school in England compare with the top five percent in school in the United States? Is it true that if more students are allowed through to the pre-university year, this will mean a lowering of "standards" for the "best" students? Since the degree of retentivity varies greatly from country to country, it is obvious that a comparison of international percentiles referring to the

---

[2] Some aspects of this problem have also been taken up in the IEA international publication (Husén, *et al.*, 1967) by the present author and others.

composite distribution of pre-university mathematics (and separately non-mathematics) students is not fair to the highly retentive systems. Therefore, it is necessary to go one step further and calculate the proportions of a *total age group* reaching various levels of achievement. It can be appreciated that a higher proportion of students in full-time schooling in a low retentive system are likely to reach, say, the international 95th percentile than in a high retentive system, but that when the same two countries are compared in terms of the *total age group* reaching the 95th percentile, the reverse may be true. Calculating the proportion of a total age group reaching certain "standards" (in terms of international percentiles) introduces the concept of "how many students are brought how far" in a particular system. It is possible to develop this line of thought and calculate an "achievement yield" of particular groups of students. This takes into account the percentage of an age group reaching a particular level of achievement, and is not simply a comparison of means between countries irrespective of the differing percentages of an age group making up the population being compared. Furthermore, it is possible to compare the "increase" in yield between a point where one hundred percent of an age group are in school (in this study, 13-year-olds) and the pre-university year. Ideally, it would be desirable to measure the "total yield" of achievement of a system. This, however, would require measuring achievement of all those dropping-out of school at the points at which they drop out. Another approach would be the longitudinal, measuring student accomplishment at the beginning and at the end of a given school year or stage.

Differentiation

Differentiation is a term used to describe the policy of grouping students by some particular criterion into different schools or into different classes within schools (Husén, 1962). In selective systems of education, students are separated, usually somewhere between the ages of ten and twelve, on the basis of ability and/or achievement, into separate school types. The more able students go to a selective academic school (*grammar school, lycée, gymnasium,* etc.) and the others continue in a form of elementary school (*modern school, école primaire, Volksschule,* etc.). This type of differentiation is sometimes known as "organizational differentiation" or "interschool grouping." When a similar form of grouping is practised within schools (grouping students by ability or achievement into classes) this is sometimes known as "educational differentiation" or "intraschool grouping."

In the twelve countries participating in the IEA study, there was more diversity between countries than within any one country in the forms and amounts of differentiation employed. Previous studies have implied that the more differentiation practised either within a system or within a school the larger will be the range of achievement; at the same time, there is other evidence (Marklund, 1962, Svensson, 1962, and Husén *et al.*, 1967) to suggest that the mean scores of "bright" students are, in the long run, much the same whether they have been subjected to the policy of differentiation or not, but that "duller" students achieve more when in a non-differentiated system of education or school than in a differentiated one. However, in any system of education, it can thus be argued that it is the achievement of one hundred percent of an age group which is as important, if not more important, than the achievement of a small élite. It is, therefore, of interest to examine the range of scores on an achievement test in relation to the amount of inter- and intra-school grouping practised in various systems of education. If it is true that larger ranges of scores are associated with the amount of differentiation practised, then educational policy makers, planners and administrators should be aware of this when planning policy. It is also of interest to know the relationship of inter- and intra-school grouping, both together and separately, with variability of achievement. For example, if it is planned to change from a selective to a comprehensive system of education, but it is expected that intra-school grouping will be practised in the comprehensive school, then what will be the approximate change in the variability of achievement? Alternatively, if intra-school grouping is not practised, then what might be the change in the range of achievement of a year group?

Related to the aspects of inter- and intra-school grouping is that of grade promotion versus age promotion. Some systems of education insist on students reaching a certain level of achievement before being allowed to progress to the next grade; this results in certain proportions of an age group being one or two grades behind the majority of their contemporaries. Other systems allow a total age group to progress as an age group through the school. It is to be expected that a grade system will have a smaller range of achievement within any one grade, but a larger range over any one age group. On the other hand, there will be an interaction effect between the age-grade progression (the promotion system which is in itself a form of grouping) and the amount of intra-school grouping practised within a grade or age group. Is it possible, for example, that within one year group in England with age grouping, but with streaming within an age group, the range of scores will be larger than in a system with grade grouping but no streaming?

The diversity of differentiation practised in the IEA study has made it possible for these questions to be examined to some extent, i.e., the relationships between various forms and degrees of differentiation and the standard deviation of scores.

Specialization and Age of Entry to School

Two other aspects of school organization where diversity exists between systems but not within systems are those of *specialization* (the practice of gradually dropping subjects or not dropping them, so that by the pre-university year only a few subjects are studied, or as many as in the early years of secondary school) and mandatory age of entry to school.

In England and Scotland, students in the penultimate and ultimate secondary school years study an average of three or four subjects only; in the United States, students in twelfth grade take three or four "solids," but it is theoretically possible that in eleventh grade they could have taken three different "solids." In many Western European countries nine or more subjects are studied through to the end of secondary school. In those countries where only few subjects are studied, there has been much discussion as to whether students should study more subjects. Those in favour of studying more subjects have pointed out that it is early enough to begin specializing at the university, and that at school a more general education should be given, since with the speed of technological change in today's world, many persons will have to be retrained several times in their lifetimes for new jobs, many of which do not even exist today. Furthermore, the fact that specialization takes place in the last years of school has a backwash effect, with the result that many students who drop-out of school before reaching the pre-university year have already dropped some subjects and in some cases are studying clusters of subjects which are arts or science biassed. Those in favour of specialization argue that it is important to concentrate on only a few subjects, since this keeps up "standards" of achievement in the pre-university year, that the universities require this specialization and that by studying a subject in depth, students are more capable of appreciating higher thought processes and that their achievement will be of higher level than those who study more subjects.

Thus it is of interest to compare the achievement of pre-university students from different countries according to whether specialization is practised or not. In general, within a country where, on average, few subjects are studied, it is difficult to examine the problem, since it is the "brighter" students who tend to study more than the average number of subjects. It should not be forgotten, however, that there are difficulties in making a straight comparison between countries on this variable, since differences between the groups of students exist which are of importance, notably that the average age of terminating the pre-university year is different from country to country and that the percentages of an age group going through to the pre-university year also differ.

England and Scotland have a mandatory *age of entry* to school of five years, Sweden and Finland of seven years and the other countries in the IEA study of six years. The median age of entry differs slightly from the mandatory age, but not sufficiently to require a different categorization in terms of the average length of schooling up to a particular point later in the systems. This particular diversity in educational practice has been mentioned earlier in this chapter as an illustration of the advantages of international educational research over national research. However, within some countries there is some small variation and interesting national studies have been carried out (Pidgeon, 1965). Those who support an earlier age of entry to school maintain that early entry makes early learning possible and that students who enter earlier will learn more than those who enter later; furthermore, it is easier for them to learn social adjustment to their peers at an earlier age, and that for "culturally deprived" children the deprivation can best be compensated by bringing the children to school earlier.

In this study, it is possible to compare the achievement of 13-year-olds in twelve countries and relate this to the mandatory age of entry to school. It is also possible to compare the relative achievement in various socio-economic status groups on the same variable. Do, for example, low socio-economic status group 13-year-old students have higher achievement scores in those countries where they begin school at five years of age than in those countries where they begin at six or seven?

It has been shown that when pre-university students' mathematics scores are adjusted for differences in age and retentivity in the different systems, the differences in scores between countries are much the same as at the 13-year-old stage (Husén *et al.*, 1967). This being so, it is interesting to add other features of school organization to that of age of entry and examine to what extent school organizational differences can account for the differences in score. It is not likely that this will be very great, since, on the basis of previous knowledge (Peaker, 1967) it is known that school and teacher variables account for a relatively small amount of the variance of scores. Nevertheless, it is of interest to those concerned with school organization to be aware of the effects of their policies.

Summary

Comparative education as a discipline has now advanced to the stage where it is necessary to carry out cross-national empirical studies of not only the input (independent) variables to systems of education, but also the "outcomes" (dependent variables) of the systems. Data collected in international studies are of special value:

1. when one wishes to study the relationship between certain variations in educational practice and educational achievement, but the practices one wishes to compare are not well represented within a single country.

2. when it is desirable to test the generality or universality of a relationship that has been found in some country.

Furthermore, international surveys of educational systems have certain advantages over small-scale controlled experimental studies. First, they involve replication and secondly, the practices being studied exist in their natural contexts with all the concomitant philosophies and value systems as they exist in practice. In a controlled experiment, it is often extremely difficult to control variables such as teacher attitude (philosophy) and once it is carried out, it requires replication.

The International Project for the Evaluation of Educational Achievement (IEA) has recently undertaken a study of mathematics achievement in twelve different school systems (Husén *et al.*, 1967). The data presented in this book come from the IEA study. The educational practices examined are those where there is considerable diversity between countries and considerable uniformity within countries.

The first practice is that concerning the differing proportions of an age group continuing through to the pre-university year (retentivity). It is intended to examine the differences in "standards" of performance associated with differing degrees of retentivity in terms of average performance, fixed international standards performance and "yield," the latter being a measure of how many students in certain defined populations are brought how far in terms of achievement within any one system.

The second practice is that of differentiation. Students are differentiated into different school types (inter-school grouping) and into different groups within schools (intra-school grouping) to differing degrees formally on the basis of ability and/or achievement. It is possible to examine the association between these two forms of differentiation and the spread of achievement scores. Further, practices differ between countries as to how students are grouped in connection with promotion policies; some countries have a system of grade promotion and others a system of age promotion. It is possible to examine the spread of scores in connection with these forms of grouping and in turn the relation between these two and the relation between spread of achievement scores and intra-school grouping.

The third and fourth practices concern the number of subjects studied in the pre-university year and the mandatory age of entry to school. It is possible to compare the mathematics scores of students from countries where nine or more subjects are studied with students' scores from countries where only three or four subjects are studied. The mandatory age of entry to school ranges from five to seven years of age in the countries participating in the IEA project. Is earlier mandatory age of entry to school associated with higher achievement scores at age 13 in general, or only for some social groups? Are there other school organizational features which account for differences in score between countries at the 13-year-old level?

All of these problems are those on which some light can be shed from the results on an international study, but which would be difficult to examine within a single nation. However, it must be remembered that these results refer only to mathematics achievement; it would require further research to check these results in other subject areas.

II. SUMMARY OF THE RESEARCH *

It has been possible to use the data collected in the first phase of the research carried out by the *International Project for the Evaluation of Educational Achievement* (IEA) to examine problems of school organisation where there is considerable diversity of practice between systems. It would be difficult to examine some of these problems directly by experiment, for reasons that are plain enough. But where diversity of practice already exists across countries,

---

* Full details of the data and the results of examining each of the four problems stated are given in Chapters 5, 6, and 7 of the study by Postlethwaite—Editors' note.

it is possible to compare practices, each of which is operating in its natural setting, i.e. within the context of the philosophy, traditions and attitudes inherent in its genesis. It is obvious that these variables which are of extreme importance in education would be extremely difficult, not to say impossible, to control in a specially designed experiment.

The IEA has constructed international mathematics tests and administered them to representative samples of students from four populations in full time schooling: (a) all 13-year-olds, (b) all students in the grade where most 13-year-olds are to be found, (c) all pre-university mathematics students and (d) all pre-university non-mathematics students. Questionnaires to collect background information were also constructed and administered to the students tested, their mathematics teachers and their school principals. The data were filed on to magnetic tape and data analysis was carried out in the University of Chicago Computation Center. The data presented in this monograph have been culled from the IEA data.

The first practice to be examined was that of retentivity—the inverse drop-out rate of a system of education. The proportion of an age group still in school in the pre-university year varied for those students studying mathematics from four percent in Belgium to eighteen percent in the United States and for those not studying mathematics from three percent in the Netherlands to fifty-two percent in the United States.

The *average* level of mathematics performance of pre-university students is lower in those countries with larger percentage of an age group still in school at the pre-university level. This is true for both students studying mathematics and those not. However, the performance of the best students is much the same in all systems. However, when the achievement "yield" (mean score multiplied by the proportion of an age group in school) of the pre-university students is examined, it can be seen that by increasing the retentivity of a school system, it is possible for a system to have both a high overall yield and an undiminished élite yield. Germany and Belgium have relatively high yields at the 13-year-old grade level and relatively low yields at the pre-university level.

These facts are of interest particularly in those European systems of education where the possibility of increasing retentivity is being examined and where many strong rearguard actions are being fought mainly concerning the maintenance of academic standards. In future research, it should be possible not only to refine the measurement of "acquired yield" and indicate this in various subject areas, but also to compare "acquired yield" with "required yield" (cf. Dahllöf, 1963). The final decision of whether or not to increase the retentivity of a system will be based on economic, political and many other factors.

The second set of practices to be examined concerned differentiation—inter-school grouping, and within the field of intra-school grouping, the practices of ability grouping and age versus grade promotion. Unfortunately, no adequate measure of the extent of inter-school grouping exists (in future research, suitable measures should be created; a possible lead might be the coding used for School type Selectivity in Pidgeon *et al.*, 1967). However, a scrutiny of the data available for 13-year-olds and equivalent grade populations suggests a positive relationship between the standard deviations of scores and inter-school grouping. Grade promotion systems have smaller standard deviations than age promotion systems; furthermore, the greater the degree of grade repeating, the smaller the standard deviation. The more ability grouping practised in a system, the larger the standard deviation of scores. However, when the amount of ability grouping practised was partialled out of the relationship between grading and the standard deviation of scores, there was no relationship for the 13-year-olds' scores (i.e., those who, in grade systems, are spread across several grades).

Thus, inter- and intra-school ability grouping is associated with large standard deviations. From other knowledge, it would seem that it is the lower social groups (culturally disadvantaged children) who are mainly responsible for the wide standard deviation by having low scores. In a non-differentiated system, they tend to score higher, thus reducing the size of the standard deviation. Although the range of scores required within a society must be determined on other than purely educational grounds by that society, there are strong arguments for the creation of a non-differentiated system, if the assumption is made that it is the duty of society to give every opportunity to each child to develop to his maximum. It is, however, pointed out that the problem of change in the area of differentiation is not merely that of taking an administrative decision for change, but that of changing the attitudes, particularly of the teachers, within the society—*de jure* abolition of a practice does not mean that *de facto* it will not exist (cf., inter-school grouping in Japan). Furthermore, it should be realised that if inter-school grouping is abolished, but intra-school grouping remains, the standard deviation of achievement scores will not be much reduced.

The third practice to be examined was that of specialization (the number of subjects studied) in the pre-university year. . . . The conclusion is that specialization, in the sense of restricting the number of subjects studied in the pre-university year, is not necessarily related to higher scores in mathematics.

The fourth practice was that of mandatory age of entry to school . . . there is not much to choose between entry at 5 years of age and entry at 6 years of age but lower scores at 13 years of age are associated with entry at 7 years of age. When the performance of 13-year-old students from different social groups is examined, it would appear that students from higher social groups benefit more from early entry to school than do students from lower social groups, but it is difficult to draw firm conclusions, because of the heterogeneity of scores within each of the age of entry groups.

It is clear that to make the mandatory age of entry to school earlier (e.g. from six to five) will not in itself improve performance; it is what happens in that extra year which is important. This is particularly true for the children of blue-collar workers. It is the qualitative differences which must now be the subject of more systematic research.

An examination of other variables likely to account for differences between countries in the mathematics scores of 13-year-olds revealed the importance of the student's opportunity to learn the mathematics involved in the tests (as rated by the mathematics teachers). This is related to some extent to the qualitative differences mentioned in the paragraph above. It will be of particular interest to mathematics educators to examine the statistics of each item in each of the countries and to consider why 13-year-olds in some countries can perform well on the item while their counterparts in other countries perform only poorly.

Of the other variables examined, important ones seem to be the pre-service training of the teachers and the number of hours of total homework (not just mathematics homework).

Although the first object of any inquiry of this kind must be to find evidence of association there is a further, more difficult, question. When evidence of association has been found how is it to be interpreted? Evidence of association is necessary if causal relations are to be inferred, but it is not enough. When we find an association between the amount of rainfall and the growth of crops we infer that it is the rainfall that causes the growth and not vice-versa. But when we find an association between interest in mathematics and performance in mathematics there may be a difference of opinion whether it is the interest that promotes the performance or the performance that promotes the interest.

In this study the author has presented the evidence of association, and has gone on to use the evidence to make those inferences which seem to him most likely. He recognises that in the last resort the interpretation must depend upon memory, introspection, and testimony and these may differ from one interpreter to another. These are grounds for caution in interpretation. They are not grounds for refraining from the attempt to interpret.

This study, and the parent study (Husén *et al.*, 1967), are first attempts at quantitative international surveys of educational achievement. At the outset many novel problems of measurement, representation and control were encountered. In the later stages there were problems of interpretation. It is to be expected that as time goes on more progress will be made in dealing with these difficulties, and that some of the conclusions reached on the present evidence may need revision as better evidence accumulates. But it may not be unduly sanguine to hope that some, at any rate, of the conclusions will stand.

BIBLIOGRAPHY

ANDERSON, C. A. "Methodology of Comparative Education," *International Review of Education*, Volume VII, No. 1, 1961.

BEREDAY, G. F. Z. *Comparative Method in Education*. New York: Holt, Rinehart and Winston, 1964.

CARROLL, J. B. "Research on Teaching Foreign Languages" in: *Handbook of Research on Teaching*, edited by N. L. Gage. Chicago: Rand McNally & Co., 1963.

DAHLLÖF, U. *Kraven på Gymnasiet*. Stockholm, 1963.

HARBISON, F. and MYERS, C. A. *Education, Manpower and Economic Growth: Strategies of Human Resource Development*. New York: McGraw-Hill, 1964.

HUSÉN, T. *Problems of Differentiation in Swedish Compulsory Schooling*, Stockholm: Svenska Bokförlaget, 1962.

HUSÉN, T. "The Relation between Selectivity and Social Class in Secondary Education." In: *International Journal for the Educational Sciences*. Volume I, pp. 17–27. Pergamon Press, Ltd., 1966.

HUSÉN, T., et al. *International Project for the Evaluation of Educational Achievement. Phase I: International Study of Achievement in Mathematics: A Comparison of Twelve Countries*. Volumes I and II. Stockholm: Almqvist and Wiksell, and New York: John Wiley & Sons, Inc., 1967.

KISH, L. *Survey Sampling*. New York: John Wiley & Sons, Inc., 1965.

MARKLUND, S. *Scholastic Attainments as Related to Size and Homogeneity of Classes*. Kungl. Stockholm: Skoloverstyrelsen, 1962.

PEAKER, G. F. "Appendix IV in Volume 2 of Children and their Primary Schools," *A Report of the Central Advisory Council for Education* (England) H.M.S.O., January, 1967.

PIDGEON, D. A. "Date of Birth and Scholastic Performance." In: *Educational Research*, Volume VIII, No. 1, 1965.

PIDGEON, D. A. (ed.) *Achievement in Mathematics. A National Study in Secondary Schools*. N. F. E. R., 1967.

SVENSSON, N.-E. *Ability Grouping and Scholastic Achievement*. Stockholm: Almqvist and Wiksell, 1962.

A COMPARATIVE STUDY OF
ATTAINMENTS IN FRENCH

Elizabeth Halsall

Using a sample of three countries (Holland, Belgium, and England), the author investigates the relation of attainment in French to three possibly explanatory variables: teaching methods, proximity to language frontier, and policy of contact with French-speaking people. The data lead the author to several important conclusions, some empirically based, others more speculatively based.

THOUGH it may not be apparent to the outside observer the educated English suffer from an inferiority complex about their lack of skill in foreign languages. Frequently on returning from abroad the exasperated English traveller writes to the newspapers to complain about his own lack of competence in some foreign tongue or the obtuseness of British firms unwilling to conduct their business in any language but English. Naturally enough the main target for abuse is the modern language teacher and in modern language circles in Great Britain much soul-searching consequently takes place. New methods are under constant discussion and demands are made for extra teaching time. But until recently no attempt had been made to supplement impressionistic judgments by scientific study and to try and determine the reasons for this blind spot in the British.

Before a research project could be set up a close analysis needed to be made of all that is implied by the question: why are the British poor at modern languages? Clearly it implies a comparison with other nations who are good at them; it also implies the existence of criteria of comparison inherent in the further question "What constitutes command of a language?" The project would therefore bestraddle two research fields not previously linked, that of comparative education on the one hand and that of linguistics and modern language methodology on the other. Since no useful comparisons could be made without the employment of standardised tests these two disciplines would have to make use of techniques in another research field, that of educational testing and statistics. The need to acquire competence in three research fields explains in part why the research project took such a long time to complete. To the worker the study still seems essentially exploratory and its main interest to lie in the problems encountered and the methods by which solutions or partial solutions were reached.

REPRINTED FROM *International Review of Education*, 9 (1963), 41–59, © 1964 by Elizabeth Halsall.

The countries chosen for comparison with England were Holland and Belgium (Flemish-speaking areas) where attainments in modern languages are reputed to be high.

A survey of the educational systems of these countries was carried out in 1956–7, much of it by on-the-spot discussion with those most competent to give advice on aspects relevant to the problems encountered. Without this field study many crucial errors would have been made; it was an indispensible part of the project. Face-to-face discussion and later personal observation of lessons were particularly useful in working out definitions of terms used in each of the three countries in somewhat different senses.

For a testing programme to be carried out it was necessary to establish criteria of attainment, to find pupils in the three countries who could be assumed to be of comparable linguistic aptitude and to establish some hypotheses on which to set up the research design.

The relevant literature distinguishes four, perhaps five, aspects of attainment in language-learning: (1) the ability to understand the spoken language; (2) the ability to understand the written language; (3) the ability to speak the language; (4) the ability to write the language; (5) the ability to translate to and from the language, whether orally or in writing. The cultural skills which form part of the mental equipment the modern linguist hopes to pass on—for example, the understanding of a different way of life and outlook—though important, were taken no account of. At present there exist no valid tests of these skills and the skills themselves have not yet been adequately studied. To many translation will seem of doubtful value as a method of learning a language but its value as a subsidiary aim cannot be questioned until the present confusion as regards international languages is replaced by general agreement on one international language which every educated man will have at his command. Modern linguists are united in considering the other four skills as indispensible elements of attainment in language, though each of them could be further subdivided into its diverse aspects. All five criteria were used in creating or selecting tests.

The attempt to find pupils in the three countries who were of comparable linguistic aptitude called for searches in the fields of both linguistics and comparative education. In so far as it has been possible to distinguish an aptitude for languages, a large component of it appears to be the capacity for verbal reasoning as shown by verbal intelligence tests. On the whole, however, the best prognosis tests have been shown to be tests in the target language of a type similar to the skill envisaged or, more accurately, to the method of language learning used on the course to be followed: thus, if the method used is an oral one the best test of future success in the language will be an oral test. An investigation of methods used in Holland and Belgium showed general adherence to translation in Holland and to an oral method in Belgium, by contrast with a "mixed" method in England. If tests in the target language had been used as aptitude tests each country would have required a different type of test; the standardisation of the Belgian and Dutch tests would have been necessary since no standardised oral or translation tests existed and the problem of their comparability would still remain to be faced. Consequently it was decided to rely on intelligence quotients as shown by verbal intelligence tests as the best measures of linguistic aptitude for this piece of research since the capacity for verbal reasoning has been shown to be an important element in this aptitude.

It was therefore proposed that each pupil in the schools chosen should be given an intelligence test in his own language standardised on pupils of his own national group and that the scales for each national test should be made comparable to each other. (As a point of method it should be stated that a test standardised in one language and used with the aid of translated versions to test the intelligence levels of the pupils of the three national groups would have produced untrustworthy scores for two of the groups owing to a hidden linguistic factor operating to their advantage or disadvantage). The proposed procedure could not, however, be carried out as in one country there was feeling against intelligence tests in some schools which had agreed to cooperate. Reliance had therefore to be placed for all three countries on background material on intelligence levels of pupils in different types of schools, with, in appropriate circumstances, information from teachers' ratings of pupils for general intelligence. In Belgium the excellent studies by Coetsier and Mortier were used and in Holland those of Luning Prak and Carpaij. In England material on IQ level of pupils was asked for from all schools and furnished by some; some local education authorities gave useful information and other evidence was gleaned, on the basis of various assumptions, from scrutiny of the Ministry of Education List 69 which deals with the numbers and proportions of pupils in various types of school. Some of the data was inevitably defective and the procedure merely the best that could be found.

The field survey of the educational systems of the three countries indicated that pupils from certain types of schools could be compared for attainment in French. In the account of each type of school given below reference is made to its general aims and to the IQ level of its pupils, since educational objectives and pupil potential necessarily affect attainment.

In Holland three types of secondary [1] school were studied:

a. The Gymnasium, a classical school with a science section aiming strictly at university and pursuing theoretic studies; the average IQ level of its pupils is 125 (Carpaij scale: Mean of test 101.5, Standard Deviation 16.0).[2]

b. The Hogereburgerschool, sometimes referred to as the HBS, which has a divided aim; some of its pupils go to the university but more go to jobs that will lead to executive positions in industry. The curriculum is rather more practical than that of the Gymnasium and the school attracts on the whole slightly less able pupils, with an average IQ of 122. The Gymnasium and the HBS often exist together as separate courses in the same school, the Lyceum, which then roughly corresponds to the British grammar school in IQ levels and aims of course. In the experiment the Lyceum and the grammar school were compared.

c. The Uitgebreid Lager Onderwijs or Ulo school, preparing pupils for minor

---

[1] Secondary school = any school attended after the age of 12 in Holland and Belgium, after the age of 11 in England.

[2] H. Carpaij. Proeve van didactische leiding van het Volksonderwijs, No. 156. Opvoedkundige Brochuren reeks Tilburg.

executive and clerical posts, e.g. as well-qualified shipping and export clerks. The IQ levels of schools of this type average out at 113 on the Carpaij scale to compare with an average IQ of 115.5 (Moray House test: Mean of test 100; Standard Deviation 16.0) for comparable classes from English schools taking part in the testing programme. However, IQ levels appear to vary appreciably from Ulo school to Ulo school; still the exam at the end of the course acts as a sifting and standardising factor with regard to the intelligence levels of pupils. The aim of the course is very different from that of the English secondary modern school: three modern languages are learned by most of the pupils to a level not very much below that of the English public examination, the General Certificate of Education, Ordinary level, under the pressure of Holland's need of clerks qualified to write and read business letters in three languages.

In Belgium two types of school were studied:

a. The Athénée or Collège, a school similar in type to the English grammar school since it prepares pupils for university studies and for executive and lower executive positions; the athénée is a state school, the collège a denominational school.

b. The École moyenne or Rijksmiddelbareschool, originally a school intermediate in type between the athénée and the elementary school but developing into an imitation of the athénée. Unlike that of the athénée, its course lasts only three years instead of six, but pupils may transfer to the athénée at the end of the course. In small towns with no athénée there appears to be little difference in IQ levels as between that of the école moyenne and that of the athénée of a large town. In towns with an athénée there is probably some, though not a great, difference between the IQ levels of the athénée and the école moyenne, reflecting a social difference; middle class pupils and possibly others tend to opt for the athénée if they can get in.

That the difference in IQ level between the two types of school is not appreciable is shown by the fact that the same courses occur in both and that when Coetsier [3] and Mortier [4] studied IQ levels in these schools they studied them as they showed themselves in the two types of courses offered by both the athénée and the école moyenne, that is the "latine" course and the "moderne" course, and not on a school basis.

The IQ levels in Belgian schools, both for the "latine" and the "moderne" courses, showed a wider range and a lower mean than in the English grammar school or the Dutch lyceum:

Average IQ "latine"   course: 119
Average IQ "moderne" course: 117

(Terman Individual Scale equivalents of the Coetsier Scale; Terman Mean of test 100, S.D. 16.0.)

The courses appear to contain both pupils who would be in English grammar schools or Dutch lycea and also those who would be in the top stream of English secondary modern schools or in Dutch Ulo schools.

[3] Dr. Leo Coetsier, Nieuwe Normen bij het Intelligentie Onderzoek;
[4] Victor Mortier. Intelligentie Onderzoek en Leerprognose, Uitgeverij Caecilia Boekhandel, Deinze, 1945.

In England also two types of school were used in the experiment:

a. The Grammar school, preparing an élite for universities and above average pupils for executive and lower executive positions. Only one foreign language is studied as a main language; a second foreign language is usually an option. We may contrast the language position in the English grammar school with that in the Dutch lyceum and the Belgian athénée where three are usually demanded. The average IQ level is about 123.5 for most grammar schools.

b. The Secondary Modern school, attended by most of the rest of the school population other than handicapped or sub-normal children. French is taken only by the more intelligent pupils and that not in all schools. As in the grammar schools pupils are divided ("streamed") according to intelligence and attainment. Hence the more intelligent pupils work together as a class, the less intelligent also being kept together.

Other types of school in each country were surveyed to check their suitability for investigation but were rejected as being atypical or in other ways not comparable.

Comparison of the intelligence levels of the schools described showed that there was greater similarity between Dutch and English schools than between Belgian and English schools or between Belgian and Dutch schools. The mean score of IQ in Dutch lycea approximates to that in English grammar schools; the same is probably true of the Dutch Ulo school and the most intelligent stream of the secondary modern school. As regards Belgium, to make the results of the testing programme comparable, the pupils had to be regrouped into two groups, one of higher intelligence and one of lower (according to teachers' ratings for general intellectual ability). When this process was completed and another which will be mentioned later, it seemed probable that the intelligence ranges and means of the two groups would be roughly equivalent to those of the English grammar school and the Dutch lyceum on the one hand and the English top secondary modern stream and the Dutch Ulo school on the other. The results of tests of attainment in French could therefore be compared.

Before hypotheses could be established on which to set up the research design a search had to be made for factors in the national situation of each country which seemed to promote or discourage good levels of attainment in modern languages, with special reference of course to French. Apart from purely organisational factors such as the length of the course, the age of beginning it, the work demanded and so on there appear to be two main groups of factors which affect attainment: the methods used in teaching a subject and the motivation of the pupils in learning it.

We will consider motivation first. There are naturally many personal aspects of motivation but in a comparative study attention is focussed on national aspects of incentive. Four of these call for remark: the incentive provided by trade and commerce, by historical and political factors, by the status of the mother tongue and by mass media such as the film. Searches showed that in the years preceding the study around 60% of the foreign trade of Holland and Belgium was carried on with French, English or German speaking countries, of which probably a minimum of 10% was with French-speaking countries. The character of British trade was very different, being largely with countries speaking English as a mother tongue or as a "lingua franca." Historical and political factors weigh heavily in favour of good standards of French in Holland and Flanders. The Dutch court spoke French until this century and the language has permeated the national life in a way unknown in England. In Belgium half the nation speaks French as a mother tongue. Moreover, both the Flemish and the Dutch speak a language of only minor international status. English, on the other hand, is now so widely spoken that even foreign scholars find it advantageous to write their articles in English, about half of the scientific periodicals extant appearing in this language. Also, few Dutch and Flemish films are made. Hence, for all these reasons the English appear to have far less incentive to study French than the Dutch or the Flemish.

However, none of these factors, as described, could be studied in isolation from each other or from the complex of many factors together making up the national situation in foreign language learning. It was necessary to look for some aspect of one or all of them whose potency varied within the national framework, making it susceptible of isolated study. For example, since the direction of trade provided an incentive, there was clearly a factor of geographical position and of contact with the foreign language. This factor one would expect to be more powerful in Holland and Belgium along the linguistic border with French-speaking areas than at a distance from it. It would therefore be of interest to compare levels of attainment in schools in Dutch and Belgian areas near to and far from the linguistic border, on the assumption that the further away children live from the border the less incentive they have to work at French. The nearest equivalent study for England would be a comparison of results in schools pursuing a consistent policy of visits to France and exchanges of English and French pupils with those of schools not doing so. In this report this factor is termed the geographical factor; schools were asked to cooperate in the study whose geographical situation or, in the case of England, whose policy made them particularly suitable for investigation.

Methods used in teaching a subject and the aims of teaching it, in so far as they are in line with the methods, will clearly influence the results attained. An attempt was therefore made to isolate a teaching methods factor by taking within a given country schools which taught according to different methods, so as to bring out, for example, the effect of two different methods at work in the same context. This attempt failed. It was found that, though teaching methods differ, in some cases sharply, from country to country, they vary relatively little within a country amongst the majority of teachers. Where they do vary there is a strong chance that the teacher or the school is untypical of the country. This is especially true of Belgium because of its centralised system of administration and inspection which improves the career prospects of teachers who conform to the officially approved method. The effect of teaching method, in so far as it could be studied, had to be studied in combination with other, mainly organisational, factors that could not be entirely disassociated from it, e.g., years of French, hours of work, etc.

This combined factor has been termed the national or country-to-country factor.

The provisional research design, which aimed at studying the effects of both motivation and teaching method, by isolating them, had been as follows:

		BELGIUM				
HOLLAND		FLEMISH AREAS		ENGLAND		
Motivation		Motivation		Motivation		Teaching
Near language frontier	Far from language frontier	Near language frontier	Far from language frontier	Policy of much contact	Policy of little contact	method
School 1 (Near, oral)	School 2 (Far, oral)	School 1 (Near, oral)	School 2 (Far, oral)	School 1 (Contact, oral)	School 2 (No contact, oral)	Oral or direct Method
School 3 (Near, gr: tr:)	School 4 (Far, gr: tr:)	School 3 (Near, gr: tr:)	School 4 (Far, gr: tr:)	School 3 (Contact, gr: tr:)	School 4 (No contact, gr: tr:)	Grammar-translation method
School 5 (Near, mixed)	School 6 (Far, mixed)	School 5 (Near, mixed)	School 6 (Far, mixed)	School 5 (Contact, mixed)	School 6 (No contact, mixed)	Mixed method

All the schools would have had to be of the same type, e.g. schools of the same general type as the English grammar school. To study factors in schools of the same type as the Dutch Ulo school or rather amongst pupils of the same intelligence levels as Ulo school pupils would have meant doubling the research design.

With the above design the following factors could have been studied:—

1. The aspect of national motivation influenced by close contact with the language. In each country School 1 would have been compared with School 2, School 3 with School 4, School 5 with School 6.

2. The methods factor. In each country School 1 would have been compared with School 3, School 3 with School 5, School 5 with School 1.

3. The total national factor. School 1 in Holland would have been compared with School 1 in Belgium and School 1 in England, and so on.

The doubling of the research design would have demanded that 36 schools in all should offer themselves for testing. Even without it efforts would have to be made to keep all other factors, e.g. the boy-girl factor or the town-country factor, constant in very varying national contexts.

In the event the final research design was to bear the scars of battle. Study of the methods factor in isolation had to be abandoned. Partly owing to national or denominational differences of policy with regard to single sex or mixed schools three mixed and two girls' schools had to be accepted. The need to fulfill essential conditions of the research project for the study of the motivational or geographical factor made it essential in Belgium to choose schools far from the linguistic frontier which were in small towns and therefore not subject to the strong French influences felt by schools in towns such as Ghent or Antwerp. Schools in small towns inevitably draw on the country areas; in addition, in Belgium the town-country factor is in this research context an even greater potential source of difficulty because country pupils often do not study French at the primary school and town pupils do. Also, in both Holland and Belgium, though not usually in England, the schools in large towns draw a proportion of their pupils from the surrounding countryside. In the results of testing both the boy-girl factor and the town-country factor had to be subjected to statistical analysis. Moreover, since conditions had to be investigated and schools approached concurrently the design had to be adapted partly, within the general framework, to fit the schools that were available. It seemed better to gather more information and have a slightly less tidy research design rather than the reverse.

The final research design was as follows:

HOLLAND		BELGIUM FLEMISH AREAS		ENGLAND	
Grammar-translation method		Oral-direct method		Mixed method	
Motivation		Motivation		Motivation	
Near language frontier	Far from language frontier	Near language frontier	Far from language frontier	Policy of much contact	Policy of little contact
School 1 (Lyceum- type school)	School 2 (Lyceum- type school)	School 1 (Lyceum- type school)	School 2 (Lyceum- type school)	School 1 (Lyceum- type school)	School 2 (Lyceum- type school)
School 3 (Lyceum- type school)	School 4 (Ulo- type school)	School 3 (Lyceum- type school)	School 4 (Ulo- type school)	School 3 (Lyceum- type school)	School 4 (Ulo- type school)
School 5 (Ulo- type school)	School 6 (Ulo- type school)	School 5 (Ulo- type school)	School 6 (Ulo- type school)	School 5 (Ulo- type school)	School 6 (Ulo- type school)
Holland Lyceum-type school = Gymnasium + Hogereburgerschool		Belgium Lyceum-type school = Athénée [5] Ulo-type school = Ecole moyenne [5] or Rijksmiddelbareschool		England Lyceum-type school = Grammar school Ulo-type school = More intelligent classes of secondary modern school	

[5] For reservations as regards intelligence levels in these schools see above.

The motivation or geographical factor would be studied by comparing within each country School 1 and School 3 with School 2, School 5 with School 4 and School 6. The national or country-to-country factor would be studied by comparing School 1 in Holland with School 1 in Belgium and School 1 in England and so on, as originally intended, but in this revised design it could not be isolated from the methods factor.

The next question to be answered was: what classes in the schools were to be tested? Ideally one would have wished to test the classes at the end of the French course, its end product. However by the end of the sixth year the differences of emphasis on various aspects of French language study both within the three countries and as between them, in line with the varying national aims in education, were so great as to render such a choice inadvisable. To achieve maximum comparability between the pupils of the three countries it was decided to test the 2nd and 3rd year of the Dutch and Belgian schools and the 3rd and 4th year of the English, when the pupils would be approximately the same age, Dutch and Belgian pupils transferring to secondary education at 12+. In this way the age factor would be eliminated. As most of the Dutch and Belgian pupils had already done a year's French in the primary school the actual level of attainment in French was more comparable than was apparent. These pupils were really in their 3rd and 4th year of French, like the English pupils, and some had done even more; this would tend to compensate for those who had done none.

In view of the agreed aims of modern language teaching the pupils were set the following tests:

a. A reading comprehension test, the Educational Testing Service of the United States kindly giving permission for the use of the reading section of Form R of the Cooperative French Test.

b. A listening comprehension test (ETS Cooperative French Listening Comprehension Test).

c. A test of translation into French from the mother tongues. As no standardised test of ability to translate basic language structures existed, one was created. The French version was composed first and was translated by nationals of the countries concerned into the mother tongue. These forms were administered to a pilot group of pupils from each country from both lyceum-type and Ulo-type schools and the resultant scores were statistically analysed by the method of Upper and Lower Thirds to eliminate defective items. The final form of the test was then incorporated in the testing programme.

d. A composition based on a picture. A picture was chosen rather than a title so as to provide the pupil with the concrete detail that enables the examiner to mark in a more reliable and standardised way. The picture told a story and the pupils were instructed in their own language to divide up their account of it into certain specified sections, again with reliability of marking in view. The compositions were then marked according to a rating technique that has been shown to be statistically fairly reliable.

e. An oral test given by the investigator to the twenty best pupils in each school group. The test was not standardised. A list of questions was prepared based on a picture presented to the pupil. A basic mark was given for each answer, with reduction of marks for errors on a standard scale and with increases of marks above the basic minimum for more fluent, idiomatic or otherwise exceptional answers.

In addition, two questionnaires were administered. The first was a motivation questionnaire designed to study the motivation of each individual pupil. It was constructed by Professor Hamley of the London University Institute of Education according to the Thurstone-Chase method of measuring attitudes; its title is "The Attitude of Schoolchildren to Learning French." The second questionnaire was designed to gather information on the pupils' general and linguistic background. It was composed by the worker on an impressionistic basis, but as factually as possible.

The tests and questionnaires were administered in March, 1957, by the French teachers of the pupils concerned. The motivation questionnaire was, however, administered by other teachers in the relevant schools so as to encourage pupils to reveal their real feelings; the oral test was given by the investigator, to promote standardisation of marking.

When the data had been thoroughly inspected it became clear that, although the testing had been done on an age-level basis, average ages of classes showed a tendency to rise in the Dutch and Belgian schools above those in the English schools. The reason for this phenomenon is to be found in the methods of selection within secondary schools for the respective countries. In England within a given year group of a school pupils are separated into classes of different levels of ability. If a pupil falls behind the work of his class he is moved into a lower one in the same year. He is only rarely kept down and made to repeat the work of a class for a second year. This selection of pupils into streams of ability is not usually practised in Holland and Belgium; instead about 25% of the pupils of a given class are kept down at the end of the year and made to repeat the work. As they are a year older than the new entrants to the class they tend to raise the average age level of the class they are kept down in and to depress its average intelligence level slightly, since, on the whole, the least intelligent pupils are kept down. This difference of approach in methods of selection within schools, the one empirical and child-centred, the other subject-centred and imposing standards set by reference to academic needs, needs to be reckoned with in any study in the field of comparative education that involves educational testing and statistics. In the present study it was found that when the pupils who had repeated a class were separated from the main group the average age level of Dutch and Belgian classes dropped to about the same as for English schools. In the case of the Dutch schools the IQ level probably rose a little but not demonstrably to a significantly higher level than that of the equivalent English schools. In the case of Belgian schools the further re-grouping according to intelligence had to be carried out in addition before one could be reasonably certain that the groups in each country were comparable.

Now that the groups in the three countries appeared to be comparable for age and IQ level and probably nearly comparable for years of French the statistical analysis of the data could be undertaken. Inspection of scores showed enough difference between the performance of the two year groups to make it necessary to separate them for analysis. Statistical analysis showed some apparent difference between the scores of boys and girls. Inspection of the pattern of these differences made it clear, however, that they were due not to a difference of sex but to a difference of school. Since the analysis was being conducted on the basis of difference between schools no special procedure needed to be followed to make allowance for this. There was just enough difference between the performances of town and country children to make it prudent to separate them before the main analysis was begun. Separation of pupils of different year levels and of town and country children made it possible to neutralise differences due to these two factors. The resultant groups, which were often small in a particular school, could now be compared: Belgian 2nd Year Town children with Dutch 2nd Year Town children and their English equivalents; Belgian 2nd Year Country children with Dutch 2nd Year Country children and their English equivalents; and the similar groups in the 3rd Year. The results of these groups were now analysed for a statistically significant difference of average scores.

The following conclusions were reached:

1. The geographical factor, *in so far as it operated within a particular country*, appeared to be of negligible importance. Indeed one or two schools far from the linguistic border had significantly higher scores for attainment than those near the linguistic border. There are two possible explanations for this feature of the results. The teaching in these particular schools was more efficient than in the schools near the linguistic border; or, pupils and/or teachers in these schools were conscious of being at a disadvantage and made greater efforts. If the latter interpretation is the correct one it underlines the importance the Dutch and Flemish attach to competence in French. However that may be, one of the hypotheses on which the research design was based was disproved.

2. The national or country-to-country comparison showed a fairly general trend in favour of higher attainment in Belgium than in either of the two other countries. This trend, already clear when Belgian schools were directly compared with Dutch or English schools, was accentuated when the Belgian pupils were regrouped into the two groups of higher and lower intelligence to correspond more closely with the Dutch and English schools. In Dutch-Belgian and English-Belgian comparisons Belgium usually came first, in Dutch-English comparisons Holland came first on the whole. In the reading and listening comprehension tests the Belgian mean was higher than the Dutch or English, generally significantly so; Holland ranked first in Dutch-English comparisons. The translation test showed a trend towards Dutch superiority, Holland often, but not always, having a higher mean, sometimes a significantly higher one; in English-Belgian comparisons Belgium usually came first in this test. Honours were more even in the composition test as between Belgium and Holland, Belgium having a slight advantage perhaps in the straight schools comparison and the advantage going to Holland when the Belgian pupils were regrouped according to intelligence; again England came last. In the oral test Belgium ranked easily first; England ranked second, in the grammar schools comparisons only; even in schools close to the linguistic frontier Holland was last. This difference between Belgian and Dutch oral results had been clearly seen by the examiner as testing was taking place. As regards the motivation questionnaire Holland showed a general trend towards higher means, and therefore poorer

motivation than Belgium and England, a fair proportion of the results being significant; this was particularly true of comparisons between English grammar schools and Dutch lycea.

What do these results imply? Firstly, the principle of specific practice is seen to be at work. For over sixty years modern language teachers have discussed the "best" methods of teaching their subjects; thirty years of research have produced no very firm conclusions. What evidence there is seems to point to the idea that pupils learn exactly what they are taught. If they are taught to speak they learn to speak, if they are taught to translate they learn to translate. This result does not tell us which is the "best" and most efficient method of teaching a language. It merely tells us what kind of method produces what kind of result. We have yet adequately to define what we mean by "best" method. However, the results of this comparative study do reinforce the evidence in favour of the principle of specific practice. The Dutch method of teaching languages is a rigorous grammar-translation method with considerable emphasis on memory work and little or none in the early stages on oral command of the language. The Belgian method is oral and direct, basic structures and vocabulary being taught to a very large extent through the medium of speech; translation is employed rather infrequently and merely to check that specific material has been assimilated; composition is encouraged but not on the whole regularly practised. The English method seems to lie halfway between the two. The Dutch slight superiority in translation and the Belgian in oral work can now be seen to support the evidence accumulated by others that pupils must practise the skill they wish to develop. It may be objected that Flemish children have greater opportunities than Dutch children for speaking French outside the classroom and that their better results in oral work could be explained in this way rather than by reference to the teaching method used. However, when we compare the performances of Dutch and Flemish pupils living close to the linguistic border i.e. with nearly equal opportunities for practice outside the classroom we find a great contrast between the two groups. Two of the Dutch schools tested were in the very south of Holland, where there is continual coming and going across the frontier for business, shopping, work or pleasure i.e. geographically well placed for the improvement of oral skills. Yet the level of achievement in one of these schools could not be compared with that of Flemish schools at the same distance from the linguistic border or indeed with that of Flemish schools remote from it. The method used was grammar-translation. In the other school rather better oral results were obtained but it was the only Dutch school that really emphasised oral work. In other words teaching methods were factors in these results.

One would tend to expect that Belgian schools would do better at composition than the Dutch schools since the method encourages direct command of basic structures. However, honours were about even. How can this be explained? If one looks carefully at the Dutch method one sees that it is fundamentally a "learning by heart" method even more than a grammar-translation one. The material is of course acquired at one remove, that is by translation, but once it is in front of the pupil it is overlearned, being frequently set twice for homework. Inevitably, even when the homework has been forgotten, a certain residue will remain in the way of a feeling for basic structures, which will be of use in free composition. The fact that so much has been seen in print will also tend to raise scores in what is after all a written exercise. Here the Belgian pupils, with their oral method, will be somewhat at a disadvantage.

The superior means of the Belgian schools in listening comprehension results should also be related, in all probability, to the method used. Any oral method implies a great deal of listening to the foreign language. Their superiority in reading comprehension stems perhaps from a generalised increased competence in grasping the significance of connected pieces of language, a competence that Dutch methods would do little to promote.

One further point needs emphasis. It was not possible within the revised research design to determine whether the *general* Belgian superiority in attainment was due to the teaching method used (that is, there was no answer that could be given to the question "What is the best method of teaching a language?"), to such organisational factors as length of course and hours of work and homework or to any other possible factors, other than those discussed here. The country-to-country results were a composite of factors that still await isolation by the use of different research designs.

The motivation results occasion some surprise. Higher means are equated with poorer motivation and the data suggests, though it hardly proves, that Dutch pupils are poorly motivated towards French. If this is so, it runs counter to what apparent national incentive would lead us to expect. On the other hand the scores on the motivation questionnaire reflect both national and personal aspects of incentive and observation in the classroom suggested that Dutch pupils were not personally well motivated towards French. The teaching methods used and the contents of the textbooks did not seem to interest them a great deal. Conditions in the classroom apparently lead to poor motivation, in the country to good. That the classroom appears to have the greater influence on the results is what one would expect. On the whole, children are more interested in the here and now than in the problematical future. The less intelligent the child the more this is true: hence perhaps the greater number of significant results for the Ulo school. Too much, however, should not be made of the motivation results as between countries; they are suggestive rather than conclusive.

3. Perhaps the most interesting results for an English observer were those obtained from a comparison of pupils in the top streams of the English secondary modern schools and pupils of equivalent intelligence in Holland and Belgium. On attainment tests these differences were almost invariably significant at the 1% level; the English results were always inferior. Average differences of 20–25 marks on tests with a total range of 40–45 marks were the rule in almost every test and school tested. Belgium appeared to have better training facilities

for the teachers of these children than did Holland, but Holland did not train its teachers appreciably better than England, as far as could be judged, in respect of modern languages in this type of school. The reasons for the strikingly poorer performance of English secondary modern school pupils may well lie in the lack of prestige of these schools and children, who have "failed the 11+ examination" for entry into grammar schools, and the consequent failure to stretch these pupils to their limits. In discussion with English secondary modern school teachers one was aware of a difference of attitude, of a greater emphasis on personal rather than academic development than is to be found amongst their colleagues in Holland and Belgium who are acutely aware that for their pupils the mastering of modern languages is a "sine qua non" if they are to obtain even minor posts.

4. The methods of selection within the schools in Holland and Belgium already alluded to during the discussion on age levels produce a crop of pupils who have been kept down for a year or more and who thus have learnt French for longer than those who have been promoted in the normal manner. It had been thought possible that the presence of often large numbers of these "doubleurs" in particular classes might be distorting the true level of these classes and preventing any correct impressionistic evaluation of standards of attainment as between England and the other two countries. Such a distortion might well deceive the casual observer. Statistical analysis showed no significant difference in achievement or motivation between "doubleurs" and their classmates. Even at the non-significant level there appeared to be no indication of any general trend. Their performances were approximately the same as those of the rest of the class. This result suggests that standards set, whether from outside the school by examining bodies or inside the school by the teaching staff, are the main forces influencing performance. Any pupil not able to reach the standard of the class he would normally be promoted to is left down; he then has a chance of reaching a qualifying standard in the course of the next year.

5. A comparison was made of pupils following different curricula. In Holland results were compared as between pupils following the gymnasium course and those taking the HBS course in the same school. Each of these results was also compared with that achieved by pupils following the Ulo course in a Ulo school, in two cases out of three in the same town. The gymnasium results were usually superior and quite frequently significantly so to those of the HBS course. This superiority was marked in the translation test and bore witness to the emphasis placed on translation in Dutch schools. In a test for which the pupils were well prepared the intelligence of the gymnasium pupils enabled them to display their talents. In the motivation results there was a trend towards higher scores, some significantly higher, amongst HBS classes and therefore towards poorer motivation. The difference in attainment was less marked between HBS and Ulo pupils if indeed there was any difference at all. In the motivation questionnaire, however, Ulo pupils showed a trend towards higher

scores (i.e. poorer motivation), significantly so in a third of the cases. In almost every case the differences between the gymnasium and Ulo pupils were in favour of the gymnasium groups and the differences were very frequently significant. Again Ulo pupils showed poorer motivation. These results are largely what one would expect. The gymnasium pupils are known to be more intelligent than the other groups. We can therefore expect them to be better in both performance and motivation; since they find the work easier they do it better and enjoy it more. The similarity between the HBS and Ulo results can perhaps be explained. The Ulo curriculum contains fewer subjects than the HBS course; it is therefore possible for less intelligent pupils to do as well on a language as more intelligent pupils extended by a wider course. Poorer motivation in Ulo pupils would be associated with their lower intelligence.

In Belgium a comparison was made between the results of the pupils following the "Latine" and the "Moderne" course respectively. There was a more marked superiority of "Latine" pupils over "Moderne" pupils than had been the case with gymnasium and HBS pupils in Holland, the differences being more frequently significant. In fact the differences are more comparable with those between gymnasium and Ulo school pupils. In the motivation results "Moderne" pupils had higher scores and therefore poorer motivation though differences were rarely significant; thus as in Holland it looked as if the less intelligent pupils had poorer motivation towards learning French.

In England a statistical comparison of the results of the grammar and secondary modern schools was not even necessary as regards attainment. A significant superiority of the grammar schools could be established by inspection. Parallel results to those in Holland and Belgium were obtained from a comparison of the motivation of grammar and secondary modern school pupils; the difference was merely more marked.

To sum up, performances by pupils following different courses appeared in all countries to be related to the demands made by the courses; courses select pupils rather than pupils courses and the resulting scores were only what was to be expected. This is an international factor related to the academic demands of modern life. Poorer motivation appeared to be related to lower ability. In respect of motivation and particularly of performance English secondary modern pupils had the aspect of a depressed class.

6. In Dutch and to a greater degree in Belgian schools pupils learn some French at the primary level though it should be remembered that in both countries secondary education begins a year later than in England. The research design did not really lend itself to a study of the importance of this factor in achievement. When the numbers of those within each year and town or country group who had different numbers of years of primary school French had been separated out each resultant group was so small as to defy analysis. In the hope of gleaning some information the dubious procedure was followed of putting together all the second year town children with one year of primary school French and comparing them first with all the second year town children with

no primary school French and then with all the second year town children with two years' primary school French, school differences being ignored; the same procedure was followed with second year country children and so on. No significant difference was to be observed in the comparison. Of course no difference had been observed between pupils who had stayed down a year or more and those who had not, but the suggested reason for this result does not operate in the case of years of primary school French. Pupils learn French at the primary school according to whether there is a teacher available or not to teach them. It is possible that those who have learned some French before the secondary school level sit back and wait for those who have not learnt any to catch up. It is equally possible that pupils who have not learnt any French at the primary school make strenuous efforts to catch up. If either or both of the above are true, classes possess within themselves a force tending towards homogeneity. A third explanation for the lack of observable significant differences would be: there is a real difference of level between the groups but school differences amongst pupils within the groups are masking it.

7. A similar and equally dubious procedure was followed to study differences of achievement or motivation due to differences of social class, a study to which the research design did not really lend itself. The results appear to give some slight indication of superior achievement amongst those of higher social class, Class 1 and to a much less extent Class 2 groups doing better than groups of lower social status. In some of the Class 1 results smallness in Class 1 may be causing unreliability. In view of this result it is just possible that school differences were not masking real differences amongst pupils with and pupils without a knowledge of French on entry to the secondary school. It would, none the less, be foolish to attach much importance to the results obtained in either the last analysis or this one.

Some of the results that have been given, though of interest to the comparative educationist, are not strictly relevant to the main purpose of the investigation which was to answer the question: why are the British poor at languages? To this main question no firm answer could be given and the conclusions reached applied only to the 2nd and 3rd year of French in Dutch and Belgian schools and to the 3rd and 4th year of French in English secondary schools. Observation shows, for example, that the oral aspect of language learning is much more emphasised in Holland at a late stage in the course. The only factor studied in isolation, the local geographical or motivational factor, proved to be of no importance. The national motivational factor was embedded in a corpus of national factors which could not be statistically analysed without the elaboration of further research designs and probably of new research techniques as well. However one can make some comment on the results achieved. Although England usually came last in any comparison, the difference between the grammar school results and those of the equivalent Dutch and Belgian schools at this level was not so great as to warrant sweeping assertions that the

English are naturally poor at languages. Standards in French in the English grammar school are maintained because of academic demands imposed somewhat artificially by the universities. These demands have no organic relationship towards any subsequent needs of students other than those of modern language specialists, whereas, for example, the required reading list for any Dutch university course assumes a reading knowledge of three languages. Consequently the standards reached in modern languages at the grammar school are largely abandoned on leaving it. At the same time the striking difference between the English secondary modern school results and those of its Dutch and Belgian counterparts underline the lack of vocational incentives for the study of French in the English school, and even more the lack of a standard set by vocational needs such as are keenly felt by Dutch and Belgian pupils on the lookout for office jobs. It would appear therefore that in the last analysis standards in French are largely set by vocational needs, even when that vocational need appears in the guise of a liberal education.

QUALITY OF EDUCATION AND SOCIO-ECONOMIC DEVELOPMENT

Héctor Correa

Using a sample of Latin American countries, Correa relates school grades to a number of social and educational variables in order to investigate the question, What accounts for differences in the quality of education between nations?

SEVERAL studies have been made of the relationship between education and socio-economic development. Most of these studies take into consideration only the quantitative aspects of education. So far, few attempts have been made to analyze the relationship between the quality of education and level of socio-economic development.

Two types of indices can be used to refer to the quality of education. The first includes what can be called indices of the productivity of the educational system, for example the coefficients of retention, drop out, repetition, promotion, etc. These indices show the relationship between a given input of enroll-

REPRINTED FROM *Comparative Education Review*, 8 (June 1964), 11–16. © 1964 by the Comparative Education Review.

ment and the output of graduates. In this sense, they measure the productivity of the educational system. The second includes indices of the factors that on an intuitive basis can be assumed to determine the quality of education, such as the student-teacher ratios, student-classroom ratios, etc. These indices will be called factor-inputs indices.

Very few studies have been made of the influence of the inputs measured by the factor-inputs indices on quality of education. Most of the few studies available are made at a level of aggregation corresponding to a single institution of education.

A first step in the analysis of an educational system might be to relate by statistical methods its indices of productivity to those of factor-inputs. However, this is not the purpose of the present article.

The objective in the present case can be described as follows. First, a methodology is presented for studying the quality of education on a level of aggregation corresponding to a country or a similar macroeconomic unit. Perhaps the word "methodology" is too ambitious. Second, an analysis will be made of whether or not it is possible to speak of "quality of education" at the level of aggregation here considered. It can be said in advance that this concept is meaningful. Finally, an index of the quality of education offered in several countries is related to some of the indices of factor-inputs in the educational system and to some other socio-economic variables.

METHODOLOGY

The data to be used are the grades obtained by students from different countries attending the same school. Such statistical data have not previously been used for the purpose of analyzing the quality of the educational system at a macro level of aggregation. Several institutions sponsored by international organizations offer courses to students from different countries. There are also several universities, for instance in the U.S.A., that have large foreign student programs. The grades obtained by these students can be considered as indices of the quality of education offered in their country of origin.

Several problems must be solved at the outset. The students attending the kind of institutions mentioned above do not represent the average student in their country of origin. There might also be reason to believe that these students are not always the best qualified to be found in their countries of origin. In every country there is a process of selection, and this process is not always based on qualifications. However, as a first approximation, it will be assumed that the students in the institutions mentioned above are the best qualified in their respective countries. In this sense, their grades give an index of the best product that can be obtained with the educational methods used in their country of origin.

A second problem among students in the institutions mentioned above is that of language. For example, lack of training in English will constitute a handicap for Spanish-speaking students in American universities. This problem is not considered in this paper because the data used refer only to Spanish-speaking students in institutions where teaching is in Spanish.

Another problem that should be taken into consideration is the impossibility of comparing grades in different subjects. One has to decide whether the grades of the students can be considered as ordinal or cardinal quantities. In the book, *The Economics of Human Resources*, [1] it was argued that grades are at most ordinal quantities. That is, they give a ranking of students in the same course, in the same subject. However, the comparison of the grades of students in one subject with the grades of the same group of students in another subject is not meaningful. All that can be compared is the ranking of the same group of students in the different subjects. The ranking of a group of students in several subjects might not be consistent; that is, some students might be the best in some subjects and the worst in some other subjects.

The consistency of the rankings of a group of students in several subjects plays an important role in the present article. If the same students, except for random variations, are the best, "average," or worst in all the subjects, the rankings of the group are consistent. The Kendall test of concordance is used to test whether a set of rankings is or is not consistent.[2] If the grades are consistent, the sum of the rankings gives what Kendall considers the best index of ranking of the whole group in all the subjects considered. Thus, an idea can be obtained of which students can be classified as best, which are "average," and which are the poorest.

The problem becomes more complicated when different students in different subjects are considered. There is actually no way to compare them.

However, our interest is not just in comparing students in different subjects, but in comparing students from different countries in different subjects. Thus, for each subject or group of subjects a ranking of the countries can be made. This ranking of the countries for each subject or group of subjects is made on the same basis as the ranking of the students of the same group, in different subjects, using Kendall's method. Once the ranking of the countries is made for several groups of subjects or institutions, it must be determined whether the rankings are consistent; that is, whether the same countries appear as the best, the "average," or the worst ones in all the subjects and/or in all the institutions. If the data are consistent, an index of the quality of education in the different countries can be established. Once the index of quality is established, it is possible to compare it with several other variables.

In these comparisons, the fact that the index gives only an idea of the order of the countries according to the quality of their education must be kept in mind. Hence, nonparametric statistical methods must be used. The methods used in this article are described in Siegel [3] and Walsh.[4]

[1] H. Correa, *The Economics of Human Resources*. North Holland Publishing Co., Amsterdam 1963. Chapter 8.

[2] M. G. Kendall, *Rank Correlation Methods*. Griffin, London 1948.

[3] Sidney Siegel, *Nonparametric Statistics*. McGraw-Hill, New York 1956.

[4] John E. Walsh, *Handbook of Nonparametric Statistics*. Van Nostrand, Princeton, 1962.

DATA TO BE USED

To apply the method described above, the grades of the Latin American students in four international institutions in Santiago have been used. These institutions are the United Nations Institute for Socio-Economic Planning (courses in economic planning); the Latin American Faculty of Social Sciences (sociology); the Latin American Demographic Center (demography); and the Latin American School for Graduates of Economics of the University of Chile (general economics).

These institutions provided the grades of several groups of students in several courses held during different years. A variety of different subjects were taught in these courses. The differences are not only from institution to institution, but also in the same institutions during different periods.

The first problem to be solved was that of obtaining a ranking of the different countries in the different institutions. As described above, the best method would have been to rank the countries in each of the subjects in each of the courses of each of the institutions considered. However, this procedure did not appear feasible because not enough students from each country were enrolled in each subject in the different institutions. Despite the serious theoretical objections, the method used here was to obtain in each one of the institutions the average of the grades of all the students coming from the same country. In Table 1, the averages of the grades for each country in each of the institutions are presented along with the rankings of the different countries.

AN INDEX OF THE QUALITY OF EDUCATION

The problem of the existence of the quality at a macro level of aggregation was studied using the data in Table 1. There is no reason to believe, *a priori*, that students from Colombia, for instance, will rank in a similar way in all the institutions considered. That is, there is no reason to believe that a quality exists in the educational system of a country which will influence the students in all the different branches of the educational system. Thus, a test must be made to determine whether this quality exists. One test is to compare the ranks of the countries represented in the different institutions and to find whether, except for random variations, they are in agreement. It can be seen in Table 1 that in Uruguay, for example, there is very close agreement. The same can be said of Mexico.

Using Kendall's test of concordance it was verified that there is agreement among the ranks of the different countries ($W = 0.613$ significant at five per cent confidence level). This result is of great importance. It shows that broad statements about the quality of the educational system in a country are meaningful. This type of hypothesis should be tested on a larger scale, using the type of data presented.

The ranking of the countries by the quality of their educational systems can be obtained using Kendall's method. For this, the sum of the ranks for each

TABLE 1

Number of Students, Average of Grades by Countries, Rankings by Institutions, and Rankings of Countries by Quality of Education Offered

INSTITUTIONS* COUNTRIES	A NO.	A GRADES	A RANKING	B NO.	B GRADES	B RANKING	C NO.	C GRADES	C RANKING	D NO.	D GRADES	D RANKING	RANKING OF THE COUNTRIES
Argentina	14	8 199	1	23	8 093	2	11	7 069	2	5	7 533	3	2
Bolivia	1	6 190	12	20	6 290	8	3	5 750	6	8	5 905	10	11
Brazil	9	7 649	2	12	6 714	6	6	5 475	9	17	6 976	7	4
Central America**	3	7 084	6	8	6 911	4	16	5 463	10	27	5 796	11	7
Colombia	3	6 965	9	6	6 853	5	8	4 229	12	8	7 208	6	8
Chile	16	7 536	4	39	7 239	3	12	6 323	3	14	7 565	2	3
Ecuador	3	6 684	11	4	5 807	9	5	5 566	8	8	7 375	5	9
Mexico	3	6 822	10	1	3 714	12	5	5 256	11	7	7 415	4	12
Paraguay	1	7 000	8	3	5 714	11	4	5 645	7	7	5 910	9	10
Peru	3	7 046	7	11	7 460	7	4	5 780	4	9	5 614	12	6
Uruguay	3	7 578	3	1	8 571	1	2	7 490	1	3	9 400	1	1
Venezuela	2	7 500	5	2	5 757	10	5	5 770	5	6	6 000	8	5

* The Institutions preferred not to be identified by name.
** Central America includes Costa Rica, El Salvador, Guatemala, Honduras, Nicaragua, Panama.

country appearing in Table 1 must be computed. The country with the lowest sum is Uruguay, and according to Kendall's method this country has the best educational system. The next lowest corresponds to Argentina, which would receive the rank of 2. The ranks of the different countries appear in the last column of Table 1. These ranks are an index of the quality of the educational system in the different countries.

Determinants of the Quality of Education

The principal use of the index of quality of education presented in Table 1 is to find the determinants of that quality. First of all, it is useful to divide these determinants into those found inside and those found outside the educational system.

The variables with which the index of the quality of education is compared are presented in Table 2. As a general observation, it should be mentioned that no attempt was made to use a total correlation between the quality of education and all the variables considered. In the study made below, the correlation between the quality of education and each one of the variables considered is presented.

Determinants of Quality Inside the Educational System

The only index in Table 2 which refers to the educational system itself is the student-teachers ratios for the universities. No correlation was found between the quality of education and the number of students taught by each professor ($r_s = -0.053$ where r_s denotes Spearman's correlation coefficient). This result shows that the students-per-professor coefficient is not a good index of the quality of education. It should also be mentioned that the index of the quality of education obtained independently of the indices of the factor-inputs makes it possible to test the usefulness of these indices of factor-inputs.

In the same way, it would be useful to test, for instance, the relationship that exists between quality of education and expenditure per student, or quality of education and equipment per student. Lack of data make it impossible to present these tests.

Determinants of Quality Outside the Educational System

In this section, the quality of education is compared with three variables: total population, quality of human resources, and per capita income.

The reason for comparing the quality of education with total population is described below. In a large group of persons, there is a greater probability that persons having higher intellectual ability will appear. In this sense, the index presented in Table 1 of the quality of education might reflect only the greater intelligence of the persons with the best qualifications out of a larger group.

TABLE 2

Student-Teacher Ratios in Higher Education, Total Population,
Harbison-Myers Index of Human Resource Development,
Per Capita Gross Domestic Production

| | STUDENT-TEACHER | | TOTAL POPULATION | | HARBISON-MYERS | | PER CAPITA G.D.P. | |
	RATIO	RANK-ING	('000)	RANK-ING	INDEX	RANK-ING	US $ 1950	RANK-ING
Argentina	23.35	9	20,051	3	82.0	1	562	2
Bolivia	—	—	3,467	10	14.8	12	72	12
Brazil	4.60	1	65,317	1	20.9	11	233	7
Central America*	7.99	6	10,942	5	29.0	7	200	8
Colombia	5.34	3	14,438	4	22.6	10	285	5
Chile	—	—	7,203	7	51.1	3	325	4
Ecuador	8.46	7	3,996	9	24.4	8	142	9
Mexico	4.84	2	32,444	2	33.0	5	260	6
Paraguay	9.34	8	1,668	12	22.7	9	123	11
Peru	7.70	4	10,249	6	30.2	6	135	10
Uruguay	—	—	2,713	11	69.8	2	377	3
Venezuela	7.74	5	6,694	8	47.7	4	933	1

— not available
* For countries included in Table 1. The values appearing in the Table are averages of the
values corresponding to each country.
Sources: Student-teacher ratios: Average of all the data available in: UNESCO La Situa-
ción Educativa en América Latina. Paris, 1960 UNESCO Basic Facts and Figures.
Paris, 1961. Total population: Average of values from 1955 to 1960 in: CEPAL, Cuadrós
del Producto Interno Bruto. Mimeograph, 1962. Harbison-Myers index: F. Harbison and
C. A. Myers, Education, Manpower and Economic Growth. McGraw-Hill Book Co.,
1963. Gross Domestic Product: Same average and source as total population.

The correlation obtained between the quality of education in a country and a
number of persons in the same country was low and shows that the hypothesis
that the index of quality of education is just an index of a larger amount of intelligent persons in a larger group of people can be rejected ($r_s = 0.091$).

Once the hypothesis that just the number of persons determines the quality
of education is rejected, the following problem comes to mind. Could the number of persons plus all the process of formation of human resources be what
determines the quality of education? To find an answer to this question, a comparison was made of the index of quality of education presented in Table 1
and the Harbison-Myers index of quality of human resources.

The Harbison-Myers index of the quality of human resources is the "arithmetic total of (1) enrollment at second level of education as a percentage of
the age group 15–19, adjusted for length of schooling, and (2) enrollment at

the third level (higher) education as a percentage of the age group, multiplied by a weight of 5".[5] The relative importance that education has in the different countries follows from the definition of the Harbison-Myers index.

The value of the correlation coefficient shows that there is a close relationship between the index in Table 1 and that in Harbison-Myers ($r_s = 0.623$ significant at a five per cent confidence level).

It is useful to mention that the significant value obtained for the correlation coefficient between the index of the quality of education and the Harbison-Myers index gives a valuable basis to the Harbison-Myers index. Repeating again some ideas that have been mentioned before, it can be said that Harbison and Myers assume the existence of a quality of human resources at a macro level of aggregation, and they use several variables that could be considered as determinants of this quality of human resources to prepare an index of the quality. However, they do not present any evidence that the idea of a quality of human resources in a macro level of aggregation is meaningful. Once a proof of the existence of the quality of human resources is obtained, different indices of this quality can be prepared.

The last correlation coefficient is between per capita gross domestic product and the index of the quality of education. Again in this case, a high correlation was found ($r_s = 0.617$ significant at a five per cent confidence level).

As a summary of this section, it can be said that the quality of the product of education is more a result of socio-economic factors outside the educational system than of the inputs in the educational system itself. This statement should be studied over a larger base.

[5] F. Harbison and C. A. Myers, *Education, Manpower and Economic Growth*. McGraw-Hill, New York 1964.

POWERLESSNESS AND KNOWLEDGE: A COMPARATIVE STUDY OF ALIENATION AND LEARNING

Melvin Seeman

This study,* conducted in Sweden, replicates and extends work done in the United States on alienation and learning. The major hypothesis is that learners are less successful in those areas of study where they have little sense of their own power to affect social and political outcomes. The study, though not comparative in itself, extends the generality of findings based on one country.

O NE OF the common complaints in the social sciences is that results turn out to be singular rather than plural. Direct replications are rare; and rarer still is any sustained effort to explore the degree of generality, or the limitation, that holds for the thesis under review. The present study is part of a series of papers that seek to test a proposition in greater depth. The thesis is that an individual's generalized expectancy for control of his outcomes (i.e., his sense of powerlessness) governs his attention to, and acquisition of, information available in the environment.

It is a thesis which has important implications both for sociological interests in the mass society and for learning theory. On the learning theory side, it has been argued that the classic laboratory studies in animal and human learning have unwittingly built "external control" into their design by using a paradigm that stresses experimenter control. These studies are, in effect, investigations of learning under the condition of low personal control. Rotter and his colleagues [1] have shown that the learning pattern is, indeed, quite different when the subject's own skills (and thus his own expectancies for control) are made relevant to the learning process.

REPRINTED FROM *Sociometry*, 30 (June 1967), 105–123. © 1967 by the American Sociological Association.

---

* This work was made possible through the collaboration of many staff members of Lund University's Sociological Institute, of which Professor Gösta Carlsson is the director. My debt to them covers the full range from generous welcome, to intellectual support and financial aid. The present work itself must stand as a partial measure of my appreciation. The data analysis benefited from the skills of Mr. Gerald King of Stanford University.
[1] See, especially, Julian B. Rotter, Shephard Liverant and Douglas P. Crowne, "The Growth and Extinction of Expectancies in Chance-Controlled and Skilled Tasks," *Journal of Psychology*, 52 (July, 1961), pp. 161–177.

121

Rotter's demonstration is also relevant to sociological interests in the idea of powerlessness, for he shows that there is poorer learning under the condition of low control, and that is precisely what theorists in the mass society tradition have asserted. Mass theory argues, in substance, that the structural conditions of mass society (e.g., high mobility, rationalization of industrial processes, bureaucratization) encourage a sense of powerlessness which leads the individual to be insensitive to, and uninformed about, an environment over which he believes he has little influence.

This assertion in mass theory—that alienation, developed out of structural aspects of modern life, has learning consequences—has been typically applied to the domains of work and politics. But the thesis presumably ought to hold for other control-relevant domains of information as well (e.g., knowledge about health among the sick, or knowledge about prison and parole for the criminal). At the same time, it should be possible to show that there are limits to the association between powerlessness and poor learning, for neither learning theory nor mass society theory necessarily imply that the powerless will be less knowledgeable in *all* domains. The principle at stake is not so much that personality or response styles of an overall character emerge; it is, rather, that in some range of specifiable circumstances, motivated avoidance or learning occur.

The demonstration that the poor learning which powerlessness encourages is specific to control-relevant information would constitute a considerable gain. It would establish a theoretically-derived principle that is broadly applicable, yet generates discriminating predictions. The research of which the present work is a part has been devoted to such a demonstration. Three studies have been completed, each seeking to examine the powerlessness-learning connection in a different institutional context. The results of these studies may be readily summarized:

1. In a hospital setting, tuberculosis patients who were high in powerlessness were compared with a matched group who were low in powerlessness, the matching including not only the standard matters of age, education and social class, but also the patients' residence on the same ward in the same hospital (to control personal and institutional variance in information-giving by different doctors and hospitals). The alienated patients showed significantly poorer knowledge on a standardized true-false test concerning health matters. This differential knowledge was apparently evidenced in their ward behavior, since staff members (nurses and physicians) were in agreement concerning the low information possessed by the more alienated patients.[2]

2. Using a randomly selected sample of the male work force in Malmö (Sweden), it has been shown that the powerlessness-knowledge relationship

---

[2] Further details regarding method and results (especially results bearing on the respondent's own conception of his information level) are contained in Melvin Seeman and John W. Evans, "Alienation and Social Learning in a Hospital Setting," *American Sociological Review*, 27 (December, 1962), pp. 772–782.

applies also to political knowledge. A sixteen-item information test was administered during the interview, as was a powerlessness scale (see below). For both manual and non-manual workers, those who were high in powerlessness scored significantly lower on the objective test of political knowledge. The relationship was sustained when the appropriate controls for education, income and social class were applied.[3]

3. In a reformatory, the learning of information relevant to correctional matters was shown to be dependent upon the inmates' degree of powerlessness. Two significant features of the design in the reformatory study are noteworthy. First, several kinds of information were presented to the inmates for learning, with the essential prediction being that only the information with control-relevant content (items dealing with parole matters) would show differential learning rates. This prediction was sustained: for the more descriptive (non-control) items there were no differences in learning between those high and low in powerlessness. Second, the design encourages the belief that we are dealing with a true *learning* phenomenon. In the reformatory case, the inmates were offered a controlled body of new information, and the results therefore lend themselves to an interpretation in terms of selective attention and acquisition (rather than powerlessness which flows from inferior knowledge).[4]

These are the studies to which I sought to add further depth. That depth was achieved by incorporating three features in the present work. First, a new type of sample was employed—a sample of non-American university students (all attending Lund University in Sweden). Second, a new domain of knowledge was examined, chiefly information about nuclear warfare (the nature of atomic bombs, their radiation effects and defense against them, etc.). Third, the question of "differential learning"—i.e., the prediction (tested in the reformatory study) that powerlessness leads to poor learning only for control-relevant knowledge—was explored further.

METHOD

The Powerlessness Scale

In each of the three studies described above, a forced-choice scale similar to the one employed here measured the respondent's relative sense of mastery or powerlessness. Though the number of items varied in the several studies, in each case the choices were of the type illustrated in the following example:

A. Even if the odds are against you, it's possible to come out on top by keeping at it.

B. A person's future is largely a matter of what fate has in store for him.

[3] See: M. Seeman, "Alienation, Membership and Political Knowledge: A Comparative Study," *Public Opinion Quarterly*, 30 (Fall, 1966), pp. 359–367.

[4] M. Seeman, "Alienation and Social Learning in a Reformatory," *American Journal of Sociology*, 69 (November, 1963), pp. 270–284.

The score derived from these responses is considered an index of the individual's generalized expectancies for control, since the items cover a relatively wide range of personal and social events (with a concentration on social-political affairs such as job opportunities, war and peace, economic success, or luck and fate as determinants of one's social life). The basic instrument in the present study contained sixteen such forced-choice items on powerlessness.[5]

The Knowledge Tests

Powerlessness is not here conceived as a construct which necessarily implicates overall personality styles, intellectual capacities, or generalized withdrawal. It refers, rather, to an explicit (albeit *relatively* generalized) expectancy for personal control, an expectancy that will not necessarily manifest itself in everything that the individual does or encounters; indeed, it may be that those with a high sense of powerlessness will learn some kinds of information *more* readily than those who are unalienated. Our focus upon "differential learning" seeks to sharpen our understanding of what kind of construct and what kind of theoretical derivations are involved in the typical psychological and sociological assertions about the person's sense of efficacy, competence, or mastery.[6]

The new domains of knowledge, about which a differential prediction was made, were called "nuclear knowledge" and "cultural knowledge." They are probably best defined by their manifest content, hence the short information tests used in this study are reproduced below. The nuclear test was an extended version of the six-item form developed by Putney and Middleton (the first six items below, which were translated into Swedish).[7] For both tests, the instruc-

[5] The technical details regarding the powerlessness scale have been reported elsewhere; see the papers cited above (footnotes 1 through 4), and the summary work by Julian B. Rotter, "Generalized Expectancies for Internal Versus External Control of Reinforcements," *Psychological Monographs*, 80, Number 1 (Whole Number 609, 1966), pp. 1–28.

[6] The sociologist's interest in powerlessness and mastery (an interest that has been sustained from Karl Marx to C. Wright Mills) is paralleled by a growing interest in related ideas among contemporary psychologists; see, for example, the idea of "efficacy" in recent voting studies; the concept of "competence" as used by Robert W. White in "Motivation Reconsidered: The Concept of Competence," *Psychological Review*, 66 (September, 1959), pp. 297–333; and the phenomenological analysis of power in Fritz Heider's *The Psychology of Interpersonal Relations*, New York: John Wiley, 1958.

[7] Snell Putney and Russell Middleton, "Some Factors Associated with Student Acceptance or Rejection of War," *American Sociological Review*, 27 (October, 1962), pp. 655–667. Professor Middleton provided the data for a comparison between the Swedish and American scores, and rightly wondered whether the somewhat specialized language might not "penalize" the Swedish sample. Though our main interest is not a comparison of the knowledge levels in the two countries, it is nonetheless relevant that the data do not reflect such a penalty. The Swedish men did slightly more poorly than their American counterparts; the Swedish women, slightly better than the American women—but there was no important difference between the two countries. The test is hard for both samples, and especially so (as one would expect) for women.

Of the four added items, two (questions 7 and 9) were expressly more political than technical (as were the first six); and two others (questions 8 and 10) were taken from a

tions offered three answer alternatives (true, false, don't know); told the respondent not to guess; and, as an aid against guessing, noted that there was no need to be discouraged if all the questions could not be answered, since some difficult ones had been included. Our fundamental prediction, of course, was that the respondent's level of nuclear knowledge would correlate negatively with powerlessness, but that the cultural test score would be unrelated to alienation.

NUCLEAR TEST

1. The primary materials used in the atomic bombs dropped on Japan were derived from uranium. (True)

2. A twenty megaton bomb has the destructive force of about twenty thousand tons of TNT. (False)

3. The neutron bomb would result in less property damage than the hydrogen bomb. (True)

4. A "firestorm" is the initial flash of an atomic explosion. (False)

5. Strontium 90 concentrates in the blood like iron and quickly causes death. (False)

6. The bomb dropped on Hiroshima had a power of approximately twenty kilotons. (True)

7. To the present time (1963), four countries have carried out nuclear weapons tests; namely, France, Great Britain, the United States and the Soviet Union. (True)

8. The heat and light radiation from an explosion of a hundred kiloton atomic bomb would cause serious injury to unprotected persons within a radius of sixteen kilometers. (False)

9. The moratorium on nuclear testing between 1958 and 1961 was initiated by the Soviet Union's unilateral decision to halt its tests. (True)

10. Radioactivity from atomic fallout is very heavy immediately following the explosion, but declines quickly in the area of the explosion within two days. (True)

CULTURAL TEST

1. Johann Sebastian Bach lived until the middle of the eighteenth century. (True)

2. Between 1960 and 1961, Sweden's population increased by about 85,000 persons. (False)

3. G. Rossini, author of "The Barber of Seville," was composing at the same time as Beethoven. (True)

4. Sidney Poitier was the first Negro to receive the Oscar award, for his role in "Porgy and Bess." (False)

---

pamphlet on survival, "If War Comes," issued for civilian consumption by the Swedish government. Putney and Middleton obtained a reproducibility coefficient of .90 for their six-item scale (p. 657). For randomly selected samples of 60 men and 60 women, the reproducibility coefficients were .91 and .90 in the present study. On the total sample in the present study, the Kuder-Richardson reliability estimate for the nuclear test was .70 and .68 for the cultural knowledge test.

5. The music and libretto for "My Fair Lady" were written by Rodgers and Hammerstein. (False)

6. The film "God's Little Acre" was based upon a novel by Erskine Caldwell. (True)

7. The main figure in Carl Milles' well-known fountain in Gothenburg is Poseidon. (True)

8. The Swedish daily paper with the largest circulation is "Dagens Nyheter." (False)

9. Ezra Pound is the author of the Pisan Cantos. (True)

10. "Fröken Julie" is the title of a Swedish film directed by Alf Sjöberg. (True)

These are hard tests; and the question of difficulty brings us to an important element in the design. It may be that the tests are too hard; it is possible, after all, to construct a test that only specialists can answer, and thus one that will produce little discrimination in knowledge among college students. But whatever the absolute level of difficulty, we wanted two tests that were relatively equal in difficulty. The reformatory study was weak in this regard, and it was a weakness that the present study sought to improve upon.

It will be recalled that the reformatory study showed differential learning: powerlessness made a difference in learning about parole; but powerlessness was not related to learning of the more descriptive material (there called "reformatory knowledge") which dealt with the average age of guards, the cost of inmate care, etc.—information not calculated to be of much use for actual control of one's outcomes in the reformatory. The distinction is between control-relevant information (parole knowledge) and material which is not control-oriented (reformatory knowledge).[8] But this latter material might well have been not only less control-oriented but also easier to learn. If that were the case, one might hold that the harder parole items show the difference they do because the inmates who are low in powerlessness are also more test-wise, or more achievement-oriented in the testing situation, hence they do considerably better than the powerless inmates where test-taking skills and motivations really count—on the harder parole material, but not on the easier descriptive items.

What is needed is a demonstration of differential knowledge where the tests have been reasonably equated for difficulty. The nuclear and cultural tests were designed to be equal in difficulty (as well as similar in the number of items, and in the pattern of true or false answers), and were administered to a pre-test sample of 135 Lund University students (66 men and 69 women). These students, unlike those in the study proper, took both tests so that a

---

[8] This distinction is by no means as straightforward as it may seem; but a fine-grained exploration of it is not possible here. Suffice it to say that the emphasis here is not upon whether the given individual values the events in question (e.g., whether he is culturally inclined; concerned about his health; interested in politics; etc.) but whether the information in general has high potential utility for altering the individual's outcomes in a given domain (nuclear survival, getting well, achieving parole or the like).

direct comparison of test difficulty could be made. The results are given in Table 1, the gist of which can be summarized as follows: (1) neither the men

TABLE 1

Comparison of Test Difficulty for Pre-Test Sample of Students Taking Both the Nuclear and Cultural Tests (N = 135)

MEASURE	MEN (N = 66)		WOMEN (N = 69)	
	NUCLEAR	CULTURAL	NUCLEAR	CULTURAL
Mean Score	4.46	4.15	3.10	3.51
(Standard Deviation)	(1.5)	(1.7)	(2.2)	(2.7)
Frequency of "Don't know" responses	153	197	255	253
Mean frequency	2.32	2.98	3.70	3.67
Correlation between tests	$r = -.05$		$r = .18$	

NOTE: The comparison of mean scores on the nuclear vs. cultural test produces a t-ratio of 1.054 for the men, and .976 for the women (neither of which approaches the .05 significance level).

nor the women achieve significantly different mean scores on the two tests; (2) the two tests are also reasonably equal in difficulty if the criterion of difficulty is the frequent use of a "Don't know" response; (3) the tests yield comparable standard deviations; (4) the two tests are clearly tapping different domains of knowledge rather than general I.Q. or test-taking skills (note the low r's between the two test scores, for both men and women); and (5) as one might expect, the men do significantly better than the women on the nuclear test (but they also do better on the cultural test, preserving the equation for difficulty if the sex of the respondent is regularly taken into account).

The Samples

The sampling procedure was necessarily complicated, partially because the present study was an addition to, and carried out in close connection with, a longitudinal study of students at Lund University. Thus, the basic sample was a panel of students who had entered the university two years before (in 1960) and had been systematically interviewed at that time by the staff of the Sociological Institute. In 1962, this panel of students was interviewed again, and the present work was initiated as part of this re-interview process, though it required an additional mail response (as described below).

The effective sample from this panel comprised 343 cases (a figure which excludes those whose questionnaires were returned as undeliverable, but, for reasons which will become clear, *includes* those who presumably received the material and failed to return it). These "panel" students were divided into two sub-samples as follows:

Sample A *(the panel mailing:* N=271). All but 72 of the panel students were randomly assigned to receive the nuclear or cultural test (with some over-assignment of nuclear tests since this was the crucial knowledge in our design and the cultural test served essentially as a control). The student received a brief covering letter, a return envelope, and two instruments: (a) the nuclear *or* cultural test (but with no knowledge of such selection); and (b) a sixteen-item powerlessness scale of the forced-choice type described above. The students' names were not asked for, but there was a code number allowing for coordination with the interviews that had been conducted earlier.

Sample B *(the matched interviews:* N=72). A group of 72 male students had been selected for intensive, follow-up interviewing.[9] This group was comprised of matched groups from three different colleges: the natural sciences, the humanities, and the social sciences. There were 24 men in each of these groups, matched on such variables as examination grades (on graduation from gymnasium, an advanced equivalent of our high school), age, college record, and the like.

In addition to providing a sample from three different colleges with matched college performance, the interview sample served as a control on the test scores yielded by the mail sample. The interview group took the nuclear test under the direct supervision of the interviewer, hence their mean score provides a control against fictitiously high knowledge levels in the mail sample (achieved possibly by checking with others, using reference works, etc.). The interview group completed three instruments: the nuclear test and the powerlessness scale (both of these being the same as the mailed versions), and a political knowledge test. The latter was developed as a second variety of politically-relevant information test, presumably less specialized and technical than the nuclear test. The test was of a true-false type, essentially the same as the one used with the adult sample in Malmö (see footnote 4). The Kuder-Richardson reliability estimate for the larger Malmö sample was .73 for the political knowledge test. The items in this test referred both to Swedish and international affairs, a typical item being as follows: "Sweden's foreign minister at the present time is Östen Unden" (False).

Sample C *(the "political" non-panel females:* N=35). This extra sample took the political knowledge test, by mail. The purpose here was simply to obtain a female counterpart to the interview group (Sample B), which was all male and had also taken the political knowledge test. Since the nuclear and cultural test samples allowed for separate male and female comparisons, it seemed reasonable to obtain a similar capability for the less technical political knowledge test. The 35 females in Sample C received the powerlessness scale

[9] Mr. Bengt Gesser did the selection and the interviewing in connection with his study of attitudes toward public leadership. He graciously consented to the additional chores required by this use of his special sample for the nuclear-cultural study, and provided invaluable help in connection with the panel sample as well. His interest and his aid were much appreciated.

and the sixteen-item political knowledge test, these 35 being all of the females newly enrolled (rather than panel students) in the colleges of law or medicine.

A Measure of Behavioral Avoidance

The topic of nuclear knowledge was not chosen by chance. Sweden occupies a rather unique place in international affairs, with a warless history that reaches back into the nineteenth century and a strong present commitment to neutrality. But that commitment is a politically sensitive, not to say touchy, one; and the question of whether Sweden should become an atomic power is a matter of considerable debate. For Sweden, the tie between the nuclear question and our concern regarding powerlessness was nicely made in Kathleen Nott's recent (and critical) book on Swedish life. She writes: "In Sweden there is a great diversity of opinion about the best way to remain at peace . . . The very divergence probably reflects helplessness: nobody knows what to do about it one way or another . . . All Swedes want, in the first place, to keep out of war, and in the second not to think about the subject more than they can help." [10]

The study design allowed a preliminary test of such avoidance, and of its relation to general feelings of helplessness. The panel sample had been interviewed in the fall of 1962, and at that time a short version of the powerlessness scale (seven items, all different from those used in the later mailing) was administered. Thus, for each subject who received the nuclear or cultural test, a previously obtained powerlessness score was available (quite independently of whether the mailed questionnaire was returned or not). The prediction about behavioral avoidance was a dual one: that subjects high on powerlessness would show avoidance either by *failing to return* the nuclear test, or by putting it aside and *delaying its return*. The cultural test served as a control, for here it was predicted that the powerlessness variable would not operate to produce a delay (or failure) in return. The aim was, again, to examine the specificity of the powerlessness effect, by showing that the avoidance (response latency or failure to return) was specific to the control-relevant feature of the nuclear information test.

RESULTS

Some Design Checks

Before turning to the crucial correlations between powerlessness and knowledge, it is important to see whether the main aims of the design have been achieved. Table 2 presents the relevant data, showing how the several samples fared on the two important measures: knowledge and powerlessness.

[10] Kathleen Nott, *A Clean, Well-Lighted Place*, London: William Heineman, Ltd., 1961, p. 22. Obviously, neither the diversity of opinion nor the urge to avoid thinking about the possibility of nuclear war are uniquely Swedish; but Sweden's relation to the problem is rather special.

TABLE 2

Means (and Standard Deviations) on Knowledge and Powerlessness, for Men and Women in Various Samples

| SCORE | NUCLEAR TEST | | | CULTURAL TEST | | POLITICAL TEST | |
| | (1) | (2) | (3) | (4) | (5) | (6) | (7) |
	PANEL WOMEN (SAMPLE A)	PANEL MEN (SAMPLE A)	INTERVIEW MEN (SAMPLE B)	PANEL WOMEN (SAMPLE A)	PANEL MEN (SAMPLE A)	NON-PANEL WOMEN (SAMPLE C)	INTERVIEW MEN (SAMPLE B)
Mean Knowledge	3.29	4.48	4.46	3.75	4.08	12.70	14.11
(Standard Deviation)	(1.9)	(1.6)	(1.8)	(1.8)	(1.9)	(2.6)	(2.7)
Powerlessness	6.42	6.61	6.08	6.69	6.65	6.97	6.08
(Standard Deviation)	(3.0)	(3.2)	(3.2)	(2.6)	(3.5)	(2.9)	(3.2)
Number of Cases	69	61	63	68	35	30	63

NOTE: Since the interview sample (B) took two knowledge tests, they are represented twice in this table (thus, the powerlessness data are the same in columns 3 and 7, and the N of 63 is repeated).

The most important aspects of Table 2 are the following:

1. As in the smaller pre-test sample (see Table 1), the nuclear and cultural tests appear to be roughly equal in difficulty, both for men and for women. The women again do considerably worse than the men on the nuclear test (3.29 vs. 4.48), but their cultural scores are lower, too. Within sex, there are no significant differences in difficulty for the two tests; and the variances are similar as well.

2. The powerlessness scores are fairly comparable across the several samples. One question of concern was whether the receipt of the nuclear test would itself affect the responses of the forced-choice scale accompanying it; and apparently it did not. For example, the panel men who received the cultural test (column 5) have a mean alienation score of 6.65, and their nuclear counterparts show a mean of 6.61 (column 2).

3. The nuclear score of the interviewed men (column 3), who took the test under direct supervision, is the same as that achieved by the men who completed the test on their own and returned it by mail (4.46 vs. 4.48); thus, there is every reason to suppose that the test scores reflect the respondents' actual current knowledge and are not seriously affected by extraneous sources over which we had no control.

4. The political knowledge test shows the same expected sex difference as the nuclear test; the women do more poorly than the men on this current affairs test.

Alienation and Knowledge

The tests of our main hypotheses are contained in Table 3, where the correlations between powerlessness and knowledge, for the various kinds of information and the several samples, are presented. The results are basically supportive of the predictions that have been outlined above, including the notion that powerlessness is *not* a global variable that correlates negatively with all kinds of information. Especially for the women in Table 3, the results show an important differential quality: high powerlessness goes with low political awareness (—.35) and with low nuclear knowledge (—.18); but that is not the case for cultural knowledge (.02). Among the men, things are not quite so clear-cut, but even here the men in the interview sample yield the expected relationship in the case of nuclear knowledge (—.31); and there is again no significant connection with powerlessness for the men who took the the cultural test (.17).

Five of the seven *r*'s in Table 3 are consistent with our predictions [11] (see columns 1, 3, 4, 5, and 6). Given the control provided by the cultural test, it is hardly likely that these differential ties between knowledge and powerlessness

[11] Of the two failures, the nuclear one is probably more important (column 2, Table 3). For these college males, the political test was apparently too easy, producing a mean score of better than fourteen on a sixteen-item test, along with a low standard deviation (column 7, Table 2). This political test, however, proved more effective with a random sample of adult males in Malmö (see footnote 4 above).

TABLE 3

Correlations Between Knowledge and Powerlessness, for Several Kinds of
Knowledge, in Various Student Samples

	NUCLEAR TEST			CULTURAL TEST		POLITICAL TEST	
	(1) PANEL WOMEN (A)	(2) PANEL MEN (A)	(3) INTERVIEW MEN (B)	(4) PANEL WOMEN (A)	(5) PANEL MEN (A)	(6) NON-PANEL WOMEN (C)	(7) INTERVIEW MEN (B)
Prediction:	Negative r			No relation		Negative r	
r	−.18*	.04	−.31**	.02	.17	−.35*	.03
(N)	(69)	(63)	(57)	(69)	(35)	(30)	(59)

* p < .05 (one-tailed test).
** p < .01 (one-tailed test).

can be explained by such generalized factors as intellectual abilities, personality features, or test-taking skills and motivations. Such factors should reveal themselves in a much more consistent way across tests and samples. Yet there are, of course, factors of a related kind that may be influencing these results and ought to be taken into account. One of these is the student's faculty (college) of enrollment, an enrollment that not only represents systematic exposure to different kinds of knowledge, but also reflects (presumably) differences in the student's interest in various kinds of knowledge. The findings, however, are not substantially different when faculty is controlled for. Thus, among the women who are enrolled in the non-technical fields (humanities and social sciences), we find the significant negative relationship for nuclear knowledge sustained (−.24, p<.01); and the absence of such a relation for the cultural test (.01).

Nor is it likely that the students' general level of academic excellence is critical. Each student's grade on the so-called "student-examen" (taken roughly at age 20, before entering the university) was recorded; and these grades show very little correlation with performance on the information tests. For example, the correlations between nuclear knowledge and exam grade were −.04 for the men, and −.01 for the women. It would seem fair to conclude that the connection shown here between powerlessness and low knowledge is specific to the control-relevant material (whether nuclear or political), that it is most clearly shown among the women in our sample, and that it is not a spurious effect of general intellectual competence.[12] It is also fair to conclude that, in

[12] Formally speaking, the appropriate test would focus on the *difference* between the r's for the nuclear test as against the cultural test, since the hypothesis embodies a contrast between the control-relevant as against the non-control information. Looked at in this way, the

absolute terms, powerlessness is predicting only a small proportion of the variance in knowledge scores, since the *r*'s are generally low.

The Problem of Avoidance

It is certainly not very illuminating to say simply that Swedes try to avoid thinking about the harsh possibilities of international war. They may well do

TABLE 4

Comparison of Mean Return Time, and Correlations of Return Delay with Powerlessness, for Nuclear and Cultural Samples

MEASURE	PANEL WOMEN		PANEL MEN	
	NUCLEAR (N = 69)	CULTURAL (N = 68)	NUCLEAR (N = 63)	CULTURAL (N = 35)
Mean return time	8.27	9.07	7.58	7.30
(Standard Deviation)	(7.1)	(7.3)	(7.2)	(6.8)
Correlation with powerlessness	.10	−.01	−.06	.09

NOTE: A high score on "return time" refers to a longer delay in returning the questionnaire. Return time was scored in terms of mail deliveries so that a mean score of eight roughly equals four days.

so, and even if they do retreat more than others (which is undemonstrated), the main point is that they are said to do so because of their sense of helplessness in the situation. This motivation they presumably share with many others; it is a rule of avoidance behavior that occupies a prominent place in the literature that describes contemporary life. We sought, as a kind of coda to the present work, to make what may be called a micro-demonstration of this rule

---

data of Table 3 do not fare too badly. Among the women, the difference in *r*'s between political knowledge (−.35) and cultural knowledge (.02) is significant at the .05 level by the one-tailed test (t=1.69, df 93); and the contrast between nuclear knowledge (−.18) and cultural knowledge (.02) shows the same trend, but yields a non-significant *t* value (1.16). The combined probability, of course, that these two control-relevant tests would show the correct difference at this level of relationship is clearly significant, though these probabilities are not independent (they involve the same *r* of .02 for the "cultural women"). Among the men, the interview *r* for nuclear knowledge (column 3 in Table 3) differs significantly from the cultural *r* (−.31 vs. .17), yielding a *t* value of 2.11 (significant at the .02 level with a one-tailed test). An alternative to the correlation procedure adopted here would involve a series of analyses of variance with major attention to the interaction effect. A non-parametric analysis of variance (based upon proportions above and below the median in powerlessness) was conducted for the panel women taking the nuclear and cultural tests (in effect, another way of comparing the *r*'s of −.18 and .02). Neither alienation alone nor type of test produces a significant chi square in this analysis; but the interaction chi square (3.01) yields a probability between .10 and .05 (two-tailed).

—i.e., to show that powerlessness leads to avoidance even in the small world of everyday tasks, like responding to an inquiry from the university.

The prediction was that those who were high in powerlessness would delay in returning the nuclear test, or not return it at all; and that this pattern would not hold for the cultural test which has no social control implications. It is possible to argue, too, that if behavioral avoidance is characteristic the nuclear test should show a generally higher (later) average return date than the cultural test, regardless of individual powerlessness. The data bearing on these predictions are presented in Table 4. Neither prediction holds: the nuclear test is not put aside longer than the cultural test; and a longer response latency on it is not associated with powerlessness.

There are several possible explanations for these negative findings, including the possibility that behavioral avoidance simply does not operate in so minimal a social context as the one we have here devised and/or the fact that the material was too brief and unthreatening to evoke the need for defensive avoidance. It is possible, too, that the measure of return delay is heavily laden with other pressures which mask the avoidance effect. One of these is the pressure toward cooperation or conformity—a taking-it-for-granted that one cooperates in social research when asked to do so. There are grounds for believing that this is a rather strong sentiment in this Swedish sample, those grounds including the fact that a return rate of 85 per cent was achieved in the present study without a follow-up letter after the initial mailing.

On the assumption that cooperation pressures would show up most clearly in the flood of early returns, those received in the first five weekdays were eliminated and the correlation between return delay and powerlessness calculated for the nuclear and cultural tests (without regard to sex, given the small N's involved and the fact that powerlessness does not vary by sex in this college sample). The r for the nuclear test was .65 ($N=33$; $p<.01$) and a nonsignificant $-.33$ for the cultural test ($N=30$). These r's say that the return of the nuclear test (after the initial cooperation phase) is delayed for those who are high in powerlessness; but, as expected, this is not the case for the cultural test. These results can hardly be taken as conclusive evidence for the behavioral avoidance hypothesis; but they are suggestive and are presented as such.

The same suggestive quality holds, too, for the evidence concerning the failure to return the questionnaire. Unfortunately, too many students sent it back (sic!), and the high rate of return became an embarrassment, as the small N's for the non-returns in Table 5 testify. It must be made clear that the powerlessness scores in Table 5 derive from a different (and much shorter) scale than the 16-item form discussed thus far. They were obtained from the seven-item version that had been administered during the interviews in the previous fall (an interview that provided the base for our later mailing of the information tests and the longer powerlessness scale). These seven items were somewhat different from those in the longer version, as a factor analysis of the entire group of items indicated. The longer scale was, by design, heavily

TABLE 5

Mean Alienation Scores (Short Form) of Students Who Returned and
Did Not Return the Cultural and Nuclear Tests

PREDICTION	NUCLEAR HIGH FOR NON-RETURNS		CULTURAL NO DIFFERENCE	
	WOMEN	MEN	WOMEN	MEN
Returned	2.67	2.33	2.59	2.68
(N)	(69)	(63)	(68)	(35)
Non-returns	2.88	3.00	2.18	2.33
(N)	(16)	(3)	(11)	(3)

NOTE: An analysis of variance conducted for the data from the women's sample only (in view of the very small N's for the men) yields an insignificant F-ratio ($F = .492$; $df = 3$, 160).

weighted with politico-economic issues (i.e., "social" control over jobs, war, inflation, etc.), while the seven-item version reflected more "personal" control —i.e., the individual's sense that *his own life* is a matter of fate (sample item: A. Many times I feel that I have little influence over the things that happen to me; B. I do not believe that chance and luck are very important in my life).[13]

There are two interesting features in Table 5 (with due caution about their stability with these N's). First, both for men and women the highest alienation is found, as predicted, among those who failed to return the nuclear test (2.88 and 3.00). Second, the cultural test certainly appears to work quite differently from the nuclear one; both for men and women, the non-returns have the *lowest* alienation scores—indeed, the differences for the cultural test appear to be more dependable than the nuclear ones. Remembering that this alienation score reflects a sense of "personal" control, it may be that the low scores for the cultural non-returns reflect greater independence about a task they do not consider important.

In any event, these data are consistent with the material above regarding delayed return: (1) high delay with the nuclear test correlated with high alienation (.65), and the non-returns show the same trend in their higher

---

13 As the factor analysis would suggest, the two scales do not correlate highly: e.g., among those (men and women) who took the nuclear test, the *r* was .44 (N=150). The distinction between "personal" control and "social" control is one that must be explored further cross-culturally. It did not appear very clearly in the early work upon which the powerlessness scale was based; see, especially, Julian B. Rotter, Melvin Seeman and Shephard Liverant, "Internal vs. External Control of Reinforcements: A Major Variable in Behavior Theory," in N. F. Washburne, ed., *Decisions, Values and Groups*, Vol. II, London: Pergamon Press, 1962, pp. 473–516, and the work cited in note 5 above.

mean powerlessness; (2) high delay with the cultural test went with low alienation ($-.33$), and the non-returns show the same relatively low alienation.
Though the trends in Table 5 are in the direction predicted, the analysis of
variance (for the women only, among whom there is a reasonable N) is not
significant. Since there were only seven items in this alienation scale, an item
analysis was conducted to determine whether the results were heavily influenced by any given powerlessness response. The trends are fairly consistent but
undramatic over these items, with the exception of one choice (item 2 in our
scale) which produces a clear-cut pattern. This item is the one given as an
illustrative "personal" item (immediately above), and produced the distribution shown in Table 6. Clearly, the nuclear and cultural tests are here produc-

TABLE 6

*Frequency of Alienated and Unalienated Choices Among Women Students
Who Returned and Did Not Return the Questionnaire
(Alienation Item #2 Only)*

CHOICE ON ITEM 2	NUCLEAR TEST		CULTURAL TEST	
	RETURN	NO RETURN	RETURN	NO RETURN
Total N	69	16	67	11
Alienated Choice ("Have little influence")	28	10	28	2
Unalienated Choice ("Chance-luck unimportant")	41	6	39	9
	$p = .06$		$p = .09$	

NOTE: The indicated probabilities were computed by the Fisher exact test, and are based on a
two-tailed test. These data show a clear interaction effect: alienation is related to low
return rates on the nuclear test, but to a relatively high return of the cultural test.
Since the nearly significant trend for the cultural test was not predicted, the probabilities have been here computed independently (see footnote 12).

ing distinctively different patterns (on an alienation item to which these
students responded months before): those who failed to return the nuclear
test are more alienated; and, as before, those who failed to return the cultural
test tend to be less alienated. These findings suggest, but hardly demonstrate,
that the phenomenon of behavioral avoidance is mediated by the individual's
sense of helplessness or mastery, and that it can be observed in microcosm in
the individual's performance of his routine tasks.

SUMMARY AND CONCLUSIONS

This work was conceived as a replication whose purpose was both re-confirmation and added depth of demonstration. The re-confirmation seems rea-

sonably clear. As in the reformatory study, we find that the individual's level of alienation correlates negatively with the control-relevant information (nuclear and political), but not with all information (e.g., the cultural test). The differential learning, in this case between nuclear and cultural knowledge, is not easily attributable to differences in the difficulty of the material presented (as might have been true in the reformatory case).

It would seem that these data reinforce the observation that when we speak of powerlessness and mastery we are dealing with expectancies for control which govern the individual's learning in determinate, yet discriminating, ways. People who believe that the environment is one they can have an effect upon show that they are sensitive to potentially helpful cues about that environment whether those cues concern matters of health, of parole, or of politics. But this is not a matter of personality style, or similarly global notions about behavior, since the superiority in knowledge has specifiable limits: it applies to nuclear and political knowledge but not to cultural knowledge; it applies to parole, but not to non-parole, information. In short, alienation in the sense used here emerges as a feature of the person that can be understood only as a problem-solving, situation-bound characteristic. As with any construct that is useful, there is a degree of generality to its operation, as is shown in the variety of control-relevant information that correlates with powerlessness; but, as with any theory that is useful, it is possible to show that the construct in question yields discriminating predictions.

The added depth of demonstration has already been implied in these remarks. There is, for one, the fact that the present demonstration occurs in a cross-cultural setting and that it involves a new domain of knowledge, namely, nuclear-political information. It is, after all, in the realm of politics that mass theory has been most prominently applied; and one can say that the applications to health and criminal behavior were simply derivations from the basically political point of view embodied in mass theory.

I have sought to add depth, too, through the concern with avoidance *behavior*. That concern reflects the view that if we are to make a serious demonstration about alienation and the mass society, it will have to be much more than an intercorrelation among "paper-and-pencil" attitudes. The task is to show in a more fundamental way that the general model we are employing holds up: i.e., that structural characteristics of the society generate various brands of alienation, and that these alienative qualities of the person have determinate consequences in behavior. My purpose is to discover whether the principles embedded in that model (e.g., the learning-withdrawal principle at stake here) are correct in their essential message; hence, the present papers have concerned themselves with the person's knowledge and behavior: not with his attitudes (since it is entirely likely, and not very persuasive, that alienated persons have related attitudes—though the task of specifying such a syndrome is useful in its own right), but with what he knows and does.

In seeking to extend our effort from the knowing to the doing, it can only be said that the extension was minimally successful. The proposition that the individual's relative sense of helplessness will lead him into delay and avoidance behavior on matters that invoke his anxieties about control can hardly be said to have been demonstrated here; but the data suggest that this is so, while inviting more discriminating tests of the matter. It is impossible to say whether the weakness of demonstration flows from such simple matters as small samples, or whether it comes more from the fact that the demonstration was calculatedly sought in an undramatic (not to say miniscule) engagement of the person's everyday life. Those engagements, however, are as much a part of the alienation logic and literature as are war, voting, suicide and unhappiness at work. One of the distinguishing marks of that literature is its tendency to see contemporary society in stark and monolithic terms, with an emphasis on the pervasive quality of alienation, in the society and in the person. The rhetoric is often very persuasive; unfortunately, the principles and the limits of their application are considerably more elusive.[14]

We have sought here to examine the generality of alienation through a test of its significance for differential learning, and its manifestation in avoidance behavior. In a sense, the method employed matches the nature of the problem, for the problem of alienation carries an inescapable dual quality: it refers to large societal troubles, and to highly personal feeling and action. We have, by design, dealt with the large troubles of nuclear warfare and political life, but only as these are wedded to the individual's sense of helplessness and his daily defenses against it. Perhaps it ought not to be forgotten that the ultimate aim is an essay on man that is macroscopic enough to speak about his important troubles, and microscopic enough to be sure that what is said is more than rhetorical.

[14] There are two points which ought to receive lengthy treatment, but which can only be signalled here. First, "powerlessness" refers to a relatively generalized set of expectations; thus, we are *not* predicting from a narrow, content-specific area (say, powerlessness in politics) to its informational counterpart (e.g., political knowledge). The idea of powerlessness apparently has a stronger, broader cutting edge than that.

Second, it is a very nice question just how "control-relevant" the nuclear information test is (a point which reinvokes the caveat in footnote 8 above). Certain kinds of knowledge about nuclear bombs—e.g., their primary materials (item 1 in the test) or their power (item 6)—are dubiously "control-relevant" certainly; and I suspect that the heavily technical character of the nuclear test has something to do with the low r's obtained here (a risk that was previsioned, and which led to the addition of four items that deal more directly with controlling the bomb, or living through its effects; items 6–10). Neither the reformatory study nor the present one solves the problem of operationalizing the "control-relevant" feature, adopting rather an ad hoc observer's view of the matter.

Part 3

THE ECONOMY

RATES OF RETURN TO SCHOOLING
IN LATIN AMERICA

Martin Carnoy

The author summarizes the results of his study of length of schooling and subsequent levels of earning in Mexico and compares them with similar studies in three other Latin American countries. The differences in the relation of these two factors, he finds, are due to differences in the rates of economic growth among the respective countries. Rapid economic growth is associated with relatively higher returns for primary and university students.

ALTHOUGH recent research in human resources has generated universal interest in education as a tool of economic development, empirical results of such research have, in fact, been almost entirely restricted to highly developed economies. Rather than putting investment in education within the context of allocating scarce resources optimally, developing countries have tended to superimpose educational investment decisions somewhat haphazardly on general development goals. More often than not, educational expenditures are made with the policy implications of developed country studies in mind.[1]

The aim of this paper is to analyze rates of return to formal schooling in Latin America. The analysis attempts to draw implications for investment in schooling which are more directly applicable to less advanced stages of development. The first part of the paper presents the results of a study by the author of the market for skills in Mexico, which is the most detailed of the rate-of-return studies available for Latin America and is of particular interest because of that economy's three decades of rapid, sustained growth. In the second part of the paper, the rates of return to different levels of schooling estimated for Mexico are compared with rates to comparable levels found in independent studies for Chile, Colombia, and Venezuela, and for various years in the United States.

REPRINTED FROM *The Journal of Human Resources*, Vol. II, No. 3 (1967), 339–374, the University of Wisconsin Press, with permission of the copyright owners, the Regents of the University of Wisconsin.

---

[1] For a well stated exposition of the dangers of applying extrapolated results from a developed country to a wide range of growth patterns, see Bert F. Hoselitz, "Investment in Education and Its Political Impact," in James S. Coleman, *Education and Political Development* (Princeton: Princeton University Press, 1965).

I. The Mexican Case

The Data

The core of the Mexico study is cross-sectional sample data for 4,000 male urban wage-earners [2] taken in a period of four months (June to September) in 1963. The sample is concentrated in the three Mexican cities of Monterrey, Puebla, and the Federal District (Mexico City). The Federal District forms the largest part of the observations, with 2,399 wage-earners interviewed; 832 wage-earners were interviewed in Monterrey, and the remaining 670 in Puebla. Information was collected through a questionnaire, either in direct interviews with employees or from applications for employment in company personnel files. The questionnaire provided data on the wage or salary of the employee, the number of years of schooling he had completed, his age, his father's occupation, whether he was attending school, and, if he had completed any part of university, the discipline he had followed. In addition, employees were classified by the type of industry that employed them and the city in which they were located. An effort was made to sample proportionately to the number of males in each of the eight occupational classes for each city in the 1960 *Censo de Población*. Within each class, large (more than 50 workers) and small (less than 50 workers), foreign and Mexican, and private and government firms were sampled. Although the sample is nonrandom, since contacts were necessary to enter places of work, subsequent testing of the sample results indicates that biases of rates of return estimates arising from nonrandom selection of firms are minor.[3]

Cost data, other than income foregone (which is estimated from the sample data), originate in a study of public expenditures on formal schooling in Mexico from 1940 to 1962. Implied rent and depreciation charges on public school buildings are included in annual public expenditures by calculating the value of the stock of these buildings in any given year, based on annual construction figures, and taking 13 percent (10 percent rent plus 3 percent depreciation) of that stock. The value of school-owned land is omitted because of lack of data. Family- or student-borne tuition expenditures for private schooling are estimated by assuming that private school costs per student in any given year were equal to public school expenditures per student.

The Results

The sample data are used to estimate income [4] as a function of several independent variables, including the number of years of formal schooling, age,

---

[2] Martin Carnoy, "The Cost and Return to Schooling in Mexico: A Case Study," unpublished Ph.D. dissertation, University of Chicago, 1964. This study contains the detailed presentation of the data, as well as results of the analysis described below.

[3] *Ibid.*, p. 133.

[4] In this paper, the words "earnings" and "income" are used interchangeably; both refer to income from labor only. Rates calculated in the second section of the paper are considered to have been all estimated from labor income (earnings) data.

occupation, and father's occupation. In the second stage the sample is divided into schooling levels. The estimated equations indicate the contribution of different factors to differences in income among urban, male wage-earners and form the basis for determining what effects changes in these variables would have on income levels.

The results of the regressions indicate that education explains a significant part of income differences among Mexican wage-earners, even when other variables are included in the equations. When schooling alone is used as an explanatory variable for income, 43 percent of income variance is explained by schooling differences; when age is added as an independent variable, the schooling percentage drops to 36; and when age, city, father's occupation, industry, and attendance are added, schooling determines 29 percent of the variance. Of all the variables used, it is the largest single determinant of income differences. The division of the sampled workers into schooling categories permits regression analysis within each category. On the basis of these results, lifetime earnings streams are obtained by schooling category, and the streams are adjusted for the effect of other variables.

The age-earnings streams enter into both the cost and the benefits aspects of rate-of-return estimates. One of the most important findings of the study is that earnings foregone by students while attending school, as calculated from the earnings of young people of equal age and education not attending school, exceed annual per student institutional costs [5] as early as the fourth year of primary school, and represent about 60 percent of total expenditures on schooling from the fifth or sixth grade of primary school through university.[6] By taking the estimated costs of schooling as an investment in future earnings and the age-income stream differences as the best available estimate of the pecuniary benefits to that investment, internal rates of return to the various schooling levels can be found. Tables 1, 2, and 3 show monthly incomes derived from the sample data; Table 4, income foregone (in annual terms) for specific years of schooling and age for incomes corresponding to Table 1; Table 5, the institutional cost per student per year in 1962; and Table 6, the private and social rates of return estimated for 1963.[7]

---

[5] Institutional costs refer to public expenditures plus approximated per student private school costs.

[6] Since no adjustment has been made on earnings foregone for unemployment among school-age job-seekers, such earnings are probably overestimated, decreasingly upward-biased as the level of schooling is increased.

[7] The internal rate of return is estimated by solving the discount formula

$$0 = \sum_{i=1}^{i=n} y_i(1+r)^i \text{ for } r, \text{ where } y_i = \text{the absolute average income difference}$$

(including schooling costs as negative income) between those in proximate schooling levels; $n =$ number of periods; and $r =$ internal rate of return. The private rate is defined here as the rate to expenditures by students and their families aside from tuition. The social rate is the rate on the total pecuniary costs of schooling, private cost (again excluding tuition) plus institutional expenditures, both public and private.

TABLE 1

Age, Schooling, and Mean Monthly Income, Urban Males,
Mexico, 1963, Unadjusted

AGE	YEARS OF SCHOOLING						
	1	4	6	8	11	13	16
10	128	128					
13	138	176	215				
15–16	274	248	339	574			
18	341	406	547	668	731	794	
22	493	659	782	936	1,009	1,090	2,081
27	556	759	919	1,286	1,739	1,832	3,008
32	583	875	1,202	1,655	2,167	2,636	5,288
39	652	977	1,395	2,094	2,620	3,539	6,032
49	796	1,113	1,679	2,753	3,738	4,826	7,185
58	770	1,136	1,990	3,087	4,625	6,480	9,230

TABLE 2

Age, Schooling, and Mean Monthly Income, Urban Males,
Mexico, 1963, Father's Occupation Constant

AGE	YEARS OF SCHOOLING						
	1	4	6	8	11	13	16
10	137	129					
13	150	179	224				
15–16	320	263	346	543			
18	443	441	559	659	713	722	
22	591	695	799	918	955	997	2,060
27	662	799	938	1,250	1,618	1,720	2,958
32	680	920	1,240	1,589	1,960	2,298	5,105
39	773	1,020	1,392	2,015	2,458	3,230	5,625
49	966	1,170	1,639	2,658	3,273	4,388	6,720
58	950	1,167	2,021	2,942	3,815	5,750	8,295

The "B" and "C" rates of return in Table 6 are estimated from income streams adjusted for the father's occupation, industry, and city, and the student's attendance factor. In the "A" rates, the total income differences by age are attributed to schooling alone; thus, the rate of return to "schooling" is

TABLE 3

Age, Schooling, and Mean Monthly Income, Urban Males,
Mexico, 1963, Father's Occupation, Industry, City of
Occupation, and Attendance Constant

AGE	\\ YEARS OF SCHOOLING						
	1	4	6	8	11	13	16
10	180	160					
13	202	218	257				
15–16	424	343	376	551			
18	590	511	571	625	745	813	
22	723	689	776	868	966	1,154	1,981
27	775	764	916	1,159	1,554	1,959	3,273
32	794	873	1,184	1,498	1,836	2,601	4,744
39	868	989	1,300	1,799	2,204	3,208	5,469
49	940	1,088	1,502	2,375	3,028	3,914	6,298
58	918	1,052	1,918	2,716	3,419	5,670	7,440

partly a rate of return to other variables (which are not associated with additional schooling) as well. Adjusting for the father's occupation separates out some of the income differences resulting from these non-schooling variables, such as home environment, the father's influence in the job market, and better market information based on the parents' knowledge of job opportunities. At the same time, however, holding the father's occupation constant may remove elements of difference which are due to variations in quality of schooling. Since differences in the quality of schooling reflect disparities in the cost of education, their effect (on incomes) should not be separated from the return to schooling.

For the most part, rates of return are not greatly affected by adjustment for the father's occupation. The rate to the second, third, and fourth years is an exception to this observedly small change: when adjusted, the rate falls from 21.1 to 15.2 percent. The decrease is due to the high percentage of peasant fathers in the one year of schooling category and the much lower income that the sons of peasants with one year of schooling earn, as compared with other sons. The rates to finishing primary school and other levels, except for completion of the university, are somewhat lowered by holding the distribution of fathers' occupations constant at the mean of the total sample. Since this distribution varies greatly among schooling categories, the small effect of holding it constant implies that a change in the composition of skills of fathers of students completing any level of schooling will only slightly affect the rate

TABLE 4

*Annual Income Foregone for Specific Years of Schooling and Age,
Urban Males, Mexico, 1963 (Pesos)*

	YEARS OF SCHOOLING					
	2–4	5–6	7–8	9–11	12–13	14–16
AGE	(1)	(2)	(3)	(4)	(5)	(6)
8	260[a]					
9	533					
10	547					
11	561					
12		657				
13		712				
14			1,964			
15			2,332			
16				4,001		
17				4,255		
18				4,509		
19					5,043	
20					5,481	
21					5,919	
22						6,867
23						7,802
24						8,737
25						4,836[b]

[a] Since the age for starting work in the one-year-of-schooling category is estimated at 8.5 years, individuals with four years of schooling are considered to forego, at the age of eight, one-half of the income adjusted according to the note on column 1.

[b] Since university graduates begin to work at 25.5 years of age, they are considered to forego, at age 25, one-half the income adjusted according to the note on column 6.

Sources: Column 1—Table 1, monthly income of the one year of schooling category × 12 × 0.75 × 0.95 × 0.5. A nine-month school year equals 12 × 0.75; 0.95 equals the correction for the 5 percent of students who work full-time, and 0.5 equals the adjustment for the half-day of primary school. Incomes in between the age midpoints in Table 1 are estimated by linear interpolation. Monthly incomes of 8- and 9-year-olds are based on the projection of the linear interpolation of monthly income between 10- and 13-year-olds. *Column 2*—Table 1, monthly income of the four years of schooling category × 12 × 0.75 × 0.90 × 0.5. The correction for full-time working students is 0.90. *Column 3*—Table 1, monthly income of the six years of schooling category × 12 × 0.75 × 0.825. The correction for full-time working students is 0.825. Secondary schools and higher are considered as meeting full days. *Column 4*—Table 1, monthly income of the eight years of schooling category × 12 × 0.75 × 0.75. The correction for full-time working students equals 0.75. *Column 5*—Table 1, monthly income of the 11 years of schooling category × 12 × 07.5 × 0.70. The correction for full-time working students is 0.70. *Column 6*—Table 1, monthly income of the 13 years of schooling category × 12 × 0.75 × 0.70.

TABLE 5

Total Institutional Cost Per Student-Year, Mexico, 1963

LEVEL OF SCHOOLING	TOTAL COST (MILLIONS OF PESOS)	NUMBER OF STUDENTS (THOUSANDS)	COST/STUDENT/ YEAR (PESOS)
Primary	2,325	5,620.3	414
Secondary	1,268	607.7	2,082
University	373	100.2	3,720

of return to the investment in that level.[8] This is not to be confused with the hypothesis that those with less educated and less wealthy parents get a mean amount of schooling equal to those with more influential families. That hypothesis is not true: the mean schooling of wage-earners in the sample with unskilled fathers is five years; those with employed (white-collar workers) fathers, nine years; and those with professional fathers, 11 years.

The adjustment for city, industry, and attendance removes elements of income differences attributable to changes in the distribution of those variables among educational levels. If the correction of the rates involves separating out factors which have nothing to do with additional schooling, as may be the case, for example, with trade unionism in certain industries, then the rates under adjustment "C" are the rates of return to schooling devoid of non-schooling effects of the variables used. It is possible that holding these variables constant, however, also separates out skill effects in different cities and industries. If that were the case, then the "C" adjustment underestimates the rate of return to schooling.

[8] An alternative way of looking at this is to compute rates by father's occupation. This has been done, for two large changes in the amount of schooling taken, in the following table on rate of return by father's occupation and years of schooling in Mexico, among urban males, for 1963:

FATHER'S OCCUPATION

YEARS OF SCHOOL-ING	PEASANT	UNSKILLED	SKILLED	WHITE COLLAR	COMMERCE	PROFES-SIONAL
8–1	26.6	22.0	22.2	11.4	28.4	19.1
11–4	26.1	18.4	17.0	19.4	23.0	22.3

Except for the sharp drop between eight years and one year of schooling in the rate of return for those with white-collar worker fathers, there is not a great difference in the rates. What differences there are do not fall into any pattern of rising or falling with social level of father's occupation.

TABLE 6

*Private and Social Internal Rates of Return by Year of Schooling,
Urban Males, Mexico, 1963 (Percentage)*

YEARS OF SCHOOLING	PRIVATE RATE			SOCIAL RATE		
	A[a]	B	C	A	B	C
2–4	21.1	15.2	5.2	17.3	12.8	4.6
5–6	48.6	44.9	32.1	37.5	34.5	26.8
7–8	36.5	31.0	24.0	23.4	20.6	17.1
9–11	17.4	15.2	16.8	14.2	12.3	13.2
12–13	15.8	14.6	22.4	12.4	11.4	16.7
14–16	36.7	39.5	34.6	29.5	31.5	27.9

[a] *A* represents the internal rate of return computed from the monthly incomes in Table 1;
B represents the internal rate of return computed from the monthly incomes in Table 2;
C represents the internal rate of return computed from the monthly incomes in Table 3.
Source: Tables 1, 2, 3, and 4, plus direct costs borne by students.

II. COMPARISON OF RATES OF RETURN AMONG LATIN AMERICAN COUNTRIES AND THE UNITED STATES

Studies on a number of other Latin American countries estimate rates of return to three or more levels of schooling for a given year. Although these estimates lack the detail of the Mexican study, they provide useful comparisons with patterns of rates in both Mexico and the United States. Latin American rates, as they appear in the original studies, are presented in Table 7.

To make the Mexican rates more directly comparable with the results for the other countries, the two rates to primary schooling are weighted by the percent of total costs per student of primary schooling incurred at each of the two levels. The weighted average of the social rates is 25 percent. Similar operations on secondary and university schooling yield average social rates of 17 and 23 percent, respectively. Weighting Chilean and Colombian general secondary and technical or special secondary schooling produces an average rate to Chilean secondary schooling of 22 percent, and to Colombian, 25 percent.[9]

The rates in Table 7 are representative of a rather broad range of development and rates of educational investment. Meaningful analysis of the rates, therefore, must be made in the context of variations in the demand for and

[9] Before proceeding to an analysis of the rates, it is also worth noting that they contain an upward bias because they are not corrected for unemployment at each level. This bias may be partially offset by a downward bias from greater under-reporting of earnings by higher level graduates relative to those at the next lowest level. In addition, earnings foregone have been omitted from the costs of primary schooling in all three countries but not Mexico. Whereas such an omission probably affects the rate to primary schooling little in Chile, it could considerably lower both the Colombian and Venezuelan estimates.

TABLE 7

Internal Rates of Return to Schooling: Mexico 1963; Chile, 1959; Colombia, 1961; and Venezuela, 1957 (Percent)

MEXICO			CHILE		COLOMBIA		VENEZUELA	
YEARS OF SCHOOLING	PRIVATE	SOCIAL	YEARS OF SCHOOLING	SOCIAL[a]	YEARS OF SCHOOLING	PRIVATE[b]	YEARS OF SCHOOLING	SOCIAL[c]
2–4	21.1	17.3	1–6[d]	24	1–5	20	1–6[e]	82
5–6	48.6	37.5	7–9[f]	29	6–11[g]	19	7–11	17
7–8	36.5	23.4	7–12[h]	17	6–11[i]	30	12–15	23
9–11	17.4	14.2	13–17	12	12–17	19		
12–13	15.8	12.4						
14–16	36.7	29.5						

[a] Rates are for males and females. [b] Includes tuition. If institutional expenditures in private and public schools are considered equal, these rates are directly comparable to social rates for other countries. Rates for urban males only. [c] Rates are probably for urban males only. [d] Average schooling = 5.5 years. [e] Rate for primary graduates over illiterate urban workers. [f] "Special" secondary schooling (average = 8.5 years). [g] Technical secondary schooling. [h] General secondary schooling (average = 11.5 years). [i] General secondary schooling.

Sources: Mexico—Martin Carnoy, "The Cost and Return to Schooling in Mexico: A Case Study," unpublished Ph.D. dissertation, University of Chicago, 1964; Chile—Arnold C. Harberger and Marcelo Selowsky, "Key Factors in the Economic Growth of Chile," presented to the conference at Cornell University on the "Next Decade of Latin American Development," April 20–22, 1966 (mimeo.); Colombia—Guillermo Franco Camacho, *Rendimiento de la Inversión en Educación en Colombia* (Bogotá: CEDE, Universidad de los Andes, July 1964); Venezuela—Carl Shoup, *The Fiscal System of Venezuela* (Baltimore: Johns Hopkins Press, 1959).

supply of skills among the four economies. Table 8 shows a number of proxy variables that serve as a reference plane for the rates.

The policy implications to be drawn from the four sets of observations in Tables 7 and 8 are tenuous at best; but despite the limited number of points, patterns emerge from which hypotheses can begin to be constructed.

1. The average level of rates is high in all four countries, relative even to the high rate of return to physical capital which predominates in Latin America. It can be argued that the rates are high *because* the rate of return to physical capital is high.[10] This hypothesis may be valid; nevertheless, except for Venezuela, where the petroleum sector may have an exceptionally high yield to physical capital, average rates of return to schooling seem to be significantly higher than rates to physical assets. This holds true even if the Chilean schooling rates are corrected for possible biases (see below).

Although large differences exist in the growth of demand for skills (as indicated by over-all growth rates of gross domestic product [GDP]/capita or by growth of the manufacturing sector) and in the supply of skills—average investment in schooling during the periods covered is 165 Mexican pesos per capita in Mexico and 278 pesos in Chile—the average rate of return to schooling is about the same in Mexico, Chile, and Colombia (20 percent) and only increases radically for Venezuela (40 percent).[11] The assumption that the "true" rate to primary schooling is half that shown for Venezuela (earnings

[10] The rate of return to a wide range of investments in Mexico averaged about 14 percent in 1962. However, the source of rates—Banco Nacional de Mexico, *Mexico as a Field for Foreign Investment* (Mexico, 1965)—does not indicate whether it is gross or net of taxes. The rate to net assets in the Venezuelan petroleum industry averaged 50.3 percent before taxes between 1947 and 1963, 24.2 percent after taxes in 1947 to 1957, and 16.5 percent after taxes in 1958 to 1963. The rate in 1958 was 16.7 percent; see Venezuela, Ministerio de Minas e Hydrocarburos, *Memoria, 1964*, pp. 1–185, 191. Two independent studies made in Chile show much lower rates: Tom Davis has found that the average, real rate of return on equities in Chile has been on the order of 6 percent or less (see Harberger and Selowsky, *op. cit.*, p. 22); a study by Rolf Luders (Universidad Catolica de Chile) shows real rates of return in industrial enterprises of 8–12 percent, depending on the size of the firm.

[11] The Harberger-Selowski estimates for Chile appear seriously overestimated. They are calculated using *constant* differences in income over time between groups with proximate levels of schooling. Going back to Blitz's original work, *Algunas Características de Edad, Educación e Ingreso de la Fuerza de Trabajo* (Santiago: Universidad de Chile, Instituto de Economía, 1962), it is possible to approximate the shape of the curves of returns (income) to those taking various amounts of schooling. Making this approximation and re-estimating rates of return to primary (5.5 years) and secondary (11.5 years) schooling yield rates of return of 11.6 percent to primary and 12.3 percent to secondary schooling, instead of the 24 and 17 percent estimated by Harberger and Selowsky. Although no new estimates were made for special and university schooling, because of the greater difficulty of accurately approximating age-income profiles from Blitz's data at those levels, it can be expected that those rates, as shown in Table 7, are also biased upward. Even if special and university rates are not biased, the average rate to schooling in Chile falls from 21.8 to 15.4 percent with the inclusion of the lower primary and secondary estimates. The average is probably closer to 12 or 13 percent.

foregone are not included in Shoup's estimate of the primary rate) would lower the average rate to approximately 30 percent. These average rates suggest that, even in a country with a relatively high stock of human capital and a low over-all average growth rate, 5 percent of the domestic product is not too great an amount to invest in formal schooling; on the other hand, 5 percent of the GDP may be too low an investment in economies undergoing rapid rates of growth at this level of development.

2. The patterns of rates indicate that, if an economy grows rapidly at this stage, bottlenecks develop at the higher and primary levels (probably the last years of primary). The higher rates to primary and university education in Mexico and Venezuela relative to secondary rates in those countries and to primary and university rates in Chile and Colombia reflect these apparent bottlenecks in the two high-growth countries. The positive correlation between rates of growth of GDP in the four countries and rate of return to investment in schooling is clearest for university training. As Table 8 shows, the increase in university students in periods directly preceding the estimation of rates is about equal in all four countries (although expenditures per capita on university are not). To complete the model, we would want to know the stock of university-trained people per capita. Of the four countries, it can be assumed that Chile has the highest ratio of university graduates; *ceteris paribus*, this would contribute to the lower rate of return to that level in Chile.[12]

Rates to primary schooling also tend to be higher in those countries with higher over-all growth rates, although the Chilean rate contradicts the trend if the Harberger-Selowsky estimates are valid. The breakdown in the gross rates shown in Table 7 indicates that the highest rate to investment within the primary level, and perhaps to investment at all levels, is at the last two years of primary schooling. There is, in other words, a large premium paid in developing countries to the primary school diploma. Since rates are not broken down for the other three countries, it is possible only to guess that the major increases in incomes over illiterates in those countries also comes from completing the final years of the primary level.

The pattern of rates at the secondary level could indicate that this level, because of its large private school component in all the countries involved, may respond best to changes of rates of return. This is a very tentative hypothesis, but the relatively high growth rate of enrollment in Mexico, Colombia, and Venezuela could result from a higher response rate to expectations of demand changes. The hypothesis might also help to explain why rates of

[12] In a preliminary set of results, Irma Edelman has estimated "suggestive" shadow rates of return to secondary and university schooling in Argentina. These are of the order of 25 percent to secondary and normal school, 20 percent to commercial school, 15 percent to university dropouts, and 8 percent to university completers. It is notable that the relatively low rates to university schooling are consistent with the positive correlation between its rates of return and recent past rates of growth of GDP per capita. See Irma Edelman, "A Linear Programming Model of Education Planning—A Case Study of Argentina" (mimeo.).

TABLE 8

*Average Percent Educational Expenditures on Each Level of Schooling,
Growth Rate of Enrollment, Educational Expenditures as Percent
of GDP and GTI, Growth of GDP/Capita, and Per Capita GDP,
Various Periods and Countries*

		MEXICO	CHILE	COLOMBIA	VENEZUELA
1.	Country:				
2.	Period:	1950–62	1949–59	1952–61	1950–57
3.	Percent of educational expenditures on primary:	55	39	53	36
3a.	Primary enrollment growth rate (%):	6.4	3.0	7.5	6.0
4.	Percent of educational expenditures on secondary:	33	48	32	48
4a.	Secondary enrollment growth rate (%):	9.4	6.3	13.0	8.3
5.	Percent of educational expenditures on higher:	12	13	15	16
5a.	Higher enrollment growth rate (%):	8.2	8.8	9.1	8.1
6.	Educational expenditures/ GDP (%):	4.1	4.9	4.8	4.8
7.	Educational expenditures/ GTI (%):	27	48	27	26
8.	Average growth rate, GDP/capita:	2.9	0.9	2.1	4.1
9.	Average growth rate, manufacturing (%):	7.5	3.3	6.0	11.6
10.	GDP/capita in last year of period[a] (1961 Mexican pesos):	4,000	5,675	3,190	5,850

[a] Exchange rates are based on purchasing power parities estimated in Economic Commission for Latin America, *A Measurement of Price Levels and the Purchasing Power of Currencies in Latin America, 1960–1962,* E/CN.12/653, March 31, 1963. The official exchange rate between the Mexican peso and the U.S. dollar was 12.5 pesos per dollar in 1961. The purchasing power of the peso was about 1.67 times as high as that of the dollar, according to the ECLA study.

Sources: Rows 3, 4, and 5—those cited in Table 7, plus student figures from UN, *Statistical Yearbook,* 1952, 1959, 1965; Rows 6, 7, 8, 9, and 10—UN, *op. cit.*

return to secondary schooling in the rapidly growing countries (Mexico and Venezuela) are lower than rates of return to both primary and university training in those countries. In a rapid growth situation, private schools may be able to increase enrollment (and graduates) quickly enough to keep rates of return at that level relatively stable, while primary and university rates climb in response to the public school sector's relative inflexibility. Countries with lower rates of economic growth do not require as rapid supply adjustments to changes in demand for skills, and so such "differentiated disequilibrium" is less likely to occur. It is interesting to note that in Chile and Colombia, where secondary school rates are separated into general and special training (see Table 7), the rates to general *and* university training are higher in Colombia than in Chile.

3. Whatever its other beneficial effects, a high rate of investment in education must be accompanied by a high rate of investment in physical capital in order to generate economic growth. It is probably true, although the data in this study helps little here, that countries with a high growth rate like Mexico and especially Venezuela [13] could have had even higher rates of growth if educational expenditures had been greater relative to investment in physical capital in the periods covered.

4. Work done in the United States indicates that the equilibrium rate of return *gross* of ability factors declines with increasing amount of schooling (see Table 9). If the decline is considered as the equilibrium or "desired"

TABLE 9

Internal Rates of Return to Schooling, United States, 1949 and 1957

YEARS OF SCHOOLING	UNITED STATES A		UNITED STATES B	
	PRIVATE, 1949	SOCIAL, 1949	PRIVATE, 1949	PRIVATE, 1957
1–2		8.9		
3–6		14.5		
7–8		29.2		
9–10	12.7	9.5		
11–12	18.6	13.7	20	28
13–14	6.2	5.4		
15–16	18.7	15.6	13+	15

Sources: United States A—W. Lee Hansen, "Total and Private Rates of Return to Investment in Schooling," *Journal of Political Economy,* LXXI (April 1963), Table 3; United States B—Gary S. Becker, *Human Capital: A Theoretical and Empirical Analysis, with Special Reference to Education* (New York: National Bureau of Economic Research, 1964), Ch. 6. See also Giora Hanoch, "Personal Earnings and Investment in Schooling," unpublished Ph.D. dissertation, University of Chicago, 1965, p. 84.

pattern of rates in all countries at all stages of growth, the rates in Chile, which has recently invested the highest proportion of its product and gross physical investment in schooling and also has had the lowest economic growth rate of the countries under study, are the nearest to that equilibrium. Furthermore, those countries with the highest rates of growth seem to have overinvested in

[13] Unlike educational expenditures in the other three countries, that in Venezuela was decreasing relative to both GDP and GTI during the period covered. In 1957, educational expenditures were 4.3 percent of GDP and 12 percent of GTI.

secondary schooling relative to university training and, in the case of Venezuela, relative to primary schooling as well. Colombia, on the other hand, undergoing only a moderate rate of growth, appears to have underinvested in secondary education relative to primary.

III. Conclusions

The search for a universal rule to allocate resources to education and within education "efficiently," not surprisingly, has yielded a multiplicity of such rules, each with equally vehement support. The analysis here confirms the possibility of a variety of optima by bringing out the relationship between the average rate of return to schooling (and the pattern of rates to various levels of schooling) and general economic conditions among four Latin American countries. It appears, from the results of the various studies, that the profitability of educational investment and the rate of growth of the economy are intimately intertwined, and that the amount of resources devoted by the public sector to schooling must depend on the past and present rate of investment in physical capital.

Within the schooling sector, rates of over-all economic growth are most closely related (positively) to rates of return to primary and university levels (especially the last two years of those levels); the comparison suggests that it is these investments which may be least responsive to increases in the demand for skills and therefore require the greatest amount of attention in economies attaining rapid growth. On the other hand, if one takes the revised Chilean rates (see footnote 11), there is a negative correlation between rate of growth and rates of return to secondary schooling. Therefore, completely different patterns of investment in education may be appropriate for rapidly and slowly developing economies.

DETERMINANTS OF EXPENDITURES
FOR EDUCATION

Ian W. Paterson

Educational expenditures vary considerably among the several provinces of Canada. This intranational comparison seeks to explain these variations by reference to a large number of socioeconomic variables. Specific hypotheses are not explicitly stated or tested, but the writer creates a theoretical model in which a large number of possible relations are mapped and then examines the importance of each variable by performing a series of correlations.

THE STUDY of determinants of expenditures for education presupposes that systematic socio-economic and educational characteristics of the community work to "determine" levels of expenditures for education. This presupposition may be logically defended; for instance, one would expect levels of expenditures for education to be closely related to levels of personal income and levels of teacher salaries. Such simple logical relationships accommodate to statistical confirmation using simple correlation techniques. This statistical test, widely employed in earlier studies,[1] estimates the gross relationship between a single factor and levels of expenditure for education.

Recent American studies have achieved more precise estimates of relationships using multiple correlation techniques.[2] Such techniques estimate net relationships between a single factor and levels of expenditures with other factors being taken into account, and also estimate relationships between groups of factors and levels of expenditures. The United States, with its fifty different states, affords first-rate opportunities for multiple correlation analyses. In comparison, the small number of Canadian provinces inhibits the use of similar analyses by restricting input factors to less than ten and output results to those producing very strong relationships between factors.

A recent study by the author applies multiple correlation analyses to Canadian data.[3] The study explored socio-economic and educational characteristics of the provinces as determinants of variations in expenditure levels for public

REPRINTED FROM *Canadian Education and Research Digest*, 7 (June 1967), pp. 155–169, by permission of the author and The Canadian Education Association.

[1] See, for example, John E. Cheal, *Investment in Canadian Youth* (Toronto: MacMillan Company of Canada, 1963).

[2] See, for example, Jerry Miner, *Social and Economic Factors in Spending for Public Education* (Syracuse: Syracuse University Press, 1963).

[3] Ian W. Paterson, *An Analysis of Determinants of Education Expenditures among the Provinces of Canada, Decennially, 1941–1961* (unpublished doctoral dissertation, University of Alberta, 1967).

elementary and secondary education for the years 1941, 1951, and 1961. In this paper, major findings from the study are given together with an idea of the theoretical model developed to guide the statistical analyses.

THE THEORETICAL MODEL

A particular purpose of the theoretical model is to achieve some control of the complex of factors that are related to levels of expenditures for education. Earlier studies simplified and ordered this complex into families of factors associated with *need, ability,* and *effort*. Since these concepts have been differently defined and have sustained normative connotations, it is useful to subsume them within the broader classifications of Demographic, Socio-Economic and Political determinants, respectively.

Demographic and socio-economic determinants describe characteristics of a community which provide the raw material for, about, and upon which *political* decisions are imposed. All political actions are derivable, in some degree, from the character of a community as described in its demographic and socio-economic features. These features, then, may be considered more remote from the determination of levels of expenditures than political actions which, having evolved from these features, impinge more directly upon expenditures for education.

Demographic and socio-economic factors constitute primary determinants and, since they concern factors over which educational policy-makers have little control, may be called Non-Policy determinants. Political factors constitute secondary determinants and, since they concern factors over which educational policy-makers have some measure of tangible control, may be called Policy determinants.

This distinction between Non-Policy and Policy determinants rests on the essential point that the former are much less susceptible to influence by policy-makers than the latter. An operational time period may be defined arbitrarily to distinguish these categories. This period is of such length that constitutional constraints, such as the school leaving age, are impervious to political manipulation and are Non-Policy determinants, while factors more readily accessible to influence by policy-makers, such as levels of provincial aid, are Policy determinants.

Identified and presumed determinants of expenditures for education, derived from the literature of studies, are fitted into the theoretical model of determinants as shown in Figure 1. The model suggests that Non-Policy determinants (made up of demographic and socio-economic factors) form the basic class of factors influencing levels of expenditures. Further, it suggests that Policy determinants (made up of political factors) form an intervening class of factors influencing levels of expenditures, and that this class is itself determined by the demographic and socio-economic factors representative of the Non-Policy determinants. From this model, two groups of factors are selected for statistical analysis: Non-Policy variables and Policy variables.

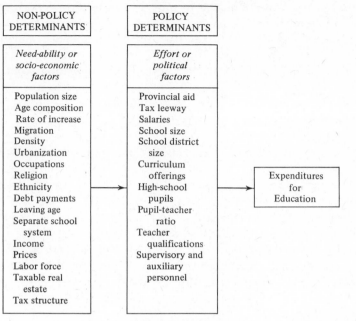

Theoretical Model of Determinants of Public Expenditures for Education.

THE VARIABLES

The dependent variable—expenditures for education—is defined as current expenditures per pupil in average daily attendance in public elementary and secondary schools. This definition specifically excludes capital outlays, debt charges, together with all public expenditures for technical, higher, adult, and pre-school education. Current expenditures are expressed in constant 1957 dollars, using three-year averages of price deflators centred on the years 1941, 1951, and 1961.

Nine Independent Non-Policy Variables

The nine independent variables reflecting Non-Policy or demographic/socio-economic factors selected for study are:

1. *School-age Population,* defined as the per cent of total population within statutory school-age limits, and designed to measure specific need for educational services;
2. *Urbanization,* defined as the per cent of population living in urban centres of 10,000 or more, and designed to measure the influence of large aggregates of people;
3. *Migration,* defined as the actual increase in population as a per cent of

natural increase, and designed to provide a ratio of provincial gains and losses in population;

4. *Education Level,* defined as the per cent of non-school population with nine or more years of formal education;
5. *Roman Catholic,* defined as the per cent of population Roman Catholic;
6. *Income Distribution,* defined as the coefficient of variation for provincial income distributions, and designed to measure the extent of income inequalities;
7. *Personal Income,* defined as personal income per capita given in constant 1957 dollars;
8. *Dependents,* defined as the number of dependents per 100 actual work-force members, given that all persons outside the actual work-force are construed as dependents regardless of age;
9. *Primary Industry,* defined as the per cent of actual work-force in primary industry, given that agriculture, mining, quarrying, fishing, hunting, logging, and trapping are construed as primary industries thereby providing a measure of occupational structure.

Six Independent Policy Variables

Six independent variables reflecting Policy or political factors are used in the study. The selection of Policy determinants was severely constrained by the availability of data, especially in the earlier years. Each of the selected Policy variables is concerned only with public elementary and secondary schools. The variables are:

1. *Enrolments Beyond,* defined as the per cent of total enrolments beyond statutory leaving ages, and designed as a measure of effort;
2. *Teacher,* defined as the number of teachers per 100 pupils in average daily attendance, to provide a measure of teacher-pupil ratios;
3. *School Size,* defined as the number of schools per 5,000 pupils in average daily attendance;
4. *School District Size,* defined as the average number of pupils in average daily attendance per school district;
5. *Salaries,* defined as the ratio of median income of family heads to average teacher salaries, and designed to contain different provincial income levels, and the relative position of teacher salaries to income levels of the provinces;
6. *Provincial aid,* defined as grants per pupil in average daily attendance given in 1957 constant dollars.

Two major statistical analyses were conducted using the variables selected to represent the major Non-Policy and Policy categories of determinants.

NON-POLICY DETERMINANTS

Multiple correlation analyses were applied to the nine independent variables chosen as indicative of Non-Policy determinants, and the dependent variable, expenditures for education, in each decennial period, 1941, 1951 and 1961. These analyses established three variables as significant determinants of levels of expenditures for education: Income Distribution, Personal Income, and Primary Industry. Together, these variables explained between 90 and 95 per cent [4] of the variance in levels of per pupil current expenditures for education. Of these, the crucial determinant was Personal Income. Alone, this factor explained between 86 and 93 per cent of expenditure variations during the years 1941, 1951, and 1961. Combined with Income Distribution and Primary Industry and holding the effects of these two factors constant, Personal Income accounted for 58 to 85 per cent of the variance in expenditure levels.

The strength of these relationships between Personal Income and levels of expenditures for education is exceptional. In the United States, economists have demonstrated similar relationships but with much less strength of association.[5] The predominant influence of Personal Income in Canada attests to the usefulness of this factor as an index of fiscal and economic capacities for educational expenditures. Representing economic capacity in terms of Personal Income implies that this factor stands for a variety of demographic and socio-economic characteristics of the community. The nature of these characteristics can be investigated with the statistical technique of factor analysis. This technique resolves interrelationships of variables into clusters of commonly-related variables. The patterning of these clusters will suggest descriptions of the national economic structure which Personal Income levels imply but do not reveal.

Income and Related Determinants

Factor analysis of the nine Non-Policy variables produced three factors, or clusters of commonly-related variables: the Dependency factor, the Rural-Urban factor, and the Roman Catholic factor. Together, these factors explained over 90 per cent of the possible variance, although individual factor contributions varied over the decennial periods. Table 1 provides the average 1941–61 provincial indexes for the variables of these factors. Provincial indexes express the variable data as percentages of the national mean. These indexes reveal which provinces increased more, and which less, than the average of all prov-

---

[4] Percentages have been adjusted downwards for small sample size by application of shrinkage formula given in Mordecai Ezekiel and Karl A. Fox, *Methods of Correlation and Regression Analysis* (New York: John Wiley and Sons, 1959), p. 301.

[5] Sherman Shapiro, *An Analysis of the Determinants of Current Public and Societal Expenditure per Pupil in Elementary and Secondary Schools* (unpublished doctoral dissertation, University of Chicago, 1962), p. 69.

inces in a given period. The indexes of Table 1 afford general descriptions of differential economic structures, but lack the detail decennial indexes would provide.

THE DEPENDENCY FACTOR. The Dependency factor consistently contributed more than one third of the variance in each period, and dominated in 1941 and 1951. Areas possessing this factor are marked by higher proportions of dependents and school-age children, wider variations in income distribution, less urbanization, lower personal incomes, and lower levels of education. Further, this factor associates with lower levels of expenditures for education.

The indexes for variables of the Dependency factor from Table 1 (column 2–7 inclusive) illustrate its explanatory power. Notable differences in provincial economies are revealed as the provinces with lower expenditure for education identify positively with the variables of this factor, while the higher expenditure provinces identify negatively with the same variables. Exceptions to these generalizations are few. Quebec exhibits a singularly high index for urbanization; Nova Scotia a higher regional index for population education levels. Saskatchewan diverges from regional expectancies widely in its urbanization level and less sharply in its income inequality and education levels.

THE RURAL-URBAN FACTOR. The contributions of the Rural-Urban factor increased in importance from 1941–61, making it the dominant factor in the later period. Those areas possessing this factor are marked by high levels of urbanization and in-migration, and lower than average proportions of the labour force in primary industry. Further, this factor associates with higher levels of personal incomes and expenditures for education. The indexes for variables of the Rural-Urban factor from Table 1 (columns 2, 5, 8 and 9) reveal that this factor clearly distinguishes only the highest and lowest expenditure provinces. British Columbia and Ontario identify positively, while Newfoundland and Prince Edward Island identify negatively, with the variables of this factor. With the exception of the primary industry variable, New Brunswick, Nova Scotia and Alberta adapt well to the variables of this factor.

THE ROMAN CATHOLIC FACTOR. The Roman Catholic factor accounted for about one quarter of the possible variance in each period, but its contribution declined consistently. Those areas possessing this factor are marked by higher proportions of Roman Catholics and school-age children, and lower education levels. Further, this factor associates with lower personal incomes and expenditures for education. The indexes for variables of the Roman Catholic factor from Table 1 (columns 2, 6, 7, and 10) indicate that this factor differentiates broadly between those provinces above and below the national levels in these variables.

These associations of factor variables with levels of personal income and expenditures for education afford insights into apparent sources of inter-provincial differences in levels of expenditures. The associations suggest that higher levels of per pupil expenditures for education tend to accompany economies characterized by higher levels of personal incomes, urbanization, education, and in-migrations; and by fewer dependents, less inequality of incomes, and

TABLE 1

Provincial Indexes for Non-Policy Determinants of Expenditures for Education
(Average 1941–61 Index)
Canada = 100

PROVINCE*	1 EDUCATION EXPENDITURES	2 PERSONAL INCOME	3 INCOME DISTRIBUTION	4 DEPEN-DENTS	5 URBAN-IZATION	6 EDUCATION LEVEL	7 SCHOOL-AGE POPULATION	8 MIGRA-TION	9 PRIMARY INDUSTRY	10 ROMAN CATHOLIC
British Columbia	150	135	86	88	161	138	75	282	51	41
Ontario	126	140	85	83	161	120	97	160	49	71
Alberta	124	118	94	90	102	113	91	103	128	60
Saskatchewan	115	108	104	95	57	91	95	20	179	71
Manitoba	112	112	94	88	121	109	86	60	98	65
Canada	*100*	*100*	*100*	*100*	*100*	*100*	*100*	*100*	*100*	*100*
Quebec	94	99	93	97	148	83	116	112	59	240
New Brunswick	83	76	100	114	68	79	114	75	93	138
Nova Scotia	80	87	109	106	85	110	117	90	80	93
Prince Edward Island	62	65	118	111	44	98	99	50	162	125
Newfoundland	50	57	115	136	51	56	110	72	102	93

* Ranked by 1941–61 average expenditures for education.

smaller proportions of Roman Catholics. This description fits the economies of British Columbia, Ontario, Alberta and Manitoba well, and Saskatchewan less precisely. Alternatively, the economies of Quebec and the Atlantic Provinces are appropriately described by the reverse of these characteristics.

INCOME ELASTICITIES. The strong association of variations in income levels with differences in levels of expenditures for education encourages computation of the income elasticity of demand for education. Income elasticity is the percentage change in expenditures associated with a one per cent change in income. The procedure used in computing elasticities involves the use of statistics produced by the multiple correlation analyses.

The national income elasticities, using one independent variable, were: .926 in 1941, .999 in 1951, and 1.116 in 1961. Elasticities computed with three and four independent variables were less. The implication from these elasticities is that, for every one per cent rise in per capita personal income, per pupil expenditures for education, nationally, increased by less than one per cent. Throughout the period, the income elasticities improve by approaching, then surpassing, one.

An indication of the responsiveness of provincial expenditures for education to a one per cent increase in provincial personal incomes derives from estimations of provincial income elasticities. These elasticities are reported in Table 2. The national elasticity of 1.091 is exceeded, or closely met, by all provinces

TABLE 2

Provincial Income Elasticities of Expenditures for Education and Average for Canada 1941–61

PROVINCE*	1941–61
British Columbia	1.093
Ontario	1.217
Alberta	1.165
Saskatchewan	.946
Manitoba	.922
Canada	*1.091*
Quebec	1.411
New Brunswick	.786
Nova Scotia	1.455
Prince Edward Island	.707
Newfoundland	.794

* Ranked by 1941–61 average expenditures for education.

except New Brunswick, Prince Edward Island, and Newfoundland. These provinces provide income elasticities which are well below the national figure. Alternatively, the elasticities for Quebec and Nova Scotia are singularly high.

These notable differences in provincial income elasticities are illuminated by comparing the decennial changes in the proportions of personal income devoted to expenditures for education among the provinces.

Income and Expenditures for Education

The data of Table 3 express per pupil current expenditures for education as

TABLE 3

Per Pupil Current Expenditures for Education as Percentages of Personal Income Per Capita by Provinces and Average for Canada 1941, 1951, 1961

PROVINCE*	1941	1951	1961
British Columbia	19.2	18.2	20.0
Ontario	15.0	16.2	16.3
Alberta	18.0	16.9	20.5
Saskatchewan	20.1	16.1	22.0
Manitoba	19.0	15.9	18.0
Canada	17.6	16.8	18.3
Quebec	15.4	16.4	18.6
New Brunswick	18.9	21.1	17.2
Nova Scotia	14.8	16.0	17.9
Prince Edward Island	19.1	15.8	15.2
Newfoundland	17.2	15.6	14.4

* Ranked by average 1941–61 expenditures for education.

percentages of per capita personal incomes within the provinces, decennially 1941–1961. While the national percentages rose from 17.6 per cent to 18.3 per cent, provincial ratios varied widely, expanding the relative ranges [6] from .301 in 1941 to .415 in 1961. These relative ranges indicate that the differences between the highest and lowest expenditure provinces increased during the period from 30 per cent to over 40 per cent.

The decennial changes in the provincial ratios are reflected in their income elasticities. The steady increases in the ratios of Quebec and Nova Scotia produce high elasticities. Alternatively, the low elasticities for Prince Edward Island and Newfoundland reflect large declines in their proportions of personal income devoted to expenditures for education. Overall increases occur in these ratios for British Columbia, Ontario and Alberta, providing each with elasticities in excess of one. The reverse applies in Manitoba and New Brunswick, while Saskatchewan's elasticity of slightly less than one reflects the sharp decline in its 1951 ratio.

[6] Relative range is the absolute range divided by the mean.

These expenditure/income ratios afford an indication of the effort made by individual provinces in current spending for education. Effort, in its simplest terms, is that proportion of wealth devoted to expenditures for education. In this regard, Ontario conspicuously produced income ratios lower than the national average in each year. Ontario's apparent effort, then was much less than its income levels would anticipate. Further, Manitoba, Newfoundland and Prince Edward Island exhibited persistently declining ratios, suggesting that their efforts were lower than the national pattern would anticipate. Although fluctuating somewhat, the ratios of the remaining provinces mark the alternative suggestion.

It may not be realistic, however, to expect each province to devote a similar proportion of its personal income to expenditures for education. It may be argued, for instance, that a high income province with low proportions of pupils to total population can more easily afford to expand its expenditure/income ratio than can a province with depressed income levels and high proportions of pupils. Furthermore, should a province in the latter category expand its ratio near to, or beyond, that of a province in the former category, then a good deal more effort has been demonstrated by the second province.

Table 4 provides the decennial proportions of pupils to total populations and the predicted expenditures per pupil, given as proportions of personal income per capita for each province (ranked by its personal income level). The predicted expenditures derive from the correlation equations between individual provincial income and education expenditure levels assessed as a whole. Hence the predictions are determined by statistical national averages in each year.

The data of Table 4 reveal that the predicted proportions of personal income spent on education move to parallel provincial income levels as the proportions of pupils in the population expand. Broadly, it would appear that the lower income provinces could afford higher expenditure/income ratios in 1941 because their proportions of pupils were generally less than those of the higher income provinces. Further, the data strongly suggest that expenditure/income ratios rise as pupil proportions decline, relatively. Consequently, the lower income provinces spent proportionally more in 1941 when their pupil proportions were generally less than the national average. The reverse applied in 1961.

The data of Tables 3 and 4 show that British Columbia, Alberta, and New Brunswick consistently spent more than predicted in spite of sharply expanding enrolment percentages. Of these, only New Brunswick's spending has declined, providing it with a low income elasticity of .786. Saskatchewan spent considerably more than predicted in 1941 and 1961, but less in 1951. In general, the effort of these four provinces is greater than their income levels and the national patterns would have anticipated. The counter conclusion emerges for Ontario, Manitoba, Newfoundland and Prince Edward Island, although the latter two ranked among the highest provinces in decennial gains for pupil enrolment. Quebec and Nova Scotia spent more than predicted in 1961, following a persistent rise in expenditure/income levels reflected in their 1.4 income

TABLE 4

Pupils in Average Daily Attendance as Per Cent of Total Population, and Predicted per Pupil Expenditures for Education as Per Cent of Personal Income per Capita, by Provinces

PROVINCE*	PUPILS IN A.D.A. AS PER CENT OF TOTAL POPULATION			PREDICTED EDUCATION EXPENDITURES AS PER CENT OF PERSONAL INCOME		
	1941	1951	1961	1941	1951	1961
Ontario	15.3	15.1	21.5	17.1	16.8	19.3
British Columbia	12.5	13.6	18.7	17.1	16.8	19.3
Alberta	17.3	16.7	21.6	17.4	16.8	18.9
Manitoba	14.9	14.8	19.6	17.4	16.8	18.8
Saskatchewan	17.2	16.7	21.2	17.6	16.8	18.5
Quebec	14.5	13.9	19.9	17.5	16.8	18.3
Nova Scotia	15.5	18.0	22.8	17.6	16.9	17.7
New Brunswick	15.5	16.7	23.3	17.9	16.9	17.1
Prince Edward Island	13.6	15.6	21.3	18.4	16.9	16.7
Newfoundland	14.6	19.3	25.9	18.9	16.9	16.3
Canada	*15.1*	*16.8*	*21.6*	*17.6*	*16.8*	*18.3*

* Ranked by 1941–61 average personal income per capita.

elasticity ratios. In terms of their initial expenditure levels, the effort of these two provinces appears more pronounced than that of Alberta and Saskatchewan.

These broad relationships between levels of personal income, proportions of pupils, and predicted expenditure/income ratios draw their validity from the unusually strong associations between levels of personal incomes and expenditures for education. Income constitutes the major Non-Policy determinant of expenditures. Further, income in its relationships with dependent socio-economic characteristics furnishes three singular clusters, or factors, of related Non-Policy determinants of expenditures for education.

POLICY DETERMINANTS

Multiple correlation analyses were applied to the six independent variables selected as indicative of Policy determinants and the dependent variable, expenditures for education, in each decennial period. Four variables emerged as significant determinants of levels of expenditures: Enrolments Beyond, Teachers, School Size, and Salaries. Together, these variables explained between 74 and 93 per cent [7] of the variance in levels of per pupil current expenditures for

[7] See footnote 4.

education. In 1941, Enrolments Beyond dominated, explaining 42 per cent of the variance by itself. In 1951, School Size was the dominant determinant, accounting for 55 per cent of the variance. In 1961, Salaries became dominant, explaining 67 per cent of the variance. These varying patterns suggest the use of factor analysis to examine the interrelationships among the variables.

Factor analysis of the six Policy variables produced two factors, or clusters of commonly-related variables. The two factors explained between 64 and 74 per cent of the possible variance. Although individual factor contributions varied sharply, one factor, named the Enrolments Beyond Leaving Age factor, dominated in each year. The other factor was named the School Size factor. Table 5 provides the average 1941–61 provincial indexes for the variables of the factors. These indexes express the variable data as percentages of the national mean, and they lack the detail of decennial indexes.

The Enrolments Beyond Leaving Age factor enlarges its contribution throughout the period, and consistently accounts for more than one third of the variance. Areas possessing this factor are marked by higher proportions of enrolment beyond statutory leaving ages, higher teacher salaries, and increased

TABLE 5

Provincial Indexes for Policy Determinants of Expenditures for Education
(Average 1941–61 Index) Canada = 100

PROVINCE*	1 EDUCATION EXPEN- DITURES	2 TEACHERS	3 SCHOOL SIZE	4 ENROL- MENTS	5 SALARIES	6 PROVIN- CIAL AID
British Columbia	150	96	44	167	72	175
Ontario	126	75	59	63	84	101
Alberta	124	101	78	157	85	119
Saskatchewan	115	113	130	144	93	108
Manitoba	112	101	93	137	88	80
Canada	*100*	*100*	*100*	*100*	*100*	*100*
Quebec	94	115	83	62	148	55
New Brunswick	83	102	110	52	100	75
Nova Scotia	80	92	112	54	101	77
Prince Edward Island	62	113	184	79	110	96
Newfoundland	50	92	107	85	122	115

* Ranked by 1941–61 average expenditures for education.

amounts of provincial aid per pupil. Further, this factor associates with higher levels of expenditures for education. The indexes for the variables of this factor from Table 5 (columns 4, 5 and 6) illustrate its explanatory power. Differences among the provinces reveal themselves as the higher expenditure provinces identify positively with the variables of this factor, while the lower expenditure provinces identify negatively. (It will be recalled that the teacher salary index affords higher indexes to lower average salaries relative to median incomes of family heads.) Exceptions to these generalizations are only Ontario with lower enrolments, Manitoba with lower provincial aid, and Newfoundland with higher levels of provincial aid.

The contributions of the School Size factor remained largely stable throughout the period, accounting for slightly less than 30 per cent of the variance. Those areas possessing this factor are characterized by smaller schools and lower pupil-teacher ratios. Further, this factor associates with lower per pupil expenditures for education. The indexes for variables of the School Size factor from Table 5 (columns 2 and 3) reveal that most provinces adapt to the variables of this factor in the anticipated directions. The lower expenditure provinces tend to associate positively with the variables of this factor, while the higher expenditure provinces tend to associate negatively. For the latter, the exceptions are Saskatchewan with smaller schools, and British Columbia with very much larger school districts. Among the lower expenditure provinces, Quebec is exceptional with its larger schools, and Nova Scotia and Newfoundland have higher pupil-teacher ratios than regional expectations would suggest.

These associations of factor variables with expenditure levels afford indications of probable sources of inter-provincial differences in levels of expenditures insofar as Policy determinants are concerned. The associations suggest that higher levels of per pupil expenditures for education tend to accompany educational environments characterized by higher levels of teacher salaries, of provincial aid per pupil, and of enrolments beyond statutory leaving ages; and by larger schools and slightly higher pupil-teacher ratios. This description fittingly applies to Alberta and British Columbia, and to Ontario, Manitoba and Saskatchewan less precisely. Alternatively, the reverse of these characteristics fits New Brunswick well, and each of the remaining provinces only a little less precisely.

The foregoing rationalization and analysis of determinants of expenditures for education in terms of Non-Policy and Policy factors marks an initial attempt to understand expenditure determinants in Canada.

EDUCATIONAL CHANGE AND ECONOMIC DEVELOPMENT

William S. Bennett, Jr.

The author tests a number of hypotheses on the relation of general and vocational education to national economic development. He employs a large sample of countries for comparison and illustrates how already published data can be used to good effect.

INTRODUCTION

Although institutional education was largely unrelated to early industrialization in the West, it is assumed that education will be important to industrial development in most areas of Asia and Africa.[1] Compared to sociologists, economists have been quite interested in this relation between economic development and education. Bowman, in a thorough recent review of the work relating economics to change in education, noted that at least since 1963 economists have been constructing empirical models of human investment in economic growth.[2] Much of this work is yet unpublished, but preliminary reports show the use of a variety of models. The newest of these include classical manpower planning techniques, cost-benefit analysis and rate of return models using linear programming.[3]

Samuel Bowles, working in Northern Nigeria, has developed an optimizing model for educational planning. The model is addressed to a number of questions including: (a) what amount of society's resources should be devoted to the educational system and (b) how the total resource use should be distributed among types of educational institutions.[4] Correa, Tinbergen and others

REPRINTED FROM *Sociology of Education*, 40 (Spring 1967), 101–114. © 1967 by the American Sociological Association.

---

[1] W. F. Moore, for example, has written, "The proportion of contemporary change that is either planned or issues from the secondary consequences of deliberate innovations is much higher than in former times," in *Social Change*, Prentice-Hall, 1963; also A. H. Halsey has noted ". . . the progressive secularization of higher learning since medieval times has increased the role of the universities as sources of technological change, until now they are beginning to occupy a place as part of the economic foundation of a new type of society," in *Social Organization and Behavior* (eds., Simpson & Simpson) Wiley: New York, 1964: or W. Form, and D. Miller, *Industrial Society*, New York: Harper & Row, 1964, p. 47.

[2] Mary Jean Bowman, "The Human Investment Revolution in Economic Thought," *Sociology of Education*, 1966, 39, 2, 111–136.

[3] *Ibid.*, pp. 131–137.

[4] S. Bowles, "Sketch of an Optimizing Model for Educational Planning," unpublished paper presented to meeting of Operations Research Society of America, 1966, Durham,

have been working toward similarly predictive models.[5] All of these seem to be improvements over the previously accepted methods of Denison, Schultz and others [6] to estimate the effect of education by an *ad hoc* analysis of the proportion of the Gross National Product not accountable in terms of measurable inputs of capital or labor.[7]

Likewise, these models offer more powerful explanations than other models, such as that of Kuznets,[8] which measure the relative amount of capital investment in education compared to other economic sectors. Kuznets, however, has uncovered some interesting relationships, including the fact that the rate of capital investment in education increased disproportionately as the American economy grew in the late 19th and 20th centuries.

With the present dearth of knowledge we cannot be too finicky about the efforts of economists to make a beginning. However, from a sociological perspective there are several potential limitations to the model building of the economists. The present discussion will limit itself to noting only two.

The first question concerns the treatment of educational output in terms pegged to the present level of integration of economy and society. For example in Bowles: "The demand functions for the outputs of the educational system . . . are specified prior to the operations of the model." [9] In short, demand for certain kinds of trained people will be computed on the basis of current demand, or at least within the framework of the current economic system. This may be a justifiable and highly useful assumption in the short run, but it seems equally possible that a new level of integration of the economy would lead to quite different demands. For example, who in England in 1740 would have been able to predict the future demand level (even 50 years hence) for iron smelters and the skills and knowledge associated with this "occupation"? Projections of income levels of iron workers in 1740 would have had little validity in predicting the productivity of iron workers at the end of the century.

North Carolina; see also "The Efficient Allocation of Resources in Education: A Planning Model with Applications to Northern Nigeria," unpublished doctoral dissertation, Harvard University, 1965.

[5] H. Correa, *The Economics of Human Resources*, North Holland Publishing: Amsterdam, Holland, 1963; J. Tinbergen, *et al.*, *Econometric Models of Education: Some Applications*, Paris: OECD, 1965.

[6] T. W. Schultz, "Education and Economic Growth," in *Yearbook of the National Society for the Study of Education*, 1961; E. F. Denison, *The Sources of Economic Growth in the United States*, Supplementary Paper No. 13, Committee for Economic Development, New York, 1961; and M. Abramovitz, "Economic Growth in the United States," *American Economic Review*, 1962, 52, 4, 762–782.

[7] T. Balogh has pointed out the particular fallacy of "assuming that education is a homogeneous input," in "The Economics of Education Planning," *Comparative Education*, 1, 1, 5–17.

[8] S. Kuznets, "Toward a Theory of Economic Growth," in R. Lekachman (ed.), *National Policy for Economic Welfare at Home and Abroad*, New York: Russell and Russell, 1961.

[9] Bowles, *op. cit.*, 1966.

A second potential shortcoming of present economic models concerns the economist's neglect of the effect of formal education on personal change. More than skills are acquired in education. One dimension of personal change, which education can affect, is the development of innovative abilities and motivation. This is not irrelevant to economics. Developing economies, via the action of individuals or small groups, must invent, innovate or adapt many *new* technologies and organizational structures to fit their local scene.

The above is not a plea to abandon efforts at economic model building. It is, however, an argument for developing some broader, if possibly less high powered, models of the relative levels of social integration in various developing nations. Specifically these models should take into account the role of education in this process, and should try to relate education to social and political variables.

The most important technique available for such investigation is the notion of systems analysis. Within the general framework of systems analysis the typical beginning is with correlational studies [10] of the interrelation of variables without prestating "cause" and "effect." In fact, since most fruitful analysis usually involves the assumption of a closed system, no one variable, neither education nor investment nor income growth, would have precedence over the other but must form an interacting system in some sort of equilibrium—usually a dynamic form of equilibrium. It is with these assumptions about the possible limitations of the current economic models that the present paper tries to begin, very crudely, a more sociological, or systems analytic, approach to the problem of education and economy.

Except for studies using gross measures of education or literacy, data on the extent of different kinds of education are still meager. There appears to be no literature which distinguishes, for example, between vocational and general education and agricultural training or between either of these and teacher training programs, the latter being a very popular distinction in the secondary or higher education systems of most developing nations. Although the "Normal School" is nearly extinct in Britain and the United States, it is very much a part of the educational scene in many less affluent nations.

EDUCATION AND DEVELOPMENT

The present article deals with the correlation between several measures of the structure of secondary education and selected aspects of economic development. It does *not* impute a causal role to either economic or educational variables. It assumes, rather, that these variables are inter-related in a complex

[10] For a particularly good introduction to the topic of systems analysis and societal process see R. Chin, "The Utility of System Models and Developmental Models," in J. L. Finkle and R. W. Gable, *Political Development and Social Change*, New York: Wiley, 1966.

manner. It will develop a set of universal propositions regarding these relationships, although it would be pretentious to call this a systems analytic model. It is hoped that future study will greatly refine and expand such a list of propositions as well as empirical findings.

A set of propositions were tested on data collected from some seventy nations (a global survey, excluding only Africa). These propositions involve a distinction between general and vocational education. Of course, there are subtle differences in the meanings of these educational concepts when applied to different nations, but generally vocational education is any course of study directly related to vocational occupations where a large part of the curriculum is devoted to learning specific skills which the student is to use immediately upon graduation. The gradation between school and shop is very slight. Vocational education usually replaces a traditional apprenticeship program of some kind. General education has no immediate occupational application but prepares the student in basic skills that can be used to learn many different occupations.

Both forms of education are probably related to development variables. Bowman and Anderson have established fairly conclusively that literacy (several different definitions) is highly related to aspects of development. Specifically, they have related income to literacy, holding available energy potential constant. Even with the contaminating variable of energy resources removed, literacy and income are still highly correlated.[11] This probably does not surprise anyone. It seems, however, a bit more problematic whether both general education and vocational education are directly related to development variables. On a still more detailed level of analysis, what is the relationship of the mix of these types of education to development? The following three general hypotheses are suggested:

Hypothesis I. The rate of general education is a function of various indices of economic development including occupational structure and population factors. The higher the indicator of development, the greater the per capita rate of general education.

Hypothesis II. The rate of vocational education is a function of various indices of economic development including occupational structure as well as population factors. The higher the indicator of development the greater the per capita rate of technological education.

Hypothesis III. The ratio between the rate of vocational education and general education (VE/GE) is a function of economic development including occupational structure and population factors.

For the educational variables, data were collected from the most recent

11 Mary Jean Bowman and C. A. Anderson, "Concerning the Role of Education in Development," in C. Geertz, ed. *Old Societies and New States*, New York: Free Press, 1963.

UNESCO volume on comparative education.[12] This volume lists enrollments for three types of education: primary, secondary and higher. These types are further broken down into such categories as secondary general, secondary vocational and secondary teacher training. In order to obtain comparable figures for a large number of nations, this study restricted itself to testing the hypotheses on secondary education statistics alone.

The data were all for one year periods, but there was some slight variability in the dates referred to. For most countries data were available for 1955–1956, and these figures were used, even though in a few cases they were not the most recent figures available. One serious source of error must be considered at this point; that is, not all countries compute "secondary education" over the same number of years. For some types of secondary education in some countries the figures cover six years, in other cases, five years, and so on.

Information is simply not available for such control. What is more important than the absolute number of years, however, is the number of students involved in this kind of training. This gives a valid estimate of a nation's investment in any given type of education. A more extensive secondary education program might be indicated by either an increase in the number of students involved or in the increased comprehensiveness for fewer students, e.g., more years of agricultural education. In either case, this would be reflected in enrollment, although, of course, the implications of these different techniques of investment would be important. The difference between investment in quantity vs. quality is critical, but it will have to await better data. In this case, the large differences found between blocks of countries would seem to lessen the importance of some minor error in estimation.

Statistics were gathered for slightly over seventy nations. A few nations were lost due to inadequate economic or demographic data, and the total sample of nations was finally reduced to sixty-nine. Inadequate data from African nations led to exclusion of this region from the sample. All other regions are represented.

Comparable data on economic and demographic conditions were gathered from Ginsburg and Berry's recent economic atlas.[13] Here four critical development variables were chosen: gross national product per capita, calories per day per capita, gross energy consumption per capita, the percent of the population increase.[14] The population variables were used both as direct measures of modernization, particularly within a given geographical or economic region, and as a control factor related to the population needs for expanded education.

[12] World Survey of Education, III, New York: UNESCO, 1961.

[13] N. Ginsburg and B. Berry, Atlas of Economic Development, Chicago: University of Chicago Press, 1961.

[14] All data on economic development or population were from 1960. This sets the date of the development figures four years later than the educational data. As far as the author is aware, these are the only statistics available. The four year gap would not seem to place any severe limitation on analysis.

TABLE 1

*Correlations * Among General Secondary Education Rates and
Three Economic Indicators † by World Region*

	GNP	CALORIES	ENERGY
World	0.395	0.493	0.418
North America and Western Europe	0.528	0.563	0.489
Eastern Europe	0.167	0.595	0.024
Latin America	0.316	0.328	0.365
Middle East and North Africa	0.164	0.341	0.082
Asia	0.183	0.603	0.645

* All correlations presented in Tables 1, 2, 3 are rank order correlations. Pearson *r* correlations in most cases tended to be slightly larger; but it was not felt that all the assumptions of Pearson *r* would be met—even with the use of log scores for the developmental variables.

† The three variables in each table are, respectively, Gross National Product per Capita; Calories per day per Capita; Gross Energy Consumption per Capita in Kilowatts.

ECONOMIC VARIABLES AND EDUCATION RATES

Hypothesis II has far stronger support than either of the others. Using any of the three measures of economic development, vocational education is most highly correlated with the economic variables. (See Table 2.)

TABLE 2

*Correlations Between Secondary Vocational Education and
Three Economic Indicators by World Region*

	GNP	CALORIES	ENERGY
World	0.775	0.734	0.780
North America and Western Europe	—0.195	—0.196	—0.016
Eastern Europe	—0.143	—0.429	—0.310
Latin America	0.434	0.367	0.332
Middle East and North Africa	0.652	0.609	0.768
Asia	0.479	0.611	0.617

The correlations between general education rates and economic variables are in the predicted direction, but are of a low order. (See Table 1.) None of the three measures of economic development account for more than 25% of the variance in general education rates. *Only for the industrial West* (North America and Western Europe) is there a consistently high correlation between general secondary education rates and economic variables.

On the other hand, Table 1 shows that for most other regions and developmental variables, the correlations are positive but quite low, between general education and development figures. Only Asia contributes strongly to the positive global correlation. Here, for two development measures, calories per day per capita and energy consumed per capita, the Asian nations show a high positive correlation between general education and development (GE). In Asia, if nowhere else in the non-western world, general secondary education is positively related to development.

This correlation (in the Asian countries) may have more to do with the cultural heritage of Asia than with any program for modernization. It is likely that Asian nations (Burma, Ceylon or India) have given an unusually great proportion of resources to status-conferring types of education. Numerous aspects of their cultural history would seem to imply this. In any case, it seems unlikely at this stage that economic development is itself dependent upon this high rate of general secondary education. It seems more plausible that the richer Asian nations simply put more money into general education. But, again, this is one of the imponderable questions of cause and effect which this article will not tackle directly.

Far more revealing are the high correlations of economic variables with vocational education. But this relationship is not universal either. Table 2 indicates that this correlation is highly dependent on the non-western nations for its size. Regional correlations for the industrialized nations of western and eastern Europe are both low negative and this is consistent across all economic variables. High correlations are found *only* for the non-western nations, particularly Asia and the Middle East-North Africa regions. That is, the correlations are most convincingly in support of Hypothesis II in the *least* developed nations.[15] At the very bottom of the economic ladder this hypothesis seems to apply most directly; there are no higher correlations anywhere in the tables covering all three hypotheses than those given in Table 2 for the poorest nations. Furthermore, these high correlations are consistent across all three developmental variables. This suggests, though it does not prove, that technological education is critical in the educational program related to development, but that after a certain point in development, Hypothesis II does not apply. The reasons for this differential relationship is perhaps clarified by looking at the *mix* of vocational and general education.

THE SECONDARY EDUCATION MIX

Attempts to relate the mix of secondary education factors to developmental variables yields peculiar results. It was predicted that the ratio between vocational education and general secondary education (VE/GE) would be *positively* related to economic development. This was advanced on the assumption

---

[15] In terms of GNP per capita, Latin America typically occupies a position intermediary to the West and Asia.

that vocational education is critical in developmental programs and that industrialization will consistently call for greater and broader technological skills —imparted through secondary education. The great concern for technical training in the United States, particularly for the "underdeveloped" segments of this industrial society, and the great concern with skilled trades (e.g. electronic technicians) would at least superficially seem to affirm this proposition. Yet, even in the United States there seems to be some rumblings in *avant garde* educationalist circles to the effect that technical and vocational education is being overstressed in relation to the needs of the economy.[16] The argument is that a highly developed economy needs people trained in generalist type skills (math, verbal skills, general knowledge, etc.). It has also been asserted that currently in the United States vocational education programs are not actually preparing people for the rapidly changing job market and fail to give people the skills or attitudes necessary for on the job training or retraining. In the U.S.A. only about 50% of the people with vocational education actually fill jobs for which they are prepared.[17]

Our data indicate that this concern that the United States had turned a corner in regard to vocational-general education mix is not unwarranted. This opinion may actually be a bit behind the facts. For although an overall low positive correlation supported Hypothesis III, rather perplexing inconsistencies appear among the regional correlations. (See Table 3.) The expected high correlation between VE/GE and development is found *only* for the poorest regions namely Asia and Middle East-North Africa. Equally high negative correlations, in contradiction to Hypothesis III, appear with the more developed regions. Latin American data reveal ambiguously low correlations which are consistent with their moderate development.

At least on the surface, this pattern of correlations, consistent over three diverse measures of economic development, suggests an unexpected curvilinear relationship between the VE/GE secondary education mix and economic development. It suggests that technological education grows disproportionately during the first stages of industrialization and then declines (again disproportionately) in later stages. It is this first phase that most of the non-western world is struggling with at the moment, while the industrialized world, including eastern Europe, seems to have embarked on a second phase in the relationship between secondary education mix and the economy.

Figure 1 presents this relationship graphically, mapping the ratio VE/GE against Gross National Product per capita. This is a freehand curve based on the slope of the regression lines obtained in the two gross correlations for all those nations below a GNP per capita of 500 dollars (log scores) and all those above this GNP figure and using the sub-averages method to rough in a curve. This is an attempt to indicate the possibility of an analytic relationship.

However, longitudinal data is badly needed to carry out a genuine analytic construction. And these must be data covering a longer and more stable span

16 *Vocational Education Act of 1963*, Office of Education Publication, OE-80034, 1965.
17 *Ibid.*

of time than the politically chaotic period of post World War II (1940–1955) which is the source of *all* available data. It is also possible that so many additional variables may affect this relationship that no analytic theory is possible.

Curves very similar to that appearing in Figure 1 could be constructed for the

TABLE 3

Correlations Among Secondary Education Ratios (Vocational Education/General Education) and Three Economic Indicators by World Region

	GNP	CALORIES	ENERGY
World	0.481	0.413	0.485
North America and Western Europe	—0.492	—0.499	—0.257
Eastern Europe	—0.481	—0.695	0.287
Latin America	0.076	—0.137	—0.031
Middle East	0.684	0.446	0.797
Asia	0.554	0.421	0.327

relationships between the other two measures of development used here (calories per capita per day and gross energy consumption) as related to the secondary education mix (VE/GE); although, in neither case is the curvilinear relationship quite so pronounced. Again, it is possible that the structures of these curves will differ in detail when better data are available. The author is convinced, however, that the general relationship mapped in Figure 1 will hold for whichever of the diverse measures of development are chosen.

Figure 1 seems to indicate that the ratio between vocational education and general education is highly related to economic development, but not related in the linear fashion which was originally predicted. Although there is considerable dispersion in the data, particularly in the region around 500 GNP per capita, the correlation for all nations below the transition point of 500 GNP per capita is fairly high ($r = 0.455$) and positive; above this "high water" mark of GNP = 500 the correlation is also convincing (—0.473), but negative in direction.[18] It can be definitely asserted, therefore, that, at least under recent world historical conditions, there is a strong tendency for vocational education to increase relative to general education up to a certain point in the development process (tentatively set at a GNP of 500 dollars per capita) and then to decline, again relative to general education rates.

However, the *if* of current historical conditions is a big one; these are cross sectional data and may reflect historical and cultural factors which combine to make up only the appearance of a universal trend. Do nations change over time

[18] It should be noted that Pearson r is used here to indicate the degree of correlation, while a rank order correlation technique is reported in Tables 1, 2, and 3. Pearson r is used in Figure 1 because the attempt is a beginning toward constructing an analytical theory relating log scores of economic growth figures to secondary education mix.

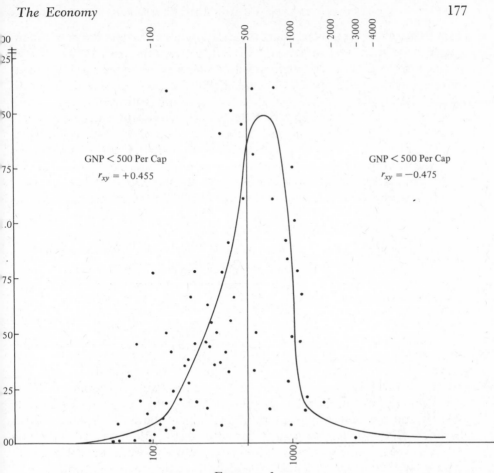

FIGURE 1

Gross National Product Per Capita (U.S. Dollars) and Ratio of Vocational Secondary Education to General Secondary Education.

in regard to secondary education mix in a fashion which is similar to that depicted in Figure 1? Unfortunately, longitudinal data are necessary to institute this control, and these data are hard to come by.

LONGITUDINAL TRENDS

Longitudinal data are, however, available back to 1940 for about 45% of the nations included in the original sample.[19] Nothing is available in the way of

[19] These data for 1940 (actually a range of dates from 1937–1940) were obtained from the files of the International Study of University Admissions, a project conducted under UNESCO auspices and directed by Frank Bowles. These data were in turn taken from published and unpublished UNESCO sources. The data were retrieved from these files with the assistance of Mary Corcoran, a research Fellow on the International Study of University Admissions.

data from any earlier period. Using these data, a table has been drawn up showing the relative changes in the ratio VE/GE between the years 1940 and 1956.
If this ratio increases in conjunction with economic development up to a point
indicated by the per capita GNP figure of 500, and then begins to decline with
further development, it follows that those nations with per capita GNP's
under 500 in 1956 should show an increase in the ratio between the dates 1940
and 1956. Likewise, those with per capita GNP's over 500 in 1956 could be expected to have decreased in ratio over the same period of time. This involves
only the assumption that all the nations have in fact undergone economic development during the period, which appears to be the case.

Table 4 bears out the assertion that the change in the ratio (VE/GE) be-

TABLE 4

*Change in Secondary Education Mix (VE/GE) Between 1940 and 1956
by Gross National Product per Capita for Thirty-Four Nations **

	A$>$Z	A$=$Z	A$<$Z	N
Low GNP	(18)	(1)	(4)	23
High GNP	(3)	(4)	(4)	11

* $x^2 = 51.17, p < .001$.

tween 1940 and 1956 is directly dependent on the level of economic development obtained by the nation in question in 1956. Using A to represent the ratio
in 1956 and Z to represent the 1940 ratio, Table 4 shows clearly that nations
with low GNP (under 500 per capita) have consistently improved their ratio
between vocational and general secondary education, while for nations with
high GNP the ratio has declined or remained roughly the same (difference of
no more than 0.1 in either direction) over the sixteen year interval. This is
completely consistent with the cross sectional data presented in Figure 1.
Again, the inadequacies of these data must be noted; yet, the trends seem irre-
futable. Nations below 500 in GNP have a distinct tendency to raise the proportion of vocational education in the secondary education mix, nations above
the point have a tendency to reduce or keep constant their proportional investment in vocational education.

CULTURAL CONTEXT

Although the relationships described above, linear or curvilinear, are relatively pronounced, it seems well to keep in mind the cultural context in which
the changes are occurring. Asia, particularly South Asia, would seem to have
some of the greatest idiosyncrasies which affect the correlations between
education and development. Asia, as has been noted earlier, has a high rate of
general education and a high rate of literacy relative to economic growth.

Burma, for example, in 1955 ranked thirty-fifth in secondary general education among all nations in this study but next to last in GNP per capita. Thailand is twenty-seventh in general education and fifty-eighth in GNP. Even India is nineteenth in general secondary education—nearly first in the non-European world—but sixty-fourth in GNP, sixty-first in calories per day, and so on among the 69 nations dealt with in this study.

This strange inconsistency between general education and industrial development would seem to be most true of the ancient Buddist-Hindu cultures of south Asia, but one should be cautious in attributing a causal relation. The social and cultural factors are undoubtedly complex. Furthermore, some Asian nations do not fit the pattern as dramatically as others.

Only two of the three economic indicators show a high correlation between development and general education (Table 1, again) in Asia. Calories per day and gross energy consumption are correlated to general education rates in Asia, whereas, GNP per capita is not. By itself, calories per day of food consumption, as an historically more stable economic measure, suggests that not Buddist-Hindu traditions, but agricultural prosperity, accounts for the greater development of general education in that part of the world. However, lacking adequate historical records of investment in education all this is the merest speculation at the moment.

In any case, general education rates tend to be relatively high in much of Asia and this carries over into the literacy levels for these countries even though general literacy figures are a poor measure of any important knowledge resources. Is this affluence in general education accompanying the world's lowest income levels a gross refutation of the hypothesis linking education to development?

Some of the doubt here may be dispelled by the data on technological education and particularly the ratio VE/GE. Table 5 is a partially filled-in chart showing the distribution of levels of economic development (three levels of GNP) as to high, medium or low rank in regard to secondary education mix (VE/GE). (In this partial chart, I have filled in those two cells which seem most interesting.) In regard to the lower one-third of the economic world (those nations below 210 in GNP per capita), we see that those poor nations, slowest in raising vocational education in proportion to general education, are predominantly Asian countries. If one can assume from Figure 1 that an increase in the VE/GE ratio is causally related to, or has some causal effect in pulling nations up into the middle ranges of economic development, it is the nations of Asia which seem to be in exactly the worst position relative to equally poor Near Eastern and Latin American nations. It is the Asian countries which are showing the lowest interest in vocational education, at least as of ten years ago.

At the same time, however, a basic dilemma of interpretation must be kept in mind for future research. At this point, one can not say for certain that there is not some third independent cultural context factor which is causing

TABLE 5

Distribution of Ranked Secondary Education Ratios (VE/GE) for Nations
High and Low in Gross National Product per Capita

		LOW GNP (BELOW 210)	HIGH GNP (ABOVE 750)
Ranked Ratios VE/GE	Highest One-third	7	Luxemburg (1194) Belgium (1015) Norway (969) West Germany (762) Denmark (913)
	Middle One-third	10	4
	Lowest One-third	Libya (90) Korea (80) Burma (52) Pakistan (56) India (72) Iran (100) Philippines (201) Thailand (100) Morocco (159) Laos (136) United Arab Republic (125) Ceylon (122) Cambodia (115)	4

both the low position of technological education and the economic problems of this region. Again, returning to Figure 1, the first (positive) part of the curvilinear relationship is highly dependent on data from Asian nations. Without the ratios for the south Asian nations, particularly, the curvilinear relationship discussed above would be less pronounced.

The data *do* highlight, however, the disadvantageous position of Asian nations and particularly their marked preference for general education over vocational education. Although the data are even more spotty concerning teacher training, it also seems that Asia has been extremely slow to invest in teacher training. This condition may magnify the problems of modernization in south and southeast Asia and exacerbate the economic misfortunes (not all locally caused) of this culturally rich area. From another perspective, D'Souza has commented on the relation between teacher salaries and the depreciation of the economic importance of education in India.[20] In many

[20] A. A. D'Souza, *Aspects of Education in India and Abroad*, Bombay: Orient Longmans, 1958, p. 65.

parts of India, for example, messenger boys make more money than school teachers.[21] This is in direct contrast to Africa where teachers seem to be getting relatively high salaries. D'Souza is himself an advocate of a rural based, technically oriented education, but his point of view is still relatively unheard of in India, except perhaps in regard to higher education.

SUMMARY AND CONCLUSION

I have tried to put the long run relationships between education and economic development into the beginnings of a propositional form. This is done not so much in the hope of establishing some kind of mathematically elegant theory, as of providing guides for badly needed research and to stimulate the collection of comparative data. It is done with an eye toward future systems analysis of the *interaction* between society and economy.

The present study found an overall low correlation between the absolute level of general secondary education per capita and indicators of economic growth. This included economic growth in all regions of the world, except Africa. There is a high positive correlation between growth in technological education and economic development. Thus, the data confirm the second hypothesis, but not the first.

However, the data concerning the mix between general education and technological education, and between general education and teacher training at the secondary school level do not bear out the third hypothesis. It was predicted that the ratio between technological education/general education (VE/GE) would be positively related to development, but this turned out to be untrue. In fact, the relationship between these two variables appears to be curvilinear. Technological education increases, relative to general education up to a theoretical maximum—apparently around the level of a Gross National Product per capita in the $500 range. But certainly many variables not dealt with in this study affect the ratio. For example, the cultural context and traditions of south Asia may help condition this curvilinear relationship.

The relationship between education and economic or social development is undoubtedly a complex one. Possibly no one theory can account for all the variables which may enter into the relationship. Likewise, no nation develops in isolation from other nations, and world events affect the necessity for educational development in any given region. The necessity for an adaptive technology in a specific field (e.g., rice cultivation) may increase the importance of some kinds of vocational education in comparison to other types of education. Or rapid social change may necessitate certain forms of general education in a nation's total educational effort over a short run period. The complexity of the total system in which these variables are embedded is staggering. ·

21 D'Souza, *op. cit.*, p. 16.

Still, global theories and global research can not be ignored. Applied concerns aside, the relationship between educational, economic and sociological variables point to numerous, untouched theoretical problems in the border areas of these disciplines. The question of a new level of societal integration in which all present relationships are altered is a real possibility. These problems pose a challenge to theory as well as to applied and basic research in all three fields.

AN INTERNATIONAL COMPARISON
OF THE TREND OF PROFESSIONAL
EARNINGS

Tibor Scitovsky

The author examines the hypothesis that, as countries grow wealthier and education becomes more accessible to larger proportions of the population, there is less disparity in income between the highly educated (the professionals) and others. He uses historical and contemporary data on the earnings of professionals and civil servants. School enrollment figures serve as a simple indicator of educational accessibility.

THE PURPOSE of this paper is to assemble and present in comparable form some of the statistics available on professional incomes in a number of Western countries. The professions selected are the law, medicine, dentistry, the higher civil service, and higher learning; the countries are Canada, Denmark, France, Germany, Norway, Sweden, the United Kingdom, and the United States. An attempt has been made to carry the data back to before World War I whenever possible.

My interest in professional incomes has been aroused by the alleged and oft-cited connection between economic growth and the advance of democracy on the one hand and the worsening economic status of the intellectual and professional classes on the other. This trend has been noted not only in the

REPRINTED FROM *The American Economic Review*, 56 (March 1966), 25–42, by permission of the author and the American Economic Association. The author is . . . indebted to many people in Denmark, England, France, Germany, Norway, Sweden, and the United States. . . . The Institute of Business and Economic Research at the University of California, Berkeley, generously provided research assistants for this and other projects; and the author owes a special debt to Mary H. Hager, his research assistant, who did the most work on this paper.

United States but in most Western countries; it explains the springing up, all over Western Europe, of organizations of intellectuals and university graduates, aimed at defending their interests and drawing the public's attention to their plight. In Canada, in the 40 years between 1911 and 1951, the income of professional people is estimated to have risen only one-quarter as fast as the income of industrial workers; in Germany, over a period half as long (1936–55), the average income of the free professions is said to have risen by half as much as the income of the rest of the economy (4, 5). The same trend, though less pronounced, is present also in Great Britain, where, between 1911 and 1956, the average income of the liberal professions has risen by two-thirds of the rise in the national income per head of occupied population. . . .

Perhaps the first person to notice and analyze this phenomenon was Alexis de Tocqueville. In his *Democracy in America* he remarked and speculated upon the lesser disparity in the United States than in France, and in the France of his day than in that of Napoleon, between the salaries of high civil servants and that of office messengers.[1] He explained the difference in these disparities by differences in the degree of democracy—more democracy in America than in France, and more democracy in the France of 1833 than in that of 1810. According to Tocqueville, an aristocracy tends barely to allow a subsistence minimum to office messengers but to vote high salaries for the high offices of State, positions which they or their children might occupy and benefit from; whereas the people, when they govern, are generous toward the humbler public officers but envious of and niggardly toward the higher ranks. He might have found his explanation even better confirmed had he known that by the mid-twentieth century these income disparties were to decline very much further in France but change little in America; and had he also known that, of the Western countries, the British pay the highest and the Swiss the lowest salaries to their high civil servants (Table 1).

Tocqueville's political argument might be carried a little further. In aristocratic and feudal societies, great disparities between the salaries of high and not-so-high civil servants have also served to restrict entry to the profession and make it a preserve of the well-to-do. For the way to the high offices of State leads through the middle ranks; and if the pay in these is insufficient to enable officials to maintain the standard of living expected in their station, then the way to the higher ranks is blocked to all but those who at this early stage can supplement their pay out of private income. An example of this has been until not so long ago a branch of the civil service in Germany and other Central European countries—the academic profession. A university professor earned as high an income as the highest ranking civil servant; but he attained this income and the accompanying high prestige late in life, and

---

[1] Cf. Vol. II, Ch. 5, pp. 77–81 in the 2nd English edition (London 1836); p. 221 of the new French edition.

TABLE 1

Civil Service Salaries (in National Currency and as Multiples of the Lowest Salary)

COUNTRY	OFFICE	1834 NATIONAL CURRENCY	MULT.	1875 NATIONAL CURRENCY	MULT.	1915 NATIONAL CURRENCY	MULT.	1955 NATIONAL CURRENCY	MULT.
United States	Under Secretary of the Treasury	—		6,000	7.1	—		17,500	5.4
	Chief Clerk	2,000	3.3	4,000	4.7	4,000	3.0	14,800	3.6
	Messenger	600	1	840	1	1,320	1	3,200	1
France	Directeur Général des Finances	20,000	13.3	25,000	14.6	25,000	12.8	2,490,000	5.1
	Huissier	1,500	1	1,700	1	1,950	1	488,000	1
United Kingdom	Permanent Head	—		1,920	32.0	1,950	23.5	4,623	15.9
	Sorter	—		60	1	83	1	291	1

Sources: United States, 1834, A. de Tocqueville, *Democracy in America*, London, 1836; 1875 and 1915, U.S. Bureau of the Census, *Official Register of the United States*, 1955, U.S. Civil Service Commission, Form 490, August 1956, "The Pay Scales of the Classification Act of 1949, as amended, and Prior Pay Scales of the Classification Act of 1932, as amended." For 1955 the GS-18 classification was taken as equivalent to the chief clerk whose post had been abolished. France: 1834, A. de Tocqueville, *op. cit.* (at this time the Directeur Général des Finances had the title of Secrétaire Général des Finances); 1871 and 1914, Statistique Générale de la France, Rapport . . relatif aux échelles des traitements, remises et indemnités fixes des fonctionnaires, agents, sous-agents et ouvriers de l'Etat remunérés au mois. *Journal Officiel*, Annexes 1911, p. 1495; 1955, André Tiano, *Le Traitement des Fonctionnaires*, Paris 1957. United Kingdom: 1876–1950, G. Routh, "Civil Service Pay, 1875–1950," *Economica*, August 1954.

until then held the position of *Privatdozent*, a title with no, or virtually no, income. Hence the need in those days and in those countries for a private income as a prerequisite for an academic career.

The political factors, however, tell only part of the story of civil service pay and are no help whatever in analyzing the earnings of the free professions. For a full explanation of the level and trend of professional incomes we need economic explanations as well. The most important of these, probably, is the increasing availability of higher education and its diminishing cost to the individual. This, too, has to do with democracy, of which it is one of the main aims and achievements; but it is democracy exerting its influence through economic channels. The increasing availability of higher education has increased the supply of people eligible for the professions and has thus tended to lower professional incomes (Table 2).[2]

It is true that, hand-in-hand with the increasing availability of education, educational requirements for eligibility to the professions have also been raised, tending to restrict supply. Where of old anyone could hang out a shield and practice his profession, now diplomas, licenses, and many years of training are required. Mostly this represents a welcome protection of the public; in some cases the desire to raise incomes by restricting numbers has also played a part. Both factors have probably been present in medicine in the United States, where alone among the countries considered, the limited number and capacity of the medical schools and their strict admission requirements have reduced the ratio of physicians to total population over the past 60 years. In all other countries and all other professions considered in this study, the relative number of professional people has increased over time.

The importance of the supply of professional training is also suggested by an international comparison of these two quantities, shown in the scatter diagram of Figure 1. Along the vertical axis is measured the salary of a highly paid natural scientist, the head of the national meteorological service, expressed as a multiple of an office-messenger's pay; along the horizontal axis is measured a rough index of the supply of professional training, the number of students enrolled in universities and institutes of technology per 100,000 of population. The correlation is striking and could go a long way toward explaining the very great national differences in salary differentials.[3]

---

[2] The increasing supply of trained and educated people is also attributed to technical progress increasing the *demand* for training and education. Neutral and uniform technical progress raises all earnings in proportion and hence raises the return on education, expressed as the (absolute) difference in earnings between the skilled and the unskilled. If education is among the uniformly progressing industries, the gap between the cost and return on education is widened, thus raising the demand for it (1, pp. 53ff.).

[3] On the other hand, the correlation could also be explained by the much greater international mobility of natural scientists than of office messengers, which would account for the much lesser absolute differences in the earnings of natural scientists. It seems likely that earnings in mobile occupations should be roughly the same in different countries, while in immobile occupations they should be quite different, higher in rich and lower in poor countries.

TABLE 2

Students Enrolled in Universities per 10,000 Inhabitants

YEAR	UNITED STATES (1)	CANADA (2)	GREAT BRITAIN (3)	FRANCE (4)	GERMANY (5)	SWEDEN (6)	NORWAY (7)	DENMARK (8)
1900	31.3							
1909					10.1			
1910	38.6						9.0	
1911								
1913					12.9			
1914				10.5		11		17.4
1915								
1920	56.6					13	9.1	
1929		30			20.0			22.5
1930	89.4		13.3	17.7		16	16.8	25.2
1935	94.4	32			11.8	19		
1936				17.6				
1939	113.4			19.1			17.7	27.9
1940						18		
1941		32						33.0
1945								
1947		64		31.7		20		
1948	179.0							
1950	176.4				22.9		22.3	31.1
1951				33.0		25		
1952		45						
1953			19.8					
1954						29		
1955			19.7					
1956	154.4	45		36.1	26.5			28.9
1957							16.3	

(1) *Sources:* F. Edding, *Die Ausgaben für Schulen und Hochschulen im Wachstum der Wirtschaft*, Pt. II, Kiel 1957, p. 94; *Biennial Survey of Education in the United States*, "Statistics of Higher Education," 1957–58, p. 7. Coverage: "Institutions with courses creditable toward bachelors' or higher degrees," including less than 3 per cent "Technical Institutions and semiprofessional schools" such as teachers' training colleges, etc. Figures are for full- and part-time undergraduate and graduate students.

(2) *Sources:* F. Edding, *op. cit.*, p. 43; For later years: Canada, Bureau fédéral de statistique, *Apercu biennial sur l'enseignement au Canada*, Pt. II, Relevé de l'enseignement supérieur, 1950/52, pp. 56–57; 1956, Canada, Bureau of Statistics, *University and College Enrollment*, Fall 1955, p. 5. Coverage: Universities and colleges other than teachers' training colleges. According to the English version of the Biennial Survey used by Edding, figures are for full-time students throughout while its French version describes them as including part-time enrollments for the postgraduates; however, the possible error is small, postgraduate enrollment being roughly 5 per cent of undergraduate enrollment before 1952 and 7 per cent in 1952. For the 1956 figure, there is no indication whether part-time enrollment is included or not.

(3) *Sources:* F. Edding, *op. cit.*, p. 81; United Kingdom, Central Statistical Office, *Annual*

Abstract of Statistics 1960 (No. 97), p. 100. Coverage: Full- and part-time university students taking courses.

(4) *Sources:* F. Edding, *op. cit.,* p. 35; Annuaire Statistique de la France, Rétrospectif, 1961, p. 67. Coverage: "Enseignement supérieur public, effectif des étudiants français et étrangers."

(5) *Sources:* 1956, *Statistisches Jahrbuch für die Bundesrepublik Deutschland,* 1957, p. 94; 1950, *ibid.,* 1952, pp. 70–71; 1935, *Statistisches Jahrbuch für das Deutsche Reich,* 1936, pp. 544 and 549; 1929, *ibid.,* 1930 pp. 454–60; 1913, *ibid.,* 1914, pp. 316–21; 1909, *ibid.,* 1910, pp. 276–78. Coverage: Universities, "Technische Hochschulen" and other types of "Hochschulen," excluding teachers' training institutions. The 1956 and 1950 figures are for "Immatrikulierte Studenten," and the earlier figures for "Studierende" excluding "Hoerer and Hospitanten" which gives a fairly consistent time series.

(6) *Sources:* F. Edding, *op. cit.,* p. 59; 1947, Sweden, *Statistisk Arsbok,* 1949, pp. 275–76. Coverage: "Institutions of Higher Education" which means Universities and various types of "Högskolorna."

(7) *Sources:* 1957, Norway, *Statistisk Årbok,* 1959, p. 251; 1950 and 1939, *ibid.,* 1953, p. 254; 1930, *ibid.,* 1931–32, p. 163; 1920, *ibid.,* 1920, pp. 183–84; 1910, *ibid.,* 1911, p. 175 and *ibid.,* 1910, p. 146. Coverage: "Universities and Equivalent Institutions."

(8) *Sources:* 1956, Denmark, *Statistisk Årbog,* 1957, p. 235; 1950, *ibid.,* 1951, p. 223; 1945, *ibid.,* 1947, p. 180; 1940, *ibid.,* 1941, p. 165; 1935, *ibid.,* 1937, pp. 153–54; 1930, *ibid.,* 1933, pp. 132–33; 1915, *ibid.,* 1920, p. 174. Coverage: The tables were for "Students in Institutions of Higher Education, Senior Vocational Schools, etc." and some of the enrollment figures had to be subtracted out to obtain a coverage that seemed reasonably comparable to that in the other European countries considered.

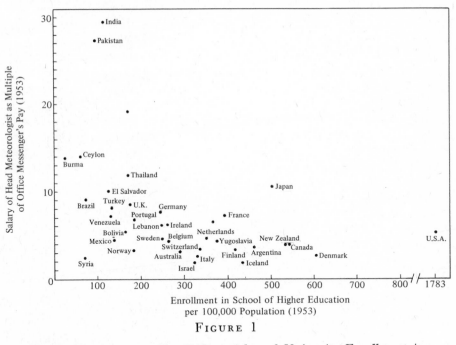

FIGURE 1

The Relation Between Pay Differentials and University Enrollment in Different Countries.

Having discussed the influences on professional incomes from the supply side, we must now turn to those exerted on the side of demand. First, the rise in real incomes that results from economic growth tends to raise demand for most consumers' goods and services, including professional services. Second, the increasing complexity of our civilization has created a demand for a whole range of new professions and occupations that require extensive scientific and technical training and thus compete with the older professions for the available supply of highly educated and trained manpower. These two factors tend to boost professional incomes and thus to counteract the depressing effect of the increase in supply.

A third factor, but one likely to exert a downward pull on the demand for professional services, is the probable lag in the productivity of professional people. The rise in incomes tends to raise the demand for goods and services because the prices of these rise either not at all or more slowly than incomes. The faster rise of earnings than of prices measures the rise in the productivity of labor; and unequal advances in the productivity of different industries and activities create changes in the structure of prices, in the pattern of demand, and also in the structure of incomes and earnings. In fields where the productivity of labor has made the greatest strides, product prices fall the most relatively to earnings and the prices of other products; in fields where labor productivity has not risen at all, product prices remain unchanged in relation to earnings in the same field but rise in relation to the prices of other products.

The productivity of professional people is notoriously very difficult to measure, because changes in the quality of professional services, in medicine for example, can be major and must be taken into account. In many professions, however, these changes cannot have been great, and productivity is likely to have advanced less than that of most other types of labor. If this is so, and if this trend has not been counterbalanced by increasing disparity in the length of the working week of professional people and others, then one would expect the prices of professional services to have risen relative to the prices of most other goods and services; and this relative rise to have discouraged demand for the services of professional people. This force, then, goes counter to the stimulating effect of rising real incomes on the demand for professional services.[4]

Yet another factor very different from those so far discussed but believed to have a great influence on professional incomes is inflation. The incomes of the professional groups here considered are determined to some extent by tradition. The members of these professions traditionally believe and like others to believe that they are rendering essential public service, the price of

---

[4] One is unduly tempted in this connection to focus attention on the relation between the prices of professional services and the average level of money incomes, expecting demand for these services to rise if their prices fall and to diminish if their prices rise in relation to average incomes. The logic of this argument is best seen in the simple case of a parallel rise in money incomes and the prices of professional services. If the prices of other goods and services stand still or increase more slowly, *real* incomes will rise and stimulate the demand for professional services; on the other hand, the slower increase of other prices implies a rise also in the *relative* price of professional services, which discourages the demand for them. There is no reason to expect these contrary forces to offset each other exactly.

which is determined by factors other than their bargaining power in the market place. This tradition inhibits them and their professional organizations in seeking to maximize their incomes and explains why these respond sluggishly to market forces and may have a range of indeterminacy within which they do not respond at all. Hence the belief that inflation lowers the real incomes of the professions.

This argument is probably valid at a time of small price increases or at the beginning of an inflationary period, and especially with respect to salaried professionals. The experience of more severe and more prolonged inflation, however, shows that market forces protect the interests of the so-called fixed-income earners as well as those of any other group. France's civil service (which includes teachers and professors) is protected no less effectively than organized labor by an escalator clause linked to the cost-of-living index; and in Chile, white-collar workers and the professions are supposed to be among the beneficiaries of inflation.

Prolonged inflation might nevertheless hurt the salaried professional groups whenever market forces are against them. For their salaries, once set, are not likely to be reduced in response to a fall in demand or rise in supply, and may remain at a higher level than the forces of supply and demand would justify. In such cases, an inflationary price rise may be necessary for market forces to exert their downward pressure on the real incomes of these groups. In other words, inflation can hurt fixed-income earners by *enabling* market forces to overcome the downward rigidity of salary scales.

While it is easy to list factors that influence the demand or supply of professional services, it is difficult to appraise their relative importance. All I could do and have done was to give data on the earnings and numbers of people in the free professions, in an attempt to furnish the coordinates of the point of intersection between supply and demand curves.[5] A third bit of information, the length of the working week, was not available; but a guess at least can be made. U. S. data for a part of the period suggest that the secular shortening of the working week was largely confined to workers and clerks. Business-men, managers, officials, and professional people work a longer week and one that has not become appreciably shorter over the years. In relative terms, therefore, compared to the rest of the occupied population, the length of the professional person's working week has increased—and the trend was probably similar in the other countries too.

II

In an international comparison of this type, the main problem is to obtain comparable data. National differences in the availability, the sources, the

[5] No data are given on the number of people on university faculties and in the civil service, owing to the difficulty of obtaining comparable series on comparable definitions. The same difficulty explains why the income data are confined to only one rank in the hierarchy; and it seemed meaningless to give the number of persons in that single rank.

derivation, and the definition of the data were so great that an originally more ambitious project had to be cut down drastically. The number of countries, professions, detail, and types of data covered is much smaller than originally contemplated; and many compromises had to be made in presentation for the sake of better comparability. To compare professional earnings over time and between nations, it would have been desirable to express them as multiples of an over-all national average of personal incomes per employed population—we had to settle instead for multiples of *national* income per *occupied* population or labor force. Another interesting comparison would have been that between the absolute levels of professional real incomes in different countries; but official exchange rates would have been too crude and misleading, purchasing power equivalents were available only for a single year, so here, too, we had to settle on a mere fragment of what was originally contemplated, the few data contained in Tables 3 and 4. We also hoped to

TABLE 3

*Average Earnings of European Professionals as a
Percentage of the Purchasing Power Equivalent
of United States Professionals for 1955* [a]
(European weights)

COUNTRY	PHYSICIANS	DENTISTS	LAWYERS	PROFESSORS	CIVIL SERVANTS	PER CAPITA INCOME
Denmark	43		62	58	39	49
United Kingdom	67	79	81	110	141	55
Norway	36		67	72	43	62/51
France	65	114		80	52	53
Germany	47	49	84	123	110	57

[a] Where 1955 data were unavailable, comparisons were based on 1950 data. These are in italics. Purchasing Power Parity rates were calculated from Tables 5 and 8 of Milton Gilbert, *Comparative National Products and Price Levels,* Paris 1958.

   Earnings data are from the unpublished appendix tables. Earnings of free professionals in Denmark, Norway, and Germany have been increased by 20 per cent, in the United Kingdom by 10 per cent, for an estimated understatement of income.

   The estimate for dentists' earnings in France is probably too high.

present data on all ranks of academic faculties and professional civil servants but the difficulties of international comparability proved insurmountable— hence the limitation of data to full professors and the highest ranking permanent civil servant.

Despite such compromises and narrowing of the scope of the study, full comparability of the data has not been achieved. The most important of the unresolved difficulties in this respect stems from differences in the provenance of the earnings data of the free professions. In the United States, estimates of the professional earnings of physicians, dentists, and lawyers are based on

TABLE 4

Average Earnings of European Professionals as a
Percentage of the Purchasing Power Equivalent
of United States Professionals for 1955 [a]
(U.S. weights)

COUNTRY	PHYSICIANS	DENTISTS	LAWYERS	PROFESSORS	CIVIL SERVANTS	PER CAPITA INCOME
Denmark	34		42	46	31	39
United Kingdom	51	61	62	83	106	42
Norway	26		49	54	32	46/37
France	46	81		57	37	37
Germany	31	28	58	84	75	39

[a] The notes of Table 3 apply *pari passu* also to this table.

questionnaire surveys, with the respondents assured of anonymity and guaranteed against disclosure of the information furnished. The French estimates are derived partly from tax, partly from other data, reconciled and rendered comparable by correcting for an estimated 33 per cent understatement of income in tax returns. In the other five countries, the estimates are based on income tax statistics without correction for understatement and are likely therefore to be too low—in a ratio presumably different for the different countries and perhaps also for different dates. For tax evasion probably increases with the burden of taxation, which is on the increase everywhere; and it is likely to be less important in a well-policed country like England, where payments into a physician's bank account are a source of information on his gross professional receipts.

It seemed impossible to correct the data for such differences; but their order of magnitude may be gauged by the discrepancy between U. S. income-tax and questionnaire-survey data in the few years for which both are available.[6] The income tax data are consistently lower, by about 18 per cent for lawyers and physicians and 13 per cent for dentists. It is unlikely that the whole discrepancy is due to tax evasion. For 1949, the Audit Control Program of the Internal Revenue Service showed an average discrepancy between net profits "reported" and "disclosable by audit" of 4 per cent for lawyers, 6.5 per cent for physicians, and 7.5 per cent for dentists (3, Table 5).[7] While this is not a full measure of tax evasion, the earnings hidden even from audit

[6] Net earnings of sole proprietorships and partnerships as shown in Schedule C of the income-tax return are available on a per capita basis for 1947 and 1953 and can be estimated with a small margin of error for a few other years for which the number of partners in partnerships is not available.

[7] The percentages in the text are based on the higher figure, while those in Table 5 of the work just cited are based on the lower "net profits reported."

TABLE 5

*Professional Earnings of Physicians as Multiples
of Per Capita Income of Occupied Population*

YEAR	UNITED STATES	UNITED KINGDOM	FRANCE	GER-MANY	CANADA	DEN-MARK	NORWAY	SWEDEN
1911		5.4						
1913								7.2
1915						4.8		
1920								5.9
1921						3.9		
1927		(4.1)		3.7				
1929	2.9			4.3				
1930	3.2					(4.9)	3.9	4.2
1935	3.4			5.3				
1936–1938		(5.2)						
1938				4.6				
1939	3.2		3.3				(3.2)	
1940						3.1		
1947					2.9			
1948	3.2						2.2	
1950	3.3			2.7				
1951	3.2		3.9				(1.5)	
1952		4.3			2.6			
1954						3.0		
1956	3.8	4.3	4.8	2.6	2.9			
1958	4.2							

would hardly explain the rest of the discrepancy. A more careful and comprehensive enumeration of deductions for tax purposes than for estimating one's income for general information may be part of the explanation; furthermore, the questionnaire surveys, with their low response rates, are believed to have an upward bias, due partly to the reluctance of the less successful professionals to admit, even anonymously, their lack of success, partly to their being less likely to have the secretarial help or leisure needed for answering questionnaires.

In addition to the above derivational differences, there also remain in the data a number of definitional differences. Not only are statistics differently collected in different countries, there are international differences also in the way in which salaries are paid, pension funds set up, and professions defined and separated from neighboring professions. Each of these differences has created problems, none of them serious but many insoluble—at least with the limited resources available to this study.

The data on the earnings of the free professions refer, whenever possible, to independent practitioners only; but in some cases they are over-all averages for the entire profession, which includes independent practitioners and salaried employees. The discrepancies so introduced are probably slight. In the United States, where earnings data are available on both definitions for a part of the period, the earnings of independent professionals fall below in depression and exceed in prosperity the average earnings of the entire profession, by a negligible 1 per cent or less for dentists and lawyers, by up to 7 per cent for physicians.

Another problem, only imperfectly resolved, was to find a comparable rank in the civil service. The obvious choice, a cabinet minister, was ruled out by great national differences in the importance of fringe benefits and the difficulties of evaluating them. We adopted the rank immediately beneath him, which minimized these difficulties but at the cost of lesser international comparability. England's permanent under-secretary and Germany's *Staatssekretär* were natural choices: they are the officials immediately below cabinet rank and at the same time also the highest-paid permanent civil servants. In France, the *secrétaire général* was an uneasy compromise; in the other countries, we have chosen the highest-paid officials outside the cabinet, even when they were political appointees.

International comparability remained an imperfectly resolved problem also in the case of professors. Many changes over time and great national differences in the ranks below the full professor forced us to omit them; but even at the professor's rank there are important differences between Europe and America. Professorial chairs are fixed in number and attained only by the select few at most European universities; in America the number of chairs is not limited and the professorship is a rank all faculty members can and most do attain in time. The data compensate for this difference in a crude way, because national averages of professorial earnings in all other countries are set beside U. S. averages that relate only to the 39 best and highest-paying institutions.

A further difficulty only partly resolved stems from the fact that civil servants—and this includes university professors on the Continent—are paid a fixed salary in some countries; in others their basic salary is augmented by rent, cost-of-living, and family allowances. In these latter cases we have taken, whenever possible, the earnings of a married man with two children, living in the capital.

In Europe, university professors usually receive extra pay for examinations. The difficulties of obtaining reliable and complete data on this extra pay forced us to exclude it from our data. Accordingly, the professional earnings of professors in the European countries are somewhat understated in the tables.[8] In Germany, professors also receive *Kolleggelder*, fees for each student

---

[8] Examination fees may be quite an important source of income in some countries. In Germany, where the rector (president) receives a percentage of all examination fees paid at his university, there used to be a saying (before World War I) at the University of Berlin that a year's tour of duty as rector was worth a villa in Gruenewald, Berlin's most exclusive residential district.

enrolled in their courses. Earnings from these used to be quite high in the days when all student fees went to the faculty. In the last decades of the last century, a popular professor could earn as much as 100,000 marks (about $100,000 in today's purchasing power), or 70 times the then-average income of the occupied population. This golden age of the German professor came to an end with legislation of 1898 (and of 1918) which gave him a fixed salary but diverted a part of student fees to the general upkeep of his university. But even today, *Kolleggelder*, the professor's share of student fees, amount to DM5.00 ($1.25) for each semester hour per student enrolled; and, with classes of a thousand or more not uncommon, a popular lecturer, or one whose courses are required, can easily double his basic salary (2).[9] Unfortunately, data from which to estimate average earnings from these fees are not available. Often the university guarantees a man's minimum proceeds from *Kolleggelder*; and we have taken the average of this minimum *Kolleggeldgarantie* as our estimate of the average of the actual *Kolleggelder*, although this must clearly be an underestimate.[10]

The earnings of civil servants and professors include the employee's and exclude the employer's contribution to pension funds; [11] and no adjustment was made for the fact that Germany deducts no employee contribution and pays pensions equal to a man's basic salary.

III

The basic data assembled for this study, the time series of net earnings in the different professions and of numbers in the free professions, are shown, separately for each country, in a series of appendix tables not printed here but available in the series of appendix tables published in the French version of this paper in *Analyse et Prévision* (Tome 1, No. 3, March 1966). These tables also contain benchmark data on total and occupied population and national income. The exact definition of each series, the sources of the data, their nature, the way of their derivation, and the assumptions on whose basis some of them had to be estimated are all stated in considerable detail in the footnotes to these tables. This seemed desirable, because the best thing this paper can, and I hope will, accomplish is to draw attention to the existence of these data and to stimulate and facilitate the task of a more ambitious undertaking to collect, render comparable, and publish the kind of data

[9] This book and correspondence with its author were the main source of information about German university professors.

[10] The share of *Kolleggelder* in average earnings as shown for 1952 and 1956 (in the appendix table) is about 10 per cent.

[11] However, the government's contribution to physicians' and dentists' pension funds under Britain's National Health Service *was* included in professional earnings so as to render them comparable to physicians' and dentists' earnings in other countries, where the government does not subsidize their pension plans.

assembled here as a very modest one-man undertaking on an incomplete scale. Estimates made on an exceptionally rough basis or derived from such estimates are within parentheses in both these and all other tables.

The time trends of net professional earnings are shown in this paper as multiples of national income per head of occupation, separately for each occupation in Tables 5 through 9. They are based on the raw data and

TABLE 6

Professional Earnings of Dentists as Multiples
of Per Capita Income of Occupied Population

YEAR	UNITED STATES	UNITED KINGDOM	FRANCE	GER-MANY	CANADA	DEN-MARK	NORWAY	SWEDEN
1914								5.9
1922								4.9
1927		(3.5)		2.5				
1929	2.4			2.7				
1930	2.7						2.4	3.7
1935	2.3			2.8				
1936–1938		(4.1)						
1938				2.6				
1939	2.4							2.8
1947					2.3			2.5
1948	2.0							
1950	2.0			2.1				2.3
1952	2.5	3.8			1.8			
1954								2.2
1955	2.6							
1956		3.3	5.5	1.9	2.1			
1958	2.8							

estimates contained in the unpublished appendix tables. Before looking at these, it is worth considering an international comparison in absolute terms. Tables 3 and 4 show the average net earnings of Europeans, expressed as a percentage of the purchasing-power equivalent of the earnings of the their U.S. colleagues, for the year 1955, in a few cases for 1950 (the italicized figures in the tables)—the only years for which purchasing-power equivalents are available. Table 3 is based on European, Table 4 on U.S. expenditure patterns; and if it is true, as is sometimes asserted, that the expenditure pattern of professional people resembles more nearly that of the average European, then Table 3 is the more relevant of the two. Both of them show that it pays to be a high civil servant in England, a university professor in

Table 7

Professional Earnings of Lawyers as Multiples
of Per Capita Income of Occupied Population

YEAR	UNITED STATES	UNITED KINGDOM	FRANCE	GER-MANY	CANADA	DEN-MARK	NORWAY	SWEDEN
1911		(7.3)						
1915						5.8		
1921						(3.9)		
1927		(7.0)		6.3				
1929	3.1			5.8				
1930	3.4					(4.4)	3.9	3.9
1935	4.0			4.5				
1936–1938		(7.5)						
1938				4.4				
1939	3.3						3.0	
1940						3.5		
1947					3.0			
1948	2.3							
1950	2.2			2.8			2.2	
1952	2.1				2.2			
1954						2.6		
1956	2.3	3.2		2.9	2.6			
1958	2.4							

Germany, and a physician in the United States.[12] They also show that the economic advantage of the professional over the average man is decidedly greater in England then elsewhere, owing, probably, to the lesser availability in England of academic training and the much smaller proportion of academically trained people.

Another striking fact, shown by these tables and even more by Tables 5 through 9; is the contrast between the limited range within which the free professions', and the very great range over which civil servants', professional earnings vary over time as well as between different countries. A tentative explanation might be that market forces have and always had full scope in determining professional earnings; whereas setting the salaries of high public officials is substantially a political decision.[13] The very high economic status

[12] The German professor's position is even more favorable than appears from the tables, because the data probably understate his income from Kolleggelder, take no account of his exceptionally generous pension plan and exclude (as in the case of other European professors) his examination fees.

[13] Market forces reassert themselves and force a raising of salary scales when these are set too low; they do not prevent their being set too high.

Table 8

Professional Earnings of Professors as Multiples
of Per Capita Income of Occupied Population

YEAR	UNITED STATES	UNITED KINGDOM	FRANCE	GER- MANY	CANADA	DEN- MARK	NORWAY	SWEDEN
1897				7.3				
1904	3.8							
1910	3.7						4.7	
1914			8.5					
1915						8.5		
1920	2.1						1.3	3.1
1921		3.8						
1927				5.6				
1929		5.4						
1930	3.7		8.9				3.7	4.2
1935	4.4				5.9	4.6		4.2
1936			8.6					
1936–1938		5.6						
1938				5.3				
1939	4.3		5.7				2.8	
1940						3.9		2.5
1941					3.0			
1945						2.7		
1947		3.8	3.8		2.3			1.7
1948	2.1						1.6	
1950	2.0			5.9		2.3		
1951			3.2					1.7
1952	1.9	3.8	3.1		1.8			
1955								2.4
1956	1.9	3.8	2.9	4.1	2.0			
1957							2.1	
1958	2.1							

of high civil servants in England, Germany, and France is probably best explained by Tocqueville. In these countries, society seems to accord high civil servants a higher status than they enjoy elsewhere for reasons that probably lie in their political traditions and class structure.

Coming now to the shape of the time series in Tables 5 through 9, they confirm the general impression of a downward trend of professional earnings in relation to the over-all average of per capita national income. All the long series, i.e., all those that go back to before World War I, show a marked downward trend, with those for high civil servants registering the greatest

TABLE 9

Professional Earnings of Civil Servants as Multiples
of Per Capita Income of Occupied Population

YEAR	UNITED STATES	UNITED KINGDOM	FRANCE	GER-MANY	CANADA	DEN-MARK	NORWAY (a)	NORWAY (b)	SWEDEN
1900	7.8								
1910	6.1						5.3		
1911		17.8							
1913				14.8					
1914			10.3						
1915						7.1			
1920	3.2						1.4		4.4
1921		15.4				3.9			
1927				10.3					
1929		15.2		10.1	8.2				
1930	6.1		11.1				3.9	6.0	5.9
1935	8.2			10.6		5.2			6.0
1936			10.5		11.0				
1936–1938		15.2							
1938				7.8					
1939	7.1		7.3				2.9	4.5	
1940						4.4			
1941					6.4				3.7
1945						3.0			
1947		8.8	4.5		5.9				2.5
1948	2.8								
1950					8.4	2.5	2.1		
1951		4.0							2.1
1952	3.9	8.5	3.9		4.1				
1954								2.0	
1955		3.9				2.6			2.6
1956	3.5	8.9	3.7	6.7	4.1				
1957							2.1	2.3	
1958	4.1								

Column (a) refers to the earnings of the *Ekspedisjonsjef*, until 1930 Norway's highest ranking permanent civil servant. Column (b) shows the relative earnings of the *Departementsrod*, the new highest rank established in 1930.

decline. The shorter series show the same downward trend, with the important exception of physicans in the United States. Data on their average professional earnings go back only to 1929 and show a rise. How this series would look if it could be carried back to 1913 I do not know; but it is worth noting that the number of physicians per population in the United States has been declining at least since 1900, while in all the other countries it has been rising. The data on French physicians' earnings also suggest an upward trend; but here the data are too few, the period too short, and the estimates too crude to attach significance to this finding. In general, however, the downward trend of professional incomes is the least pronounced and least well established in the medical profession. Perhaps the great advance in medicine and the resulting greatly increased demand for physicians' services account for this; an important additional factor in the United States probably is the restriction of entry to the profession.

To explain the prevalence of the downward trend, a number of factors were listed at the beginning of this paper. Some of these, such as the increasing supply of education and educated people, would tend generally to mitigate inequalities of income; others, such as the slower than average rise in the productivity of professional people, would explain a fall in the relative earnings of professionals only. This raises the question to what extent the decline in the economic status of the professions is peculiar to them and to what extent it is part of a general trend toward lesser inequalities of income. Could it be that professional people have more or less maintained their relative position on the income scale and that the fall in their relative earnings merely reflects the general compression of the entire income scale? To answer this question, we would need to know much more than we now know. What scanty information is available on income distribution by size is summarized in Table 10 and does suggest a general reduction in inequalities of income over time. It is impossible, however, to attach much significance or even

TABLE 10

Gini Index of Income Inequality by Size

YEAR	UNITED STATES	UNITED KINGDOM	GERMANY	SWEDEN	DENMARK
1935				.54	
1936	.47		.49		
1938		.43			
1939					.50
1945				.48	
1946	.41				
1949		.42			
1950	.40		.45		
1952					.44
1954				.38	
1955		.41			

Sources: Selma Goldsmith, G. Jaszi, H. Kaitz, and M. Liebenberg, "Size Distribution of Income Since the Mid-Thirties," *Rev. Econ. Stat.*, Feb., 1954. *Economic Survey of Europe in 1956*, Economic Commission for Europe, United Nations.

credence to such evidence, because this information is only available for two periods which are too close together and not very comparable, the first period being one of massive unemployment, the second one of full or overfull employment in most of the countries considered. Data on secular changes in the inequality of incomes within each of the professions would also be helpful; but they will have to be collected by a future and more ambitious project. I very much hope that this paper will facilitate its coming.

REFERENCES

1. G. S. BECKER, *Human Capital*. New York 1964.
2. A. BUSCH, *Die Geschichte des Privatdozenten*. Stuttgart 1959.
3. M. FARIOLETTI, "Some Income Adjustment Results from the 1949 Audit Control Program," Conference on Research in Income and Wealth, *Studies in Income and Wealth*, Vol. 23, *An Appraisal of the 1950 Census Income Data*, Princeton 1958, pp. 239–84.
4. J. F. HABERER AND F. L. KIM, "The Economic Position of Canadian Scientists and Engineers," *Canadian Mining and Metal. Bull.*, Oct. 1956, 721–25.
5. G. WOLFF, "Der Anteil der freien Berufe am Sozialprodukt," *Das Geistige Kapital*, March 1956, 34–36.

Part 4

SOCIAL
DIFFERENTIATION

EDUCATIONAL CHANNELS AND ELITE MOBILITY: A COMPARATIVE ANALYSIS

Joel Gerstl

and Robert Perrucci

This comparison of intergenerational mobility into one elite occupation, engineering, in Britain and the United States reveals contrasting patterns and indicates some of the mechanisms, including education, that explain the differences. Changes in recruitment into engineering during the past forty-five years indicate increasing rigidity in the United States and a pattern of increasing fluidity in Britain. In addition, high status origins are more highly related to professional success in the United States than they are in Britain. The advantages of cumulative evidence based on comparisons of particular occupational and educational institutions are suggested.

THERE CAN be little question that a major emphasis in recent literature concerning national contrasts of social mobility has been (as exemplified in the work of Lipset, Bendix and Zetterberg [1]) on the convergence of patterns in countries at an advanced stage of industrial development. Much as in the area of occupational prestige ratings,[2] the interest in similarities has involved a neglect of divergent trends. As S.M. Miller has concluded, "There probably is more convergence in rates than most people had believed. But this does not mean that the actual convergence is overwhelming; if we were able to approach the data without the background of decades of speculation, we would probably be concerned with the variation in the rates." [3] Perhaps now that we have gotten past the decades of speculation it is time to consider the divergences that do occur, and, even more important, to attempt to account for such divergences.

One area where the evidence for convergence of mobility patterns is especially ambiguous, is that of movement into the upper rungs of the occupational hierarchy—the managerial and professional categories called elites.

REPRINTED FROM *Sociology of Education*, 38 (Spring 1965), 224–232. © 1965 by the American Sociological Association.

[1] Seymour Martin Lipset & Reinhard Bendix, *Social Mobility in Industrial Society* (Berkeley, University of California, 1959).

[2] Cf. Joel E. Gerstl & Lois K. Cohen, "Dissensus, Situs & Egocentrism in Occupational Ranking," *British Journal of Sociology* XV (September, 1964) pp. 254–261.

[3] S.M. Miller, "Comparative Social Mobility," *Current Sociology*, IX, No. 1 (1960), p. 58.

While some of the explanation for social mobility may not require a consideration of formal education channels,[4] the area of elite mobility in any society[5] is intimately connected to the structure of education. Certainly, for established professions, access to the formal educational channels is a prerequisite for entry. An examination of the connection between elite mobility and educational channels provides data for detailed international comparisons, and illuminates the mechanisms involved.

Before proceeding to our comparative analysis there are several theoretical and methodological problems that must be considered. While these considerations are relevant to all mobility investigations they are especially crucial for comparative analyses.

Two areas with especially great theoretical implications are: (1) the distinction between *forced mobility* (due to changes in occupational structure) and *pure mobility* (due to the interchange of individuals between status categories);[6] and (2) boundary problems, especially the use of the simple manual-nonmanual split as versus finer status categories such as elites. Use of the latter often leads to asymmetrical findings resulting from a larger number of status categories and from attention to downward as against upward mobility.

Miller's reinterpretation of the Lipset-Bendix-Zetterberg data indicates the crucial differences that alternative mobility measures produce. The asymmetrical nature of mobility rates—that a nation may be high in one measure of mobility and low in another—may be due not only to methodological shortcomings but may well be an accurate reflection of different rates which warrant a theoretical explanation.

The difficulty of separating forced and pure mobility confounds the explanation of trends that appear. In total mobility studies one can seldom know how much of the change can be explained by shifts in the occupational structure. (Rogoff's study[7] is a rare exception in specifically attempting to partial out the effects of changes in the occupational structure.)

It is possible that with a focus on different indices of mobility, such as the movement from manual to nonmanual as compared with movement into elite categories, the amount of variation resulting from untested assumptions may be progressively reduced. For example, if samples of university graduates are compared, variations in rates that might be due to education, values, or aspirations can be more readily explained. While this narrowing of focus in-

[4] Cf. C. Arnold Anderson, "A Skeptical Note on the Relation of Vertical Mobility to Education," *American Journal of Sociology*, LXVI (May, 1961), pp. 560–570.

[5] See, e.g., Robert M. Marsh, "Values, Demand and Social Mobility," *American Sociological Review*, 28 (August, 1963), pp. 565–575.

[6] Saburo Yasuda, "A Methodological Inquiry into Social Mobility," *American Sociological Review*, 29 (February, 1964), pp. 16–23.

[7] Natalie Rogoff, *Recent Trends in Occupational Mobility*, Glencoe, The Free Press, 1953.

creases the precision of comparative statements, it does limit the population to which conclusions may be extended. But it may well be that the methodological difficulties of comparative analysis require a building up of smaller studies of limited scope, rather than the broad national comparisons which obfuscate many of the details that should be taken into consideration.

As a contribution to the accumulation of case studies in comparative mobility, we are concerned with changes over time in the recruitment into one elite occupation in Great Britain and the United States. The specific occupation for which we have comparable information is that of the engineer [8]—an elite by dint of professional standing, with similar social prestige in the two countries.[9]

The general framework for this comparison is necessarily the total mobility pattern for the two countries involved. Three separate indices of upward mobility in Britain and the U.S. from Miller's analysis are shown in Table 1. The rates of intergenerational movement from manual to nonmanual categories are very similar for the two countries. However, consideration of movement into elite occupations from either the manual or middle-class level shows the two to have dissimilar patterns. Britain has much less mobility into elite occupations than does the United States.

Part of this difference is due to the relative size of the elite category and is thus not only a reflection of the amount of individual movement or pure mobility. In America, with larger elite strata, there is a structural push toward a higher rate of mobility into the elite. In addition, the mechanisms for gaining access to elite occupations are very different in the two societies. The contrast is that of contest and sponsored mobility,[10] seen most dramatically in the proportions gaining access to higher education.

While the U.S. has high rates of mobility in terms of all three indices shown in Table 1, the British rate of upward movement is comparable only for the short manual to nonmanual move and relatively low for entry into the elites. Can one conclude from this that the U.S. is more open than Britain? Other findings suggest that the answer to a question such as this is by no means clear-cut. In considering patterns of downward mobility, for example, which Miller suggests may be a better indicator of fluidity than is upward mobility, there is much *more* movement from nonmanual to manual in Britain than in the United States. Contradictory evidence is also provided by Yasuda's comparison of intergenerational *pure* mobility rates among various coun-

[8] The American findings are reported in Robert Perrucci, "The Significance of Intra-Occupational Mobility: Some Methodological and Theoretical Notes, Together With a Case Study of Engineers," *American Sociological Review*, 26 (December, 1961), pp. 874–883. The British findings are reported in Joel Gerstl, "Social Origins of Engineers," *New Society*, 36 (6 June, 1963), pp. 19–20.

[9] Gerstl & Cohen, *op. cit.*

[10] Ralph H. Turner, "Sponsored and Contest Mobility and the School System," *American Sociological Review*, 25 (December, 1960), pp. 855–867.

TABLE 1

Upward Mobility Rates for Great Britain and the United States *

	MANUAL INTO NONMANUAL	MIDDLE CLASSES INTO ELITE I AND II	MANUAL INTO ELITE I AND II
Great Britain	24.8	8.6	2.2
United States	28.8	19.8	7.8

* Adapted from Miller, *op. cit.,* Tables III, VI, and XI.

tries, which shows Britain to be considerably more open than the United States.[11]

Some implications of the asymmetry in these mobility indices, and another comparison of U.S. and British rates of mobility may be provided, in examining the social origins of university trained engineers in the two countries. We shall look also at the relationship between social origins and success in one's career. This comparison, restricted to one occupational category, has several advantages. Variations due to ability, amount of training, and aspirations are to some extent limited by the university backgrounds of subjects in both samples. Also, changes in occupational structure will have similar effects in each group. Accordingly, we will be approaching an estimate of pure mobility.

Changes in recruitment over time are shown in Table 2, which shows the social origins for three periods of graduation of U.S. engineers and three age cohorts in the British group. The American sample indicates an uneven tendency toward a higher proportion of the recent engineers coming from high status fathers, while the British sample reveals a trend in the opposite direction. The more recent U.S. engineers are increasingly the sons of professionals (21 per cent to 30 per cent). Younger British engineering graduates, on the other hand, are less likely to be the sons of professionals than are their older colleagues (52 per cent to 28 per cent). The increasing proportion of high status sons moving into engineering in the U.S. seems to have paralleled the upgrading of engineering as a profession. The increasing emphasis upon mathematics and the physical sciences as necessary for engineering has also enhanced its respectability. In addition, these prerequisites for engineering as a career are more likely to be a part of the high school curriculum of the high status son than of the low status son. A similar pattern of upgrading the engineering profession does not seem to have occurred in Great Britain, despite the continued concern regarding recruitment into the profession. This may account for the lack of attraction which engineering in Britain has for sons of professionals. The contrasting status of engineers in the two countries is indi-

[11] Yasuda, *op. cit.,* p. 19.

TABLE 2

Social Origins of British and American Engineers
for Selected Time Periods

UNITED STATES SAMPLE *	ENGINEER'S PERIOD OF GRADUATION		
Father's occupation:	1911–1930	1931–1940	1941–1950
Professional-semi-professional	21.1	32.0	29.7
Clerical and sales	22.9	25.2	25.5
Skilled and semi-skilled	30.1	23.3	20.9
Unskilled	25.9	19.5	23.8
	(498)	(640)	(1329)

BRITISH SAMPLE **	ENGINEER'S YEAR OF BIRTH		
Father's occupation:	Before 1917	1918–1927	1928 and after
Professional-executive	51.8	40.9	28.0
Middle white collar	25.5	39.8	41.9
Manual	22.7	19.3	30.1
	(110)	(176)	(93)

* Adapted from Perrucci, *op. cit.*
** Adapted from Gerstl, *op. cit.*

cated by the one-way flow of the "brain drain," England constantly losing personnel to the U.S.

While there has been little change in recruitment patterns for American engineers in the two most recent time periods, the amount of upward mobility for the British has been steadily increasing. Interestingly, for the most recent engineers, the proportion coming from professional backgrounds is similar for the two countries. The total pattern that emerges with respect to changes over time is one of declining mobility in American recruitment as contrasted with increasing mobility in Britain.[12]

It is, of course, possible that the relatively small shifts in recruitment that have occurred in the U.S. sample (as compared to the British sample) may be due to changes in the proportion of the labor force in various occupational categories. Thus, the increasing proportion of engineers coming from profes-

[12] It should be emphasized that the comparison in this paper is restricted to engineers with university degrees in the U. S. and Great Britain. The non-university engineers in Great Britain are primarily composed of persons of manual and middle-class origins. Little is known, on the other hand, of the origins of many of the technical institute graduates in the U. S. who are often functionally classified as engineers.

sional origins would be due simply to an increasing proportion of the labor force who are professionals. An examination of the occupational structure over the last half-century in the U.S. does not indicate that our changing patterns of recruitment are only reflections of the changing composition of the labor force. Between 1910 and 1960 there has been a steady increase in the proportion of the labor force in professional occupations and in clerical and sales occupations. Our recruitment data show similar increases in the proportion of engineers having fathers of professional and clerical and sales occupations. However, census data also indicate that there has been a sizable increase in the proportion of the labor force in skilled and semi-skilled occupations. Our recruitment data, on the other hand, indicate that the largest recruitment *decline* has occurred among sons of skilled and semi-skilled fathers. An additional consideration is that for this same time period of 1910–1960 the number of engineering graduates coming out of the universities has gone from approximately 1,000 to 36,000.[13] Thus, the marked growth in engineering enrollments has not come from any increased recruitment of manual working-class sons to this occupation.

We may hazard a few guesses as to the continuation of these recruitment trends for the two countries in question. The increasing proportion of recruitment from manual strata in Britain is likely to continue. The changes in British education beginning with the 1944 Education Act concerning secondary education, are only now affecting higher education as indicated in the Robbins report.[14] On the other hand, the trend of increasing recruitment from high status origins in the U.S. will probably continue considering the apparent flow of high calibre students into engineering and science. It would appear that even the increased manpower needs for engineers, as suggested by several personnel projections, will not necessarily increase the recruitment of lower class youth, since the increased needs will occur in management and basic research functions, while traditional engineering functions will remain stable. In this connection, we would suggest that it is the traditional engineering image that would most likely attract the mobile lower class youth,[15] while the basic research and managerial functions would require academic knowledge and social skills that are differentially distributed in the class structure. Thus, the lower class youth in the U.S. is disadvantaged both by the lack of social supports and inducements to undertake science oriented curricula, and by the absence of such programs in the schools he is most likely to attend.

A refinement in the analysis of the degree of mobility attained may be introduced by considering the degree of success achieved in professional engineering careers. Clearly, not all engineers are of equal status. If success is

[13] Joseph M. Pettit and James M. Gere, "The Evolution of Graduate Education in Engineering," *Journal of Engineering Education*, 54 (October, 1963), pp. 57–62.

[14] *Lord Robbins' Committee: Report on Higher Education*, London, HMSO, 1963.

[15] See Martin Trow, "Some Implications of the Social Origins of Engineers," *Scientific Manpower 1958*, National Science Foundation, pp. 67–74.

independent of social origins, this would be an additional indicator of the openness of the social structure.

As access to the means for mobility (i.e., engineering training) becomes wider, differential rewards are more likely to be related to social origins. For access to training operates as a screening mechanism which, if highly rigorous, is more likely to result in equal treatment once the initial hurdle is passed. Since university entrance is much more selective in Britain than in the U.S., we would expect that this is the stage at which the crucial sorting out process takes place. Just as almost all British entrants to university survive through their final year while Americans do not, so the success of British graduates in the same field should be more independent of their social origins than it is in the U.S.

The comparison of Tables 3 and 4 would indicate that this expectation is sustained. Table 3, reveals the strong relationship between level of present job and the social origins of American engineers. In each of the time periods shown, whatever the length of their working experience, sons of professionals are more likely to occupy the high prestige administrative and technical jobs in engineering. While Table 4 is not directly comparable because of the absence of specific time comparisons, the successful British engineer may be viewed as equivalent to those in the high status administrative and technical positions in the American sample. All British engineering graduates are seen to have good chances of success, what ever their origins. Although those of manual origins do somewhat less well, there is no difference between sons of professionals and those from middle-class backgrounds.

Our most general finding emerging from the comparison of one elite level occupation in two countries, both in terms of changing patterns of recruitment over time and in the relation of social origins to degree of success, suggests the degree of fluidity in Britain to be greater than in the U.S. This does not by itself refute the conclusion of the broad similarity of trends in industrialized countries. It may well be, for example, that the pattern for other occupations is very different and may off-set trends that apply in the case of engineers. However, the importance of engineering as indicative of patterns for elite occupations must not be underestimated. For, engineering is the single largest professional category in an industrial society (excluding teaching, of course, which is primarily female). Furthermore, it is likely that engineering is the one profession most open to entry, engineers tending to have lower status origins than members of other professions.[16] In addition, once entry to the engineering profession is realized, success should be more susceptible to intrinsic career criteria than in other professions. For example, in medicine and law, family influence, as manifest in contacts and financial aid in starting

[16] Although education has the largest proportion of students of lower socioeconomic origins in a comparison of ten undergraduate academic fields, engineering has a very similar pattern and is not significantly different from education. See, e.g., James A. Davis, *Great Aspirations*, Chicago, Ill.: National Opinion Research Center, Report No. 90, March, 1963.

TABLE 3

Present Job Position of American Engineers by Father's Occupation and Period of Graduation *

Present Job Position	Professional Semi- Professional	Clerical and Sales	Skilled Semi- Skilled	Unskilled
PERIOD OF GRADUATION				
1911–1930				
High Administrative Position	40.9	29.8	24.0	29.4
High Technical Position	30.5	34.2	33.3	27.9
Low Technical Position	28.5	36.0	42.7	42.6
	(105)	(114)	(150)	(129)
1931–1940				
High Administrative Position	26.3	18.0	11.4	18.4
High Technical Position	28.3	34.8	32.9	25.6
Low Technical Position	45.4	47.2	55.7	56.0
	(205)	(161)	(149)	(125)
1941–1950				
High Administrative Position	12.6	6.5	8.6	5.4
High Technical Position	20.2	18.0	16.5	15.4
Low Technical Position	67.1	75.5	74.8	79.2
	(395)	(339)	(278)	(317)

* Adapted from Perrucci, *op. cit.*

a practice, is much more relevant than it is in the organizational world of the engineer.[17] It is in this respect that engineering is most exemplary of "careers

[17] Of course, bureaucratic careers also exist in law and medicine albeit in smaller proportions. See, e.g., Jack Ladinsky, "Careers of Lawyers, Law Practice, and Legal Institutions," *American Sociological Review*, 28 (February, 1963), pp. 47–54.

TABLE 4

Social Background and Success of British Engineers *

	PROFESSIONAL-EXECUTIVE	WHITE COLLAR	MANUAL
Successful **	67.0	66.0	55.0
Unsuccessful	33.0	34.0	45.0
	(154)	(138)	(87)

* Adapted from Gerstl, *op. cit.*
** Success is defined by attainment of median income for one's age group.

open to talent." These considerations apply equally to engineers in Britain and in the U.S.

If such findings as ours are combined with attention to patterns of asymmetry (both of manual to nonmanual mobility as versus elite recruitment and of upward versus downward mobility) and with such methodological refinements as those of Yasuda, the types and directions of variations in mobility rates would appear to warrant further attention. Certainly more consideration needs to be given to the mechanisms which allow or constrain occupational movement.

Education which all too frequently is treated merely as an indicator of social position is obviously one of the most crucial of these mechanisms. When education is treated as an indicator, the significance of where, how and for what end one is educated tends to be lost. In the case of the engineers for example, to treat all engineers as equal merely because they hold a B.S. degree is misleading. The particular school attended, the level of performance, the field of specialization, and managerial versus technical orientation are all related to degree of success in one's field.[18]

Perhaps a useful direction for future research might include detailed comparisons of particular occupational groups which would serve to highlight the mechanisms and variations which tend to receive little attention in the context of gross international contrasts.

[18] For examples of these variations see James A. Davis, "Intellectual Climates in 135 American Colleges and Universities: A Study in 'Social Psychophysics,'" *Sociology of Education*, 37 (Winter, 1963), pp. 110–128; and Peter I. Rose, "The Myth of Unanimity: Student Opinions on Critical Issues," *Sociology of Education*, 37 (Winter, 1963), pp. 129–149.

POTENTIAL ELITES IN GHANA AND THE IVORY COAST: A PRELIMINARY COMPARISON

Remi P. Clignet
and Philip Foster

This study examines patterns of social recruitment in two highly selective systems of secondary education in two adjoining African states with differing colonial and educational traditions but similar economic conditions and sociocultural changes. Marked differentials occur between two groups of sampled students of roughly equivalent academic status in the two areas. Ghanaian students are uniformly drawn from higher socioeconomic groups than their Ivory Coast counterparts. However, in relation to population characteristics, the two systems appear to function in a similar manner. Furthermore, both groups are characterized by a considerable degree of uniformity concerning career aspirations, expectations, and perceptions of future roles.

I N SPITE of a growing body of literature dealing with the emergent elites of the new African states, it must be confessed that we know very little about them. There is sometimes a tendency to speak of them as if they were homogeneous in character; yet much material concerning their social origins, their aspirations, and their value orientations remains extraordinarily impressionistic.

Further, the term "elite," although frequently used, is very ambiguous. An elite may be defined in terms of its common possession of a single attribute or set of objective attributes. Thus, in the African context, we could regard as members of an elite all individuals who have achieved a given minimal level of education or income or who are engaged in particular occupations. This definition has shortcomings if we are concerned with elites in terms of their decision-making abilities (political or otherwise) or their capacity to act as generalized reference groups for the remainder of the population.[1] Thus, in the following pages, when we examine the characteristics of two samples of

REPRINTED FROM *American Journal of Sociology*, 70 (November 1964), 349–362, by permission of The University of Chicago Press.

[1] For example, if education is used as the criterion of elite membership, it is clear that the two groups of students we compare below constitute part of the national elite. They certainly fall well within the top 1 per cent of the population in level of schooling. However, we do know that a substantial proportion of these groups will enter primary-school teaching or low-grade clerical work. Neither of these two occupations enjoys very high prestige or status within either country.

secondary-school students in the Ivory Coast and Ghana, we shall treat them as "potential elites." Their schooling provides a necessary, but not sufficient, qualification for them to assume key positions in their societies.

In most contemporary African states, employment opportunities within the modern economic sector are dominated by the demands of government and other public agencies. This bureaucratization of the employment structure confers a high premium upon educational qualifications (usually as measured by examination success) for access to elite roles. Recruitment policies of the larger firms in the private sector also present the same characteristics.

Furthermore, in many areas, explosive rates of growth in the output of the schools are associated with a very sluggish development of job opportunities in this modern sector. This has very rapidly raised the minimal educational qualifications necessary to enter most occupations. Thus, a post-primary education becomes a critical factor in occupational success, and in no country in Africa south of the Sahara do more than 2 per cent of any age cohort enter any form of secondary institution.[2] We therefore feel justified in regarding African secondary schools as "elite reservoirs" whose graduates will fill most positions of power and authority in the next few decades. A crucial problem of research is, therefore, to examine the social composition of secondary-school populations and to ascertain to what extent recruitment patterns are fluid or constricted.

A second step is to analyze how this recruitment function is affected by the residue of colonial experience. For example, although a great deal has been written about differences between French and British colonial policies, no empirical evidence exists with respect to contrasts in processes of elite selection within areas formerly governed by the two colonial powers. We have, therefore, attempted to compare the characteristics of a sample of secondary-school students in Ghana, an ex-British territory, with those of a similar group of students in the formerly French Ivory Coast. These countries provide a good opportunity for controlled comparison insofar as they are largely similar in terms of a whole range of characteristics but differ with respect to certain key variables.[3]

Some Comparisons Between Ghana and the Ivory Coast

First, there are substantial similarities in the economies of Ghana and the Ivory Coast.[4] Although the latter is rather the less developed of the two, both

[2] Clearly, we refer here to the African population only and exclude the Union of South Africa, where levels of education among Africans are considerably higher than for the rest of the continent.

[3] The particular appropriateness of Ghana and the Ivory Coast for a comparison of this type has already been noted by R. J. Harrison Church, *West Africa: A Study of the Environment and of Man's Use of It* (3rd ed.; London: Longmans, Green, & Co., 1961), p. 344.

[4] The best general sources for the background of the two areas are, for Ghana: D. E. Apter, *The Gold Coast in Transition* (Princeton, N.J.: Princeton University Press, 1955);

countries rank highest in income per capita among the nations of West Africa, with a level of between $150 and $200 per annum. The comparative prosperity of the two states is, in large measure, attributable to an extensive development of profitable cash crops in the southern and central portions of the respective territories. The occupational structure of both countries is relatively more complex than those of other West African states (with the possible exception of Senegal).

These over-all economic similarities are reinforced by the fact that the pattern of sociocultural change in both areas has followed similar lines. European penetration was initially effected from the coastal zone with the gradual incorporation of other traditional groupings in the central and northern areas at a later date. Thus maximal change has occurred in the southern and central areas of both nations; and it is in these that the exchange economy is most developed, processes of urbanization most advanced, and formal education most in evidence. In contrast, the populous northern areas are, in both cases, far less developed, with a greater emphasis on subsistence farming, lower levels of urbanization, and a more limited diffusion of formal education. Both territories are divided into a largely Christian south and a predominantly Islamic north.

There are equally striking similarities in terms of ethnic composition. Since these nations are adjacent to each other, the Akan peoples of southern and central Ghana are closely related to the Anyi and Baoule groups of the southeastern and central Ivory Coast. Further, the Ewe of Ghana and the Kru groups of the Ivory Coast, though belonging to different ethnic clusters, do manifest substantial similarities in their pattern of social organization and stand in similar relationship to the Akan peoples of both areas. Last, some of the Voltaic peoples of northern Ghana are represented in the Ivory Coast, and there are parallels between their culture and that of the nuclear and peripheral Mande of the latter nation.

Given these substantial similarities between the two countries, we must now indicate in what respects they diverge. Clearly, their patterns of administration were and are rather different. Traditionally, the French tended to develop a system of direct and internally centralized administration which was, in turn, closely integrated with their West African Federation and the metropole itself. Conversely, the British relied to a greater extent on indirect rule (particularly in Ashanti and the northern areas) and developed a less centralized pattern of administration which also de-emphasized the direct links between Ghana, the other areas of British West Africa, and the metropole.

More important, although the pattern of French penetration in the Ivory Coast substantially paralleled British expansion in Ghana, it always lagged

---

and for the Ivory Coast: Ministère des Finances des Affaires Economiques et du Plan Service de la Statistique, *Inventaire économique et social de la Côte d'Ivoire* (Abidjan: 1960).

behind it. Thus, by the end of the nineteenth century, the British had effectively incorporated most of the territories that now constitute contemporary Ghana, and in the southern zone, in particular, the European impact was already considerable. By contrast, the French were not able to establish effective administration in some areas until after the close of the first World War.

THE SCHOOL SYSTEMS

Since educational diffusion is a corollary of European overrule, it is clear that this "staggered" development of the two areas had considerable implications for the growth of their educational systems. By 1950, Ghana, with a population of roughly 5 million, had 281,000 individuals enrolled in formal schools at all levels, while the Ivory Coast, with an estimated population of 3.2 million, could point to only 35,000 persons enrolled. During the last decade the difference at the primary-school level has been closing, owing to massive investment by the government of the Ivory Coast in primary education.[5] However, at the secondary-school stage the contrast between the countries remains formidable and needs further examination.

The school system in the Ivory Coast consists of a six-year primary sequence followed by a highly differentiated system of secondary studies. In 1963 there were a little under 300,000 students in primary schools compared with less than 20,000 in all kinds of post-primary institutions. These post-primary schools vary greatly in prestige, ranging from Centres d'Apprentissage offering a four-year terminal program of vocational training to the academic and technical Lycées which provide access to university studies. It is the latter group of institutions which concerns us here, since they are the crucial segment of the whole system so far as processes of elite formation are concerned.

The Ghanaian system is much larger. By 1960, there were already 512,000 pupils in the six-year primary schools and, most strikingly, no less than 225,000 in all types of post-primary education. The vast majority of the latter were in so-called middle schools: these provided a terminal four-year sequence for most pupils but also acted as feeder institutions to a small group of highly selective public secondary schools which offered a five-year course.[6] In 1960 there were over 14,000 students in these latter institutions which are, in fact, generally comparable to the Lycées and Collèges of the Ivory Coast. It is clear, therefore, that a comparison of potential elites in the two nations can

[5] This is not to suggest that primary-school expansion in Ghana has been negligible. On the contrary, it has been substantial, but the maximum growth rate has now been passed and the system continues to grow at a slower pace.

[6] This figure excludes some 6,000 pupils enrolled in private secondary schools in Ghana. However, these institutions are, for the most part, at such a low level that they are usually more comparable to middle schools. It is noteworthy, also, that public secondary schools in Ghana are not, for the most part, "government" schools but are institutions often founded by voluntary agencies but now overwhelmingly aided from government funds.

be most effectively made by contrasting Ghanaian secondary-school students with their counterparts in the Lycées of the Ivory Coast.

However, this ignores the crucial problem of obtaining comparable groups when the cycle of secondary studies is so different. With this in mind, it was decided to compare Ghanaian pupils in the final year of their five-year basic secondary course with Ivory Coast Lycée students preparing the first part of their *Baccalauréat* examination.[7] This constitutes a crucial cutoff point in both systems. In Ghana, approximately 60 per cent of the students successfully pass the General School Certificate examination at the end of five years, but of these successful candidates, only about one-third enter the sixth forms which prepare directly for the university. In the Ivory Coast, just under 40 per cent of the candidates pass the first *Baccalauréat* successfully at the first attempt and enter for the one-year course preparing for the second *Baccalauréat*, which is preparatory to university study and is thus roughly similar to the Ghanaian sixth form.

The two samples discussed in the following pages are, therefore, very comparable in terms of level of study and type of school and were drawn as follows.[8] The Ghanaian sample, consisting of 775 fifth-form boys drawn in 1961 from twenty-three secondary institutions, constituted just over 45 per cent of the entire male fifth-form population in the secondary schools at that time. Correspondingly, the Ivory Coast sample of male students sitting for the first part of the *Baccalauréat* was drawn in 1963 from the eight institutions which prepare for this examination. The sample comprised 259 cases or 82 per cent of all pupils at this educational level in the Ivory Coast.[9] At this stage the Ghanaian system contains over five times as many students as that of the Ivory Coast.

This suggests that the two systems can only be contrasted not in terms of

[7] Generally, the curriculum at this level in both systems is not highly specialized, though there is more "streaming" by subject groups in the Ivory Coast.

[8] In 1961, Ghana had forty-six secondary schools with fifth-form classes. The twenty-three schools selected for investigation were randomly drawn from this list stratified by region, type, and size. In the case of the Ivory Coast, the smaller size of the system made it possible to attempt a total coverage at the *Baccalauréat* level. However, 18 per cent of students were not reached, owing to temporary absence from classes. Girls were excluded from this comparison in view of their small number at this level in the Ivory Coast. Also, since their backgrounds are very different from those of boys, they certainly would have distorted the picture as far as Ghana is concerned.

[9] In practice, Ghanaian students have completed anywhere between thirteen and fifteen years of education before reaching the fifth-form level. This is because selection for secondary school can be from any one of the middle-school years. Conversely, the Ivory Coast students have theoretically completed twelve years of education. Therefore, we might expect the latter group to be younger than the Ghanaians. In fact, the reverse is the case. Ivory Coast students average 20.3 years of age and Ghanaian students, 19.2. This is due to the far greater incidence of doubling classes in the Ivory Coast system (47 per cent of the sample had doubled one or several previous classes) and the fact that children probably start schooling later than in Ghana.

two colonial prototypes but also in terms of their relative level of growth and "maturity."

Social Background of Potential Elites

We must first consider the ethnic characteristics of these two groups of students. This is no idle academic problem in the context of contemporary African politics. With the advent of independence, ethnic minorities increasingly demand equal access to key institutions in the new states. In particular, they claim that they have obtained less than their "fair share" of crucial roles, owing to their lack of opportunities to obtain school places.[10] In both Ghana and the Ivory Coast, such inequalities in educational provision have been very evident.

Table 1 illustrates the pattern of differential ethnic recruitment into secondary schools in the two areas. To simplify the picture, we have divided both nations into three general ethnic zones (southern, central, and northern) and classified the numerous groups into one or the other of these categories. Further, to facilitate comparison, we have provided crude selectivity indexes by computing the ratio between a group's representation in the general population and its representation in the sample.

It might have been expected that in the smaller and less-established system of the Ivory Coast, inequalities in ethnic access between north and south would be more marked. In fact, this is only partially true. To be sure, in Ghana, the variations between the southern and central groupings which were substantial at all levels of education up to 1945 seem to have been largely eradicated, while in the Ivory Coast they are still very apparent. In this context it is important to note that the central portion of Ghana includes the major cocoa-producing areas and constitutes the economic heartland of the nation. The gap between economic development of southern and central Ghana is proportionally less than that between the corresponding zones of the Ivory Coast. Though the northern areas of both countries are very similar in their level of development, northern Ghanaians are far less successful in getting into post-primary education of this type than are their Ivory Coast counterparts. This is in spite of the fact that the far greater size and maturity of the Ghanaian educational system might have led us to expect a greater access of northern groups into the secondary schools. Not only are there proportionally more places available in Ghanaian secondary institutions but these places are geographically more diffused throughout the country. This suggests that the growth of an educational system does not quickly even up ethnic inequalities.

There has historically been a close relationship in Africa between the growth of the schools and the development of towns; it was usually within

[10] For Ghana, this point is discussed more fully in Philip Foster, "Ethnicity and the Schools in Ghana," *Comparative Education Review*, VI (October, 1962), 127–35.

TABLE 1

Ethnic Background of Sampled Students in Relation to Ethnic Charac-teristics of Populations of Ivory Coast and Ghana

	IVORY COAST			GHANA		
ETHNIC GROUPS	PER-CENTAGE * OF POPU-LATION	PER-CENTAGE OF SAMPLE	SELEC-TIVITY RATIO	PER-CENTAGE † OF POPU-LATION	PER-CENTAGE OF SAMPLE	SELEC-TIVITY RATIO
Southern	31.2	50.5 (131)	1.6	47.0	64.2 (498)	1.4
Central	30.2	21.3 (55)	0.7	20.7	28.2 (218)	1.4
Northern	34.2	20.5 (53)	0.6	30.7	6.3 (49)	0.2
Other	4.4	6.2 (16)	1.4	1.6	1.2 (9)	0.8
No answer	—	1.5 (4)	—	—	0.1 (1)	—
Total	100.0	100.0 (259)	—	100.0	100.0 (775)	—

* Computed from Ivory Coast, Ministère du Plan, *Inventaire économique de la Côte d'Ivoire, 1947–1956* (Abidjan, 1958), p. 26.
† Computed from Gold Coast, *Census of Population, 1948* (Accra, 1950), pp. 367–69. These figures are not entirely reliable and no data are yet available from the 1960 census concerning the present ethnic composition of the population.

urban centers that a demand for formal schooling was first manifest. The growth of an exchange economy and the development of new Western-type occupations, access to which was often dependent on formal educational qual-ifications, stimulated an early desire for education. Moreover, urban children tended to adjust more rapidly to the requirements of the schools. Both Ghana and the Ivory Coast have, therefore, long been faced by persistent and sharp differentials between urban and rural levels of primary schooling. It is interest-ing to examine these differentials at the secondary-school level (Table 2). This table indicates the nature of this relationship in the two territories, using the rather crude measure of community size as an index of urbanization. We also have attempted to show an almost identical degree of drift of the stu-dents in both samples from the smaller villages to the very largest towns.[11]

[11] Actually, this movement is very complex and involves not only direct migration from the very smallest to the very largest centers, but also a multiplicity of small-scale move-ments to towns slightly larger than the place of birth. It also correlates in some measure with a migration from the northern and central areas to the coastal zone, though this is more marked in the Ivory Coast.

Table 2

Background of Sampled Students in Relation to Size of Birthplace and Present Residence

POPULATION OF TOWN OR VILLAGE	DISTRIBUTION OF IVORY COAST POPULATION *	BIRTHPLACE OF SAMPLED STUDENTS	SELECTIVITY RATIO	PRESENT RESIDENCE OF SAMPLED STUDENTS	SELECTIVITY RATIO	DISTRIBUTION OF GHANAIAN POPULATION †	BIRTHPLACE OF SAMPLED STUDENTS	SELECTIVITY RATIO	PRESENT RESIDENCE OF SAMPLED STUDENTS	SELECTIVITY RATIO
Below 5,000	82.3	62.5	0.8	48.6	0.6	77.0	38.1	0.5	26.8	0.3
5,000–9,999	4.3	11.6	2.7	12.4	2.9	6.0	14.3	2.4	12.1	2.0
10,000–49,999	3.7	10.8	2.9	13.9	3.8	9.3	24.4	2.6	26.7	2.9
Above 50,000	9.7	7.3	0.8	20.8	2.1	7.7	19.4	2.5	33.3	4.3
Not born in or not resident in Ivory Coast or Ghana	—	6.9	—	3.1	—	—	3.5	—	0.6	—
No answer	—	0.8	—	1.2	—	—	0.3	—	0.5	—
Total	100.0	99.9	—	100.0	—	100.0	100.0	—	100.0	—

* Computed from Ivory Coast, Ministère du Plan, *Inventaire économique de la Côte d'Ivoire, 1947-58* (Abidjan, 1960), p. 37.
† Computed from Ghana, *Population Census, 1960*, Advance Report of Vols. III and IV.

219

It is clear that Ghanaian students come from a more urban background in terms of both birth and residence than do their Ivory Coast counterparts. This is understandable enough in view of the rather higher levels of urbanization in Ghana as a whole. However, this tells us very little about how the two educational systems function in terms of selection when the residential characteristics of the population as a whole are taken into account. In spite of the fact that Ghanaian students are more urban in background, it could still be concluded a priori that the relationship between secondary-school selection and urban origin is looser in Ghana than in the Ivory Coast; such a pattern would not be surprising since the Ghanaian secondary-school system offers far more places in relation to population. Conversely, it could be suggested that the smaller the system, the sharper the differentials are likely to be—a pattern found in so many Western countries. However, these two assumptions seem hardly tenable in this instance. If anything, the urban/rural differentials are rather more marked in Ghana than in the Ivory Coast, particularly if we look at the pattern of recruitment from the very smallest and the very largest communities. Ivory Coast enrolments from the smallest centers are proportionally larger than in Ghana. Also, there is in Ghana a linear relationship between size of birthplace or place of residence and secondary-school access—the larger the town, the greater the proportional representation of students from these centers. This is not duplicated in the Ivory Coast; students born or resident in the very largest towns (Abidjan and Bouaké) are actually less well represented in the system than those from medium-sized communities.

We are somewhat puzzled by these unexpected disparities. Very tentatively we suggest that they may be due to differences in the geographical dispersion of towns and secondary schools in the two countries. Thus Abidjan is the only highly urbanized center in the Ivory Coast, and the overwhelming bulk of secondary schools are concentrated there. These are essentially national institutions recruiting from the whole country. Since, however, the rate of growth of the population of Abidjan has expanded faster than the school system, students coming from this city are proportionally disadvantaged as compared with individuals from other areas.

In Ghana, conversely, there is a more even dispersion of both schools and urban centers. Although secondary institutions theoretically draw upon a national population, they tend to recruit on a far more regional basis.[12] It could have been hypothesized that, under such conditions, rural boys would be proportionally more favored than their Ivory Coast counterparts. Yet this is clearly not the case—far from evening up urban/rural contrasts, the geographic diffusion of educational facilities and towns has tended to sharpen differentials.

---

[12] For example, within the investigated schools located in Abidjan, only 18 per cent of the sampled students actually lived in that city. By contrast, in the investigated schools of Accra and Kumasi, no less than 40 per cent of sampled students were permanent residents.

Thus we can see that, with respect to both ethnicity and urbanization, the growth of an educational system does not necessarily, in the short run, lead to a lessening of differentials in recruitment. When, however, we examine the family backgrounds of the two groups of students in terms of paternal occupation, the picture seems to conform more closely to our expectations (Table 3). First, it is evident that although Ghana and the Ivory Coast are alike in so many other respects, their occupational structures are very different. To be sure, both are peaked and constricted at the summit, but there is in Ghana a much greater level of growth and differentiation at the higher occupational levels. The greater maturity of the economic structure of Ghana is reflected in the fact that the proportion of students from "white-collar" backgrounds is about double that in the Ivory Coast and the offspring of skilled workers and artisans are relatively more numerous in the Ghanaian group. Conversely, the children of farmers and fishermen form a larger proportion of the enrolment in the Ivory Coast sample.

However, if we relate these figures to the population base, it is apparent that the Ivory Coast system tends to favor the selection of children of professional and clerical workers to a far greater degree than does the Ghanaian system. In terms of this variable, the expansion of the Ghanaian system has tended to produce a more open pattern of recruitment than that prevailing in the Ivory Coast.

Let us finally take a look at the educational backgrounds of the fathers of our two groups of students (Table 4). As we might expect, it shows a pattern very similar to that in the preceding table and reflects the much more substantial development of formal education in Ghana. Well over half of the fathers of the Ghanaian pupils have gone beyond primary school as against just over 10 per cent of the Ivory Coast fathers. In fact, 4 per cent of Ghanaian fathers have completed a university education, while there is not one example of this in the Ivory Coast sample. Indeed, nearly all Ivory Coast fathers in the "above-primary" category only went as far as the "École Primaire Supérieure," while almost half of the Ghana fathers in this category had gone even beyond middle school.[13]

Unfortunately, the selectivity ratios for the two systems cannot be computed for parental education, since no data exist concerning the educational level of adult males in the Ivory Coast. We do know that, in Ghana, the education of the fathers of our students is very much higher than that prevailing among the adult male population. Indeed, the gradient among selectivity ratios is far steeper than it is for either urban/rural or occupational characteristics, indicating the rather greater importance of paternal education in in-

[13] In the Ivory Coast, the structure of the educational system did not allow Africans to pursue regular secondary studies of the metropolitan type before 1928. Correspondingly, although it was difficult for Africans to undertake such studies in the Gold Coast before 1928, opportunities did exist; by that time there was a very small but highly significant group of second- or third-generation university graduates.

TABLE 3

Paternal Occupations of Sampled Students Compared with Occupations of Adult Male Population in Ghana and Ivory Coast
(Per Cent)

OCCUPATIONAL GROUP	IVORY COAST			GHANA		
	ADULT MALE POPULATION *	SAMPLED STUDENTS	SELECTIVITY RATIO	ADULT MALE POPULATION †	SAMPLED STUDENTS	SELECTIVITY RATIO
Professional, higher technical and administrative	0.3	7.7 (20)	25.7	1.5	20.8 (161)	13.9
Clerical and allied (including teachers)	1.7	10.0 (26)	5.9	5.4	15.6 (121)	2.9
Private traders and businessmen	3.3	6.9 (18)	2.1	3.8	11.0 (85)	2.9
Skilled workers and artisans	0.9	3.1 (8)	3.4	11.8	10.6 (82)	0.9
Semiskilled and unskilled workers	7.0	1.2 (3)	0.2	13.4	1.5 (12)	0.1
Farmers and fishermen	86.3	67.9 (176)	0.8	62.8	37.4 (290)	0.6
Other (including police and uniformed services)	0.5	2.3 (6)	4.6	1.3	0.6 (5)	0.5
No answer	—	0.8 (2)	—	—	2.5 (19)	—
Total	100.0	99.9 (259)	—	100.0	100.0 (775)	—

* Computed from UNESCO, *Première mission du groupe de planification de l'éducation en Côte d'Ivoire* (Paris: UNESCO, 1963), p. 19; and from UNESCO, *Situation et perspectives de l'emploi dans le cadre du plan décennal de développement, 1963*, Table IIH. (Mimeographed.)

† Computed from Ghana, *Population Census, 1960*, Advance Report of Vols. III and IV.

fluencing secondary-school access.[14] We have little doubt that the situation is much the same in the Ivory Coast. We do know that the fathers of our students are more highly educated than the adult males of Abidjan for whom

[14] The Ghanaian selectivity ratios vary from 0.4 for students with uneducated fathers to 13.0 for students whose fathers had attended university or its equivalent.

data do exist, and it is certain that this latter group is far better educated than the bulk of the Ivory Coast male population.[15] We would hazard that the selectivity gradients by level of paternal education are probably even steeper than those for Ghana.

Let us now draw together our previous discussion. It is clear enough that there are considerable differences in the social backgrounds of these two very significant groups of students. Ghanaian pupils, in general, are more "acculturated" than their Ivory Coast counterparts in terms of certain background characteristics. They are much more likely to be drawn from the larger urban centers and to come from families with higher occupational and educational backgrounds. Further, in terms of religious affiliation, Ghanaian students are overwhelmingly Christian (less than 5 per cent are Moslem) while over 15 per cent of the Ivory Coast group are Moslems.

However, if we compare the characteristics of pupils with those of the general population, it seems clear enough that both systems function in a similar manner. To be sure, certain differences are apparent; the French schools are much more selective in terms of occupational background, though urban/rural differentials are a little less marked. Indeed, what is surprising about the Ivory Coast system is that it seems to be about as fluid in its recruitment patterns as is the Ghanaian system, in spite of its very limited size. We suspect that part of the explanation may lie in the fact that Ivory Coast secondary schools are normally free while even in the public schools of Ghana, substantial tuition and boarding fees are still charged.[16]

However, what is outstanding about these systems is that both recruit from very broad segments of the population. Selection is undeniably skewed in favor of particular groups, but it is noteworthy that almost 70 per cent of Ivory Coast students and nearly 40 per cent of Ghanaian students come from farming families in which parents are overwhelmingly illiterate. A great deal has been made about the "exclusive" and "aristocratic" nature of elite academic institutions of the French or British type in Africa. The plain fact is that they are by no means exclusive in their clientele and draw upon able individuals from most ethnic and socioeconomic groups. This suggests that the elites of the two territories are likely to be extraordinarily heterogeneous in terms of social origin for some time to come.[17] In this sense, the functional differences between British- or French-type educational systems are minimal. Such differ-

[15] See République de la Côte d'Ivoire, *Recensement d'Abidjan, 1955* (Abidjan, 1960), p. 37.

[16] About 50 per cent of the Ghanaian students had bursaries and scholarships, but in most cases these only covered a part of tuition and subsistence costs.

[17] It is possible that patterns of recruitment may become more constricted in the future. However, we do not believe that this will be the case in Ghana (see Philip Foster, "Secondary Schooling and Social Mobility in a West African Nation," *Sociology of Education*, XXXVII [Winter, 1963], 165–71). Correspondingly, in the Ivory Coast, two recent administrative decisions have limited access to the second cycle of studies and imposed subsistence costs on students. It will be interesting to see what effect these regulations will have.

TABLE 4

Comparison Between Paternal Levels of Education of
Sample Students in Ivory Coast and Ghana
(Per Cent)

LEVEL OF EDUCATION	IVORY COAST	GHANA
None	65.3	32.4
	(169)	(251)
Some primary school	14.6	7.3
	(38)	(57)
Completed primary school	4.6	2.1
	(12)	(16)
Above primary school	12.4	52.9
	(32)	(410)
No answer	3.1	5.3
	(8)	(41)
Total	100.0	100.0
	(259)	(775)

ences as do occur are largely explainable in terms of the absolute size of the educational systems and the different socioeconomic profiles of the two nations.

Of course, it is interesting to speculate whether existing fluidity in access to secondary schooling will continue to increase or will diminish in the future. It is possible to argue that, as the number of educated elites increases, they will be able to command differential access into the schools for their children, with the result that patterns of recruitment will become more restricted. This argument has considerable force, but we would suggest, however, that elites will not be able to effectively monopolize access to secondary schooling since they are not in a position to resist or even control mass demand for education. Indeed, they themselves are ideologically committed to the provision of mass schooling at all levels.

SOME COMPARISONS CONCERNING ACADEMIC AND OCCUPATIONAL ASPIRATIONS

We may now examine how these two groups of students differ in their perceptions of their academic prospects and future occupations. This is a crucial area for research, for within the context of these slowly developing economies the possibility always arises of blocked educational and occupational mobility for later cohorts of students.

First, it is quite evident that many students in both samples tend to hold quite unrealistic expectations concerning their educational prospects. The chances of a Ghanaian fifth-form student's entering the pre-university sixth form are about one in five; in the Ivory Coast, two out of five move from the first to the second *Baccalauréat* level. However, 49 per cent of the Ivory Coast students and 37 per cent of the Ghanaians felt "certain" that they would be able to continue their full-time studies; a further 40 and 48 per cent, respectively, felt that they had an extremely good chance of so doing. Virtually no student in either sample wished voluntarily to discontinue his schooling. This is a remarkable level of commitment to a continuing education, a commitment, it must be added, which is closely linked to the occupational and status benefits supposedly imparted to schooling. However, the fact is that the educational structures of both nations are sufficiently constricted to make these hopes unrealistic; and, unless educational expansion at lower levels of the system is paralleled by an increase in the number of places available at the more advanced stage, the number of frustrated pupils is likely to increase.

Given the fact that students consistently overestimate their educational chances, what can we say about their career aspirations? Students were asked to state the job they would most like to enter if they were entirely free to choose. Table 5, therefore, really represents a profile of those jobs believed to be the most desirable within the contemporary occupational structure of the two countries.

Clearly, student aspirations are virtually identical in both samples. Most individuals aspire to professional or semiprofessional careers, as one might expect in the light of their progress so far in the educational system. Even more informative is the high proportion of students in both countries who are oriented to scientific and technological occupations. There is a persistent myth that academic secondary schools in West Africa have been busy producing a non-technologically oriented, literary elite who are committed to careers in the administration.[18] This is clearly not the case, for individuals attracted to essentially administrative functions comprise well under a fifth of the sample in both cases. It is also apparent that these students do not want to become clerks, as we are so often informed.

There are some interesting additional features. A high level of choices for medicine reflects the very high status traditionally accorded this occupation in both nations, and, indeed, this has historically been one of the only professional jobs available to Africans. Conversely, the other professional occupation that has been traditionally held in such esteem in West Africa, that of law, is chosen by very few contemporary students. Only 4 per cent of the Ghanaian and less than 2 per cent of Ivory Coast pupils are interested in legal careers, whether in the administration or in private practice. One may speculate whether disinterest in this occupation, which is still very highly rated in

---

[18] For a typical view see Judson T. Shaplin, "A Sea of Faces," *Bulletin of the Harvard Graduate School of Education*, VI (Summer, 1961), 4.

TABLE 5

Occupational Aspirations of Sampled Students
(Per Cent)

OCCUPATION *	IVORY COAST	GHANA
Medicine	20.5	17.3
	(53)	(134)
Other professional	15.1	18.5
	(39)	(143)
Higher administrative	15.8	19.4
	(41)	(150)
Science and technology	39.4	28.7
	(102)	(222)
Clerical	1.5	4.4
	(4)	(34)
Primary-school teaching	1.5	5.0
	(4)	(39)
Uniformed services	2.3	4.5
	(6)	(36)
Other and no answer	3.9	2.2
	(10)	(17)
Total	100.0	100.0
	(259)	(775)

* Occupational categories which are not self-explanatory are as follows: *Other professional:* university professors and secondary-school teachers (in both the Ivory Coast and Ghana the latter group is accorded professional ranking), economist, statistician, etc. *Higher administrative:* Executive posts within the public administration or larger commercial enterprises. For convenience, we have also included politics and law within this category. *Science and technology:* This includes a wide spectrum of occupations. Typical are pharmacy, engineering, surveying, agricultural research, veterinary work, etc. *Primary-school teaching:* In Ghana, this also includes middle school teaching, which is ranked almost identically with primary-school teaching in occupational ratings made by students. *Uniformed services:* Police and military.

terms of prestige and income in both countries, largely reflects the para-political position of the legal profession. Law may be remunerative; it also carries with it certain "occupational hazards." [19] This judgment would tend to be supported by the fact that very few students envisage a career in politics. In fact, less than 1 per cent of Ivory Coast pupils and only 1.5 per cent of

[19] The marked "legalism" of both metropolitan powers toward the end of the colonial period insured both high income and occupational security for members of the legal profession. The politicization of bureaucratic structures since independence has greatly limited the legal practitioner's autonomous role.

Ghanaians even remotely contemplate political careers. This casts doubt upon some contemporary observations by political scientists concerned with Africa who argue that a high degree of political orientation characterizes potential elites. To be sure, up to the independence period, fluidity in political developments did make a political career attractive to a large number of individuals in the educated and semieducated cadres. However, at present, in both areas the stabilization of the existing regimes has led to the virtual monopolization of higher and intermediate political positions by cohorts educated in the previous period. Furthermore, careers in opposition politics are, for very obvious reasons, not attractive under present conditions.

Both groups, but especially students in the Ivory Coast, have therefore shifted their career aspirations to professional occupations very often of a scientific or technological variety, but with a very heavy emphasis on occupational security. Thus, in both samples, when students were asked what constituted the most crucial factor in determining their occupational choice, security was ranked far higher than prestige, congenial conditions of employment, pay, or promotion opportunities. Further, students were asked what type of job they could *expect* to get if they were unable to continue with their studies beyond their present class. Their answers evidence characteristics very different from their occupational aspirations (Table 6).

TABLE 6

Occupational Expectations of Sampled Students
(Per Cent)

OCCUPATION	IVORY COAST	GHANA
Medicine	0.0	0.0
Other professional	0.3	1.6
	(1)	(12)
Higher administrative	1.9	0.1
	(5)	(1)
Scientific and technological	6.7	8.2
	(17)	(63)
Clerical	25.5	49.8
	(66)	(386)
Primary-school teaching	51.4	34.5
	(133)	(267)
Uniformed services	4.6	4.5
	(12)	(35)
Other and no answer	9.6	1.3
	(25)	(11)
Total	100.0	100.0
	(259)	(775)

Very few students actually anticipate entering professional or semiprofessional occupations, while the few who expect to pursue scientific and technological careers can envisage only low-level employment as laboratory assistants or agricultural demonstrators. Overwhelmingly, both groups expect to enter only two types of occupation: clerical work and primary-school teaching, both of which are accorded only moderate ratings in terms of prestige and perceived income.[20] There is, however, an interesting reversal between the two samples regarding these two occupations. We suspect that greater Ivory Coast emphasis on primary teaching reflects the rather recently higher rate of expansion in the primary system and the subsequent increase in job openings.

The table shows one thing very clearly; these students have no illusions as to the occupational currency of their education. They have attended school for anywhere between eleven and fifteen years and lie within the top 1 per cent of the population so far as educational experience is concerned. Yet, given their present level of schooling, they expect no more than clerical work or primary-school teaching. The unfortunate thing is that they are probably right.

A great deal is made of the so-called insatiable need for educated personnel in these developing areas. However, it is quite evident that the definition of "need" often depends upon an implicit comparison being made between the educational and occupational profiles of developed areas and those of Africa. However, to use Western profiles as "templates" for African development is quite unjustifiable, since in terms of the market situation in many African states the demand for educated personnel is quantitatively and qualitatively very limited. Thus in both the Ivory Coast and Ghana the bulk of new employment opportunities generated over the last few years have been in low-level teaching and clerical jobs. The paradoxical situation arises that, in spite of the limited diffusion of education in both countries, even a relatively long schooling does not guarantee high-status employment. To put it another way, the combination of limited job opportunities and a growing educational system leads to a sharp drop in the occupational returns for a given level of schooling.

These students therefore display a mixture of optimism and hardheadedness as regards their occupational future. They certainly overrate their chances of continuing their education and tend to aspire to a cluster of occupations, entry into which is essentially determined by their ability to obtain access to

[20] Students in both samples were asked to rank an identical list of twenty-five occupations ranging from professional to unskilled jobs. In the Ivory Coast, "primary-school teacher" was ranked ninth in terms of prestige and thirteenth in terms of perceived income. The corresponding Ghanaian rankings were nineteenth in both cases. In Ghana, in particular, the primary-school teacher is ranked only at about the level of a motor-car mechanic or petty trader. "Government clerk" was ranked fifteenth in terms of prestige and fourteenth in terms of perceived income in the Ivory Coast. By contrast, the Ghanaian group ranked this occupation eleventh in both cases. It is interesting to note that the reversed nature of the rankings corresponds to the differential job expectations of the two samples.

further studies. However, they are extraordinarily realistic in estimating what kinds of occupation their *present* level of education will enable them to enter.

In these respects the two samples are very much alike, and they also tend to give similar responses concerning employer preferences and location of work. The traditional domination of job opportunities by government in both areas is reflected in a substantial preference for occupations within the public sector: over 69 per cent of Ivory Coast and 84 per cent of Ghanaian students would prefer to work for the government. However, significant differences do occur. More of the Ivory Coast sample would prefer to be self-employed (11 per cent as against 4 per cent), while only 12 per cent of Ghanaians would choose to work for a private employer, as against 18 per cent of the Ivory Coasters. At present, Ghana is rather more committed to the development of the economy along socialist lines, and openings in the public service are proportionately more numerous and more differentiated than in the Ivory Coast.[21]

Furthermore, both groups express a strong preference for employment in the largest urban centers within which the elites are overwhelmingly concentrated; almost 70 per cent of the students in both countries wish to reside in such major towns as Abidjan, Accra, and Kumasi. However, a markedly higher proportion of Ghanaians express a preference for working in rural areas (29 per cent as against 8 per cent). This is surprising in view of the more urban background of Ghanaian students.

SOME CONCLUDING OBSERVATIONS

Our initial problem in this paper was to indicate the part played by secondary schools in processes of elite recruitment in two new African nations. There are certainly distinct differences in the social background of secondary-school pupils as between Ghana and the Ivory Coast, and certain contrasts are apparent in some aspects of recruitment. Yet the evidence demonstrates that both systems tend to operate in a rather similar manner. In spite of a very limited number of places and formidable academic barriers to entry, the secondary schools of both nations draw upon very broad segments of the national populations. To be sure, the chances of achieving secondary-school access vary considerably as between subgroups but this does not imply that the majority of students come from privileged socioeconomic or ethnic minorities.

There has been some recent speculation regarding the political implications of the widening gap between African elites and the masses. In the case of these two countries, this concern is not justified. Post-primary education, insofar as it plays a critical role in elite formation, is still available to young people from the most "humble" circumstances and is not the prerogative of a

---

[21] Probably about 60 per cent of employment within the modern sector of the Ghanaian economy is with some form of public agency, while in the Ivory Coast this figure is approximately 25 per cent.

predetermined group. In this sense, the contact between the potential elite and the masses is very marked. However, in another respect, the prolonged educational experience of this minority does set it apart from the rest of the population. How effectively secondary schooling generates a feeling of common identity among its beneficiaries is beyond the scope of this paper. It could well be that formal education creates patterns of affiliation that transcend other social and ethnic loyalties. It is only in that kind of context that we can talk meaningfully of a "gap" between the elite and the mass.

Furthermore, both groups of students are remarkably similar with respect to the nature and level of their aspirations and expectations. Moreover, both face a very restricted range of occupational opportunities. In effect, secondary education up to this level no longer allows automatic access to high-status occupations and roles. Its importance has come to lie in the degree to which it feeds into higher education. Completion of the fifth form or the first *Baccalauréat* now only enables individuals to enter occupations that up to a decade ago were filled mainly by primary- or middle-school leavers. Preoccupation with job security among students may well reflect their difficulties with respect to employment.

Most of the new African states share a primary commitment to economic development plus a belief in the key role to be played in this respect by the educated cadres. Yet we have seen that both samples are oriented toward government employment in the largest urban centers and attach overwhelming importance to occupational stability. Such individuals, we suggest, are not highly likely to emerge as potential innovators in the field of economic development. At the present time, indeed, African entrepreneurs are usually far less educated than members of the bureaucracy. Insofar as the latter group tends usually to limit the autonomy of economic activities, it will be interesting to see to what extent effective communication can be maintained between bureaucratic and entrepreneurial elites with very different levels of formal education.[22]

---

[22] For an interesting discussion of the relationships between bureaucratic and entrepreneurial elites in the new nations, see S. N. Eisenstadt, "Problems of Emerging Bureaucracies in Developing Areas and New States," in Bert F. Hoselitz and Wilbert E. Moore (eds.), *Industrialization and Society* (The Hague: UNESCO and Mouton, 1963), pp. 167–68.

ECONOMIC, POLITICAL AND SOCIAL DETERMINANTS OF MOBILITY: AN INTERNATIONAL CROSS-SECTIONAL ANALYSIS

Thomas G. Fox
and S. M. Miller

The authors identify five variables, including education, which are likely to influence social mobility. They carefully specify the limitations imposed on their analysis by weaknesses in the data, difficulties of intercountry comparison, and the primitive state of explanatory theory in the area. They conclude that, of the five variables tested, differences in national educational level are the most important for explaining differences in upward *social mobility.*

R ECENT national comparative studies of intergenerational occupational (social) mobility have shown considerable variations in the rates of outflow from manual to nonmanual strata (upward mobility) and from nonmanual to manual strata (downward mobility).[1] One of the authors was associated with an unsuccessful attempt to find simple dominating relationships between patterns of social mobility and various economic indicators.[2] The results suggested that although economic factors may be important, they are not uniquely significant in influencing mobility patterns. Therefore, it would be well to expand the analysis of mobility determinants by exploring an intricate complex of social and economic forces that might influence mobility.

The present paper extends the analysis in two ways: (1) it investigates a complex of possible economic, social and political determinants of social

REPRINTED FROM *Acta Sociologica*, 9 (1966), 76–93, by permission of the authors. This report is one of a series supported by Grant G-25124 of the National Science Foundation to the Syracuse University Youth Development Center. Principal Investigator: S. M. Miller.

[1] S. M. Miller, *Comparative Social Mobility: A Trend Report and Bibliography*, Current Sociology IX, No. 1 (1960), the entire issue; Seymour M. Lipset and Reinhard Bendix, *Social Mobility in Industrial Society* (Los Angeles and Berkeley: University of California Press, 1959), p. 26; Thomas Fox and S. M. Miller, *Intra-Country Variations: Occupational Stratification and Mobility*, in Stein Rokkan and Richard L. Merritt, eds., *Comparing Nations* (New Haven: Yale University Press, 1966).

[2] S. M. Miller and Herrington Bryce, *Social Mobility and Economic Growth and Structure*, Kölner Zeitschrift für Soziologie, Summer, 1962. Sonderheft 5.

mobility; (2) it employs the techniques of multiple regression and partial correlation analysis. Unfortunately, the analytical study of comparative social mobility is still in the infant stages of development and no reasonably well-developed hypotheses exist which specify the "crucial" intersocietal determinants of mobility. Consequently, several economic, political and social variables have been selected from the ponderous mobility literature for the statistical analysis. The inadequacies of much basic data, the tortuous realigning of occupational categories to achieve some semblance of comparability, and the distortions of the statistical techniques require the recognition that the analysis can only be regarded at best as suggestive.

With these limitations in mind, it will be seen that five mobility determinants—gross national product (GNP) per capita, education, political stability, urbanization, achievement motivation—in concert account for more than 80 percent of the manual and nonmanual outflow mobility variance among twelve nations.

We deal with only one form of social mobility—intergenerational occupational change—and only one gross type of movement—manual and nonmanual outflow. Preferably, the association of mobility and its five possible determinants should be studied over time in a number of countries. At the moment, though, a longitudinal analysis is difficult because at the empirical level it is almost impossible to specify the time interval between generations. We are not dealing with cohorts but with mixed generational groupings. While we speak of the fathers' and sons' generations, the sons have a considerable age range (depending on the sampling decisions of each study) and only share the one characteristic of being someone's son. The fathers, of course, vary greatly also in age and share only the characteristic of being someone's father. Indeed, if a father and his son were both included in the sample, we would have reports on two fathers and two sons extending over three generations! Furthermore, mobility data are scarcely available over time.

Consequently, we have to rely on cross-sectional investigation. A number of nations are studied at *approximately* the same point in time. We assume that the results are revealing about changes over time.

THE MOBILITY VARIABLES

We utilize only manual-nonmanual outflow rates to simplify the analysis. Manual outflow, or upward mobility, gives us the proportion of sons of manual fathers who have gained nonmanual occupations. Conversely, nonmanual outflow, or downward mobility, is the proportion of sons of nonmanual fathers engaged in manual occupations. These are the two dependent variables. A more complete analysis would delineate the height of movement by distinguishing between short-range and long-range mobility and would use a more intricate classification than manual-nonmanual.

The basic intergenerational mobility data underlying this study are derived from numerous individual mobility studies as comparatively reanalyzed by Miller.[3] All nations for which we have roughly comparable mobility data available for the period 1949 to 1957 are utilized in this study. Geographically, the countries range from Japan to the United States and Great Britain—including much of Western Europe and Hungary. The basic mobility data are presented in columns (1) and (2) of Table 1.

THE MOBILITY DETERMINANTS

The dates for the values of the five independent variables center somewhere near the median time period of the total mobility cross-section. The values of the independent variables are based primarily on the compilation and evaluation of data by the Yale University Political Data Program.[4]

The five independent variables have been selected because they cover most of the explicit or implicit suggestions about the determinants of the rates of mobility in a nation. They have particular significance in the process of industrialization, which is partially revealed in the occupational changes portrayed by mobility rates. If we can discern which of the variables—economic, industrial, political, demographic and motivational—have great impact, singly or in concert, we may be able to point out some of the important elements in speeding up the pace of industrialization. We now turn in more detail to the independent variables shown in Table 1.

Economic Development

One of the major hypothesized determinants of mobility is the level of economic development. The relationships can be developed as follows. Rising levels of economic development are dependent on technological progress. Technological progress in the more economically advanced nations has been associated with a decline in the demand for many types of manual labor and an increased demand for nonmanual labor. As the relative size of the nonmanual strata increases, we would expect rising levels of economic development (and technological progress) to induce higher levels of upward mobility (outflow from the manual strata to the nonmanual) and declining levels of downward mobility (nonmanual outflow to the manual strata). In the context of our cross-sectional analysis, we should find higher levels of upward mobility associated with higher levels of economic development, and lower levels of downward mobility associated with higher levels of economic development.

[3] S. M. Miller, *op. cit.*, Table 1, p. 30. The modes of mobility analysis are discussed in Chapter I.

[4] Bruce M. Russett, *et. al.*, *Handbook of Basic Political and Social Data for Cross-National Comparisons* (Yale University Political Data Program). (Partial draft, mimeographed, 1963.)

TABLE 1

Summary of Data Used in Analysis of Mobility Determinants

NATION	(1) MANUAL OUTFLOW MOBILITY a (X_1)	(2) NONMANUAL OUTFLOW MOBILITY a (X_2)	(3) GNP PER CAP. (1957 U.S. $)b ($X_3$)	(4) PRIM./SEC. ENROLLMENT AS % OF POP. AGED 5–19c (X_4)	(5) POLITICAL STABILITY d (X_5)	(6) PER CENT OF POPULATION IN LOCALITIES OVER 20,000 e (X_6)	(7) ACHIEVEMENT MOTIVATION f (X_7)
Denmark	24.1	36.8	1057	72	1	44.8	0
Finland	11.0	24.0	794	70	0	31.2	0
France (II)	29.6	26.9	943	76	0	33.3	1
Great Britain	24.8	42.1	1189	80	1	66.9	0
Hungary	14.5	27.5	490	66	0	37.0	0
Italy	8.5	34.4	516	50	0	30.3	0
Japan	23.7	29.7	306	73	0	43.1	0
Netherlands	19.6	43.2	836	68	1	49.8	0
Norway	23.2	28.6	1130	70	1	32.8	0
Sweden	25.5	27.7	1380	71	1	40.8	0
United States (II)	28.7	22.6	2577	81	1	52.0	1
West Germany	20.0	29.0	927	73	0	55.1	1

Sources:

a Levels of mobility are from S. M. Miller, "Comparative Social Mobility," *Current Sociology*, IX, (1960), Table III, p. 34.

b Income data converted into 1957 U.S. dollars are from Mikoto Usui and E. E. Hagen, "World Income," (Center for International Studies, Massachusetts Institute of Technology; Cambridge, Mass.: 1959) as cited by Bruce M. Russett, *et. al.*, "Handbook of Basic Political Data for Cross-National Comparisons," (Yale University Political Data Program; New Haven: 1963). (Partial Draft, mineographed.) Income data for Hungary refers to Net Material Product; that for Finland is for Gross Domestic Product at Factor Cost.

c Enrollment data is derived from United Nations, *Compendium of Social Statistics, 1963*, as calculated by Russett, *et. al., op. cit.* The figures are for enrollment only, not attendance.

d This is a dummy variable. The value 1 is given nations classified as politically stable democracies; politically unstable democracies and dictatorships are assigned 0. The classification of all nations except Japan are from Seymour Martin Lipset, *Political Man* (Garden City, New York: Doubleday and Co., Inc., 1960), Table I, p. 49. Following Lipset's criterion for Europe, Japan is classified as 0.

e These figures, generally, are for the years 1955–1960 and were compiled by International Urban Research of the University of California at Berkeley, as reported by Russett, *et. al., op. cit.*

f This is a dummy variable. Classification 0 is for nations with negative values on McClelland's index of n achievement motivation. Cf. David C. McClelland, *The Achieving Society* (Princeton, New Jersey: Van Nostrand, Inc., 1961), pp. 461–62. (Also reported in Russett, et. al., op. cit.).

As Harvey Leibenstein has pointed out, there is no clear-cut conceptualization of economic development.[5] For an approximate measure of the level of economic development for each nation we will use the value of GNP per capita. This is a more representative measure of the level of economic activity than, say, the value of GNP alone, which does not relate the value of economic output to the size of a nation's population. (Of course, neither measure of economic activity is an adequate measure; for example, they place no value on changes in leisure time.) Leibenstein, defending his own use of the value of per capita output as an index of the level of economic development, argues that "development implies the enhancement of the economy's power to produce goods and services per capita, for such enhancement is the prerequisite to raising standards of living." [6] Without expressing output in per capita terms there exists no a priori reason that the nation with the highest absolute level of economic output is the most highly economically developed, in Leibenstein's sense.

Education

Most sociologists engaged in mobility studies agree that education is an asset to the upwardly mobile, but there is no agreement on the relative importance of education. A number of conflicting findings are reported, leaving the relationship of mobility to education unclear. C. Arnold Anderson, for example, after examining mobility and education data for three countries (Great Britain, Sweden, United States) notes that a considerable amount of upward mobility occurs independently of formal education.[7] After a rather lengthy comparative study, his conclusion was that formal education is not an important determinant of mobility. Gösta Carlsson, on the other hand, in his study of social mobility in Sweden, remarks that although education was a relatively unimportant mobility determinant in the past, theoretically it should become increasingly important in the future.[8] Seymour M. Lipset and Reinhard Bendix, notwithstanding the conclusions of Anderson and Carlsson, find that education is a crucial factor in the intergenerational mobility process.[9]

In terms of gross association, we expect that upward mobility should be an increasing function of education and downward mobility a decreasing function. Higher levels of education probably mean that manual sons have greater opportunity to gain the educational credentials important for occupational advance. On the other hand, access to formal educational facilities is easiest for

[5] Harvey Leibenstein, *Economic Backwardness and Economic Growth* (New York: John Wiley and Sons, Inc., 1963), p. 8.

[6] *Ibid.*, p. 10.

[7] C. Arnold Anderson, *A Sceptical Note on the Relation of Vertical Mobility to Education*, American Journal of Sociology, LXVI (May, 1960), pp. 560–70.

[8] Gösta Carlsson, *Social Mobility and Class Structure* (Lund, Sweden: C. W. K. Gleerup, 1958), p. 137.

[9] Seymour M. Lipset and Reinhard Bendix, *op. cit.*, p. 197. Cf. Otis Dudley Duncan and Robert W. Hodge, *Education and Occupational Mobility: A Regression Analysis*, American Journal of Sociology, LXVIII (May, 1963).

sons of non-manual fathers who, in addition to having an economic advantage over "blue-collar" workers, probably enjoy social and motivational advantages as well. This would mean that with higher levels of education, we might expect less downward mobility.

Educational levels are extremely difficult to incorporate into any international comparison. Indices of literacy and newspaper circulation were not found to be discriminating enough for analytical purposes.[10] Data available on college enrollment in different nations are subject to such ambiguous interpretation that they were not deemed appropriate. Instead, we use primary and secondary school enrollment as a percentage of the population aged 5 to 19. Statutory enrollment requirements among these nations generally apply over the age range 7 to 14,[11] so that the indicator is not overly biased due to differential educational legislation with respect to age. (But the age distribution of the age range 5 to 19 can vary from country to country.)

Urbanization

Another important mobility determinant is believed to be urbanization. Within a nation, rates of mobility are higher in the metropolises than in the nation as a whole.[12] Extending this finding to the international scene, one would expect levels of mobility to be higher in the more urbanized nations and lower in the less urbanized nations.

The most logical urbanization indicator is the proportion of the population living in "cities". For this purpose, the percentage of the population living in localities of 20,000 and over is used, as compiled by International Urban Research of the University of California.[13] We would prefer to use, say, the percentage of populations living in cities of 50,000 or 100,000 population or more. Unfortunately, useful comparable data of this sort are not available. Because it is difficult to justify using the term "metropolitan" for a city of only 20,000 population, our index of urbanization must remain unsatisfactory on many grounds.

Political Stability

Different types of national political systems may exercise important effects upon mobility opportunities. We have resorted to one dimension of political structure and behavior—political stability—because of the unavailability of indicators of other forms of political life. The impact of political stability is unclear. Under some conditions, politically stable democracies may produce high rates of both upward and downward mobility; yet revolutionary regimes

[10] Cf. Bruce M. Russett, et. al., op. cit.
[11] Cf. United Nations, A Preliminary Report on the World Social Situation (1952).
[12] Cf. Bertram Hutchinson, Urban Social Mobility Rates in Brazil Related to Migration and Changing Occupational Structure, America Latina, Vol. VI, No. 3 (Julho–Setembre de 1963), pp. 47–62; Seymour M. Lipset and Reinhard Bendix, op. cit., pp. 203–26.
[13] Cited by Bruce M. Russett, et. al., op. cit.

(particularly after wartime devastation) may induce high upward mobility by eliminating the old guard.

Several indices of political stability are available: [14] deaths from domestic group violence per million population, votes in national elections as a percentage of the voting age populations, and the number of chief executives of a nation divided by the number of years that a nation has been independent. All are subject to ambiguous interpretation. It was therefore decided to use Lipset's special classification of nations into politically stable democracies and unstable democracies and dictatorships, despite our hesitations about it. His criterion for stable European democracies is ". . . the uninterrupted continuation of political democracy since World War I *and* the absence over the past twenty-five years of a major political movement opposed to the democratic 'rules of the game.'" [15] This variable is a qualitative one. As can be noted in Table 1, it is incorporated into the statistical models as a dummy variable having the value 1 for politically stable democracies and the value 0 for unstable democracies and dictatorships.[16]

Achievement Motivation

Motivation is frequently suggested as a determinant of mobility. We have therefore made use of McClelland's well-known index of achievement motivation as an indicator.[17] It is often suggested that nations characterized by a strong feeling of a need to achieve have high levels of both upward and downward mobility. Conversely, low-mobility nations are thought to have populations with low motivation to achieve.

Anticipating some curvilinear relationships in the use of this variable, the index of achievement motivation is incorporated into the linear statistical models as a dummy variable. Those nations having a positive value on the achievement motivation index were assigned the value 1; nations having a negative value were denoted 0. Also, by using a qualitative variable which eliminates the problem of curvilinearity, problems of the relative ordering of nations on the motivational indicator have been avoided.

SIMPLE CORRELATIONS

Although our principal interest is in the multivariate analysis of the determinants of intergenerational mobility among twelve nations, it is useful to ex-

[14] Cf. *Ibid*.

[15] Seymour M. Lipset, *Political Man* (Garden City, N. Y.: Doubleday and Co., 1960), p. 48.

[16] For a technical discussion of the use of qualitative or dummy variables within the context of multiple regression and correlation analysis, see Mordecai Ezekiel and Karl A. Fox, *Methods of Correlation and Regression Analysis*, 3rd. ed. (New York: John Wiley and Sons, Inc., 1959), Ch. 22.

[17] As reported in Bruce M. Russett, *et. al., op. cit.*

amine first the gross relationships between each of the mobility variables and the five independent variables.

The simple correlation coefficients for manual outflow and nonmanual outflow mobility with each of the independent variables are given in the first two rows of Table 2.

TABLE 2

Matrix of Simple Correlations Among All Variables

VARIABLES	x_3	x_4	x_5	x_6	x_7
X_1 Manual Outflow Mobility	.569	.803	.503	.417	.451
X_2 Nonmanual Outflow Mobility	−.270	−.149	.385	.475	−.441
X_3 Gross National Product per Capita	1.00	.571	.626	.372	.487
X_4 Primary and Secondary School Enrollment		1.00	.373	.593	.444
X_5 Political Stability			1.00	.443	−.192
X_6 Population in Localities over 20,000				1.00	.199
X_7 Achievement Motivation					1.00

Manual outflow mobility is positively related with each of the five independent variables. All of the simple relationships appear to be substantial. The relationship between manual outflow and education emerges with overwhelming importance ($r = .80$) as a potential source for explaining manual outflow mobility variance in the international cross-section.

Nonmanual outflow mobility, as shown in Table 2, does not seem too closely related with any of the independent variables (although the directions are as presumed). The negative and virtually insignificant association with GNP per capita and education might suggest that little importance be attached to these hypothesized mobility determinants in the explanation of international variations in the amount of downward mobility. The highest degree of simple correlation occurs between nonmanual outflow and the measure of urbanization, but the correlation is not very great ($r = .48$) compared with those found in the upward mobility analysis.

As will later become apparent, the net relationship between nonmanual outflow and each of the five mobility determinants is not even roughly approximated by the simple correlation coefficients which are estimates of gross association.

Inspection of the last five rows and columns of Table 2 shows considerable statistical interaction among the independent variables. For example, the correlation between political stability and urbanization is substantial ($r = .44$). The high degree of interaction among the independent variables means that some statistical difficulty will be encountered in the multivariate analysis in attempts to identify net relationships.

Multiple Regression and Correlation Results

The multivariate cross-sectional analysis of the determinants of mobility shows that the five independent variables collectively do account for most of the observed variations among the twelve nations. As estimated by the coefficient of multiple determination presented in the last column of Table 3, the five mobility determinants collectively explain 83 per cent of the variance in manual outflow mobility and 86 per cent of the nonmanual outflow variance. Given the assumed complexity of the mobility process and the historical, cultural, economic and political differences among the nations, the five independent variables together offer a remarkably good explanation of international variations in the extent of upward and downward mobility across the "white-collar/blue-collar" divide.

The net of partial regression coefficients and coefficients of multiple determination are given in Table 3. A complete summary of the partial correlation coefficients and beta coefficients for both nonmanual and manual mobility are presented in the middle and lower panels of Table 4. For comparative purposes, the simple correlation coefficients between the dependent mobility variables and the five independent variables appear in the upper panel of Table 4.

Before turning to a detailed scrutiny of our statistical estimates, a few short comments on statistical tools may be of some value. The partial correlation coefficients measure the linear association between the dependent variable and *one* independent variable, when the *linear* effects of the other independent variables upon the dependent mobility variables have been held constant. Similarly the beta coefficients or, as sometimes called, the standardized net regression coefficients, show the impact of one standard deviation change in an independent variable upon the standard deviation of the dependent variable, holding constant the direct *linear* effects of the other independent variables. Thus, the partial correlation coefficient is a measure of the "closeness" of a net relationship, whereas the beta coefficient is an estimate of the "relative importance" of a net relationship.[18] While partial correlation analysis is easily subject to distortion, it is useful in attempts to sift out the effects of one of many influences on a phenomenon.

We turn now to a more detailed examination of the results of the multiple regression and correlation analysis portrayed in Tables 2 and 4.

GNP per Capita

With respect to manual outflow mobility and the level of economic development, Table 4 clearly shows an important shift when we control for the

---

[18] Tests of significance and reliability have not been reported because our data do not conform to the rigid requirements of simple random sampling, homogeneous variances, and other conditions necessary for the application of conventional confidence intervals.

TABLE 3

Net Regression Coefficients and Coefficients of Multiple Determination: Manual and Nonmanual Outflow Mobility with All Independent Variables for Twelve Nations

Dependent Variables	Constants	INDEPENDENT VARIABLES — NET REGRESSION COEFFICIENTS					Coefficient of Multiple Determination R^2
		GNP per Capita (1957 U.S. dollars) X_3	Primary and Secondary School Enrollment as % of Pop. Aged 5–19 X_4	Political Stability X_5	Percentage of Pop. in Localities over 20,000 X_6	Achievement Motivation X_7	
X_1 Manual Outflow Mobility	−14.433	−.006 (.004)	.587 (.207)	10.656 (4.534)	−.170 (.135)	9.248 (4.576)	.829
X_2 Nonmanual Outflow Mobility	−45.467	−.011 (.003)	−.369 (.185)	12.011 (4.051)	.371 (.120)	.423 (.409)	.863

Figures in parentheses are the "unbiased" standard errors of the net regression coefficients.

TABLE 4

Summary of Correlation and Regression. Analyses of Manual and Nonmanual Mobility Determinants in Twelve Nations

Dependent Variables	INDEPENDENT VARIABLES				
	X_3	X_4	X_5	X_6	X_7
Simple Correlation Coefficients					
Manual Outflow Mobility	.57	.80	.50	.42	.45
Nonmanual Outflow Mobility	−.27	−.15	.39	.47	−.44
Partial Correlation Coefficients					
Manual Outflow Mobility	−.52	.76	.69	−.46	.64
Nonmanual Outflow Mobility	−.77	−.63	.77	.78	.39
Beta Coefficients					
Manual Outflow Mobility	−.55	.70	.83	−.29	.63
Nonmanual Outflow Mobility	−.98	−.43	.94	.63	.28

other variables: While the partial correlation (−.52) is only slightly lower than the simple correlation (.57), the direction of the net relationship changes. The corresponding beta coefficient (−.55) for this variable—also negative— is large but is not the most important manual outflow determinant. The magnitude of the relationship between upward mobility and the level of economic development is not surprising, but the negative net relationship is unexpected. The implication, though tenuous, is that lower levels of manual outflow mobility are associated with higher levels of economic development when the influence of the other independent variables is held constant. This might suggest that a nation with high GNP per capita and ranking low on the other variables tends to be rigid in class structure. But this must remain even more tentative than our other conclusions because of the unreliability of the estimates of the net relationships among these variables (see Table 3).

Nonmanual outflow mobility is much more closely related to the five independent variables than is suggested by the simple correlation coefficients in Table 2. The partial correlation (−.77) between downward mobility and the level of economic development is substantial and negative. As measured by the data coefficient (−.98), the level of economic development has the greatest effect upon downward mobility. Higher levels of GNP per capita are closely and importantly associated with lower levels of downward mobility. Substantial economic development safeguards the positions of those in the higher level occupations.

Education

Manual outflow mobility is more closely associated with education than with any of the other independent variables: the positive partial correlation (.76) between these variables is quite large. In terms of the beta coefficient, education turns out to be the second most important source in the explanation of variations in upward mobility among the twelve nations (beta = .70).

Nonmanual outflow or downward mobility is negatively related to education. This mobility determinant, as estimated by the partial correlation (−.63), is considerably more closely related to downward mobility than suggested by the simple correlation coefficient (−.15). Thus, the net relationship between nonmanual outflow and education is greatly underestimated when only the gross association is examined. Although these two variables have a close net relationship, the beta weights show that education is not as important with respect to downward mobility as GNP per capita and some of the other determinants.

Higher proportions of the school-aged population enrolled in primary and secondary schools are positively and closely related to higher levels of upward mobility and negatively and less importantly related to downward mobility. Accessibility to educational opportunities exerts considerable positive influence over manual outflow, but is less important to—but related with—lower levels of nonmanual outflow mobility.

Political Stability

After accounting for the other independent variables, both manual and nonmanual mobility are closely and positively related with politically stable democracies. The partial correlation coefficients between political stability and manual outflow (.69) and nonmanual outflow (.77) point up the closeness of the relationships. In terms of the beta coefficient weights, this determinant is most important in the explanation of manual outflow mobility differentials among nations. Political stability is the second most important independent variable with respect to nonmanual outflow, falling only slightly behind the economic variable.

Inclusion of the dummy variable for political stability into the statistical models aids greatly in the estimation of net relationships for both upward and downward mobility with each of the other four mobility determinants. The introduction of this previously neglected qualitative factor increases the reliability of the other net and beta regression coefficients.

The results support the view that political stability is of great importance in assuring high rates of access to the better occupational levels of society for those originating in manual families and in preventing nonmanual sons from having an assured inheritance of their fathers' levels. "Political stability," in Lipset's classification, is highly correlated with democratic practices; in turn, democratic political practices may affect or facilitate social fluidity.

The alternative view that instability leads to the possible emergence of new groups is inadequately tested because we do not have a sufficient number of countries in which vast change occurred in a significant time period before the collection of mobility experiences.

Urbanization

The estimated net relationship between manual outflow and urbanization is similar to that evident between the former and GNP per capita. Neither the partial correlation ($-.46$) nor the beta ($-.29$) is very large; in particular, the low value of the beta coefficient shows that urbanization, as measured, contributes but little in the overall explanation of manual outflow mobility variance among the twelve nations. More disturbing is the fact that the sign of both is negative. The city mobility studies have reported mobility to be rather high but perhaps this is due to education or some other factor rather than to urbanization effects. In any case, the relationships are not strong enough to be considered statistically valid.

On the other hand, urbanization appears quite important with respect to nonmanual outflow. Higher levels of urbanization are positively related to higher levels of downward mobility (partial correlation $= .78$) and is a relatively important determinant (beta $= .63$) of downward mobility. While urbanization does not appear to facilitate upward movement, it does affect the likelihood of downward mobility.

Again, we wish to emphasize the provisional nature of these findings. We have earlier noted that our index of urbanization is far from completely satisfactory. The results might be drastically altered if we had a more representative index of national degrees of urbanization.

Achievement Motivation

The index of achievement motivation emerges as a significant factor with respect to upward mobility, but it is of no great importance in terms of downward mobility. The prevalence of a feeling of a need to achieve is closely (partial correlation $= .64$) and importantly (beta $= .63$) associated with higher levels of manual outflow mobility; it is more dominant than either education or political stability.

Conversely, positive feelings of a need to achieve are not significantly related to the level of nonmanual outflow mobility. Both the beta ($.28$) and the partial correlation ($.39$) are relatively small. This variable could probably be dropped as a determinant of nonmanual outflow mobility.

Overall, motivation appears of importance in terms of upward mobility but offers little as a source of explanation in international variations in downward mobility rates.

JOINT EFFECTS

In this section, the statistical models for explaining mobility variations among twelve nations will be altered by deleting some of the less important independent variables.

Manual Outflow

The five independent variables—gross national product per capita, education, political stability, urbanization, and achievement motivation—together explain 83 per cent of the manual outflow variations among the twelve nations in this cross-section. Table 5 shows what happens to the various coefficients used in our analysis when one or more of the independent variables is excluded.

When the least important manual outflow determinant, urbanization, is dropped from the analysis, R^2 (line 1', Table 5) shows that the other four independent variables will explain 79 per cent of the manual outflow variance. If only achievement motivation is deleted, the overall explanatory power of the four remaining variables is much weaker; R^2 (line 1") falls from 83 per cent to 71 per cent of the variance accounted for, and the social economic variable becomes insignificant. When urbanization and political stability together are eliminated, the three remaining independent variables together yield an R^2 (line 1''') of only .67.

The five independent variables in concert are capable of accounting for most of the upward outflow mobility among nations. Although singly some do not appear as important, when all are incorporated within the manual outflow estimating model, each appears to make a noticeable contribution in the total explanation of international manual outflow mobility differentials.

Nonmanual Outflow

The five independent mobility determinants account for 86 per cent of the nonmanual outflow variance. Table 6 illustrates the statistical effects of discarding some of the determinants of downward mobility.

The contribution of the achievement motivation index in explaining downward variance is minimal; when this determinant is deleted, R^2 (line 2', Table 6) only falls to 84 per cent of the variance explained. If only the variable for political stability is omitted, the four remaining variables account for only 66 per cent (line 2") of the nonmanual outflow variance. When political stability and urbanization are dropped, (line 2''') the explanatory power of the model falls off radically—only 21 per cent of the variance in nonmanual outflow mobility is accounted for by variations in GNP per capita, education, and achievement motivation.

Of all the mobility determinants, only the achievement motivation index appears to be of little or no importance in the overall explanation of nonmanual outflow variation among nations. The other four independent variables, which have varying degrees of unreliability, are of prime importance in statistically accounting for the downward mobility variance.

TABLE 5

*Manual Outflow Mobility: Regression Equations and Partial and Multiple
Correlation Coefficients with Different Combinations of Independent
Variables for Twelve Nations*

ESTIMATING EQUATIONS FOR X_1	INDEPENDENT VARIABLES					CONSTANT TERM	COEFFICIENT OF MULTIPLE DETERMINATION R^2
	X_3	X_4	X_5	X_6	X_7		
	Simple Correlation Coefficients						
	.57	.80	.50	.42	.45		
	Partial Correlation Coefficients						R^2
1	−.52	.76	.69	−.46	.64		.829
1′	−.41	.68	.59	—	.55		.789
1″	−.001	.73	.37	−.26	—		.714
1‴	.182	.69	—	—	.12		.667
	Beta Coefficients						
1	−.55	.70	.83	−.29	.63		
1′	−.43	.56	.67	—	.54		
1″	−.001	.81	.29	−.19	—		
1‴	.14	.69	—	—	.79		
	Net Regression Coefficients						
1	−.006 (.004)	.587 (.207)	10.656 (4.534)	−.170 (.135)	9.248 (4.577)	−14.433	
1′	−.005 (.004)	.471 (.194)	8.571 (4.399)	—	8.020 (4.659)	−13.545	
1″	*	.682 (.242)	3.646 (3.503)	−.112 (.157)	—	−24.156	
1‴	−.002 (.003)	.581 (.215)	—	—	1.160 (3.543)	−21.944	

* Not important enough to show.
— Indicates variable omitted.
Figures in parentheses are for unbiased standard errors of the net regression coefficients.

TABLE 6

Nonmanual Outflow Mobility: Regression Equations and Partial and Multiple Correlation Coefficients with Different Combinations of Independent Variables for Twelve Nations

ESTIMATING EQUATIONS FOR X_2	INDEPENDENT VARIABLES					CONSTANT TERM	COEFFICIENT OF MULTIPLE DETERMINATION R^2
	X_3	X_4	X_5	X_6	X_7		
Simple Correlation Coefficients							
	−.27	−.15	.39	.47	−.44		
Partial Correlation Coefficients							
2	−.77	−.63	.77	.78	.39		.863
2′	−.78	−.56	.79	.79	—		.839
2″	−.25	−.41	—	.76	−.45		.663
2‴	−.11	.10	—	—	−.38		.207
Beta Coefficients							
2	−.98	−.43	.94	.63	.28		
2′	−.73	−.39	.69	.67	—		
2″	−.20	−.39	—	.84	−.34		
2‴	−.13	.11	—	—	−.43		
Net Regression Coefficients							
2	−.011 (.003)	−.369 (.185)	12.011 (4.051)	.371 (.120)	.423 (.409)	45.467	
2′	−.008 (.003)	−.326 (.181)	8.805 (2.621)	3.977 (.118)	—	41.019	
2″	−.002 (.003)	−.324 (.268)	—	.501 (.163)	−.505 (3.827)	35.935	
2‴	−.001 (.005)	.096 (.331)	—	−6.347 (5.456)	—	27.300	

— Indicates variable omitted.

Figures in parentheses are for unbiased standard errors of the net regression coefficients.

CONCLUSIONS

Overall, the five independent variables—GNP per capita, education, political stability, urbanization, achievement motivation—together yield an extremely good statistical explanation of manual and nonmanual outflow variance in the international cross-section. But the quality of the empirical "inputs" in this study are such that of necessity our findings must remain tenuous. Even neglecting limitations intrinsic to our statistical mode of analysis, the basic data for the five determinants of mobility have such large errors that the statistical reliability of most of the net regression coefficients is rather weak. Consequently, our ability to point out the relative significance of individual determinants of mobility is weak.

In general, our conclusions corroborate those of the earlier study.[19] Economic factors are important, but they are not unique determinants of mobility nor do they operate in any simple way.

The education variable emerges as the individually most important and ostensibly reliable determinant of manual outflow mobility. Higher levels of upward mobility are associated with higher levels of education, as measured. The relationship of manual outflow mobility to political stability and achievement motivation is fairly close, but we do not have sufficient statistical confidence in the estimated relationships to conclude that the positive relationships are important. The level of economic development does not emerge as important with respect to upward mobility, nor does the variable for urbanization.

The determinants of downward (nonmanual outflow) mobility have been more fully identified than for upward mobility. Higher levels of economic development are closely and importantly associated with lower levels of downward mobility. Nonmanual outflow mobility is considerably greater under conditions of politically stable democracies than in nations characterized by unstable democracies and dictatorships. Urbanization is also closely and positively related to downward mobility. The three determinants, political stability, the level of economic development, and urbanization, all appear as very important determinants of nonmanual outflow mobility. Of the other two determinants, achievement motivation is of little importance, and education does not appear more than distantly related to downward mobility.

Comparative mobility studies have a number of weaknesses. A rigorous and methodologically satisfactory study of intersocial determinants of mobility must await the collection of intergenerational mobility data of a much higher quality than is currently available. Unfortunately, high quality data collected at approximately the same point in time are not within immediate sight. We probably will get new national studies from time to time with, hopefully, suf-

[19] S. M. Miller and Herrington Bryce, *op. cit.*

ficiently detailed occupational categorization to facilitate international comparisons. Unfortunately, our statistical technology has not been adequately developed for mobility studies. Most important perhaps is the great need for theoretical work which will elucidate the process of mobility as a *national* and not only as an individual phenomenon.

This study points up how little we know of macro-level patterns. The fact that mobility differences among nations can be attributed to such a complex of socioeconomic factors suggests that many of our statements about economic development ignore the possibilities of alternative, competitive and substitute routes of change and the complicated interplay of variables. The impact of any variable may depend on other conditions in the society. For example, high levels of education may have different effects on mobility when economic development is high or when it is low. The general social "freeing up" of society—as with urbanization or political stability—may make downward mobility more likely without any other changes taking place. If the study of social mobility is to realize its potential contribution to the analysis of society as a whole and to the process of economic development, we must turn to the assessment of leads, lags, multiplier and compounding effects of the variables influencing social change.

Part 5

THE CULTURE

DELIBERATE INSTRUCTION AND HOUSEHOLD STRUCTURE: A CROSS-CULTURAL STUDY

John D. Herzog

Do all societies strive with equal formality to transmit to their children cultural beliefs and norms? If not, what are some of the social and psychological conditions that determine whether such deliberate instruction is offered? These are two of the questions that direct this exploratory study. The author develops numerous hypotheses and proceeds to test them against data from a large number of societies.

INTRODUCTION

THIS IS A study of the functions which different forms of "education" serve in different types of cultures. It departs considerably from the frame of reference in which education is usually discussed by educators, sociologists, and even anthropologists. Hopefully, the reader will not be distracted by this from thoughtful consideration of the data and of the interpretations offered.[1]

Throughout this paper, the term "instruction" has been used in preference to "education." The former has been little used by anthropologists, and perhaps will connote roughly the same thing to most readers. But "education," as a concept and as a label, has been badly abused by anthropologists, who have meant different things by it at different times.

Early anthropologists, such as Hambly (1926), used the term to refer to virtually everything that happens to children. In a later period, psychoanalytically-oriented fieldworkers such as Erikson (1950) requisitioned it to cover the early socialization of the child in the household of his birth, a process which might be better subsumed under the categories "child training" and "child care." In addition, many anthropologists analyzing "education" for audiences of educators have used the occasion to discuss aspects of socialization which only very loosely might be considered educational. Herskovits'

REPRINTED FROM *Harvard Educational Review*, 32 (Summer 1962), 301–342. Copyright © 1962 by the President and Fellows of Harvard College.

---

[1] This research was initiated with the encouragement of John W. M. Whiting, who first recognized that "deliberate instruction" might be a fruitful cross-cultural variable. The author wishes to thank William R. Charleson, Roy G. D'Andrade, Robert L. Munroe, and Dr. Whiting for their many theoretical and methodological suggestions. Robert L. Munroe aided in the reliability check during a period when time was very precious to him; the author is much indebted. Finally, the author is appreciative of the encouragement and advice of his wife, Dorothy S. Herzog.

251

cogent discussion (1943) of Dahomean child training, under the title "Education and Cultural Dynamics," is an example.[2] This conceptual fuzziness has not forwarded anthropology's contribution to the understanding of education or of other aspects of socialization, nor has it convinced many educators that anthropology has much to say to them.

The present author wishes to steer clear of these shifting sands. Therefore, the term "instruction" has been used throughout, except in a few instances where variation of terminology seemed stylistically desirable.

By "deliberate instruction" we mean that process by which an adult, or at least a person of a senior age grade, takes a child or a group of children aside and attempts verbally to communicate to them certain ideas, skills, and facts. Such communication must take place on the initiative of the adult, and not be requested by the children, nor be the adult's response to a misdemeanor or omission by the child (which might be better called "scolding"). The motivation of the adult's behavior in such instances would seem to be the feeling that children need to be told certain things directly, or they will not learn them and thus not grow up to be culturally acceptable adults. Examples of deliberate instruction with which Western readers are familiar are the school, the catechism, and parental lectures to children.

By "cultural beliefs and norms" we refer to the ideas about "the good," "the true," and "the beautiful" which are explicitly or implicitly part of every culture, and which serve to regulate and integrate behavior in it. Examples are religious beliefs and practices, ideas of morality, obligatory etiquette, cosmology, ethics, genealogies, history and traditions, literature and mystical writings or sayings, poetry and songs. Such ideas are in theoretical apposition to the knowledge and techniques which are used to ensure physical survival and comfort, and which may be regarded as the *technical* knowledge of a society. It is clear that a society could not long survive without a well-developed and efficiently communicated technical apparatus; it is less clear (although probably no less true) that a society could not survive without a well-developed and efficiently communicated apparatus of beliefs and norms. It is with the communication of this latter body of beliefs and norms that this paper is exclusively concerned.

Finally, this study is concerned only with instruction which does *not* lead to occupational specialization, although, of course, the same instruction may lead to specialization in one society, but not in another. The only instruction with which we shall be dealing is that which ideally, at least, is available to all members of one or both sexes in a society; or if not generally available to all members, does not produce vocational or professional advancement for the "graduate." We are concerned, in other words, with "general education."

Admittedly, the distinction between technical knowledge (and communica-

---

[2] Herskovits' subsequent discussion (1949, Chapter 19) of "enculturation" and its various aspects ("education", "schooling", "training", etc.) is, however, one of the clearest confrontations of the subject to be found in the anthropological literature.

tion of it) and beliefs and norms (and instruction in them) is an arbitrary one, although in making it, we follow Kluckhohn (1949). But the factors which probably influence the manner in which knowledge of both types is communicated seem quite different. Technical training might be best provided "on the job." Children could then watch, imitate, receive informal advice, and practice under the direct supervision of an experienced adult. Only if technical knowledge and skills are generally exercised beyond the ken of children—as in our American society and, for example, in many hunting and fishing economies—is deliberate instruction at some stage required. Thus, we should expect to find the presence and absence of technical instruction to be highly correlated with the settings, with respect to children, in which the predominant subsistence activities are carried out. Mead (1943) speaks to this same point. Unfortunately, this line of thought has not been tested in this paper.

Deliberate instruction in beliefs and norms, or "regulatory training" in Kluckhohn's terminology (1949:206), is intuitively not so simple to predict. Some readers may be surprised to learn that there are societies which do not make any deliberate attempt to instruct their children in beliefs and norms. The Lau of Fiji are a good example:

> The people do not believe in educating children. Small children are said to be without minds. . . . Bigger children are watery souled. It is generally believed that it is useless to teach them anything, and that schools ought to be for big boys, almost young men. . . . The education of Fijian children therefore consists in picking things up as they go along by example. . . . Their ignorance is extraordinary. . . . The children pick up tales, but tell them most unintelligently. . . . On the other hand, children pick up practical knowledge very early, because they begin to help their parents—boys, their fathers; girls, their mothers —at an early age, through their own sweet will, more as a game at first. Gradually this develops into regular and real work until at the age of fifteen or sixteen they are enrolled among the adults so far as work is concerned.[3]

Similarly, Du Bois reports that among the Alorese

> . . . Children are not so much debarred from adult activity as given no role in it. This means that such learning as goes on is largely in terms of restrictive discipline and absorption, rather than permissive discipline or deliberate training. . . . Neither sex has any ritually or socially recognized crisis rites to dramatize the passage from childhood to adulthood. It is basically an individual and personal transition that must be made.[4]

Neither of these authors means to imply that the children do not learn the beliefs and norms of their societies. They do learn, of course, but they do

[3] Arthur M. Hocart: *Lau Islands, Fiji;* Bernice P. Bishop Museum, Bulletin 62 (Honolulu: 1929). P. 146. (In HRAF.)
[4] Cora Du Bois: *The People of Alor* (Minneapolis: University of Minnesota Press, 1944). Pp. 47, 80. (In HRAF.)

so through methods other than direct tuition: imitation, reward and punishment, and identification.

On the other hand, a culture may go to great pains to ensure that norms and beliefs are meticulously transferred. Our own elaborate school system attests to this. But the insistence on instruction may lead to the use of forms very different from those with which we are acquainted. Among the Papago, for example,

> Young people were ceaselessly trained in the moral code. . . . The moral code must be gone over and over. . . . The father was generally the speaker, though the mother might take her turn, especially with the girls. The time was chosen when the family were all lying in the dark on their sleeping mats, . . . often in the hours before dawn. There was a special method of speaking: a low, insistent monotone. . . . These speeches have an effect that is almost hypnotic. . . . This constant, though unaggressive repetition of principles must have had the effect of producing a unity of sentiment in the community as profound as it was unconscious.[5]

The Somali have developed another means by which deliberate instruction in beliefs and norms can be provided. Most Somali live in nomadic bands, but a few live in permanent settlements called *jama'a*, which are both agricultural and religious centers. The *jama'a*

> act as training centres for the devouts (*wadaad*), usually described as "bush teachers" or "bush preachers," who wander about from camp to camp through the bush, stopping now and then to hold classes where at least some rudimentary knowledge of theology is imparted. In these transitory bush schools children are taught prayers and verses from the Koran and generally acquire the ability to read and write Arabic. Children receive a thorough grounding in the Koran and their familiarity with Koranic texts remains with them throughout their lives.[6]

The main point here is that cultures vary widely in the extent to which norms and beliefs are taught by deliberate instruction. Some verbalize ideals infrequently, and encourage learning by other techniques. Some expect parents to do much lecturing; others utilize specialists of various sorts, to whom the children report for such purposes. Still others organize dramatic initiation ceremonies in which the emotional element greatly outweighs the intellectual. The objective of this paper is to suggest some of the social, structural, and psychological conditions under which deliberate instruction is, and is not, offered.

[5] Ruth M. Underhill: *Social Organization of the Papago Indians*; Columbia University Contributions to Anthropology, No. 30 (N.Y.: 1939). P. 163. (In HRAF.)

[6] I. M. Lewis: "Sufism in Somaliland: A Study in Tribal Islam—I and II"; *Bulletin of the School of Oriental and African Studies*, University of London. Vol. 17, pp. 581–602; Vol. 18, pp. 145–160. P. 14, HRAF pagination.

Previous Research

"Deliberate instruction" has received little sustained attention from anthropologists. Two or three factors contribute to this situation. First, anthropologists have until recently concerned themselves mostly with "primitive" cultures in which specialized institutions of instruction usually do not exist. Firth, for example, in his highly regarded ethnography of the Pacific island of Tikopia, reports that

> the observer is impressed almost immediately by the absence of any institutionalized education. The training of children is a private affair, and is very largely a function of the kinship situation, the parents of the child playing the most important part as instructors.[7]

Second, almost all anthropologists who have specialized in the study of socialization and personality development have been heavily influenced by Freudian ideas, and to a lesser extent, by general behavior (learning) theory. Neither theoretical orientation assigns to deliberate instruction a very significant role in the overall socialization of the child.

Finally, it is possible that anthropologists have steered away from consideration of deliberate instruction in part because of the grandiose claims regarding its importance made by early twentieth century social scientists and philosophers, and in the contemporary period by many educators, politicians, and social reformers. Durkheim, for example, felt that the social function of "education" (by which he meant "schooling") is to

> . . . arouse in the child (1) a certain number of physical and mental states that the society to which he belongs considers should not be lacking in any of its members; (2) certain physical and mental states that the particular social group (caste, class, family, profession) considers, equally, ought to be found among all those who make it up. [Without this education, society] would break down into an incoherent multitude of little fragments in conflict with one another. (1956:70, 79)

Sentiments similar to Durkheim's can be found in almost every contemporary textbook on education, including those by comparative educators, who might be expected to be more cautious. Many anthropologists of the present generation may feel that their role is that of providing antidotes for such oversimplifications.

The general position of anthropology, at least until recently, is well represented by the following words of Linton:

[7] Raymond Firth: *We, the Tikopia* (London: Allen and Unwin, 1936). P. 147. (In HRAF.)

The conscious training of the individual undoubtedly influences the content of his personality, making for the establishment of particular habits and attitudes. It also influences the more superficial aspects of personality organization by setting certain concrete goals for the individual's attainment and directing his energies toward these. However, its influence is too intermittent and forms too small a part of the total influences to which the individual is subjected for it to have much effect on the deeper organization of personality. To put it concretely, conscious training can develop almost anyone into a fairly successful businessman or craftsman, but it cannot make him an extrovert. . . . [Conscious] training always looms large in the minds of the society's members. Our own naive belief in universal education as a panacea is a case in point. However, this conscious training receives its high rating mainly because it is the only aspect of cultural conditioning of which the society is conscious . . . . (1936:475-6)

We do not mean to imply in any way that those subjects which the "psychological anthropologists" have studied do not deserve attention. We feel that it is time that learning and teaching of a more cognitive nature be scrutinized, also. Such study would have two purposes: the determination of the actual impact which "conscious training" does have on children, and the discovery of the conditions under which a society resorts to this technique of socialization.

It is encouraging that during the past decade increased attention has been paid by anthropologists to the first of these goals. The so-called "complex societies" have slowly fallen within the purview of anthropology, and a chapter on "education" is to be found in most books of the "community study" genre. (See, for example, Service and Service, 1954:227-238.) There is an increasing tempo of anthropological writing on broadly conceived educational issues (Cf. Spindler, et al, 1955, and Mead, 1951), although much of this is impressionistic. Anthropologists have moved from their discovery of the psychiatric hospital as a "small society" (Cf. Caudill, 1958, and Rappoport, 1960) to a similar view of the American college (Cf. various articles in Sanford, ed., 1962). It would be only a short further step to a similar view of elementary and secondary schools. Finally, many ethnographers are nowadays sent to the field with instructions to report on the cognitive, as well as the emotional, training systems of their "tribes." (Cf. Whiting, et al, 1955)

But there is no emerging "tradition" of comparative anthropological study of deliberate instruction in the second sense mentioned above. It is therefore not surprising that one of the major cross-cultural generalizations tested in the present study was suggested by a historian, Bernard Bailyn, whose provocative ideas will be discussed under Theoretical Orientations and Results. Before discussing Bailyn's proposal, however, we will outline the methodological and theoretical antecedents of this study.

METHODOLOGY

The cross-cultural method employed in this paper is described in detail in several of the sources listed in the bibliography: Whiting, 1954; Whiting and Goethals, 1957; Whiting and Whiting, 1960; Moore, ed., 1961. The cross-cultural method has been developed to exploit ethnographic materials in the testing of generalizations about human behavior. The method supplements the controlled laboratory of the psychologist with the "natural laboratory" of man's numerous group solutions to the basic problems of living.

The cross-cultural method is *not* synonymous with what is frequently called the "comparative" approach. The cross-cultural method stipulates that all judgments about data be objective and operational; that societies to be studied be chosen so far as possible by criteria unrelated to the major foci of research; and that generalizations be stated, and samples selected, in such ways that they are amenable to simple statistical tests of significance. In such research, the single society, or a particular aspect of it, is the "unit." The typical comparative analysis does not meet these conditions, usually for good and valid reasons.

There are, of course, severe limitations to this kind of research. Certain areas of the globe are poorly covered in the anthropological literature. Excellent ethnographies abound with lacunae on topics which may be of interest to the researcher but which did not occur to the original fieldworker. The complications introduced by the diffusion of traits from society to society must be faced. Thus, one of the major problems of cross-cultural research is that of framing the "suitable" question, one for which answers are generally available in the anthropological literature.

The feasibility of cross-cultural research has been greatly increased in recent years by the continued expansion and widespread availability of the Human Relations Area Files (HRAF). These Files contain minutely cross-indexed ethnographic accounts of several hundred cultures, distributed systematically throughout the world, and chosen for inclusion by experts in the various geographical areas. Given a suitably phrased question, the Files will yield information in a fraction of the time required for library research.[8]

In carrying out this study, the writer went through the relevant portions of the Files on individual cultures and typed out all statements dealing with the presence and absence of instruction in beliefs and norms. A total of 111 separate files (and, in a few cases, books) was consulted in this manner. Sixty-nine of the societies were chosen by a group of graduate students who did a preliminary survey of "religious education" long before the present hypotheses were developed. (Constantine, *et al*, 1961) Thirty-four societies were later added to complete a standard cross-cultural sample frequently used to test hypotheses at the Laboratory of Human Development, and for

---

8 For a fuller discussion of the Files, see Moore, ed., 1961.

which numerous ratings on other subjects are available. A final eight societies were deliberately chosen at one point to increase geographical coverage and to add a few "complex" societies, which appeared to be few in number.

A rating sheet was then devised. This sheet divided deliberate instruction into three categories, for theoretical reasons which will later be evident. The divisions are as follows:

Type I: deliberate instruction by *kin*, with or without change of residence.

Type II: deliberate instruction by *non-kin*, *without* change of residence required.

Type III: deliberate instruction by *non-kin*, *with* change of residence required.

An example of Type I instruction is the Papago case previously quoted; of Type II, the Somali example, or our own schools; of Type III, the practice of the Mende of Sierra Leone, who traditionally required pubescent boys and girls to live and participate in separate "bush schools" for periods up to three or four years in duration. Type III instruction usually (but not always) takes place as a part of, or connected with, initiation ceremonies— of which more later.

The rater (i.e., the present writer) then made for each of the three categories a summary rating which combined his judgment of whether or not deliberate instruction in cultural beliefs and norms was practiced and his judgment as to its universality for all children of at least one sex. If he was doubtful about either criterion, his summary judgment was marked as "inferred." The rater also judged whether change of residence was required to receive the instruction, and whether the instruction was provided by kin or non-kin. This second group of decisions obviously led to the placement of any recorded instruction in one of the three types; if the rater was doubtful about either of them, the summary judgment was again marked as "inferred." Later examination of the ratings showed that there were no important differences in the distribution of the "inferred" and the "stated" cases; they have therefore been combined in the analyses which follow. (They are discriminated in the Appendix list of ratings, however.) Thus, with respect to deliberate instruction of each of the three types, there are three possible ratings: Present, Absent, and Not Ascertainable.

It was possible to make ratings (i.e., Present or Absent) for at least one type of instruction for 96 of the 111 societies in the original sample. Specifically, 79 Present or Absent ratings were made for Type I, of which 47 were of instruction present; 90 ratings were made for Type II, of which 42 were of instruction present; 81 ratings were made for Type III, of which 27 were of instruction present.

The present study deals almost exclusively with Type II, deliberate instruction by non-kin without change of residence, and Type III, deliberate instruction by non-kin with change of residence required. Type I instruction seems to vary most closely with Type II instruction. However, the scoring of it was intuitively unsatisfactory, and discussion of it has been avoided throughout this paper. A separate study is indicated.

All of the ratings were made by the present writer. While this is not methodologically desirable, financial limitations precluded the hiring of a neutral coder. Most of the ratings were made in ignorance of the scores which the societies had obtained on the various independent variables; in fact, certain of these had not been selected when the ratings were being done. In addition, a reliability check was done on a sample of ten societies. The per cent agreement for Type I was 80 per cent; for Type II, 90 per cent; and 80 per cent for Type III. This level of agreement was judged sufficient for the present introductory effort. If there are errors of judgment in the ratings (and there probably are), they are probably not systematically biased. Random errors "tend usually to prevent a relationship from appearing in the data rather than to create a relationship where one does not exist." (McClelland, 1961:24; see also Ferguson, 1959: Chapter 18) The fact that we have achieved relatively high degrees of significance using our very gross measures provides added weight for the findings.

The geographical distribution of the societies in the final sample of 96 is shown in Table 1. Also shown is the rating for presence and absence of Type II instruction.

TABLE 1

Geographical Distribution of the Sample, and Type II Instruction

	TYPE II INSTRUCTION			
Geographical Area *	PRESENT	ABSENT	NOT ASCERTAINABLE	TOTAL NUMBER OF SOCIETIES
Africa (Sub-Sahara)	1	16	1	18
Circum-Mediterranean	12	1	0	13
East Eurasia	13	6	1	20
Oceania	5	10	1	16
North America	9	6	2	17
South America	2	9	1	12
Totals:	42	48	6	96

* These subdivisions correspond to those in the *World Sample, q.v., infra.*

The 96 societies include representatives of 58 of the 60 culture areas into which Murdock has divided the world in his *World Ethnographic Sample* [9]; only Caucasia and Northwest Europe are unrepresented. Six of the 58 culture areas are represented by three societies each, the rest by one or two.

It is evident from Table 1 that Type II instruction is distinctly *not* a Sub-Saharan trait. Nor does it occur very frequently in South America, although the sample here is small. But it cannot be said that such instruction is a unique characteristic *of* any particular area. Almost all Circum-Mediterranean cultures have it, but so do 65 per cent of the East Eurasian, 58 per cent of the North American, and 31 per cent of the Oceanian. The distribution around the world is sufficiently widespread that the hypothesis of diffusion cannot account satisfactorily for all of it. The situation on the continent of Africa (in the table split into Sub-Saharan and Circum-Mediterranean regions) is revealing. South of the Sahara, only one of seventeen societies has Type II instruction; north of the Sahara, only one of six does not. This, despite the many centuries of intercourse between the two areas.

These considerations lead us to discard the diffusion hypothesis and encourage us to hope that by examining the structures of the societies which do and do not practice instruction, we will gain some notion as to the circumstances which lead to its presence.

THEORETICAL ORIENTATION

The basic theoretical orientation of this study regards the institutions of a culture first as "maintenance systems," through which the culture makes its ecological adjustments; and second as "cultural solutions" to the psychological problems which the maintenance arrangements produce. The maintenance systems of a society are the basic procedures through which its members obtain nourishment, shelter, and protection. These usually require that each member act in a prescribed manner on certain specific occasions, both for his own good and for that of the group. For example, if a man wishes protection from his enemies, he must know who among his fellows is bound to defend him, as well as the culturally-approved forms of argumentation, law, and physical combat. If he wishes food, he must follow the customary techniques by which it is produced, distributed, and consumed.

But the maintenance systems of a society also affect its techniques of child training, and thus the processes of socialization which its children experience. Different processes of socialization lead to the pre-eminence of different issues and problems for the growing child, as well as for adults. For example, main-

[9] The *World Sample* provides ratings on approximately 30 variables, such as household structure, form of marriage, type of subsistence economy, degree of political integration, etc., for some 565 societies distributed throughout the world. The *World Sample* is a basic tool of cross-cultural research. It was first published in Murdock, 1957; it is reprinted, with corrections, in Moore, ed., 1961.

tenance arrangements which place a mother, a father, and their children out in the woods, in virtual isolation from other such households (the classic American frontier pattern), have obvious implications for personality development. The over-burdened father and mother will make strong demands on their children to learn to do things for themselves, and to help their parents, as soon as possible; the issues of independence and responsibility will loom large for the children, and presumably will continue to in later life.

Thus, maintenance systems and socialization practices interact to form the society's non-subsistence institutions, or "projective systems" [10]: those customs and beliefs which are *not* directly involved in the satisfaction of basic biological needs, but which often are as obligatory and unquestioned for members of the society as the maintenance practices, since they provide the approved means of satisfying psychological needs. Maintenance systems influence the nature of the projective institutions which a society may have; but the psychological outcomes of the society's child-training also strongly influence the nature of these institutions. Archetypical projective systems are religious beliefs and customs, group ceremonials, ethnotheories of disease, and the like. The basic assumption of this paper is that the various types of deliberate instruction are, at least in certain respects, projective solutions for certain of the psychological needs of the children from societies of different sorts.

The theoretical orientation which has just been presented is a very brief summary of views stated much more explicitly in Whiting and Child (1953), Whiting and Whiting (1960), and Whiting (1961), to which the reader is referred for further clarification. The orientation must be stated in more operational terms to admit of cross-cultural research, however, and it is to this task that we now turn.

The formulation which led to the selection of many of the specific variables used in this study has been called the "status envy hypothesis." (Whiting and Burton, 1961) This is a theory of child development in which the central concept is the child's envy of persons who control resources which the child himself would like to control. The theory postulates that the child practices, in phantasy or play, the role or roles of those persons who control the resources (such as food, freedom from pain, warmth, and affection). The covert practice of the envied role provides the basis for the otherwise mysterious process of identification. When the child has matured sufficiently, and has been practicing a role ultimately open to him, he is able to enter it and perform up to cultural expectations relatively quickly.

The general theoretical orientation regarding maintenance and projective systems, and the status envy hypothesis, are brought together when we realize that different maintenance systems provide vastly different household

[10] The reader will note that this usage of the term "projective" does not completely parallel its more customary usages in psychology and education. See the explanation of this use in Whiting and Child, 1953: Chapter 6, and Whiting, 1961:356.

personnel, from the point of view of the child, with whom to interact and identify. The situation in which the infant lives and sleeps exclusively with his mother in a hut all of their own contrasts strikingly with the situation in which the infant is raised as a co-inhabitant of a house with numerous grandparents, parents, uncles, aunts, and siblings. In the first instance, the mother is the controller of virtually all resources desired by the child; in the second, numerous persons mediate them and are available as objects for identification. Thus, different maintenance systems provide different constellations of "significant others" in the life of the child; these varied patterns lead to emphasis upon different psychological issues in the lives of both children and adults. These issues will be "solved," we predict, in characteristically different ways by societies with characteristically different maintenance systems. The various forms of deliberate instruction are one of the classes of solutions which societies may employ.

The status envy hypothesis, and the various empirical studies relating to it, have been discussed at length by its originator in a number of recent or forthcoming publications: Whiting (1960a), Whiting and Burton (1961), Whiting (1961), and especially Whiting, Fischer, *et al* (forthcoming). The theory places great, although not exclusive, emphasis on "early learning," suggesting that the identifications formed by the infant in his natal household have a profound influence on his later psychological development.

There are two empirical studies which also influenced the direction of this research. The first is a graduate seminar report (Constantine, *et al*, 1961) which showed, for a sample of 69 societies, a high correlation between the degree of political integration of a society and the presence and absence of what was called "religious education" (essentially, Type II instruction). This finding was replicated by the present author in an earlier paper (Herzog, 1961), and in Table 2 is reproduced using the enlarged sample and revised definitions of the present study.

A similarly strong relationship exists between Type II instruction and Mur-

TABLE 2

Political Integration and Type II Instruction

POLITICAL INTEGRATION *	INSTRUCTION		
	PRESENT	ABSENT	
States over 100,000 in population (S)	17	5	
States 1500–100,000 in population (L,M)	11	14	$\chi^2 = 14.16$
Dependent societies and peace groups (D,P)	2	4	(d.f.$=3$)
Autonomous communities under 1500 population and absence of political integration (A,O)	9	25	
			$p < .005$

* Ratings of political integration are taken from Column 15 of the *World Sample*. See Appendix: Code E.

dock's measures of social stratification (Column 14); socially stratified societies tend to have instruction, while classless societies do not.

These are not startling conclusions, although they had not been previously documented. Table 2 is, as one frank colleague remarked, merely a "statistical verification of things we already know intuitively." The really interesting question remains both unasked and unanswered: what are the *reasons* for the strong correlation between instruction and cultural complexity? This paper provides some possible answers.

The second study to which this research is closely related is that of Bailyn (1960). Bailyn, a specialist in American history, was interested in tracing the historical origins of universal public elementary education in the United States. His examination of the social history of England and the American colonies during the period when the public schools (i.e., Type II institutions) were beginning, led him to conclude that the most important cause of their establishment was change in the composition of, and functions discharged by, the household. "The family group familiar to the early colonists" in England, he says, "was a patrilineal group of extended kinship gathered into a single household. . . . It was these patriarchal communities that shouldered most of the burden of education." (1960:15-16) In the colonies, however, these traditional arrangements proved untenable. The prestige of the parents was diminished in the hostile and unfamiliar environment; the availability of free land encouraged youths to strike out on their own and to resist the teachings and advice of their parents. The nuclear household became the predominant household form of the society.

As early as 1640, Bailyn records, it was realized that this new form of household was "failing in its more obvious educational functions." (26) "The fear of brutish decline" affected colonists in all areas of America; their response to it, especially in New England, was "a rapid enhancement of the role of formal schooling." (27) What the family was no longer able to provide, a revitalized public teaching institution was given to do.

Bailyn's interpretation of the American experience is well-documented and persuasive. It seems reasonable that societies living in large family groups which include several mature generations will be able to use the personnel of the household to instruct their young, while societies with nuclear households might find this difficult and resort, when possible, to institutionalized instruction outside the home.[11] This proposition is relatively easy to test by cross-cultural methods and is the first hypothesis explored in the following section.

RESULTS

The Bailyn hypothesis specifies that societies with households with numerous adults do *not* have Type II instruction, and that societies with households with two or less adults *do* have instruction. The World Sample

[11] It should be emphasized, in fairness to Bailyn, that this formulation of the generalization is ours, and not his. It does appear to accord with his thinking, however.

provides us with a workable estimate of household composition for the cultures in our sample. Murdock's categories (Column 7) can be conveniently grouped for our purposes into four major household types [12]:

extended households (Murdock's *s*, *e*, and *l*), in which three or more adults, customarily belonging to two or more generations of the same family, live under the same roof along with their children;

nuclear households (Murdock's *n*), in which a man and his wife customarily live in the same house, with their children;

polygynous households (Murdock's *p* and *q*), in which a polygynously married man and his two or more wives customarily live in the same house, with their children;

mother-child households (Murdock's *m*), in which a mother and her children occupy a house all their own, the father having his own separate house or residing in a communal men's house.

The results of the test of the association between these variables are shown in Table 3.

TABLE 3

Household Type and Type II Instruction

HOUSEHOLD TYPE	INSTRUCTION		
	PRESENT	ABSENT	
Extended	20	8	$\chi^2 = 13.52$
Nuclear	11	11	
Polygynous	5	7	$p < .005$
Mother-child	6	21	

The hypothesis is *not confirmed*. In fact, its opposite is supported, and at a high level of significance. The *number* of people in the household seems directly, rather than inversely, related to the presence of instruction outside of it.

It is conceivable that household structure and political integration are intercorrelated, and that we have discovered nothing new in the association shown in Table 3. This possibility is explored in Table 4.

Putting the two maintenance system variables together shows clearly that they are *not* redundant. Only *mother-child* societies are relatively unaffected by political complexity: no matter how complex they may be, they rarely

[12] Communal household societies are ignored in this instance. Only one, the Siriono, who have neither Type II nor Type III instruction, occurs in the present sample.

TABLE 4

Political Integration, Household Type, and Type II Instruction

POLITICAL INTEGRATION	HOUSEHOLD TYPE	INSTRUCTION	
		PRESENT	ABSENT
High (S, L, M)	Extended	13	3
	Nuclear	9	1
	Polygynous	3	2
	Mother-child	3	13
Low (D, P, A, O)	Extended	6	5
	Nuclear	1	10
	Polygynous	2	5
	Mother-child	2	8

have Type II instruction.[13] On the other hand, societies with *nuclear* households are greatly affected by political complexity, and this difference is significant beyond the .002 level, by Fisher's Exact Test. *Extended* and *polygynous* household societies are moderately affected by political integration, but the differences are not significant. A general conclusion which we can draw from this data is that with respect to Type II instruction, political integration affects the household groups dissimilarly.

Though Bailyn is borne out in his feeling that household composition is related to Type II instruction, the specific association which he appears to assert is not a common one, cross-culturally. A second look at his English and American data seems called for.

Bailyn's conclusion that the nuclearization of the family in America was associated with a "veritable frenzy" of interest in schools (28) is consonant with the cross-cultural evidence; in fact, the complex nuclear household colonies are exactly the type of society *most* likely to have such a child-training institution, according to Table 4.[14] The public elementary school is, of course, only one of the several forms which such instruction may take; in our nine complex-nuclear societies with instruction, the most frequent form which such teaching assumes is the church-school. Actually, Bailyn notes that

[13] They have Type III instruction when they are complex, however, and tend not to when they are simple, as shown in Table 5, *infra*. This relationship approaches, but does not quite reach, statistical significance (Fisher's Exact Test).

[14] The societies in this group are the Amhara, Balinese, Burmese, Bulgar, Lebanese, Malays, Makassarese, modern New Englanders, and Tuareg. The only complex, nuclear household society lacking Type II instruction is the Trobrianders. The Trobrianders are nominally nuclear; but many women are married polygynously to the chiefs and live in essentially mother-child households. Perhaps then, they are not genuine exceptions to the general association.

the motive of much early American schooling was religious, indeed sectarian; he declares that what gave education "its greatest importance and its characteristic form was its position in the emerging pattern of American denominationalism." (1960:39)

However, Bailyn's assertions about the lack of instruction in extended-household England are not consonant with the cross-cultural findings. Certainly the England of Elizabethan times was a complex "state"; certainly the household, as Bailyn describes it, was "extended." We would expect some sort of Type II instruction to have existed. And apparently a variety of Type II instruction did exist, although Bailyn (rightly, for his purposes) chooses to de-emphasize its importance in the overall socialization of the child. The church, he says, played "a role as formal educator exercised through institutions of pedagogy which it supported and staffed." (18) Bailyn is not explicit as to the nature and distribution of these institutions, but Curtis (1948), one of the sources upon whom Bailyn relies, states:

It is very difficult to assess the provision of primary education. . . . No systematic study . . . has yet been made, and such a research would be a stupendous task. However, there are clear indications that primary education was more widespread than was formerly believed. . . . We know that the Church included the instruction of the young as one of the duties of the incumbent of the parish and that the "school" was frequently held on the church porch or in a room above the porch. How far this instruction went beyond the teaching of religion and morals depended upon the individual clergyman. (pp. 101, 104)

There also seems to have been numerous schools preparing boys for the grammar schools; much of the curriculum of these was religious.

Clearly, this church-sponsored teaching meets the definition of Type II instruction which we originally proposed for our cross-cultural rating system. It would thus conform to the trend delineated in the sample. Probably the Bailyn hypothesis should be reformulated to refer only to the *relative* importance of Type II instruction in extended, and in complex-nuclear, societies. Perhaps the "tone" of Type II education is different in nuclear and extended households, and it is this difference which Bailyn has discovered. We shall return to this point some pages forward, but we shall not be able fully to clear it up; additional research is necessary.

Thus far, we have dealt only with Type II instruction: instruction by non-kin without change of residence. Certain types of societies characteristically do not employ this sort of child-training: the mother-child group stands out. Let us now take a look at these aberrant societies. What kind of instructional procedures, if any, do they use?

A consideration of the place of Type III instruction—instruction by non-kin with change of residence required—is obviously called for. Table 5 reports the relationship among political integration, household type, and Types II and III instruction.

Table 5 is a complicated table, in which several statistically significant relationships exist. The most important, however, is the association among the

TABLE 5

Political Integration, Household Type, and Types II and III Instruction

POLITICAL INTEGRATION	HOUSEHOLD TYPE	INSTRUCTION			
		NEITHER PRESENT	TYPE II ONLY	TYPE III ONLY	BOTH PRESENT
High (S, L, M)	Extended	3	12	1	1
	Nuclear	1	7	0	2
	Polygynous	2	2	0	1
	Mother-child	4	1	9	2
Low (D, P, A, O)	Extended	5	5	0	1
	Nuclear	11	1	1	0
	Polygynous	4	0	3	2
	Mother-child	6	0	2	2

TABLE 6

Political Integration, Household Type, and Types II and III Instruction

POLITICAL INTEGRATION	HOUSEHOLD TYPE	INSTRUCTION		
		TYPE II ONLY	TYPE III ONLY	
High	Extended and Nuclear	19	1	p<.002 (Fisher's)
	Polygynous and Mother-child	3	9	
Low	Extended and Nuclear	6	1	p=.008 (Fisher's)
	Polygynous and Mother-child	0	5	
All	Extended and Nuclear	25	2	$\chi^2=22.19$ p<.001
	Polygynous and Mother-child	3	14	

various forms of household and the two types of instruction. Overwhelmingly, when *some* form of instruction is offered, Type II is employed by extended and nuclear societies, and Type III is favored by mother-child societies and, to a lesser extent, polygynous household societies. This generalization holds under conditions of both high and low political integration. Table 6 displays the relevant figures from the bigger table. (Those societies in which *both* Types II and III occur have been left out of Table 6, although the overall relationship is almost as strong [significant at the .005 level] when they are included as contradicting the general hypothesis.)

Table 5 also shows that mother-child and polygynous societies are somewhat more likely to employ both types of instruction than are extended and nuclear societies, *if* instruction is employed at all. This relationship, which does not quite reach the .05 level of significance, is shown in Table 7.

TABLE 7

Household Type and Types II and III Instruction

| | INSTRUCTION | | |
HOUSEHOLD TYPE	TYPE II OR III	BOTH PRESENT	
Extended and Nuclear	27	4	$\chi^2 = 3.35$
Polygynous and Mother-child	17	7	$p > .05$

A third interesting relationship is that between political integration and the presence and absence of *any* kind of instruction. As Table 8 shows, politically complex societies tend to have instruction, no matter what form of household is typical of them; simple societies do not.[15]

Furthermore, the mother-child-polygynous group is as likely to have *some* sort of instruction as the extended-nuclear. (See Table 9)

There are, then, four relatively clearcut conclusions to be drawn from inspection of the relations among household structure, political complexity, and types of instruction:

1. Politically complex societies, no matter their household type, tend to

[15] The form of presentation of Table 8 disguises certain significant differences between extended and nuclear household societies of low political complexity. These have already been pointed out in the discussion following Table 4 and will be re-examined in the Interpretation.

use deliberate instruction; politically simple societies get along without it.

2. When some form of instruction is offered, Type II is employed by extended and nuclear societies, and Type III is employed by mother-child societies. Polygynous societies are intermediate.

TABLE 8

Political Integration, Household Type, and Instruction

POLITICAL INTEGRATION	HOUSEHOLD TYPE	INSTRUCTION		
		NONE	SOME (II, III, OR BOTH)	
High	Extended and Nuclear	4	23	N.S.
	Polygynous and Mother-child	6	15	
Low	Extended and Nuclear	16	8	N.S.
	Polygynous and Mother-child	10	9	
All	High	10	38	$\chi^2 = 14.90$
	Low	26	17	$p < .001$

TABLE 9

Household Type and Instruction

HOUSEHOLD TYPE	INSTRUCTION		
	NONE	SOME	
Extended and Nuclear	20	31	
Polygynous and Mother-child	16	24	N.S.

3. Mother-child and polygynous societies are somewhat more likely than nuclear and extended to employ concurrently both Type II and Type III instruction.
4. With regard to Type II instruction, societies with different household types are affected dissimilarly by political integration.

Other significant relationships exist in the data of Table 5: some of these will be discussed in the next section. But the preceding are our most straightforward results. They raise, for this writer, more vital questions than they answer. Why do complex societies require some sort of instruction? Why is household structure so strongly associated with the type of "education" employed by a society? Is it possible that Type II instruction "solves" a particular psychological problem for the children who experience it, and Type III another? If so, how do societies with neither type of instruction (notably, the simple mother-child and nuclear ones) manage to cope with these psychological issues?

Given the present data, these are questions which can only be answered by interpretation and by citing relevant studies by other investigators. Nonetheless, some possible answers will be put forward in the following pages, with the full knowledge that they are highly speculative and that much additional research is called for.

INTERPRETATION

The question regarding the association between political complexity and instruction initially seems simple to answer. Complex societies require instruction in beliefs and norms to prevent their dissolution into Durkheim's "incoherent multitude of little fragments," or the "incipient savagery" (Bailyn, 1960:28) which the American colonists feared.

Parsons, in a sophisticated analysis of the functions of the school class in American society (1959), makes a similar point. One of the main functions which he lists is the "internalization of a level of societal values and norms that is a step higher than those [the child] can learn in his family alone." (309) This is not the only "outcome" of instruction which Parsons discusses, but it is a central one. The major "cultural" function of instruction, in Parsons' view, is the attainment of consensus on "values and norms."

The deficiency of this argument is that it converts a well-known correlation into an assertion of causality. All that we really know is that complexity and instruction are usually coincidental. Could we not as well argue that instruction "causes" complexity?

This last notion is unfamiliar but not difficult to present plausibly. Let us suppose that certain maintenance systems predispose a society to employ a version of deliberate instruction. In this event, two further developments are implied. First, the beliefs, norms, and "discoveries" of the society will be communicated more exactly and efficiently to younger generations than if less specific techniques were used. Second, instructional specialists may develop who are particularly adept at the communication of beliefs and norms. Under these circumstances, the "cultural heritage" of a society will grow, a greater command over the environment will ensue, and political and social development will at least become more probable.

It may be objected that this alternate formulation is undemonstrable. But we must insist that the complexity-leads-to-instruction argument is equally undemonstrable, or at least undemonstrated. If deliberate instruction is necessary for cultural continuity in complex societies, how do the ten complex societies without deliberate instruction (in Table 5) hang together? Why do as many as seventeen of the simple societies instruct their children, if "complexity" is the determining variable?

It might be argued also that instruction in *technical* knowledge might lead to the development of sociocultural complexity, but that instruction in beliefs and norms could hardly do so. This argument is not convincing. Far more basic for the long-range development of a culture than bits and pieces of technical knowledge is the attainment and communication of an appropriate "world view," or cosmology, from which specific "discoveries" can be generated and understood. The technological revolution of the Western world is traceable not to any specific technical or scientific "inventions," but to the development of scientific philosophy and method, which, in turn, led to specific advances in technology.

We are deliberately stating the case for the instruction-produces-complexity hypothesis in an extreme manner. We are trying to establish it as a reasonable alternative to the argument more frequently heard. We acknowledge that neither view can be regarded as "correct." In order to demonstrate the validity of one or the other, some third factor must be shown regularly to intervene between complexity and instruction. If such a factor could be found, the direction of the relationship between complexity and instruction might be grasped.

We furthermore agree that cultural complexity is "caused" by many factors in addition to, and probably more important than, instruction. We are quite unable to refute (and uninterested in doing so) those theories which trace cultural development to ecological adaptation (Steward, 1955); to the need, stemming from conquest or cultural amalgamation, for the transmission of an arcane "great tradition" (Redfield, 1953); to basic psychological needs, such as that for "achievement" (McClelland, 1961); or even to abstract cyclic processes (Toynbee, 1947). None of these (except perhaps the last) is antithetical to the point of view we wish to present.

We will try to show that the psychological resultants of child-rearing in societies with certain types of households predispose these societies, no matter their complexity, to employ deliberate instruction. Those societies which employ instruction to "solve" the psychological problems of their children have a head start, at least, on the road toward sociocultural complexity, and it is therefore not surprising to find that the majority of them are, indeed, complex.

To establish the reasonableness of this position, we shall try to do two things: 1) demonstrate that household structure affects patterns of child-training and/or the psychological development of the child; 2) show a relationship between these psychological issues and the use by cultures of the several forms of deliberate instruction.

Let us first examine the possible psychological needs of children in mother-child cultures. The characteristic instruction in such societies is Type III. Furthermore, such instruction is usually offered as a part of male or female initiation ceremonies.[16] Specifically, fifteen of the mother-child societies have Type III instruction, or both Type II and Type III instruction; in thirteen of them (Azande, Fang, Gusii, Hausa, Kikuyu, Lovedu, Moundu, Mende, Mossi, Thonga, Wolof, Yao, Yokuts), the instruction is provided in the course of male initiation ceremonies, or in both male and female initiation ceremonies. In one of them (Bemba) the instruction is provided only in a girls' initiation rite; and in the case of the Aztecs, it is provided in a form parallel to male rites and very similar to a Western boarding school. One can also say, after reading the descriptions of these rites, that in most cases the specifically instructional elements are only very minor parts of the ceremonies.

Of the twelve mother-child societies without Type III instruction, six (Ainu, Callinago, Nuer, Tallensi, Tanala, Tiv) have initiation ceremonies entirely lacking elements of instruction, as we have defined it; one (Somali) has both a male initiation ceremony and Type II instruction at another time and place; three (Ashanti, Chukchee, and Ganda) have no initiation ceremonies of any sort; and two (Lolo and Rajput) cannot be rated as to presence or absence of initiation rites, due to inadequate information. In other words, Type III instruction implies the presence of male or female rites, but rites need not always include Type III instruction.

The most common features of initiation ceremonies are seclusion from the opposite sex (usually requiring temporary change of residence to an initiation camp or "bush school"); ritual recognition of sexual identity and maturity; and the infliction of physical pain by the initiators (usually in the form of genital operations).

The function of male rites and analogous institutions has been discussed at length in Whiting, Kluckhohn, and Anthony (1958), Whiting and Burton (1961), and Whiting, Fischer, et al (in preparation). Whiting's view is that the rites are collective efforts to resolve the characteristic psychological problem of males in mother-child societies: sexual identity. Whiting notes that such ceremonies occur almost invariantly in societies in which 1) mother and

---

[16] Information about initiation ceremonies is taken from unpublished data at the Laboratory of Human Development.

child are each other's chief companions for the first two or three years of the child's life and, in particular, sleep together to the exclusion of the father, who sleeps in his own hut or in a communal men's hut; 2) the child grows up in a community controlled by his father's male relatives (patrilocal residence). Such conditions are quite characteristic of the fifteen mother-child household societies with Type III instruction: all but the Yokuts have mother-child sleeping (concerning the Aztecs, sleeping data are not available), and all are patrilocal except the Bemba (married couples live near the husband's mother's brother) and the Yao (matrilocal).[17]

Whiting's thesis, derived from the status envy formulation, is that in such societies the mother is virtually sole mediator of resources for her infant. Under such circumstances, the child's primary identification is made with her, or at least with the female role. But as boys, especially, grow up they learn that men also control resources significant to them, and that increasingly they themselves will be expected to "act like men." This later learning conflicts with their original identification; the initiation rite is an attempt to erase the primary identification and to substitute for it a more appropriate sex-role choice. The rites are, essentially, a period of concentrated manipulation of resources by the men, such that the boys come to envy and to identify with them.

If the status envy interpretation of the function of male initiation ceremonies is correct, we should not be surprised that their instruction components are often minimal or nonexistent. There are much more dramatic techniques available, such as circumcision and tests of endurance, through which to accomplish the "brain-washing." Yet certain societies demonstrate that instructional aspects are not necessarily minor. In the *Poro* (boys') and *Sande* (girls') ceremonies of the Mende, both technical and "regulatory" instruction were prominent. In the *telpuchcalli* schools of the Aztecs, boys of fifteen and older received instruction in religion and warfare. But both these examples are atypical.

Our main point—that mother-child household, patrilocal societies have initiation ceremonies and Type III instruction in order to cope with sex identity problems—is apparently threatened when we note that twelve societies having *other* household types also have Type III instruction. But it is significant that five of them, despite their household structure, have both mother-child sleeping and patrilocal residence (Aranda, Bulgarians, Gond, Riff, and Wogeo); probably the Murngin should also be included. Two of the others (Ojibwa and Pavasupai) have only female rites, much like the Bemba; and concerning two (Kung and Malay) sleeping arrangement data are not available. Thus, only the Thai and Papago rank as genuine exceptions.

[17] Data regarding sleeping arrangements are taken from unpublished materials at the Laboratory of Human Development. Data regarding marital residence are taken from Column 8 of the *World Sample*.

There are also five mother-child societies which have neither male initiation ceremonies nor Type III instruction. Concerning the Lolo, very little information of any sort is available; the judgment regarding Type III instruction is very tentative. Another, the Chukchee, is one of the mother-child sleeping, matri-biased societies which Munroe (1961) has shown rarely have initiation ceremonies. The Ashanti, Ganda, and Rajput are troublesome exceptions; but each has a pattern of change of residence for young boys, at various ages, which permanently takes the boy out of the household of his mother and thus may serve as a functional equivalent of an initiation ceremony and/or Type III instruction.

Thus, most of our "bush and boarding schools" (Type III instruction) occur in mother-child household societies in which the residence pattern is patrilocal. It seems reasonable, drawing on our own evidence and that of the various Whiting papers, to conclude that their major function is that of resolving the cross-sex identity problems of the adolescents who participate in them.[18]

We have already discussed six of the polygynous household societies with Type III instruction (Aranda, Havasupai, Murngin, Ojibwa, Riff, and Wogeo) from the standpoint of their similarity and dissimilarity to mother-child societies. The small number of polygynous societies in the sample (14) and their widespread distribution throughout the cells of Table 5, make it very difficult to demonstrate the validity of any assertion which might be offered about them. In general, polygynous societies with a low degree of political integration seem to have many of the characteristics of mother-child societies and to employ Type III instruction; some of those with a high degree of integration have the attributes of nuclear or extended household societies, and Type II instruction. Beyond this inadequate statement we do not wish to go at present. Further study of the child-training customs of these fourteen societies is clearly needed.

In focusing attention on extended and nuclear households, and the type of instruction which they employ, we are opening up new territory. Rarely has "education" been regarded as a "projective institution." What possible psychological—as opposed to cultural, vocational, and allocational—needs can "schooling" possibly serve? Let us see if we can answer this question first with respect to extended households.

In the 1959 paper previously cited, Parsons suggests that "the system of formal education is the child's first major step out of primary involvement in his family of orientation." (300) In the classroom, the child becomes subject to "universalistic expectations," (303) increasingly similar to those which he will experience as an adult, and which contrast with the "particularistic" (303) treatment he experiences from his parents, especially his mother. The

---

[18] Whether or not they actually accomplish their aim, of course, is another question currently under study by members of the staff of the Laboratory of Human Development.

main goal toward which the school child works, and with respect to which he is judged, is "achievement," or "relative excellence in living up to the expectations imposed by the teacher as an agent of the adult society." (304) To the extent that the child is successful in replacing the personalized values and ideals of his home with the values and ideals of the larger community and school, he is judged "good."

Parsons goes on to say that the child learns achievement motivation by means of a "process of identification with the teacher," (306) a process through which the teacher's (society's) goals become the child's. Children differ, however, with regard to their ability to identify with the teacher and thus to achieve. They differ largely in the degree to which they have become independent of their parents. The "independent" child has identified with his parents in learning things to please them; making the switch to the teacher, *in loco parentis*, is not a difficult feat. The "dependent" child, however, has identified with the "child-role" (307) in his household of orientation and in school aligns himself not with the teacher but with his peer group. He thus achieves a low degree of mastery over the universalistic role relationships of his society and is sorted by the machinery of the school into the less demanding curricula and walks of life.

What Parsons seems to be saying, in our terminology, is that the characteristic psychological problem of most American children is that of relative mastery of the behavior which will be appropriate for them as adults. "Sex role" has already been "psychologically stamped in" (300) by the time children reach school; what remains problematic is the issue of *growing up*. Children who have identified with the "child-role" may never grow up, psychologically.

Let us review now what is known about child training in extended households, especially with relation to its possible import for independence-dependence. Almost by definition, in such households one or several adults are constantly available to tend the child and to minister to his needs. By and large, husband and wife occupy the same house and eat and sleep together. But cross-cultural research has revealed certain specific socialization practices characteristic of extended households. Whiting (1961) found that societies of this type treat their infants significantly more indulgently than either nuclear or mother-child societies. Whiting (1959) had earlier reported that the same societies wean their infants and begin independence training relatively late. McClelland (1961) adds that societies with extended and nuclear households tend to have more achievement imagery in folktales than polygynous and mother-child societies, and suggests that children in them receive more "emphasis on independent achievement" (374) than children in societies with low n Achievement scores. Also, Whiting (1959) found that aggression training (i.e., training for impulse control) is significantly stricter in extended households than in the other types. Finally, "transition anxiety"—anxiety occurring in the child during the shift of status from infant to child—is significantly lower in extended households than in nuclear (Whiting, Chasdi, *et al.*, in press), as we might have expected from the foregoing.

Under such circumstances, we would *not* expect problems of cross-sex identification to arise. The child interacts with both men and women and can observe, in particular, that his father controls numerous resources, directly or through his mother, that the child himself desires. The initial identification of the child will be with "parent" or "adult," not merely with "mother" or "woman."

On the other hand, the role of the infant might seem highly desirable to the growing child, once infancy is left behind. The older he gets, the more disabilities he suffers: less indulgent care, weaning, pressure to act on his own, demands that he control his aggressive impulses. If a younger brother or sister arrives, he can observe the latter enjoying all the prerogatives he himself used to enjoy. Status envy, we would predict, is directed toward this earlier state; it is as inappropriate a basis for learning adult role behavior as cross-sex identification.

However, the problem of altering this orientation does not seem so complex. The child's primary identification in infancy is with the adult role; the troublesome circumstances leading to the inappropriate age choice occur later, and can be affected by methods less extreme than those of the mother-child societies. We submit that one of the techniques employed by extended household societies to deal with this psychological problem is Type II instruction.

Schooling says to the extended household child, in a sense, "Your dreams of returning to infancy are nonsense. We are going to show you the way the world really operates, and you had better do as we say." It proceeds to do so by taking the child out of his indulgent household for a portion of the day and placing him in the hands of a task-oriented, relatively impersonal teacher. It is striking that most of the teachers in Type II instruction are men. Some twenty extended household societies have a total of 29 separate instances of Type II education; 21 of the 29 instances involve only male teachers. The function of these teachers, according to the status envy hypothesis, is to manipulate resources, such as freedom from pain, social prestige, and freedom of mobility, so that the child's fixation of his infancy is broken and an awareness of the power and privileges of adults, especially men, is produced.

Impressionistically at least, Type II instruction in extended household societies has a very different flavor from such instruction in nuclear societies. "Rote learning" is emphasized; the status differential between teacher and pupil is relatively larger; a variety of levels of achievement is not recognized, as a rule, all students striving to meet the same tradition-decreed goals.[19]

[19] These comments are admittedly subjective. Perhaps some indication of their validity may be obtained from the following passages, describing Type II instruction in extended household societies:

"Generally speaking, education is a private affair and has been so considered from the

This is exactly what we would expect to find if, as Parsons indicates, "the most important single predispositional factor with which the child enters the school is his level of *independence*." (300) If he is independent, he is able to "achieve"; if he is dependent, as should be most products of extended households, individual initiative along adult-approved lines will be slight and the child will depend either on the teacher for detailed instructions, or upon his peers who will join with him in resisting the efforts of the teacher to make them into adults.

Earlier, we suggested that Type II instruction is only *one* of the techniques by which extended household societies deal with their problem of dependence. Nerlove (1962) has recently shown that such societies also employ a type of initiation ceremony in dealing with this problem. Using a method similar to content analysis,[20] she found in a sample of 49 North and South American tribes that extended (and polygynous) societies hold initiations in which the theme is the breaking away of the adolescent boy from his household of origin and in which the boy acquires in turn a mystical guardian spirit. Furthermore, such rites are usually undertaken singly, rather than in groups as in mother-child societies; this is consonant with our finding that only three of 28 extended household societies have Type III instruction, which would be difficult to provide if the boy is at the same time to be isolated. Mother-child societies, Nerlove found, stress the recognition of gender identity, the acquisition of a tribal or ancestral totem, and the incorporation of boys in the male group, in their initiation ceremonies. The correspondence between the basic themes and techniques of the ceremonies of both groups, and the psychological problems which we have maintained are characteristic of the groups, is quite striking.

Indirect evidence that Type II instruction is particularly "needed" by extended household societies is provided in Table 10. Among all societies with a low degree of political integration, only those with extended households

---

first. Every village has its little room, always in a private house, where the boys sit on the floor with their large-print books of Chinese characters before them, and, as they sway back and forth with half-shut eyes, they drone out the sounds of the ideographs, not in unison, but each for himself." Homer B. Hulbert: *The Passing of Korea*. N.Y.: Doubleday, Page & Co., 1906. (In HRAF.)

"Unless the parents are well-to-do and can employ a private tutor or guardian, their boys are sent to the village mosque schools, or to the house of some local citizen who has a private school. An enterprising teacher, who is almost always an attendant at a mosque and leads the prayers there, thus forms a fair-sized school. It is open to boys only. . . . I have never ceased wondering how fifty to sixty boys from five to fifteen, could learn their lessons. . . . Early attendance at the school is encouraged and the boy who has taken his lesson from his teacher immediately after the morning prayer, is the first to get off from class, sometimes before noonday prayer." 'Ali Shah Sirdar Ikbal: *Eastward to Persia*. London: Wright and Brown, 1930. (In HRAF.)

[20] This "content analysis" technique could also be applied to the material taught in Types II and III instruction. Unfortunately, this was not possible for the present paper. The author is indebted to Roy G. D'Andrade for this suggestion.

TABLE 10

Household Type and Type II Instruction *

	INSTRUCTION	
HOUSEHOLD TYPE	TYPE II PRESENT	NO INSTRUCTION PRESENT
Extended	6	5
Nuclear	1	11

p=.024
(Fisher's Exact Test)

* Societies of Low Political Integration.

tend to employ Type II instruction at least as often as they employ no instruction at all. It would be superfluous to compare extended households with mother-child or polygynous in this respect, but the comparison between extended and nuclear is of interest.

Once again, the societies which are apparent exceptions to the general rule are of interest. Among the politically simple societies, five extended household societies do not have instruction. Three of them employ change of residence techniques which seem to serve as substitutes: the Tlingit believe that "if a boy were brought up at home where he is apt to be petted and spoiled more than is good for him, he would not make a strong man," [21] so they send him at adolescence to his uncle's house; the Lepcha send some, but far from all, boys to the lamaseries for a period; and the Mundurucu formerly required boys of a young age to remain for two years in virtual confinement in the men's house. Araucanian parents and grandparents are among the most enthusiastic devotees of Type I instruction in the sample; also, the boy was traditionally sent to visit the cacique on set occasions to demonstrate his skill in etiquette and rhetoric. Only the Tupinamba seem to have employed no readily observable alternative to Type II instruction in this group.

Among the extended household societies of high political integration, four do not have Type II instruction. The Gond have already been discussed: while their household structure is extended, their sleeping arrangements and residence rules are similar to those of societies employing Type III instruction, which, in fact, they do also. The Samoans have elaborate youth organizations, one each for the boys and girls, which serve definite socialization, if not instructional, purposes. The Yoruba data on child-training are meager, and the rating for Type II instruction is actually "Not Ascertainable," not "Absent." Only the Lau Fijians seem genuine exceptions in this group.

These various items at least tend to support the view that the basic psycho-

[21] Florence Shotridge: "The Life of a Chilkat Indian Girl," *The Museum Journal*, Vol. 4. Philadelphia: The University Museum, 1913. P. 101. (In HRAF.)

logical issue of extended household societies is dependency, or "growing up," and that Type II instruction is one means by which this problem is handled. More conclusive evidence is not available.

The final group of societies is the nuclear. We have seen that these societies overwhelmingly employ Type II instruction when they are politically complex, and just as overwhelmingly do not employ it when they are simple. Why should this be?

Let us first review what is known about child-training in nuclear households. In the first place, mother and father normally sleep and eat together; according to our previous formulations, this should lead to an appropriate, or at least to a not *in*appropriate, primary identification by the child. Furthermore, nuclear household societies wean their infants earlier than societies of all other types, begin independence training at a significantly younger age, and are relatively lenient in permitting children to display aggressive behavior. (Whiting, 1959) The "transition anxiety" of their children, perhaps as a consequence, is significantly higher than that of extended household children. (Whiting, Chasdi, *et al.*, in press) They stand relatively high in *n* Achievement scores, as reported earlier (McClelland, 1961); with respect to infant indulgence they are intermediate. (Whiting, 1961)

Under these conditions, we predict that adulthood is the envied role for the child. The adults of both sexes relatively early give and withhold resources which the child wishes, and consume them in his presence. The child does not bask in an idyllic childhood, nor has he a debilitating sexual identity problem with which to contend. Rather, his goal is to become an adult as quickly as possible and to gain for himself the advantages of this status. But society is constantly putting obstacles in his way, which he must progressively surmount if he is ever to be considered an adult. The characteristic problem of the nuclear boy and girl is, in a word, *achievement*.

Parsons suggests that in the United States the organizing principle of the classroom is achievement. The successful student is the one who identifies with his teacher as he has previously identified with his parents. In other words, a complex nuclear society such as ours "exploits" the natural proclivities of its children by setting before them a series of learning tasks of everincreasing difficulty. The more of them the child accomplishes (i.e., graduates from high school, attends college, and so forth), the more privileges he will eventually enjoy. Clearly, the motivation of the children in a nuclear school is very different from that of the students in an extended household school; probably the difference in "atmosphere" which we earlier discussed may be traced to this contrast.

But we still have not explained the difference between simple and complex nuclear household societies in the use of instruction. On the one hand, it is obvious that "artificial" learning situations are not needed in *any* nuclear societies to the extent that they are in others, since nuclear children presumably have neither sex identity nor "generation" problems to resolve.

Additionally, in a *simple* nuclear society, the boy or girl usually can accompany one or both parents into all social settings, and is probably pressed into economic service as soon as he or she is capable of being useful. Beliefs and norms can be taught by the parents themselves, either in context or during specially set aside intervals. Since these nuclear-raised children are eager to learn all attributes of adulthood as quickly as possible, and since all attributes are readily visible to them, no special Type II institutions are necessary.

This formulation is supported by the data in Table 11, which shows that nuclear societies of low political complexity are significantly less likely than other societies to employ either Type II or Type III instruction. In our basic terminology, they have no projective "need" for it.

TABLE 11

Household Type and Instruction *

| | INSTRUCTION | |
| | TYPES II, III, | |
HOUSEHOLD TYPE	OR BOTH	NONE
All others	15	15
Nuclear	2	11

$\chi^2 = 4.55$
$p < .05$

* Societies of Low Political Integration.

Simple nuclear societies also tend to be less likely to employ Type I instruction—deliberate instruction by kin—than other types of societies. Our measure of Type I instruction is admittedly unsatisfactory, but the tendency shown in Table 12 further emphasizes a surprising fact: nuclear societies of

TABLE 12

Household Type and Type I Instruction *

| | INSTRUCTION (TYPE I) | |
HOUSEHOLD TYPE	PRESENT	ABSENT
All others	10	5
Nuclear	4	7

N.S. (Fisher's Exact Test)

* Societies of Low Political Integration.

low complexity fail to employ the socialization techniques for which they are uniquely fitted.

Why, then, do societies of this type so unanimously employ Type II instruction when they are politically complex? For a possible answer, we shall have to go far afield.

In 1951, Murdock and Whiting suggested that the role of women in the subsistence and ritual activities of a culture might have important implications for child care and personality development. They pointed out that the interactions of mother and child in a society in which women are largely responsible for a demanding field agriculture are likely to be very different, in quantity and quality, from those of mother and child in a society in which the women have few chores to perform beyond housework and in this are assisted by the numerous members of an extended family. They reported a small study which supported these views: in a sample of twenty societies, those in which the women participated minimally in "economic activities" were higher in "initial dependency and indulgence" (33) than those in which the women had a demanding economic role. Unfortunately, the authors do not tell us if the observed differences were statistically significant, and the study was apparently not pursued further.

This item is extremely suggestive, however, in relation to our current problem. Is it possible that the economic role of women in complex societies with nuclear households is less demanding than the economic role of women in simple nuclear societies? If so, may not the increased "initial dependency and indulgence" which the stay-at-home mothers provide be the answer to the riddle?

Although there is no very satisfactory way of obtaining, quickly, measures of initial dependency and indulgence for each of the 21 nuclear household societies in our sample, there is now available a technique for measuring the role of women in the subsistence economy. This was originally devised by Heath (1958); it was later refined by Brown (1961). Involved is a quantification of the ratings in Columns 2, 3, 4, and 5 of Murdock's *World Sample*, which contain information about the use of agriculture, animal husbandry, fishing, and hunting and gathering, and the extent to which women participate in these activities, for each of the 565 societies. Brown's formula permits the derivation of a single figure representative of women's role in subsistence pursuits.[22]

Table 13 shows the interrelationship of political integration and role of women for the societies in the sample, divided by household type. Significance levels reported are calculated by Fisher's Exact Test.

The *only* household group for which there is a significant correlation is the nuclear, although the strong tendency in the same direction among the polygynous societies should not be overlooked. The reason for large effect

[22] For a detailed explanation of the formula, see Brown (1961). Heath (1958) is more generally available, but lacks certain refinements developed by Brown. Using the formula, Brown found an association between high role of women in subsistence and the presence of female initiation rites.

TABLE 13

Political Integration, Role of Women, and Household Type

		ROLE OF WOMEN							
		HIGH	LOW	HIGH	LOW	HIGH	LOW	HIGH	LOW
Political	High	9	9	2	8	1	4	9	7
Intergration	Low	3	8	11	2	7	2	4	6
		N.S.		$p = .002$		N.S.		N.S.	
		Extended		Nuclear		Polygynous		Mother-child	

among the nuclear household societies is not immediately clear: it is possible that in *complex* nuclear societies the division of labor along sex lines is more extreme than most anthropological investigators [23] have realized, and that the blurring of occupational boundaries (so far as sex is concerned) in Western industrial society is an altogether unique phenomenon. Certainly "occupational specialization" is characteristic of "developing" societies, according to sociologists and economists.

The relationship among political integration, role of women, and Type II instruction, for nuclear household societies, is shown in Table 14. Despite the crudeness of our measure of role of women, the association is clear.

The table shows that nuclear household societies with a high degree of complexity do not involve their women in subsistence pursuits, and at the same time employ Type II instruction; it shows the reverse for nuclear societies with low complexity. It seems highly probable that women who are not involved in subsistence work spend at least part of their "free" time with their children; at any rate, from Murdock and Whiting's report, we know that such women are more likely to indulge their children than are their chore-burdened opposites.

In other words, complex nuclear households have several of the attributes of extended households, and it is plausible that children from them possess the same or similar problems as children from genuine extended households. If the children possess the same problems, the culture might be forced to resort to the same type of solution for them: Type II instruction. Such instruction would, in turn, become enmeshed with two sets of issues for nuclear children: dependency *and* achievement. The role of the school in the lives of such children will be, we predict, correspondingly large.

The exceptions to the general pattern with respect to instruction are only

[23] Barry, Bacon and Child (1957) argue that weak differentiation in sex-role training and sex-typed behavior is characteristic of nuclear household societies. Their large sample includes very few *complex* nuclear societies, however.

TABLE 14

Political Integration, Role of Women, and Type II Instruction *

POLITICAL INTEGRATION	ROLE OF WOMEN	INSTRUCTION (TYPE II)		
		PRESENT	ABSENT	
High	Low	8	0	
	High	1	1	$\chi^2 = 16.93$
Low	Low	0	2	(d.f. = 3)
	High	1	10	p < .001

* Nuclear Household Only

three in number among the nuclear societies. The Trobrianders (complex nuclear without Type II instruction) have already been discussed: many of their children are raised in mother-child households, and the resulting sexual identity problem is apparently solved by the change of residence pattern for which Malinowski provided the classical description. The Karen are politically simple; they are recorded as having Type II instruction, but what they have is extremely unstructured, consisting of village elders who teach such boys as are interested something of the lore of the community. Finally, the Kung (a simple nuclear society) have Type III instruction rather than Type II; this exception is not easily explained.

We also note that our interpretation is consonant with Parsons' statement that dependence-independence is the single most important predispositional factor for success and failure in American schools. It reinforces our feeling that schools in extended household societies have an "atmosphere" different from schools in nuclear societies: nuclear children, despite the degree of indulgence and dependency which they probably have experienced, come to the classroom more eager to achieve, more interested in clearing away the barriers to adulthood, than their "pure" extended household peers.

Finally, this interpretation suggests a further reason for the flowering of universal public education in the United States, which we earlier discussed in relation to the Bailyn hypothesis. Certainly the *composition* is not the only aspect of household arrangements which has changed since Elizabethan times. In that period, and in Frontier America, women were the economic equals of, or complements for, their husbands. But as the country prospered and became more complex, women were increasingly relieved of their subsistence tasks, and the home and children became their chief responsibility. Under these conditions, we suggest, the twin problems of achievement and dependency became salient, and America's response with Type II instruction was both quick and vigorous.[24]

CONCLUSIONS AND IMPLICATIONS

At the end of the section on Results, we asked several complicated questions. We will now offer some tentative answers.

One of the questions had to do with possible problems which Types II and III instruction "solve" for children in different societies. We have theorized that these instructional forms *do* answer specific needs. We first reviewed Whiting's evidence that mother-child children experience *gender identity conflict*, and that Type III instruction and the other aspects of initiation ceremonies with which it is meshed are attempts to lessen this conflict. We next examined extended household societies and ventured that *dependence* is a major problem in them, and that Type II institutions serve in some way to wean the child from dysfunctional beliefs and values to universalistic norms more appropriate for the adult world. We concluded that nuclear household societies develop *achievement* needs in their children, and that special institutions of instruction are not ordinarily necessary for them; but that under certain conditions of cultural complexity, dependency also becomes an issue for nuclear household children, and Type II instruction is then widely utilized.

It must be admitted, however, that we have not adduced very convincing evidence as to why mother-child societies use Type III instruction to accomplish their ends, and other societies use Type II. Rather vaguely, we suggested that Type III instruction and initiation ceremonies deal with an inappropriate early identification, while Type II institutions have the somewhat "easier" job of altering an identification process which occurs at a later stage. The difference here is between what Whiting and Burton (1961) have labeled "identification" and "identity"; this is a complex issue, which we would like to avoid in the present paper.

A second question concerned those societies recorded as having no instruction. We suggested that simple nuclear societies do not need it because the children have a built-in motivation to learn adult behavior. We also pointed out that Type III instruction is a minor, perhaps dispensable, part of a powerful emotional experience for boys in mother-child societies, and that such societies without instruction far from ignore the training of their children.

---

[24] Since the above was written, the author has come upon additional remarks by Parsons which seem generally supportive of the present interpretation of the nuclear household in modern industrial society. In particular, Parsons claims that there has been "a trend within the family to *increase* the dependency of the young pre-oedipal child, particularly on the mother . . ." (110) See Talcott Parsons: "Youth in the Context of American Society," *Daedalus*, XCI, 1 (Winter, 1962), pp. 97–123; especially pp. 110 and 114–15.

In passing, we also indicated that an occasional alternative to Type II or III instruction is a permanent change of residence, such as the Tlingit and the Trobrianders practice, in which the child is separated from his natal household.

The final question concerned the relationship between political integration and instruction. We argued that deliberate instruction might logically be regarded as a possible "cause" of complexity. Only with respect to nuclear household societies can this question be discussed interestingly. Among these, a low role of women is associated with both Type II instruction and cultural complexity. It is possible to argue that subsistence arrangements which permit mothers to stay at home with their children lead to the establishment of Type II instruction, which in a nuclear society might rapidly affect cultural development. However, the question is not really answered, and it is very doubtful that it can be.

With respect to educational practice, this study raises some basic issues. Beyond an inexact concern about children from "broken homes," it has not been customary to view the structure of the households from which students come as relevant to the practice of education. This study suggests that the constellation of household personnel may be a crucial factor in determining the success or failure of a child in various sorts of educational institutions.

This study also sheds some light on the difficulties which many "slum" children have in adjusting to the typical public school. It is well known that many such children come from homes in which the father is no longer present, or lacks status; in other words, from mother-child households. The basic problems of these children cannot be dealt with effectively in the regular program of the "day" school.[25] Proposals are frequently made to re-establish the Civilian Conservation Corps, or to set up boarding units as parts of public school systems. These seem quite realistic strategies, considering the cross-cultural evidence, for meeting both the emotional and intellectual needs of the relatively large mother-child minority in Western society.

There are also implications in this study for educators engaged in the ticklish work of aiding underdeveloped nations to build modern systems of education. If the findings herein presented are correct, the transplantation of Western forms of education to new soil is far more delicate a task than is usually realized, even by those who advocate "awareness" of cultural differences. For example, a progressive-minded educator who wishes to establish a "modern" school in an extended household, dependency-minded village in Afghanistan has very inappropriate raw material with which to carry out this venture. Similarly, those who would shut down the costly "English-model" boarding schools which exist in West Africa should ask themselves whether

[25] In support of this, see Miller (1958) and Rohrer and Edmonson (1960).

they can provide the mother-child students with substitutes which will serve both emotional and intellectual purposes as well as the originals do.

Throughout this paper, occasional reference has been made to further research which might well be carried out. There are four specific projects which seem particularly promising.

The first involves a series of *in*-cultural tests of the hypotheses developed in this cross-cultural survey. In almost every community in the United States and elsewhere several or all of the major household types exist where there are children who participate in various instructional activities. Their behavior in these activities can be observed and analyzed, and their personalities can be studied for evidence of the various "problems" which we have postulated. *In*-cultural replication and elaboration of cross-cultural studies are always desirable.

Second, the "content analysis" of the subjects taught in the various instructional institutions could be carried out. In this way, the alleged differences in "atmosphere" between the nuclear and extended Type II institutions might be demonstrated or disproved.

Third, Type I instruction should be restudied, employing a more sensitive, better calibrated rating system. Type I instruction would seem to be the variety involving the most people, and thus the most promising potential projective system. It is regrettable that the data regarding Type I were not available for this study.

Finally, efforts should be made to devise a rating system, or series of systems, for the interaction of mother and child during the day. Quite crucial to many theories of child development are the quality and amount of contact which mother and child have; but the daylight hours are virtual blanks on the cross-cultural chart at present. Our success in using the role of women in the subsistence economy as an indirect measure of mother-child interaction suggests that a less circuitous rating might be even more productive.

REFERENCES

A. *Theoretical*

1. BAILYN, BERNARD. *Education in the Forming of American Society*. Chapel Hill, North Carolina: University of North Carolina Press, 1960.
2. BARRY, HERBERT, III, M. K. BACON, AND I. L. CHILD. "A Cross-Cultural Survey of Some Sex Differences in Socialization," *Journal of Abnormal and Social Psychology*, LIII, 3 (Nov., 1957), pp. 327–32.
3. BROWN, JUDITH K. "A Cross-Cultural Study of Female Initiation Rites." Ed. D. thesis, Harvard Graduate School of Education, 1961.
4. CAUDILL, WILLIAM. *The Psychiatric Hospital as a Small Society*. Cambridge, Massachusetts: Harvard University Press, 1958.
5. CONSTANTINE, ALEXAKOS, M. BROWN, W. CHARLESON, AND J. CLARK. "Religious Education." Cambridge, Massachusetts: Harvard Graduate School of Education, 1961. (Mimeographed.)

6. CURTIS, S. J. *History of Education in Great Britain* (4th edition). London: University Tutorial Press, 1957.

7. D'ANDRADE, ROY GOODWIN. "Father-Absence and Cross-Sex Identification." Ph.D. thesis, Department of Social Relations, Harvard University, 1962.

8. DURKHEIM, EMILE. *Education and Society.* Translated by Sherwood G. Fox, Glencoe, Illinois: Free Press, 1956.

9. ERIKSON, ERIK. *Childhood and Society.* New York: Norton, 1950.

10. FERGUSON, GEORGE A. *Statistical Analysis in Psychology and Education.* New York: McGraw-Hill, 1959.

11. GOETHALS, GEORGE AND J. W. M. WHITING. "Research Methods: The Cross-Cultural Method," *Review of Educational Research,* XXVII, 5 (Dec., 1957), pp. 441–48.

12. HAMBLY, W. D. *Origins of Education among Primitive Peoples.* London: Macmillan, 1926.

13. HEATH, DWIGHT B. "Sexual Division of Labor and Cross-Cultural Research," *Social Forces,* XXXVII, 1 (Oct., 1958), pp. 77–79.

14. HERSKOVITS, MELVILLE J. "Education and Cultural Dynamics," *American Journal of Sociology,* XLVIII, 6 (May, 1943), pp. 109–21.

15. HERSKOVITS, MELVILLE J. *Man and His Works.* New York: Alfred J. Knopf, 1949.

16. HERZOG, JOHN D. "Religious Education and Socio-Cultural Complexity: A Cross-Cultural Study." Paper read at American Anthropological Association meetings, Philadelphia, Pennsylvania, November, 1961.

17. KLUCKHOHN, CLYDE. *Mirror for Man.* New York: McGraw-Hill, 1949.

18. LINTON, RALPH. *The Study of Man.* New York: Appleton-Century-Crofts, 1936.

19. McCLELLAND, DAVID. *The Achieving Society.* Princeton, New Jersey: Van Nostrand, 1961.

20. MEAD, MARGARET. "Our Educational Emphasis in Primitive Perspective," *American Journal of Sociology,* XLVIII, 6 (May, 1943), pp. 5–11.

21. MEAD, MARGARET. *The School in American Culture.* (The Inglis Lecture, Harvard University, 1950.) Cambridge, Massachusetts: Harvard University Press, 1951.

22. MILLER, W. B. "Lower Class Culture as a Generating Milieu of Gang Delinquency," *Journal of Social Issues,* XIV, 3 (1958), pp. 5–19.

23. MOORE, FRANK W. (ed.). *Readings in Cross-Cultural Methodology.* New Haven, Connecticut: Human Relations Area Files Press, 1961.

24. MUNROE, ROBERT L. "Some Studies of Cross-Sex Identity." Paper read at American Anthropological Association meetings, Philadelphia, Pennsylvania, November, 1961.

25. MURDOCK, GEORGE P. "World Ethnographic Sample," *American Anthropologist,* LIX, 4 (August, 1957), pp. 664–87. Also reprinted, with corrections, in Moore (23).

26. MURDOCK, GEORGE P. AND J. W. M. WHITING. "Cultural Determinants of Parental Attitudes: The Relationship between Social Structure, Particularly Family Structure, and Parental Behavior." In Milton J. E. Senn (ed.), *Problems of Infancy and Childhood.* New York: Josiah Macy, Jr., Foundation, 1951. Pp. 13–80.

27. NERLOVE, SARA BETH. "A Cross-Cultural Study of Male Initiation Rites in North and South America." Senior Honors thesis, Department of Anthropology, Radcliffe College, 1962.
28. PARSONS, TALCOTT. "The School Class as a Social System: Some of Its Functions in American Society," *Harvard Educational Review*, XXIX, 4 (Fall, 1959), pp. 297–318.
29. RAPOPORT, ROBERT. *Community as Doctor*. Springfield, Illinois: Charles C Thomas, 1960.
30. REDFIELD, ROBERT. *The Primitive World and Its Transformations*. Ithaca, New York: Cornell University Press, 1953.
31. ROHRER, J. H. AND M. S. EDMONSON. *The Eighth Generation*. New York: Harper, 1960.
32. SANFORD, NEVITT (ed.). *The American College*. New York: Wiley, 1962.
33. SERVICE, ELMAN AND HELEN S. SERVICE. *Tobati: Paraguayan Town*. Chicago: University of Chicago Press, 1954.
34. SPINDLER, GEORGE D. (ed.). *Education and Anthropology*. Stanford, California: Stanford University Press, 1955.
35. STEWARD, JULIAN. *Theory of Culture Change*. Urbana, Illinois: University of Illinois Press, 1955.
36. TOYNBEE, A. J. *A Study of History*. Abridgment of Vols. I-VI by D. C. Somervell. New York: Oxford University Press, 1947.
37. WHITING, JOHN M. "The Cross-Cultural Method." In Gardner Lindzey (ed.), *Handbook of Social Psychology*. Cambridge, Massachusetts: Addison-Wesley, 1954.
38. WHITING, JOHN M. "Cultural and Sociological Influences on Development," In *Maryland Child Growth and Development Institute*. Baltimore, Maryland, 1959. Pp. 5–9.
39. WHITING, JOHN M. "Resource Mediation and Learning by Identification." In I. Iscoe and M. Stevenson (eds.), *Personality Development in Children*. Austin, Texas: University of Texas Press, 1960. Pp. 112–26.
40. WHITING, JOHN M. "Social Structure and Child-Rearing: A Theory of Identification." (Mona Bronsman Sheckman Lectures, Tulane University, New Orleans, Louisiana, 1960). Manuscript.
41. WHITING, JOHN M. "Socialization Process and Personality." In Francis L. K. Hsu (ed.), *Psychological Anthropology*. Homewood, Illinois: Dorsey Press, 1961. Pp. 355–80.
42. WHITING, JOHN W. M. AND ROGER BURTON. "The Absent Father and Cross-Sex Identity," *Merrill-Palmer Quarterly*, VII, 2 (April, 1961), pp. 85–95.
43. WHITING, JOHN W. M., ELEANOR H. CHASDI, HELEN F. ANTONOVSKY, AND BARBARA C. AYRES. "The Learning of Values." In Egon Z. Vogt and E. M. Albert (eds.), *People of Rimrock*. Cambridge, Mass.: Harvard University Press, 1960.
44. WHITING, JOHN W. M. AND I. L. CHILD. *Child Training and Personality*. New Haven, Connecticut: Yale, 1953.
45. WHITING, JOHN W. M., I. L. CHILD, W. W. LAMBERT, *et al*, *Field Guide*

for a Study of Socialization in Five Societies. Cambridge, Massachusetts: Laboratory of Human Development, Harvard University, 1955. (Mimeographed.)

46. WHITING, JOHN W. M., J. L. FISCHER, R. G. D'ANDRADE, AND R. L. MUNROE. Manuscript on the status envy hypothesis, in preparation.

47. WHITING, JOHN W. M., RICHARD KLUCKHOHN, AND ALBERT ANTHONY. "The Function of Male Initiation Ceremonies at Puberty." In Eleanor Maccoby, Theodore Newcomb, and Eugene Hartley (eds.), *Readings in Social Psychology* (3rd edition, revised). New York: Holt, 1958. Pp. 359–70.

48. WHITING, JOHN W. M. AND BEATRICE B. WHITING. "Contributions of Anthropology to the Methods of Studying Child Rearing." In P. H. Mussen (ed.), *Handbook of Research Methods in Childhood Development.* New York: Wiley, 1960. Pp. 918–44.

B. Ethnographic Sources

Ethnographic data was obtained from the Human Relations Area Files in all cases except:

Americans (modern New England)	Okinawans
Gusii	Rajput (Khalapur)
Mixtecans (Juxlahuaca)	Tarong (Ilocano)

which are contained in Beatrice B. Whiting (ed.), *Child Rearing in Six Societies.* New York: Wiley, and:

Ainu Murdock, G. P. "The Ainus of Northern Japan." In *Our Primitive Contemporaries.* New York: Macmillan, 1934. Pp. 163–91.
Shinichiro, Takakura. "The Ainu of Northern Japan, A Study in Conquest and Acculturation." Translated and edited by John A. Harrison. *Transactions* of the American Philosophical Society, New Series, L, 4 (April 1960).
Bali Covarrubias, Miguel. *Island of Bali.* New York: Alfred A. Knopf, 1938.
French Wylie, Laurence. *Village in the Vaucluse.* Cambridge, Mass.: Harvard University Press, 1957.
Havasupai Spier, Leslie. "Havasupai Ethnography," *Anthropological Papers* of the American Museum of Natural History, Vol. XXIX, 3, 1928. Pp. 80–408. (Now in HRAF also.)
Navajo Leighton, Dorothea, and Clyde Kluckhohn. *Children of the People.* Cambridge, Mass.: Harvard University Press, 1946.
Serbs Halpern, Joel M. *A Serbian Village.* New York: Columbia University Press, 1958.

Societies consulted for which it was not possible to make any ratings regarding deliberate instruction (all HRAF):

Albanians	Kachin	Samoyed
Andamanese	Kalmyck (Europ.)	Semang
Buryat	Koryak	Tapirape
Georgians	Lāpps	Toda
Iban	Lur	Yakut

APPENDIX

Codes

A. *Culture area:* numbers correspond to the 60 culture areas listed in Murdock's *World Sample.*
B. *Type I instruction:*
    P—stated presence
    (P)—inferred presence
    A—stated absence
    (A)—inferred absence
    N—not ascertainable

C. *Type II instruction:*
Same code as B.

D. *Type III instruction:*
Same code as B.

E. *Political integration:* (from Murdock's Column 15, *World Sample*)
    A—autonomous local communities, not over 1500 in population
    D—dependent societies lacking any political organization of their own
    L—little states, between 10,000 and 100,000 in population
    M—minimal states, between 1500 and 10,000 in population
    O—absence of any political integration, even at the local level
    P—peace groups transcending local community, where basis of unity is other than political
    S—states, over 100,000 in population

F. *Household:* (from Murdock's Column 7, *World Sample*)
    c—communal households
    e—extended family households
    l—lineal family households
    m—mother-child households
    n—nuclear family households
    p—polygynous family households
    q—qualified polygynous family households
    s—stem family households
    Letters in parentheses indicate corrections of, or additions to, the *World Sample* ratings.

G. *Role of women in the subsistence economy:*
    1—0-54   ⎫
    2—55-74   ⎬ Low
    3—75-94   ⎪
    4—95-104 ⎭

    5—105-114 ⎫
    6—115-139 ⎬ High
    7—140-169 ⎪
    8—170-194 ⎭

Ratings

SOCIETY	A	B	C	D	E	F	G
Afghans	21	P	(P)	N	M	l	1
Ainu	23	P	(A)	(A)	D	m	4
Aleut	41	P	(P)	A	A	e	4
Alor	33	A	A	A	A	n	7
Americans	16	N	P	N	S	n	1
Amhara	11	(A)	P	(A)	S	n	4
Aranda	34	P	(P)	P	A	p	7
Araucanians	57	P	A	A	A	l	4
Ashanti	6	P	A	A	S	m	3
Atayal	31	(A)	N	(A)	O	n	6
Aymara	56	(A)	(A)	(A)	D	n	5
Azande	9	(A)	(A)	P	L	m	6
Aztec	50	P	(A)	P	S	m	2
Bali	32	(P)	(P)	(A)	L	n	2
Bemba	3	A	A	P	S	m	5
Bulgarians	18	N	P	(P)	S	n	5
Burmese	29	N	P	A	S	n	4
Caingang	60	(A)	(A)	N	O	p	6
Callinago	52	P	(A)	(A)	A	m	2
Carib	53	P	(A)	(A)	A	p	7
Chukchee	23	(A)	(A)	N	A	m	3
Comanche	45	P	N	(A)	P	p	5
Crow	45	P	(A)	A	M	q	5
Cuna	51	P	P	A	M	e	2
Fang	5	P	A	P	A	m	6
French	15	(A)	P	(A)	S	s	5
Ganda	5	P	(A)	A	S	m	5
Gond	27	(A)	(A)	P	M	e	6
Gusii	4	(A)	(A)	P	A	m	6
Hausa	12	A	(P)	P	S	(m)	2
Havasupai	44	P	(A)	P	A	p	2
Ifaluk	36	P	(A)	A	A	n	6
Ifugao	31	P	A	(A)	O	n	8
Iranians	21	N	P	N	S	l	4
Iroquois	47	(A)	P	(A)	L	e	8
Karen	29	N	(P)	N	A	n	5
Kaska	41	(A)	(A)	A	O	n	6
Kazak	22	N	(P)	(A)	S	l	7
Khasi	29	(P)	N	N	M	s	4
Kikuyu	4	P	P	P	A	m	7
Koreans	24	(P)	(P)	(A)	S	s	5
Kung	1	P	A	P	A	n	6
Kurd	20	N	(P)	N	M	p	3
Lau	38	A	A	A	M	l	3
Lebanese	20	N	P	N	S	n	1

Ratings

SOCIETY	A	B	C	D	E	F	G
Lepcha	25	P	(A)	(A)	D	l	5
Lolo	24	N	(A)	N	A	m	4
Lovedu	2	(P)	A	P	L	m	4
Makassarese	33	N	(P)	N	L	n	2
Malays	30	(A)	(P)	(P)	S	n	3
Marquesans	40	(A)	(P)	(A)	M	(e)	1
Mataco	58	(A)	N	(A)	A	n	2
Mbundu	2	(A)	(A)	(P)	L	m	6
Mende	6	(A)	(A)	P	L	m	5
Mixtecans	50	(A)	(P)	(A)	—	(e)	—
Mosquito	51	(A)	(P)	(A)	M	e	7
Mossi	7	(A)	(A)	(P)	S	m	3
Mundurucu	54	(A)	(A)	(A)	A	e	4
Murngin	34	(A)	(A)	P	A	p	7
Nambicuara	59	P	(A)	A	A	n	6
Navajo	48	P	(A)	(A)	A	(n)	3
Nootka	42	P	(P)	A	M	e	4
Nuer	10	P	(A)	A	P	m	6
Ojibwa	46	P	(P)	(P)	A	p	6
Okinawa	24	(P)	P	N	D	s	4
Paiute	44	P	N	(A)	A	p	6
Papago	49	P	(P)	(P)	A	l	4
Pomo	43	P	(P)	A	A	l	5
Pukapuka	39	(A)	A	A	A	n	8
Rajput	26	A	(P)	(A)	—	m	—
Riff	14	N	(P)	P	M	p	1
Rwala	20	N	(A)	(A)	L	p	1
Samoans	39	(A)	(A)	(A)	M	e	7
Serbians	18	N	(P)	N	S	l	6
Siriono	55	P	(A)	A	A	c	2
Somali	11	N	P	N	L	m	5
Tallensi	7	(A)	(A)	A	A	m	2
Tanala	28	A	A	(A)	M	m	3
Tarong	31	N	P	(A)	—	n	—
Telugu	27	P	(P)	(A)	D	l	3
Thai	30	N	P	P	S	s	4
Thonga	2	(A)	(A)	P	L	m	7
Tibetans	25	P	(P)	(A)	S	p	4
Tikopia	39	(A)	A	A	A	n	7
Tiv	8	P	(A)	A	M	m	4
Tlingit	42	P	(A)	A	A	l	2
Trobriand	37	P	A	A	M	n	6
Tuareg	13	P	(P)	(A)	M	n	1
Tupinamba	60	(P)	(A)	(A)	A	e	8
Vietnamese	30	P	P	(A)	S	l	5

SOCIETY	Ratings						
	A	B	C	D	E	F	G
Wogeo	35	P	(A)	(P)	O	p	4
Wolof	12	N	(P)	P	S	m	7
Yao	3	P	(A)	P	M	(m)	6
Yokuts	43	P	(P)	P	A	m	2
Yurok	42	P	P	A	O	l	3
Yoruba	6	(P)	N	A	S	e	3

IMAGE OF THE TEACHER BY ADOLESCENT CHILDREN IN FOUR COUNTRIES: GERMANY, ENGLAND, MEXICO, UNITED STATES

H. H. Anderson,

G. L. Anderson,

I. H. Cohen,

and F. D. Nutt

The authors describe children's perceptions of the teacher in a four-country sample. They then relate the pupils' responses to selected cultural variables in an attempt to account for differences.

A. PURPOSE

This report is based upon the *Lost Composition*, one of the eleven *Anderson Incomplete Stories* which were administered to over 9,000 fourth- and seventh-grade children in the seven countries of Germany, England, Norway, Sweden, Finland, Mexico, Puerto Rico, and continental United States, during the period from 1952–1957. The purpose of the research was two-fold: to develop and test an instrument that would be sensitive to cross-national similarities and differences, and to examine children's responses in the light of certain hypotheses.

REPRINTED FROM *The Journal of Social Psychology*, 50 (May 1959), 47–55. © 1959 by the Journal Press. Presented at the meetings of the Midwestern Psychological Association, Detroit, Michigan, May 3, 1958.

B. MATERIALS AND PROCEDURE

The Lost Composition

The children were asked to write a completion to the following story:

Betty often handed in her homework composition late to the teacher. This time it was an especially important composition and she had, moreover, finished it. On the way to school she lost her composition book and could not find it anywhere.
What does Betty say to her teacher?
What does the teacher say?
Think about these questions and finish this story with a few sentences.

The children's story completions in other languages were translated into English. The reliability of translation has been studied by Geierhaas (11) and shown to be adequate. From the content of the children's stories, a coding manual of 118 categories has been prepared and each protocol has been coded into categories. Independent coders of this story, using these content categories, demonstrated percentages of agreement of 89.1 and 90.09.

In coding the story completions distinction has been made between "check items" and "code items" (6). A group of check items contains mutually exclusive categories in one of which each story must be checked. A code item is a category which is used only when the corresponding item appears in the child's story. In the coding manual for this story there are three sets of check items which provide answers to the questions: (a) Who initiated the contact, the child or the teacher? (b) Did the child tell the truth? (c) Did the teacher believe the child? The analysis presented in this paper is based on the three sets of check items and on 13 coding categories of punishment.

As shown in Table 1, the subjects were 3,178 seventh-grade children from

TABLE 1

Numbers of Seventh-Grade Children Responding to Story Number 6,
The Lost Composition, *of the* Anderson Incomplete Stories

LOCATION	ABBREVIATION	NUMBER
Karlsruhe, Germany	Kar.	621
Hamburg, Germany	Ham.	471
Munich, Germany	Mun.	325
Mexico City	Mex.	866
Birmingham, England	Bhm.	397
Knoxville, Tennessee	Knx.	214
Benton Harbor, Michigan	BnH.	284
		3178

Karlsruhe, Hamburg, and Munich, Germany; Birmingham, England; Mexico City; Benton Harbor, Michigan, and Knoxville, Tennessee.[2] These locations were chosen for this report because it was assumed that, among our samplings, Germany (14) and Mexico (10, 13) represented the more dominative and authoritarian cultures and England and the United States represented the more integrative or democratic cultures.

It was further assumed that there will be found examples of integrative relating in the most dominating or authoritarian cultures and examples of domination in the presumed democratic cultures, as indeed our own research has already suggested (3, 4, 5, 12).

C. HYPOTHESES

The hypotheses grew out of previous research on democratic and dictatorial teacher-child relations in American school rooms (1, 2, 7, 8, 9). It was assumed that the same differences in child behavior reported in American dominative and integrative school rooms would be found to exist in more extensive samplings of dominative and integrative cultures.

The over-all hypothesis concerning Creativity in human relations is that democratic or integrative relationships facilitate Creativity and that dominative or authoritarian relationships restrict it.

The principal hypotheses of the cross-national research program that concern this story are:

1. Children brought up in a more dominating or authoritarian culture are different in their interpersonal relations from children in less dominating (more democratic) cultures.

2. In the *Lost Composition* story, valid communication will be lower in dominating cultures, that is, children in dominating cultures will show lower

[2] We are grateful for the cordial coöperation of many persons in the several locations in which we have gathered data. Specific acknowledgments for assistance in Karlsruhe and Hamburg, Germany; Birmingham, England; Knoxville, Tennessee, and Mexico have been made in previous reports (3, 6).

For assistance in Munich, Germany, we are grateful to Städt. Oberschulrat Ederer, Professor Dr. Philip Lersch, Director, and Dr. Heinz-Rolf Lückert, Psychologisches Institut, University of Munich, and to the university students who served as members of our research team: Flne. Ilse Garbsch, Doris Hoberg, Beate Liller, Ilsabe Reese, Gabriele Schiller, Christel Zumsande, and Herren Hermann Brandstätter, Erich Harrer, Ludwig Krause, Lothar Schubert.

For permission to gather data in Benton Harbor, Michigan, we wish to thank Mr. Meryl A. Bird, Superintendent of Public Schools, and the principals of the public and parochial junior high schools. The data were gathered by Mary Ann Daugherty, Maryanne L. Myers, and Justin Lee Smith, who were recipients of Social Science Research Council Undergraduate Research Stipends, 1956, for work on this study, and H. H. Anderson.

A private grant has accelerated the coding and interpretation of the cross-national data as part of a five-year program of research in the area of Creativity.

frequencies of telling the teacher the truth and higher frequencies of telling the teacher a lie.

3. Children in dominating cultures will be less ready to face reality and will thus show lower frequencies of the child's initiating contact with the teacher.

4. In the *Lost Composition* story, children in more dominating cultures will show the following characteristic images of the teacher: (*a*) More stories will have the teacher initiate the contact with the child. (*b*) More stories will have the teacher disbelieve the child. (*c*) More stories will have the teacher punish the child.

Conversely, the image of the teacher in stories from more integrative or democratic cultures will show significantly lower frequencies in these characteristics.

D. RESULTS

Table 2 shows that over four-fifths of the children in each location wrote

TABLE 2

Mutually Exclusive Percentages of Children Indicating which Member of the Teacher-Child Interaction Initiated the Contact

CHILD INITIATED — % (CAT. 21–1)	TEACHER INITIATED — % (CAT. 21–2)	NO INFORMATION — % (CAT. 21–3)
Kar. 87.9	Ham. 11.5	BnH. 9.5
BnH. 87.7	Mex. 11.1	Knx. 8.4
Mun. 87.4	Kar. 9.3	Mun. 7.7
Knx. 86.4	Bhm. 8.3	Mex. 6.1
Bhm. 85.6	Knx. 5.1	Bhm. 6.0
Ham. 83.6	Mun. 4.9	Ham. 4.9
Mex. 82.8	BnH. 2.8	Kar. 2.7
Chi^2 not sig.	Chi^2 sig. .01	Chi^2 sig. .01

stories in which the child initiated contact with the teacher. The Chi-square test revealed no significant differences between locations. The remaining children either had the teacher initiate the contact or gave no information from which the initiation of the contact could be inferred. Although the frequencies of stories in which the teacher initiated the contact were very low, the percentages were significantly different between locations. Three of the four samplings which have been assumed to come from more dominating or authoritarian cultures were highest in teacher-initiated contacts. The Munich sampling which fell between Benton Harbor and Knoxville represents an exception to our hypothesis.

Table 3 shows that 83 per cent or more of the children in each location had Betty tell the teacher the truth; the range of percentages is very small, though the over-all Chi-square was significant at the .05 level. Less than 13

TABLE 3

Mutually Exclusive Percentages of Total Children Indicating Whether the Child Told a Truth or A Lie

TRUTH — % (CAT. 23–1)	LIE — % (CAT. 23–2)	NO INFORMATION — % (CAT. 23–3)
Mex. 89.5	Kar. 12.7	Knx. 9.8
Bhm. 89.2	Mun. 8.9	BnH. 9.2
BnH. 88.0	Ham. 8.1	Ham. 6.8
Ham. 85.1	Bhm. 6.3	Mun. 6.8
Knx. 85.0	Knx. 5.1	Mex. 6.8
Mun. 84.3	Mex. 3.7	Bhm. 4.5
Kar. 83.6	BnH. 2.8	Kar. 3.7
Chi² sig. .05	Chi² sig. .01	Chi² sig. .01

per cent in each location had Betty tell the teacher a lie. Although the percentages were small, the differences between locations were significant. Consistent with the hypothesis, the three German locations were highest in having Betty tell a lie. Not consistent with the hypothesis was the Mexico City sampling which fell between Benton Harbor and Knoxville at the bottom.

In Table 4, the mutually exclusive check items of *Teacher believed,*

TABLE 4

Mutually Exclusive Percentages of Total Children Indicating Whether the Teacher Believed or Did Not Believe the Child's Story, Regardless of Whether it Was the Truth or a Lie

BELIEVED — % (CAT. 22–1)	DISBELIEVED — % (CAT. 22–2)	NO INFORMATION — % (CAT. 22–3)
Knx. 53.7	Kar. 48.9	BnH. 26.1
Bhm. 52.1	Ham. 47.6	Knx. 25.7
BnH. 50.7	Mun. 44.6	Mex. 22.2
Mun. 42.5	Mex. 42.1	Kar. 20.3
Ham. 36.9	Bhm. 32.2	Bhm. 15.6
Mex. 35.7	BnH. 23.2	Ham. 15.5
Kar. 30.8	Knx. 20.6	Mun. 12.9
Chi² sig. .01	Chi² sig. .01	Chi² sig. .01

Teacher disbelieved, and *No information* each differentiated between locations at the .01 level.

The hypothesis was that in an integrative or democratic culture there would be higher expressions of confidence in the child by the teacher as indicated by high frequencies of the item, *Teacher believed*. In Table 4, the children's images of the teacher consistently support this hypothesis. The three allegedly more democratic samplings were not significantly different from each other in percentages of stories in which the teacher believed the child. They were, however, significantly different at the .01 level from the three German samplings, and from the Mexico City sampling at the .05 level.

In the *Teacher disbelieved category*, Knoxville and Benton Harbor, lowest in percentages, were not significantly different from each other, yet were each significantly different at the .01 level from all other samplings. Karlsruhe, Hamburg, and Munich, highest in *Teacher disbelieved*, were not significantly different from each other, yet in turn were each significantly higher at the .01 level than the three samplings from the hypothesized democratic locations.

The ratios of percentages of *Teacher believed* to *Teacher disbelieved* ranging from Knoxville (2.9) to Karlsruhe (.54), were for all samplings consistent with the hypotheses. The ratio was highest, that is, higher percentages of *Teacher believed* than of *Teacher disbelieved*, in the democratic samplings of Knoxville, Benton Harbor, and Birmingham in that order. The relationship was reversed, that is, the frequency of *Teacher believed* was lower than the frequency of *Teacher disbelieved*, in the more dominating samplings of Munich, Mexico City, Hamburg, and Karlsruhe.

There was no systematic relationship between the teacher's belief or disbelief and the child's having told the truth or a lie.

Tables 5 and 6 are based upon categories of the teacher's punishing the child. Punishing is defined as: threatening, scolding, admonishing, advising, hitting, referring to the child's past unsatisfactory behavior or reputation, giving an inferior mark, assigning extra hours, assigning extra work, depriving of recreation, expelling or isolating, a negative statement of the teacher's unpleasant thought or act, or generically punishing. These represent the range of punishment items found in the story completions. The category of "Teacher has child rewrite the composition" was not included in the composite punishment category for two reasons, even though it was a frequently used category. Many children did not perceive this as punishment, and also, rewriting the composition was assumed to be a teacher's legitimate expectation of a school child. To simplify presentation and interpretation of data, Tables 5 and 6 give percentages of children in each location who wrote one or more of the punishment items.

Since more than four-fifths of all children produced stories in which a truth was told, only these stories are used in the punishment tables. To include children telling a lie would introduce a small though confounding variable. We asked the following questions of the data: when the child told the truth, what percentages of teachers were reported to have punished? What percentages when the teacher believed the child? What percentages when the teacher did not believe the child?

The rank order percentages of children who perceived the teacher as punishing are given in Table 5. Mexico City was highest in rank order with

TABLE 5

Of Those Stories in Which the Child Told the Truth, Percentages in Which the Teacher Was Perceived as Punishing Regardless of Whether the Teacher Believed or Disbelieved the Child

LOCATION	%
Mex.	69.7
Bhm.	68.4
Ham.	60.8
Mun.	57.7
Kar.	47.2
BnH.	44.0
Knx.	32.4
Chi^2 sig. .01	

69.7 per cent of the stories having one or more punishing items. Mexico City and Birmingham were significantly higher than all other locations, although not significantly different from each other. Knoxville was lowest in frequency, significantly lower than all other locations, including Benton Harbor at the .05 level. The low ranking of Knoxville and Benton Harbor and the higher ranking of the German and Mexico City samplings were consistent with the hypotheses. Birmingham's high position was consistent with reports of "canings" and of other physical punishment in some of the other stories.

Another perspective of punishment is given in Table 6 which shows the percentages of punishment when the teacher believed and when the teacher disbelieved the child's story. In all locations more teachers were perceived as punishing when they disbelieved than when they believed. The largest difference was in Benton Harbor, where nearly twice as many teachers were perceived as punishing when they disbelieved as when they believed. Hamburg showed the least difference: as many teachers believed and punished as disbelieved and punished.

Table 6a shows the rank order percentages of teachers who believed the child but nevertheless punished. Mexico City was significantly higher than all other locations except Hamburg and Birmingham. Knoxville and Benton

TABLE 6

Of those Stories in Which the Child Told the Truth, Percentages in Which the Teacher Was Perceived as Punishing When the Teacher Believed the Child, and When the Teacher Disbelieved the Child

(a) TEACHER BELIEVED AND PUNISHED *		(b) TEACHER DISBELIEVED AND PUNISHED *	
Mex.	64.0	Bhm.	84.4
Ham.	59.9	Mex.	76.0
Bhm.	57.8	Mun.	63.6
Mun.	50.4	BnH.	60.6
Kar.	40.1	Ham.	60.1
BnH.	33.8	Kar.	54.2
Knx.	33.3	Knx.	37.8
Chi² sig. .01		Chi² sig. .01	

* Rank order correlation 6a — 6b. $r = .643$; $p = .13$, not significant.

Harbor, lowest, were significantly lower than all others except Karlsruhe. Table 6b shows rank order percentages of teachers who disbelieved and punished. Birmingham and Mexico City were significantly higher than all other locations. Knoxville, again lowest, was significantly lower than all others except Karlsruhe. Benton Harbor was relatively high, in this unique instance, significantly higher than Knoxville.

Rank order percentages in Tables 5 and 6 were generally consistent with the hypotheses with the exception of Benton Harbor which was relatively high in punishment when the teacher disbelieved.

E. SUMMARY AND CONCLUSIONS

1. The purpose of the research program, of which this report is a part, was to develop and test an instrument that would be sensitive to cross-national similarities and differences, and to examine children's responses in the light of certain hypotheses about integrative and dominative cultures. The story-completions to one of the *Anderson Incomplete Stories* given by 3,178 children in Germany, England, Mexico, and the United States were analyzed to determine the children's image of the teacher.

2. The story involved a child with a reputation for handing in homework late to her teacher, who this time completed her composition on time, but lost it. Content categories were established to determine: (*a*) Who initiated the contact, the child or the teacher? (*b*) Whether the child told the truth or a lie? (*c*) Whether the teacher believed or disbelieved the child? (*d*) Whether the teacher punished the child in any way?

3. The hypotheses tested were that responses from children in a more

dominating or authoritarian culture will be different from those of children in a more integrative or more democratic culture. Specifically, that in more dominating cultures there will be relatively higher frequencies of the teacher's initiating contact with the child, of the child's telling a lie, of the teacher's disbelieving the child, and of the teacher's punishing the child.

4. For purposes of this research the samplings from Hamburg, Karlsruhe, and Munich, Germany, and from Mexico City were assumed to come from more dominating or authoritarian cultures; samplings from Benton Harbor, Michigan; Knoxville, Tennessee; and Birmingham, England, were assumed to come from less authoritarian, that is, from integrative or more democratic cultures.

5. In all locations there were more child-initiated contacts than teacher-initiated contacts, and more truths than lies told. The hypotheses regarding teacher-initiated contacts and lies told were supported with but minor exceptions. In the more dominative or authoritarian locations, without exception the children wrote stories in which the teacher more frequently did not believe the child; conversely, in the more integrative or democratic samplings without exception the children wrote stories in which the teacher more frequently did believe the child. The hypotheses regarding punishment were supported with some exceptions: *e.g.*, Birmingham, which was higher than expected, and Karlsruhe, which was lower than expected.

6. It is concluded that the *Anderson Incomplete Stories* is an instrument sensitive to cross-national similarities and differences, and that children reared in allegedly more authoritarian and dominating culture hold images of the teacher that are significantly different from those held by children in less dominating, that is, more integrative or democratic cultures.

REFERENCES

1. ANDERSON, H. H. Domination and social integration in the behavior of kindergarten children and teachers. *Genet. Psychol. Monog.*, 1939, 21, 287–385.
2. ANDERSON, H. H. Domination and socially integrative behavior. In R. G. Barker, J. S. Kounin, and H. F. Wright (*Eds.*), *Child Behavior and Development: A Course of Representative Studies.* New York: McGraw-Hill, 1943. (Pp. 459–483.)
3. ANDERSON, H. H., & ANDERSON, G. L. Children's perceptions of social conflict situations: A study of adolescent children in Germany. *Amer. J. Orthopsychiat.*, 1954, 24, 246–257.
4. ANDERSON, H. H., & ANDERSON, G. L. Cultural reactions to conflict: A study of adolescent children in seven countries. In G. M. Gilbert (*Ed.*), *Psychological Approaches to Intergroup and International Understanding: A Symposium of the Third Interamerican Congress of Psychology.* Austin, Texas: Published for the Interamerican Society of Psychology by the Hogg Foundation for Mental Hygiene, Univ. Texas, 1956. (Pp. 27–32.)
5. ANDERSON, H. H., & ANDERSON, G. L. A cross-national study of teacher-child

relations as reported by adolescent children. Paper presented at the Fifth Interamerican Congress of Psychology, National University of Mexico, Mexico City, December, 1957.

6. ANDERSON, H. H., ANDERSON, G. L., DAUGHERTY, M. A., MYERS, M. L., SMITH, J. L., & MASON, J. E. Dominative and Integrative teacher-child relations in five countries as reported by adolescent children. Paper presented to the Psychology Section, Michigan Academy of Science, Arts, and Letters, Wayne State University, Detroit, Michigan, March 22, 1957.

7. ANDERSON, H. H., & BREWER, H. M. Studies of teachers' classroom personalities: I. Dominative and socially integrative behavior of kindergarten teachers. Stanford, Calif.: Stanford Univ. Press, 1945.

8. ANDERSON, H. H., & BREWER, J. E. Studies of teachers' classroom personalities: II. Effects of teachers' dominative and integrative contacts on children's classroom behavior. Stanford, Calif.: Stanford Univ. Press, 1945.

9. ANDERSON, H. H., BREWER, J. E., & REED, M. F. Studies of teachers' classroom personalities: III. Follow-up studies of the effects of dominative and integrative contacts on children's behavior. Stanford, Calif.: Stanford Univ. Press, 1946.

10. DIAZ-GUERRERO, R. Neurosis and the Mexican family structure. *Amer. J. Psychiat.*, 1955, 6, 411–417.

11. GEIERHAAS, F. G. Problems of reliability in evaluating story completions about social conflict by German adolescent children. Master's thesis, Michigan State Univ. Library, East Lansing, 1955.

12. HEBER, R. F. A cross-national comparison of children's judgment of parent-child conflict in Germany, England, Finland, United States, and Mexico. Master's thesis, Michigan State Univ. Library, East Lansing, 1955.

13. DE LEONARD, C. C. Some psycho-cultural defense reactions of Mexican Indians. In G. M. Gilbert (*Ed.*), *Psychological Approaches to Intergroup and International Understanding: A Symposium of the Third Interamerican Congress of Psychology*. Austin, Texas: Published for the Interamerican Society of Psychology by the Hogg Foundation for Mental Hygiene, Univ. Texas, 1956. (Pp. 50–56.)

14. MCGRANAHAN, D. V. A comparison of social attitudes among American and German youth. *J. Abn. & Soc. Psychol.*, 1946, 41, 245–257.

NATIONAL MOTIVES PREDICT
PSYCHOGENIC DEATH RATES
TWENTY-FIVE YEARS LATER

Stanley A. Rudin

This study uses McClelland's achievement motivation scores, derived from content analysis of children's stories from sixteen countries, and relates them to psychogenic death rates. The author finds that the need for achievement, as seen in children's stories, predicts death rates resulting from ulcers and hypertension, and power motivation scores predict rates resulting from murder, suicide, and cirrhosis of the liver twenty-five years later. The study illustrates what can be done by relatively simple statistical manipulation of extant data, once an ingenious and well-considered hypothesis has been developed.

McCLELLAND and his colleagues [1] have found a number of significant positive correlations between the motive for achievement (referred to as "need for achievement" and defined as the motive to excel in comparison with some abstract standard of excellence at the performance of some task) in a nation and its actual performance in economic productivity. This motive is measured by content analysis of imaginative literature; the criteria of economic productivity have varied. Several studies have been done on past and present societies; the results of all are in essential agreement. The reliability and validity of this method for predicting the behavior of individuals and small groups have been demonstrated elsewhere.[1,2]

The purpose of this study was to investigate the possibility that the need for achievement might produce undesirable psychological effects in a society as well as desirable ones, and to study the effects of other motives prevalent in a society in relation to criteria of mental health or psychological disorder (hereafter referred to as psychomorbidity).

In one of McClelland's studies,[1] children's books of stories from about the year 1925 from 22 nations—all relatively modern, Western or Westernized, and within the temperate zone so as to control for extremes of climate and poverty—were content analyzed and each country assigned a score on the need for achievement. The stories were those selected for use in schools for

REPRINTED FROM *Science*, 160 (May 1968), 901–903. © 1968 by American Association for the Advancement of Science. Additional data (Table 2) supplied by the author.

¹ D. McClelland, *The Achieving Society* (Van Nostrand, Princeton, N.J., 1961).

² J. Atkinson, Ed., *Motives in Fantasy, Action, and Society* (Van Nostrand, Princeton, N.J., 1958); D. McClelland, J. Atkinson, R. Clark, E. Lowell, *The Achievement Motive* (Appleton-Century-Crofts, New York, 1953).

children to practice reading. Children's stories were chosen for these reasons: (i) previous research on primitive tribes had shown significant relationships between contents of myths and actual achieving behavior; children's stories, many of which derive from an oral tradition, seem to be an approximation of myths and legends in advanced civilizations, (ii) they usually have existed in rather standard form for at least a generation, (iii) they are imaginative and aim both to interest and instruct the child, (iv) they are usually not restricted to one social class and hence reflect the "popular culture" of the day, (v) they are not likely to reflect transient external events since children are not usually considered old enough to care about such things, (vi) they were available, and (vii), as Margaret Mead is reputed to have said, "A society must get its values over to its children in terms so simple even a social scientist can understand them." While undoubtedly children learn values directly from the readers themselves to some extent, it is assumed here only that these reading books reflect the motives and values of the society at that time. Two measures of economic growth from 1929 to 1950 were obtained by using the relative increase in production of electricity per capita and the relative increase in national income per capita. The 1925 need-for-achievement scores predicted the increase in electricity output per capita significantly better than chance (rho $= .53$, $P < .01$) and the correlation with per capita income gain was in the right direction although not significant (rho $= .25$).[3]

There is a general belief among psychologists, however, that hard-driving achievers are likely to suffer from psychogenic ailments such as neuroses, ulcers, and hypertension; while derived originally from clinical observations, there is strong experimental support for such assumptions.[4] McClelland's scores from 1925 were therefore related to several indices of psychomorbidity from about 1950 to 1953. The year 1950 was chosen for several reasons. (i) McClelland and his co-workers had found national motive scores to predict economic productivity in modern societies over about a 25-year time span; hence, I inferred that whatever social psychological processes were at work affecting that behavior would also affect the behavior I was interested in. (ii) Social scientists generally regard about a 30-year time period as constituting a "generation"; that is, if a whole generation of children are taught certain motives and values, then the behavioral manifestations of them will be most numerous when that generation of children has reached maturity and

[3] The measure of correlation used was the Spearman rank-difference correlation rho $= 1 - [\Sigma 6\, d^2/(N^3 - N)]$, where $d =$ the difference between ranks of the scores of the two variables and $N =$ the number of cases. This statistic was used throughout the present study also. See S. Siegel, Nonparametric Statistics (McGraw-Hill, New York, 1956), pp. 202–212.

[4] J. Brady, R. Porter, D. Conrad, J. Mason, J. Exptl. Anal. Behav. 1, 69 (1958); L. Berkowitz, Aggression: A Social Psychological Analysis (McGraw-Hill, New York, 1962).

are actually running the society. In this case, the stories were mainly for children about 10 to 15 years of age; 25 years later, at ages 35 to 40, they might reasonably be expected to be acting out their values and setting the trend of the whole society at that time. (iii) By their late 30's people are physically weak enough to begin dying off of psychogenic ailments, yet are not so old that degenerative diseases play a significant role in causes of death.

As measures of psychomorbidity, death rates probably due largely or substantially to psychological factors were selected. Although other indices might appear more directly relevant, such as admissions to mental hospitals per capita, such data either do not exist for all countries, are not readily accessible, or might vary greatly in meaning from one country to the next. Thus, in one country sparsity of population and a rural economy would permit mild chronic psychotics to exist marginally, whereas they could not in an industrialized nation of high population density. Also, national methods of diagnosis and definitions of categories used in gathering such statistics are not always comparable.

The United Nations has since about 1948 compiled death rates according to International Statistical Classification from the published reports of many member states. The *Demographic Yearbook* for 1954[5] was therefore consulted. Five cause-of-death categories were selected that seemed to have psychological factors as the primary or underlying causes: murder, suicide, alcoholism (as measured by deaths due to cirrhosis of the liver), ulcers, and hypertension (high blood pressure) without mention of heart disease. While some deaths due to cirrhosis of the liver are certainly not due to alcoholism, and some deaths due to ulcers and hypertension are probably due to as-yet unknown genetic and other factors, I assumed either that these factors would remain relatively constant from one country to the next and that the component due to psychological factors would contribute the major part of the variance, or that they would be unrelated to the psychological causes.

Of McClelland's original 22 countries studied, causes-of-death data were available for 17, and motivational scores for the year 1925 were to be had for only 16 of these countries. Death rate scores were obtained by following three rules: (i) if the rate for only one year is given, use it; (ii) if the rates for two or more years are given, use the average; and (iii) no figures labeled "provisional" shall be used. The next problem was to determine whether these were all separate measures of psychomorbidity, or whether some common factors ran through them. All five measures were therefore correlated with one another, and the resultant intercorrelations, shown in Table 1, demonstrate that the data fall neatly into two clusters:

---

[5] Statistical Office of the United Nations, *Demographic Yearbook, 1954* (United Nations, New York, ed. 6, 1954), table 30, pp. 558–587.

TABLE 1

Correlations (rho) Among Psychogenic Death Rates, About the Year 1950.
N (Number of Countries) = 17.

CAUSE OF DEATH	SUICIDE	CIRRHOSIS OF THE LIVER	ULCERS	HYPERTENSION
Homicide	.44	.40	−.10	−.25
Suicide		.49	.19	−.36
Cirrhosis of the liver			−.30	−.28
Ulcers				.54

murder, suicide, and alcoholism correlate highly with one another, while ulcers and hypertension do not correlate with the three preceding measures (in fact, there is a tendency toward small negative correlations) but do correlate highly and significantly with each other ($P < .02$). To cross-validate, the death rates for about 1960 [6] were obtained in the same way and the intercorrelations were calculated. There were minor and insignificant changes in the pattern of intercorrelations. In view of the small number of countries studied and the clarity of the results, a factor analysis was deemed superfluous.

The cluster comprising murder, suicide, and alcoholism was termed "deaths due to aggressiveness and acting-out," with aggressiveness here very broadly defined as a tendency to act out emotional impulses and to take an active, manipulative approach toward the world. Deaths in the other cluster, comprising those due to ulcers and hypertension without mention of heart disease, were labeled "deaths due to inhibition."

McClelland [1] has also provided data on the 1925 motivational scores of 16 of these countries (all except Switzerland) for a need or motive besides that of achievement, namely the need for power, defined as the desire to dominate others, to influence others, to have a decision-making position over others, or the desire to direct the behavior of others.

Two hypotheses were then formulated on the basis of the above interpretation of the death rate clusters and the definitions of the need for achievement and the need for power: (i) the need for achievement in 1925 will correlate positively with the 1950 death rate cluster due to inhibition, but will not be correlated with the death rate cluster due to aggressiveness; and (ii) the need for power in 1925 will correlate positively with the 1950 death rate cluster due to aggressiveness, but will not be correlated with the death rate cluster due to inhibition. Death-rate-cluster scores were obtained by ranking the countries studied on each death rate, summing ranks within a cluster, and re-ranking the summed ranks. [See Table 2]

[6] Statistical Office of the United Nations, Demographic Yearbook, 1960 (United Nations, New York, ed. 12, 1960), table 19, pp. 552–569.

TABLE 2

Psychogenic Death Rates per 100,000 Population (1950)

	YEAR	HOMICIDE	SUICIDE	CIRRHOSIS OF LIVER	HYPERTENSION	ULCERS	RANK: AGGRESSIVENESS	RANK: INHIBITION
Republic of South Africa (European Population)	1951	3.00	10.1	8.8	6.5	4.6	6	13.5
Canada	1952/3	1.15	7.2	4.7	7.2	5.0	11	11
U.S.A.	1951	4.90	10.4	9.8	8.6	5.5	3	8
Japan	1952	2.10	18.5	7.3	9.3	19.9	2	3.5
Belgium	1952	.70	13.1	5.9	10.6	5.8	10	7
Denmark	1951/2/3	1.18	23.5	5.9	4.05	7.4	4	10
Finland	1952	3.30	17.6	2.5	2.9	4.8	8	17
France	1952	.70	15.4	22.8	7.4	3.1	7	13.5
Germany (Western)	1952	.90	17.6	9.2	4.9	7.0	5	9
Ireland	1951/2	.40	2.4	2.2	17.2	8.4	17	2
Netherlands	1952/3	.55	6.4	3.1	4.8	5.0	16	15
Norway	1952	.40	6.9	3.4	5.3	3.8	15	16
Sweden	1951	.60	16.2	3.1	16.1	8.6	12	3.5
Switzerland	1952	1.26	21.5	11.8	4.4	6.7	1	12
England (incl. Wales)	1952	.70	9.9	2.6	18.2	12.3	14	1
Australia	1952	1.60	10.6	4.7	16.3	6.8	9	5
New Zealand	1952	1.00	10.1	3.0	8.8	7.5	13	6

For national motive scores see D. McClelland, *The Achieving Society*, Appendix II, pp. 461–463.

The results are shown in Table 3. Both hypotheses are regarded as confirmed, the rho of .66 between the need for achievement and deaths due to inhibition being significant beyond the .01 point (one-tailed test); and,

TABLE 3

*Correlations (rho) Between 1925 Motives and 1950 Death Rate Clusters,
Death Rates, and Other Behavior. N (Number of Countries) = 16.*

BEHAVIOR	MOTIVE	
	NEED FOR ACHIEVE- MENT	NEED FOR POWER
Aggressiveness cluster	−.11	.42
Murder	.03	.22
Suicide	−.09	.51
Cirrhosis of liver	−.31	.13
Inhibition cluster	.66	−.02
Ulcers	.57	.20
Hypertension	.52	−.18
Film attendance *	.55	−.05
Books published *	−.48	.02

* N = 15; see text.

although the correlation between the 1925 need for power and the 1950 death rate cluster due to aggressiveness (rho = .42) just misses the required rho of .425 to be significant at the .05 level (one-tailed test), it is deemed high enough to confirm the hypothesis, especially since the correlation with suicide alone was .51, with P < .05.

The logic of "construct validity" as elaborated by Cronbach and Meehl [7] is used here. Since I inferred previously that suicide, murder, and alcoholism constitute a cluster called "deaths due to acting-out or aggressiveness," I can go one step further and assume that each separate death rate of the cluster is simply one manifestation of a generalized behavioral tendency, the separate death rates being influenced at times by local conditions. Now I can argue that one death rate is only one sample behavior of the cluster, just as one item is merely one sample of what is tested on an intelligence test. Admittedly, this train of thought is tenuous and opens the door to unrestricted speculation. It can, however, be held in check if other behavioral tendencies which look as if they should correlate with those in the construct

[7] L. J. Cronbach and P. Meehl, *Psychol. Bull.* 52, 281–302 (1955).

on theoretical grounds do so. As will be discussed below, evidence of this nature is available for the inhibition death rate cluster; to date, however, the only evidence bolstering the construct validity of the aggressiveness cluster is a significant correlation between the 1950 aggressiveness death-rate cluster and the 1950 divorce rate. This correlation is reasonable, since people who are aggressive should have difficulty living with one another. Since divorce rate was not selected in advance and its correlation predicted, however, it is admittedly a weak buttress and requires future validation.

The construct validity of the inhibition cluster obtains support from two other correlations. After a hard day achieving, the resident of a country high in the need for achievement will probably seek escape and eschew recreation demanding some intellectual effort. The number of books produced per capita and attendance at motion pictures per capita were therefore calculated from data from about 1955–1958 furnished in another United Nations publication.[8] As can be seen in Table 3, the results were as hypothesized: the 1925 need-for-achievement scores correlated (rho) —.48, with $P < .05$ (one-tailed test) with books produced per capita about 1955–1958, and (rho) .55, $P < .05$, with per capita attendance at films over the period about 1955–1958, the only years for which data were available. This was, of course, before television was widely in use. It is interesting to note that the United States is one of the nations highest on both the aggressiveness cluster and the inhibition cluster, one of the lowest on book production, and one of the highest on film attendance.

Aside from demonstrating that a high need for achievement is not the unmixed blessing it might be assumed to be, these results help clarify the meaning of the two scores. I interpret the need for achievement as a tendency to postpone immediate gratification to attain greater future gratification, to inhibit emotional impulses, and generally to maintain a "Protestant ethic" with emphasis on hard work, sobriety, and concrete results. While detracting somewhat from his inference that a society high in the need for achievement is most fortunate, these results generally support and strengthen McClelland's overall interpretation of the need-for-achievement score.

The need for power is seen as correlated with the acting out of impulses and with a manipulative, aggressive attitude toward other people. I infer also a loss of humane values and a willingness to engage in violence (as exemplified in murder and suicide). Possibly the high alcoholism rate reflects a high anxiety level in countries high in the need for power.

[8] Statistical Office of the United Nations, *Statistical Yearbook, 1960* (United Nations, New York, 1960). The number of books produced per country is given in table 178, pp. 594–597; the number of persons attending motion picture theaters is given in table 183, pp. 605–606. To obtain the rates used in this study, these numbers were divided by the population of the country in 1958, the year to which most of these data are applicable. The number of countries used in these computations was reduced to 15, since data on the Union of South Africa were lacking.

A weakness of this study is its failure to correlate the 1925 motivation scores with death-rate-cluster scores for more years, say from 1926 to 1980. The only data I can offer are correlations of the 1925 motivation scores with 1960 death rate clusters; they were slightly lower and insignificant, but only barely. The problem is that not enough time has elapsed, nor is enough data available, to fill in the gaps. McClelland has also given motivation scores for many more countries for 1950; there are no relationships between these scores and those for death rate clusters for about 1960; however, none would be expected until death rates from about 1975 are available. The ideal future cross-validation study would take the 1950 motivation scores and correlate them with the death rate clusters for every year from 1950 to, say, A.D. 2050.

In addition, other behavioral indices must be added to the cluster (for example, number of hours watching television per capita for the inhibition cluster, crime rates and number of riots for the aggressiveness cluster) including other death rates if possible, since recently available drugs appear to control ulcers and hypertension.

Part 6

NATIONAL DEVELOPMENT

DOES EDUCATION ACCELERATE
ECONOMIC GROWTH?

David C. McClelland

In this study, as in the other articles in this section, education is viewed as one of many social and cultural variables affecting a nation's total growth and development. Here, the author investigates the relationships among school enrollment, educational stock, achievement motivation, rate of economic growth, and level of educational development in a global sample of countries. He notes the policy implications of his findings.

FACED by the desire of new nations to develop rapidly, economists and other planners have become intensely interested in the economic impact of investments in education. They often are forced into considering the problem by the low level of skills of all types in the countries they are trying to help and advise. What good does it do to develop a plan for a system of public health care if there are no doctors, nurses, or medical assistants in the country? How can a factory be operated without the skilled labor to man it? How can the skilled labor be taught without teachers—and the teachers without an institution to train them? The questions, once started, are endless, but for the planner they boil down to one very broad issue: what is the return on investments in education, as compared with other investments?

The problem is always one of priorities for the planner. Everything is in some sense desirable—from new roads to new health services or new factories —but before he decides to give a high priority to education, he must have some idea of the rate of return from various types of development of human resources.

Economists have tried to make contributions to this problem in a variety of ways. Schultz and his co-workers [1] have calculated that in the United States "expenditures on education have increased over 100 times from 1900 to 1956 —on high school education for instance from $81 million in 1900 to $10,944

REPRINTED FROM *Economic Development and Cultural Change*, 14 (April 1966), 257–278, by permission of The University of Chicago Press. The author is indebted to Professors J. R. Myers, R. M. Hamlin, A. Curle, and A. J. Meyer of Harvard University for advice and encouragement in preparing this report and also to Mr. Barclay Hudson, who helped him particularly with the statistics it contains.

---

[1] T. W. Schultz, "Investment in Human Capital," *American Economic Review*, LI (March 1961), 1–17; and "Reflections on Investment in Man," *Journal of Political Economy*, LXX, No. 5 (October 1962 supplement), 1–8. See also S. J. Mushkin, ed., *Economics of Higher Education* (Washington: GPO, 1962).

million in 1956." [2] Since gross national income was also increasing many times over during the same period, it seems reasonable to argue that at least some of this increase must be attributable to increased skills in the labor force, making education a productive investment, rather than simply a consumption item. Denison and Correa [3] have attempted, in fact, to determine what shares of the increase in gross national product in the U. S. can be attributed to the usual types of capital formation, arguing that the large increase left unaccounted for in this way might legitimately be attributed to improvements in human resources. The trouble with such a residual approach is that any theorist can lay claim to the "x" factor—the variable that produced the greater increase in GNP than can be accounted for in any of the usual ways. It is hard to think of a way to allocate properly the portion of this unknown input that can be assigned to education, or to research, or to better health, or to other factors not usually included in such computations.

Some of the same objections apply to another method of trying to determine the economic benefits of education through its effect on the life-income streams of the persons educated. That is, it is obvious that college graduates earn more than high school graduates, and it is a straightforward computational problem to estimate the cost of their education (outlay plus income foregone) as an investment, the return on which is the increased income received over the average productive lifetime of college graduates.[4] The difficulty lies in proving how much of the increased income is due strictly to the educational input and how much to other factors associated with college-going, such as higher socio-economic status or greater intelligence. It is difficult to conceive of a natural experiment in which young people of varying backgrounds and IQ's were assigned at random to go or not to go to college in order to isolate the effects of college-going *per se*. Even if this social experiment might be approximated—as it might for trade school-going—it would be hard to be sure that income differentials were really adequate measures of relative contribution to national economic growth and to estimate what the returns to the individual or the economy might have been if the same capital had been invested in other ways.[5]

[2] F. Harbison and C. A. Myers, *Education, Manpower, and Economic Growth* (New York: McGraw-Hill, 1964), p. 6.

[3] E. F. Denison in *The Residual Factor and Economic Growth* (Paris: OECD, 1964). H. Correa, *The Economics of Human Resources* (Den Haag: Brukkerij Pasmans, 1962).

[4] See Mushkin, *op. cit.*

[5] While the Russian analyst Strumilin is quite sophisticated in demonstrating the very large income returns to investments in education, he leaves out of consideration entirely the possibilities that (a) the return may have been due in part to other factors like social position of family, and (b) the return on the same amount of money invested in something other than education needs to be taken into account. S. G. Strumilin, "The Economic Significance of National Education," in E. A. G. Robinson and J. E. Vaizey, *The Economics of Education* (New York: St. Martin's Press, 1966).

Even to put the question this way suggests the inadequacy of this approach. It doesn't seem to touch the root of the matter—which is somehow to show what kind of educational investment should be made to promote growth of the economy as a whole. Other theorists have abandoned the cost-benefit approach in favor of a simple manpower requirements analysis. They start with the relationships existing among nations at different stages of development between, say, the number of secondary school graduates and gross national income.[6] They then determine where a particular country is on the national income scale, project where it wants to be in a few years' time (in terms of planned annual increases in GNP), and estimate on the basis of the experience of other countries how many secondary school students it should be educating now. This is a variant of a rational planning approach which estimates how many firms or institutions of what kind are needed to produce a given planned national income, goes from there to an estimate of how many of what kinds of employees will be needed to operate these firms, and from there to the kinds and costs of education needed to train those employees.

The difficulty with this logical approach is, basically, that it assumes what still needs to be proved. It assumes that because there is now a high correlation between level of education and national income, the one *caused* the other. That is, if the level of education may have been the *result* of economic growth, how can one recommend to an underdeveloped country that it should set up a given level of education to help produce the growth? One cannot even go very easily from the kinds of people employed in factories in developed countries to a recommendation that one will need the same kinds of people in the same numbers in a developing country. Nor can one assume that the developing countries will need to spend the same amount on education as other countries are spending to reach the same level of productivity. The "logical" approach to determining the need for educational expenditures gets no closer to solving the basic problem than any of the other approaches.

Is there no way to get a better fix on the problem of how much education contributes to economic growth? After all, one solid inescapable fact remains: among contemporary nations, there is a sizable correlation between human resource development and GNP. For example, Harbison and Myers[7] report correlations among 75 nations between GNP per capita and primary school enrollment of .67, between GNP per capita and secondary school enrollment of .82, and between GNP per capita and third level enrollment of .74. Curle[8]

[6] Cf. J. Tinbergen and H. Correa, "Quantitative Adaptation of Education to Accelerated Growth," *Kyklos* (1962).

[7] *Ibid.*

[8] A. Curle, "Education, Politics, and Development," *Comparative Education Review*, VII, No. 3 (1964), 226–45.

reports a similar correlation (r = .64) between per capita income and post-primary enrollment. He has also pushed the analysis a bit further by showing that greater wealth is associated with a greater percentage of the national income invested in education (r = .53) and that spending more money on education is associated with a higher post-primary enrollment ratio (r = .61). In his words, "This, of course, does not of itself demonstrate anything except that rich nations tend to spend proportionally more on education than poor ones," [9] but such a substantial relationship is certainly a challenge to study carefully the processes by which it happened. That is, did increases in educational investment precede rapid rates of economic growth, or were rapid increases in wealth followed by increased spending on education? Or did both occur together? These are the critical questions of social dynamics that cry out for an answer.

Curle practically alone has sought to pursue these matters a little, although it was not his primary purpose. He correlated levels of investment in education and of post-primary enrollment in the middle 1950's with average percent growth rates in income per capita between 1954 and 1959. He found no relationship. That is, the countries that were stressing education more were not growing faster economically during the same time period, so far as these measures are concerned.

But the whole problem clearly needs more detailed study. Consider the question of lag-time, for example. Isn't it likely that increased educational inputs would have an economic impact, not during the time in which they are made, but 10 or even 20 years later, when the better educated stock reaches its peak of influence in the labor force? Some data accumulated by Kaser [10] suggest that this may be the case. For instance, in the Netherlands, both annual percentage increases in GNP per capita and secondary enrollment remained fairly low and stationary from 1900 to 1930. Between 1930 and 1938, secondary enrollment nearly tripled: the effect in national income was unobservable immediately—perhaps because of World War II. But then in 1960, a good 25 years later, when these secondary school pupils would be in their early forties, GNP per capita showed the largest percentage increase it had shown since 1900 in the Netherlands. Other such instances can be found in other countries for which he presents time series, but obviously a systematic study needs to be made, to be certain one is not basing a generalization on a biased sample of cases.

The present investigation was undertaken to see what information could be extracted from available statistics as to the relations that have existed between changes in educational inputs and economic outputs among countries in the course of their recent development (1930 to 1960). In other words, the

[9] *Ibid.*, p. 227.

[10] M. C. Kaser, "Education and Economic Progress: Experience in Industrialized Market Economies," in Robinson and Vaizey, *op. cit.*

goal is to get behind the static relationship and try to discover the dynamics of the changes that brought it about. Anyone who has looked into this field at all knows how extraordinarily difficult it is to get figures that mean anything—particularly figures reflecting *changes* over time that are comparable from one country to another. So it will be necessary at the outset, before presenting the findings, to define rather carefully the measures employed.

ECONOMIC DEVELOPMENT

Most studies employ "gross national product, as an annual rate of growth and per capita, . . . as the best available measure of economic progress" despite "the shortcomings of this procedure" because "no alternative is feasible." [11] There is no need to review the shortcomings of the measure here—the weakness of equating currencies through exchange rates corrected for inflation, the non-comparability of national accounts, the relative unavailability of income figures at the exact times and places needed, etc.—but two difficulties need particularly to be discussed, as they are less widely appreciated.

The first arises from the fact that economic development, properly speaking, is a multivariate concept. In addition to referring to total income, it also includes notions of productive capacity, infra-structure, income distribution, etc. Thus, there are instances in which national income figures alone violate our total conception of what development means—as in the case of Kuwait, for example, where average income per capita has recently been higher than in the United States. Most of these cases involve countries where rich oil reserves or other precious natural resources have been discovered and exploited by foreign companies. In all of them, measures of national income show high levels and rates of economic growth which do not reflect "development" in the other senses in which the term is used (e. g., productive capacity). For example, Algeria ranked 3rd out of 55 countries in economic growth in the 1954–59 period, on the basis of its average percentage increase in income per head. It does not seem to make sense in terms of our present problem to ask whether investments in education, say in Kuwait or Algeria, led to their high rates of economic development, defined in the narrow sense of increases in wealth. It appears preferable to find some other indicator or indicators of development which reflect more representatively its multivariate nature and which consequently might be expected to be influenced by investments in education.

In another place,[12] I have argued that electricity consumed provides a convenient, rough, but reasonably accurate estimate of rate of development

[11] *Ibid.*
[12] D. C. McClelland, *The Achieving Society* (Princeton: Van Nostrand, 1961).

in this more general sense. It has, of course, great technical measurement advantages over national income figures, because statistics on electric power consumption are readily available for practically every country in the world, in internationally comparable units, for exactly comparable time periods. The figures are more "believable," in the sense that fewer errors are made in computing them. Furthermore, production and consumption figures are for all practical purposes equal, which avoids complications introduced when indexes are used relating to materials that can be overproduced, stock-piled, and used gradually over time.

Conceptually, electric power consumed also has some advantages. It enters into most categories in an input-output table (except agriculture in traditional societies). It is widely used in the public sector (for lighting streets, trans-portation, etc.); it enters into nearly all kinds of manufacturing. Yet it is also a home consumption item (lighting, radio, toasters, etc.). The fact that it plays little role in traditional subsistence agriculture is not a major disadvantage from the planner's standpoint, since most countries are trying to move the agricultural sector into a more advanced stage in which electric-ity is used, as in food processing. Electricity seems to be as important in countries operating at the highest as well as the lowest economic levels: that is, there seems to be no obvious cut-off point—as there would be for many indicators—above or below which it becomes wildly unrepresentative of the functioning of the economy. Furthermore, it is hardly ever imported in significant amounts, but is produced, distributed, and consumed locally. This implies a certain level of technical knowledge locally that is one of the variables in what is meant by "development"—a "know-how" which in con-trast is not necessarily implied by a rich oil strike exploited by a foreign company. In short, electricity consumed ought to be a pretty good index of development in countries varying widely in internal economic structure. Such a hypothesis is firmly supported by the fact that Kwh consumed per capita correlated .86 in the mid-'fifties with estimates of income per capita in 40 countries.[13] The agreement is very close except for the countries which are rich in natural resources like oil, and a case can be made for the fact that electricity is a better index of development in its multivariate sense in such countries.

This is not to argue that the electricity measure has no flaws. It would obviously be better to combine a number of such measures in an over-all index to remove the bias a single measure introduces in particular cases. For in-stance, where hydroelectric power can be readily generated, in countries like Norway and Canada, the measure overestimates the level of development in the multivariate sense.

It is necessary therefore to remove the initial capacity of the country to

[13] Cf. *ibid.*, p. 87.

produce electricity. This we would want to do anyway, since our interest is in *gains* rather than in absolute levels. But absolute gains are highly correlated with initial levels in electricity production as in other economic indicators: this is what is sometimes meant by saying that the rich get richer. In order to correct for starting level, economists regularly convert absolute gains to percentage gains to compare the rates of gain of different countries. This leads to the second technical difficulty with the traditional method of measuring economic growth: percentage changes are often *negatively* correlated with starting levels. Converting to percentages "overcorrects" for a positive correlation and introduces a negative one. That is, a country starting at a low level is likely to have a larger percentage increase than one starting at a high level. It is possible to remove such a correlation by determining how much better or worse a country is doing in comparison with what it might be expected to do on the basis of the over-all regression of absolute gain on initial starting level. When converted to log units, plots of electricity consumed in 1929 times gain in consumption from 1929–1950 and again for the 1952–1958 period show remarkable linearity. Thus, it is possible to use a linear regression equation to see what gain in electrical output a country would typically have shown between 1929–50, given its starting level in 1929. Its actual gain is compared with the predicted gain to see whether it is an "over-" or "under-achiever" compared with the average trend line. The degree of either positive or negative deviation in standard score units becomes the measure of growth rate.[14] This method essentially compares a country's rate of growth with the rates of other countries starting at the same level (as defined by the over-all regression function). It is used here in preference to the more traditional and very similar multiple and partial regression mode of analysis, because it allows for greater flexibility in plotting residuals (see below).[15]

[14] Some readers may wonder whether countries which are richly endowed with coal and usable water power will not tend to show more rapid rates of growth in production of electric power. The resource base is of course highly correlated with *levels* of production of electric power (cf. *ibid.*, p. 51), but the advantage of the rate measure adopted is that it removes the influence of initial level. That is, it answers the question of whether a country has performed better or worse than expected, *given its starting level* (which is very much influenced by its natural resources). To double-check on whether in fact the influence of resource base had been removed, a correlation was run for 23 countries between a combined measure of coal produced plus usable water power (1947–50) and our measure of rate of gain in electric power produced (1952–58). The correlation is only +.13, which is negligible and nowhere near significance. As expected, removing the effect of initial level of electricity production also removes the effect of resource base on this measure of *rate* of growth.

[15] In what follows it must be understood that terms like "economic growth" or "economic development" refer to this electricity measure—which, though empirically and conceptually correlated with income figures, may be considered too narrow an index to be described in such general terms. Readers who are bothered by this may prefer to think of the results obtained in terms of some such concept as "technological growth."

EDUCATIONAL INPUTS

The stress a country puts on education may be measured in a variety of ways—by literacy rates, by expenditures on education, or by enrollment figures at various levels of instruction. For practical purposes, enrollment figures must be used because of the scarcity of other data. Among such figures, primary enrollments seem less likely to be important for economic growth for a variety of reasons. On the one hand, correlations of economic levels with primary school enrollment ratios are lower than with secondary enrollment ratios. On the other, primary school attendance has a doubtful relationship to significant improvements in the labor force or even to literacy itself. That is, the marginal product of a primary school education would seem likely to be low, because skilled artisans may function practically as well without being literate. Furthermore, primary school attendance is not enough by itself to lift a person to the level of being able to perform jobs characteristic of the middle class. For these reasons post-primary education seems likely to be the more important input for economic growth *on the average*, as Curle has concluded.[16] However, it seems wise to go further than he did and break down these figures into second and third level enrollment ratios, because the latter may turn out to be particularly important for recent economic advances in highly developed countries.

Next, it is necessary to distinguish between educational stocks and flows. A *stock* is the number of people in a country of a given age group at a particular time with, for example, at least some secondary education. Usually a stock must be considered in relation to the level of development of a country. That is, if one is interested in whether a more educated population accelerates economic growth among poor as well as among rich countries, comparisons must be made *within* rather than across these groups. Britain can be compared with France, and India with Tunisia, but cross-level comparisons would be meaningless. In short, the educational stocks must be corrected for the base, just as the economic outputs must be.

A *flow* is a change—an increase or a decrease—in enrollment ratios between one period in time and another—a change which must be corrected for starting level, just as changes in economic outputs are corrected, not by using percentages, but by comparing countries which start at the same level. An *enrollment ratio* is the number of students enrolled in a given type of education in a given year relative to some population base and is neither a stock nor a flow by itself. Changes in such enrollment ratios may be used to calculate flows or estimate stocks among adult segments of the population.

Unfortunately, secondary school enrollment ratios published by UNESCO are not usable, for several reasons. Their intent is to estimate the percentage of a given age category—say, 15 to 19—in secondary school, but we suspect

16 Curle, *op. cit.*

something is peculiar about the index when we discover that in 1960 it is 122 percent for the United Kingdom, or that in Yugoslavia it decreased from 53 percent in 1950 to 22 percent in 1960. At first glance one wonders how Britain can educate more than exist in an age class, or why Yugoslavia is apparently falling off so rapidly in the stress it is putting on education. Obviously the ratios must be carefully analyzed to see whether a cross-nationally meaningful index can be developed from their constituent parts.

First, consider the *numerator*—the number of students enrolled in secondary schools in a given year. The difficulty is that different countries define "secondary" in different ways—as beginning anywhere from the fifth to the tenth year of schooling. Thus, the figures for Czechoslovakia refer to the pupils enrolled in grades 10 through 13, whereas in Austria they refer to grades 5 through 12. Obviously Austria will appear to be giving many more students a secondary education than Czechoslovakia. To correct for this it was decided to call the first six years of education (after nursery school and kindergarten) primary and everything between that and higher education secondary.[17] Thus, two years of enrollments had to be subtracted from Austria's total and three years added to Czechoslovakia's. Unfortunately, this had to be done for many years very crudely, simply by obtaining the average secondary enrollment per year, as defined by the country, and then adding or subtracting this figure as often as needed to bring the total to what it would be if the first six years were arbitrarily assigned to primary education. This gives a higher score to countries providing more years of secondary education (though most give 12 years in all of primary plus secondary), but this was considered correct, in the sense that such countries were in fact educating their people more. Further refinements in terms of adjustments for lengths of the school year, quality of education, or number of graduates simply could not be made with the data available. So our measure is simply exposure to education beyond the sixth year and prior to entrance into university education.

The *denominator* cannot readily be a given age group according to UNESCO practice, because the resulting index is not unidimensional. There are two ways to get a high ratio: one is to have a "good" school system which promotes children efficiently according to age and enrolls a high percentage of them in secondary school. The other is to have a "bad" school system which may not enroll nearly as many of the correct age group in secondary school but which has a lot of over-age children or adults enrolled in secondary school. Thus, paradoxically, it is possible for the index to go down, as it did in Yugoslavia, as the school system improves. That is, the denominator may stay the same (age group 15–19), but the numerator goes down (fewer students 20 and over), because the school system has "caught up" with itself. At the very least, the index does not

---

[17] See M. Debeauvais, "The Balance between the Different Levels of Education," in Robinson and Vaizey, *op. cit.*

show what it is supposed to show—namely, the percentage of persons in a given age group who are going to school. It seems better to compute a less ambiguous index by using the total population as the denominator as UNESCO has done for higher education.

SAMPLE OF COUNTRIES

In the tables that follow, the aim was always to include all the countries on which data were available for the indexes and time periods under consideration. However, there were also two general restrictions on the sample set in the initial study: [18] (1) tropical countries (lying between the Tropics of Cancer and Capricorn) were excluded, because it was believed (probably erroneously) that climate and the different diurnal distribution of light and dark might make the electricity measure less valid for such countries; and (2) very small countries like Iceland, Luxembourg, and Malta were excluded, because it was believed the electricity index again might be less reliable for such countries, i. e., more subject to one or two major events like establishing a single new factory. Electricity figures were generally available for all countries not excluded in this way, so that further exclusions occurred because the educational data were not available.

EDUCATED STOCK AND ECONOMIC GROWTH

Having decided on our measures and the sample, we can now test the hypothesis that the level of educational stock in a country is related to subsequent rates of economic growth. The most adequate test is provided by the data assembled in Table 1, because only in this case was it possible to estimate an educational stock from secondary enrollment figures published for the 1930's. Ideally, one would like to see whether countries with more adults with a secondary school education developed more rapidly than countries with fewer such adults, but the figures available are more approximate than that. Secondary school enrollments (including technical and normal schools) are published by UNESCO for each year from 1930 to 1939. It is not, of course, possible to tell how many *individuals* are represented by these figures, but their sum does give a very rough indication of the number of secondary school years of education to which adults in a country at the peak of their influence (age 30 to 40 in 1950) had been exposed 10 to 20 years earlier. Thus one can say that in 1950 there were about 281 school years of secondary education available among adults aged 30 to 40 per 1,000 Canadians, as compared to 193 school years per 1,000 Swedes. So far as this age group was concerned, the Canadians would seem to be somewhat better educated than the Swedes.

[18] McClelland, *op. cit.*

TABLE 1

Countries Classified by Economic Level and Educated Adult Stock
in 1950 and by Rate of Economic Growth, 1952–58

ECONOMIC LEVEL: ELECTRICITY PRODUCED, 1950	EDUCATED ADULT STOCK, 1950 [a]	ECONOMIC GROWTH RATE, 1952–58 [b]
A. Kwh/cap > 1000		
England	500 [c, d]	+ .17
U.S.	415	+ .47
Canada	281 [e]	+ .06
Australia	227 [f]	+ .42
Norway	220	− .77
Sweden	193 [f, g]	− .64
New Zealand	184	− .29
Finland	128	− .08
B. Kwh/cap between 400 and 900		
Denmark	345 [c]	− .89
Netherlands	292	− .15
Austria	157 [f]	+ .38
Czechoslovakia	154 [c]	+ .23
France	152 [d]	− .24
Japan	144	− .04
Italy	110	− .57
Chile	108	−1.81
C. Kwh/cap between 100 and 300		
Ireland	153 [g]	− .41
Poland	130 [c, h]	+1.26
Hungary	76	− .62
Argentina	56	− .56
Portugal	54	+ .76
Spain	47 [c, i]	+ .01
D. Kwh/cap < 100		
India	35 [j]	+1.12
Pakistan	34 [j]	+2.75
Turkey	31	+1.38
Iraq	21 [d]	+ .29
Tunisia	16 [k]	−1.87
Syria	16 [d]	− .25

[a] Estimated years of secondary education available among adults age 30 to 40 per 1,000 inhabitants in 1950. Total years of secondary education given in the 10-year period 1930–39 (age group 30 to 40 in 1950) divided by population in 1950. Figures from

UNESCO, *L'éducation dans le monde. II. L'enseignement du second degré (1963)*. Secondary education is defined to include general, technical, and normal education beyond the 6th year and before university or higher education. It does not matter whether the education is given in what the country may call a primary or a secondary school. Thus, in Austria the "primary" school is limited to 4 years followed by approximately 8 years of secondary or technical education. One-fourth of the enrollment figures for the secondary schools is subtracted as belonging to the age period called primary in other countries. On the other hand, in Czechoslovakia the "primary" school is 9 years long, so that the equivalent of 3 years of enrollments must be added to the Czechoslovakian figures for secondary school enrollment. Both public and private school enrollments are included.

b Deviations in standard score units of gains in electricity produced over gains predicted from regression of 1952 production level on 1952–58 gains (see McClelland, *op. cit.*, p. 100).

c Estimate based on interpolation or extrapolation from existing annual figures.

d Estimate for private schools added based on ratio of public to private enrollments at other time periods.

e Figure only approximate because of complications in the school system in the province of Quebec.

f Estimate for technical school enrollments added based on ratio of general to technical enrollments at other time periods.

g Underestimate due to unavailability of enrollments in first and second years of secondary education given in some primary schools.

h Very approximate. The boundaries of Poland were quite different in 1950 from what they were in 1930–39. The assumptions have been made that most people educated in Poland in the 1930's would gravitate to what is now Polish territory and that the losses in educated stock due to the war (and particularly the Jewish extermination policy) have to some extent been compensated for by the addition of former German territories where the secondary education rate was probably higher.

i Probably an overestimate because of inability to assess full effects of decreases in school enrollments, deaths, and emigration resulting from the Spanish Civil War.

j Education figures are for India and Pakistan combined; they have been partitioned approximately on a population basis—82.5 percent to India, and 17.5 percent to Pakistan.

k Because of substantial emigration of Europeans in the mid-fifties after Tunisian independence, it is estimated that only half of the 40 percent of secondary school years given to Europeans in the 1930's was available in the 1950's.

To find out if being better educated affects the rate of economic growth, the countries are classified as explained earlier according to their economic level, using the electricity measure previously discussed. A country is classed as more or less educated depending on whether it is above or below the median in years of secondary schooling per 1,000 inhabitants *within a group of countries* roughly at the same economic level. One can quarrel with the groupings of individual countries into economic levels A, B, C, or D on the basis of the electricity measure (e. g., both Finland and Chile seem somewhat overrated as to their levels), but it was made objectively with the main criterion being the desire to include an even number of countries within each grouping, so that no bias could be involved in dividing the countries into the more or less educated categories.

Obviously, in any case the relationship is a fairly strong one. The better educated countries in 1950 (those above the median in education for their economic level) develop faster in the 1952–58 period at nearly every level, and the over-all trend is highly significant. Ten or 71 percent of the relatively better educated countries developed at an above average rate, as compared with three or 21 percent of the relatively less educated countries ($\chi^2 = 7.03$, $p < .01$). One can think of the relationship in terms of absorptive capacity or needs of the economies at various levels of development. For countries at the lowest levels of development (Kwh/cap < 100 in 1950), obviously the need for highly educated people (engineers, technicians, etc.) is much less than for highly industrialized countries like the U. S. or Sweden. Nevertheless, *within each level* of development, the better educated countries tended to develop faster subsequently.

It is important to note, however, that if the same table is prepared using secondary enrollment figures for 1950 (see Table 5) instead of educational stock figures, the relationship does *not* hold, as Curle's results had already foreshadowed.[19] Apparently, as one would expect, lag is important in educational investments. It is the secondary enrollments for the 1930's that are related to rates of economic growth in the 1950's. The rate of such enrollments in the 1950's should not (and does not) relate to immediate rates of growth, because the young people are not yet active in the labor market: their influence should be felt in the late 1960's and the 1970's. To restate the obvious conclusion which these findings support: education is a long-term investment from the economic point of view.

It is desirable to check the finding shown in Table 1 with different sets of figures, to make certain it is not just an accidental product of manipulation of existing figures. Unfortunately, secondary enrollment figures are not available for a very large sample of countries before 1930, so we must use a less satisfactory approximation of the educational stocks available during the other time period (1929–50) for which we have estimates of rates of economic growth. In this case, secondary enrollment at the start of the period (1930) provides a better estimate of educated stock than it does in 1950, for two reasons: (1) the economic growth period (1929–50) is much longer, so that at least some of the secondary school graduates from the early 1930's will have become actively employed before its end in 1950; and (2) enrollment rates in 1930 are almost certainly more closely correlated with earlier rates (1920) than are enrollment rates in 1950, because in recent years educational enrollments have more often than formerly been manipulated as a means of achieving national policy goals. At any rate, Table 2 was prepared to check the same relationship found in Table 1, but for a different economic growth period and using the 1930 enrollment rates as an approximation of the education stock available during the 1929–50 growth period.

Once again the relationship is highly significant: the more educated countries at a given economic level developed more rapidly than the less educated countries.[20] Eight or 80 percent of the better educated countries developed

---

[19] Curle, *op. cit.*

[20] Obviously, Sweden seems very much out of line with the over-all trend, having developed rapidly despite a rather low level of secondary school enrollment. This should serve to emphasize the approximate quality of all estimates in these tables. There may be errors in many individual estimates, so that one should pay attention only to over-all trends, not to individual cases.

TABLE 2

Countries Classified by Economic Level (1929)
and Secondary School Enrollment Ratios (1930)
and by Rate of Economic Growth, 1929–50

ECONOMIC LEVEL: ELECTRICITY PRODUCED, 1929	SECONDARY SCHOOL ENROLLMENT PER 1,000 INHABITANTS, 1930 [a]	ECONOMIC GROWTH RATE, 1929–50 [b]
Kwh/cap > 800		
U. S.	44.3	+1.86
Canada	31.8 [e]	+1.73
Sweden	18.8 [f, g]	+3.17
Norway	18.7	− .03
Kwh/cap 150 to 500		
England	50.2 [c, d]	+1.65
Denmark	40.5 [e]	+ .14
Netherlands	32.2	− .10
Australia	26.2 [f]	+1.13
New Zealand	21.4	+1.86
Japan	15.7	− .44
Finland	14.0	+ .74
Austria	13.8 [f]	− .12
France	10.3 [d]	− .55
Chile	10.0	− .43
Italy	6.8	− .62
Kwh/cap < 150		
Ireland	12.4 [g]	+ .33
Hungary	6.5	− .26
Poland	5.1 [e]	+ .03
Argentina	4.9	− .61
Spain	4.4	− .63
Portugal	4.3	− .52

[a] Estimated number of persons in secondary school per 1,000 inhabitants when secondary school is defined as in Table 1 except that normal school enrollments are not here included.

[b] Deviations in standard score units of gains in electricity produced per capita over gains predicted from regression of 1929 production level on 1929–50 gains (see McClelland, *op. cit.*).

[c] And following (see Table 1).

at an above average rate, as compared with only two or 18 percent of the less educated countries ($\chi^2 = 5.58$, corrected for small sub-class numbers, $p < .02$). Since the correlation between rates of economic gain between the earlier and the later periods is insignificant, this can be considered an independent replication of the finding shown in Table 1. In both time periods, the amount of secondary education available among adults made a significant difference in the rate of economic growth, as reflected in the electrical output measure.

Interaction Between *n* Achievement, Educational Levels, and Economic Growth

Previous work has shown that the achievement orientation of important élites in a country, as determined by content analysis of children's textbooks, is significantly related to subsequent economic growth.[21] This raises the question as to whether educational level is just an aspect of the general mobilization for achievement, or whether it is an independent variable contributing to economic development in its own right. The simplest way to shed light on the question is to cross-classify the data in Tables 1 and 2 by the *n* Achievement level of the countries concerned. The main results of this procedure are given in Table 3. One can see that *n* Achievement is not

Table 3

Average Economic Growth Rates Among Countries
Classified According to n *Achievement and Secondary*
Education Levels for Two Time Periods

| | | AVERAGE ECONOMIC GROWTH RATES [a] | | |
| | | 1929–50 | | 1952–58 |
CLASSIFICATION	N	MEAN	N	MEAN
High both in *n* Achievement [b] and secondary education level [c]	6	+1.14	7	+.83
High on only one of the two variables	6	+ .66	12	+.17
Low in both variables	5	− .18	8	−.49

a Deviations of actual over predicted gains in electricity produced, expressed in terms of standard scores.
b Based on stories in children's textbooks (see McClelland, *op. cit.,* pp. 90, 100).
c Using the same classifications for relatively high and low stocks of secondary education shown in Tables 1 and 2.

significantly related to secondary education level, because the cases are fairly evenly divided among the four cells in the two-by-two table, yet we know from previous analyses that each is significantly related to economic growth. Furthermore, they obviously combine to produce the most rapid average growth rates of all. Countries which are high in both *n* Achievement

21 McClelland, *op. cit.*

and educated stock grow significantly faster in both time periods than countries which are high in only one of the two factors. The p values are less than .10 and .025 for the earlier and later time periods (Mann-Whitney U tests, one-tailed).

What is involved in such an analysis can be seen more clearly from Table 4, which lays out the data using higher rather than secondary education figures for 1950. The university figures have three advantages for our purposes over secondary enrollments: (1) they are available for more countries; (2) they are probably more accurate, because there is less ambiguity about what university education is across countries; and (3) there should be less time lag in getting such students actively into the labor force and contributing to acceleration of immediate rates of economic growth (1952–58). At any rate, higher education enrollments bear an even closer relation to rates of economic growth in the 1950's than secondary education does. In an analysis of variance corrected for disproportionality, the F value for educational level (representing the means of $+.49$ vs. $-.51$) is 7.22, $p < .02$, and for n Achievement it is 6.06, $p < .05$. Again, the countries which were high in both factors rank higher in growth rates than countries which were high in only one factor ($p = .02$, Mann-Whitney U test).

To interpret these findings a little, high achievement motivation predicts economic growth; more knowledge (as represented by more education) predicts economic growth, but motivation plus knowledge predicts growth better than either motivation or knowledge alone. Such a conclusion certainly makes eminently good sense. All the achievement motivation in the world, without knowledge (as in some preliterate tribes),[22] should have little effect on economic growth, and vice versa: it should take more than a highly educated populace to produce rapid economic growth. The people have got to *want* to achieve, to care about putting their knowledge to productive uses.

SOURCES OF INCREASED EDUCATIONAL FLOWS

In three independent analyses, two involving secondary and one higher education, it has been found that more education leads to faster growth within groups of countries at approximately the same level of economic or technological development. The obvious next question is how some countries happened to be higher in educational stocks at a given moment in time. Certainly, to reach a higher level of education, a country must have had a period of fairly rapid expansion of its educational system—in short, a period of above-average educational flow. Thus, the problem is to discover what variables are associated with more rapid educational flows.

A logical hypothesis would be that higher n Achievement would lead a country to expand its educational system more rapidly, so that it will be in a better position to develop economically. The idea is supported by the fact

[22] *Ibid.*

Table 4

Rate of Economic Growth (1952–58) as a Function
on n Achievement (1950) and Higher Education
Enrollments Relative to Economic Level (1950)

ENROLLMENT IN HIGHER EDUCATION PER 100,000 INHABITANTS RELATIVE TO
ECONOMIC LEVEL (1950)
RELATIVELY HIGH (1950) [a]   RELATIVELY LOW (1950) [a]

	RELATIVELY HIGH (1950) [a]			RELATIVELY LOW (1950) [a]	
High n Achievement (1950)[b] (2.10 or more)	Aa U.S.S.R.	+1.62[c]	A	W. Germany	+ .53
	A U.S.	+ .47	B	France	− .24
	A Australia	+ .42	C	Portugal	+ .76
	A Canada	+ .06	C	Spain	+ .01
	B Israel	+1.18	D	Tunisia	−1.87
	C Ireland	− .41	D	Syria	− .25
	C Argentina	− .56			
	D Bulgaria	+1.37			
	D India	+1.12			Mean gain high n Achievement = +.49
	D Turkey	+1.38			
	D Pakistan	+2.75			
	Mean gain = +.86			Mean gain = −.18	
Low n Achievement (1950) (below 2.10)	A New Zealand	− .29	A	England	+ .17
	A Finland	− .08	A	Belgium	−1.65
	B Netherlands	− .15	A	Norway	− .77
	B Japan	− .04	A	Switzerland	−1.92
	B Italy	− .57	A	Sweden	− .64
	C Poland	+1.26	B	Denmark	− .89
	C Uruguay	− .75	B	Austria	+ .38
			B	Chile	−1.81
			C	Hungary	− .62
			C	Mexico	+ .12
			D	Iraq	+ .29
			D	Algeria	− .83

Mean gain low n Achievement = −.46

Mean gain = −.09   Mean gain = −.68
Mean gain for relatively high   Mean gain for relatively low
levels of university education = +.49   levels of university education = −.51

a The countries were first grouped by economic level in terms of Kwh electricity per capita produced in 1950, as in Table 1. Group A includes all countries with a Kwh/cap electricity production above 1,000 in 1950; group B all countries with an electricity production between 400–900 Kwh/cap in 1950; group C all countries with an electricity production between 100–300 Kwh/cap in 1950; group D all countries with an electricity production below 100 Kwh/cap in 1950. The countries within a group were then listed according to the enrollment per 100,000 inhabitants in higher education in 1950 (see Table 6). Those countries in which the enrollment was above the median for their economic level were classified as "relatively high" in higher education enrollment, and vice versa.

b These are n Achievement scores obtained from children's textbooks about 1950. For an explanation, see McClelland, *op. cit.* High n Achievement scores are 2.10 or more achievement images per story in the sample of stories coded.

c Positive and negative deviations in standard score units from the regression of the gain in electricity produced between 1950 and 1958 and initial level of electricity production in 1952. Positive scores indicate better than average expected gains in production, negative scores the reverse (see McClelland, *op. cit.*, p. 100).

that 1925 n Achievement levels are significantly correlated with 1950 secondary educational stocks ($r = .44$, $N = 17$, $p < .05$) and by the fact that, as Table 4 shows, 1950 n Achievement levels come close to being significantly related to higher education enrollment rates in 1950 ($\chi^2 = 2.90$, $p < .10$). It would seem logical to assume that these correlations of n Achievement with educational levels would have come about by n Achievement having produced a higher educational flow earlier.

However, this simple idea turns out to be untrue, at least so far as secondary education flows are concerned. Table 5 assembles the data necessary to check the hypothesis, by grouping countries according to their starting secondary enrollment rates (1950), their gains in secondary enrollment rates (1950 to 1957), and their n Achievement levels in 1950. The countries have to be grouped according to starting enrollment rates to remove, as usual, the correlation between base rates and size of gain. No correlation exists for starting rates of 20 per 1,000 or more, but below that point gains are distinctly smaller, making it necessary to compare countries in the same starting categories. The table shows that in each category of starting level (except the lowest) it is the countries with *low* n Achievement in 1950 which have above-median rates of secondary educational expansion between 1950 and 1957. For the way the countries are divided in Table 5, only four, or 28 percent, of those with rapidly expanding secondary education establishments were high in n Achievement in 1950, as compared with 11 or 69 percent of those with slowly expanding secondary schools ($\chi^2 = 4.8$, $p < .05$). The significance of this result varies somewhat, depending where the median breaks are made, so that such an unexpected result gains real credence only when we discover that it also tended to hold for the earlier period. That is, only three, or 33 percent, of the countries showing above-median gains in secondary school enrollments between 1930 and 1950 were high in n Achievement around 1925, compared with six, or 75 percent, of the countries showing below-median gains in secondary education. The difference does not quite reach the 5 percent level of significance, but taken together with the previous finding, it makes one entertain seriously the notion that high levels of n Achievement have led in the past to a relative neglect of secondary education. One cannot even escape this conclusion by arguing that the countries high in n Achievement were already so high in secondary education level that they did not need to expand it more. For, if we consider in Table 5 only those countries which did "need" more secondary education, in the sense of being below average in 1950, the relationship is still inverse between n Achievement level and secondary education expansion.

What does then account for marked increases in the flow of secondary education? None of the other national psychological characteristics like "other-directedness" or concern for affiliation [23] has any predictive power.

[23] *Ibid.*

How about wealth? After all, Curle has shown [24] that wealthier countries tend to spend a greater percentage of their income on education, and the more they spend, the higher the post-primary enrollment tends to be. There is some support for this hypothesis in the top portion of Table 5, which lists the income per capita for each country in Clark's International Units about 1950. In the top category, the countries which show larger gains in secondary enrollment between 1950 and 1957 are by and large those that can better afford more education ($r = .42$, $p < .05$, $N = 18$). However, the few cases on which income estimates are available at the bottom of Table 5 do not support the hypothesis, and also, it is only weakly supported for the earlier time period. That is, if wealth for the countries in Table 2 as of 1938 [25] is related to secondary enrollment gains between 1930 and 1950, the resulting rank order correlation is only .11 ($N = 19$, not significant). However, the low correlation may be due to irregularities in reporting data in the postwar period. For example, the UNESCO figures we have been using show that one of the wealthiest countries, England, actually experienced a *decrease* in the secondary enrollment rate from 1930 to 1950. However, alternative figures compiled by Kaser show that the English rate *more than doubled* during the same time period. If Kaser's figures for England are used, obviously the correlation would be much higher. If England is omitted on the grounds of conflicting data, the r goes up to .24. But it is, of course, not permissible to choose a set of data from another source to support another hypothesis. Rather, it has seemed preferable to stick to one source (the UNESCO figures) throughout, on the grounds that the method of reporting is more likely to be consistent. All we may properly conclude is that there is weak support for the hypothesis; that in the past, wealthier countries have tended to expand secondary education more rapidly, but it seems highly likely that some as yet unmeasured factor will turn out to have greater predictive power than wealth itself. Here, as elsewhere, money is just a means to an end; a country will use it for education only if it is interested in education.

Nevertheless, we can still get a rough idea of how wealth and secondary education end up so highly correlated. There obviously have been ebbs and flows in interest in education and achievement in these countries since 1900. Apparently, when a country is interested in achievement, it tends to concentrate more on productive activities, on business, than on "service" or welfare functions such as more secondary education for the masses. During this period the country tends to develop rapidly economically, especially in those countries which have developed secondary or higher education previously to a fairly high level (Tables 3 and 4). Its rapid economic growth increases its wealth, which it then tends to spend more on secondary educa-

[24] *Op. cit.*
[25] Figures from W. S. Woytinsky and E. S. Woytinsky, *World Population and Production* (New York: Twentieth Century Fund, 1953).

TABLE 5

Countries Classified by Level of Secondary School Enrollment (1950), Gain in That Enrollment 1950–57, and n Achievement Level (1950)

COUNTRY	SECONDARY SCHOOL ENROLLMENT, 1950 a	GAIN IN SECONDARY ENROLLMENT, 1950–57 b		N ACHIEVEMENT LEVEL, 1950 c (+ = ABOVE MEDIAN)	WEALTH (IU/CAP/ 1950) d
A. Rate > 20/1000					
Netherlands	51.0	19.0		1.48	500
New Zealand	41.0	16.5		2.05	885
Czechoslovakia	19.5	15.5		—	326
Australia	33.0	14.4		2.38+	723
Denmark	57.2	14.3	Above	1.05	616
Sweden	32.8 e	12.8	median	1.62	628
Finland	21.9	11.2	gain	1.52	345
France	23.3	10.7		2.38+	490
Belgium	48.6 f	10.4		.43	509
England and Wales	48.3	9.0		1.67	598
U. S.	43.1	8.9		2.24+	1162
W. Germany	41.8	8.2	Below	2.14+	362
Ireland	22.8 g	8.1	median	2.29+	438
Norway	30.8	7.4	gain	1.71	466
Japan	87.3	7.3		1.29	197
Canada	30.5 h	7.0		2.29+	809
Italy	20.2	6.1		1.33	238
Bulgaria	22.7	3.6		2.24+	210
B. Rate 10 to 20/1000					
Chile	17.9	8.9	Above	1.19	264
Hungary	15.6	8.4	median	1.81	139
Austria	13.0 i	6.5	gain	1.86	251
India	11.2	6.0		2.71+	
Spain	10.1	5.1	Below	2.33+	394
Argentina	12.9	3.4	median	3.38+	368
Syria	11.6 g	2.5	gain	2.10+	
C. Rate 10/1000 and below					
Portugal	8.2	5.0	Above	2.10+	146
Turkey	5.1	4.8	median	3.62+	
Iraq	6.9	4.5	gain	1.95	
Tunisia	9.3	2.2	Below	2.14+	
Pakistan	9.9 j	2.1	median	2.29+	
Mexico	4.5	1.4	gain	1.57	

a Number of secondary students (defined as in Table 1) in general and technical schools per 1,000 inhabitants enrolled in 1950. From UNESCO, *op. cit. L'éducation dans le monde. II. L'enseignement du second degré, 1963.* Adult education is included which is classified as belonging to this level.
b Secondary enrollment ratios for 1957, minus those for 1950, defined as in Table 1.
c Based on stories in children's textbooks around 1950; see McClelland, *op. cit.*
d Estimates of income per capita in internationally comparable units. See C. Clark, *The Conditions of Economic Progress,* 3rd ed. (London: Macmillan, 1957).
e Underestimate due to unavailability of enrollments in first and second years of secondary education given in some primary schools.
f Estimate based on interpolation or extrapolation from existing manual figures.
g Includes estimate for private technical school enrollments.
h Figure only approximate, because of complications in the school system in the Province of Quebec.
i Estimate for technical school enrollments added, based on ratio of general to technical enrollments at other time periods.
j Approximate, includes some primary education given in secondary school establishments, but does not include private technical school enrollments.

tion, particularly if its n Achievement level has fallen. The type cases here are Sweden and Denmark, which were quite high in achievement orientation in 1925, showed little interest in expanding secondary education in the 1930's, but at the same time developed economically at an above-average rate.[26] Both countries had dropped sharply in n Achievement level by 1950, and both subsequently (1952–57) showed great interest in expanding secondary education (Table 5), using the wealth acquired in the earlier period for this purpose. At the same time, they developed economically more slowly than average. In short, one can argue that in the past, secondary education has tended to expand rapidly *after* a wave of high n Achievement and rapid economic growth, not before it or at the same time.

However, rapid expansion of higher education in the 1950's is quite another matter. Table 6 assembles the facts which clearly show that n Achievement level is *positively* associated with rapid expansion of higher education ($\chi^2 = 4.98$, p $<$ .05), just as it was *negatively* associated with rapid expansion of secondary education in the same time period. Furthermore, rapid gain in higher education enrollments is also significantly associated with technological growth (1952–58). Twelve or 67 percent of the countries with relatively high gains in third level enrollments showed above average gains in technological growth, as compared with five or 29 percent of those with relatively low gains in third level enrollments ($\chi^2 = 4.98$, p $<$ .05). Here educational expansion seems to be part of the wave of high n Achievement and economic growth, rather than an alternative that follows it, as in the case of secondary education. An explanation for this apparent paradox may be found in the fact that higher education, particularly in the 1950's, has come to be seen as contributing more directly and immediately to technological growth than secondary education. That is, the modern industrial machine has become so complex, requiring as it does high-level technical knowledge of everything from jet engines to chemical processing to digital computers, that it has become fairly obvious to all nations striving for

26 McClelland, *op. cit.,* p. 90.

TABLE 6

Countries Classified by n *Achievement Level (1950)*
and by Gain in Higher Education Enrollment (1950–60)

1950 LEVEL AND 1950–60 GAIN IN HIGHER EDUCATION ENROLLMENT
PER 100,000 INHABITANTS

	GAIN RELATIVELY HIGH [a]			GAIN RELATIVELY LOW [a]		
	COUNTRY	1950 LEVEL	1950–60 GAIN	COUNTRY	1950 LEVEL	1950–60 GAIN
High n	U. S.	1,511 [c]	472 [d]	Ireland	296	66
Achievement [b]	U. S. S. R.	689	429	Canada	594	51
(1950)	Australia	441	415	Spain	267	− 8
	Bulgaria	381	387	Pakistan	93	72
	Argentina	480	347	Tunisia	51	13
	France	325	342			
	W. Germany	257	271			
	Israel	445	255			
	Turkey	118	137			
	Syria	89	134			
	Portugal	161	111			
	India	112	108			
Low n	Netherlands	603	320	Finland	359	170
Achievement	Belgium	234	312	Denmark	402	168
(1950)	Austria	358	288	Hungary	264	139
	Japan	470	280	New Zealand	742	97
	England	209	275	Sweden	346	92
	Mexico	111	147	Uruguay	484	57
				Poland	477	57
				Switzerland	341	57
				Norway	217	41
				Italy	520	−159
				Iraq	91	82
				Algeria	59	11

a There is no relationship between gain in enrollment and starting enrollment level in 1950, so long as the latter is above 200/100,000 inhabitants. Below that point, gains are much lower. So classification as to relatively high or low has been made within these two groups of countries starting at different levels. For countries below the lines in the table, the gains are high or low compared to other countries starting at roughly the same low level in 1950.

b These are n Achievement scores obtained from children's textbooks about 1950. For an explanation, see McClelland, *op cit.*

c Number of students enrolled in institutions of higher learning per 100,000 inhabitants in 1950. From *UN Compendium of Social Statistics: 1963.*

d Gain in number of students enrolled in institutions of higher learning per 100,000 inhabitants between 1950 and 1960.

achievement that they must produce more of the people who know about these things if they are to develop rapidly. On the other hand, these same countries apparently view continued expansion of secondary education, beyond the levels already attained, as less obviously connected with immediate increases in productivity, and as more of an expense item with important welfare and political overtones. Our data support the somewhat different view that expansion of secondary education has not just been a welfare investment, but one which has in the long-run accelerated economic growth (Tables 1 and 2).

Policy Implications

So far, the analysis has been largely theoretical, aimed at tracing as carefully as possible the connections which have existed between investments in education and rates of economic growth. Is there any way the findings can be made more meaningful to development planners? One of the first questions they would want answered is whether investments in education pay off at a high rate. After all, the data so far have only shown that some very vaguely defined "higher" levels of investment in education have been associated with more rapid economic growth, as measured by an electric power index which does not convey a very obvious idea of how much a country has benefited from the investment. Obviously, the additional education costs something. Was the return on the cost high or fairly low? Can a rate of return be estimated?

Since costs of education are in monetary terms, national increases in electric power consumed must be converted into the same units to calculate a rate of return on educational investments. This can be done, because electricity use bears a fairly close relationship to national income figures. For crude estimation purposes, it is not necessary to employ the regression equation relating the two variables. Instead, knowing from the more precise electric power data that education does make a difference in rate of growth, and that electric power changes are related to income changes, we may simply use the much cruder estimates of income per capita changes in the same time period to estimate the effects of education in monetary terms. The estimates for income per capita for different countries for various years in the 1950's have unfortunately been made by different people, using different methods of calculation, so that one feels considerable doubt about the wisdom of using the data to compare economic growth rates. Nevertheless, Table 7 has been prepared as carefully as possible, using differences between estimates of national incomes per capita available for two time periods, 1953 [27] and 1957–58.[28] What it purports to show is the effect in dollar

[27] M. H. Watkins and E. E. Hagen, *Estimate of World Income, 1953* (Cambridge: MIT Center for International Studies, 1956).

[28] Harbison and Myers, *op. cit.*

TABLE 7

Gains in National Income per Capita (1953 to 1957–58)
for Countries Investing Relatively More
or Relatively Less in Higher Education (1950)

RELATIVELY HIGH INVESTMENTS IN HIGHER EDUCATION (1950)			RELATIVELY LOW INVESTMENTS IN HIGHER EDUCATION (1950)		
THIRD LEVEL ENROLLMENT/ 100,000 [a]	COUNTRY	INCOME/CAP GAIN, 1953 TO 1957–58 [b]	THIRD LEVEL ENROLLMENT/ 100,000 [a]	COUNTRY	INCOME/CAP GAIN, 1953 TO 1957–58 [b]
A [c] 1,511	U. S.	$669	A 234	Belgium	$479
A 594	Canada	631	A 346	Sweden	470
A 441	Australia	395	A 257	W. Germany	445
A 359	Finland	344	A 217	Norway	413
A 742	New Zealand	342	A 209	England	259
B 445	Israel	276	B 325	France	343
B 603	Netherlands	236	B 402	Denmark	309
B 520	Italy	209	B (200)	Chile	129
C 480	Argentina	124	C 267	Spain	51
C 484	Uruguay	53	C 111	Mexico	19
Mean 618		$328	257		$302

a From UN Compendium of Social Statistics: 1963.
b Values for 1953 from Watkins and Hagen, op. cit., and for 1957–58 from Harbison and Myers, op. cit.
c Economic level of the country determined by electric power index, as explained in Table 4.

terms of the greater investments in higher education, demonstrated in Table 4 to have a significant impact on economic growth. Unfortunately, data on only 10 countries in each category of educational input were available, but they are pretty well matched for other variables like economic level and n Achievement. Thus, we can have a more reasonable hope that the average difference in rate of income gain is due to the large average difference in investments in higher education, rather than to other factors. Great caution should be exercised in interpreting the income gains of any particular country. There are wide margins of error for any given estimate. Consider Belgium, for instance. Kaser [29] reports an income per capita figure for 1947 of $900 and for 1958 of $1,200 (which agrees with the Harbison-Myers estimate). The UN estimate for 1949 is only $582, which seems fairly consistent with the Watkins-Hagen figure for

29 Kaser, op. cit.

1953 of $716, but not particularly with the figure in Ginsburg[30] for 1956 of $1,015. Possibly annual variations were this great, but more probably methods of computation differed. The point is that the value for Belgium's gain in income per capita given in the table is quite arbitrary: it could be off by one hundred or two hundred dollars. The only virtues of the estimates are that they were obtained consistently from the same sources, in the expectation that the errors would be randomly distributed and that the averages for 10 countries should be considerably more stable and meaningful.

According to these admittedly crude estimates, the countries investing more heavily in higher education in 1950 had a greater return in income, roughly equivalent to $26 a head over a seven or eight year period, or $2,600,000 per 100,000 people. The cost of higher education varies considerably from country to country, having been around $210 a student per year in the Netherlands, $420 in Germany, and $1,000 in the U. S. in 1950.[31] Suppose we take a high median figure of $800 a student: how much did it cost the countries emphasizing higher education more to obtain this higher income? On the average, they educated 361 more university students per 100,000 inhabitants than the countries investing less heavily in higher education—which at a cost of $800 a student comes to roughly $290,000. To this "out-of-pocket" cost should be added some "foregone income" cost, since the students were not working during their year of study in 1950. Again, suppose we assign a high average annual income figure to each of them, of $2,000. This would bring the total average cost of educating around 360 extra university students per 100,000 inhabitants to roughly $1,000,000, as compared with an average return of $2,600,000 per 100,000 inhabitants 7 or 8 years later. According to such estimates, the return in a single year was at least two-and-one-half times the 1950 cost, representing a yield on the investment of over 12 percent a year at compound interest. Obviously, such a calculation is extremely crude and "wobbly," in the sense that removing either the U. S. or Canada from the high educational investment column would suggest a negative rather than a positive payout from educational investments. Furthermore, one can quarrel with many individual estimates in the table, such as the figure for third level enrollment in the United States, which doubtless included many students who would be classified as being in second level education in European countries. All that can be said for the calculation is that it represents an honest and conservative attempt to estimate the return on investments in third level education, on the average, using standard figures on as many countries as possible, in order to average out "other factors" which might have been responsible for the greater average gain in income in one

[30] N. Ginsburg, *Atlas of Economic Development* (Chicago: University of Chicago Press, 1961).

[31] Estimates based on figures given in F. Edding, "Expenditure on Education," in Robinson and Vaizey, *op. cit.*; and Kaser, *op. cit.*

group, rather than the other. It will have served its purpose if it stimulates others to make a more thorough estimate along similar lines. So far as it goes, it tends to support a growing conviction on the part of development planners that the rate of return on educational investments may be fairly high.

It can reasonably be objected, however, that this rate of return applies particularly to developed countries like the United States and may not be as applicable to underdeveloped countries where the issue is of critical significance. There are two questions that need answering—one having to do with whether an underdeveloped country can really expect any such rate of return, and the other having to do with target levels of secondary and higher education that are necessary to produce such rates of return. As for the first question, it should be remembered that the real weight of the argument rests on the electric power index, not on income per capita measures, which are much less reliable and impossible to get in any very meaningful way in underdeveloped countries. So far as the electric power index is concerned, the data in Tables 1, 2, and 4 strongly suggest that education makes itself felt as much or more at the lowest levels of development as it does at the highest levels.[32] It may not be possible to estimate the rate of return of investments in higher education among poor countries in monetary terms, but the electric power data give one no reason to believe that it would be less.

The second question remains: how can an underdeveloped country expect to get any such rate of return from investments in higher education if it does not have the secondary and primary school graduates to do the many other jobs that require less education? Isn't it putting the cart before the horse to talk about investing in university education before the base of the educational pyramid has been strengthened?

What a development planner needs is some kind of a crude estimate of the rate at which he should be educating second and third level students in order to enjoy some of the economic benefits that appear to accrue from such investments in education. The estimate for secondary education is difficult to arrive at, because of the lag problem. That is, we can ask at what rates underdeveloped countries like India and Turkey were educating secondary students in the 1930's, on the assumption that what they did then must have been sufficient to permit fairly rapid growth in the 1950's. However, these estimates, which come out to 3 per 1,000 inhabitants, are certainly too low, because of the rapid growth of technological knowledge and the growing demand for better educated people. After all, a country wants to educate enough secondary school students not for its current needs, but for its needs 20 years from now. It remains to make some estimates based on Table 5.

[32] Unfortunately, the lowest levels measured do not include many countries just beginning development, so the generalization may not hold for them. Here one must rely on the more detailed analysis of educational priorities by stage of development prepared by Harbison and Myers, *op. cit.*

Obviously, there are a number of underdeveloped countries listed which were developing rapidly in the 1950's (India, Bulgaria, Turkey, Pakistan) which had been educating secondary students at a rate of only a 10 to 20 per 1,000 inhabitants. Assuming that they want to educate for a rapidly expanding economy with growing demands for educated people, it seems wise for such countries to set as a goal the upper limit of this range, namely, 20 secondary school students for every 1,000 inhabitants. Countries even less developed than the ones we have been considering, such as the new African nations, will have to be satisfied with a lower figure in the immediate future, but even they should move towards this as soon as possible.[33] Another consideration is that a number of countries have, in the recent past, at any rate, developed quite rapidly at fairly high technological levels with a secondary enrollment ratio in the 20 to 25 per 1,000 range. Thus, a country can be somewhat reassured that it need not be left completely behind in the race for development if it does not pour *more* of its scarce resources into education than is necessary to raise the secondary enrollment ratio to about 20 per 1,000. Obviously, the figure will vary from country to country, depending on the population pyramid and other local conditions, but it is useful to have an approximate figure to shoot at. One further advantage derives from the fact that a plot of number of teachers employed in secondary schools vs. number of students enrolled for a large number of countries shows an amazingly constant ratio of one teacher employed for every 20 students. Thus, we arrive at the convenient manpower requirement figure of one secondary school teacher needed for every 1,000 inhabitants in a country.

As for higher education, we are on somewhat surer ground. Examination of the third level enrollment ratios (1950) of underdeveloped countries that developed rapidly in the 1950's (Table 6) yields an average figure of about 200 per 100,000, which seems both safe in terms of future manpower needs and achievable for backward countries. It also has the advantage of standing in a ratio to the number of secondary school students—namely 1 to 10—which comes very close to the ratio describing the line of best fit for the plot of second against third level enrollments in a large sample of countries. The ratio varies between 1 to 12 and 1 to 8 as between the Anglo-Saxon and Scandinavian educational systems, where secondary education is more widespread, and the Latin educational systems, which educate fewer people at the secondary level but send more of them on to higher education. At any rate, sending one secondary school graduate out of every ten on to a university education seems to have been adequate in a number of countries that have developed rapidly economically. It is worth noting an eventuality that these ratios suggest might be

[33] Harbison and Myers deal in greater detail with the particular educational needs of countries at different stages of development. All that is attempted here is a crude over-all estimate for an "average" underdevelopd country.

dangerous—namely, a too-rapid expansion of higher education at the expense of secondary education, so that the ratio falls to something like 1 to 5. This may produce "unemployed intellectuals," since the rest of the population is not educated to the point where they can use their high level skills. Thus, the 2 per 1,000 third level to 20 per 1,000 second level students is not only a target to aim for, it is also a guide as to a balanced relationship which should probably not be wildly overreached, if a country wants to maintain optimum conditions for economic growth.

All of these estimates are obviously subject to all sorts of errors—not the least of them being the danger of predicting for the future in terms of the past. Nevertheless, it has seemed better to make some estimates, however crude, for the simple reason that decisions about educational investments have to be made on some basis in all the developing countries. And certainly it seems better to base those judgments on what information can be gathered about the experience of other nations developing in the recent past. This experience suggests that (1) countries investing more heavily in education have tended to develop more rapidly; (2) the return on higher education investments may be as high as 12 percent, compounded annually, under average conditions; and (3) adequate educational goals for underdeveloped countries to set for rapid economic development are 20 students in secondary school and 2 students in higher education for every 1,000 inhabitants in the country.

EDUCATION, POLITICS AND DEVELOPMENT

In another global study, economic, social, and political variables are related to one another. Large masses of data are used systematically to discuss a number of hypotheses concerning these variables.

CONTEMPORARY attention is so concentrated on the role of education in development, that we are inclined to forget its capacity to stunt growth.[1] Yet in most societies for most of recorded time, education has been a reactionary force rather than a progressive one. Education, often closely associated with religion, has tended rather to hallow antiquity than to promote innovation. It has usually been the prerogative of the ruling group, endowing them with the skills to maintain their hegemony and perpetuating the values upon which it rested.

REPRINTED FROM *Comparative Education Review*, 7 (February 1964), 226–245. © 1964 by Comparative Education Review. This article is taken from a paper prepared for a seminar conference held at Boston University during the summer of 1963, sponsored by the Comparative Administration Group of the American Society for Public Administration.

---

[1] There is good evidence that affluent countries spend more on education than poor ones, but this by no means indicates that they are rich *because* of their investment in education. One might as well argue that rich owe their wealth to the fact that they spend more than poor ones on champagne and fur coats for their wives. In order to demonstrate that education has contributed to national wealth we may either follow the controversial approach of T. W. Schultz, which is acceptable neither to all economists for one set of reasons, nor to all educators for another; or we may correlate educational expansion with subsequent changes in the rate of economic growth over a period of time (assuming, of course, that it will take some years for education to achieve an economic impact). We may be able to trace this relationship in certain countries, and even in groups of countries at specific periods. For example, there is a positive correlation at the .02 level between the size of post-primary enrollment of 36 countries in 1938 and their rate of economic growth during the next decade. This tendency is not reproduced, however, during the post-war period, during which somewhat unreliable statistics are available for a much larger and more economically varied group of nations. This is obviously not to say that education has had no positive impact on the economy, but to suggest that it is very hard to isolate specifically educational factors from political, social, economic and other elements in the growth process. But it must be admitted in addition that some forms of education are far more conducive to development than others.

EDUCATION, EQUALITY AND THE SPIRIT OF INNOVATION

Even today it may be argued that some aspects of certain educational systems serve rather to retard than to promote growth. One authority [2] attributes much of Britain's failure to match continental economic growth to the traditionalism in which aspects of her system are shrouded.

This is not to be wondered at. The elite of the world have, for the most part, tended to be satisfied with their position of wealth, power and status. They saw no need for radical change and it would have been peculiar indeed if they had espoused a system which threatened to over-turn their world. To the modernisers, education is a means of actualising more and more of the world's potential brain-capacity, of bringing this great semi-tapped resource to bear upon the world's problems. But this means disrupting the older, more static habits of mind, and it introduces competition for those who had previously derived security from those very attitudes. This was not the aspect of education which was popular in the past. It is not popular today in some countries where a ruling minority has much to lose if power—even if only intellectual power—becomes the prerogative of the majority.

But of course all learning, even the most classical scholasticism, carries the germ of growth. In some parts of the desert, seeds which have lain dormant through years of drought begin to sprout after rain. In the same way, new social circumstances can stimulate germination in even the most arid educational systems. Such a change was the emergence of nationalism in nineteenth century Europe. The drive to establish new types of political entity was closely associated with the founding of national education systems. These systems spread to classes of people who had seldom enjoyed educational opportunities and began to give to education an innovational character. Education began to rival birth as a qualification for positions of prestige. As more people became more educated, so a technological society took shape in which education became more and more important. To some, its importance was as a stepping stone, previously not available, to authority of the traditional type. For the majority, however, education became the tool by which a new class was created which was neither aristocracy nor peasantry, and in which skill and knowledge counted far more than inherited status. Thus, in Europe especially, the innovating element in education was closely associated with its social role. Where its function was egalitarian, it stimulated growth: where oligarchical, it buttressed the status quo. It need hardly be said that education's shift from a "maintaining" to a "changing" function was neither steady nor consistent. If in some of the older countries it still serves to preserve privilege, in some of the newer it helps to create a new, exclusive, and even repressive elite.

The rise of nationalism in the European sense was not, of course, the only circumstance to give new force and direction to education. In Japan, for

[2] John Vaizey, *Education for Tomorrow*, London: Penguin Books, 1962, pp. 21–29.

example, the development of education in the Meiji period followed a highly realistic appraisal of the country's economic position *vis-à-vis* the Western world once that country's isolation was ended. This view was formalised in an Imperial (and therefore divine) rescript that was pursued with unquestioning loyalty. Nevertheless, even in this context, the levelling tendencies of an innovating education were not to be resisted indefinitely. For a variety of reasons, among which education must be included, the social structure of Japan is different, specifically more egalitarian, than it was at the dawn of the century.

The U.S.A. has not had such rigidities to erode. The mere removal to the New World implied, in many people, a breaking down of traditional social adhesions. However it was essential that education should have a progressive character. There was no status quo to preserve; on the contrary, a new society had to be built and a diversity of peoples welded into one. Above all, perhaps, the ideology which sanctioned this welding was to be promoted and perpetuated.

Except in Japan these processes have all been relatively slow and haphazard. They have resulted from a galaxy of decisions and policies, often contradictory, frequently impractical, but having this much in common, that they reflected the changing quality of society. In this respect they may be contrasted with the educational character of many Latin American states. In these countries, so prone to revolution, so dominated by the jockeying for position of dominant cliques rather than evolution, the isolation and ossification of the educational system is inseparable from the stagnation of society.

The official policy of most countries is now to support education, laying stress on its economic and cultural importance. So many clarion pronouncements to this effect have been made that no administration, whatever its inner feelings, dares lag unduly for fear of losing face. Moreover, many nations, as we shall see, have good reason for sincere belief in the role of education in their development.

RELATIONSHIPS BETWEEN EDUCATION, POLITICS AND DEVELOPMENT

If, as already suggested, there is any relationship between an educational system capable of promoting innovation and a social move in the direction of egalitarianism, then it is reasonable to suppose that there may be various types of connection between education, development and political structure. In order to explore these connections a sample was constructed containing all those countries about which information was available regarding the percentage of national income invested in education, and domestic fixed capital formation as a proportion of total expenditure on gross national product. The latter approximates what may be thought of as savings, and will subsequently be referred to as such: as we shall shortly see, this was considered as the most reliable single indicator of purposefulness in development (and indeed there is a fairly close correlation in Table 1 between rank orders for savings and for rates of economic growth[a]). The countries concerned were also rated on a somewhat crude dichotomy of "Competitive" or "Non-competitive" politically. For those countries for which the information was available, rank orders were given for rates of infant mortality (as possibly reflecting the same type of concern—or unconcern—for human material as does education), post-primary educational enrollment, per capita income, and rate of economic growth. (These will all be found in Table 1, together with the correlations etc. derived from them. Levels of significance will only be referred to in the text in general terms, but letters in the text refer to similarly designated calculations in Table 1.)

The first implication is of some relationship between education and economic development. Indeed, there is a high correlation between per capita income and the percentage of national income invested in education.[b] This, of course, does not of itself demonstrate anything except that rich nations tend to spend proportionately more on education than do poor ones. It was considered that the developmental value of education, if any, might be revealed by relating both investment in education and post-primary enrollment ratios (which are generally considered as having most relevance to development capacity) to rates of economic growth. None of these relationships had any statistical significance, however. It is true that there were some countries, Japan for example, in which high investment in education and rapid economic growth appeared to be connected. But in others, such as Venezuela prior to 1958, very speedy economic expansion was matched with extremely low investment in education; in yet others, such as Norway, high investment in education accompanies negligible economic growth. In fact, the average investment in education of the ten countries which had the lowest rate of economic growth was slightly higher than that of the twelve which had the highest— and both were above the mean.

It would indeed be rash to attempt any precise definition of the role of education and development. Nevertheless, as we shall consider later, it is not inconceivable that with the global absence of relationships there are similarities, often to be defined in terms of political ideology or social structure, between education and economic development in smaller groups of countries.

A further hypothesis relating the possible innovating role of education in European industrialisation, is that those countries which are striving to achieve development may be likely to invest most in education. This does not mean that they have yet achieved a high per capita income, nor does it mean that their expenditure in education is necessarily helpful to that end. It simply suggests that those countries which are attempting to innovate and to expand their economies are likely also to be those in which some egalitarian processes are at work, and which believe in the importance of human resource development.

The rate of savings is not, of course, the only means of judging the seriousness of the development intent. Another is the possession of a sound develop-

TABLE 1

Correlations Between Education, Politics and Development

	SAVINGS AS PERCENTAGE OF GNP	RANK ORDER OF SAVINGS	INVESTMENT IN EDUCATION AS PERCENTAGE OF NATIONAL INCOME	RANK ORDER OF INVESTMENT IN EDUCATION	INFANT MORTALITY PER 1000 LIVE BIRTHS	RANK ORDER OF INFANT MORTALITY	PER CAPITA GNP, RANK ORDER	POLITICAL SYSTEM	POST-PRIMARY ENROLLMENT RATIO, RANK ORDER	RATE OF ECONOMIC GROWTH, ABOUT 1954–1959 RANK ORDER
Algeria	25.5	10.5	3.3	28	117.9	47	43	NC	39	3
Argentina	21.0	23.5	2.5	43	59.1	32	24	C	25	53.5
Australia	27.0	7	2.2	47.5	19.5	5	5	C	6	11
Austria	23.7	14	3.9	17.5	22.9	21	19	C	15	14
Barbados	27.4	6	3.4	26.5	66.4	33	—	C	—	6
Belgium	17.5	36	5.6	4	26.2	13	10	C	8	50.5
Brazil	16.3	41.5	2.6	42	170	52.5	33	C	32	19.5
Br. Guiana	22.5	17	3.7	20	60.9	34	29	NC	45	48
Burma	19.6	29.5	3.6	23.5	130.3	50	52	NC	37	29
Canada	26.5	8	4.5	10	27.3	14	2	C	11	37
Ceylon	12.8	52	4.6	8.5	57.5	31	47	NC	—	37
Chile	8.7	56	2.4	44.5	127.9	49	41	C	28	53.5
Colombia	18.4	32	2.1	49	99.8	43	28	NC	38	37
Congo (L)	18.2	33	5.1	7	143	51	49	C	49	49
Costa Rica	17.9	34	4.0	16	80.3	40	30	C	29	41
Cuba	17.6	35	3.4	26.5	—	—	26	NC	36	52
Cyprus	15.8	45	4.3	12	30.0	17	25	C	16	55.5
Denmark	19.1	31	2.9	38.5	22.5	9	14	C	13	34
Dom. Rep.	15.8	45	1.6	54.5	—	—	36	NC	40	41
Ecuador	14.1	50	1.7	53	105.8	45	37	NC	35	31
Finland	29.9	4	6.3	2	19.8	6	13	C	12	32.5
France	17.4	37	3.0	36	26.1	12	9	C	18	29
Germany (W)	24.0	12	3.6	20	33.7	22	15	C	1	7
Ghana	19.7	28	1.5	56	113.1	46	45	NC	48	8
Greece	25.5	10.5	1.6	54.5	40.1	23.5	35	NC	21	19.5
Guatemala	12.0	53	2.4	44.5	91.7	42	42	NC	41	21.5
Iceland	31.1	3	3.1	33	13.3	1	8	C	4	32.5
Israel	23.4	15	3.0	36	29.8	16	18	C	22	5
Italy	22.5	19.5	3.2	30	40.1	23.5	22	C	17	15.5
Jamaica	21.5	22	2.3	46	51.0	29	32	NC	—	9
Japan	31.4	2	5.7	3	29.8	16	18	C	22	5
Korea	11.4	55	4.2	14.5	63.1	36	50	NC	19	29
Luxemburg	23.3	16	1.9	51.5	31.5	20	6	C	27	44

TABLE 1 (Cont.)

	SAVINGS AS PERCENTAGE OF GNP	RANK ORDER OF SAVINGS	INVESTMENT IN EDUCATION AS PERCENTAGE OF NATIONAL INCOME	RANK ORDER OF INVESTMENT IN EDUCATION	INFANT MORTALITY PER 1000 LIVE BIRTHS	RANK ORDER OF INFANT MORTALITY	PER CAPITA GNP, RANK ORDER	POLITICAL SYSTEM	POST-PRIMARY ENROLLMENT RATIO, RANK ORDER	RATE OF ECONOMIC GROWTH, ABOUT 1954–1959 RANK ORDER
Malta	19.8	27	4.4	11	31.4	19	—	NC	—	15.5
Mauritius	21.0	23.5	3.5	25	69.5	37	—	NC	—	57
Mexico	15.7	47	1.4	57	75.1	39	40	NC	46	24.5
Netherlands	23.9	13	5.2	6	15.4	2	17	C	10	26.5
New Zealand	19.6	29.5	3.7	20	22.8	10	3	C	9	17.5
Nigeria	11.9	54	1.9	51.5	62.9	35	51	C	50	37
Norway	27.8	5	5.5	5	18.5	4	12	C	23	47
Panama	17.0	38	3.9	17.5	57.1	30	27	NC	24	41
Peru	15.8	45	2.9	38.5	103.4	53	44	NC	34	45.5
Philippines	8.5	57	3.2	30	73.1	38	39	C	14	24.5
Portugal	16.9	39	2.0	50	88.5	41	38	NC	33	37
Puerto Rico	20.5	25	7.4	1	43.1	26	20	C	2	21.5
Rhodesia S & N	22.4	18	3.6	23.5	—	—	46	NC	—	12
South Africa	20.2	26	3.1	33	126.8	48	23	NC	44	13
Switzerland	21.7	21	3.1	33	20.8	7	4	C	26	26.5
Tanganyika	15.0	49	3.0	36	170	52.5	—	NC	47	36
Thailand	15.4	48	2.7	40.5	41.7	25	48	NC	31	40.5
Trinidad	31.8	1	2.7	40.5	45.4	28	—	NC	—	40.5
Turkey	16.7	40	2.2	47.5	—	—	31	NC	43	47.5
U. K.	16.1	43	4.2	13	22.1	8	11	C	7	13
U. S. A.	16.3	41.5	4.6	8.5	25.2	11	1	C	3	8.5
Venezuela	26.3	9	4.1	14.5	45.1	27	16	C	42	14.5

Rank order correlations

a. Savings and rate of economic growth: N = 57, Rho = .38, t = 3.00, p = .01.
b. Per capita income and percentage of national income invested in education: N = 52, Rho = .53, t = 4.41, p = .001.
c. Savings and per capita income: N = 52, Rho = .61, t = 3.00, p = .01.
d. Savings and investment in education: N = 57, Rho = .26, t = 2.00, p = .05.
e. Savings and investment in education in Latin American and Caribbean countries: N = 18, Rho = .44, t = 1.96, p = .02.
f. Investment in education and per capita income in Latin American and Caribbean countries: N = 18, Rho = .44, t = 1.96, p = .1.
g. Savings and infant mortality: N = 53, Rho = .42, t = 3.29, p = .01.
h. Per capita income and infant mortality: N = 48, Rho = .75, t = 7.68, p = .001.

i. Savings and post-primary enrollment: N = 49, Rho = .59, t = 4.39, p = .001.
j. Savings and primary enrollment: N = 57, Rho = .43, t = 3.54, p = .001.
k. Investment in education and post-primary enrollment: N = 49, Rho = .61, t = 5.08, p = .001.
l. Investment in education and primary enrollment: N = 57, Rho = .40, t = 3.24, p = .01.
m. Per capita income and post-primary enrollment: N = 49, Rho = .64, t = 5.76, p = .001.
n. Infant mortality and post-primary enrollment: N = 47, Rho = .64, t = 5.58, p = .001.
o. Infant mortality and investment in education: N = 53, Rho = .34, t = 2.34, p = .05.
p. Infant mortality and rate of economic growth: N = 53, Rho = .03, t = .21, no significance.

χ^2 *Distributions*

q. Political system and investment in education: χ^2 = 6.82, p = .01.
r. Political system and infant mortality: χ^2 = 15.0, p = .001.
s. Political system and savings: χ^2 = 2.88, p = .1.

ment plan, a criterion which has been employed by certain agencies in determining whether or not to give assistance. Now, however, most countries have a plan, and there is no fully adequate way of discriminating between good and bad plans. In any case it would be virtually impossible on a global scale to do what is more important, to discover whether or not the plans are being consistently followed. Another measure is to determine how much of a nation's expenditure is, from the point of view of development, frivolous. It may be argued that heavy expenditures on armed forces shows a lack of interest in development, but clearly some countries are under much greater political pressure to arm than are others. If, however, one is to take more variable criteria, an elaborate analysis of each economy would be called for, a task which would occupy a substantial volume.

A country's savings proportionate to its wealth are taken as more significant of its drive to develop rather than is its wealth.[c] It is true that it is harder for poor countries to save than for rich ones, and that therefore there is likely to be some correlation between per capita GNP and savings. It is also true that many countries are all the wealthier simply because they *have* saved. This increases the likelihood that there will be a relationship between the proportion of savings to gross national product, and the volume of that product per capita. Nevertheless, it is possible for some countries, such as Japan, to have a very high rate of savings coupled with a relatively low per capita GNP, while others, such as New Zealand, have, relative to other countries, a much higher per capita GNP than savings. It has been pointed out that savings will include capital expenditure on education, and thus some relationship between savings and expenditure on education is inevitable. But capital expenditure on education tends to be a small proportion of the whole. Moreover, as we shall shortly see, there are other means of relating the educational effort (e.g. through school enrollments) to savings.

It was found that there was some relationship between savings and investment in education.[d] However, a smaller group of Latin American and Caribbean countries showed a higher relationship.[e] It is interesting that in this case there was a much less significant relationship between investment in education and per capita GNP than for the whole sample.[f] This suggests that in the relatively more homogeneous sample a general principle emerges with greater sharpness.

A further assumption was made that countries which invest in the education of their people will also look after their welfare in other respects. The most obvious of these is health, and the most accurate single measure of effective work in health was taken to be the level of infant mortality. The relationship between savings and infant mortality level was significant.[g] But the relationship between high per capita income and low infant mortality was exceptionally close.[h]

It was also predicated that countries which were seriously pursuing development would have larger school enrollments, particularly at post-primary level. The relationships between both post-primary and primary enrollment and savings were significant.[i, j] The relationships, as might have been expected, were of equal significance between enrollment and investment in education.[k, l] The relationship between per capita GNP and post-primary enrollment shows a similar situation.[m] There appears to be a slightly greater commitment to post-primary education in the countries both investing most in education and having the largest volumes of savings. Correlations not previously referred to in the text are: infant mortality level with, respectively, post-primary enrollment,[n] investment in education,[o] and rate of economic growth.[p]

The inference which may be drawn is that savings and per capita GNP (which are clearly apt to be related in the majority of cases) are dominating factors in relation to social development (i.e. education and health as understood in various ways). The hypothesis that, on a global scale, educational development is related to savings is not disproved, indeed some correlation is shown; but it is subordinated to economic indicators of a particular country's condition. The fact that educational development (both investment and enrollment) is correlated with economic growth suggests that we should view these relationships as being at least partly within the realm of what is thought to be appropriate, rather than what is more causally related (as low infant mortality and high per capita income). We are, in fact, probably justified in suggesting that countries most concerned to develop pay most attention, *inter alia*, to education.

The next assumptions to be examined were those concerning the relationship between political structure on the one hand with education, savings and health on the other. The same criteria for the latter three variables were employed, but arbitrary distinctions were made between "high" and "low." A high rate of savings was reckoned as over seventeen per cent of expenditure on GNP. A high proportion of national income invested in education was reckoned to be three per cent. A low rate of infant mortality was reckoned to be less than fifty per thousand live births. The political rating employed was adapted from Almond and Coleman.[3] Their assessments of Competitive, Semi-competitive, and Authoritarian were applied to those countries which were common to their sample and the present one. The author made his own assessment of those which were not in the Almond and Coleman sample. This, however, did not present much difficulty, because the majority were European countries of obvious political complexion. In order to give adequate numbers, however, Semi-competitive and Authoritarian were taken together and referred to (as they will be throughout) as non-competitive. The relationship between high educational investment and competitive politics was significant.[q] Even more significant was the relationship between low infant mortality and competitive politics.[r] The relationship between savings and competitive politics is, however, of borderline significance.[s] There is thus some slight suggestion that the countries which enjoy competitive political systems are also those which save most: the fact that they invest most in their human resources seems to be fairly self-evident.

When Almond and Coleman published their tentative hypothesis that there was some tendency for greater degrees of development to be associated with competitive forms of government, several critics pointed out that the richer countries could "afford" to be democratic, or that democracy was something

TABLE 2

Comparison of Egalitarian and Non-Egalitarian African Countries in Terms of Per Capita Income and Educational Expenditure per Person (US dollars)

| | EGALITARIAN | | | NON-EGALITARIAN | |
COUNTRY	EXPENDITURE PER PERSON	PER CAPITA INCOME	COUNTRY	EXPENDITURE PER PERSON	PER CAPITA INCOME
Egypt	5.0	133	Angola	0.3	70
Ghana	3.5	135	Ethiopia	0.6	54
Guinea	3.0	58	Liberia	1.6	103
Nigeria	1.3	70	South Africa *	1.7	381
Tunisia	6.0	131	S. Rhodesia **	1.0	134
Average	*3.8*	*105*	*Average*	*1.0*	*148*

* Non-European only.
** Combined for S. and N. Rhodesia and Nyasaland.

which "happened" (though obviously not always) when nations reached a certain stage of prosperity. This might come about for all sorts of reasons. One would be, for example, that development depends greatly on the activity of

[3] James S. Coleman, "Conclusion: The Political Systems of the Developing Areas," and Appendix; Gabriel A. Almond and James S. Coleman, editors, *The Politics of the Developing Areas*, Princeton, New Jersey: Princeton University Press, 1960. pp. 532–582.

entrepreneurs; that entrepreneurs are frequently persons of a class to whom society denies traditional status, which accounts for their election of entrepreneurial activity as a means of advancement; and that once they have achieved success they wish to consolidate and improve through education the position of their children. The writer suggests, however, that emphasis on education tends to be an integral part of the policy of nations which are striving for development, and that investment in education is not merely a by-product of development already achieved. (As has already been said it is outside the present frame of reference to attempt to demonstrate the extent to which education actually promotes development.) But it is now apparent that this emphasis on education, and hence on development, is associated with political orientation. There is a relationship among nations' attitudes towards human beings, their rates of development, and the character of their politics.

Socio-Political Typologies and Their Educational Corollaries

Despite the existence of some fairly close correlations between development effort, political system, and human resource development policy as manifested in educational statistics, a glance at the figures in Table 1 reveals a number of exceptions. Some of these may at least in part be accounted for by confusions in educational policy. But in others there may be factors not taken into account by the rather crude global measures employed here.

It seems possible that calculations based on Almond and Coleman's typology omit a variable which has considerable bearing upon a nation's development of its human resources. This is the extent to which it is egalitarian in the sense of offering the possibility for anyone, irrespective of class, race, tribe, religion or any other ascribed qualities, to attain the highest positions in the land, so that no one is excluded by the accident of birth from educational opportunities or from the advantages which these opportunities might bring.

A glance at various aspects of national economic and educational performance on a regional basis gives some preliminary grounds for supposing that egalitarianism is a significant feature. Of the twenty independent Latin American states, the seven which may be considered as relatively more competitive and egalitarian than the rest have an average per capita expenditure on education of $15.4 and an average per capita income of $416. The others are not only poorer (per capita income averages $191), but also spend proportionally much less on education per capita ($3.9).

In Africa the five least egalitarian (and most non-competitive) countries are compared with an equal number which are egalitarian, some being competitive and others non-competitive politically (Table 2).

Similar tendencies may be noted in relation to a group of Middle Eastern countries (Table 3).

It has already been noted that the countries with the highest per capita incomes tend to have the greatest amount of education. To that extent the

TABLE 3

*Comparison of Middle Eastern Countries in Terms of Per Capita
Income and Proportion of the Population in Post-Primary Education*

| | EGALITARIAN | | | NON-EGALITARIAN | |
COUNTRY	PROPORTION OF POPULATION IN POST-PRIMARY EDUCATION	PER CAPITA INCOME	COUNTRY	PROPORTION OF POPULATION IN POST-PRIMARY EDUCATION	PER CAPITA INCOME
Cyprus	3.75	374	Iran	.63	100
Egypt	2.45	133	Iraq	1.05	195
Israel	3.14	540	Jordan	2.50	96
Lebanon	2.35	269	Saudi Arabia	.05	166
			Syria	1.69	111
			Turkey	.77	276
			Yemen	.04	50
Average	2.92	290	*Average*	.96	142

The per capita income for Yemen is a very crude estimate. The rather extraordinary case of Kuwait is excluded from these comparisons. With a per capita income of $2500 and an expenditure on education per person of $144—both the highest figures in the world—only .62 of the total population are in secondary education.

above figures are not unexpected. At the same time it has been particularly noted by one authority [4] that the economic vigor of the egalitarian group—though lacking the oil wealth of Iran, Iraq and Saudi Arabia—has been closely associated with their commitment to education.

In Europe it is significant that the three countries which perhaps most markedly combine non-competitive politics with a non-egalitarian society have easily the lowest per capita expenditure on education. With a European average of $34, Greece spends $5, and Portugal and Spain $4 each.

It is not, of course, enough to evaluate educational systems in terms of their size and cost. In the ensuing pages an attempt has also been made to characterise them in terms of quality and function. The criteria for making such judgments vary so widely from one country to another,[5] since, apart from the question of establishing standard measurements, information on such vital matters as teacher qualifications is hardly ever comparable. The element of subjectivity in these judgments predominates even after the available evidence has been considered. The main qualitative issues on which the judgments were made include the existence of education planning procedures leading to presumed careful decisions, and the professionalism of the educational sys-

[4] A. J. Meyer, *Middle Eastern Capitalism: Nine Essays*, Cambridge: Harvard University Press, pp. 1–17.

[5] For a useful discussion of this difficulty see *Manual of Educational Statistics*, UNESCO, 1961.

tem, including measures taken to train and retrain teachers, and to revise and evaluate the curriculum. Other factors include the presence of a unitary educational system, as is normally the case in egalitarian societies, or a dual or segregated system as it frequently is in non-egalitarian ones. Three potential roles for education are also considered: *traditional*, which implies an emphasis on maintaining the traditional values of a static society; *economic*, which implies particular emphasis on technical education and various techniques of gearing the output of the educational system to the needs of the economy for skilled personnel; *political*, which implies the use of the school system to implant a political ideology in the young. The extent to which these functions obtrude on what might be termed *general* education, or education for its own sake, depends upon the socio-political context.

While most democracies (or competitive systems) espouse egalitarian ideals, many non-competitive societies also practice them. Pre-eminent among these are the communist countries and the mass party states such as Ghana and Egypt. It is equally true that there are some countries possessing competitive political systems which are socially non-egalitarian. This occurs when elements of the social structure, despite the constitution, create barriers against the progress of certain elements of the population. India with its caste system, the segregated southern states of the USA, and Brazil, especially the northeastern region where the non-egalitarian social system is in marked contrast to the democratic constitution, may all be cited as examples of competitive political associated with non-egalitarian social systems.

There are also, of course, non-competitive political systems having non-egalitarian social structures. These include such traditional oligarchies as Ethiopia and Afghanistan as well as South Africa, Peru, Iran, and Venezuela before the last change of administration.

This suggests the existence of four types of societies: competitive egalitarian; competitive non-egalitarian; non-competitive egalitarian; and non-competitive non-egalitarian.

The first hypothesis to consider is that a country's degree of egalitarianism affects its educational policy regardless of whether or not its political system is competitive. It will not be possible to compare figures on a global basis as was done in the previous grosser calculations, since egalitarianism is a matter of degree. England, for example, is highly egalitarian when compared with many less affluent but still democratic countries. On the other hand, it is much less egalitarian than a similarly prosperous country like France. In addition, although it will be maintained that egalitarian countries spend more on education than non-egalitarian ones, comparisons can be made only among countries of approximately the same per capita income. For this reason it is seldom possible to consider both developed and underdeveloped countries in the same context. Indeed, even within Africa, non-egalitarian (but wealthy) South Africa spends four times as much on education per capita as egalitarian (but much poorer) Ghana. (It must be admitted, however, that the greater part is spent on the education of the white population.) Therefore, except for using the European communist countries for purposes of illustration, we shall concentrate henceforth on the underdeveloped areas. Most of the sample is drawn from the countries cited in Table 1, together with a few others for which it was possible to obtain the requisite information, but about which data needed for previous calculations were not available.

The findings may be summarized as follows:

A. *Politically competitive, egalitarian.* This category would include USA, Canada, New Zealand, most countries of Western Europe, Puerto Rico, Trinidad, a few—such as Uruguay—of Latin America, and a handful in Afro-Asia. Most of these nations are long established and wealthy. They have a high rate of economic growth and of post-secondary enrollment. Infant mortality is low. These are, for the greater part, the countries in which the rise of education and of industrialism was associated with nineteenth century nationalism. This is essentially the pattern of the developed nations of the world, embodying not only the values which are dear to the Western world, but the great resources with which they may be realised and maintained.

Omitting the countries of Europe, Australia and North America, it is remarkable how successful economically many of those have been in contrast to the less developed areas which are both less competitive politically and less egalitarian socially. Israel, Japan, Puerto Rico, Jamaica and Trinidad have all registered the most notable economic successes while at the same time investing heavily in education (see Table 1). Nigeria, which apart from the more feudal Northern Region is an outstanding example among the new African states of egalitarian democracy, has, despite its great poverty, a surprisingly satisfactory rate of economic growth. Nigeria is also remarkable for the constructive steps being taken to plan and to develop the educational system.

The educational systems of these countries have the following attributes:

1. They are unitary. That is to say, there are not parallel systems, as in South Africa for white and black, or as in England for "upper" and "lower" classes. There are, of course, private schools, but these are not so numerous or so organised as to create a different educational caste.

2. They are carefully planned by specially established agencies either in the Ministry of Education, or a planning organisation, or both. This planning relates not only to the logistics of educational expansion, but also to national man-power needs.

3. Their quality is high. Teachers are adequately trained, or efforts are being made to train them; they receive in-service training; their professional associations are supported and encouraged. Adequate machinery exists for the evaluation and revision of the curriculum.

The function of these systems may be described as both general educational and economic. They promote education both for its own peculiar role of "leading out" the capacities of the individual, and for its contribution to the economic needs of the country.

B. *Politically competitive, non-egalitarian.* There are perhaps greater divergencies among these countries than in any of the other types, because the extremely varied elements within their social systems give rise to the non-egalitarian elements. In India it is the caste system which acts counter to the spirit of equality enshrined in all democratic constitutions; in Brazil, pre-revolutionary Pakistan, and several other countries, it is the oligarchy of landlords and aristocrats; in the U.S. South it is prejudice on the part of a dominant racial group which has also great local political power. It is, of course, extremely hard to estimate the extent to which the non-egalitarian qualities of different countries have affected national performance. It is apparent, however, that countries of this type are characterised neither by the economic progress nor the high investment in education which is common among those in the competitive egalitarian group.

The most important question to ask about any non-egalitarian society is the extent to which governmental power resides in the hands of the non-egalitarian elite. In pre-revolution Pakistan the elite were the rulers and all workings of government, though democratic in constitution, were permeated with their non-egalitarian attitude, until in the end democracy withered and died. An entirely different situation exists in the Philippines, where the social elite do not have political power. In the case of Pakistan a non-egalitarian society subverted the constitution, but in the Philippines the democratic constitution is not directly affected by inequalities in the society, although these to some extent impair the effectiveness of government action.

i. India. The population of India is so vast, and its problems are so complex, that it would be absurd to isolate the socio-religious caste factor as being pre-eminent. Nevertheless, about 40% of her population is denied a large measure of social mobility because of caste, and the effects of denying to the country full use of its reservoir of brainpower cannot but be enormous. Government policy in this respect is enlightened, but in many places the barriers of caste are almost as rigid as ever. The following figures are interesting:

Economic growth rate	3.5
Per capita GNP	$72
Infant morality per 1000 live births	145.9
Post secondary enrollment ratio	1.88
Percentage of national income invested in education	1.7
Per capita expenditure on education	$2.0

ii. Philippines. Despite a period as an American colony and subsequent independence, the elite of Spanish descent have retained their economic if not their political supremacy. The Chinese mercantile class, by reason of its wealth, also constitutes something of a social oligarchy. The concentration of so much power in the hands of a racial minority, even on a non-political basis may be related to the educational structure. While the children of the social elite are sent to expensive schools and, in many cases, to Universities overseas, the remainder attend national institutions, many of which have extremely low standards. More than 250,000 students are enrolled in higher education, an amazingly large number for a population of 28,000,000 in which there is an illiteracy rate of thirty per cent. But the social barriers mean that qualifications obtained through local education are insufficient in job competition with persons educated abroad who also have the influence of rich connections behind them.

The rate of economic growth has been adequate: 5.6 per cent, but savings have been low, 8.5. Infant mortality is 73.1 per 1000 live births. Public expenditure on education per head is $6.

iii. Brazil. This country contains many of the contradictions to be expected in a country in which the democratic theory of government is offset by the extreme non-egalitarian character of the social structure in certain areas. Brazil is relatively wealthy and spends a very large amount on education per head, $32 (being second only to Venezuela in Latin America), but her achievement in other respects is very mediocre:

	BRAZIL	WORLD MEAN
per capita income	$262	$200
infant mortality	120	84–5
primary enrollment	34	42
post-primary enrollment	1.40	2.29

Despite the differences among these countries, certain common features in their educational systems may be noted:

1. They are usually dual, there being one school structure—which is private —for the elite, and another—which is government-supported—for the masses. The quality of the education offered to the elite tends to be superior to that available to the average citizen. (This is even the case in England.)

2. Although in some countries, such as India, a consistent effort is made in planning, there is less homogeneity with regard to planning in this group than in either of the egalitarian groups.

3. These systems also vary considerably in their quality. The effectiveness of state education may be reduced by the loss of good teachers to the more lucrative private schools. In the Philippines state education is excellent but exiguous, and the use of education in job competition with the privately educated elite has led to the proliferation of a vast number of fourth-rate private institutions offering almost worthless qualifications. Thus in a rather unusual sense the non-egalitarian character of the society is associated with a disastrous decline in the standards of education.

To the general and economic functions of education must be added a third, the traditional, by which the private systems of non-egalitarian societies attempt to maintain the status and values of a particular group.

C. *Politically non-competitive, egalitarian.* Countries of this character are

mostly members of the Soviet bloc and certain of the "uncommitted" Afro-
Asian nations, such as Ghana, Egypt and Indonesia.

i. Communist countries. Table 4 compares in various economic and educational respects a group of European communist countries and an equivalent
number of non-communist nations randomly selected, in that they were alpha-
betically the first eight European nations in a sample. (This table is intended
to be suggestive rather than in any sense statistically significant.)

The most outstanding inference from Table 4 is the exceedingly high growth

TABLE 4

Comparison of European Non-communist and Communist Countries

COUNTRY	PER CAPITA GNP	RATE OF ECONOMIC GROWTH	INVESTMENT IN EDUCATION AS % OF NATIONAL INCOME	EXPENDITURE PER CAPITA ON EDUCATION IN DOLLARS	PROPORTION OF TOTAL POPULATION IN POST-SECONDARY EDUCATION
Competitive Politically					
Austria	532	6.1	3.9	18	3.81
Belgium	1015	2.3	5.6	46	4.80
Denmark	913	3.8	2.9	34	3.99
Finland	941	4.0	6.3	38	4.10
France	1046	4.3	3.0	32.5	3.39
W. Germany	762	7.4	3.6	27	7.34
Greece	239	5.7	1.6	5	3.17
Iceland	1146	4.0	3.1	50	5.92
Average	824	4.7	3.8	31	4.57
Communist					
Bulgaria	285	9.5	3.9	30	2.90
Czechoslovakia	543	7.5	—	53	1.88
E. Germany	[984]	9.7	5.0	78	1.38
Hungary	387	5.9	2.9	18	1.51
Poland	468	8.8	4.8	19	2.41
Rumania	320	10.3	—	28	1.82
U.S.S.R.	682	10.5	7.1	120	4.35
Yugoslavia	297	10.7	2.8	10	4.58
Average	496	9.1	4.4	45	2.60

rate of the communist countries (the average rate, for what this is worth, is
approximately double that of the non-communist sample). Next, the communist countries are considerably poorer per capita than the rest. The USSR,
most powerful of the communist countries, is out-ranked in wealth by seven
of the other group. Nevertheless, so far as these limited figures can tell us,

proportionate investment in education is higher. However, the communist countries, with the exception of Czechoslovakia, East Germany and USSR, were extremely "undereducated" until recently, and except in USSR and Yugoslavia, post-primary enrollments do not compare with those of the other sample.

In view of the close correlation, on a global scale, between per capita income and expenditure on education it is perhaps more significant to contrast in Table 5 these communist countries on a basis of paired comparisons with

TABLE 5

Non-communist and European Communist Countries: Paired Comparisons *

	PER CAPITA INCOME	RATE OF ECONOMIC GROWTH	EXPENDITURE PER CAPITA ON EDUCA-TION—U.S. $	INFANT MORTALITY PER 1000 LIVE BIRTHS
Bulgaria	285	9.5	30	41.5
Turkey	276	5.9	10	(50)
Czechoslovakia	543	7.5	53	22.7
Israel	540	9.0	25	29.8
E. Germany	[984]	9.7	78	38.8
United Kingdom	998	2.6	36	22.1
Hungary	387	5.9	18	43.9
South Africa	381	6.3	10	107
Poland	468	8.8	19	54.9
Italy	442	6.0	16	40.1
Rumania	320	10.3	28	71.0
Colombia	330	3.7	12	99.8
U.S.S.R.	682	10.5	120	35
Netherlands	708	4.4	32	15.4
Yugoslavia	297	10.7	10	82.2
Malaya	298	2.2	8	68.9

SUMMARY	HIGHEST EXPENDITURE ON EDUCATION	HIGHEST RATE OF ECONOMIC GROWTH	LOWEST INFANT MORTALITY RATE
Communist countries	8	6	4
Non-communist countries	0	2	4

* It must be remembered that the communist system of accounting presents some difficulties in comparison with other non-communist nations. Possibly the similarities in per capita income would not be so great, nor the differences in growth rates so marked, if identical systems of accounting were employed. The per capita income figures for East Germany are highly tentative. The figures for per capita expenditure in U.K. apply only to England and Wales. The infant mortality figures for Turkey are estimated.

those in the non-communist world which are closest to them in per capita income.

Since, as we have already seen, per capita income correlates highly with these variables, it might have been expected that scores would have been evenly distributed, as they are indeed for health. It is hard not to draw the conclusion that this type of country places great value on education, both as a political and an economic tool. It is hard to say how far this commitment to education is responsible for their high rate of economic growth. It is interesting that only the lowest two in terms of rate of growth are exceeded by their country of comparison. In each case the latter has, for the non-communist world, a high rate of growth; in fact Israel ranks among the first three or four. It is interesting that infant mortality figures do not follow the same pattern and would not appear, in the communist countries, to be subject to the same influences that have affected high expenditure on education.

The case of China is interesting, even though reliable statistics on a number of matters unfortunately are not available. Starting from approximately the same economic base as India, per capita income has increased between 1950 and 1959 by 100 per cent: in India by only 12–15 per cent.[6] (The Chinese rate of growth has indeed been one of the fastest in the world: 12.1.) Over the same period absolute real investment in China was quintupled, and in India only doubled. These differences can, of course, be explained in many ways. But in no sense can they be said to represent any insuperable superiority of the democratic system, especially if flawed by inequalities. It is noteworthy that the immense economic growth has been accompanied by an equally dramatic educational expansion. School enrollment increased between 1949 and 1959 from 25 to 171 million. Plans are made involving the enrollment of 300,000,000 persons in education institutions (with an increasing emphasis on higher education) and many millions more in literacy classes.[7]

Both Russians and Chinese, but especially the latter, treat education with great seriousness as an economic, and still more as a political, weapon. The Russians spend more per person on education than any other country except Kuwait. Specific political outlook is associated with both rapid economic expansion and a concentration on education. It would appear that the Western nations have something of a lead in size of both their economies and their educational systems, but are fairly rapidly losing it. The problem is whether the non-communist nations, and in particular the underdeveloped ones with which we are concerned, can match the vigor of the communist countries without copying their ideology.

[6] These figures are taken from Wilfred Malenbaum and Wolfgang Stolper, "Political Ideology and Economic Progress," World Politics, vol. XII, no. 3 (April 1960), pp. 413–421.

[7] These figures are taken from John Wilson Lewis, Education and the Chinese Polity: Themes in Development, a paper prepared for the Lake Arrowhead Conference on Education and Political Development, June 25–29, 1962. Mimeographed. Pp. 19, 21.

ii. Non-communist countries. Ghana is an egalitarian, non-communist nation. Since this country achieved a measure of self-government in 1952 (it became fully independent five years later), the most strenuous efforts have been made to expand education, as the following figures [8] indicate:

ENROLLMENT IN GOVERNMENT AND ASSISTED SCHOOLS	1951	1960
primary schools	234,000	477,000
middle schools	66,175	147,000
secondary schools (excluding Achimota)	2,776	15,119

Recurrent expenditure on education increased from £G 1,561,304 in 1951 to £G 6,471,838, while expenditure by local authorities grew from £G 700,691 in 1954 to £G 1,592,143 in 1956. The enrollment in teacher training colleges grew from 1,437 in 1954 to 4,055 in 1958. In 1961 attendance at primary school was made compulsory and, though enrollment figures are not available, it was anticipated that the first year intake of 124,000 in 1960 would be more than doubled to give a total of around 744,000 in primary education.

Although these figures cannot be correlated with significant changes in rate of economic growth or infant mortality, they indicate a surprisingly vigorous attempt to expand education.

Per capita income, $135, is the highest in Africa, except for South Africa.

The education systems of these countries tend to be:

1. Unitary
2. Carefully planned and closely geared to the country's need for skilled manpower.
3. Of high quality.

Although general education is not neglected, there is greater stress on the economic function than in any other type, while the political role of education is also given prominence.

D. *Non-competitive politically, non-egalitarian.* These cover a wide range, from such "old-fashioned" dictatorships as Paraguay and the Dominican Republic under Trujillo, to the "traditional oligarchies" of Afghanistan and Ethiopia, by way of "colonial and/or racial oligarchies" such as South Africa, Angola and, to some extent, Peru. They vary greatly in the size of the ruling group (in South Africa, for example, it is twenty per cent of the total population; in the Dominican Republic it was a single family with its toadies); and the political structure (again in South Africa, there is political competition *within* the ruling white population; in others there is complete autocracy). There are also a number of countries whose status is in some doubt, which

---

[8] These figures are taken from an unpublished work on the development of the labor force in Ghana by David Williams.

are gradually moving in the direction of genuine democracy coupled with a truly open society. A surprisingly large number of the non-competitive, non-egalitarian societies, including many which are not classified by Almond and Coleman as "colonial or racial oligarchies," are divided along lines of race. These include many Latin American countries, Sudan, Afghanistan, Ethiopia, Liberia (in the sense that the ruling group is of an entirely different background and stock, though Negro, from the rest), Nepal, Burma, and several others. Most of these countries are extremely poor. This is not surprising: they are countries which have neglected their human resources because, they have, for the most part, been completely unconcerned about them. Though this is changing now in places, one cannot make up rapidly for such neglect.

The countries in this category as a whole accept, for a variety of reasons ranging from Ethiopian traditionalism to the sophisticated philosophy of Apartheid, the principle of social difference based on race, class, caste, or language. Those in the ruling group are not prepared to accord to those they rule full political rights or social opportunities for educational betterment. Their position is extremely logical, if one assumes the attitude of a group which is prepared to keep another in subjection. Education makes people restless and dissatisfied if they are in a position of inferiority: only the rich and powerful whom it confirms in their authority can receive education unmoved. Moreover, a ruling group can live extremely well on the sweated labor of even completely ignorant workers. The nation as a whole would no doubt profit if the labor force were better equipped, but national considerations are not necessarily the concern of the oligarchy, which is contented with things as they are, and fears that a change would diffuse economic benefits and education more widely, thus weakening their position.

South Africa has perhaps grappled with situations with more ingenuity, albeit perverted, than any other nation. It has even recognised the importance of certain levels of education for the Bantu. Per capita GNP in South Africa ($381) is double that of any other African nation and well above the world mean. South Africa and Venezuela under the recent Jimenez dictatorship are the only countries in this category to have achieved real prosperity. Both have had considerable mineral resources. South Africa has the additional advantage of long settlement by a vigorous and large white population, and a generally well-endowed terrain. But although South Africa is a prosperous country, as shown by per capita income and the growth rate of 6.3, her wealth is ill-distributed, as might be expected from her political structure. This is dramatically illustrated by contrasting infant mortality rates between the white population (27.6) and the black (126.8). The rates of post-primary enrollment for the population as a whole (0.71) are also well below the world mean. This is especially significant in view of the fact that the white proportion of the population is as intensively educated as almost any other in the world: one in every seventy-five white South Africans is receiving higher education, as compared with one in every two hundred and fifty in Britain.

A few other countries in this category have achieved considerable economic growth, though not yet a high per capita income, through mineral extraction. These include the now disintegrated Central African Federation and the Congo in the days of Belgian colonization. Territories like Angola, which lacked mineral resources, have remained miserably poor and pitiably ignorant in spite of centuries of colonization. The literacy rate in Angola is about five per cent and the primary enrollment ratio about one per cent: perhaps the lowest in the world. We should distinguish, however, between countries settled permanently by Europeans having a personal interest in promoting prosperity for themselves, and those temporarily colonized by officials and others chiefly concerned to maintain order and to collect taxes. In the former there has often been an almost inevitable diffusion of some prosperity—the South African Bantu are richer than those of neighboring countries.

Venezuela provides an interesting example of the changes related to a dramatic reversal of political power. When in 1958 President Betancourt replaced Jimenez, the policy toward education almost immediately altered radically. Even more interesting is the change in the health picture (Table 6).

Only careful analysis of future trends will suggest possible ways in which the alteration of social policy has affected the economy. It is clear, however, that such alterations are inextricably associated with political changes.

The thesis that these countries spend little on education should be tempered by three observations:

i. They may indulge in educational "conspicuous consumption." Trujillo, for example erected splendid university buildings, a great museum, and other educational edifices. These, however, contributed little to the educational needs of his people, serving only as show pieces to prove to visiting dignitaries that he was addicted to culture.

ii. Popular pressure, through UN conferences and other means, can stimulate some expansion of education. Here we can only try to estimate how sincere and effective this has been.

TABLE 6

Venezuela: Changes in Educational and Health Expenditure

	1956	1957	1958	1959	1960	1961
GNP	17,930	20,506	22,488	23,176	—	—
Savings	28.89	26.52	28.99	26.30	—	—
Percent of NI spent on ed.	—	—	—	1.1	—	4.1
Expenditure per head on ed. (local currency)	—	—	28	58	117	117
Expenditure per head on ed. (U.S. dollars)	—	8.4	—	35	70	70
Infant mortality	67.3	65.8	63.9	55.3	45.1	—

iii. Statistics may sometimes show high expenditure on education. In some cases these are known to have been falsified.

To sum up, countries of this type cannot be expected to invest much in education. Most are very poor, and the ill-distributed wealth of a few of them comes from some particular national advantage, such as oil or other natural resources.

General features of the educational systems of these societies are:

1. They are dual in the wealthier countries, such as South Africa and Peru. In the poorer nations, such as Afghanistan, there is virtually no education except for the scions of the elite.
2. There is little planning of education as a whole.
3. The quality of education tends to be low, except sometimes for what is given to the elite minority.

The function of education in these countries is mainly traditional, though in some respects and in some cases attempts have been made to introduce an economic function within this general pattern. For example, the Belgian regime in the Congo organized relatively wide-spread education of a simple technical type (but virtually nothing above this level) in the dual attempt to maintain stability and to exploit the country's resources.

The characteristics and functions of educational systems in the four socio-political systems considered in this section are summarised in Table 7.

TABLE 7

Summary of Characteristics and Functions of Educational Systems

TYPE OF POLITICAL SYSTEM	FORM OF EDUCA-TIONAL SYSTEM	PLANNING APPROACH	QUALITY	FUNCTION
Competitive Egalitarian	Unitary	Strong	Good	Economic
Competitive Non-Egalitarian	Dual	Fairly strong	Varied, usually good for elite	Economic; Traditional
Non-Competitive Egalitarian	Unitary	Strong	Good	Economic; Political
Non-Competitive Non-Egalitarian	Dual, or Unitary if only for elite	Weak	Poor	Traditional

EDUCATION AND DEVELOPMENT IN EGALITARIAN AND NON-EGALITARIAN SOCIETIES

Up to this point both developed and underdeveloped countries have been considered. Now an attempt will be made to see whether the typology developed in the last section has any significance when applied to a sample composed only of underdeveloped countries (i.e. one excluding the nations of Western Europe, North America and Australasia. The sample is shown in Table 8, specific calculations are referred to, as previously, by letters in the text).

TABLE 8

Relation Between Political Systems and Development

(A) NON-EGALITARIAN COUNTRIES

	PLANNING ORGANIZA-TION	QUALITY AND EFFICIENCY	PER CAPITA EXPENDITURE IN U.S. DOLLARS	PER CAPITA INCOME IN U.S. DOLLARS	PERCENTAGE OF NATIONAL INCOME IN EDUCATION
Afghanistan	1	1	1	54	0.2
Algeria	3	3	—	—	3.3
Angola	1	1	—	—	2.6
Brazil	1	2	32	262	2.6
British Guiana	1	1	—	—	3.7
Burma	1	1	1	52	3.6
Ceylon	1	2	5	122	4.6
Chile	1	2	10	180	2.4
Colombia	2	2	14	330	2.1
Dominican Republic	1	1	4	205	1.6
Ecuador	2	2	3	204	1.7
Ethiopia	1	1	0.6	54	—
Greece	1	2	5	239	1.6
Guatemala	2	2	3	179	2.4
India	3	2	1	72	1.7
Iran	1	1	5	100	—
Iraq	1	1	11	195	—
Korea	1	1	2	80	4.1
Laos	1	1	2	—	—
Liberia	1	1	1	103	—
Mauritius	2	2	—	—	3.5
Mexico	2	2	5	178	1.4
Pakistan	2	1	0.6	56	1.2
Panama	2	2	13	350	3.9
Philippines	3	2	6	201	3.2
Portugal	1	2	4	201	2.0
Rhodesia & Nyasaland	1	1	—	—	3.6
Saudi Arabia	1	1	5	166	—
Turkey	1	2	5	276	2.2
Vietnam	1	1	2	133	—
Yemen	1	1	—	—	—
Average	*1.45*	*1.55*	*5.18*	*166*	*2.57*

TABLE 8 (Cont.)

(B) EGALITARIAN COUNTRIES

	PLANNING ORGANIZA-TION	QUALITY AND EFFICIENCY	PER CAPITA EXPENDITURE IN U.S. DOLLARS	PER CAPITA INCOME IN U.S. DOLLARS	PERCENTAGE OF NATIONAL INCOME IN EDUCATION
Argentina	2	2	9	374	2.5
Barbados	3	3	—	—	3.4
Bolivia	1	1	1	66	—
Costa Rica	2	2	14	307	4.0
Cuba	2	2	18	361	3.4
Cyprus	3	3	17	374	4.3
Congo (L)	1	1	4	98	5.1
Egypt	3	2	6	131	—
Ghana	2	2	4	135	1.5
Israel	3	3	28	540	3.0
Jamaica	2	2	—	—	2.3
Japan	3	3	16	240	5.7
Malta	2	3	—	—	4.4
Mexico	2	2	5	178	1.4
Nigeria	3	1	0.7	21	1.9
Puerto Rico	3	2	—	—	7.4
Tanganyika	2	1	0.6	61	3.0
Trinidad	2	3	—	—	2.7
Tunisia	2	2	7	133	3.4
Venezuela	2	2	39	762	4.1
Average	2.25	2.10	11.74	255	3.53

χ^2 Distributions

t. Political system and combined rating for planning and educational quality: $\chi^2 = 15.23$, p = .001.

u. Political system and investment in education: $\chi^2 = 2.18$, p > .10.

v. Political system and per capita expenditure on education: $\chi^2 = 4.37$, p = between .05 and .02.

w. Political system and per capita income: $\chi^2 = .41$, p > .90

Working with the relatively limited sample of underdeveloped countries it has not been possible to explore the four-fold division of systems with extensive statistics. There has been only a handful of competitive countries which were non-egalitarian, and of non-egalitarian ones which were competitive politically. The calculations which follow refer, therefore, only to a straight comparison between egalitarian and non-egalitarian systems. When the politics of the newer African states are consolidated and their social policies have been continuous long enough, however, they may yield a body of statistics that will enlarge evidence about the non-competitive egalitarian group. Such movements as the Alliance for Progress might also introduce egalitarian opportunities to Latin America, without eliminating the old guard, thus enlarging the competitive non-egalitarian group. It may be observed *en passant* that one of the problems of this type of study is the recent spread of decolonisation. Almond and Coleman [9] based some of their calculations on three colonial groups—French West and Central Africa, and Ruanda-Urundi. These three have now become 16 sovereign states, whose political status is entirely different even though their economic situation has scarcely changed. Likewise, Hagen [10] correctly revises one of the Coleman and Almond tables by classing Venezuela as politically competitive rather than authoritarian—but the statistics he employs relate to the period when Venezuela was still under a dictatorship.

The dichotomy of egalitarian and non-egalitarian is frail, especially when an attempt is made to evaluate quality in defining educational variables. For present purposes this has been done by awarding scores on a three point scale (good, average, poor) to each country for planning (i.e. capacity for rational decision-making) and quality (i.e. teacher training competence and curriculum regulation):

		PLANNING; AVERAGE SCORE	QUALITY; AVERAGE SCORE
Egalitarian countries	(20)	2.20	2.10
Non-Egalitarian countries	(30)	1.44	1.47

The egalitarian countries' scores are very significantly higher than those of the non-egalitarian groups.[(t)]

It was clearly necessary, however, that these highly personal ratings should be measured against something more tangible. For this purpose, two measures were employed: the amount spent per capita on education, and the proportion of national income invested in education. Although there may be exceptions, it is in general to be expected that countries spending more on education will have better educational systems. The mean for investment in education in all underdeveloped countries of the world was calculated (three per cent) and the egalitarian and non-egalitarian groups compared in this respect.

Proportionately more of the egalitarian than of the non-egalitarian countries have investments above the world mean, but the difference is of marginal statistical significance.[(u)] However, there is a fairly marked difference between the average percentages invested: egalitarian countries 3.58; non-egalitarian countries 2.62.

In terms of money spent per capita, the egalitarian group is superior. Taking the world mean for underdeveloped countries ($6) the proportion of egalitarian countries above the mean is significantly higher than in the non-egali-

9 Almond and Coleman, *op. cit.* p. 542.

10 Everett E. Hagen, "A Framework for Analysing Economic and Political Change," Robert E. Asher et al, *Development of the Emerging Countries: An Agenda for Research*, Washington, D. C.: The Brookings Institution, 1962.

tarian group.[v] Average expenditures also show a marked difference: egalitarian countries, $11.62; non-egalitarian countries, $5.70.

The significance of this finding might be largely vitiated however, if the egalitarian countries proved to be much wealthier than the rest, because their expenditure might be a function of wealth rather than of their socio-political structure. For this calculation the world mean of $200 was employed since it provided a relatively even division of the sample. The distribution of per capita income between egalitarian and non-egalitarian countries proved, however, to be random [w] which suggests that egalitarianism, rather than national wealth, is the important corollary of high per capita expenditure on education. It must be recognised that the average per capita income, is higher in egalitarian than in non-egalitarian societies, $255 against $173, but this seems not seriously to weaken our contentions concerning the important role of egalitarianism in the promotion of education. Indeed, it is plausible that egalitarian societies also lay more firmly the groundwork for economic growth.

It is not easy to offer any firm evidence for the various orientations of education which are mentioned. Traditionalism can only be assessed through such unquantifiable means as a study of the textbooks, curriculum and similar features.

The political role of education can be judged by a considerable body of literature on the egalitarian and non-competitive societies, but this, too, is hardly amenable to statistical treatment. It is possible, however, to obtain some support for assessment of the economic role of education. The percentage of the population enrolled in secondary vocational education was taken for all those countries in Table 8 for which it was available (15 egalitarian and 24 non-egalitarian). The non-egalitarian percentage was .14, the egalitarian was .80, more than five times as much.

REFERENCES

Save where specific mention is made to the contrary, statistical material is derived from the following sources:

Post-primary school enrollment: UNESCO, *World Survey of Education III, Secondary Education*. New York: International Document Service, 1961.

Primary school enrollment: UNESCO, *World Survey of Education II, Primary Education*. Paris: UNESCO, 1958.

Education administration, different systems: UNESCO, *World Survey of Education, Handbook of Educational Organisation and Statistics*. Paris: UNESCO, 1955; also *Educational Planning*, International Bureau of Education and UNESCO, publication no. 247, 1962.

Infant mortality: *Demographic Yearbook, 1961*. New York: United Nations, 1962.

Investment in education (percentage of national income devoted to education): *Basic Facts and Figures, 1961*. Paris: UNESCO, 1962.

Savings (the proportion of gross fixed capital formation to expenditure on gross national product, mostly for 1960, but in a few instances for 1959 or 1958):

Yearbook of National Accounts Statistics, 1961. New York: United Nations, 1962.

Rate of economic growth: *Yearbook of National Accounts Statistics, 1961.* These are mostly given in the Yearbook over a period of about 1954–1959. Where not given, they have been calculated for the same period.

Per capita income: Norton Ginsberg, *Atlas of Economic Development.* Chicago and London: University of Chicago Press, 1961.

Per capita expenditure on education: *International Yearbook of Education, Vol. XXII, 1960.* Paris: UNESCO, and Geneva: International Bureau of Education.

Political systems: categories derived from Gabriel A. Almond and James S. Coleman, eds., *The Politics of the Developing Areas,* Princeton, New Jersey: Princeton University Press, 1960.

In a few instances, *e.g.* in the case of information regarding Venezuela, data have been obtained from earlier issues of one or other of the periodical United Nations publications.

NATIONAL POLITICAL DEVELOPMENT:
MEASUREMENT AND ANALYSIS

Phillips Cutright

The author devises an index of political development based upon a rigorous empirical definition of the term. He then compares levels of political development among a global sample of countries and their relation to education and other variables.

L ARGE scale comparative studies of national political systems offer the social scientist a methodology of great analytic power if only proper use can be made of the material at hand. In this article we examine in some detail a single sociological effort to apply the comparative method to national political systems.

Perhaps the best known and most articulate effort by a sociologist to deal

REPRINTED FROM *American Sociological Review,* 28 (April 1963), 229–245. © 1963 by the American Sociological Association. It is a pleasure to acknowledge the support of the Faculty Research Committee of Dartmouth College. A Ford Foundation Public Affairs grant to Dartmouth College also aided the execution of this research. I was greatly stimulated by and am indebted to Robert A. Dentler for his advice, encouragement and helpful criticism during the initial and final stages of the study. Robert Sokol gave the manuscript a careful reading. My thanks to Robert Van Dam, Lawrence Stifler, Kimberly Holtorff and the other students who helped in the collection of some of the materials. The views expressed here in no way reflect the opinion of the Social Security Administration.

empirically with a large number of contemporary national political systems is that of Seymour M. Lipset [1] who establishes two groupings of national political systems, stable and unstable democracies, and popular and elite based dictatorships. He then poses the question: What differences in national economic development might explain why a nation would be in one group and not in the other? [2] To answer this question he offers a number of indicators of wealth, industrialization, education, and urbanization. (He does not combine indicators to form a scale of wealth or industrialization, or economic development, although development forms one-half of the central theme of the paper. The other half, "democracy," is not scaled either.)

Lipset presents the statistical means for the nations in each of the two political groups (stable democratic as opposed to all other forms of government) in two areas of the world, the English-speaking and European areas and the Latin American area. A sample of his analysis of these means is instructive: Among the English-speaking and European stable democracies the average number of telephones per 1,000 persons (a "wealth" indicator) is 205 compared to only 58 per 1,000 in "European and English-speaking unstable democracies and dictatorships." Similar differences favoring democratic nations is revealed for all of the indicators of wealth, industrialization, urbanization and education

[1] Seymour M. Lipset, "Some Social Requisites of Democracy: Economic Development and Political Legitimacy," *American Political Science Review*, 53 (March, 1959), pp. 69–105. See also Lyle W. Shannon "Is Level of Development Related to Capacity for Self-Government?" *American Journal of Economics and Sociology*, 17 (July, 1958), pp. 367–82, and a follow-up study also by Shannon, "Socio-economic Development and Demographic Variables As Predictors of Political Change," *Sociological Quarterly* III (January, 1962), pp. 27–43. Leo F. Schnore's "The Statistical Measurement of Urbanization and Economic Development," *Land Economics* XXXVII (August, 1961), pp. 229–245, contains an assessment of the relationship among a number of different non-political indicators of national development we will use in this paper.

[2] Ratings by a single expert or by panels of experts, averaging the opinions of judges concerning their opinions on the condition of the press, political freedoms, etc., are of less value than a more objective indicator of political development. Careful examination of Russell H. Fitzgibbons, "A Statistical Evaluation of Latin American Democracy," *Western Political Quarterly*, 9 (1956), pp. 607–19, as well as Lipset's attempt to place nations in "democratic" or what amounts to "undemocratic" clusters, reveal the problems of this method of subjective evaluation. The shift in the rank order (by experts) of the Latin American nations across time periods allows the person using the index to take his pick of the democratic and undemocratic nations. A more crucial point is the lack of agreement among raters concerning the rank order and, with larger numbers of nations, the necessity to abandon subjective evaluations and turn to objective indicators—what expert can be in intimate contact with the political histories of all the nations of the world and also be willing or able to order them on simple scales, let alone multiple dimensions? We can devise statistical and objective methods of measuring political development, just as the economist does when he asks about energy consumption per capita and not what an expert believes the whole economy of a nation has been doing over the past year. This implies that we can also remove ourselves from the world of ethnocentric judgments about the goodness or evil of political systems and turn to other aspects of political systems in order to understand them.

among the English-speaking and European groups and, also, among Latin American democracies and non-democracies.

Lipset seeks to show the effect of economic development on national political systems. This statistical effect is given as proof that a strong relationship exists. However, comparison of means between two groups may show a difference without telling us the strength of the association between the independent variables that are presumably responsible for the observed difference between the two groups. Thus Lipset notes that stable democracies have 205 telephones per 1,000 persons compared to only 58 per 1,000 in non-democratic nations and infers that there is a "strong" relationship or association between this indicator of national wealth and the type of political system observed.

To give a little more depth to his claims, Lipset presents the ranges for each indicator. Here some curious findings appear. The first and most obvious is that the means between the two types of national governments differ, yet the spread in the values on almost every indicator is so extreme that it appears that it would be very difficult to place a single nation in either the democratic or non-democratic category knowing, for example, only its score on the number of telephones. In the European and English-speaking stable democracies a nation may have from 43 to 400 telephones per 1,000 population while a European dictatorship may have as few as 7 or as many as 196 per 1,000. One wonders about the stable European democracies that have only 43, 60, 90, 130, 150 or even 195 telephones. How do they manage while dictatorial European nations can at the same time have as many as 196 per 1,000? More striking is the case of Latin American *democracies* in which the average number of telephones is 25 and the range is from 12 to 58. The number of telephones in Latin American democracies seems paltry when compared to the number of telephones in European dictatorships. European dictatorships have, on the average, double the number of telephones (and "wealth" and "economic development") of Latin American democracies.

Such a peculiarity can exist for a number of reasons. The first may be a failure to develop a scale of "democracy" that could approximate the scale on which all the independent variables are defined. A nation is either democratic or it is not, according to the Lipset scoring system. It makes little difference that in the verbal discussion of national political systems one talks about shades of democracy if, in the statistical assessment, one cannot distinguish among nations. However, one cannot distinguish among national political systems without a scoring system that assigns values to different nations according to some stated criteria. Although Lipset states his criteria he does not differentiate between France and Albania, Brazil or Chile. We would be better able to assess his descriptive statistics if the dependent variables—the national political system—had been indexed or scaled.

A second reason is a lack of adequate conceptualization of national political systems. A value laden curiosity about democracies and dictatorships is no substitute for theoretical focus. A theoretical focus means one has a hypothesis to test using a set of predicting variables that are "given" by the theoretical scheme. Lipset seeks to test the hypothesis that democracy will flourish in nations where wealth is distributed rather equally and in which large masses of starving or near starving farmers and workers are not dominated by an elite of wealth and aristocracy. Do populations with a relatively high standard of living possess the "self-restraint" necessary to sustain "democratic institutions?" Do impoverished masses languish under an elite dictatorship which further re-presses them or do they support tyrants (in which they give popular support to a dictatorship) who repress them? Lipset makes no distinction between the varieties of "democratic" or non-democratic political systems. His working hypothesis asks only whether or not a significant difference on each economic indicator exists between nations with two types of political characteristics. When the hypothesis is confirmed he explains the finding through discussion of what people want or what the effects of education might be on self-restraint.

The concept of social change does not appear in Lipset's analysis of his data but he refers to studies by Schnore and Lerner in which statistical assessment of the interdependence of many of the same indicators used by Lipset is demonstrated and, in the case of Lerner, some links between education, com-munication, urbanization, economic development and individual political participation are tentatively established.[3] Lerner's analysis is, however, re-stricted to the Middle East.

RESEARCH OBJECTIVES AND HYPOTHESIS

In the first part of this paper we develop an index of political development. The index of political development is operationally defined. The concept that guided construction of the index can be stated simply—a politically developed nation has more complex and specialized national political institutions than a less politically developed nation. Degree of political development can be mea-sured and each nation can be placed on a continuum of development, which will allow it to be compared with any other nation in the world. Operationally we bank heavily on the role played by political parties in national political life in measuring political development.[4]

[3] See Daniel Lerner, *The Passing of Traditional Society,* Glencoe: The Free Press, 1958.

[4] The index is, of course, heavily dependent upon available data. The selection among alternative items for the index was guided by the coherent interpretation of Max Weber's political sociology as given by Reinhard Bendix, *Max Weber: An Intellectual Portrait,* Garden City: Doubleday, 1960.

The primary source for the materials used in this study was the *Political Handbook of the World: Parliaments, Parties and Press,* published annually for the Council on Foreign Relations, New York: Harper and Brothers, from 1940 through 1961. Needed supple-mentary checks were secured by reference to the *Encyclopedia Britannica* and other reference works. Nations included for study are listed in Table 2. With the exception of nations located in Africa, nations recognized by the United Nations as being "independent" na-

The principal hypothesis tested is that political institutions are interdependent with educational systems, economic development, communications systems, urbanization, and labor force distribution. A nation's economic system can develop only if its educational system keeps pace, if people concentrate in urban areas, if communication and transportation systems emerge and if changes occur in family and social life that induce people to fit into the demands of the unfolding system. Schnore has measured the interdependence among certain of these factors.[5] But to test the hypothesis that political institutions are not set apart from the rest of a society's social institutions we must construct an index of political development and then test the hypothesis by assessing the association between political development and other measures of national systems.

CONSTRUCTING AN INDEX OF POLITICAL DEVELOPMENT

The following items were selected and given the weights indicated. The time period covered by the data is 1940 through 1960. The score each nation received for the first year was added to the score it received the following year to get a cumulative total score.

A scheme for scoring the nations (in which high scores mean high develop-

---

tions in the 1960 *Statistical Yearbook* were included in this study. A few very small nations (Monaco, Liechtenstein, Andorra) were omitted. Nearly 100 per cent of the populations of all continents except Africa are thus included. The decision to omit Africa was based on the well known statistical effect of artificially inflated relationships when a large number of the cases cluster at one or both ends of the regression line. Including African nations would have inflated our correlations because they would have clustered in one corner of the scattergram. Until we develop a more sensitive measure of political development and also accumulate accurate information on the social and economic conditions in most African nations it seemed reasonable to exclude them from this initial study. A total of 77 independent nations are included.

[5] For a matrix of rank order correlations of a number of indicators of these variables see Schnore, *op. cit.*, p. 236. Schnore's correlations tend to be slightly higher than product moment correlations using the T scoring method, but slight differences in the case base included may account for such differences.

See also Alex Inkeles, "National Character and Modern Political Systems," Francis L. K. Hsu, editor, in *Psychological Anthropology*, Homewood, Illinois: The Dorsey Press, 1961, pp. 172–208. He reviews various approaches to this topic and cites studies which suggest connections between national character and modern political systems. However, no conclusions can be drawn from this body of work in part because it lacks a standard measure of political systems against which different national characters might be associated. For a definite point of view on the subject of the importance of personality to social change generally and economic and political change in particular, see Everett E. Hagen, *On the Theory of Social Change*, Homewood, Illinois: The Dorsey Press, 1962. Hagen's theory has the virtue of being testable but he presents little supporting evidence himself—again, in part, because the evidence simply does not exist. In rejecting economic theories of social change Hagen swings to psychological explanations, but does not completely bypass sociological perspectives.

ment) should penalize each nation for political instability which represents "backsliding" and reward it for achieving or retaining more complex political forms of organization. Points for any one year were awarded in the following manner.

1. *Legislative Branch of Government*

   Two points for each year in which a parliament existed in which the lower or the only chamber contained representatives of two or more political parties and the minority party or parties had at least 30 per cent of all seats. One point for each year in which a parliament existed whose members were the representatives of one or more political parties, but where the "30 per cent rule" was violated. No points for each year no parliament existed or for years when either of the above types of parliaments was abolished or discarded by executive power. Parliaments whose members are not members of political parties are given a zero. Parliaments that are not self-governing bodies (e.g., the mock parliaments of colonial governments) are given a zero.

2. *Executive Branch of Government*

   One point for each year the nation was ruled by a chief executive who was in office by virtue of direct vote in an open election where he faced competition or was selected by a political party in a multi-party system, as defined by the conditions necessary to get 2 points on the legislative branch indicator above. If the parliament ceased being a multi-party parliament because of executive action, the chief executive stopped getting points. One half point each year the chief executive was not selected by virtue of his hereditary status but was selected by criteria other than those necessary to attain one point as given above. Colonial governments receive one half point per year. No points if the nation was governed by a hereditary ruler.

It is possible for a nation to acquire no points, one half or 1 point depending on the selection of the chief executive. The combined index has a range of zero to 3 points per year. Over the 21 year period of our study it would be possible for a nation to have a total raw score between zero and 63 points.

RELATIONSHIP OF POLITICAL TO OTHER MEASURES OF NATIONAL DEVELOPMENT

This study began with the aim of measuring the degree of association between political development and other types of socio-economic development. The objective was a statistical assessment of the degree of association between educational development, urbanization, communication development, economic growth and labor force characteristics and the measure of political development.[6] A statistical statement of the proportion of the variation around the mean of the political development index that could be accounted for by covariation with selected independent variables was also sought. Finally, if the association was reasonably close one might build a prediction equation which would describe for each nation whether its level of political development was commensurate with the values it had on the independent variables in a prediction equation.

Of the several independent variables considered, the communications development index [7] had a Pearson zero order association with political development of .81.[8] The communications development index is tightly related to an index of economic development (.95) but is a better predictor of political development than is economic development.[9] The communications index reflects the ability and the need of national systems to maintain differing types of communication systems depending on the varying degrees of literacy of their population and varying levels of integration of the economic and social order.

The relationship between national communications development and political development may be seen in graphic form in Figure 1.

[6] Social-economic statistics used in this report were drawn from the last reporting year from the following United Nations sourcebooks: *Demographic Yearbook, 1960, Statistical Yearbook, 1960,* and *Report on the World Social Situation, 1957. The Yearbook of Labor Statistics, 1960,* was the source for labor force statistics.

Statistical assessment followed T scoring of all data. A simple technique for computing the T score is given in Allen E. Edwards, *Statistical Methods for the Behavioral Sciences,* New York: Holt, Rinehart and Winston, 1954. For a single item, T scoring of the raw data will yield a mean of 50 and a standard deviation of 10. If we add items together to form an index, four items with a sum of 200 represents a subject (or nation) with an average index score. All single item indicators and combined indices in this paper have been T scored. The original T scoring was done for all independent and territorial political divisions in the world (excluding most Pacific Island dependent territories) for which data was available. Thus the T score for newsprint consumption is based on a case base of 93 and not the 77 nations reported here. This fact accounts for the small departures in Table 1 of means and standard deviations one would expect from T scoring.

[7] The communications development index is formed by summing the T scores a given nation received on newspaper consumption, newsprint consumption, telephones and the number of pieces of domestic mail per capita. If one or two indicators of the four were missing we took the average of the two or three available indicators and added their scores to estimate the total index score. Five of the 77 nations had less than two communications indicators and their scores were estimated and used in the prediction equation developed later in the paper.

[8] Variables considered but not included in the matrix because of high intercorrelations with variables in the matrix were an economic development index and the industrial labor force index. Economic development was measured by combining the T scores for a given nation of per capita measures of: energy consumption, steel consumption, income in U.S. dollars and the number of motor vehicles. These items are all highly intercorrelated: See Schnore, *op cit.,* p. 236.

[9] Product moment correlation of communication development against political development was .81 compared to .68 for economic development against political development.

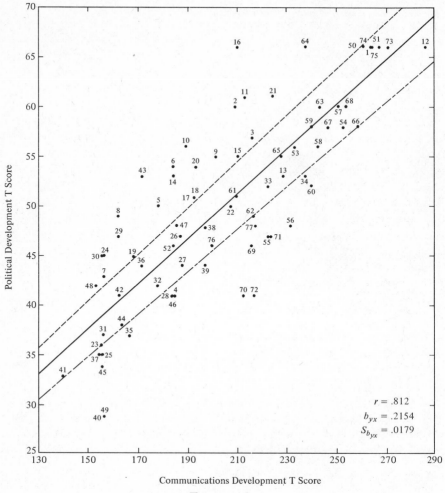

FIGURE 1

Relationship of Communications Development to Political Development. (See Table 2 for the identification of each nation by its number shown here.)

This scattergram makes the correlation coefficient more meaningful. The communication development scores on the horizontal axis increase from left to right. The political development scores are on the vertical axis and increase vertically.

The most striking thing about the Figure 1 is the steady increase in the level of political development as the level of communication development increases. The main diagonal is the *regression line*. If every nation's scores were such as to put it exactly on that line, the correlation coefficient would be 1.00. We see, however, that some nations are above the line and some are below. What is the difference? A nation below the line is politically under-developed relative to its given level of communication development.[10] The difference between the communication index scores that the politically over-developed nations (above the line) really have and what they would have if they were on the regression line may represent the extent of possible imbalance in the social system of the nation.

Nations below the line face alternative routes to the line. They can increase their level of political development and rise vertically to the line or they can decrease their communications and move to the left until they meet the line—maintaining or perhaps decreasing their level of political development. Such movements as this may seem unlikely to people living in a society in which communication systems are believed to increase steadily, but alternative (even "impossible") movements can occur during revolutions, civil wars and terri-torial occupation by a foreign power, or through economic disasters. Internal social change may be violent or not, but in any case should result in movement of predictable direction.

Mathematical models have been considered [11] which might be applied to data like these to test the notion that there will be movement toward the line. Empirical testing would be the only way to state whether nations do in fact increase or decrease either variable in order to come into equilibrium. How-ever, if measurements are made each year for a period of years, the movement of nations can be precisely plotted. If empirical tests do not show nations moving toward their equilibrium point, then it is also possible that the same test will reveal different equilibrium points for nations in different socio-eco-nomic conditions. We have conveniently assumed a common set of equilib-rium points rather than several (one could have had several equilibrium points simply if different clusters of nations had different regression lines, a possibility to be explored in later research).

The inability of our index to actually distinguish for every nation the refine-ments of political development, the missing data and substitution of estimates

---

[10] Our use of the terms politically over- or under-developed should not be understood as a judgment of what the nation should have from a moral or ethical point of view. A politically underdeveloped nation lacks sufficient points which it could obtain only if it met the criteria set by our political development index. In severe cases it may lack any political party or even a parliament. Our statements of whether or not a nation is under-developed or overdeveloped are not made with sole reference to its score of the political development index—a nation is either high, low or in between on the index. This judgment is made with reference to the political development score the nation should have *relative* to its level of communications development. Thus a nation with a one party system may actually be overdeveloped politically relative to its communications system or its level of urbanization and other measures of national growth.

[11] See James S. Coleman, "The Mathematical Study of Small Groups," in Herbert Soloman (ed.), *Mathematical Thinking in the Measurement of Behavior*, Glencoe: The Free Press, 1960, pp. 26–30.

for five communication scores, the mis-reporting of political information—all of these types of error exist and should be considered before refined explanations of minor deviations from the line are attempted.[12] For the benefit of students who may wish to consider these possibilities, the nations that lie between the two broken lines in Figure 1 may be considered as being off the regression line because of measurement and other errors; hence attention may be devoted to nations that are outside the bands for deviant case analysis or comparison of extreme cases on either side of the line.

Accounting for National Political Development

Inspection of the matrix of correlations in Table 1 reveals a high degree of association between each predicting variable and political development.[13] But the variable most closely associated is the communications development index. If taken alone it accounts for 65 per cent of the variation of the political development scores around the mean.

Computation of a multiple correlation coefficient using all four independent variables simultaneously reveals a multiple R of .82. Thus a total of 67 per cent of the observed variation around the mean of the dependent variable is associated with covariation in the independent variables. This compares with the 65 per cent of variation that could be associated using communications as a single predictor.

---

[12] In Figure 1 we have drawn broken lines on either side of the regression line we actually observed for the 77 nations. For these data the sample estimate of the standard error of the regression coefficient can be applied to describe what is a "small" and what is a "large" departure from the regression line. The broken lines on each side of the regression line represent the range of alternative regression lines that would be likely to occur if we were drawing a sample of 77 from a larger population. Although these statistical conditions are not met in this case, the use of a high and a low estimate of alternative regression coefficients establishes a hypothetical band which may help us sort out errors of measurement and other types of error that may result in moving a nation several points away from the line when actually it should be closer to it. Measurement errors may also place a nation on the line when it ought not to be there, but this is less likely than the former movement which decreases correlations.

[13] When intercorrelations are high it becomes impossible to give exact meaning to the size or sign of the beta weights in the prediction equation. This is a favorable pastime of some sociologists but inspection of the correlations and beta weights in Table 1 should make them hesitate to partial out variation to any specific independent variable in a multiple regression analysis. Since I have indulged in this statistical fantasy myself, I feel obliged to bring it to the attention of my colleagues. The use of partial correlations to produce meaningful correlations when intercorrelations are high is also doubtful. Removing the effect of "communication" and then seeing what the partial is between education and political development would reveal a partial of near zero, but this certainly would not mean that education was not a vital factor. Partial correlation is a way of finding out what added gain one may expect by including certain variables in a multiple regression equation, but it tends to over-simplify our conception of the world under some conditions. It is what might be called an "anti-systems" statistic, albeit an occasionally useful one.

TABLE 1

Matrix of Correlations of National Measures of Political Development, and Levels of Communication, Urbanization, Education and Employment in Agriculture: N = 77

	2	3	4	5	MEANS	S.D.
1. Communication	74	88	−86	81	204.5	36.4
2. Urbanization	—	77	−75	69	49.9	8.2
3. Education		—	−78	74	105.8	16.7
4. Agriculture			—	72	53.1	10.5
5. Political Development				—	49.9	9.7

$\tilde{Y} = 3.7 + 172X_1 + .232X_2 + .003X_3 − .014X_4$
Ry .1234 = .82
Modified prediction equation used:
$Y = 1.97 + .1789X_1 + .2274X_2$
Ry .12 = .82

The communications index summed the T scores of newspaper readers per capita, newsprint consumption per capita, the volume of domestic mail per capita and the number of telephones per capita.

The urbanization index is the T score of the proportion of the population of the nation living in cities over 100,000. The education index was formed by combining T scores of literacy with T scores of the number of students per 100,000 enrolled in institutions of higher education, and the proportion of the economically active labor force employed in agriculture was also T scored.

Political development scores were T scored.

Correlations in this matrix use estimated values when no data was available. Although political development values were available for each nation, urban data was missing in 2 of the 77 cases, communication scores in 5, education lacked 4 national scores and agriculture was missing in 18 cases. Estimates were based on the regression of a known value for a nation on the unknown, using regression weights for all of the nations on which data was available. These estimates were then used in the prediction equation.

The fact that the communication index is highly correlated with the education index, and its .95 correlation with economic development, reveals the highly interdependent nature of national social organization. Thus, the score a nation receives on communications development is itself highly dependent on the national level of educational development, urbanization, labor force movement out of agricultural employment, and economic development. That communications and not economic development, urbanization or education best accounts for the political development of a nation is significant. It should not obscure, however, the essential interdependence of this matrix of characteristics which collectively give a distinctive profile to any given nation and collectively interact to yield political outcomes which in turn interact to yield further changes in the independent variables themselves.

USING THE PREDICTION EQUATION TO FULL ADVANTAGE

Political development scores can be used in several ways. We can make a simple statement about the relative position of any nation regarding its political development by comparing the index score of one country with scores of other nations. We can extend the power of such comparison considerably, however, if we use a "prediction equation" to predict what the score of any nation on political development "should be" on the basis of its "complete" profile of national development.[14]

When this calculation is done the predicted value of political development can be compared to the actual value of any nation. If we subtract the predicted value from the actual value we get a number that represents the error of prediction. If the error is positive, the nation has a higher than expected political development score.

For example, the actual political development T score for Canada is 66 and its predicted value is 61.5. The difference is +4.5. Canada has a larger than predicted political development score. On the other hand, Argentina has an actual political development value of 53, but a predicted value of 57.4, with a negative residual of —4.5. Argentina's actual political development is less than expected on the basis of its communications and urbanization scores.

These errors may tell us much about some of the factors that influence political development. One such factor is revealed in Table 2 which groups nations according to their geographic location. The size of the average net residual error for the 12 nations in North America, was a positive 5.2. The table also shows that of the 12 nations in North America, 10 had positive residuals. The situation is similar for South America. There, average net residuals reveal greater than predicted political development—an average error of more than three T score values. Looking over the table as a whole, it is clear that nations located in the Western Hemisphere enjoy a considerable advantage in their political development over nations located in Asia or Europe.[15]

We might speculate that the absence of international conflict over the long history of North and South America has resulted in far greater benefits for their political development than we anticipated. Our common stereotype of Latin political instability is subject to some re-evaluation when seen from the world perspective. Far from being unstable, the prediction equation suggest that they are not only relatively stable but relatively more developed than *comparable nations* around the world. The absence of international conflict may well be one of the crucial variables to consider as a background to understanding the political development of nations. Of course, in the absence of international conflict within the Western Hemisphere it is impossible to

[14] The new beta weights in the prediction equation show, however, that no gain in prediction would come from using education or agricultural labor force scores and for that reason we use a modified prediction equation which is shown in Table 1. It yields a multiple R identical with that given by all four predictors. Only communication development and urbanization scores are used to calculate the expected political development values for the 77 nations.

[15] The U.S.S.R. is considered to be in Europe and New Zealand and Australia in Asia for the convenience of presentation as well as their geographic location.

differentiate among nations within the hemisphere. Little can be said about the relation of war to political development because such conflicts do not exist. (*Anything* that does not exist in the Western Hemisphere but does exist in other areas of the world can be invoked as an "explanation" of the direction of the residual values!) [16] In fact a number of Asian nations received their independence largely through the indirect effects of World War II. The Asian nations that have more complex political organization than predicted are India, Indonesia, Burma and the Philippines. These achieved independence *after* the war was over. Most *long run independent* Asian nations have *lower* than predicted political development. There are, in short, no single factor explanations of political development. The presence or absence of international conflict on the territory of a nation, and other violent conflict may, if protracted, influence the development of nations; and complex social systems are especially vulnerable to such changes. Changes that disrupt socio-economic life may be expected to disrupt other aspects of the national system. We might hypothesize the amount of disruption would be related to the degree of complexity of organization and interdependency within a given nation.[17]

When we compare the predicted with the actual score and find that a nation has departed from its predicted values, we can view it as being under some pressure to move toward the predicted score on political development (or social development). The student interested in mass movements, political change or revolution may have seen in the preceding discussions a means of locating nations that may be experiencing deep strains in the socio-political system.

For example, theories of political change which view mass movements as the carriers of political change usually portray such action as taking place when the political institutions are not "adequate" in form or function and are sufficiently out of phase with other areas of national development to set up the conditions that allow traditional bonds of allegience of the masses to the elites and to existing political institutions to be broken in a mass upheaval. The meaning of the deviation from the "multiple" regression line formed by a set of predicted political scores may be translated in terms of its possible measurement of pressures on certain social classes, economic, or power-elite groups. Kornhauser regards the historic development of na-

---

[16] See Hagen, *op. cit.*, pp. 185–199 for a statement of social mechanisms that intervene to produce conditions favorable to political development as a consequence of conquest in war or other factors that led to a "withdrawal of status respect" from elite and non-elite groups in the afflicted society. His comments would seem to apply particularly well to certain Asian nations and the consequences of World War II for their political development.

[17] Greater depth of analysis of the variation among nations within continents can be achieved by subtracting out the "bias" effect (the mean of the net residual errors of prediction) that being located on a particular continent gives to a nation, and each nation can then start out on equal terms for further analysis. For example, we could subtract 5.2 from each *actual* score of the North American nations and 3.5 from each South American nation. In similar vein, we could add 1.5 to each Asian nation and 1.8 to each European nation.

TABLE 2

Residual Error of Prediction of Political Development:
*by Continent and Nation **

North America	Y-Ỹ			Y-Ỹ
1. Canada	4.5	38. Lebanon		−3.0
2. Costa Rica	8.1	39. Mongolia		−5.0
3. Cuba	3.9	40. Muscat		−8.5
4. Dom. Republic	−4.8	41. Nepal		−1.5
5. El Salvador	6.7	42. Pakistan		0.6
6. Guatemala	8.2	43. Philippines		10.8
7. Haiti	5.4	44. Thailand		−2.6
8. Honduras	8.5	45. S. Arabia		−9.8
9. Mexico	4.6	46. Syria		−6.2
10. Nicaragua	9.4	47. Turkey		2.0
11. Panama	8.4	48. Viet Nam		1.0
12. United States	−0.1	49. Yemen		−8.5
		50. Australia		1.7
South America		51. N. Zealand		3.0
13. Argentina	−4.5			
14. Bolivia	7.2	*Europe*		
15. Brazil	3.7	52. Albania		1.6
16. Chile	12.7	53. Austria		−1.4
17. Colombia	1.5	54. Belgium		0.0
18. Ecuador	2.9	55. Bulgaria		−5.4
19. Paraguay	2.2	56. Czechoslovakia		−6.2
20. Peru	6.6	57. Denmark		−0.5
21. Uruguay	5.2	58. Finland		−1.1
22. Venezuela	−2.8	59. France		1.3
		60. W. Germany		−6.7
		61. Greece		0.7
Asia		62. Hungary		−4.1
23. Afganistan	−3.2	63. Iceland		1.2
24. Burma	5.7	64. Ireland		9.8
25. Cambodia	−4.2	65. Italy		−0.1
26. Ceylon	2.1	66. Luxembourg		−3.2
27. China	−0.9	67. Netherlands		−1.8
28. Fed. of Malaya	−4.4	68. Norway		1.0
29. India	6.4	69. Poland		−6.9
30. Indonesia	5.8	70. Portugal		−9.8
31. Iran	−4.6	71. Romania		−5.7
32. Iraq	−2.5	72. Spain		−12.7
33. Israel	−3.5	73. Sweden		3.2
34. Japan	−6.3	74. Switzerland		4.8
35. Jordan	−4.1	75. United Kingdom		1.0
36. Rep. of Korea	−1.0	76. Yugoslavia		−1.2
37. Laos	−3.8	77. U.S.S.R.		−5.3

* Numbers in front of each nation identify it in Figure 1. Standard error of estimate of
    residuals: Sy .x = ±5.60
Adopted from Edwards, *op. cit.*; p. 162.

tional social systems in terms of its rate of development (i.e., rate of urbanization, industrialization, transformation of the educational institutions, and the complexity of the economy and communications systems) in relation to political behavior of certain segments of the population that are affected by rapid change.[18] Other theorists focus on the importance of changes in national character before the economic transformations which lead to political disequilibrium can occur.[19]

The method presented in this paper makes a *prediction* about which nations should experience political movements of a specific type (either toward increasing complexity or decreasing complexity). Theories of change can then be tested against what actually happens. This frees us from the primary and very legitimate criticism leveled against most political change theorists: that they are talking about something that is past and done with. The explanations suffer from *ex post facto* explanation.

Taking Asia as an example, we have already noted the political character of India (6.4) the Philippines (10.8) Burma (5.7) Indonesia (5.8). These are the only Asian nations whose positive errors of prediction are larger than one standard deviation ($s_{y.x} = +5.60$) of the residuals. Changes *have* been occurring in these nations, and the more dramatic of these changes are political. Burma and Indonesia have turned away from complex political organization and have abandoned multi-party politics. They may move toward the regression line not only by increasing their socio-economic development scores (a problematic event) but by decreasing their level of political development (a certainty). When they reach the line, the strain to reestablish more complex political forms may return, providing socio-economic development continues.

The pressures in India and the Philippines toward similar political "backsliding" may also be strong and whether they will follow the same path taken by the Burma and Indonesia is problematic. If rapid economic-social development can occur they may achieve political stability.[20]

[18] William Kornhauser, *The Politics of Mass Society*, Glencoe: The Free Press, 1959. See also the discussion by Joseph R. Gusfield, "Mass Society and Extremist Politics," *American Sociological Review*, 27 (February, 1962), pp. 19–30.

[19] Hagen, *op. cit.*, and Inkeles, *op. cit.*

[20] Philippine deviation may be partially explained by this observation. "While Washington officials and Ambassador Spruance took great pains to maintain neutrality between the candidates, they made it clear to the Philippine government that the conduct of the election was of vital concern to the United States. Had the Liberal Administration been returned to power by means of fraud and violence, it would have been in no position to bargain successfully for badly needed economic assistance and for the much desired revision of the Bell Act!" *Internal pressures* for an honest election, however, are also cited. Willard H. Elsbree, "The 1953 Philippine Presidential Elections," *Pacific Affairs*, XXVII, (March,

For the case-study oriented student of social change, this technique supplies a basis on which to pick cases on more than "expert" testimony. Here is a tool for locating deviant cases if one wishes to compare different types of nations in detail to see the institutional mechanisms or other national characteristics that allow a nation to wander far from the regression line for many years. He might wish to contrast, for example, Ireland (9.8) with Spain (—12.7), or Chile (12.7) with Argentina (—4.5).

In tracing out of the social correlates of the political development of nations, one need not wait for the future. The design used here could be taken back to 1930. One might calculate the residual values at five year intervals and recalculate the deviations, observing the differences among different types of nations. Continued up to 1960, the last sample of points and deviations would look approximately like our own.[21] Such an analysis might reveal cut-off points in social-economic development beyond which change in the political system is apparently unavoidable. It could reveal a cut-off point further down the scale where complex political institutions cannot stand for long. Such a longitudinal study could get at the interaction between political and other institutions in the society. It could measure some of the non-economic aspects of economic growth that trouble students of underdeveloped nations. Does the existence of complex (given their level of socio-economic development) political organization in Latin American States give them an advantage over their politically backward counterparts in Europe and Asia? What are the effects of sustained political development on other systems within the nation that may allow it to "take off" to new heights of social growth or plunge it into revolution and political traditionalism? What differences in national character sustain political change, economic change or traditionalism, and how is national character affected by increasing levels of organizational complexity in nations? [22]

1954), p. 13. It is, however, interesting to note that representation in the Philippine lower House conformed to our definition of multi-party representation only during the first decade of independence, and has violated the "30 per cent rule" of minority party representation since 1957. In India the Congress Party's majorities also override the 30 per cent rule.

[21] Space restrictions prohibit more than mention of the statistical problems of treating change over time: for example, one would need measures of both political and non-political values. It is possible to study development without reference to a nation's relative position in the world. This is the approach usually followed by the case study worker. For a fascinating treatment of the single nation case study which is relevant to many of the concerns of this paper see James C. Davies, "Toward a Theory of Revolution," *American Sociological Review*, 27 (February, 1962), pp. 5–19.

[22] For one example of changes induced by industrialization see Alex Inkeles and Peter H. Rossi, "National Comparisons of Occupational Prestige," *American Journal of Sociology*, LXI (January, 1956), pp. 329–339, a study of ranking of occupations by inhabitants of six nations. Rankings are highly correlated. The authors interpret this as an outcome of the industrial occupational system and the centralized national state.

Summary

This report developed some of the possible applications of an index of political development for 77 independent nations in all continents except Africa. (Africa was omitted for statistical considerations.) Knowledge of the level of the development of the communications system of a nation accounts for 65 per cent of the variation in scores around the mean of the political development index. A multiple regression equation which added educational development, agriculture labor force and degree of urbanization to the communication index as predictors of political development raised the level of explained variation to 67 per cent ($Ry.1234 = .82$).

The matrix of high intercorrelations among a variety of indicators of the specialization and level of development of different aspects of national social-economic and political life supported the idea that social systems are indeed systems—that is, their parts are interdependent. The concept of interdependence and the statistical method of this study led us to consider the existence of hypothetical equilibrium points toward which each nation is moving. It is possible for a nation to be politically overdeveloped or underdeveloped, and we suggest that either political or non-political changes will occur to put the nation into equilibrium.

The extent to which a nation diverges from its predicted level of political development was considered and possible ways to utilize these errors of prediction were discussed. Finally, the ability of social scientists to test theories concerning revolution, mass movements and political change was considered.

EDUCATION AND POLITICAL DEVELOPMENT: THE LATIN AMERICAN CASE

W. Raymond Duncan

How does education bring about change in the structure and culture of politics? Special attention is given to Mexico in this study of Latin America.

PUBLIC education conditions political action in developing societies. Literacy tends to produce individuals who are apt to follow election campaigns, who have political information, and who may feel themselves capable of influencing governmental decisions. It thereby creates a wider range of participants in political life.[1] Literacy also propels people toward various skills which in turn lead them to interest groups, parties, civil service, and other institutions. This specialization of labor diversifies the structure of political action, moving it toward modern forms.

The way in which individuals participate within modern institutions is shaped by the culture of politics defined as attitudes toward authority and leadership. These attitudes are formed in the home and church, in the workplace and school. Teachers and textbooks operate in this dimension to build the sense of national unity and to legitimize specific decision-making patterns that may range from democratic to totalitarian. Examples abound. Under Meiji leadership after 1890, Japanese leaders devised a new blend of filial piety, the samurai ethic, and obedience to the emperor as the curriculum for political indoctrination in the schools. In postwar Germany, American leaders attempted to de-Nazify and reeducate Germans to "democracy." When the French departed Laos, Laotian leaders printed secondary textbooks for the first time in the Lao language—a major effort toward building attitudes of national consciousness. More vivid evidence is found in countries that have experienced recent social revolution. In the non-Western

REPRINTED FROM *The Journal of Developing Areas*, 2 (January 1968), 187–210. © 1968 by Western Illinois University.

[1] See Gabriel A. Almond and Sidney Verba, *The Civic Culture–Political Attitudes and Democracy in Five Nations* (Princeton, N. J.: Princeton University Press, 1963); also Karl Deutsch, "Social Mobilization and Political Development," *Political Science Review*, IV (September 1961), 493–514, where literacy, an indicator of social mobilization, is isolated as a force that expands the politically relevant sector of the population; Daniel Lerner, *The Passing of Traditional Society* (London: Free Press, 1958), pp. 57–64; Edward Shils, *Political Development in the New States* (Gravenhage, Netherlands: Mouton, 1962), pp. 17–19.

world, Russia and China have placed enormous emphasis on public education as a means to control the rate and direction of political development within the parameters of variant Marxist-Leninist ideologies. Among the revolutionary elites of post-colonial states, those in Guinea, Mali, Ghana, Algeria, Egypt, and Indonesia soon changed the school curriculum to "indigenize" its content along specific ideological lines.[2] However, there are limitations to education as a means to change radically the political culture.

In Latin America the traditional political culture is one of authoritarian decision-making, centralized control by a limited political elite, and dominant-submissive interpersonal relationships between the leaders and the led. Available evidence suggests that this underlying attitude-set is present at a time when more literate people have progressively entered the political arena through diversified modern institutions. As a tentative hypothesis, then, it can be argued that the structure of politics changes more rapidly than the culture of politics. If this assessment is correct, and it must be admitted that it is contrary to currently accepted theory based on investigations in regions other than Latin America, then traditional attitudes will for decades continue to shape the decision-making processes within developing political institutions.

The difficulty with contemporary theories that evaluate education and political development is a tendency to equate increasing literacy with early change in underlying attitudes toward authority. The implication is that educated individuals in developing areas replace their particularist, ascriptive, and diffuse attitudes with universalist, achievement, and pragmatic attitudes, the *sine qua non* of modernism.[3] The thesis of this article is that while education brings with it certain kinds of structural change examined below, it does not necessarily produce corresponding changes in the traditional culture of politics.

[2] Selected studies of education and political development include Herbert Passin, "Japan," in *Education and Political Development*, ed. James S. Coleman (Princeton, N. J.: Princeton University Press, 1965), pp. 304–12; on Russian education, several English works are available: *Soviet Commitment to Education* (Washington, D.C.: U.S. Department of Health, Education and Welfare, 1959); Jeremy R. Azrael, "Soviet Education," in *Education and Political Development*, pp. 233–71; George Z. F. Bereday, *et al.* (eds.), *The Changing Soviet School* (Boston, Mass.: Houghton Mifflin, 1960). On Chinese education see Stewart Fraser (ed.), *Chinese Communist Education: Records of the First Decade* (Nashville, Tenn.: Vanderbilt University Press, 1965); C. T. Hu, "Communist Education: Theory and Practice," *China Quarterly*, X (April–June 1962), 84–97; Theodore H. E. Chen, "Elementary Education in Communist China," *Ibid.*, 98–122.

[3] See Alfred Stephen, "Political Development Theory," *Journal of International Affairs*, XX, No. 2 (1966), pp. 224, 228. See also, Russell H. Fitzgibbon and Kenneth J. Johnson, "Measurement of Latin American Political Change," *American Political Science Review*, IV (September 1961), 515–26 where the assumption that modern institutional development is paralleled by modern attitudes seems implicit.

LITERACY AND STRUCTURAL CHANGE

In Latin America increased literacy can be correlated with interest group and political party formations, with widened election participation, with fewer insurrections, and with expansion of middle sectors desiring modernization. These changes in the structure of politics opened new channels for wider participation and established in some cases an institutional framework to accommodate on a permanent basis peaceful transitions of political power.

Political Parties and Civil-Military Relations

Of the ten Latin American countries with over 65 percent literacy, relatively wide participation in politics occurs through interest groups, elections, and political parties (see Table 1). Argentina is well known for its large labor movement inaugurated by Juan Domingo Perón, and six republics have modern indigenous parties devoted to social reform, industrialization, and national development: the Colorado party of Uruguay, the Party of the Institutionalized Revolution (PRI) of Mexico, the National Liberation party of Costa Rica, the Christian Democratic party of Chile, the Communist party of Cuba, and the Democratic Action party of Venezuela. These modernizing parties of the 1960's range within individual party systems from the dominant single party type in Mexico to the two-party system of Uruguay and the multiparty variety in Chile.[4] They aggregate diversified interests and help to insure regular and frequent elections according to constitutional norms and procedures, another index of modernization.

In the six countries mentioned above, high literacy rates and modern party systems appear to be related to fewer coups d'etat and less military intervention in civilian political affairs. Uruguay has not experienced a successful insurrection in the twentieth century, and Mexico, Chile, and Costa Rica have civilian-dominated governments. The military in Venezuela appears at present content to allow the Democratic Action party to run the government, and its nonintervention during the tense days of the December 1963 presidential election are positive signs for civilian predominance. In Cuba the new military is well under the control of Fidel Castro who has defeated military counterrevolution from the old professional army through a rebuilt

---

[4] The Christian Democrats defeated in September 1964 the Popular Action Front (FRAP), a Communist and Socialist coalition, by a vote of 56.6 percent to 38.5 percent in an election that produced an 87.41 percent turnout of the registered electorate. It must be said that while more than one party operates in Mexico, the PRI clearly dominates the political system. The PRI itself, however, is composed of three major groups (labor, farm, and popular) which compete for power within the party. Presidential candidates must be acceptable to these groups, one factor which helps produce a party no longer governed by the traditional "strongman" as in the past.

TABLE 1

Literacy, Political Parties, and Coups d'Etat [a]

1945–1964

COUNTRY	YEAR OF CENSUS	LITERATE PERCENTAGE OF POPULATION	MODERN INSTITUTIONALIZED PARTY	NO. OF COUPS BETWEEN 1945–1964
Argentina	1960	91	None [c]	2
Uruguay	1963	90	Colorados	0
Costa Rica	1963	84	National Liberation Party (PLN)	1
Chile	1960	84	Christian Democrats (CD)	0
Cuba	1953 [b]	78	Communist (PCC) [d]	2
Paraguay	1962	74	None	4
Panama	1960	73	None	2
Ecuador	1962	67	None	3
Venezuela	1961	66	Accion Democratica (AD)	3
Mexico	1960	65	Party of the Institutionalized Revolution (PRI)	0
Colombia	1951	62	None	2
Peru	1961	60	Popular Alliance for Revolutionary Action (APRA)	2
Dominican Republic	1956	60	None	1
Nicaragua	1963	50	None	0
Brazil	1950	49	None	4
El Salvador	1961	49	None	3
Honduras	1961	45	None	2
Bolivia	1950	32	National Revolutionary Movement	4
Guatemala	1950	29	None	2
Haiti	1950	10	None	3

a Literacy rates (ages fifteen years and over) for the years noted are from the *Statistical Bulletin for Latin America,* produced by the Economic Commission for Latin America (ECLA) (New York: United Nations, 1966), III, No. 2, p. 36. The number of coups are cited by Martin C. Needler, "Political Development and Military Intervention in Latin America," *American Political Science Review,* LX (September 1966), 616–26.

b The literate percentage of Cuba's population is undoubtedly higher since 1953, given Castro's emphasis on adult literacy campaigns after the January 1959 Revolution. For instance, out of a total population of 6,933,253 in 1961, some 707,000 illiterates (presumably over fifteen years of age) were taught to read and write in that same year. See Richard R. Fagen, *Cuba: The Political Content of Education* (Stanford, Calif.: Stanford University Press, Hoover Institution, 1964), p. 11.

c Several institutionalized parties are not included in this column because they are more traditional than modern, e.g., Conservatives and Liberals in Colombia. Others are too small to command widespread participation, e.g., the Socialists of Chile. "Modern" means dedicated to social reform, industrialization, and national development.

d After the January 1959 Revolution.

armed forces, tight party organization, and personal control since January 1959. These six countries experienced a total of only six coups between 1945 and 1964 in contrast to eleven that occurred in the four weak-party states (Argentina, Paraguay, Panama, Ecuador) that have over 65 percent literacy. In the ten republics below 65 percent literacy, twenty-three coups occurred (see Table 1).

These statistics suggest that a high literacy level, though insufficient in itself, is a necessary condition for less military intervention in civil affairs. The second basic condition appears to be development of a countervailing institution (the political party) able to aggregate interests, provide competent political leadership, and channel funding for economic development. The decline of the military acting as a civilian political institution can be a central index of modernization when it means redirection of scarce money and manpower from nonproductive military to productive economic investments; Costa Rica, Chile, and Mexico are cases in point. In contrast, Brazil allocates twice as much money to military spending as to education—a reflection of the role the military plays in Brazilian politics (see Table 2). The problem of building countervailing institutions vis-à-vis the military is endemic in Latin America, given its authoritarian and violent history in which the military played a central role in maintaining political stability in the absence of legitimate political institutions after the wars of independence. Moreover, the importance of the military in transitional politics as a symbol of international power and prestige makes it a potent competitor with other national institutions for allegiance and loyalty.

Literacy and Middle Sector Expansion

Literacy is a stimulant to expansion of the middle sectors in Latin America by providing an educational base for semiprofessional and professional status, higher income, and social and political mobility. The ten countries with over 65 percent literacy have a higher percent of their labor forces in intermediate and senior grades of industrial employment than the ten countries of lower literacy levels, and Argentina with the highest literacy has the largest industrial management group.[5] Not surprisingly, most countries with over 65 percent literacy have a higher per capita income than those under 65 percent and are also more urbanized (see Table 3).

The political importance of the middle sector groups lies in the goals and aspirations which they tend to express. According to J. J. Johnson, who has written extensively on middle sector formation in Latin America, these individuals identify closely with the nation-state as opposed to local enclaves, want more public education in their countries, desire industrialization through state planning and intervention in the economic process, and tend to substitute the political party for the family as the center for political

[5] Colombia and Brazil are exceptions. See Table 2.

TABLE 2

*Investments by Latin American Governments in
Education and Defense
1961–1965* [a]

COUNTRY	YEAR	PERCENTAGE OF FEDERAL BUDGET INVESTED IN EDUCATION	PERCENTAGE OF FEDERAL BUDGET INVESTED IN DEFENSE
Argentina	1962	10.7	16.5
Uruguay	1961	2.9 [b]	8.5
Costa Rica	1965	28.1	3.1
Chile	1964	14.4	8.8
Cuba	. . . .	. . .	. . .
Paraguay	1964	19.0	23.1
Panama	1964	17.9	. . .
Ecuador	1964	14.5	13.1
Venezuela	1965	12.2	10.6
Mexico	1964	24.4	10.5
Colombia	1965	12.5	24.4
Peru	1963	24.7	20.9
Dominican Republic	1964	13.9	20.2
Nicaragua	1964	17.0	15.3
Brazil	1964	5.8 [c]	14.0
El Salvador	1965	24.2	11.0
Honduras	1964	22.1	11.9
Bolivia	1963	24.4 [d]	11.8
Guatemala	1964	. . .	11.0
Haiti	1965	11.2	26.0

a Figures from "Situacion económica: Producto e Ingreso Nacionales y Finanzas," in *América en Cifras 1965* (Washington, D.C.: Unión Panamericana, Instituto Interamericano de Estadística, Organizacion de los Estados Americanos, 1965), pp. 103–28. These statistics may be misleading insofar as they do not indicate the breakdown of federal expenditures into primary, secondary, university, technical, or teacher training sectors of education. They are nevertheless useful as a guide to governmental commitment to education in the process of nation-building.
b Includes investments in other "social" projects. *Ibid.,* p. 125.
c Includes investment in "cultural" sector. *Ibid.,* p. 105.
d Includes investments in "fine arts." *Ibid.,* p. 104.

thought and action.[6] From the middle sectors have come the twentieth century leaders of the military, intellectual, and political world who give direction to social change and national government. Gustavo Diaz Ordaz of Mexico, Eduardo Frei of Chile, José Figueres of Costa Rica, Fernando

6 John J. Johnson, *Political Change in Latin America* (Stanford, Calif.: Stanford University Press, 1966 ed.), pp. 1–14.

TABLE 3

Literacy and Middle Sector Formation in Latin America [a]

COUNTRY	LITERATE PERCENTAGE OF POPULATION	PER CAPITA INCOME (U.S. DOLLARS AT CURRENT PRICES)	PERCENTAGE OF LABOR FORCE IN INTERMEDIATE AND SENIOR GRADES OF EMPLOYMENT IN SECONDARY SECTORS	PERCENTAGE OF LABOR FORCE IN AGRICULTURE	PERCENTAGE OF URBAN POPULATION
Argentina	91	799.0	35.9	25.2	68
Uruguay	90	560.9	33.0	21.7	81
Costa Rica	84	361.6	22.3	54.7	36
Chile	84	452.9	21.4	29.6	66
Cuba	78	516.0	21.7	41.5	55
Paraguay	74	193.2	14.2	53.8	35
Panama	73	371.0	15.2	49.8	47
Ecuador	67	222.7	10.5	53.2	39
Venezuela	66	644.5	18.2	41.3	61
Mexico	65	415.4	16.9	57.8	50
Colombia	62	373.4	21.0	53.9	48
Peru	60	268.5	. . .	62.5	41
Dominican Republic	60	313.2	. . .	69.6	28
Nicaragua	50	288.4	. . .	67.7	37
Brazil	49	374.6	15.2	50.5	37
El Salvador	49	267.5	10.5	63.2	35
Honduras	45	251.7	4.5	93.1	25
Bolivia	32	122.3	7.6	49.4	37
Guatemala	29	257.7	7.7	74.9	30
Haiti	10	149.2	3.0	83.2	17

[a] The per capita income figures are for 1961, from *The Economic Development of Latin America in the Post-War Period* (New York: United Nations, 1964), p. 51. Note that income distribution in Latin America is very uneven. Vast numbers of people receive amounts far lower than the average per capita income, and a privileged few enjoy incomes far higher. The other columns are from *Social Aspects of Economic Development in Latin America,* ed. Egbert de Vries and Jose Medina Echavarria (Paris: UNESCO, 1963), I, 90–91.

Belaúnde Terry of Peru, and Romulo Betancourt of Venezuela are middle sector representatives. If more middle sector groups means more interest in and more dedication and leadership toward modernization, then literacy again is a central impetus for change.

EDUCATION AND TRADITION

The foregoing examples suggest a clear connection between literacy and structural change. With the exceptions of Argentina, Ecuador, Panama, and

Paraguay, relative high literacy appears to be correlated with modern indigenous political parties, less military intervention in civilian government, and regular and frequent elections to effect legitimate, peaceful transitions of political power. Uruguay, Chile, Mexico, and Costa Rica are cases in point; the Venezuelan and Cuban examples are too new to make an affirmative judgment though events since 1958 in Venezuela and since 1959 in Cuba (at least as far as a modernizing party is concerned) suggest a similar correlation. Since low literacy in ten of the republics is accompanied by the virtual absence of modernizing parties, a high frequency of military interventions, and a limited middle sector, the evidence tends to support this approach to structural modernization through literacy.[7]

The central issue is not that institutional development is stimulated by increased literacy, but that the attitudes which condition political behavior within developing institutions must be examined more critically. Too often the assumption is that where interest groups, political parties, and elections exist, they reflect modern attitudes such as pragmatism, equalitarianism, achievement, and high national identification. This assumption can mislead one into believing that increased literacy not only builds the base for modern institutional development but also tends to change traditional, underlying attitudes toward authority, with the implication that "democratic" attitudes are being formed. If we are to understand the functions performed by political institutions in Latin America, the nature of relationships between leaders and followers, and the direction of evolving political systems, it is imperative to probe beyond institutional change into the cultural world of attitudes, values, and beliefs that shape interpersonal political action.

Limited studies of Latin American political cultures show a persistence of traditional attitudes in spite of modern institutional evolution and increasing literacy. One source of evidence is the work of John Gillin, a social anthropologist, which focuses upon ethos components in modern Latin America.[8] Gillin argues that Latin American attitudes and values are essentially personalistic (focusing upon inner unique differences between people), paternalistic, transcendental, fatalistic, attach great weight to hierarchy, and stress emotion as fulfillment of self. These attitudes and values, which encourage social and political inequality in terms of opportunity and

[7] One could debate these correlations on the basis of Argentina alone, which does not fit this model of development even though it has the highest literacy in Latin America. Continued military intervention, instability, mass labor discontent, and no effective party leadership makes Argentina a unique contrast to the general pattern. Another unique case is Bolivia at the other end of the literacy spectrum: low literacy but with a relatively strong party from 1952 until late 1964 when President Victor Paz Estenssoro was overthrown by the military, led by General René Barrientos, Vice-President.

[8] John F. Gillin, "Some Signposts for Policy," in *Social Change in Latin America Today*, ed. Richard N. Adams, *et al.* (New York: Harper, 1960), pp. 14–62; Gillin, "Ethos Components in Modern Latin American Culture," in *Contemporary Cultures and Societies of Latin America*, ed. Dwight B. Heath and Richard N. Adams (New York: Random House, 1965), pp. 503–17.

status, are operative in most sectors of society (from illiterate to literate) and help to explain traditional perceptions and expectations at work within institutions. The dynamics of interpersonal political action in Latin America include dominant-submissive relationships between leaders and the led that often result in personalist autocratic leadership by *caudillos* (political bosses) and *caciques* (local leaders).[9] Other traditional values linked to authoritarian leadership include *machismo*, expressions of manliness and action-orientation, and *paternalism*, the expectation of "protection" by individuals in higher stations of life over others in lower positions.[10] These feelings, emotions, and beliefs that stress *people* rather than offices and impersonal institutions help to explain the oligarchical as opposed to democratic leadership that often prevails in Latin America and partially accounts for continued executive predominance in political life despite constitutional provisions for separation of powers and checks and balances. That educated people interact within these cultural parameters suggests that education per se has not significantly changed traditional perceptions and expectations. This hypothesis is supported by a study by Frank Bonilla and Kalman Silvert on education and national identification in which the authors found surprisingly low identification with the nation-state among highly literate and participant individuals in Argentina, Mexico, Chile, and Brazil.[11]

Other Sources of Evidence

These sources suggest that traditional values continue to shape perceptions and expectations of individuals in Latin America both during and after their attainment of higher levels of education.[12] The following list is by no means complete.

First, conservative and tradition-bound groups fall at both ends of the class spectrum of Latin American societies. They are likely to be illiterate unpoliticized Indians or *campesinos* (peasants) of the lower classes, or well-educated landholding or commercial elites of the upper classes. That educative conservative groups cling to the status quo and oppose major social

---

[9] Gillin, "Ethos Components in Modern Latin American Culture," pp. 509–11.

[10] *Ibid.*; also, Gillin, "Some Signposts for Policy," pp. 36–38.

[11] Kalman Silvert and Frank Bonilla, *Education and the Social Meaning of Development: A Preliminary Statement* (New York: American Universities Field Staff, 1961), mimeographed. In another article by Silvert, "Some Propositions on Chile," *American University Field Staff Report*, West Coast of South America Series, XI, No. 1 (1964), he states that "the coexistence of a strong national modern community and at the same time a resistant traditional one is not unique in Chile." The key point is that such a traditional community is often well educated and highly politicized, which is what Gillin stresses.

[12] For application of this thesis to other areas, see Donald E. Weatherbee, "Traditional Values in Modernizing Societies," *Journal of Developing Areas*, I (October 1966), 41–54. Also, Ann Ruth Willner, "The Underdeveloped Study of Political Development," *World Politics*, XVI (April 1964), 481–82, where she stresses continuity of traditionalism in modern politics.

and economic reforms suggests little direct correlation between high educational attainment per se and modern Western values. In the political sphere the educated conservative elites long dominated the system of national decision-making, sometimes opposing widened secular and public educational opportunities for the broad mass of society. Their influence is clearly visible today. They can virtually stop the process of change in some countries (Haiti, Honduras, Ecuador, El Salvador, Nicaragua) and impede it in other republics. For example, reformist presidents were elected in Chile and Colombia in 1964 and 1966, but they face stiff opposition from conservatives who are politically powerful bankers or congressmen in the national legislature.

Second, the phenomenon of national *caudillos* supported by educated members of society in postwar Argentina, Brazil, Colombia, Venezuela, and Peru suggests that authoritarian values are operative in educated Latin Americans just as they were in educated Germans and Italians during the 1930's and 1940's. While the political styles of Juan Perón in Argentina (1946–55), Rojas Pinilla in Colombia (1953–57), Pérez Jiménez in Venezuela (1948–58), and Manuel Odría in Peru (1948–56) were different, they were all dictators initially supported by a sizable portion of the literate population—urban workers in Argentina and educated large landholders and businessmen in Colombia, Venezuela, and Peru.[13] Lesser known subnational *caciques* are in turn supported by both literate and illiterate people in rural Argentina, Colombia, Venezuela, and Peru, which helps to account for the politically passive and inarticulate rural populations in these countries.

Third, in Argentina, Brazil, and Ecuador, the traditional intervention of the military in civilian affairs has not been perceptively reduced by increased professionalization, institutionalization, and leveling of the socioeconomic status of the officer corps. During a period when the officer corps are receiving more technical education in military colleges and when expansion of public education has given the lower classes increased opportunity to qualify for military schools, military insurrections have increasingly taken the form of attempts by the possessing classes to maintain the status quo. Moreover, postwar insurrections have been increasingly directed against constitutionally elected presidents and have become more violent as popular resistance to military intervention develops.[14] Higher educational attainment among the

13 See Tad Szulc, "The Dictators," in *Latin American Politics*, ed. Robert D. Tomasek (New York: Doubleday, 1966), pp. 41–55. For an excellent study of the wide appeal of General Gustavo Rojas Pinilla in Colombia, see Vernon L. Fluharty, *Dance of the Millions: Military Rule and the Social Revolution in Colombia, 1930–1956* (Pittsburgh, Pa.: University of Pittsburgh Press, 1957), pp. 130–58. The political setting leading to the Odría administration is examined by James L. Payne, *Labor and Politics in Peru* (New Haven, Conn.: Yale University Press), pp. 48–56.

14 Martin C. Needler makes these points in his recent article, "Political Development and Military Intervention in Latin America," *American Political Science Review*, LX (September 1966), 616–26.

officer corps and expanded educational opportunities in the public schools have not resulted in increased reform orientations or democratic attitudes within the military. J. J. Johnson, long a student of civil-militarism in Latin America, sums up the position by stating that the "role of the armed forces has not changed basically under the impact of the massive transformation [where education is a key link in the transformation] that has taken place since World War I." [15]

Fourth, since the conquest, the upper classes of Latin American societies have accorded prestige and status not to manual work, industry, and trading, but to artistic and intellectual efforts. This traditional tendency has led to the study of the social sciences and medicine in higher education rather than the physical sciences or engineering.[16] This contempt for manual labor, imitated by the middle sectors of society, suggests the absence of the Western Protestant Ethic identified so closely with thrift, industry, and economic development in the United States.[17]

Traditional distaste for manual work, beyond its immediate significance for Latin American industrial development, led to serious political repercussions in both the Cuban and Mexican revolutions. Most of the revolutionary leaders in Mexico and Castro in Cuba devoted major effort toward the construction and inculcation by radio, television, and textbooks of revolutionary national ideologies which stress the importance of work, achievement, struggle, and austerity for all members of society. Cuban textbooks, magazines, and newspapers (e.g., Granma, Rebel Youth, The World, and Sierra Maestra) continually idealize the workers in education, agriculture, and industry.[18] During the Lázaro Cárdenas and Lopez Mateos periods in Mexico, government-printed textbooks focused upon work themes for all Mexican citizens.[19] Frequently the best workers in Cuba have become na-

[15] John J. Johnson, The Military and Society in Latin America (Stanford, Calif.: Stanford University Press, 1964), p. 101. See also pp. 102–4, 106. He discusses particularly the military in Brazil, Chile, Argentina, Venezuela, Ecuador, El Salvador, and Honduras.

[16] Thomas Roberto Fillol develops this thesis and applies it to Argentina in his Social Factors in Economic Development: The Argentina Case (Cambridge, Mass.: M.I.T. Press, 1961), pp. 16–18.

[17] The impact of traditional values and attitudes in Latin America on entrepreneurship is well explored by Seymour Martin Lipset in "Values, Education, and Entrepreneurship," in Elites in Latin America, ed. Lipset and Aldo Solari (New York: Oxford University Press, 1967), pp. 3–60.

[18] Evidence to support this point can be gleaned from the translations on Cuba by the Joint Publications Research Service (JPRS), Washington, D.C. See also Richard R. Fagen, "Mass Mobilization in Cuba: The Symbolism of Struggle," Journal of International Affairs, XX, No. 2 (1966), pp. 254–71; and Fagen, Cuba: The Political Content of Adult Education (Stanford, Calif.: Hoover Institution, Stanford University, 1964).

[19] Textbooks during the Cárdenas period strongly emphasized socialism based upon Marxist ideology. See Secretaría de Educación Pública, Comisión Editora, "Serie S.E.P.," 3rd year text. Socialism began to disappear from primary textbooks after 1940 and "democratic" themes reappeared.

tional heroes and are rewarded with free trips to China and the Soviet Union. These Cuban and Mexican emphases upon work in the new revolutionary ethics are designed to establish new patterns of national thought and participation; the need for them accentuates the tenacity of traditional cultural attitudes.

Fifth, high educational attainment has not significantly modified the extreme individualism and the deep respect for authority between leaders and subordinates within the upper echelons of organized political life. As in the past, respect and authority is conferred more upon the *person* occupying an office or position than upon the office or position itself. Since it is often well educated individuals who reach the upper echelons of political and economic organizations, the implication of *personalist* relationships is great. As Tomás Robert Fillol argues:

Since it is not the job or office that is the object of respect and value but the person who occupies it, and since having reached a higher position, his value orientations lead him to assume that he *Is* superior to his subordinates, the individual in a position of authority will not be likely to have self-doubts regarding the justification of such authority. He will tend to be more or less autocratic. Furthermore, since subordinates *Are* inferior, and thus not to be trusted in the performance of their functions, and since any failure or inadequacy in the socially acceptable performance of his job will reflect *personally* upon himself and his family, he will naturally be reluctant to delegate his authority and responsibilities.[20]

The upshot of these interpersonal relationships is limited sharing of effective decision-making power, fewer alternative choices available to political leaders, limited cooperation and dialogue between members of different political parties, and stifled development of impersonal institutionalized problem-solving based upon compromise, bargaining, and reason—even though the political actors may be well educated.[21]

Sixth, a kind of informal education occurs when individuals become urbanized. They experience new relationships, are exposed to the demonstration effect of modern urban living, are available for recruitment into

[20] Fillol, *Social Factors in Economic Development*, p. 19.

[21] *Ibid.* See also Fluharty, *Dance of the Millions*, pp. 165–67; Ernst Halperin, *Castro and Latin American Communism* (Cambridge, Mass.: M.I.T. Press, 1963), pp. 2–3, where he discusses the absence of a *homo burocraticus* mentality in Latin America. Interpersonal relations within political parties, based upon traditional attitudes and values, is examined by Robert E. Scott, "Political Parties and Policy Making in Latin America," in *Political Parties and Political Development*, ed. Joseph LaPalombara and Myron Weiner (Princeton, N.J.: Princeton University Press, 1966), pp. 331–67, see particularly pp. 338–40. The development of increased participation in political structures without corresponding development of effective organizations and institutions is the subject of Samuel P. Huntington, "Political Development and Political Decay," *World Politics*, XVII (April 1965), 386–430. On a similar theme, see Robert E. Scott, "Political Elites and Political Modernization," in *Elites in Latin America*, pp. 117–45, especially p. 121.

organized labor groups and political parties, and can listen to candidates at election time. The remarkable findings of studies conducted on urban working classes in Latin America is that education acquired through exposure to modern urban life brings little apparent revolution of rising expectations or deep explosive social discontent.[22] Rather, traditional authoritarian and paternalist attitudes often persist. Recent election returns from the slum urban areas of Lima, Caracas, Santiago, and Valparaiso illustrate the point: The shantytown districts of Lima favored General Manual Odría, the most conservative of four presidential election candidates in 1963; the shantytown vote during the Venezuelan presidential elections of 1963 in Caracas went to Arturo Uslar Pietri, a conservative intellectual and representative of business interests; the shantytowns of Santiago and Valparaiso supported Eduardo Frei over Salvador Allende, the Marxist candidate, in the 1964 Chilean presidential elections. These election returns suggest a continuity of traditional values in spite of new social-cultural experiences.

The Mexican Case

In order to investigate these contemporary political attitudes in Mexico, a questionnaire was devised and administered in Mexico City in 1964. The purpose of the questionnaire was to assess the relative impact of levels of education (a) on the authoritarian orientation so evident in the structure and culture of the Mexican political system, (b) on the formation of modern political attitudes associated with democratic egalitarianism, and (c) on the role and function of education as understood by the respondents to the questionnaire. Conclusions reached from such a questionnaire, while certainly neither final nor conclusive evidence, do indicate the direction and force of education in shaping Mexico's political culture. Evidence from this independent research in Mexico City can be linked with recent information gathered by Verba and Almond in connection with their study on *The Civil Culture*, and by Silvert and Bonilla in their work on *Education and the Social Meaning of Development*, to form a growing picture of education and attitude change in Mexican politics.[23]

Questionnaire Results

The questions asked, methodology followed, and correlation coefficients obtained are included in the Appendix of this study. In summary, the find-

[22] Daniel Goldrich, "Toward the Comparative Study of Politicization," in *Contemporary Cultures and Societies of Latin America*, pp. 363–66.

[23] For other relationships between education and attitude formation, see Gabriel A. Almond and Sidney Verba, *The Civic Culture* (Princeton, N. J.: Princeton University Press, 1963); and Kalman Silvert and Frank Bonilla, *Education and the Social Meaning of Development* (New York: American Universities Field Staff, 1961).

ings suggest that increasing levels of education within the sample did not correlate significantly with decreasing authoritarian attitudes. Second, the correlation coefficient between increasing levels of education and the modern political attitude scale was not significant (.0351), indicating that more education did not make the subjects of this sample more "modern" in their political perceptions. In short, increased education did not appear to accentuate the subjects' attitude toward democratic egalitarianism as defined within the framework of the questions asked (see Table 8 of Appendix).[24] Indeed, for the employees of the Bank of Mexico, who had the highest level of education as a working class, the correlation coefficient was negative, rather than positive (see Table 8).

The low impact of education as a direct socializing experience affecting authoritarian values is related probably not only to attitude-formation in the family but also to the process of education itself. The Almond and Verba project revealed that the Mexican subjects felt little freedom to discuss unfair treatment in the school and rarely discussed problems with their teachers in comparison with citizens of the United States.[25] This pattern of authority in the school is also indicated by this survey, for in response to question one, teachers were the only occupational group to show a positive correlation between higher levels of education and increased strength of authoritarian attitudes.[26] The pattern characterized by rare discussion of problems and feeling of restraint in school decreased in the Almond-Verba study as higher levels of education were achieved. But given the heavy "dropout" rate of students before they reach higher levels, the basic pattern of authority in the school is highly significant.

The Mexican Case Summarized

Limited quantitative evidence gathered in Mexico indicates that authoritarian perceptions of the self in relation to others operate in the political system and condition relations between leaders and followers at all levels of political activity. This conclusion is confirmed by Mexican writers and spokesmen. Francisco González Pineda, in his *El Mexicano: Su Dinamica Psicosocial* (1959) and *El Mexicano: Psicologia de Su Destructividad* (1961), describes Mexican attitudes toward authority which result in a compulsive attraction to strong personalist rule (*caciquismo*) in the form of a national president who serves as a kind of temporary "absolutist monarch" through a dominant single party that provides for "hereditary power" changed

[24] Almond and Verba found in relation to citizens of the United States, Britain, Germany, and Italy, that Mexican citizens expected less equal treatment by their governmental bureaucracy and the police. *The Civic Culture*, p. 108.

[25] *Ibid.*, pp. 332–33.

[26] Question one reads as follows: Every decent person should have a feeling of love, gratitude, and respect for his parents. See Appendix.

each six years.[27] In a work by Dr. Vincente Suarez Soto, *Psicologia Abismal del Mexicano*, the author describes, as did Samuel Ramos in the 1930's, the deep sense of inferiority that pervades the Mexican people producing in part general indecision and uncertainty resolved by a dominant president.[28] The upshot of authoritarian values and attitudes, as one Mexican senator explained it on the Senate floor on 6 September 1961, is "oligarchical rule." He said,

I wish to affirm vigorously and courageously that an oligarchy supported by the people governs in Mexico, an oligarchy that has made possible the leading of the nation into development . . . . the difference between the Mexican elite and others is that ours is a revolutionary minority, while others in Latin America are of a military, clerical, large agricultural, or of a simple industrial financial type, and (as) conservative minorities they hold back from becoming revolutionary minorities . . . . [they] do not think about the problem of transforming their people, but merely about development of properties and of their own businesses.[29]

The perseverance of these traditional authoritarian attitudes is all the more meaningful to development theory insofar as the indices of development are present in Mexico: urbanization, increasing literacy, mass media expansion, widening middle sectors, and an operative indigenous political party to accommodate the increasing number of literate people after the 1910 revolution. Before the 1910 revolution, Mexican leaders could claim only limited participation in the tightly controlled dictatorship of Porfirio Diaz (1876–1910). During these years, when 85 percent of the population was illiterate, the labor sector remained undiversified and failed to organize into functional interest groups or national parties. After 1920, when literacy began to spread in Mexico, labor became more and more diversi-

[27] Both works published in México, D. F., by Editorial Pax-Mexico, Asociación Psicoanalitica Mexicana, A. C. See p. 53 in former and pp. 202–3 in latter.

[28] (México, D. F.: Secretaría de Educación Pública, Instituto Federal de Capacitación del Magesterio, 1962), I, 142–43, of a two-volume work.

[29] Quoted by Frank R. Brandenburg, *The Making of Modern Mexico* (Englewood Cliffs, N. J.: Prentice-Hall, 1964), p. 3. Brandenburg, long a student of Mexican political development, concludes that Mexico is ruled by an elite which he calls the "Revolutionary Family." It is composed of the men "who have run Mexico for over half a century, who have laid the policy-lines of the Revolution, and who today hold effective decision-making power" (p. 3). This group includes the incumbent president, the president-elect (one every sixth year), several very wealthy individuals (or labor union leaders), and a few powerful national and regional political leaders. Other influential individuals of the political elite represent vested interests in finance, commerce, private industry, and agriculture (p. 4). Also, the closed procedure of selecting new presidents further illustrates limited political decision-making within the PRI hierarchy (pp. 145–50). For other views on centralized decision-making in Mexico, see Robert E. Scott, *Mexican Government in Transition* (Urbana, Ill.: University of Illinois Press, 1959), pp. 197–293. On the same theme, see Raymond Veron, *The Dilemma of Mexico's Development* (Cambridge, Mass.: Harvard University Press, 1963), p. 131.

fied and the base of political participation was extended in the 1930's to include first rural and factory workers followed by white-collar workers, teachers, civil servants, professionals, and intellectuals in the 1940's.[30] Through large interest groups these people began to participate in national politics through the large dominant Mexican party with its labor, farm, and popular interest group sectors. The party of the revolution, today called the Party of Institutionalized Revolution (PRI), became more and more institutionalized and began to provide the political machinery for selection and election of a new and different president each six years, for attainment of broad social reforms, and for communicating new national symbols (heroes, slogans, songs, poems) designed to build national identification and to stimulate national integration and development. The PRI became the mechanism for wider sharing in governmental life.

The time frame of increasing literacy, labor diversification, and interest group formation with the PRI is illustrated in Tables 4 and 5. These statistics are not meant to suggest that increased literacy was the single determinant of later political and economic modernization. They do suggest that because increasing literacy and labor specialization occurred concurrently with interest group formation and their incorporation in the party structure, literacy was a vital impetus for politicization. They further suggest that middle sector expansion directly affects Mexican political development, for it has produced expansion of the PRI's popular groups (CNOP, see Table 5)—a distinctly middle sector organization composed of teachers, civil servants, professional women, small industrialists, and intellectuals. As an outgrowth of increasing literacy, the CNOP grew from its inception in 1943 to 1,848,000 members by 1959 at a time when the percentage of the literate population increased from 37 percent in 1940 to 70 percent in 1960. By 1964 this federation reached a 3,122,000 membership, making it the largest grouping in PRI. In short, the rise in levels of literacy has brought a major structural change within the dominant single party, where the largest division of participants is found in the middle sector organization, CNOP, rather than in the divisions of less educated individuals, the labor groups (CROM, CGT, CTM, and CNC). While vastly increased participation and social mobilization (Deutsch's term) occurred, persistent traditional authoritarian attitudes continued to shape political interaction.

CONCLUSION: IMPLICATIONS FOR RESEARCH

Traditional values and attitudes in Latin America are in part the product of the Iberian conquest which brought with it paternalist-political and

---

[30] This is not to suggest that education *produces* industry but that increased education, during a time of industrialization, stimulates labor diversification as skills become more sophisticated. Education is of course a vital base for sustained industrialization. The chief concerns of this paper are relationships between education and political deyelopment rather than the stimulants to increased education, of which industry can be one.

TABLE 4

Increasing Literacy and Labor Diversification 1940–1960 [a]

YEAR	POPULATION	LITERATE PERCENTAGE OF POPULATION	AGRICULTURE		INDUSTRY		SERVICES [b]	
			NO. OF WORKERS	PERCENTAGE	NO. OF WORKERS	PERCENTAGE	NO. OF WORKERS	PERCENTAGE
1900	13,607,272	15	—	—	—	—	—	—
1910	15,160,369	22	—	—	—	—	—	—
1930	16,552,722	29	—	—	—	—	—	—
1940	19,653,552	37	3,831	63.3	836	13.8	1,117	18.4
1950	25,791,017	66	4,824	58.3	1,222	14.8	1,774	21.4
1960	34,923,129	70	6,342	52.8	1,868	15.5	3,065	25.5

[a] Figures for population and literacy percentages are computed from Mexican *Anuarios Estadísticos* for the relevant years. If *Anuarios* were not available, Jose I. Iturriaga's *La Estructura Social y Cultural de México* (México, D. F.: Fondo de Cultura Economica, 1951) contains similar statistical data. Figures in the "Agriculture," "Industry," and "Services" columns are from Ramón Ramirez, *Tendencias de la Economía Mexicana* (México, D. F.: Escuela Nacional de Economía, Universidad Nacional Autonoma de México, 1962), p. 19.

[b] "Services" include transportation, communications, commerce, finance, and civil service occupations.

TABLE 5

Formation of Interest Group Sectors [a]
(Participate through PRI)

YEAR FORMED	INTEREST GROUP	MEMBERSHIP (1958)
1918	Regional Confederation of Mexican Workers (CROM)	35,000
1922	General Confederation Workers (CGT)	25,000
1936	Mexican Confederation of Laborers (CTM)	1,500,000
1938	National Farmers' Federation (CNC)	2,500,000
1938	Federation of Government Employees' Unions (FSTSE)	300,000
1943	National Federation of Popular Organizations (CNOP)	1,848,000 [b]

[a] From Robert E. Scott, *Mexican Government in Transition*, pp. 166–67.
[b] Figure includes FSTSE membership.

religious authoritarianism accompanied by a rigid social hierarchy.[31] These conditions were not conducive to self-government during the colonial period and did not prepare the Latin American elites for independence. Instead, traditionalism produced authoritarian political systems where followers tended to transfer power completely rather than delegate it temporarily to their leaders, and where the idea that man is responsible for his own world never really took root.[32] Independence brought no legitimate substitute political institutions. Thus, anarchy ensued after independence had been won. Traditionalism in Latin America, not a solid foundation for the growth of democratic institutions as we know them in the United States, continues to condition the entire process of political development in spite of increasing literacy and expanding education.

To conclude that literacy can be correlated with various forms of increased engagement in politics, but not always with fundamental change in underlying attitudes toward authority, has future research implications. First, political development theory (or theories) must be applied carefully to individual Latin American polities if flaws in the theory are to be ascertained, reworked, and modified to fit reality. This task is essential in the continuing search for a general theory of political development. To date,

[31] For a fascinating approach to traditional attitudes formation in Latin America, see Richard M. Morse. "The Heritage of Latin America," in *The Founding of New Societies,* ed. Louis Hartz (New York: Harcourt, Brace and World, 1964), pp. 123–77. The Indian and Negro heritages are also important in forming the weaker complements to dominant Iberian values. The mixture of whites and Indians has produced the mixed-blood *mestizo,* the man perhaps most achievement-oriented in Latin America today.

[32] *Ibid.,* pp. 172–173. The implications of these attitudes for democratic government, which requires specific historical experiences, is examined by Zevedei Barbu, *Democracy and Dictatorship: Their Psychology and Patterns of Life* (New York: Grove Press, 1959), pp. 12–23.

most development theory is based upon research in the new nations of Africa and Asia, not upon Latin American evidence dating back to the colonial period and conditioned by a substantially different cultural setting.

Second, as new and productive uses of quantitative statistical analysis are devised, qualitative intuitive assessments based upon accurate and reliable information must not be given short shrift. If central links between political structures and political cultures, between institutions and values are to be discussed intelligently, then study of unquantifiable information should be geared to human judgment about social and political interrelationships.

Third, the decision-making and conflict-resolution process *within* emerging modern institutions should be a major concern. These processes include leaders, subordinates, issues, alternatives, ideologies, procedures, unwritten rules, and custom. They also involve political socialization (i.e., learning of attitudes toward authority in the home, school, and church) which we know in the case of Mexico is authoritarian with obedience and respect for authority as key values. In-depth study of these forces would help to expand the understanding of decision-making within modern institutions. In spite of the growth of modern parties and increased politicization cited in the six countries with high literacy, the important elements of personalism, *machismo, caciquismo,* and paternalism continue to shape the pattern of developing decision-making processes. One impact of traditionalism occurs in the broad spectrum of Latin American labor movements which have been organized and injected into the political system not from below as social mobilization increased but from above by strong leaders building a base of political power, e.g., Cárdenas in Mexico, Perón in Argentina, Vargas in Brazil. Another impact of traditionalism is on the heavy commitment to equitable redistribution of the national income through state direction of the economy. This ideological objective suggests a strong element of historic paternalism and raises serious questions about economic development paralleled with social welfare programs (Uruguay is the classic case) which divert scarce funds from capital formation. These examples indicate that the pattern of political development in Latin America will be markedly different from that in the United States or Britain even though the indices of development —urbanization, literacy, mass media circulation—appear to be similar.

APPENDIX: STUDY OF MEXICAN ATTITUDES TOWARD POLITICS AND EDUCATION

The questionnaire consists of forty-two items. Twelve of these questions are divided into two groups: eight items on personal information such as sex, age, place of birth, and level of education achieved, and four general questions on the role of the Mexican school. The thirty remaining questions are divided into three equal groups of ten questions covering (a) authoritarianism, (b) modern political attitudes, and (c) education in Mexico. Each of these ten-question sets constitutes an opinion-attitude scale which is designed to reflect the respondent's opinion-attitude toward each item or statement within the scale.[33] Five of the thirty questions are "turned-around" and were later scored in reverse to obviate the tendency of a respondent to fall into a "set" pattern of agreement or disagreement with all items. The questionnaire was pre-tested, and several items were deleted or changed to make them more discriminating. The questions are of course "mixed" on the questionnaire to prevent the relations between questions from becoming too obvious.

The subjects were given a wide choice of responses, ranging from strong agreement, through moderate agreement, slight agreement, undecided, slight disagreement, moderate disagreement, to strong disagreement. The subjects were asked to circle one of the numbers under each statement which registered their attitudes: $+3$, $+2$, $+1$, 0, -1, -2, and -3. Unmarked items were given the intermediate score of 4. These responses were converted into scores as follows: $+3$ became 7, $+2$ became 6, $+1$ became 5, 0 and unmarked items became 4, -1 became 3, -2 became 2, and -3 became 1. All "turned-around" items were scored in reverse order, with -3 equal to 1, etc.

These raw scores were then transferred to IBM cards, as was all background information, such as levels of education achieved, etc. This method was used to facilitate IBM determination of the correlation coefficients between the various groups of items in the questionnaire. A correlation coefficient is the mathematical expression of the degree of covariation that exists for any two variable items. The key point is that when there is no similarity between variables, the correlation is zero; when there is perfect similarity, the correlation is $+1$; and when there is perfect dissimilarity, the correlation is -1.[34] Correlation coefficients allow the investigator to gain information on the relationship between two basic variables, as in this questionnaire, the relationship between levels of education and political attitudes reflected in the opinion scales.

The Opinion-Attitude Scales

The Authoritarian Attitude Scale, one of the three scales employed in this research, consisted of the following questions:

[33] This method of integrating several opinion-attitude scales into a single questionnaire was originated by Rensis Likert. See "A Technique for the Measurement of Attitudes," No. 140 in *Archives of Psychology*, ed. R. S. Woodworth (New York: Columbia University Press, 1932), and Rensis Likert and Gardner Murphy, *Public Opinion and the Individual* (New York: Harper, 1938). The opinions reflected in this questionnaire also reflect political attitudes; the two are intimately related. See Gordon W. Allport, "The Composition of Political Attitudes," *American Journal of Sociology*, XXXV (September 1929), 225, and Bernard Fensterwald, Jr., "The Anatomy of American Isolationism and Expansionism," *Journal of Conflict Resolution*, II (September 1958), 280–310.

[34] Fensterwald, "The Anatomy of American Isolationism and Expansionism," p. 296.

1. Every decent person should have a feeling of love, gratitude and respect for his parents.
4. Most people who fail to get ahead in life simply don't have enough willpower.
7. What this country needs is fewer laws and agencies and more courageous, tireless, devoted leaders whom the people can put their faith in.
10. Too many people today are living a soft life; we should look for the fundamental principles that require force and work.
13. The most important virtues that children can learn in the home are obedience and respect for authority.
16. No insult to honor should ever go unpunished.
19. It is good to spend money to construct schools, but in reality Mexico is spending too much to educate *campesinos* who aren't going to get ahead in life.
22. People can be grouped into two categories: weak and strong.
25. No normal, reasonable and respectable person could ever think of hurting a friend or parent.
28. It is essential for effective work that our bosses outline in detail what is to be done and precisely how to do it.

These questions were so stated that persons with strong authoritarian attitudes would be expected to agree with them.[35]

The Modern Political Attitude Scale, the second of three attitude scales, was composed of the following questions:

2. If a person wants to get ahead in life, it is better to have money than ability.
5. If a man works hard, is resourceful and creative, he can be very successful.
8. The way to resolve conflict between the different interest groups is through compromise.
11. If one wants to be successful in his profession, it is more important to be clever and imaginative than to be from a "good family."
14. In spite of industrialization and progress in education, the basic relationships among Mexicans are static and do not require a constant adjustment.
17. Mexicans possess many rights, the principal of which is equality before the law.
20. Personalism (*personalismo*) ought to rule in politics.
23. Through science we can hope to discover many things now unknown to the human mind.
26. In spite of what people say, the best way of telling the importance of people is through their family background.

[35] The questions on the Authoritarian Attitude Scale were taken from T. W. Adorno, *et al., The Authoritarian Personality* (New York: Harper, 1950), pp. 226–27, 231, 237.

29. It is not necessary that the program for progress of the nation be made from alternative courses of action.

Negative answers to questions 2, 14, 20, 26, and 29, and positive answers to all other questions were scored as modern political attitudes.

Attitudes on education as a central force for Mexican national development were placed into the following Functions of Education Attitude Scale:

3. Mexico should have a definite kind of educational system in order to reach its political and social goals.
6. Of all the roads to national development, formal and controlled education is the best.
9. If all men knew how to read and write and were well-educated, they would act reasonably and peaceably in their relations with each other.
12. A good system of education in Mexico ought to be controlled by the government and not left to chance.
15. Justo Sierra was right when he said that Mexico would be democratic if the importance of democracy were taught through the schools.
18. We can predict the social development of a country if we examine its system of education.
21. It is important that Mexicans have a uniform education in the schools if they want to avoid internal political conflict.
24. One of the principal functions of the schools is to teach its students patriotism and a sense of civil responsibility in order that they may fit into Mexican society.
27. It is through a good system of education that Mexico can increase the number of citizens that believe in the ideals of democracy.
30. A country that has various systems of different education will only produce people that will later disagree politically.

Positive answers to these questions indicate several kinds of attitudes relative to education. Strong agreement with all the questions suggests that the respondent believes that education should be controlled by the government (a part of the authoritarian syndrome), that through education democratic values can be transmitted from teachers and textbooks to students, and that education is the central force in Mexican national development.

Composition of the Sample

The questionnaire was distributed to 149 white-collar workers in the Federal District of Mexico.[36] Seventy-eight subjects, or 52 percent of the sample,

[36] Admittedly, 149 respondents is a very small base on which to build a theory. This case study, therefore, is not designed to erect a general theory. It does offer quantitative data for reaching tentative estimates of the limitations of education as an input to political development (in the realm of attitudes toward authority) and suggests that the rate of change in political cultures may be far slower than originally judged by political scientists.

worked for the Sears Roebuck Company. Thirty-two subjects, or 21.5 percent of the sample, worked for the Bank of Mexico. Seventy-nine subjects (53 percent) were male while seventy (47 percent) were female. The range in age was from eighteen to sixty-two years.

The educational background of the sample was rather disparate. Fifty-one subjects (34 percent) had completed university training, while twenty-one subjects (14 percent) had begun but had not finished university studies. Thirty-five (24.5 percent) had completed normal school for teachers or preparatory school for the university. Seventeen subjects (11 percent) had completed secondary training, while sixteen (10.5 percent) had begun secondary studies but had not finished. Another interesting statistical breakdown is related to the time period during which the subjects attended primary school. Thirty-eight subjects (26 percent) were educated during the thirties when socialist primary education was promoted in the public schools. Nineteen subjects (13 percent) received their primary instruction before the socialist era, and forty-eight (32 percent) went to primary school after the socialist era. These subjects were publicly educated, while the remaining forty-four (29 percent) were educated in private schools.

Questionnaire Results

Results from the questionnaire indicate moderate agreement with the authoritarian questions, where the mean score for seven of the ten authority questions was over five. In the authority scale, attitudes of disagreement were registered as a mean score on questions 7, 19, and 22. On the Modern Political Attitude Scale, mean scores for agreement and disagreement were split evenly, five and five. The breakdown of mean scores is given below, where the score can be compared to the specific question. The strongest agreement was registered by the total sample in the education scale where eight of ten mean scores were over five and two mean scores were over four. This would have been a likely prediction of the education scores, if the authoritarian scores were moderately high, since the questions on education were closely related with strong governmental control and with the authoritarian syndrome of opinions.[37] The pattern of mean scores for the total sample is shown in Table 6.

Other data from this study suggest that higher levels of education reduced the authoritarian attitudes only slightly; that is, as educational levels increased, authoritarian attitudes decreased relatively little. A correlation coefficient of –.3139 between higher levels of education and the authoritarian attitude scale (totals of ten authoritarian questions) illustrate the point. Secondly, the correlation coefficient between increasing levels of education

---

[37] Agreement most probably reflects the de facto educational policy of the Mexican government, which approximates the elements embodied in the questionnaire.

TABLE 6

Mean Scores of the Three Opinion-Attitude Scales

AUTHORITARIAN ATTITUDES		MODERN POLITICAL ATTITUDES		ATTITUDES TOWARD EDUCATION	
QUESTION	MEAN SCORE	QUESTION	MEAN SCORE	QUESTION	MEAN SCORE
1	6.892	2	2.832	3	5.986
4	5.637	5	6.483	6	5.859
7	3.510	8	6.107	9	5.744
10	5.711	11	6.241	12	5.348
13	5.872	14	3.315	15	5.959
16	5.342	17	5.610	18	6.355
19	1.691	20	1.617	21	4.503
22	3.422	23	6.765	24	6.395
25	6.543	26	2.389	27	5.912
28	5.348	29	3.617	30	4.718

and the modern political attitude scale was not significant (.0351), indicating that more education did not make the subjects of this sample more "modern" in their political perspectives. Further, as levels of education increased, the authoritarian attitudes built into the education scale decreased only slightly, as they did in the authoritarian attitude scale itself. The correlation coefficient between increasing education and the education scale was a slightly significant −.2881. The authoritarian scale and education scale were related in terms of a correlation coefficient of .4758, suggesting that as people in the sample were more authoritarian they believed that education should be controlled, be oriented to a specific policy, and be designed to inculcate democratic values through control of Mexico's younger generations. Of course, this is a broad generalization based upon analysis of limited information; certainly exceptions to the generalization would exist within the total sample.

In order to investigate other relationships emerging from this study, subgroups were extracted from the total sample and then correlated with increasing education. These correlations are given in Tables 7 and 8. In general, the following tables indicate a weak relationship between increased (or higher) levels of education and decreased authoritarian attitudes. A notation of "ns" in the following tables signifies that the correlation coefficient was "not significant" (between .2000 and −.2000). Mean answers included in the tables are denoted by the "m" columns.

The relationships between the three scales and increased educational levels is summarized in the following table:

TABLE 7

Correlation Coefficients Between Increasing Education and the Authoritarian Attitude Scale

A

QUESTION	MALE	M	FEMALE	M	TEACHER	M
1	−.2055	6.950	ns	6.826	.3998	6.593
4	ns	5.462	ns	5.840	ns	5.937
7	−.2844	3.212	−.3075	3.855	ns	3.156
10	ns	5.387	ns	3.855	ns	5.500
13	ns	5.712	−.2905	6.057	ns	5.593
16	ns	5.262	ns	5.434	.2259	5.093
19	ns	1.512	ns	1.898	−.3729	1.843
22	ns	3.062	−.2801	3.840	ns	3.437
25	ns	6.437	ns	6.666	ns	6.156
28	ns	5.150	−.2776	5.579	ns	4.750

B

QUESTION	BANK OF MEXICO	M	SEARS ROEBUCK	M
1	ns	6.923	ns	7.000
4	−.3154	5.461	ns	5.623
7	ns	3.205	−.3775	3.844
10	ns	5.666	−.2445	5.805
13	ns	5.717	−.2518	6.051
16	−.2529	5.358	ns	5.415
19	ns	1.820	ns	1.157
22	−.2423	3.025	−.2276	3.584
25	ns	6.538	ns	6.701
28	−.2013	4.974	ns	5.792

C

QUESTION	EDUCATED BEFORE AND AFTER CÁRDENAS PERIOD [a]	M	EDUCATED DURING CÁRDENAS PERIOD	M
1	ns	6.802	ns	6.975
4	ns	5.816	ns	5.550
7	−.4008	3.352	ns	3.800
10	−.2338	5.704	ns	5.800
13	−.2230	5.507	ns	6.425
16	ns	5.225	ns	5.200
19	−.2380	1.690	ns	1.600
22	−.2557	3.774	ns	2.750
25	ns	6.338	ns	6.725
28	ns	5.366	ns	4.925

[a] Those subjects educated before or after the Cárdenas period were placed together in a separate group and correlated with levels of education.

TABLE 8

Correlation Coefficients Between Increasing Education
and the Three Scales

	AUTHORITARIAN ATTITUDE	MODERN POLITICAL ATTITUDE	ROLE OF EDUCATION
Males	−.2372	ns	−.2561
Females	−.2949	ns	−.2501
Bank of Mexico	ns	−.2380	ns
Sears Roebuck	−.3369	ns	ns
Teachers	ns	ns	ns
Education Before or After Cárdenas Period	−.4832	ns	−.4059
Education During Cárdenas Period	ns	ns	ns

THE CORRELATES OF EDUCATIONAL
EFFORT: A MULTIVARIATE
ANALYSIS

Walter I. Garms, Jr.

This paper postulates a set of factors clustered into three groups as determinants of educational effort by nations. These groups are the ability to support education, the expectations of the population for education, and the governmental framework and attitudes. A set of multiple regressions shows the most important explanatory variables for educational effort to be (1) kilowatt-hours of electricity produced per capita, a measure of economic development and therefore of ability to support education; (2) school enrollment as a percentage of school-age population, a measure of the expectations of the population of the country for education; (3) governmental style of the country. The multiple regression also shows that several variables which might reasonably be expected to affect educational effort actually make little or no independent contribution.

INTRODUCTION

Although there has been a good deal of interest in the use of education by nations to help achieve economic progress, relatively few studies have investigated educational effort across nations. In addition, previous studies of educational effort by nations have tended to use bivariate procedures, even though the basic conception may have been a multivariate one. Svennilson, Edding, and Elvin plotted school enrollment ratios against gross national product per capita for 20 European countries, the United States, and the U.S.S.R. A rough line of regression through their scatter-plot seems to indicate that countries with higher gross national product per capita have higher enrollment ratios, but they reported no correlations.[1] Harbison and Myers devised a scale of "human resource development" and gathered data for 75 countries on 14 variables which they believed to have some connection with this scale. They obtained a 14 by 14 correlation matrix from these measures, but confined their statistical analysis to comments on individual simple correlations in this matrix.[2]

REPRINTED FROM *Comparative Education Review*, Vol. 12 (October 1968), pp. 281–290, by permission. © 1968 by Comparative Education Review.

[1] I. Svennilson, F. Edding, and L. Elvin, *Targets for Education in Europe in 1970*, Policy Conference on Economic Growth and Investment in Education (Paris: O.E.C.D., 1962), pp. 71–73.

[2] Frederick Harbison and Charles A. Myers, *Education, Manpower, and Economic Growth* (New York: McGraw-Hill, 1964).

Curle gathered information on 6 variables for 55 countries. He computed rank order correlations between each pair of these measures, and chi-square measures between type of political system and several of the measures. Among other things, he found a significant rank order correlation between per capita income and percentage of national income invested in education. This finding bears directly upon the substance of the study reported here, but because it is a bivariate analysis there is no control for the effect of other variables.[3]

McClelland examined the relationship between school enrollment in a base year and subsequent economic growth rate. Within groups of countries at approximately the same economic level, he found a strong correlation between these measures.[4] Edding found a correlation of 0.992 in 1954 between per capita income and per capita education expenditures for 18 countries.[5] Although this extremely high correlation would appear to rule out any other variable, there is in fact a statistical artifact operating here. The extremely wide spread of per capita incomes among nations, and the fact that per capita education expenditures cannot exceed per capita income, guarantee a high correlation. A more appropriate variable to investigate is *effort*, rather than absolute level of expenditure.

All of the studies mentioned used essentially bivariate procedures. The study to be reported here presents a theoretical framework which assumes multiple causality of educational effort by nations and then applies multivariate statistics in an attempt to test the framework.

THE HYPOTHESES

The general hypothesis of this study is that public effort for education by nations will depend upon three factors: (a) the ability to support education, (b) the expectations of the population for education, and (c) the manner in which the government utilizes the ability and expectations of the population in providing support for education. Each of these factors may be thought of as having one or more facets, resulting in a series of hypotheses regarding the independent contribution of each to the determination of public educational effort by nations. The dependent variable to be predicted is relative educational effort by nations, which will be defined operationally as percentage of national income publicly spent for education.

[3] Adam Curle, "Education, Politics, and Development," *Comparative Education Review*, 7 (February 1964), pp. 226–245.

[4] David C. McClelland, "Does Education Accelerate Economic Growth?" *Economic Development and Cultural Change*, 14 (April 1966), pp. 257–278.

[5] Friedrich Edding, *Internationale Tendenzen in der Entwicklung der Ausgaben für Schulen und Hochschulen* (Kiel, 1958), p. 157 ff., quoted in Seymour Sacks, "Present Patterns and Historical Trends in Educational Expenditures: The Constraints on the Planning for Education in Developed Nations" (Maxwell Graduate School, Syracuse University, 1967). (Mimeographed.)

A. Ability

It is not immediately clear what the effect of differences in per capita income is apt to be on the percentage of that income spent on education. *It is here hypothesized that, other things being equal, greater per capita national income will result in a greater percentage of this income spent for education, because discretionary income tends to rise more rapidly than total income.* The finding of Curle mentioned above tends to support this hypothesis, but it should be recalled that his was a simple correlation and did not hold other factors constant. The hypothesis goes contrary to the situation among states in the United States, where the poorest states make the greatest relative effort for education. Teacher mobility among states and some degree of national consensus about the amount of public education to be offered make the situation among states in the United States different than is here hypothesized among nations. Note that this is not a hypothesis of a simple correlation of income with educational effort ignoring other factors, but of a partial correlation when other factors are held constant. The same is true of the other hypotheses.

B. Expectations

Expectations of the population for education may be thought of in terms of a quantity facet and a quality facet, with the quantity facet representing the number of children to be educated in proportion to the population and the quality facet representing expectations for the quality of education to be offered each child.

The hypothesis for the quantity facet is that the higher the proportion of the population to be educated, the higher will be national educational effort.

Expectations of quality will tend to be influenced primarily by the amount of education of the adult population and by various needs which arise through urbanization. In general, parents who are more educated will expect more and better education for their children, both as a means for economic advancement and as an end in itself. Urbanization implies a market economy which requires more skills be taught in the schools than are necessary in the subsistence economy often found in rural areas. In addition, children who are useful in simple jobs on the farm are often a burden in the city, and city dwellers may well expect the schools to perform a custodial function. Thus, *with regard to quality expectations, it is hypothesized that public effort for education will increase with increasing level of education of the adult population and with increasing urbanization.*

C. Government

This factor is hypothesized to be of considerable importance among nations, in spite of results that seem to indicate the opposite in school districts of the United States. James, Kelly, and Garms found that none of the factors of governmental arrangements which they measured made a significant difference in expenditure on education by larger school districts in the United States.[6] Campbell and his associates made similar findings in their study.[7] However, the differences in governmental arrangements are much less pronounced among school districts of the United States than among the governments of the nations of the world. Additionally, the form of governmental arrangements in both of these studies was considered to be attitudinally neutral. The factor was viewed as having a mediating effect upon school expenditures; that is, it either facilitated or hindered the expression of the primary factors. As such, no directional hypothesis for these mediating variables could be formulated with confidence. In the present study, on the other hand, the government factors are viewed as primary, rather than mediating, variables. They reflect not only the form of the government, but the attitudes of those who run it. There are definite directional hypotheses.

The first facet of the government factor has to do with the attitude of the government, through its organization and its leader, toward education as an instrument of national policy. Although governments, like most other social phenomena, come in an almost infinite variety, defying measurement on a scale, categorization is possible. The facet of governmental attitude is here presented as a classification of governments into (a) those which are fairly broadly representative of the people, (b) those which are not broadly representative and which have mobilized the resources of the country toward the achievement of some national goal or goals (typically, the goal of economic development), and (c) those which are not broadly representative and are oriented primarily toward preserving the *status quo* of a ruling class. These categories of governmental attitude will be called "representative," "mobilizational," and "*status quo.*" While such a classification, like all simple classifications of complex phenomena, is arbitrary and obscures many minor differences, it appears conceptually sound. An actual classification of governments into these categories (to be discussed later) indicates that it is possible, without great uncertainty, to put every government in this study into one, and only one, of these categories.

It is presumed that where the government is broadly representative, the leaders of the country will fairly accurately reflect the wishes of the population as a whole, and educational effort will primarily be determined by the factors of ability and expectations. It seems probable, however, that the leaders of a country with a non-representative government are less influenced

---

[6] H. Thomas James, James A. Kelly, and Walter I. Garms, *Determinants of Educational Expenditures in Large Cities of the United States,* U. S. Department of Health, Education, and Welfare Cooperative Research Project No. 2389 (Stanford, California: School of Education, Stanford University, 1966).

[7] Alan K. Campbell, "The Socio-Economic, Political, and Fiscal Environment of Educational Policy-Making in Large Cities," Paper presented at the meeting of the American Political Science Association, New York, September, 1966.

by the citizens of the country and more influenced by their own goals for the nation. *When such a country is mobilized toward some national goal, it is hypothesized that the leaders will recognize the need for trained manpower to reach that goal and that educational effort and expenditures will be higher than would be predicted from the ability and expectations factors alone.* Where a non-representative nation is oriented toward maintenance of the *status quo* of a ruling class, it is expected that the rulers will not be interested in broadly educating a populace which might then rise against them. Therefore, *it is hypothesized that educational effort in the* status quo *nations will be lower than would be predicted from ability and expectations factors alone.*

The second facet of the government factor is the extractive capability of the government: the extent to which the political system can extract resources from the environment for public purposes.[8] *It is hypothesized that the higher the extractive capability of the government, the higher the public effort for education.*

The Sample

The unit of analysis for this study must be the nation, because the theoretical framework postulates effects of certain political arrangements which are national in scope. For the same reason, only independent nations could be used and, of these, only those that had been independent long enough that educational effort would reflect that nation's ability, expectations, and government rather than the policies of a former colonial ruler. Extremely small nations were eliminated, and it was also necessary to eliminate nations for which information could not be obtained on all of the variables.

The base year for the study is 1963. The sample consists of all independent nations in that year which had been independent for at least six years, had a population of at least 100,000, and for which data could be obtained on all variables. This restricts the sample to a total of 78 nations. Raw data on each variable for each nation are given in Table 1, as are data sources.

The conditions imposed result in some unfortunate exclusions. Forty-one nations, most of them African, have become independent since 1957, and thus are excluded. Eleven nations, among them mainland China, had to be excluded for lack of data on all variables. Five independent nations were excluded as too small for consideration. The results should be interpreted in the light of these exclusions.

Variables were selected which could be measured in comparable fashion for the nations in the sample and which were believed reasonably to represent the concepts of the theoretical framework.

---

[8] For a comprehensive definition and discussion of extractive capability, see Gabriel A. Almond and G. Bingham Powell, Jr., *Comparative Politics: A Developmental Approach* (Boston: Little, Brown and Co., 1966), p. 195 ff.

1. Dependent Variable

The dependent variable representing educational effort is public educational expenditures as a percentage of national income (abbreviated subsequently *EXP/NI*). Data on public educational expenditures in local currency are available for all countries in the sample, but national income in local currency is not available for the communist countries. These countries use net material product, a measure which cannot be made comparable with national income because of different accounting concepts. It was necessary to find educational expenditures per capita in U.S. dollars in order to be able to compare them with available estimates of national income per capita in U.S. dollars. Total public expenditures on education were used, but because of wide swings in annual capital expenditure the average for the years 1962–1964 was used. In converting to U.S. dollars, the free exchange rate was used if there was one. If not, the official rate was used. For communist countries the non-commercial rate calculated by the Statistical Office of the United Nations was used if quoted; otherwise the basic rate was used.

2. Ability to Support Education

One cannot use national income per person as an independent variable measuring financial ability because it has already been used as a divisor in the dependent variable. Instead, the measure of ability chosen is kilowatt hours of electricity produced per capita (*KWH*). This measure has been used for the same purpose by McClelland because of the availability of the data for all countries, the fact that electricity is everywhere measured in identical units, that it cannot be stockpiled, that it is not imported in significant amounts, and that its rate of production is highly correlated with national income per capita.[9]

3. Expectations for Education

a. *Quantity facet.* Two complementary variables are used to measure the quantity facet of expectations for education. The first is the percentage of the population aged five to nineteen years (abbreviated *5–19*). This is a direct measure of the number of children who are roughly at school-attending age. The second is the enrollment ratio (*ENROLL*). The ratio used is a ratio of the number of students attending all first and second level education as a percentage of the population in the age group which is eligible for first and second level education in each country. This adjusted ratio takes account of the fact that first and second level education start and end at different ages in different countries. Taken together, these two variables represent the total quantity of education required. The percentage of the population

[9] David C. McClelland, *The Achieving Society* (New York: The Free Press, 1967), pp. 85–87.

TABLE 1

Data for the Variables, by Country[a]

NATION	AVERAGE PUBLIC EXPEND. PER CAP. ON EDUC. (U.S. $) 1962-64[h]	AVERAGE NATIONAL INCOME PER CAP. (U.S. $) 1962-64[i]	PUBLIC EXPEND. ON EDUC. AS % OF NATIONAL INCOME 1962-64[j]	KWH ELECT. PRODUCED PER CAP. 1963 (000,000)[k]	PER CENT POPULAT. AGE 5-19 1963[l]	SCHOOL ENROLLMENT RATIO, 1ST AND 2ND LEVEL 1963[m]	DAILY NEWSPAPER CIRCULATION PER 1,000 1963[m]	PER CENT POPULATION IN CITIES OVER 100,000 1963[l]	GENERAL GOV'T REVENUE AS % OF GNP 1963[n]	GOV'T STYLE 1963[o]
Afghanistan	$ 0.40	$ 75	0.53	12	33.1[q]	9	4	3.4		S
Albania	14.86	204[p]	7.28	146	33.1	106	49	8.4		M
Argentina	19.27	550	3.50	573	28.7	73	146	41.3		R
Australia	48.32	1,375	3.51	2,682	27.9	90	348	58.9	22.4	R
Austria	35.71	850	4.20	2,571	21.1	68	244	38.3	34.1	R
Belgium	81.25	1,125	7.22	2,050	22.6	114	285	18.5	25.2	R
Bolivia	2.68	112	2.39	89	38.4[q]	50	23	9.9	15.9	R
Brazil	3.48	225	1.55	365	36.9	58	54	18.9		R
Bulgaria	26.15	325	8.05	889	25.1	89	151	14.9		M
Burma	1.57	75	2.09	23	34.2[q]	51	9	5.6	15.7	M
Cambodia	4.69	112	4.19	15	32.7[q]	42	8	7.0		M
Canada	120.52	1,625	7.42	6,463	30.5	80	223	44.5	26.2	R
Ceylon	6.30	112	5.63	38	34.1	80	35	4.8		R
Chile	10.73	450	2.38	684	34.5	78	118	37.3	22.2	R
China (Taiwan)	5.26	162	3.25	441	37.7	79	64	28.0	19.9	R[r]
Colombia	6.59	275	2.40	349	36.9[q]	60	52	37.7	10.5	R
Costa Rica	17.11	325	5.26	385	38.7	84	75	24.0	16.0	R
Cuba	14.58	275	5.30	424	33.2[q]	74	70	27.6		M
Czechoslovakia	32.37	750	4.32	2,140	26.9	87	272	14.1		M

Denmark	100.17	1,375	7.29	1,491	25.1	86	341	22.4	29.0	R
Dominican Rep.	6.05	187	3.24	128	38.3	65	27	12.2		R
Ecuador	4.00	162	2.47	105	37.7	57	52	18.5	23.2	R
El Salvador	6.12	225	2.72	125	37.2	54	47	10.3		S
Ethiopia	0.55	25	2.20	8	41.0ᵃ	5	2	2.9		S
Finland	86.01	1,125	7.65	2,603	29.5	82	359	16.5	29.4	R
France	47.85	1,375	3.48	1,844	24.5	94	245	17.8	36.2	R
Germany, Eastᵇ	64.45	698ᵖ	9.23	2,765	20.0	78	126	21.8		M
Germany, F. R.ᶜ	47.85	1,375	3.48	2,556	20.0	87	315	33.3	36.8	R
Ghana	9.52	187	5.09	64	33.3	52	31	7.7		M
Greece	8.99	450	2.00	374	25.4	71	121	12.6	22.0	R
Haiti	0.99	75	1.32	17	35.5	24	6	5.8		S
Honduras	4.07	187	2.17	55	39.3	49	20	7.1	9.2	R
Hungary	33.89	650	5.21	958	25.2	81	167	24.1		M
Iceland	51.00	1,375	3.71	3,546	30.7	105	443	0.0		R
Indiaᵈ	2.04	75	2.72	66	34.1	38	12	7.8	12.0	R
Indonesia	0.38	75	0.51	13	32.4	44	11	9.8		M
Iran	7.17	187	3.83	41	34.1	40	7	20.5		S
Ireland	28.77	650	4.43	1,018	28.8	91	240	19.1	22.8	R
Israel	59.61	850	7.01	1,327	33.0	83	143	32.4	28.7	R
Italy	39.50	650	6.08	1,413	23.7	62	111	26.0	31.3	R
Japan	34.28	550	6.23	1,671	29.5	86	416	44.7	22.9	R
Jordan	6.75	187	3.61	62	38.5	68	27	14.6	24.9	R
Laos	1.84	75	2.45	7	36.2ᵃ	23	12	8.6		S
Lebanon	9.31	275	3.39	284	28.5ᵃ	74	76	33.1		S
Liberia	4.36	137	3.18	177	29.0	20	3	0.0		R
Libya	13.41	162	8.28	99	33.3	51	5	22.4		R
Luxembourg	45.65	1,375	3.32	4,242	20.4	64	369	0.0	32.8	R

TABLE 1 (Cont.)

NATION	AVERAGE PUBLIC EXPEND. PER CAP. ON EDUC. (U.S. $) 1962-64h	AVERAGE NATIONAL INCOME PER CAP. (U.S. $) 1962-64i	PUBLIC EXPEND. ON EDUC. AS % OF NATIONAL INCOME 1962-64j	KWH ELECT. PRODUCED PER CAP. 1963 (000,000)k	PER CENT POPULAT. AGE 5-19 1963l	SCHOOL ENROLLMENT RATIO, 1ST AND 2ND LEVEL 1963m	DAILY NEWSPAPER CIRCULA-TION PER 1,000 1963m	PER CENT POPULATION IN CITIES OVER 100,000 1963l	GENERAL GOV'T REVENUE AS % OF GNP 1963n	GOV'T STYLE 1963o
Mexico	$ 9.80	$ 375	2.61	353	37.8	68	115	21.7		R
Mongolia	0.04	75	0.05	143	26.8	57	88	19.5		M
Morocco	6.73	162	4.15	92	37.4	36	17	18.9		R
Nepal	0.40	75	0.53	1	33.3	18	1	1.3		S[s]
Netherlands	69.68	1,125	6.19	1,753	28.1	89	284	31.9	32.3	R
New Zealand	57.54	1,625	3.54	3,532	29.3	90	401	16.5	25.9	R
Nicaragua	4.47	225	1.99	163	39.7	49	54	15.3		S
Norway	79.19	1,125	7.04	10,761	25.1	86	388	19.3	36.4	R
Panama	18.07	375	4.82	277	36.2	70	76	26.4	17.5	R
Paraguay	3.10	187	1.66	54	38.5	65	12	16.8		S
Peru	8.35	225	3.71	310	36.2	68	39	17.6		S[t]
Philippines	4.69	137	3.42	139	38.3	76	18	10.7	12.5	R
Poland	31.96	550	5.81	1,204	30.3	90	146	21.9		M
Portugal	5.36	275	1.95	476	27.1	65	64	12.7	19.8	S
Rumania	19.44	325	5.98	621	26.4	82	168	14.5		M
South Africa[e]	15.84	375	4.22	1,631	34.5	69	57	18.0	19.5	R
Spain	5.86	450	1.30	833	25.4	67	153	29.2	14.2	S[u]
Sudan	5.09	75	6.79	13	34.9[q]	14	5	2.3		M
Sweden	89.99	1,625	5.54	5,349	22.8	77	499	19.0	38.6	R
Switzerland	82.09	1,625	5.05	3,815	22.9	63	365	19.2	23.9	R
Thailand	2.71	112	2.42	31	36.5	55	12	7.2		S

Tunisia	10.64	187	5.69	82	33.6	58	26	10.4		R
Turkey	6.51	225	2.89	132	34.1	55	51	10.0		R
U.S.S.R.	63.96	850	7.52	1,835	27.1q	97	216	26.3		M
U.A.R.f	6.59	137	4.81	159	35.1	48	15	27.0		M
United Kingdomg	68.90	1,375	5.01	3,227	22.2	93	488	34.9	27.1	R
U.S.A.	153.31	2,625	5.84	5,341	28.6	100	337	28.5	26.7	R
Uruguay	14.00	450	3.11	609	26.0	71	314	46.4	27.9	R
Venezuela	27.54	750	3.67	831	36.7	83	78	34.2	25.2	R
Vietnam Rep.	1.52	75	2.02	26	27.3q	57	59	10.2	20.7	M
Yugoslavia	15.54	325	4.78	710	28.1	84	72	8.9		M

a Data are for the year or years indicated at the top of the column, or for the nearest available year. Of the 741 items of data, 108 are not for the year indicated. Of these, all but 13 are within three years of the year indicated. b Includes West Berlin. c Includes East Berlin. d Includes Kashmir. e Excludes Southwest Africa. f Includes Egypt, but not Syria. g Includes England, Scotland, Wales, and Northern Ireland. h Excludes England, Scotland, Wales, and Northern Ireland. h Excludes Southwest Africa. f Includes Egypt, but not Syria. g Includes England, Scotland, Wales, and Northern Ireland. h Expenditure data and population data used to compute this column are from Unesco, *Statistical Yearbook, 1965.* Currency exchange rates are from U.N., *Statistical Yearbook, 1965.* See text for method of calculation of average expenditure. i Source: U.N., *Estimates of Per Capita Income in United States Dollars* (New York: United Nations, 1966) (dittoed), except where noted. The figure shown is the midpoint of the range given in that publication. j Calculated from the first two columns. k Source: U.N., *Statistical Yearbook, 1965.* l Source: U.N., *Demographic Yearbook,* various years, except as noted. m Source: Unesco, *Statistical Yearbook, 1965.* n Source: U.N., *Yearbook of National Accounts Statistics, 1965.* o Source: Arthur S. Banks and Robert B. Textor, *A Cross-Polity Survey* (Cambridge: The M.I.T. Press, 1963). R = representative; M = not representative, mobilizationally oriented; S = not representative, *status quo* oriented. See text for explanation of coding method. p An estimate prepared by taking a ratio of the 1957 Usui and Hagen G.N.P. figures for Bulgaria, Czechoslovakia, Hungary, Poland, Rumania, and U.S.S.R. to the 1962–1964, U.N. national income figures for these countries. This ratio was then applied to the Usui and Hagen figures for Albania and East Germany to give a 1962–1964 national income estimate for these two countries. See Mikoto Usui and E. E. Hagen, *World Income, 1957* (Cambridge: M.I.T. Center for International Studies, 1959). q Data missing from *Demographic Yearbook,* or categorized in such a way that the percentage aged 5–19 could not be calculated from the data. Percentage was calculated from data in Unesco, *Statistical Yearbook, 1965,* by dividing total enrollment at first and second levels by unadjusted enrollment ratio at first and second levels to give an imputed population aged 5–19. r Not coded by Banks and Textor. Coded representative for purposes of this study. s Coded non-representative, but system style unascertainable by Banks and Textor. Coded *status quo* for purposes of this study. t Coded non-representative, but representative character unascertainable by Banks and Textor. Coded *status quo* for this study. u Coded non-representative but with system style ambiguous by Banks and Textor, with a note that it was ruled by a junta. Coded *status quo* for this study. u Coded non-representative but with system style ambiguous by Banks and Textor, with a note that system might be termed "decayed mobilizational." Coded *status quo* for this study.

which is of school age does not rapidly fluctuate as a result of political control. The enrollment ratio, on the other hand, represents a political decision by the nation on how broadly it shall educate. In a sense, then, the enrollment ratio is a political variable as well as an expectations variable. It is classified under expectations because it is not in itself a direct measure of political arrangements or attitudes, but is a resultant of them, and because it does help to measure quantity of education expected.

b. *Quality facet.* The quality facet of expectations for education is also measured by two variables. The first, newspaper circulation per 1,000 inhabitants (*NEWS*) is a proxy for level of education of the adult population. A measure, such as is used by the United States Census, of median years of schooling of the adult population, would be preferable, but is not available for most countries. Newspaper circulation, on the other hand, should be a better measure of education than a simple measure of literacy. Definitions of literacy vary greatly from country to country making inter-country comparisons of questionable value.

The second quality variable is percentage of population living in cities of over 100,000 (*CITIES*), used as a measure of urbanization. No measure of urbanization is ideal, for it is usually impossible to define a geographical line which separates an urban from a rural area. There is also no measure of urbanization universally used. The measure used here is reported by most countries and presumably correlates highly with any other consistent measure of urbanization which might be used.

4. Government

The first governmental variable is the categorization of governments into three groups according to style of operation and attitude, as discussed above. The categorization is based upon the data in Banks and Textor.[10] All countries classified by them as polyarchic or limited polyarchic were considered to have a representative government for the purpose of this study. Countries coded under the above method as not representative were categorized by system style. A non-representative country with a mobilizational or limited mobilizational style was coded mobilizational; a non-representative country with a non-mobilizational style was coded *status quo.* Of the 78 nations in the study, 47 are classified as representative, 18 are mobilizational, and 13 are coded *status quo.*

The second governmental variable is general government revenue, both national and local, as a percentage of gross national product (*GOV REV*), used as a measure of the extractive capability of the government. Unfortunately, this measure is available for only half the countries in the sample. It was used in a separate regression, but could not be used with the entire sample of 78.

[10] Arthur S. Banks and Robert B. Textor, A *Cross-Polity Survey* (Cambridge: The M.I.T. Press, 1963).

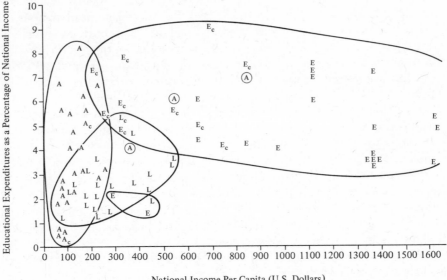

FIGURE 1

Comparison of Educational Effort by Nations.

STATISTICAL ANALYSIS

A scatterplot of educational effort against national income per capita (Figure 1) is illuminating. Countries in different geographical areas are indicated by different letters, and communist nations by subscripts. Some of the interesting things indicated by the plot are the following:

1. Almost all of the Asian and African nations have less than $200 national income per capita, and within this group there seems to be no clear relationship between wealth and educational effort. There is wide range in effort, but no clear basis for saying that it increases or decreases with wealth. The three of these nations which have substantially more wealth per capita than the rest (note the circled A's on the diagram) are, in order of increasing wealth, South Africa, Japan, and Israel.

2. There also appears to be no clear relationship between wealth and educational effort for the European nations, but for a different reason. Here there is wide variation in wealth, but the percentage of national income spent for education shows considerably less variation than in the Asian and African nations. The exceptions to this are three relatively poor, but non-

communist, European nations (Greece, Portugal, and Spain), where educational effort is only about one-third that for other European nations.

3. Latin American nations as a group tend to make only about half as much effort for education as do European nations. In this group of countries there is some tendency for educational effort to rise as ability rises.

4. The communist countries show no unusual pattern of educational effort.

This plot of countries makes it appear that there is a real difference between countries with low ability and those with high ability. Consequently, regressions were done not only on the entire 78 nation sample, but also on samples of high ability countries and low ability countries. The low ability sample consisted of 39 nations with less than $300 national income per capita. The high ability sample consisted of 49 nations with more than $200 national income per capita. It was necessary to have the samples overlap in this way in order to have enough cases in the low ability sample and to have more than one *status quo* country in the high ability sample.

A fourth sample, consisting of the 39 countries for which data on general government revenue as a percentage of national income were obtainable, was also tested. Unfortunately, the conclusions from this sample can not be generalized about as easily as those for the first three samples because the sample excludes most low income countries, most non-representative countries, and all communist countries. Extractive ability of the government should be an important variable; it is unfortunate that insufficient data are available for a conclusive test of its effect.

The problem of including in a multiple regression equation a categorical variable, such as the categorization of governments used here, is solved by employing dummy variables. For the three categories it is necessary to have two dummy variables, which were called *MOBIL* and *STAT QUO*. Countries were coded to these variables as follows:

	VALUE ASSIGNED TO VARIABLE	
TYPE OF COUNTRY	MOBIL	STAT QUO
Representative	0	0
Mobilizational	1	0
Status Quo	0	1

Thus, a regression coefficient found for the variable *MOBIL* will apply only to mobilizational countries, since all others have a zero value for the variable. The value of the regression coefficient for the variable *MOBIL* indicates the amount by which its educational effort will be higher than would be expected on the basis of its ability and expectations alone. Similarly, the regression coefficient for *STAT QUO* indicates the amount by which educational effort in *status quo* countries is different than would be expected on the basis of other variables alone. Coding of representative countries with a zero for both of these variables amounts to an assumption that their form of government will not affect systematically the amount of educational effort. While we have thus used two dummy variables to represent a three-fold categorization of governments, conceptually this is only a single variable.

The correlation matrix for the 78 nation sample is shown as Table 2. The results of the multiple regressions for the samples are shown in Table 3. The "standard regression coefficient" (also called the "beta weight") is computed from the regression coefficient by multiplying it by the ratio of the standard deviation of the independent variable to that of the dependent variable. The "variance attributable to variable" is the product of the standard regression coefficient and the simple correlation of the variable with EXP/NI. These products sum to R^2, the total variance explained by the regression. Thus, the relative effects of the variables are best judged by the size of the numbers in this column.

From these tables, we may test the hypotheses which were proposed earlier.

A. *Ability*

The first hypothesis, that ability to support education (measured by KWH) will positively affect educational effort, is strongly supported for all nations and for rich nations, but is not significantly supported for the poor nations. Note that the percentage of the variance in EXP/NI attributable to KWH for the three samples is 14, 13, and 1 respectively. Other things being equal, countries with higher incomes tend to spend a greater percentage of that income on education.

B. *Expectations for Education*

1. Percentage of population of educable age (5–19). The hypothesis that this variable will positively affect educational effort, other things being equal, is not supported in any of the samples. This is indicated by the negative standard regression coefficient when the prediction was for a positive one. However, the size of the coefficient is such that we can have little confidence that it is different from zero. It appears that the relative number of children to be educated is not a significant factor in explaining national educational effort.

2. Percentage of eligible population enrolled in school ($ENROLL$). The hypothesis of a positive effect of this variable upon educational effort is strongly supported for all 78 countries and for the high income and low income countries separately.

3. Education of adult population ($NEWS$). This hypothesis is not supported. The effect appears to be negative rather than positive. Possible reasons for this finding will be discussed below.

4. Urbanization ($CITIES$). This hypothesis is not supported significantly, although the sign of the regression coefficient is positive as hypothesized.

TABLE 2

Correlation Matrix for All 78 Countries

	EXP	EXP/NI	NI	KWH	5–19	ENROLL	NEWS	CITIES	MOBIL	STAT QUO
EXP	1.00	.61	.93	.80	-.57	.59	.78	.37	-.12	-.33
EXP/NI		1.00	.40	.42	-.36	.51	.37	.24	.22	-.44
NI			1.00	.80	-.60	.61	.86	.39	-.22	-.32
KWH				1.00	-.54	.46	.76	.27	-.15	-.27
5–19					1.00	-.45	-.69	-.26	-.17	.33
ENROLL						1.00	.64	.47	.04	-.47
NEWS							1.00	.41	-.17	-.35
CITIES								1.00	-.18	-.28
MOBIL									1.00	-.21
STAT QUO										1.00

TABLE 3

Effects of the Independent Variables Upon EXP/NI

INDEPENDENT VARIABLE	REGRESSION COEFFICIENT	STANDARD REGRESSION COEFFICIENT	SIMPLE CORRELATION WITH EXP/NI	VARIANCE ATTRIBUTABLE TO VARIABLE

A. Sample: All 78 nations. Multiple R = .63. Significance of regression = .998.

KWH	.00039	.34	.42	.14
5–19	−.01811	−.05	−.36	.02
ENROLL	.03004	.34	.51	.17
NEWS	−.00270	−.18	.37	−.07
CITIES	.00531	.03	.24	.01
MOBIL	.87378	.18	.22	.04
STAT QUO	−1.00549	−.19	−.44	.08

Total variance explained = .39

B. Sample: 49 nations with more than $200 national income per capita. Multiple R = .71. Significance of regression = .998.

KWH	.00036	.37	.36	.13
5–19	−.02449	−.07	−.32	.02
ENROLL	.04494	.33	.54	.18
NEWS	−.00225	−.16	.26	−.04
CITIES	.01060	.06	.01	.00
MOBIL	1.68668	.35	.43	.15
STAT QUO	−.88003	−.14	−.41	.06

Total variance explained = .50

C. Sample: 39 nations with less than $300 national income per capita. Multiple R = .58. Significance of regression = .94.

KWH	.00184	.13	.05	.01
5–19	−.01867	−.04	−.00	.00
ENROLL	.04363	.50	.32	.16
NEWS	−.04744	−.62	−.07	.04
CITIES	.02205	.11	.12	.01
MOBIL	.53114	.13	.20	.03
STAT QUO	−.97681	−.25	−.37	.09

Total variance explained = .34

D.   Sample: 39 nations with GOV REV data. Multiple R = .73.
Significance of regression = .998.

KWH	.00023	.28	.55	.15
5–19	.06717	.22	−.27	−.06
ENROLL	.03954	.34	.59	.20
NEWS	.00110	.09	.54	.05
CITIES	−.00225	−.01	.25	.00
MOBIL	−.59996	−.07	−.28	.02
STAT QUO	−1.05505	−.15	−.31	.05
GOV REV	.05601	.23	.52	.12

Total variance explained = .53

C. Government

1. Governmental style (MOBIL and STAT QUO). The hypothesis that there will be a difference in educational effort among representative, mobilizational, and status quo countries is supported in all three cases, although less strongly for the poorer countries. A separate test of significance, in which the variables MOBIL and STAT QUO were tested simultaneously (because they are conceptually one variable) gave significances of .98, .98, and .85 for the all-nation, rich nation, and poor nation samples respectively.

2. Extractive capability (GOV REV). A separate regression of 39 countries for which data on GOV REV were available (see D in Table 3) indicates that the extractive capability of the government has some significance as a variable. Care should be used in generalizing the results of this regression, however, because of the rather systematic exclusion of poor countries, non-representative countries, and communist countries.

Three main determinants of educational effort by nations were postulated: ability (represented by KWH), expectations (represented by 5–19, ENROLL, NEWS, and CITIES), and government (represented by MOBIL, STAT QUO, and GOV REV). In the sample of all 78 countries, these three factors account respectively for 14 per cent, 13 per cent, and 12 per cent of the total variation in the dependent variable (see Table 3). For the rich nations, the percentages are 13 per cent, 16 per cent, and 21 per cent. For the poor nations the factors account for 1 per cent, 21 per cent, and 12 per cent respectively. In the separate sample of nations for which GOV REV data are available, the factors account for 15 per cent, 19 per cent, and 19 per cent of the total variance. Thus, with the exception of the ability factor in the sample of poor nations, it appears that the three factors of ability, expectations, and government have about equal effect on educational effort, at least when the factors are measured with the variables used here.

An analysis of residuals (actual effort less predicted effort) for the sample of all 78 nations indicates that the regression equation predicts educational effort within plus or minus 50 per cent for four-fifths of the countries. The countries for which the regression equation predicts low by more than 50 per cent are Denmark, Ethiopia, Finland, Iran, Laos, Libya, Tunisia, and Sudan. Those for which it predicts high by more than 50 per cent are Afghanistan, Brazil, Burma, Indonesia, Mongolia, Nepal, Spain, and Vietnam Republic. While it might be possible to make specific hypotheses for the deviation of individual countries, it is difficult to imagine a single unmeasured variable that would improve the prediction for all or most of them. The suspicion is high that measurement errors in the data used may be responsible for the large deviations of many of these nations.

It is interesting to speculate on the reasons for the negative findings. Surprisingly, according to this analysis, if two nations existed that were identical in all respects except that one had a higher proportion of its population between the ages of 5 and 19 than did the other, there would be no significant difference in their educational effort. One possibility is that the condition which brings about a high percentage of people 5 to 19 years old is a high birth rate. But a high birth rate is closely connected with ability since increasing population can cancel the effect of economic growth, leaving the same or lower national income per capita. The simple correlation of *5–19* and *KWH* in the 78 nation sample is −.54. Thus, it may be that *KWH* provides an adequate measure of the variable *5–19*, leaving little remaining variance for *5–19* to explain. It is also possible that, for this variable with a rather small variance, measurement errors prevent a significant finding.

Similarly, it may be that urbanization is not a separate variable, but is another way of measuring the same thing measured by the enrollment ratio. It is also possible that increasing urbanization brings increased demands for all kinds of public expenditures and that school expenditures may be slighted in favor of more immediately pressing needs for streets, police, fire protection, and similar things. A further possibility is that urban residents may spend more for education in the private sector, which is not measured by the data of this study.

The most surprising finding is the rather strong negative coefficient of the variable *NEWS*, measuring education of the adult population. This appears to indicate that, other things being equal, a nation whose adult population is more highly educated will spend a smaller percentage of its national income on education. The reason for this may have much to do with the high correlation of *NEWS* and *KWH*. A possible interpretation is that as education of the adult population increases, economic status increases faster than percentage of income spent on education. The variable *KWH* tends, as it were, to "overpredict," and *NEWS*, with its negative coefficient, counterbalances this overprediction. *NEWS* is then acting as a "suppressant variable," and its partial effect must be viewed in this context. The action of this suppressant variable is shown in the last column of Table 3, where *NEWS* is shown making a negative contribution to the explanation of variance in Samples A and B. The variable 5–19 performs a similar role in Sample D.

Multivariate analysis has the major advantage over bivariate analysis of showing the relative effects of several variables simultaneously. A researcher using bivariate analysis might have looked at the simple correlation of —.36 between proportion of population aged 5 to 19 and educational expenditures as a percentage of national income. He would have come to the conclusion that educational effort is inversely proportional to the number to be educated. The multivariate analysis shows that this variable cannot be considered an important determinant of educational effort. In addition, multivariate analysis points to the relative explanatory value of those variables which are important.

Of course, no correlational analysis can prove causality. However, a showing of strong partial effects can give powerful support to a theoretical framework which presents a reasonable basis for causality and which includes all those variables that might reasonably be effective determinants.

This study was a cross-sectional one because of data limitations. More research on a longitudinal basis would be very desirable in order to make firmer causal inferences. In addition, the negative findings of the study need more investigation and clarification. Further possible variables (McClelland's n—Achievement is an example) should be investigated.

TABLE 4

Effect of Independent Variables Upon EXP/NI (Summary)

THEORETICAL FACTOR	VARIABLE	HYPOTHE-SIZED EFFECT	ACTUAL EFFECT			
			ALL 78 NATIONS	49 RICH NATIONS	39 POOR NATIONS	39 WITH GOV REV DATA
Ability	KWH	+	+**	+**	Nil	+*
Expectations						
Quantity	5–19	+	Nil	Nil	Nil	+
	ENROLL	+	+**	+**	+**	+**
Quality	NEWS	+	–	–	–	Nil
	CITIES	+	Nil	Nil	Nil	Nil
Government						
Governmental Style	MOBIL	+	+*	+**	+	Nil
	STAT QUO	–	–**	–	–*	–
Extractive Ability	GOV REV	+				+

Effects, the significance of which is less than .75, have been reported as Nil.
* Significance more than .90.
** Significance more than .95.